murach's
Java
programming

5TH EDITION

Joel Murach

murach's Java programming

5TH EDITION

Joel Murach

MIKE MURACH & ASSOCIATES, INC.

4340 N. Knoll Ave. • Fresno, CA 93722

www.murach.com • murachbooks@murach.com

Editorial team

Author: Joel Murach

Writer: Mary Delamater

Editor: Anne Boehm

Production: Maria Spera

Books for Java programmers

Murach's Java Servlets and JSP (3rd Edition)

Murach's Android Programming (2nd Edition)

Books for database programmers

Murach's MySQL (2nd Edition)

Murach's Oracle SQL and PL/SQL for Developers (2nd Edition)

Murach's SQL Server 2016 for Developers

Books for web developers

Murach's HTML5 and CSS3 (3rd Edition)

Murach's JavaScript and jQuery (3rd Edition)

Murach's PHP and MySQL (2nd Edition)

Books for .NET programmers

Murach's C# 2015

Murach's ASP.NET 4.6 Web Programming with C# 2015

Books for Python programmers

Murach's Python Programming

For more on Murach books,
please visit us at www.murach.com

Printed in the United States of America

10 9 8 7 6 5 4 3 2 1
ISBN: 978-1-943872-07-7

Contents

Expanded contents

Section 2   Object-oriented programming

Chapter 10   More object-oriented programming skills

Section 3   More essential skills

Chapter 11   How to work with arrays

Chapter 18 How to get started with Swing

Section 6 Advanced skills

Introduction

Since its release in 1996, the Java language has established itself as one of the leading languages for object-oriented programming. Today, Java continues to be one of the most popular languages for application development, especially for web and mobile applications, like Android apps. And that's going to continue for many years to come, for several reasons.

First, developers can obtain Java and a wide variety of tools for working with Java for free. Second, Java code can run on any modern operating system. Third, Java is used by many of the largest enterprises in the world. Fourth, Java's development has always been guided by the Java community. As a result, the Java platform is able to evolve according to the needs of the programmers who use the language.

Who this book is for

This book is for anyone who wants to learn the core features of the Java language. It works if you have no programming experience at all. It works if you have programming experience with another language. It works if you already know an older version of Java and you want to get up-to-speed with the latest version. And it works if you've already read three or four other Java books and still don't know how to develop a real-world application.

If you're completely new to programming, the prerequisites are minimal. You just need to be familiar with the operation of the platform that you're using (like Windows, Mac OS X, or Linux) so you can perform tasks like opening, saving, printing, closing, copying, and deleting files.

What version of Java this book supports

This book shows how to use Java SE 9, which includes JDK (Java Development Kit) 9. However, since all versions of Java are backwards compatible, the code and skills presented in this book will work with later versions too. Besides that, this book clearly identifies when Java introduced its most recent features. That way, you can avoid these features if you want your code to work with earlier versions of Java.

What IDEs this book supports

This book supports two of the most popular IDEs (Integrated Development Environments) for working with Java, NetBeans and Eclipse. Both of these IDEs are available for free and run on all operating systems.

To support both IDEs, the printed pages show how to use NetBeans, and the download for this book includes a PDF file that shows how to use Eclipse. In addition, this download includes the source code for this book formatted for both NetBeans and Eclipse. As a result, it's easy to use either IDE with this book.

How to get the software you need

You can download all of the software that you need for this book for free from the Internet. To make that easier for you, appendix A shows how to download and install this software on Windows, and appendix B shows how to download and install this software on Mac OS X.

How this book helps you learn

Like all our books, this one has features that you won't find in competing books. That's why we believe that you'll learn faster and better with our book than with any other. Here are just some of those features.

- Unlike many Java books, this book shows you how to use an IDE to develop Java applications. That's how Java programming is done in the real world, and that by itself will help you learn faster.

- Unlike many Java books, this one focuses on the Java features that you will use every day. As a result, it doesn't waste your time by presenting features that you probably won't ever need.

- To help you learn how to develop applications at a professional level, this book presents complete, non-trivial applications. For example, chapter 15 presents a Product Manager application that uses presentation classes, business classes, and database classes to implement the three-tier architecture. You won't find complete, real-world applications like this in other Java books, even though studying these types of applications is the best way to master Java development.

- The exercises at the end of each chapter give you a chance to try out what you've just learned. They guide you through the development of some applications, and they challenge you to apply what you've learned in new ways. As a result, you'll gain valuable, hands-on experience in Java programming that will build your skills and your confidence.

- All of the information in this book is presented in our unique paired-pages format, with the essential syntax, guidelines, and examples on the right page and the perspective and extra explanation on the left page. This helps you learn more while reading less, and it helps you quickly find the information that you need when you use this book for reference.

How our downloadable files help you learn

If you go to our website at www.murach.com, you can download all the files that you need for getting the most from this book, in both NetBeans and Eclipse format. These files include:

- All of the applications presented in this book

- The starting code for the exercises that are at the end of each chapter

- The solutions to the exercises

These files let you test, review, and copy the code. In addition, if you have any problems with the exercises, the solutions are there to help you over the learning blocks, which is an essential part of the learning process. For more information on downloading and installing these files, please see appendix A (Windows) or appendix B (Mac OS X).

Support materials for instructors and trainers

If you're a college instructor or corporate trainer who would like to use this book as a course text, we offer a full set of the support materials you need for a turnkey course. That includes:

- Instructional objectives that help your students focus on the skills that they need to develop

- Dozens of projects that let your students prove how well they have mastered those skills

- Test banks that let you measure how well your students have mastered those skills

- A complete set of PowerPoint slides that you can use to review and reinforce the content of the book

To learn more about our instructor's materials, please go to our website at www.murachforinstructors.com if you're an instructor. Or if you're a trainer, please go to www.murach.com and click on the *Courseware for Trainers* link, or contact Kelly at 1-800-221-5528 or kelly@murach.com.

Companion books

When you finish this book, you'll have all of the Java skills that you need for moving on to web or mobile programming with Java. Then, if you want to move on to web programming, *Murach's Java Servlets and JSP* will show you how to use Java servlets and Java Server Pages to develop professional web applications. Or, if you want to move on to Android programming, *Murach's Android Programming* will get you started with that.

Please let us know what you think of this book

When we started the first edition of this book, our goals were (1) to teach you Java as quickly and easily as possible and (2) to teach you the practical Java concepts and skills that you need for developing real-world business applications. We've tried to improve on that with each subsequent edition, and as this 5th edition goes to press, we hope that the book is more effective than ever before. Many of the improvements have come from the feedback we've received from our readers, so if you have any comments about this book, we would appreciate hearing from you at murachbooks@murach.com.

Thanks for buying this book. We hope you enjoy reading it, and we wish you great success with your Java programming.

Joel Murach
Author

Anne Boehm
Editor

Section 1

Essential skills

This section gets you started quickly with Java programming. First, chapter 1 introduces you to Java applications and shows you how to use an IDE to work with Java projects. Then, chapter 2 shows you how to write your first Java applications. When you complete these chapters, you'll be able to write, test, and debug simple applications of your own.

After that, chapter 3 presents the details for working with the eight primitive data types. Chapter 4 presents the details for coding control statements. Chapter 5 shows how to code methods, handle exceptions, and validate data. And chapter 6 shows how to thoroughly test and debug an application. In addition, it shows how to deploy an application.

These are the essential skills that you'll use in almost every Java application that you develop. When you finish these chapters, you'll be able to write solid programs of your own. And you'll have the background that you need for learning how to develop object-oriented programs.

1

An introduction to Java

This chapter starts by presenting some background information about Java. This information isn't essential to developing Java applications, so you can skim it if you want. However, it does show how Java works and how it compares to other languages.

After the background information, this chapter shows how to use the NetBeans IDE (Integrated Development Environment) to work with a Java application. For this book, we recommend using NetBeans because we think it's the best and most intuitive IDE for getting started with Java.

However, Eclipse is another great IDE for working with Java applications, and many programmers prefer it. As a result, the download for this book includes a PDF file that shows how to use Eclipse with this book instead of NetBeans. So, if you want to use Eclipse, you can use this PDF file whenever you need to learn how to perform a task with Eclipse.

An overview of Java

In 1996, Sun Microsystems released a new programming language called Java. Today, Java is owned by Oracle and is one of the most widely used programming languages in the world.

Java timeline

Figure 1-1 starts by describing all major releases of Java starting with version 1.0 and ending with version 1.9. Throughout Java's history, the terms *Java Development Kit* (*JDK*) and *Software Development Kit* (*SDK*) have been used to describe the Java toolkit. In this book, we'll use the term *JDK* since it's the most current and commonly used term.

In addition, different numbering schemes have been used to indicate the version of Java. For example, Java SE 8 or Java 1.8 both refer to the eighth major version of Java. Similarly, Java SE 9 and Java 1.9 both refer to the ninth major version of Java. The documentation for the Java API uses the 1.x style of numbering. As a result, you should be familiar with it. However, it's also common to only use a single number such as Java 6.

This book shows how to use Java 9. However, Java is backwards compatible, so future versions of Java should work with this book too. In addition, most of the skills described in this book have been a part of Java since its earliest versions. As a result, earlier versions of Java work with most of the skills described in this book.

Java editions

This figure also describes the three most common editions of Java. To start, the Standard Edition is known as *Java SE*. It's designed for general purpose use on desktop computers and servers, and it's the edition that you'll learn how to work with in this book. For example, you can use Java SE to create a desktop application like the ones presented in section 4.

The Enterprise Edition is known as *Java EE*. It's designed to develop distributed applications that run on an intranet or the Internet. You can use Java EE to create web applications.

The Micro Edition is known as *Java ME*. It's designed to run on devices that have limited resources, such as mobile devices, TV set-top boxes, printers, smart cards, hotel room key cards, and so on.

With some older versions of Java, Java SE was known as J2SE (Java 2 Platform, Standard Edition). Similarly, Java EE was known as J2EE (Java 2 Platform, Enterprise Edition). If you are searching for information about Java on the Internet, you may come across these terms. However, they aren't commonly used anymore.

Java timeline

Year	Month	Release
1996	January	JDK 1.0
1997	February	JDK 1.1
1998	December	SDK 1.2
1999	August	Java 2 Platform, Standard Edition (J2SE)
	December	Java 2 Platform, Enterprise Edition (J2EE)
2000	May	J2SE with SDK 1.3
2002	February	J2SE with SDK 1.4
2004	September	J2SE 5.0 with JDK 1.5
2006	December	Java SE 6 with JDK 1.6
2011	July	Java SE 7 with JDK 1.7
2014	March	Java SE 8 with JDK 1.8
2017	July	Java SE 9 with JDK 1.9

Java editions

Platform	Description
Java SE (Standard Edition)	For general purpose use on desktop computers and servers. Some early versions were called J2SE (Java 2 Platform, Standard Edition).
Java EE (Enterprise Edition)	For developing distributed applications that run on an intranet or the Internet. Some early versions were called J2EE (Java 2 Platform, Enterprise Edition).
Java ME (Micro Edition)	For devices with limited resources such as mobile devices, TV set-top boxes, printers, and smart cards.

Description

- The *Java Development Kit (JDK)* includes a compiler, a runtime environment, and other tools that you can use to develop Java applications. Some early versions were called the Software Development Kit (SDK).

- Java was originally developed and released by Sun Microsystems. However, Oracle bought Sun Microsystems in April 2010.

Figure 1-1   Java timeline and editions

How Java compares to C++ and C#

Figure 1-2 compares Java to C++ and C#. As you can see, Java has some similarities and some differences with these languages.

When Sun's developers created Java, they tried to keep the syntax for Java similar to the syntax for C++. That way, it would be easy for C++ programmers to learn Java. In addition, they designed Java so its applications can be run on any computer platform without needing to be compiled for each platform. In contrast, C++ needs to be compiled for each platform.

Java was also designed to automatically handle many operations involving the allocation and de-allocation of memory. This is a key reason why it's easier to develop programs and write bug-free code with Java than with C++.

To provide these features, early versions of Java sacrificed some speed (or performance) when compared to C++. However, improvements in later versions of Java have greatly improved Java's speed. Now, Java runs faster than C++ in some contexts, and its performance is adequate in most contexts.

When Microsoft's developers created C#, they used many of the best ideas of Java. Like Java, C# uses a syntax that's similar to C++. In addition, C# handles memory operations automatically.

C# can run on any platform that has a runtime environment for it. However, Windows is the only operating system that fully supports a runtime environment for C#. As a result, C# is primarily used for developing applications that only need to run on Windows.

Java runs faster than C# in most contexts. However, the performance of C# is adequate in most contexts.

Operating systems that support Java

Windows

Mac OS X

Linux

Most versions of UNIX

Most other modern operating systems

A note about Android

- The Android operating system doesn't support Java in the same way as most operating systems. However, you can use all Java 7 language features and some Java 8 features to write the code for Android apps.

Java compared to C++

Feature	Description
Syntax	Java syntax is similar to C++ syntax.
Platforms	Compiled Java code can run on any platform that has a Java runtime environment. C++ code must be compiled once for each type of system that it is going to be run on.
Speed	C++ runs faster than Java in some contexts, but Java runs faster in other contexts.
Memory	Java handles most memory operations automatically, but C++ programmers must write code that manages memory.

Java compared to C#

Feature	Description
Syntax	Java syntax is similar to C# syntax.
Platforms	Like Java, compiled C# code can run on any platform that has a runtime environment for it.
Speed	Java runs faster than C# in most contexts.
Memory	Like Java, C# handles most memory operations automatically.

Figure 1-2   How Java compares to C++ and C#

Types of Java applications

You can use Java to write almost any type of application (also known as an app or a program). In this book, you'll learn how to develop desktop applications. However, you can also use Java to develop web applications and mobile apps.

Two types of desktop applications

Figure 1-3 shows two types of *desktop applications* that you can create with Java. This type of application runs directly on your computer.

The easiest type of desktop application to create is known as a *console application*. This type of application runs in the *console*, or *command prompt*, that's available from your operating system. The console provides an easy way to get input from the user and to display output to the user. In this figure, for example, I entered three values in the console application, and the application has performed a calculation and displayed the result. When you're learning Java, it's common to work with console applications until you have a solid understanding of the Java language.

Once you have a solid understanding of the Java language, you can create a desktop application that uses a *graphical user interface* (*GUI*). In this figure, for example, the GUI application performs the same tasks as the console application. In other words, it gets the same input from the user, performs the same calculation, and displays the same result. However, the GUI application is more user-friendly and intuitive.

Since developing the GUI for an application requires some significant Java coding skills, this book doesn't present a GUI application until section 4. Until then, this book uses console applications to teach the basics of Java.

A console application

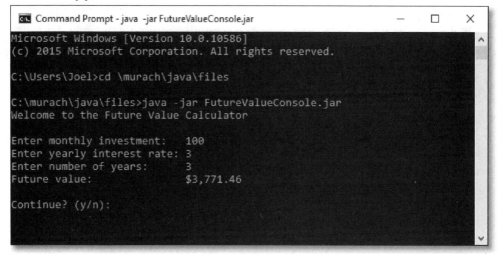

A GUI application

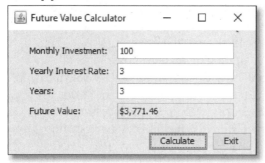

Description

- A *console application* uses the console to interact with the user.
- A *GUI application* uses a *graphical user interface* to interact with the user.

Figure 1-3   Two types of desktop applications

Web applications and mobile apps

In the early days of Java, which were also the early days of the Internet, one of the most exciting features of Java was that you could use it to create a special type of web-based application known as an *applet*. An applet could be stored in an HTML page and run inside a Java-enabled browser. With tightening security restrictions in recent years, applets are effectively obsolete. As a result, we don't cover them in this book.

However, many *web applications* still rely on servlets. A *servlet* is a special type of Java application that runs on the server and can be called by a client such as a web browser. This is illustrated by the first screen in figure 1-4. To start, when the user clicks the Calculate button, the web browser on the client sends a request to the servlet that's running on the server. This request includes the user input. When the servlet receives this request, it performs the calculation and returns the result to the browser, typically in the form of an HTML page.

In this figure, the servlet doesn't access a database. However, it's common for servlets to work with a database. For example, suppose a browser requests a servlet that displays all unprocessed invoices that are stored in a database. Then, when the servlet is executed, it reads data from the database, formats that data within an HTML page, and returns the HTML page to the browser.

When you create a servlet-based application like the one shown here, all the processing takes place on the server and only HTML, CSS, and JavaScript is returned to the browser. That means that anyone with an Internet or intranet connection, a web browser, and adequate security clearance can access and run a servlet-based application. To make it easy to store the results of a servlet within an HTML page, the Java EE specification provides for *JavaServer Pages* (JSPs). As a result, it's common to use JSPs with servlets.

You can also use Java to develop *mobile apps*, which are applications that run on a mobile device such as a smartphone or tablet. In particular, Java is commonly used to write the code for apps that run on Android devices. For example, this figure shows a mobile app that was developed with Java.

An app works much like a traditional application. However, the user interface has to be modified so that it's appropriate for a mobile device. In this figure, for example, the user interface has been modified to work with a touch-screen device that has a small screen and no keyboard. As a result, the user can use the keypad that's displayed onscreen to enter numbers and can press the Done button on this keypad to perform the calculation.

The Android operating system includes its own virtual machine that supports a subset of Java, including all features of Java 7 and some features of Java 8. As a result, if you use Java to develop Android apps, you can't use all of the features of Java, especially the newest ones. That's because the Android virtual machine is not a Java virtual machine. In other words, the Android virtual machine can't run compiled Java code, and a Java virtual machine can't run compiled Android code. Still, you can use most features of Java to write code for Android apps, and it's easy enough to compile that code so the Android virtual machine can run it.

A web application

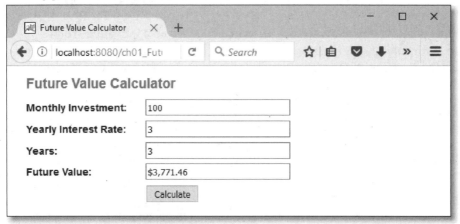

A mobile app

Description

- An *applet* is a type of Java application that runs within a web browser. In the past, it was possible to run applets in most web browsers. Today, fewer and fewer web browsers support applets, so they are effectively obsolete.

- A *servlet* is a type of Java application that runs on a web server. A servlet accepts requests from clients and returns responses to them. Typically, the clients are web browsers.

- A *mobile app* uses a mobile device such as a smartphone or tablet to interface with the user.

- The Android operating system supports a subset of Java, including all features of Java 7 and some features of Java 8.

Figure 1-4   Web applications and mobile apps

An introduction to Java development

At this point, you're ready to see the source code for an application. You're ready to learn how Java compiles and interprets this code. And you're ready to be introduced to some of the IDEs that you can use to develop this type of code.

The code for a console application

When you develop a Java application, you start by entering and editing the *source code*. To give you an idea of how the source code for a Java application works, figure 1-5 presents the code for the console version of the Future Value application shown in figure 1-3.

If you have experience with other programming languages, you may be able to understand much of this code already. If not, don't worry! You'll learn how all of this code works in the next few chapters. For now, here's a brief explanation of this code.

Most of the code for this application is stored in a *class* named FutureValueApp that corresponds with a file named FutureValueApp.java. This class begins with an opening brace ({) and ends with a closing brace (}).

Within this class, two *methods* are defined. These methods also begin with an opening brace and end with a closing brace, and they are indented to clearly show that they are contained within the class.

The first method, named main(), is the *main method* for the application. The code within this method is executed automatically when you run the application. In this case, the code prints data to the console to prompt the user, accepts the data the user enters at the console, and calculates the future value. To do that, the main() method calls a second method, named calculateFutureValue(). This method calculates the future value and returns the result to the main() method.

The code for a console application

```java
import java.text.NumberFormat;
import java.util.Scanner;

public class FutureValueApp {

    public static void main(String[] args) {
        System.out.println("Welcome to the Future Value Calculator");
        System.out.println();

        // get a Scanner object to scan for user input
        Scanner sc = new Scanner(System.in);

        String choice = "y";
        while (choice.equalsIgnoreCase("y")) {

            // get input from user
            System.out.print("Enter monthly investment:    ");
            double monthlyInvestment = sc.nextDouble();

            System.out.print("Enter yearly interest rate: ");
            double interestRate = sc.nextDouble();

            System.out.print("Enter number of years:      ");
            int years = sc.nextInt();

            // convert all input values to months
            double monthlyInterestRate = interestRate / 12 / 100;
            int months = years * 12;

            // call method to calculate future value
            double futureValue = calculateFutureValue(
                    monthlyInvestment, monthlyInterestRate, months);

            // format and display the result
            NumberFormat currency = NumberFormat.getCurrencyInstance();
            System.out.println("Future value:               "
                    + currency.format(futureValue) + "\n");

            // see if the user wants to continue
            System.out.print("Continue? (y/n): ");
            choice = sc.next();
            System.out.println();
        }
    }

    private static double calculateFutureValue(double monthlyInvestment,
            double monthlyInterestRate, int months) {
        double futureValue = 0;
        for (int i = 1; i <= months; i++) {
            futureValue = (futureValue + monthlyInvestment)
                    * (1 + monthlyInterestRate);
        }
        return futureValue;
    }
}
```

Figure 1-5   The code for a console application

How Java compiles and interprets code

Once the source code has been written, you use the *Java compiler* to compile the source code into a format known as Java *bytecode* as shown in figure 1-6. At this point, the bytecode can be run on any platform that has a *Java runtime environment* (*JRE*) installed on it. A JRE includes all of the software needed to run bytecode. Among other things, this includes an implementation of a *Java virtual machine* (*JVM*). This JVM includes a *Java interpreter* to translate the Java bytecode into native code that can be understood by the underlying operating system.

Most modern implementations of the JVM have replaced the Java interpreter with a *just-in-time compiler* (*JIT compiler*). A JIT compiler is similar to an interpreter in some ways, but it actually compiles the most used parts of the Java bytecode into native code and stores this code in a cache. This improves performance significantly.

Since JREs are available for all major operating systems, you can run Java on most platforms. This is what gives Java applications their *platform independence*. In contrast, C++ requires a specific compiler for each platform.

How Java compiles and interprets code

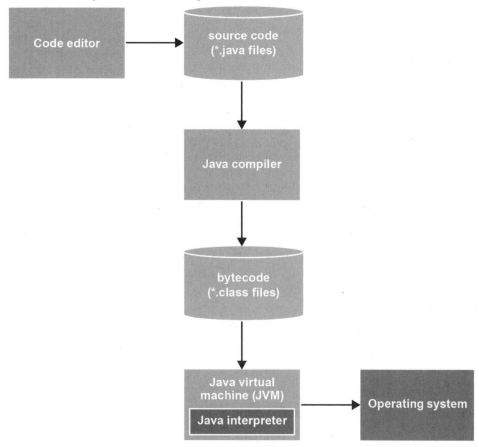

Description

- When you develop a Java application, you typically use a code editor to work with the *source code* for the application. Files that contain source code have the .java extension.

- The *Java compiler* translates Java source code into a *platform-independent* format known as Java *bytecode*. Files that contain Java bytecode have the .class extension.

- A *Java virtual machine* (*JVM*) includes a *Java interpreter* that executes Java bytecode. Most modern implementations of the JVM have replaced the Java interpreter with a *just-in-time compiler* (*JIT compiler*). A JIT compiler is similar to an interpreter in some ways, but it improves performance significantly.

- A *Java runtime environment* (*JRE*) has all of the components necessary to run bytecode including a JVM. Since JREs are available for most operating systems, Java bytecode can be run on most operating systems.

Figure 1-6   How Java compiles and interprets code

An introduction to Java IDEs

To develop Java applications, you typically use an *Integrated Development Environment (IDE)*. Although you can use a simple text editor with command-line tools, an IDE provides features that can make developing Java applications considerably easier. Figure 1-7 describes some of the features of the most popular IDEs.

All of the IDEs listed in this figure are either free or have a free edition. That makes them particularly attractive to students as well as programmers who are learning on their own. Most of these IDEs also run on all modern operating systems.

The first two IDEs listed in this figure, NetBeans and Eclipse, are two of the most popular Java IDEs. Both of these IDEs provide all of the features listed in this figure. For example, both of these IDEs help you complete your code and notify you of potential compile-time errors. They both automatically compile your code before you run it. And they both include a debugger that lets you perform standard debugging functions like setting breakpoints, stepping through code, and viewing the values of variables.

The third IDE listed in this figure, IntelliJ IDEA, isn't as popular as NetBeans and Eclipse. However, we have included it here to give you an idea of the range of IDE choices that are available for Java. In addition, other Java IDEs are available that aren't included here.

The fourth IDE listed in this figure, Android Studio, is designed for developing Android apps. It was developed by Google and IntelliJ, and is now the official IDE for developing Android apps.

Popular Java IDEs

IDE	Description
NetBeans	A free, open-source IDE that runs on most modern operating systems. NetBeans is commonly used for developing most types of Java applications, but not for Android apps.
Eclipse	A free, open-source IDE that runs on most modern operating systems. Eclipse is commonly used for developing most types of Java applications, but not for Android apps.
IntelliJ IDEA	The Community Edition of this IDE is a free, open-source IDE that runs on most modern operating systems.
Android Studio	An IDE specifically designed for Android development that's based on IntelliJ IDEA and backed by Google.

Features provided by most IDEs

- A code editor with code completion and error detection.
- Automatic compilation of classes when you run the application.
- A debugger that lets you set breakpoints, step through code, and view the values of active variables.

Description

- To develop Java applications, you typically use an *Integrated Development Environment* (*IDE*) like those listed above. All of these IDEs are either free or have free editions.

Figure 1-7   An introduction to Java IDEs

How to use NetBeans to work with existing projects

Now that you have some background information about Java, you're ready to start working with existing NetBeans projects. In particular, you're ready to learn how to open and run any of the projects for this book. You can download these projects as described in the appendixes for this book.

An introduction to NetBeans

Figure 1-8 shows the NetBeans IDE with an open Java project. In NetBeans, a *project* is a folder that contains all the files for an application. In this example, the project is named ch01_FutureValueConsole.

In the Projects window, the ch01_FutureValueConsole folder contains two subfolders: (1) Source Packages and (2) Libraries. The Source Packages folder contains the source files for the application, and the Libraries folder contains the Java *libraries* that are used by the application. In this case, the application uses just the JDK 1.8 libraries, but you can add others.

Within the Source Packages folder, the source files can be organized into *packages*. In this case, there's only one file, and it's stored in the default package. For simple applications like this, that's acceptable. However, as you develop more complex applications, it's considered a best practice to store your source files in packages as described in chapter 10.

In this figure, the application consists of a single source file named FutureValueApp.java, and this file is open in the *code editor*. Because this class contains the main() method for the application, it's called the *main class*. When you run an application, the main() method in the main class is executed by default.

As of this writing, Java 9 has not yet been released. That's why the JDK 1.8 library is used by this application, and that's why NetBeans 8.1 is used to work with this project. When Java 9 is released in July of 2017, though, you'll be able to use JDK 1.9 and NetBeans 9.0.

NetBeans with a Java project

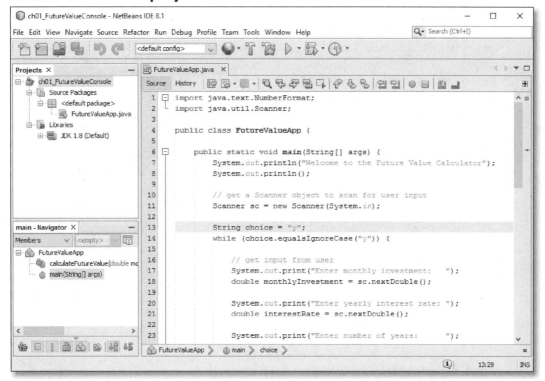

Description

- A NetBeans *project* consists of a top-level folder that contains the subfolders and files for an application.

- The Source Packages subfolder contains the .java files that make up the project. These files define *classes* that are later compiled into .class files.

- At a minimum, a project consists of a single class that contains the main() method. The main() method is the starting point for the application. The class that contains the main() method can be referred to as the *main class*.

- The .java files that make up a project can be organized into one or more *packages*. It's generally considered a best practice to organize your classes by storing each class within a package.

- The Libraries subfolder contains the *libraries* that are available to your project. These libraries contain the Java classes that you can use in your projects. By default, you can use the classes in the JDK libraries.

- The folders, files, and libraries that make up a Java project are listed in the Projects window. If this window isn't visible, you can display it by using the Window→Projects command. Then, you can expand and collapse the nodes in this window by clicking on the plus and minus signs.

- When Java 9 is released in July of 2017, you'll be able to use JDK 1.9 instead of 1.8 and NetBeans 9.0 instead of 8.1.

Figure 1-8   An introduction to NetBeans

How to open, close, and delete a project

To open a project in NetBeans, you use the Open Project dialog box shown in figure 1-9. This dialog box lets you navigate to the folder that contains the project you want to open. In this figure, for example, the Open Project dialog box shows all of the existing NetBeans projects in this folder:

`C:\murach\java\netbeans\book_apps`

To clearly indicate when a folder contains a Java project, the Open Project dialog box displays a small coffee cup icon to the left of the folder name. Then, you select the project you want to open and click the Open Project button.

When you're done working with a project, you can close it to remove it from the Projects window. To do that, you can use one of the techniques described in this figure.

You can also delete a project if you decide that you no longer want to work with it in NetBeans. Before the project is deleted, NetBeans will prompt you to confirm the deletion. Then, by default, NetBeans deletes all of the files for the project except for the source files. That way, you can work with those files outside of NetBeans if you want to. If you want to delete the source files as well, you can select the "Also Delete Sources" option in the dialog box that's displayed.

How to compile and run a project

Figure 1-9 also describes how to compile and run a project. An easy way to run a project is to press F6. Then, if the project has been modified since the last time it was compiled, NetBeans automatically compiles the project and runs the main() method in the main class.

If you want to compile a project without running it, you can use the Build command as described in this figure. You can also use the Clean and Build command to compile the project and remove any files that are no longer needed. This sometimes helps to get a project to work correctly after you have copied, moved, or renamed some of its files.

The dialog box for opening a project

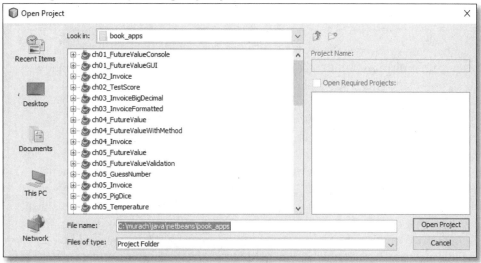

How to open, close, and delete a project

- To open a project, click the Open Project button in the toolbar or select the File→Open Project command. Then, use the Open Project dialog box that's displayed to locate and select the project and click the Open Project button.

- You can also open a project by using the File→Open Recent Project command and then selecting the project from the list that's displayed.

- To close a project, right-click on the project in the Projects window and select the Close command, or select the project and then use the File→Close Project command.

- To delete a project, right-click on the project in the Projects window and select the Delete command. When you do, you'll have the option of deleting just the files that NetBeans uses to manage the project or deleting all the folders and files for the project.

How to compile and run a project

- To run a project, press F6 or click the Run Project button in the toolbar.

- When you run a project, NetBeans automatically compiles it. As a result, you usually don't need to compile a project separately.

- To compile a project without running it, you can right-click on the project in the Projects window and select the Build command.

- To delete all compiled files for a project and compile them again, you can right-click on the project and select the Clean and Build command. This removes files that are no longer needed and compiles the entire project.

Mac OS X note

- To enable right-clicking with Mac OS X, you can edit the system preferences for the mouse.

Figure 1-9   Basic skills for working with existing projects

How to use the Output window
with a console application

When you run a console application in NetBeans, any data that's written to the console is displayed in the Output window. In addition, The Output window can accept input. This is illustrated in figure 1-10.

In this figure, the application prompts the user to enter the monthly investment amount, the yearly interest rate, and the number of years. Then, it calculates and displays the future value of this series of investments.

This application started by displaying a welcome message. Then, it displayed a prompt indicating that the user should enter a monthly investment. In response, the user typed "100" and pressed Enter. After that, the application prompted the user for two more values, and the user entered "3" for those values. Then, the application displayed the future value and asked the user if it should continue. At this point, the application is still running, and the user can enter "y" to perform another calculation or "n" to end the application.

When you're learning Java, it's common to create applications that use the console to display output and get input. Because of that, the first three sections of this book show how to code console applications. Then, section 4 of this book teaches you how to create applications that use a graphical user interface (GUI).

An application that uses the Output window for input and output

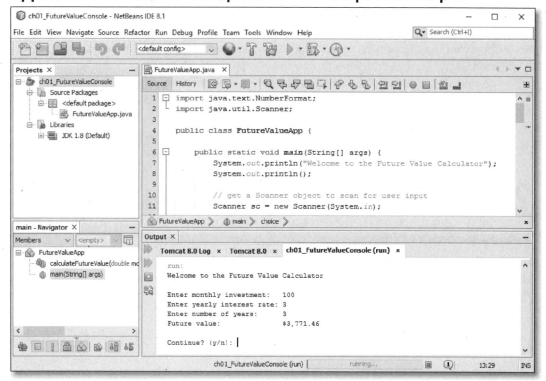

Description

- When you run an application that prints data to the console, that data is displayed in the Output window.

- When you run an application that requests input from the console, the Output window pauses to accept the input. Then, you can click in the Output window, type the input, and press the Enter key.

- In addition to displaying output and accepting input, the Output window can display other information. For example, it can display messages when the application is compiled, and it can display errors that are encountered when an application is run.

Figure 1-10   How to use the Output window with a console application

How to work with two or more projects

Up to this point, you've seen how to work with a single project in NetBeans. However, NetBeans lets you open and work with two or more projects at the same time. If, for example, you want to run some of the projects from the download for this book before you start creating your own projects, you can open those projects in NetBeans at the same time. You'll get a chance to do that in the first exercise for this chapter.

Figure 1-11 presents the skills for working with two or more projects. When you open two or more projects, all of the open projects appear in the Projects window. Then, when you open any of the files for a project, they appear in separate tabs in the main window. After you open a file, you can run the project for that file by pressing F6 or clicking on the Run Project button in the toolbar. Or, if you want to run a different project, you can select the project in the Projects window and then press F6 or click on the Run Project button.

NetBeans with two open projects

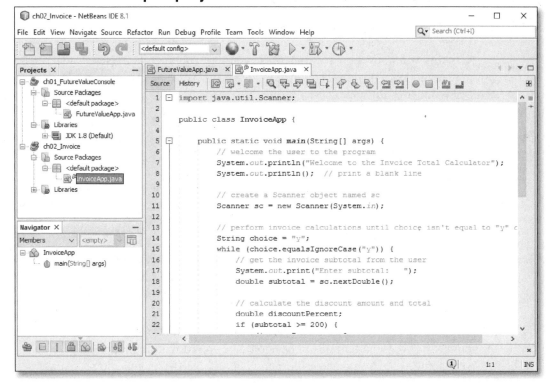

Description

- NetBeans lets you open and work with two or more projects at the same time.
- When you open multiple projects, they all appear in the Projects window.
- When you open a file for a project, NetBeans opens the file in a tab in the main window.
- To run the currently selected project, press F6 or click the Run Project button in the toolbar.
- To change the currently selected project, click on the project in the Projects window.

Figure 1-11   How to work with two or more projects

How to use NetBeans to develop new projects

Now that you know how to work with existing Java projects in NetBeans, you're ready to learn how to develop new Java projects. That's what you'll learn in the remainder of this chapter.

How to create a new project

Figure 1-12 presents the dialog boxes for creating a Java application. You use the New Project dialog box to choose the type of project you want to create. In most cases, you'll create a Java Application project as shown here. Then, when you click the Next button, NetBeans displays a New Java Application dialog box like the second one in this figure.

The New Java Application dialog box lets you enter a name and location for the project. In this figure, for example, the project name is "ch01_Test" and it will be stored in this folder:

`C:\murach\java\netbeans\book_apps`

If you install the source code for this book as described in the appendix, all of the applications presented in this book should be stored within this folder.

By default, when you create a Java application, NetBeans generates a main class with a main() method. If that's not what you want, you can remove the check mark from the "Create Main Class" option. In most cases, though, you'll leave this option checked. Then, you can enter a name for the main class. In addition, you typically want to enter a package for this class.

For the project in this figure, for example, NetBeans suggested "ch01_test.Ch01_Test". Here, "ch01_test" would be the name of the package and "Ch01_Test" would be the name of the class. However, I deleted the name of the package, and I changed the name of the class to TestApp. As a result, NetBeans created a project named ch01_Test that contains a main class named TestApp in the default package.

When this dialog box is complete, you can click the Finish button to create the project and the class that contains the main() method. Then, NetBeans creates a folder that corresponds with the project name, and it creates some additional files that it uses to configure the project.

The dialog boxes for creating a new project

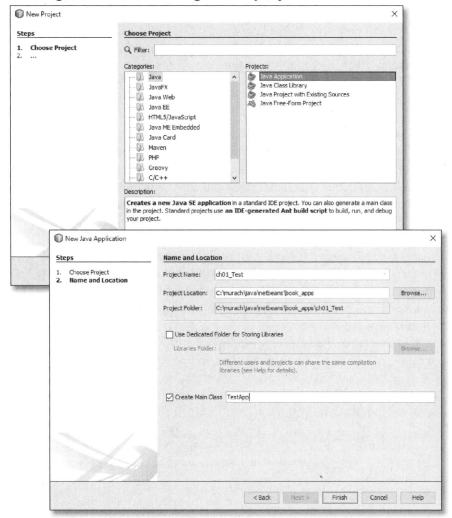

Description

- To create a new project, use the File→New Project command or click the New Project button in the toolbar to display the New Project dialog box. Then, select a project type, click the Next button, and complete the dialog box that's displayed.

- To create a Java Application project, enter the project name and location and the name you want to use for the main class. It's generally considered a best practice to enter a package name for each class.

Figure 1-12   How to create a new project

How to work with Java source code and files

When you create a new project that contains a class with a main() method, the class is typically opened in a new code editor window as shown in figure 1-13. To make it easier for you to recognize the Java syntax, the code editor uses different colors for different language elements. In addition, NetBeans provides standard File and Edit menus and keystroke shortcuts that let you save and edit the source code. For example, you can press Ctrl+S to save your source code, and you can use standard commands to cut, copy, and paste code.

When you create a project with a main class, NetBeans generates some code for you. In this figure, for example, NetBeans generated the code that declares the class, the code that declares the main() method, and comments that describe the class and method. Although you can delete or modify the class and method declarations, you won't usually do that. However, you may want to delete or modify some or all of the comments.

If the source code you want to work with isn't displayed in a code editor window, you can use the Projects window to navigate to the .java file and then double-click on it to open it in a code editor window. In this figure, for example, you could double-click on the TestApp.java file in the Projects window to open it in the code editor window.

You can also rename or delete a .java file from the Projects window. To do that, just right-click on the file and select the appropriate command. If you rename a file, NetBeans automatically changes both the name of the .java file and the name of the class. Since the name of the .java file must match the name of the class, this is usually what you want.

NetBean's code editor with the starting source code for a project

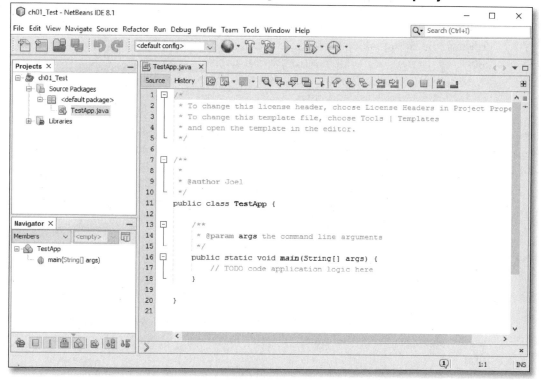

Description

- To open a .java file in the *code editor*, double-click on it in the Projects window. Then, you can use normal editing techniques to work with the source code.

- To collapse the code for a method or comment, click the minus sign (-) to its left. Then, a plus sign (+) appears to the left of the method or comment, and you can click the plus sign to display the code again.

- To save the source code for a file, use the File→Save command (Ctrl+S) or click the Save All Files button in the toolbar. This automatically compiles the file so it doesn't have to be compiled when the project is run.

- To rename a file, right-click on it, select the Refactor→Rename command, and enter the new name in the resulting dialog box.

- To delete a file, you can right-click on it, select the Delete command, and confirm the deletion in the resulting dialog box.

Figure 1-13   How to work with Java source code and files

How to use the code completion feature

Figure 1-14 shows how to use the *code completion feature*. This feature prevents you from making typing mistakes, and it allows you to discover what fields and methods are available from various classes and objects. In this figure, for example, I started to enter a statement that prints text to the console.

First, I entered "sys" and pressed Ctrl+Spacebar (both keys at the same time). This displayed a list with the System class as the only option. Then, I pressed the Enter key to automatically enter the rest of the class name.

Next, I typed a period. This displayed a list of fields and methods available from the System class. Then, I used the arrow keys to select the field named out and pressed the Enter key to automatically enter that field name.

Finally, I typed another period. This displayed a long list of method names. Then, I typed "pr" to scroll down the list to the methods that start with "pr", and I used the arrow keys to select one of the println() methods. At this point, I could press Enter to have NetBeans enter the method into the editor for me.

When you use code completion, it automatically enters opening and closing parentheses and arguments whenever they're needed. In this figure, for example, the selected println() method is followed by a set of parentheses that contains a string argument. When I inserted this method into the code editor, NetBeans inserted the parentheses and highlighted the argument so I could enter a value for it.

The code completion feature can also make it easy for you to enter values for string variables. If you type a quotation mark to identify a string value, the code completion feature automatically adds the closing quotation mark and places the cursor between the two quotes. At this point, you can enter the text for the string.

If you experiment with the code completion feature, you'll quickly see when it helps you enter code more quickly and when it makes sense to enter the code yourself. In addition, you'll see that it helps you discover the fields and methods that are available to the various classes and objects that you're working with. This will make more sense as you learn more about Java in the next few chapters.

The code editor with a code completion list

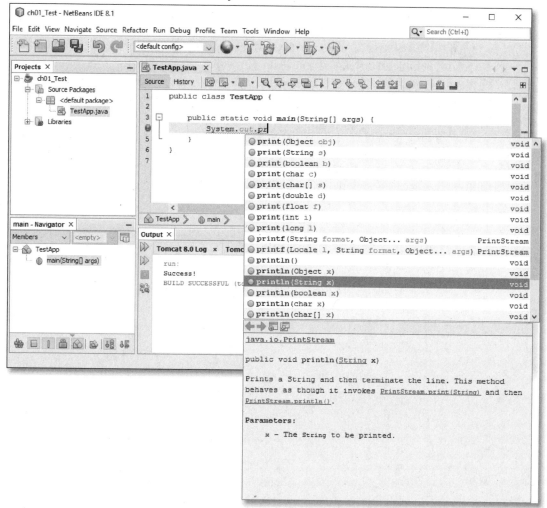

Description

- You can use the *code completion feature* to help you enter the names of classes and objects and select from the methods and fields that are available for a class or object.

- To activate the code completion feature for entering a class or object name, press Ctrl+Spacebar after entering one or more letters. Then, a list of all the classes and objects that start with those letters is displayed.

- To insert an item from a code completion list, select the item and then press the Enter key.

- If you enter the opening quote for a string value, the code completion feature automatically adds the closing quote and places the cursor between the two quotes.

Figure 1-14   How to use the code completion feature

How to detect and correct syntax errors

A *syntax error* is a statement that won't compile. As you enter text into the code editor, NetBeans displays syntax errors whenever it detects them. In figure 1-15, for example, NetBeans displays an error that indicates that a semicolon needs to be entered to complete the statement. This error is marked with a red icon to the left of the statement. In addition, the statement that contains the error is marked with a wavy red underline.

If you position the mouse pointer over the red error icon or over the statement itself, NetBeans displays a description of the error. In this figure, for example, the description indicates that NetBeans expects a semicolon at the end of the statement. As a result, you can fix the error by typing the semicolon.

The code editor with an error displayed

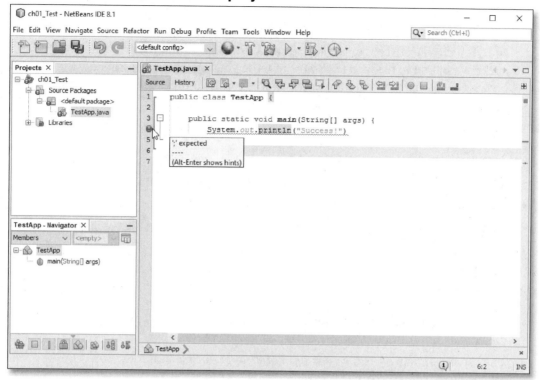

Description

- NetBeans often detects *syntax errors* as you enter code into the code editor.
- When NetBeans detects a syntax error, it displays a red error icon to the left of the statement in error, and it places a red wavy line under the statement.
- To get more information about a syntax error, you can position the mouse pointer over the error icon. Or, you can move the cursor to the line that contains the error and press Alt+Enter.

Figure 1-15 How to detect and correct syntax errors

Perspective

In this chapter, you were introduced to Java, and you learned how to use an IDE such as NetBeans to create and run a Java application. With that as background, you're ready to learn how to write your own Java applications. But first, I recommend that you familiarize yourself with an IDE such as NetBeans by doing the exercises at the end of this chapter.

Summary

- You can use the *Java Development Kit* (*JDK*) to develop Java applications.
- The *Standard Edition* (*SE*) of Java is called *Java SE*.
- You can use Java SE to create *desktop applications* that run on your computer.
- A desktop application can use a *graphical user interface* (*GUI*) or a *console* to display output and get user input. Applications that use a console to interact with the user are known as *console applications*.
- You can use the Enterprise Edition of Java, which is known as *Java EE*, to create *web applications*.
- You can use Java to write the code for *mobile apps* such as Android apps.
- The *Java compiler* translates *source code* into a *platform-independent* format known as Java *bytecode*.
- A *Java runtime environment* (*JRE*) includes all of the software needed to run bytecode.
- A JRE includes an implementation of a *Java virtual machine* (*JVM*).
- A JVM includes a *Java interpreter* to translate the Java bytecode into native code that can be understood by the underlying operating system.
- An *Integrated Development Environment* (*IDE*) can make working with Java easier by providing code completion, error detection, automatic compilation, and a debugger.
- NetBeans and Eclipse are two of the most commonly used IDEs for Java development.
- Java code is stored in *classes*. The *main class* of an application is the class that contains the *main method* (named main()), which is the starting point of the application.

Before you do the exercises for this chapter

Before you do any of the exercises in this book, you need to install the JDK and NetBeans. In addition, you need to install the source code for this book from our website (www.murach.com). For complete instructions, see the appendixes of this book.

If you want to use Eclipse instead of NetBeans, you can find an Eclipse version of these exercises in the PDF file that's included in the download for this book.

Exercise 1-1   Use NetBeans to open and run two projects

This exercise shows you how to use NetBeans to open and run two console applications.

Open and run the Invoice application

1. Start NetBeans.

2. Open the project named ch01_ex1_Invoice. On a Windows system, the project should be stored in this directory:

    ```
    C:\murach\java\netbeans\ex_starts
    ```

3. Open the InvoiceApp.java file in the code editor and review its code to get an idea of how this application works.

4. Press F6 to run the application. Enter a subtotal when you're prompted, and then enter "n" when you're asked if you want to continue.

Open and run the Test Score application

5. Open the project named ch01_ex2_TestScore. Then, open the TestScoreApp.java file in the code editor and review its code.

6. Click the Run Project button in the toolbar to run the application. Enter one or more grades when you're prompted, and enter 999 to end the application.

Run the applications again

7. Select the Invoice application in the Projects window. Then, press F6 to run this application.

8. Select the Test Score application in the Projects window and click the Run Project button to run this application.

9. Close both projects.

Exercise 1-2   Use NetBeans to develop an application

This exercise guides you through the process of using NetBeans to enter, save, compile, and run a simple application.

Enter the source code and run the application

1. Start NetBeans.

2. Select the File→New Project command from the NetBeans menu system. Then, use the resulting dialog boxes to create a Java Application project named ch01_Test that contains a main class named TestApp. On a Windows system, store the project in this directory:

    ```
    C:\murach\java\netbeans\ex_starts
    ```

3. Modify the generated code for the TestApp class so it looks like this (type carefully and use the same capitalization):

    ```
    public class TestApp {
        public static void main(String[] args) {
            System.out.println("Success!");
        }
    }
    ```

4. Press F6 to compile and run the application. This should display "Success!" in the Output window.

Use the code completion feature

5. Enter the statement that starts with System.out again, right after the first statement. This time, type "sys" and then press Ctrl+Spacebar. Then, use the code completion feature to select the System class, and complete the statement.

6. Enter this statement a third time, right after the second statement. This time, type System, enter a period, and select out from the list that's displayed. Then, enter another period, select the println() method, and complete the statement. You should now have the same statement three times in a row.

7. Run the application again. It should display the message three times in a row in the Output window.

Introduce and correct a syntax error

8. In the code editor window, delete the semicolon at the end of the first println() method. When you do, NetBeans should display an error icon to the left of the statement.

9. Correct the error. When you do, NetBeans should remove the error icon.

10. Use the File→Save command (Ctrl+S) to save the changes.

2

How to write your first Java applications

Once you've installed Java and an IDE, the quickest and best way to *learn* Java programming is to *do* Java programming. That's why this chapter shows you how to write complete Java applications that get input from a user, make calculations, and display output. When you finish this chapter, you should be able to write comparable applications of your own.

Basic coding skills

This chapter starts by introducing you to some basic coding skills. You'll use these skills for every Java program you develop.

How to code statements

The *statements* in a program direct the operation of the program. When you code a statement, you can start it anywhere in a coding line, you can continue it from one line to another, and you can code one or more spaces anywhere a single space is valid. In the first example in figure 2-1, the lines that aren't shaded are statements.

To end most statements, you use a semicolon. But when a statement requires a set of braces {}, it ends with the right brace. Then, the statements within the braces are referred to as a *block* of code. For example, the InvoiceApp class and the main() method shown in this figure both contain a block of code.

To make a program easier to read, you should use indentation and spacing to align statements and blocks of code. This is illustrated by the program in this figure and by all of the programs and examples in this book.

How to code comments

The *comments* in a program typically document what the statements do. Since the Java compiler ignores comments, you can include them anywhere in a program without affecting your code. In the first example in figure 2-1, the comments are shaded.

A *single-line comment* is typically used to describe one or more lines of code. This type of comment starts with two slashes (//) that tell the compiler to ignore all characters until the end of the current line. In the first example in this figure, you can see four single-line comments that are used to describe groups of statements. The other comment is coded after a statement. This type of comment is sometimes referred to as an *end-of-line comment*.

The second example in this figure shows how to code a *block comment*. This type of comment is typically used to document information that applies to a block of code. This information can include the author's name, program completion date, the purpose of the code, the files used by the code, and so on.

Although many programmers sprinkle their code with comments, that shouldn't be necessary if you write code that's easy to read and understand. Instead, you should use comments only to clarify code that's difficult to understand. In this figure, for example, an experienced Java programmer wouldn't need any of the single-line comments.

One problem with comments is that they may not accurately represent what the code does. This often happens when a programmer changes the code, but doesn't change the comments that go along with it. Then, it's even harder to understand the code because the comments are misleading. So if you change the code that you've written comments for, be sure to change the comments too.

An application that consists of statements and comments

```java
import java.util.Scanner;

public class InvoiceApp {

    public static void main(String[] args) {
        // display a welcome message
        System.out.println("Welcome to the Invoice Total Calculator");
        System.out.println();   // print a blank line

        // get the input from the user
        Scanner sc = new Scanner(System.in);
        System.out.print("Enter subtotal:   ");
        double subtotal = sc.nextDouble();

        // calculate the discount amount and total
        double discountPercent = .2;
        double discountAmount = subtotal * discountPercent;
        double invoiceTotal = subtotal - discountAmount;

        // format and display the result
        String message = "Discount percent: " + discountPercent + "\n"
                       + "Discount amount:  " + discountAmount + "\n"
                       + "Invoice total:    " + invoiceTotal + "\n";
        System.out.println(message);
    }
}
```

A block comment that could be coded at the start of a program

```java
/*
 * Author:   J. Murach
 * Purpose: This program uses the console to get a subtotal from the user,
 *          and it calculates the discount amount and total and displays them.
 */
```

Description

- *Statements* direct the operations of a program, and *comments* typically document what the statements do.

- You can start a statement at any point in a line and continue the statement from one line to the next. To make a program easier to read, you should use indentation and extra spaces to align statements and parts of statements.

- Most statements end with a semicolon. But when a statement requires a set of braces { }, the statement ends with the right brace. Then, the code within the braces can be referred to as a *block* of code.

- To code a *single-line comment*, type // followed by the comment. You can code a single-line comment on a line by itself or after a statement. A comment that's coded after a statement is sometimes called an *end-of-line comment*.

- To code a *block comment*, type /* at the start of the block and */ at the end. You can also code asterisks to identify the lines in the block, but that isn't necessary.

Figure 2-1   How to code statements and comments

How to create identifiers

As you code a Java program, you need to create and use *identifiers*. These are the names in the program that you define. In each program, for example, you need to create an identifier for the name of the program and for the variables that are used by the program.

Figure 2-2 shows you how to create identifiers. In brief, you must start each identifier with a letter, underscore, or dollar sign. After that first character, you can use any combination of letters, underscores, dollar signs, or digits.

Since Java is case-sensitive, you need to be careful when you create and use identifiers. If, for example, you define an identifier as CustomerAddress, you can't refer to it later as Customeraddress. That's a common coding error.

When you create an identifier, you should try to make the name both meaningful and easy to remember. To make a name meaningful, you should use as many characters as you need, so it's easy for other programmers to read and understand your code. For instance, netPrice is more meaningful than nPrice, and nPrice is more meaningful than np.

To make a name easy to remember, you should avoid abbreviations. If, for example, you use nwCst as an identifier, you may have difficulty remembering whether it was nCust, nwCust, or nwCst later on. If you code the name as newCustomer, though, you won't have any trouble remembering what it was. Yes, you type more characters when you create identifiers that are meaningful and easy to remember, but that will be more than justified by the time you'll save when you test, debug, and maintain the program.

For some common identifiers, though, programmers typically use just one or two lowercase letters. For instance, they often use the letters *i*, *j*, and *k* to identify counter variables like the ones shown later in this chapter.

Note that you can't create an identifier that's the same as one of the Java *keywords*. These 50 keywords are reserved by the Java language. To help you identify keywords in your code, Java IDEs display these keywords in a different color than the rest of the Java code. As you progress through this book, you'll learn how to use most of these keywords.

Valid identifiers

```
InvoiceApp          $orderTotal         i
Invoice             _orderTotal         x
InvoiceApp2         input_string        TITLE
subtotal            _get_total          MONTHS_PER_YEAR
discountPercent     $_64_Valid
```

The rules for naming an identifier

- Start each identifier with a letter, underscore, or dollar sign. Use letters, dollar signs, underscores, or digits for subsequent characters.

- Use up to 255 characters.

- Don't use Java keywords.

Keywords

```
boolean     if          interface   class       true
char        else        package     volatile    false
byte        final       switch      while       throws
float       private     case        return      native
void        protected   break       throw       implements
short       public      default     try         import
double      static      for         catch       synchronized
int         new         continue    finally     const
long        this        do          transient   goto
abstract    super       extends     instanceof  null
```

Description

- An *identifier* is any name that you create in a Java program. These can be the names of classes, methods, variables, and so on.

- A *keyword* is a word that's reserved by the Java language. As a result, you can't use keywords as identifiers.

- When you refer to an identifier, be sure to use the correct uppercase and lowercase letters because Java is a case-sensitive language.

Figure 2-2   How to create identifiers

How to declare a class and a main method

In the last chapter, you learned that if you use an IDE to create a project, it typically generates a *class* with a *main method* named main(). Now, figure 2-3 presents the syntax for declaring a class and a main method.

To code a class, you begin with a *class declaration*. In the syntax for declaring a class, the boldfaced words are Java keywords, and the words that aren't boldfaced represent code that the programmer supplies. The bar (|) in this syntax means that you have a choice between the two items that the bar separates. In this case, the bar means that you can start the declaration with the public keyword or the private keyword.

The public and private keywords are *access modifiers* that control the *scope* of a class. Usually, a class is declared public, which means that other classes can access it. Later in this book, you'll learn when and how to use private classes.

After the public and class keywords, you code the name of the class using the basic rules for creating an identifier. When you do, it's a common coding convention to start every word within a class name with a capital letter and to use letters and digits only. We also recommend that you use a noun or a noun that's preceded by one or more adjectives for your class names.

After the class name, the syntax summary shows a left brace, the statements that make up the class, and a right brace. It's a good coding practice, though, to type your ending brace right after you type the starting brace to prevent missing braces. When you use an IDE, the IDE typically adds the ending brace automatically after you type the starting brace and press Enter.

The two InvoiceApp classes in this figure show how a class works. The only difference between the two classes is where the starting braces for the class and the block of code within the class are placed. Although either technique is acceptable, we've chosen to use the first technique for this book.

Within a class, you code one or more *methods*, which are blocks of code that perform the actions of the program (they're similar to *functions* in some programming languages). As you know, the main method is a special kind of method that's automatically executed when you run the class that contains it. All Java programs contain a main method that starts the program.

To code a main method, you begin by coding a *main method declaration* within the class declaration as shown in the two InvoiceApp classes in this figure. Although I won't describe this declaration, you should know that all main method declarations are coded exactly as shown. You'll learn more about the keywords used by this declaration later in this book.

To make the structure of the main method clear, its code is indented within the InvoiceApp class. In addition, its ending brace is aligned with the beginning of the method declaration. If the starting brace is coded on a separate line, it is also aligned with the beginning of the method declaration. That makes it easy to see where the method begins and ends. Then, between the braces, you can see the one statement that this main method performs. This statement displays a message to the user, and you'll learn more about it later in this chapter.

The syntax for declaring a class

```
public|private class ClassName {
    statements
}
```

The syntax for declaring a main method

```
public static void main(String[] args) {
    statements
}
```

A public class named InvoiceApp that contains a main method

```
public class InvoiceApp {                       // declare and begin the class
    public static void main(String[] args){
        System.out.println("Welcome to the Invoice Total Calculator");
    }
}                                               // end the class
```

The same class with different brace placement

```
public class InvoiceApp                         // declare the class
{                                               // begin the class
    public static void main(String[] args)
    {
        System.out.println("Welcome to the Invoice Total Calculator");
    }
}                                               // end the class
```

The rules for naming a class

- Start the name with a capital letter.
- Use letters and digits only.
- Follow the other rules for naming an identifier.

Recommendations for naming a class

- Start every word within a class name with an initial cap.
- Each class name should be a noun or a noun that's preceded by one or more adjectives.

Description

- A Java application consists of one or more *classes* that start with a *class declaration*. You write the code for the class within the opening and closing braces of the declaration.
- The public and private keywords are *access modifiers* that control what parts of the program can use the class. Most classes are declared public, which means that the class can be used by all parts of the program.
- The file name for a class is the same as the class name with .java as the extension.
- A *method* is a block of code that performs a task.
- Every Java application contains one *main method* that you can declare exactly as shown above. This is called the *main method declaration*.
- The statements between the braces in a main method declaration are run when the program is executed.

Figure 2-3   How to declare a class and a main method

How to work with numeric variables

This topic shows how to work with numeric variables. It introduces you to the use of variables, assignment statements, arithmetic expressions, and two of the eight primitive data types that are supported by Java.

How to declare and initialize variables

A *variable* stores a value that can change, or *vary*, as a program executes. Before you can use a variable, you must *declare* its data type and name, and you must *assign* a value to it to *initialize* it. To do that, you can use either of the techniques described in figure 2-4.

This figure starts by summarizing two of the primitive *data types* that are available from Java. You can use the *int* data type to store *integers*, which are numbers that don't contain decimal places (whole numbers), and you can use the *double* data type to store numbers that contain decimal places.

To show how this works, the first example uses one statement to declare an int variable named counter. Then, it uses a second statement to assign an initial value of 1. However, it's often easier to declare a variable and assign an initial value in a single statement as shown by the second example. Here, the first statement declares an int variable named counter and assigns an initial value of 1. And the second statement declares a double variable named unitPrice and assigns an initial value of 14.95.

When you assign literal values to double types, it's a good coding practice to include a decimal point, even if the initial value is a whole number. If, for example, you want to assign the number 29 to the variable, you should code the number as 29.0. This isn't required, but it clearly indicates that you are working with the double type, not the int type.

If you follow the naming recommendations in this figure as you name variables, it makes your programs easier to read and debug. In particular, you should capitalize the first letter in each word of the variable name, except the first word, as in scoreCounter or unitPrice. This is referred to as *camel case*, and it's the standard convention for naming variables when you're using Java.

When you initialize a variable, you can assign a *literal* value like 1 or 14.95 to a variable as illustrated by the examples in this figure. However, you can also initialize a variable to the value of another variable or to the value of an expression like the arithmetic expressions shown in the next figure.

How to code assignment statements

After you declare a variable, you can assign a new value to it. To do that, you code an *assignment statement* that consists of the variable name, an equals sign, and a new value. The new value can be a literal value, the name of another variable as shown in this figure, or the result of an expression as shown in the next figure.

Two of the eight primitive data types

Type	Description
`int`	Integers (whole numbers).
`double`	Double-precision, floating-point numbers (decimal numbers).

How to declare a variable and assign a value in two statements

Syntax

```
type variableName;
variableName = value;
```

Example

```
int counter;          // declaration statement
counter = 1;          // assignment statement
```

How to declare a variable and assign a value in one statement

Syntax

```
type variableName = value;
```

Examples

```
int counter = 1;            // declare and initialize an int variable
double unitPrice = 14.95;   // declare and initialize a double variable
```

An example that uses assignment statements

```
int quantity = 0;           // declare and initialize an int variable
int maxQuantity = 100;      // declare and initialize another int variable

// two assignment statements
quantity = 10;              // quantity is now 10
quantity = maxQuantity;     // quantity is now 100
```

Description

- A *variable* stores a value that can change, or *vary*, as a program executes.

- Before you can use a variable, you must *declare* its data type. Then, you can *assign* a value to the variable. This value can be a literal value, another variable, or an expression like the arithmetic expressions shown in the next figure.

- Assigning an initial value to a variable is known as *initializing* a variable. It's a common practice to declare a variable and initialize it in a single statement. It's common to initialize int variables to 0 and double variables to 0.0.

- An *assignment statement* assigns a value to a variable. If the data type has already been declared, an assignment statement does not include the data type.

Naming recommendations for variables

- Start variable names with a lowercase letter and capitalize the first letter in all words after the first word.

- Each variable name should be a noun or a noun preceded by one or more adjectives.

- Try to use meaningful names that are easy to remember.

Figure 2-4   How to declare variables and assign values to them

How to code arithmetic expressions

To code simple *arithmetic expressions*, you can use *arithmetic operators* like the four operators summarized in figure 2-5. As the first group of statements shows, these operators work the way you would expect them to with one exception. If you divide one integer into another integer, the result doesn't include any decimal places. In contrast, if you divide a double into a double, the result includes decimal places.

When you code assignment statements, you can code the same variable on both sides of the equals sign. Then, you can include the variable on the right side of the equals sign in an arithmetic expression. For example, you can add 1 to the value of a variable named counter with a statement like this:

```
counter = counter + 1;
```

In this case, if counter has a value of 5 when the statement starts, it has a value of 6 when the statement finishes. This concept is illustrated by the second and third groups of statements.

If you mix integer and double variables in the same arithmetic expression, Java automatically *casts* (converts) the int value to a double value and uses the double type for the result. If that's not what you want, you can explicitly cast the double value to an int value by coding the int type in parentheses just before the double value. Then, Java uses the int type for the result. This is illustrated by the fourth group of statements.

Conversely, if you want to force Java to convert an int type to a double type, you can code the double type in parentheses just before the int type. Then, Java uses the double type for the result. This is also illustrated by the fourth group of statements.

Although it's not shown in this figure, you can also code expressions that contain two or more operators. When you do that, you need to be sure that the operations are done in the correct sequence. You'll learn more about that in the next chapter.

The basic operators that you can use in arithmetic expressions

Operator	Name	Description
+	Addition	Adds two operands.
–	Subtraction	Subtracts the right operand from the left operand.
*	Multiplication	Multiplies the right operand and the left operand.
/	Division	Divides the right operand into the left operand. If both operands are integers, then the result is an integer.

Statements that use simple arithmetic expressions

```
// integer arithmetic
int x = 14;
int y = 8;
int result1 = x + y;          // result1 = 22
int result2 = x - y;          // result2 = 6
int result3 = x * y;          // result3 = 112
int result4 = x / y;          // result4 = 1

// double arithmetic
double a = 8.5;
double b = 3.4;
double result5 = a + b;       // result5 = 11.9
double result6 = a - b;       // result6 = 5.1
double result7= a * b;        // result7 = 28.9
double result8 = a / b;       // result8 = 2.5
```

Statements that increment a counter variable

```
int invoiceCount = 0;
invoiceCount = invoiceCount + 1;              // invoiceCount = 1
invoiceCount = invoiceCount + 1;              // invoiceCount = 2
```

Statements that add amounts to a total

```
double invoiceAmount1 = 150.25;
double invoiceAmount2 = 100.75;
double invoiceTotal = 0.0;
invoiceTotal = invoiceTotal + invoiceAmount1;     // invoiceTotal = 150.25
invoiceTotal = invoiceTotal + invoiceAmount2;     // invoiceTotal = 251.00
```

Statements that mix int and double variables

```
double result9 = invoiceTotal / invoiceCount;      // result9  = 125.50
int result10 = (int) invoiceTotal / invoiceCount;  // result10 = 125
double result11 = (double) invoiceCount / 4;       // result11 = 0.5
```

Description

- An *arithmetic expression* consists of one or more *operands* and *arithmetic operators*.

- When an expression mixes the use of int and double variables, Java automatically *casts* the int types to double types. To retain the decimal places, the variable that receives the result must be a double.

- To manually cast a variable to another type, you can code the type in parentheses just before the variable.

Figure 2-5   How to code arithmetic expressions

How to work with string variables

Now that you have some basic skills for working with numbers, you're ready to learn some basic skills for working with strings. For now, these skills should be all you need for many of the programs you develop.

How to create a String object

A *string* can consist of any letters, numbers, and special characters. To declare a string variable, you use the syntax shown in figure 2-6. Although this is much like the syntax for declaring a numeric variable, a string is an object that's created from the String class when a string variable is declared. Then, the String object refers to string data. When you declare a string variable, you must capitalize the String keyword because it is the name of a class, not a primitive data type.

As you progress through this book, you'll learn a lot more about classes and objects. For now, though, all you need to know is that string variables work much like numeric variables. The difference is that string variables store a reference to a String object that contains string data. Because of that, strings are *reference types*, not primitive types.

When you declare a String object, you can assign a *string literal* to it by enclosing a string of characters within double quotes. You can also assign an *empty string* to it by coding a set of quotation marks with nothing between them. Finally, you can use the null keyword to assign a *null value* to a String object. That indicates that the value of the string is unknown.

How to join and append strings

If you want to *join*, or *concatenate*, two or more strings into one, you can use the + operator. For example, you can join a first name, a space, and a last name as shown in the second example in figure 2-6. Then, you can assign that string to a variable. When concatenating strings, you can use string variables or string literals.

You can also join a string with a primitive data type. This is illustrated in the third example. Here, a variable that's defined with the double data type is appended to a string. When you use this technique, Java automatically converts the double value to a string.

You can use the + and += operators to *append* a string to the end of a string that's stored in a string variable. If you use the + operator, you need to include the variable on both sides of the = operator. Otherwise, the assignment statement replaces the old value with the new value instead of appending the old value to the new value. Since the += operator provides a shorter and safer way to append strings, this operator is commonly used.

The syntax for declaring and initializing a string variable

```
String variableName = value;
```

How to declare and initialize a string

```
String message1 = "Invalid data entry.";
String message2 = "";
String message3 = null;
```

How to join strings

```
String firstName = "Bob";                      // firstName is Bob
String lastName = "Smith";                     // lastName is Smith
String name = firstName + " " + lastName;      // name is Bob Smith
```

How to join a string and a number

```
double price = 14.95;
String priceString = "Price: " + price;
```

How to append one string to another with the + operator

```
firstName = "Bob";                    // firstName is Bob
lastName = "Smith";                   // lastName is Smith
name = firstName + " ";               // name is Bob followed by a space
name = name + lastName;               // name is Bob Smith
```

How to append one string to another with the += operator

```
firstName = "Bob";                    // firstName is Bob
lastName = "Smith";                   // lastName is Smith
name = firstName + " ";               // name is Bob followed by a space
name += lastName;                     // name is Bob Smith
```

Description

- A *string* can consist of any characters in the character set including letters, numbers, and special characters like *, &, and #.

- In Java, a string is actually a String object that's created from the String class that's part of the Java *API (Application Programming Interface)*. The API provides all the classes that are included as part of the JDK.

- To specify the value of a string, you can enclose text in double quotation marks. This is known as a *string literal*.

- To assign an *empty string* to a String object, you can code a set of quotation marks with nothing between them. This means that the string doesn't contain any characters.

- To assign a *null value* to a string, you can use the null keyword. This means that the value of the string is unknown.

- To *join* (or *concatenate*) a string with another string or a data type, use a plus sign. Whenever possible, Java automatically converts the data type to a string.

- When you *append* one string to another, you add one string to the end of another. To do that, you can use assignment statements.

- The += operator is a shortcut for appending a string expression to a string variable.

Figure 2-6   How to create and use strings

How to include special characters in strings

Figure 2-7 shows how to include certain types of special characters within a string. In particular, this figure shows how to include backslashes, quotation marks, and control characters such as new lines, tabs, and returns in a string. To do that, you can use the *escape sequences* shown in this figure.

Each escape sequence starts with a backslash. If you code a backslash followed by the letter *n*, for example, the compiler includes a new line character in the string as shown in the first example. If you omitted the backslash, of course, the compiler would just include the letter *n* in the string value. The escape sequences for the tab and return characters work similarly as shown in the second example.

To code a string literal, you enclose it in double quotes. As a result, if you want to include a double quote within a string literal, you must use an escape sequence as shown in the third example. Here, the \" escape sequence is used to include two double quotes within the string literal.

Finally, you need to use an escape sequence if you want to include a backslash in a string literal. To do that, you code two backslashes as shown in the fourth example. If you forget to do that and code a single backslash, the compiler uses the backslash and the next character to create an escape sequence. That causes a compiler error if the escape sequence isn't valid, or it yields unexpected results if the escape sequence is valid.

Common escape sequences

Sequence	Character
\n	New line
\t	Tab
\r	Return
\"	Quotation mark
\\	Backslash

New line

String

```
"Code: JSP\nPrice: $49.50"
```

Result

```
Code: JSP
Price: $49.50
```

Tabs and returns

String

```
"Joe\tSmith\rKate\tLewis"
```

Result

```
Joe       Smith
Kate      Lewis
```

Quotation marks

String

```
"Type \"x\" to exit"
```

Result

```
Type "x" to exit
```

Backslash

String

```
"C:\\java\\files"
```

Result

```
C:\java\files
```

Description

- Within a string, you can use *escape sequences* to include certain types of special characters.

Figure 2-7   How to include special characters in strings

How to use classes, objects, and methods

So far, you've learned how to create String objects from the String class in the Java API. As you develop applications, though, you need to use dozens of different classes and objects from the Java API. To do that, you need to know how to import classes, create objects from classes, and call methods from objects or classes.

How to import classes

In the Java API, groups of related classes are organized into *packages*. Figure 2-8 shows a list of some of the commonly used packages. Since the java.lang package contains classes that are used in almost every Java program (such as the String class), this package is automatically made available to all programs.

However, to use a class from a package other than java.lang, you typically include an import statement for that class at the beginning of the program. When you code an import statement, you can import a single class by specifying the class name. Or, you can import all of the classes in the package by typing an asterisk (*) in place of the class name. Although it requires less code to import all of the classes in a package at once, importing one class at a time clearly identifies the classes you're using. As a result, it's generally considered a good practice to import one class at a time.

When you import a class, you don't have to qualify it with the package name. This is shown by the first example that creates a Scanner object. You'll learn more about how this code works in the next figure. For now, just note that the code uses the Scanner class without qualifying it.

If you don't import a class, you can still use the class in your code, but you have to qualify it with its package name each time you refer to it. This is shown by the second example that creates a Scanner object. This example performs the same task as the first example. However, you have to qualify the Scanner class with the name of the package twice. Since that can lead to a lot of unnecessary typing, you'll usually want to code an import statement for the classes you use.

In addition to the packages provided by the Java API, you can get packages from third party sources, either as open-source code or by purchasing them. You can also create packages that contain classes that you've written. You'll learn how to do that in chapter 10.

Common packages

Package name	Description
`java.lang`	Classes fundamental to Java, including the String class. In addition, it provides classes that work with the primitive data types, including the Integer and Double classes.
`java.util`	Utility classes, including the Scanner class for getting input from the console and a Date class that you can use to get the current date and time.
`java.text`	Classes for working with text, including the NumberFormat class that you can use to format numbers.
`java.time`	Classes for working with dates and times.
`java.io`	Classes that read data from files and to write data to files.

How to import a single class from a package

Syntax

```
import packagename.ClassName;
```

Examples

```
import java.util.Scanner;
import java.util.Date;
import java.text.NumberFormat;
```

How to import all classes in a package

Syntax

```
import packagename.*;
```

Examples

```
import java.util.*;
import java.text.*;
```

How to use the Scanner class to create a Scanner object

With an import statement

```
Scanner sc = new Scanner(System.in);
```

Without an import statement

```
java.util.Scanner sc = new java.util.Scanner(System.in);
```

Description

- The API for the Java SE provides a large library of classes that are organized into *packages*.

- All classes stored in the java.lang package are automatically available to all Java programs.

- To use classes that aren't in the java.lang package, you can code an import statement for a single class or for all classes in the package.

- If you don't code an import statement for a class, you must qualify the class name with the name of the package that contains it each time you refer to the class.

Figure 2-8   How to import classes

How to create objects and call methods

To use a Java class, you usually start by creating an *object* from the *class*. As the syntax in figure 2-9 shows, you typically do that by coding the class name, the variable name that refers to the object, an equals sign, the new keyword, and the class name again followed by a set of parentheses. Within the parentheses, you code any *arguments* that are required by the *constructor* of the class.

In the examples, the first statement shows how to create a Scanner object and assign it to a variable named sc. For this object, the constructor requires just one argument (System.in), which represents console input. In contrast, the second statement creates a Date object that represents the current date and assigns it to a variable named now. For this object, the constructor doesn't require any arguments. As you go through this book, you'll learn a lot more about how to use constructors to create objects. For now, you only need to be able to create a Scanner object as shown here.

When you create an object, you can think of the class as the template for the object. That's why the object can be called an *instance* of the class, and the process of creating the object can be called *instantiation*.

Once you've created an object from a class, you can *call* any of the *methods* that are available from the object. To do that, you code the object name, a dot (period), and the method name followed by a set of parentheses. Within the parentheses, you code the arguments that are required by the method.

In the examples, the first statement calls the nextDouble() method of the Scanner object named sc to get data from the console. The second statement calls the toString() method of the Date object named now to convert the date and time that's stored in the object to a string. Neither of these methods requires an argument.

Besides methods that you can call from an object, some classes provide *static methods* that can be called directly from the class. To do that, you substitute the class name for the object name as shown in the third set of examples. Here, the first statement calls the toString() method of the Double class, and the second statement calls the parseDouble() method of the Double class. Both of these methods require one argument.

As you progress through this book, you'll learn how to use dozens of classes and methods. For now, though, you can focus on the syntax for creating an object from a class, calling a method from an object, and calling a static method from a class.

How to create an object from a class

Syntax

```
ClassName objectName = new ClassName(arguments);
```

Examples

```
Scanner sc = new Scanner(System.in);  // creates a Scanner object named sc
Date now = new Date();                // creates a Date object named now
```

How to call a method from an object

Syntax

```
objectName.methodName(arguments)
```

Examples

```
double subtotal = sc.nextDouble();     // get a double entry from the console
String currentDate = now.toString();   // convert the date to a string
```

How to call a static method from a class

Syntax

```
ClassName.methodName(arguments)
```

Examples

```
String priceString = Double.toString(price); // convert a double to a string
double total = Double.parseDouble(inputStr); // convert a string to a double
```

Description

- When you create an *object* from a Java class, you are creating an *instance* of the *class*. Then, you can use the *methods* of the class by *calling* them from the object.

- Some Java classes contain *static methods*. These methods can be called directly from the class without creating an object.

- When you create an object from a class, the *constructor* may require one or more *arguments*. These arguments must have the required data types, and they must be coded in the correct sequence separated by commas.

- When you call a method from an object or a class, the method may require one or more arguments. Here again, these arguments must have the required data types and they must be coded in the correct sequence separated by commas.

- In this book, you'll learn how to use dozens of the Java classes and methods. You will also learn how to create your own classes and methods.

Figure 2-9   How to create objects and call methods

How to view the API documentation

One of the most difficult parts of using Java is learning how to use the overwhelming number of classes and methods that are available from its API. To do that, you frequently need to look up classes and methods in the API documentation.

Figure 2-10 summarizes some of the basic techniques for navigating through the API documentation. This figure begins by showing the start of the documentation for the Scanner class, which goes on for many pages. To display the documentation for this class, you click the package name (java.util) in the upper left frame. Then, you click the class name (Scanner) in the lower left frame.

If you scroll through the documentation for this class, you'll get an idea of the scale of the documentation that you're dealing with. After a few pages of descriptive information, you come to a summary of the eight constructors for the class, followed by a summary of the dozens of methods that the class offers. That's followed by more detail about these constructors and methods.

At this point, this is probably more information than you can handle. That's why one of the goals of this book is to introduce you to the classes and methods that you'll use most of the time. After you've learned how to work with those classes and methods, the API documentation should make more sense to you, and you'll be able to use this documentation to research classes and methods that aren't presented in this book.

However, it's never too early to start using the API documentation. So, feel free to use this documentation to review the classes and methods that are presented in this book and to get more information about them. Similarly, feel free to use this documentation to research any other classes or methods that you want to know more about.

The documentation for the Scanner class

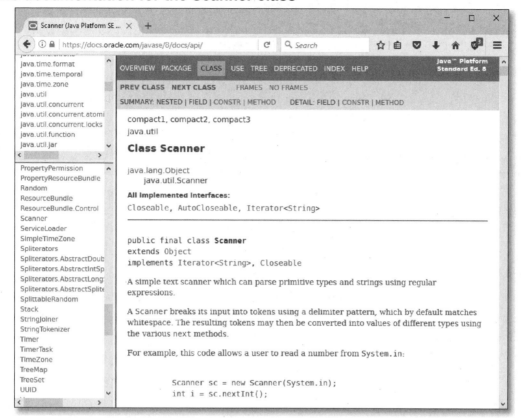

Description

- The Java SE API contains thousands of classes and methods that can help you do most of the tasks that your applications require.

- You can use a browser to view the Java SE API on the Internet. For example, for Java SE 8, you can go to this address:
  https://docs.oracle.com/javase/8/docs/api/

- To select a package, click on it in the top left frame. This displays a list of classes in the package in the lower left frame.

- To display the documentation for a class, click on it in the lower left frame. This displays the documentation for that class in the right frame.

- Once you display the documentation for a class, you can scroll through it or click on a hyperlink to get more information.

- To make it easier to access the API documentation, you can bookmark the index page. Then, you can easily redisplay this page whenever you need it.

Figure 2-10   How to view the API documentation

How to use the console for input and output

Most applications get input from the user and display output to the user. Ever since version 1.5 of Java, the easiest way to get input is to use the Scanner class to get data from the console. And the easiest way to display output is to use the System.out object to print data to the console.

How to print output to the console

To print output to the *console*, you can use the println() and print() methods of the System.out object as shown in figure 2-11. Here, System.out refers to an instance of the PrintStream class that you can use to print output to the console. Because this object is created automatically by Java, you don't have to include code that creates it in your program.

Both the println() and print() methods accept a string argument that specifies the data to be printed. The only difference between the two is that the println() method starts a new line after it displays the data, and the print() method doesn't.

If you study the examples in this figure, you shouldn't have any trouble using these methods. In the first example, for instance, the first statement uses the println() method to print the words "Welcome to the Invoice Total Calculator" to the console. The second statement prints the string "Total: " followed by the value of the total variable (which is automatically converted to a string). The third statement prints the value of the variable named message to the console. And the fourth statement prints a blank line since no argument is coded.

Because the print() method doesn't automatically start a new line, you can use it to print several data arguments on the same line. In the second example, for instance, the three statements use the print() method to print "Total: ", followed by the total variable, followed by a new line character. Of course, you can achieve the same result with a single line of code like this:

```
System.out.println("Total: " + total);
```

This figure also shows an application that uses the println() method to print seven lines to the console. In the main() method of this application, the first four statements set the values for four variables. Then, the next seven statements print a welcome message, a blank line, the values for the four variables, and another blank line.

When you work with console applications, you should know that the appearance of the console may differ slightly depending on the operating system. However, even if the console looks a little different, it should work the same.

Two methods of the System.out object

Method	Description
`println(data)`	Prints the data argument followed by a new line character to the console.
`print(data)`	Prints the data to the console without starting a new line.

The println() method

```java
System.out.println("Welcome to the Invoice Total Calculator");
System.out.println("Total: " + total);
System.out.println(message);
System.out.println();              // print a blank line
```

The print() method

```java
System.out.print("Total: ");
System.out.print(total);
System.out.print("\n");
```

An application that prints data to the console

```java
public class InvoiceApp {

    public static void main(String[] args) {

        // set and calculate the numeric values
        double subtotal = 100;          // set subtotal to 100
        double discountPercent = .2;    // set discountPercent to 20%
        double discountAmount = subtotal * discountPercent;
        double invoiceTotal = subtotal - discountAmount;

        // print the data to the console
        System.out.println("Welcome to the Invoice Total Calculator");
        System.out.println();
        System.out.println("Subtotal:         " + subtotal);
        System.out.println("Discount percent: " + discountPercent);
        System.out.println("Discount amount:  " + discountAmount);
        System.out.println("Total:            " + invoiceTotal);
        System.out.println();
    }
}
```

The console

```
Welcome to the Invoice Total Calculator

Subtotal:         100.0
Discount percent: 0.2
Discount amount:  20.0
Total:            80.0
```

Description

- Although the appearance of a console may differ from one system to another, you can always use the print() and println() methods to print data to the console.

Figure 2-11   How to print output to the console

How to read input from the console

Figure 2-12 shows how you can use the Scanner class to read input from the console. To start, you create a Scanner object by using a statement like the one in this figure. Here, the variable named sc refers to the Scanner object, and System.in is an object that you can use to get input from the standard input stream, which is typically the keyboard. Like the System.out object, the System.in object is automatically available to you. Because of that, you can use this object with a Scanner object whenever you want to get console input.

Once you've created a Scanner object, you can use its methods to read data from the console. The method you use depends on the type of data you need to read. To read string data, for example, you use the next() method. To read integer data, you use the nextInt() method. To read double data, you use the nextDouble() method. And to read all of the data on a line, you use the nextLine() method.

The examples in this figure illustrate how these methods work. Here, the first statement gets a string and assigns it to a string variable named name. The second statement gets an integer and assigns it to an int variable named count. The third statement gets a double and assigns it to a double variable named subtotal. And the fourth statement reads any remaining characters on the line.

Each entry that a user makes is called a *token*, and a user can enter more than one token before pressing the Enter key. To do that, the user separates the entries by one or more space, tab, or return characters. This is called *whitespace*. Then, each "next" method gets the next token that has been entered. If, for example, you type 100, press the spacebar, type 20, and press the Enter key, the first token is 100 and the second one is 20.

If you want to get string data that includes whitespace, you can use the nextLine() method. If, for example, the user enters "New York" and presses the Enter key, you can use the nextLine() method to get the entire line as a single string.

If the user doesn't enter the type of data that the next method is looking for, an error occurs and the program ends. In Java, an error like this is also known as an *exception*. If, for example, the user enters a double value but the nextInt() method is used to get it, an exception occurs. In chapter 5, you'll learn how to prevent this type of error.

Although this figure only shows methods for working with String objects and int and double types, the Scanner class includes methods for working with most of the other data types that you'll learn about in the next chapter. It also includes methods that let you check what type of data the user entered. As you'll see in chapter 5, you can use these methods to avoid exceptions by checking the data type before you call the method that gets the data.

The Scanner class

```
java.util.Scanner
```

How to create a Scanner object

```
Scanner sc = new Scanner(System.in);
```

Common methods of a Scanner object

Method	Description
next()	Returns the next token stored in the scanner as a String object.
nextInt()	Returns the next token stored in the scanner as an int value.
nextDouble()	Returns the next token stored in the scanner as a double value.
nextLine()	Returns any remaining input on the current line as a String object and advances the scanner to the next line.

How to use the methods of a Scanner object

```
String name = sc.next();
int count = sc.nextInt();
double subtotal = sc.nextDouble();
String cityName = sc.nextLine();
```

Description

- To create a Scanner object that gets input from the console, specify System.in in the parentheses.

- When one of the next methods of the Scanner class is run, the application waits for the user to enter data with the keyboard. To complete the entry, the user presses the Enter key.

- Each entry that a user makes is called a *token*. A user can enter two or more tokens by separating them with *whitespace*, which consists of one or more spaces, tab characters, or return characters.

- The entries end when the user presses the Enter key. Then, the first next(), nextInt(), or nextDouble() method gets the first token; the second next(), nextInt(), or nextDouble() method gets the second token; and so on. In contrast, the nextLine() method gets all of the input or remaining input on the current line.

- If the user doesn't enter the type of data that the method expects, an error occurs and the program ends. In Java, this type of error is called an *exception*. You'll learn more about this in chapter 5.

- Since the Scanner class is in the java.util package, you typically include an import statement when you use this class.

Note

- The Scanner class was introduced in version 1.5 of the JDK.

Figure 2-12   How to read input from the console

Examples that get input from the console

Figure 2-13 presents two examples that get input from the console. The first example starts by creating a Scanner object. Then, it uses the print() method of the System.out object to prompt the user for three values, and it uses methods of the Scanner object to read those values from the console. Because the first value should be a string, the code uses the next() method to read this value. Because the second value should be a double, the code uses the nextDouble() method to read this value. And because the third value should be an integer, the code uses the nextInt() method to read this value.

After all three values are read, a calculation is performed using the int and double values. Then, the data is formatted and the println() method displays the data on the console.

Unlike the first example, which reads one value per line, the second example reads three values from a single line. Here, the first statement uses the print() method to prompt the user to enter three integer values. Then, the next three statements use the nextInt() method to read those three values. This works because a Scanner object uses whitespace (spaces, tabs, or returns) to separate the data that's entered at the console into tokens.

In this figure, the console does not use bold when it displays user input. However, it does use bold for the output that's printed to console. This makes it easy to tell the difference between user input and program output, and it's a convention that's used throughout this book.

Code that gets three values from the user

```
// create a Scanner object
Scanner sc = new Scanner(System.in);

// read a string
System.out.print("Enter product code: ");
String productCode = sc.next();

// read a double value
System.out.print("Enter price: ");
double price = sc.nextDouble();

// read an int value
System.out.print("Enter quantity: ");
int quantity = sc.nextInt();

// perform a calculation and display the result
double total = price * quantity;
System.out.println();
System.out.println(quantity + " " + productCode +
                   " @ " +  price + " = " + total);
System.out.println();
```

The console after the program finishes

```
Enter product code: cshp
Enter price: 49.50
Enter quantity: 2

2 cshp @ 49.5 = 99.0
```

Code that reads three values from one line

```
// read three int values
System.out.print("Enter three integer values: ");
int i1 = sc.nextInt();
int i2 = sc.nextInt();
int i3 = sc.nextInt();

// calculate the average and display the result
int total = i1 + i2 + i3;
int avg = total / 3;
System.out.println("Average: " + avg);
System.out.println();
```

The console after the program finishes

```
Enter three integer values: 99 88 92
Average: 93
```

Figure 2-13   Examples that get input from the console

How to code simple control statements

As you write programs, you need to determine when certain operations should be done and how long repetitive operations should continue. To do that, you code *control statements* like the if/else and while statements. But before you learn how to write those statements, you need to learn how to write expressions that compare numeric and string variables.

How to compare numeric variables

Figure 2-14 shows how to code *Boolean expressions* that use *relational operators* to compare int and double data types. This type of expression evaluates to either true or false, and the operands in the expression can be either variables or literals.

In the first set of examples, for instance, the first expression is true if the value of the variable named count is equal to the literal value 5. The second expression is true if the value of the testScore variable is not equal to 0. And the sixth example is true if the value of the variable named quantity is less than or equal to the value of the variable named reorderPoint.

When you code expressions like these, you must remember to code two equals signs instead of one for the equality comparison. That's because a single equals sign is used for assignment statements. As a result, if you try to code a Boolean expression with a single equals sign, your code won't compile.

When you compare numeric values, you usually compare values of the same data type. However, if you compare values of different types, Java automatically casts the less precise numeric type to the more precise type. For example, if you compare an int type to a double type, Java casts the int type to the double type before the comparison is made.

How to compare string variables

If you want to compare strings for equality, you can't use the relational operators. Instead, you must use the equals() or equalsIgnoreCase() methods of the String class that are summarized in figure 2-14. Both of these methods require an argument that provides the String object or String literal that you want to compare with the current String object.

In the examples, the first expression is true if the value in the string named userEntry equals the literal value "Y". In contrast, the second expression uses the equalsIgnoreCase() method, so it's true whether the value in userEntry is "Y" or "y". Then, the third expression shows how you can use the not operator (!) to reverse the value of a Boolean expression that compares two strings. Here, the expression evaluates to true if the lastName variable is *not* equal to "Jones". The fourth expression is true if the string variable named code equals the string variable named productCode.

Relational operators

Operator	Name	Description
==	Equality	Returns a true value if both operands are equal.
!=	Inequality	Returns a true value if the left and right operands are not equal.
>	Greater Than	Returns a true value if the left operand is greater than the right operand.
<	Less Than	Returns a true value if the left operand is less than the right operand.
>=	Greater Than Or Equal	Returns a true value if the left operand is greater than or equal to the right operand.
<=	Less Than Or Equal	Returns a true value if the left operand is less than or equal to the right operand.

Examples of Boolean expressions

```
count == 5                 // equal to a numeric literal
testScore != 0             // not equal to a numeric literal
years > 0                  // greater than a numeric literal
i < months                 // less than a numeric variable
subtotal >= 9.99           // greater than or equal to a numeric literal
quantity <= reorderPoint   // less than or equal to a numeric variable
```

Two methods of the String class

Method	Description
equals(String)	Compares the value of the String object with a String argument and returns a true value if they are equal. This method makes a case-sensitive comparison.
equalsIgnoreCase(String)	Works like the equals() method but is not case-sensitive.

Examples

```
userEntry.equals("Y")                   // equal to a string literal
userEntry.equalsIgnoreCase("Y")         // equal to a string literal
!lastName.equals("Jones")               // not equal to a string literal
code.equalsIgnoreCase(productCode)      // equal to another string variable
```

Description

- A *Boolean expression* is an expression that evaluates to either true or false. To create a Boolean expression, you can use the *relational operators* to compare two numeric operands.

- To compare two numeric operands for equality, make sure to use two equals signs. If you only use one equals sign, you are coding an assignment statement, not a Boolean expression, and your code won't compile.

- If you compare an int value to a double value, Java casts the int value to the double type.

- To test two strings for equality, you must call one of the methods of the String object. If you use the equality operator, you may get unpredictable results. This is described in more detail in chapter 4.

Figure 2-14   How to compare numeric and string variables

How to code if/else statements

Figure 2-15 shows how to use the *if/else statement* (or just *if statement*) to control the logic of your applications. This statement is the Java implementation of a control structure known as the *selection structure* because it lets you select different actions based on the results of a Boolean expression.

The syntax summary shows that you can code this statement with just an if clause, you can code it with one or more else if clauses, and you can code it with a final else clause. In any syntax summary, the ellipsis (...) means that the preceding element (in this case the else if clause) can be repeated as many times as it is needed. And the brackets [ ] mean that the element is optional.

When an if statement is executed, Java begins by evaluating the Boolean expression in the if clause. If it's true, the statements within this clause are executed and the rest of the if/else statement is skipped. If it's false, Java evaluates the first else if clause (if there is one). Then, if its Boolean expression is true, the statements within this else if clause are executed, and the rest of the if/else statement is skipped. Otherwise, Java evaluates the next else if clause.

This continues with any remaining else if clauses. Finally, if none of the clauses contains a Boolean expression that evaluates to true, Java executes the statements in the else clause (if there is one). However, if none of the Boolean expressions are true and there is no else clause, Java doesn't execute any statements.

If a clause only contains one statement, you don't need to enclose that statement in braces. This is illustrated by the first example in this figure. However, if you want to code two or more statements within a clause, you need to code the statements in braces. In addition, it's generally considered a good practice to include the braces even if a clause only contains a single statement. That way, the braces clearly identify the block of statements for the clause. It also makes it easy to add more statements later if that becomes necessary.

If you declare a variable within a block, that variable is available only to the other statements in the block. This can be referred to as *block scope*. As a result, if you need to access a variable outside of the block, you must declare it before the if statement. In this figure, for instance, all of the examples declare the discountPercent variable before the if statement. That way, the code after the if statement can access the discountPercent variable, even if the if statement assigns a new value to it.

The syntax of the if/else statement

```
if (booleanExpression) { statements }
[else if (booleanExpression) { statements }] ...
[else { statements }]
```

If statements without else if or else clauses

With a single statement

```
double discountPercent = .1;
if (subtotal >= 100)
    discountPercent = .2;
```

With a block of statements

```
double discountPercent = .1;
if (subtotal >= 100) {
    discountPercent = .2;
    status = "Bulk rate";
}
```

An if statement with an else clause

```
double discountPercent = 0.0;
if (subtotal >= 100) {
    discountPercent = .2;
} else {
    discountPercent = .1;
}
```

An if statement with else if and else clauses

```
double discountPercent = 0.0;
if (customerType.equals("T")) {
    discountPercent = .4;
} else if (customerType.equals("C")) {
    discountPercent = .2;
} else if (subtotal >= 100) {
    discountPercent = .2;
} else {
    discountPercent = .1;
}
```

Description

- An *if/else statement*, or just *if statement*, always contains an if clause. In addition, it can contain one or more else if clauses and a final else clause.

- If a clause requires just one statement, you don't have to enclose the statement in braces. However, it's generally considered a good practice to include the braces.

- If a clause requires more than one statement, you must enclose the block of statements in braces.

- Any variables that are declared within a block have *block scope*, so they can only be used within that block. As a result, if you want to use a variable in another block of the if statement or after the if statement, you must declare it before the if statement.

Figure 2-15   How to code if/else statements

How to code while statements

Figure 2-16 shows how to code a *while statement*. This is one way that Java implements a control structure known as the *iteration structure* that lets you repeat a block of statements. However, Java also offers other implementations of this structure, and you'll learn about them in chapter 4.

When Java executes a while statement, the program repeats the statements in the block of code within the braces *while* the Boolean expression in the statement is true. In other words, the statement ends when the expression becomes false. If the expression is false when the statement starts, Java never executes the statements in the block of code.

Because a while statement loops through the statements in the block as many times as needed, the code within a while statement is often referred to as a *while loop*. Here again, any variables that are defined within the block have block scope, which means that they can't be accessed outside the block.

The first example in this figure shows how to code a loop that executes a block of statements while a variable named choice is equal to either "y" or "Y". In this case, the statements within the block get input from the console and print output to the console. This is a common way to control the execution of a program like the one in the next figure.

The second example shows how to code a loop that adds the numbers 1 through 4 and stores the result in a variable named sum. Here, a *counter variable* (or just *counter*) named i is initialized to 1 and the sum variable is initialized to zero before the loop starts. Within the loop, the first statement adds the value of i to sum, and the second statement adds a value of 1 to i.

When Java executes this code, the value of i is 1 the first time through the loop. As a result, the first time through the loop, Java adds 1 to the sum so its value becomes 1. The second time through the loop, Java adds 2 to the sum so its value becomes 3. The third time through the loop, Java adds 3 to the sum so its value becomes 6. And the fourth time through the loop, Java adds 4 to the sum so its value becomes 10. However, when the value of i becomes 5, the Boolean expression in the while statement evaluates to false, and the loop ends. The use of a counter like this is a common coding practice, and single letters like *i, j,* and *k* are commonly used as the names of counters.

When you code loops, you must be careful to avoid accidentally coding *infinite loops*. If, for example, you forget to code a statement that increments the counter variable in the second example, the loop never ends because the counter never gets to 5. Then, you have to cancel the application so you can debug your code. Fortunately, most IDEs provide an easy way to stop an infinite loop. For example, NetBeans provides a Stop button that's available from its Output window.

The syntax of the while loop

```
while (booleanExpression) {
    statements
}
```

A loop that continues while choice is "y" or "Y"

```
Scanner sc = new Scanner(System.in);
String choice = "y";
while (choice.equalsIgnoreCase("y")) {
    // get the invoice subtotal from the user
    System.out.print("Enter subtotal:   ");
    double subtotal = sc.nextDouble();

    // print the user input to the console
    System.out.println("You entered: " + subtotal);

    // see if the user wants to continue
    System.out.print("Continue? (y/n): ");
    choice = sc.next();
    System.out.println();
}
```

A loop that calculates the sum of the numbers 1 through 4

```
int i = 1;
int sum = 0;
while (i < 5) {
    sum = sum + i;
    i = i + 1;
}
```

Description

- A *while statement* executes the block of statements within its braces as long as the Boolean expression is true. When the expression becomes false, the while statement skips its block of statements so the program continues with the next statement in sequence.

- The statements within a while statement can be referred to as a *while loop*.

- Any variables that are declared in the block of a while statement have block scope.

- If the Boolean expression in a while statement never becomes false, the statement never ends. Then, the program goes into an *infinite loop*.

- Since accidentally coding an infinite loop is a common mistake, most IDEs provide a button that you can click to stop or terminate an infinite loop.

Figure 2-16   How to code while statements

Two illustrative applications

At this point, you have learned enough about Java to write some simple applications of your own. To show you how you can do that, this chapter ends by presenting two applications.

The Invoice application

Figure 2-17 shows the console and the code for an Invoice application. Although this application is simple, it gets input from the user, performs calculations that use this input, and displays the results of the calculations. This continues until the user enters anything other than "Y" or "y" in response to the Continue prompt.

The code for the Invoice application starts by displaying a welcome message at the console. Then, it creates a Scanner object named sc that's used in the while loop of the program. Although this code could create this object within the while loop, that would recreate the object each time through the loop, which would be inefficient.

Before the while statement, this code initializes a String object named choice to "y". Within the loop, the code gets a double value from the user and stores it in a variable named subtotal. After that, the loop uses an if/else statement to set the discount percent based on the value of subtotal. If, for example, the subtotal is greater than or equal to 200, the discount percent is .2 (20%). If that condition isn't true but the subtotal is greater than or equal to 100, the discount percent is .1 (10%). Otherwise, the discount percent is zero.

As you review this if statement, note that the subtotal and discountPercent variables are declared before the if/else statement. As a result, these variables are available to the rest of the code block, including the if/else statement.

When the if/else statement finishes, the code calculates the discount amount and the invoice total. Then, it displays the discount percent, discount amount, and invoice total on the console. Next, it displays a message that asks if the user wants to continue. If the user enters "y" or "Y", the loop is repeated. Otherwise, the program ends.

Although this application illustrates most of what you've learned in this chapter, it has a couple of shortcomings. First, the numeric values that are displayed should be formatted with two decimal places since these are currency values. To fix this issue, you can format numbers as shown in the next chapter. Second, if the user doesn't enter a valid double value for the subtotal, an exception occurs and the program crashes. To fix this issue, you can prevent these exceptions from occurring as shown in chapter 5.

In the meantime, if you're new to programming, you can learn a lot by writing simple programs like the Invoice program. Doing that gives you a chance to become comfortable with the coding for input, calculations, output, if/else statements, and while statements.

The console

```
Welcome to the Invoice Total Calculator

Enter subtotal:    150
Discount percent: 0.1
Discount amount:  15.0
Invoice total:    135.0

Continue? (y/n):
```

The code

```java
import java.util.Scanner;

public class InvoiceApp  {

    public static void main(String[] args) {
        System.out.println("Welcome to the Invoice Total Calculator");
        System.out.println();  // print a blank line

        Scanner sc = new Scanner(System.in);

        // perform invoice calculations until choice isn't equal to "y" or "Y"
        String choice = "y";
        while (choice.equalsIgnoreCase("y")) {
            // get the invoice subtotal from the user
            System.out.print("Enter subtotal:    ");
            double subtotal = sc.nextDouble();

            // get the discount percent
            double discountPercent;
            if (subtotal >= 200) {
                discountPercent = .2;
            } else if (subtotal >= 100) {
                discountPercent = .1;
            } else {
                discountPercent = 0.0;
            }

            // calculate the discount amount and total
            double discountAmount = subtotal * discountPercent;
            double total = subtotal - discountAmount;

            // display the results
            String message = "Discount percent: " + discountPercent + "\n"
                        + "Discount amount:   " + discountAmount + "\n"
                        + "Invoice total:    " + total + "\n";
            System.out.println(message);

            // see if the user wants to continue
            System.out.print("Continue? (y/n): ");
            choice = sc.next();
            System.out.println();
        }
    }
}
```

Figure 2-17   The Invoice application

The Test Score application

Figure 2-18 presents another Java application that should give you more ideas for how you can apply what you've learned so far. This application lets the user enter one or more test scores. To end the application, the user enters a value of 999. Then, the application displays the number of test scores that were entered, the total of the scores, and the average of the scores.

The code for this application starts by displaying the instructions for using the application. Then, it declares and initializes three variables, and it creates a Scanner object for getting input from the console.

The while loop in this program continues until the user enters a test score that's greater than 100. To start, this loop gets the next test score. Then, if that test score is less than or equal to 100, the program adds 1 to the score count, and it adds the test score to the total of the scores. Here, the if statement is necessary because you don't want to increase the score count or total when the user enters 999 to end the program. When the loop ends, the program calculates the average score and displays the score count, total, and average.

To include decimal places in the score average, this program declares the averageScore variable as a double type. In addition, the statement that calculates the average score casts the scoreTotal variable from the int type to the double type. This causes Java to automatically cast scoreCount from the int type to the double type, so it can use double arithmetic, not integer arithmetic.

To allow statements outside of the while loop to access the scoreTotal and scoreCount variables, this code declares these variables before the while loop. If these variables were declared inside the while loop, they would only be available within that block of code and couldn't be accessed by the statements that are coded after the while loop. In addition, the logic of the program wouldn't work because these variables would be reinitialized each time through the loop.

Like the Invoice application, this application has some obvious shortcomings. First, the application sometimes displays too many decimal places for the average score. Second, if the user enters data that the nextInt() method can't convert to an integer, the application crashes. However, you'll learn how to fix the first issue in the next chapter, and you'll learn how to fix the second issue in chapter 5.

The console

```
Enter test scores that range from 0 to 100.
To end the program, enter 999.

Enter score: 90
Enter score: 80
Enter score: 75
Enter score: 999

Score count:    3
Score total:    245
Average score: 81.66666666666667
```

The code

```java
import java.util.Scanner;

public class TestScoreApp {

    public static void main(String[] args) {
        // display operational messages
        System.out.println("Enter test scores that range from 0 to 100.");
        System.out.println("To end the program, enter 999.");
        System.out.println();   // print a blank line

        // initialize variables and create a Scanner object
        int scoreTotal = 0;
        int scoreCount = 0;
        int testScore = 0;
        Scanner sc = new Scanner(System.in);

        // get a series of test scores from the user
        while (testScore <= 100) {
            // get the input from the user
            System.out.print("Enter score: ");
            testScore = sc.nextInt();

            // accumulate score count and score total
            if (testScore <= 100) {
                scoreCount = scoreCount + 1;
                scoreTotal = scoreTotal + testScore;
            }
        }

        // display the score count, score total, and average score
        double averageScore = (double) scoreTotal / scoreCount;
        String message = "\n"
                + "Score count:    " + scoreCount + "\n"
                + "Score total:    " + scoreTotal + "\n"
                + "Average score: " + averageScore + "\n";
        System.out.println(message);
    }
}
```

Figure 2-18   The Test Score application

How to test and debug an application

In chapter 1, you were introduced to *syntax errors* that are detected by an IDE when you enter code. Because syntax errors prevent an application from compiling, they are also commonly referred to as *compile-time errors*. Once you've fixed the syntax errors, you're ready to test and debug the application as described in this topic. And when you do the exercises, you'll get hands-on practice testing and debugging.

How to test an application

When you *test* an application, you run it to make sure the application works correctly. As you test, you should try every possible combination of valid and invalid data to be certain that the application works correctly under every set of conditions. Remember that the goal of testing is to find errors, or *bugs*, so they're not discovered by users as they run the application.

As you test, you will inevitably encounter two types of bugs. The first type of bug causes a *runtime error*, also known as a *runtime exception*. A runtime error causes the application to end prematurely, which programmers often refer to as "crashing". In this case, an error message like the one in the first console in figure 2-19 is displayed. This message shows the line number of the statement that was being executed when the error occurred.

The second type of bug produces inaccurate results when an application runs. These bugs occur due to *logical errors* in the source code. For instance, the second console shows output for the Test Score application. Here, the final totals were displayed and the application ended before any input was entered. This type of bug can be more difficult to find and correct than a runtime error.

How to debug an application

When you *debug* a program, you find the cause of the bugs, fix them, and test again. As your programs become more complex, debugging can be one of the most time-consuming aspects of programming. That's why it's important to write your code in a way that makes it easy to read, understand, and debug.

To find the cause of runtime errors, you can start by finding the source statement that was running when the program crashed. To do that, you can start by studying the error message. For example, the first console in figure 2-19 shows that the statement at line 18 in the main() method of the InvoiceApp class was running when the program crashed. That's the statement that uses the nextDouble() method of the Scanner object, and that indicates that the problem is invalid input data. In chapter 5, you'll learn how to fix this bug.

To find the cause of incorrect output, you can start by figuring out why the application produced the output that it did. For instance, you can start by asking why the second application in this figure didn't prompt the user to enter any test scores. Once you figure that out, you're well on your way to fixing the bug.

A runtime error that occurred while testing the Invoice application

```
Output - ch02_Invoice (run)  ×                                              —
    Welcome to the Invoice Total Calculator

    Enter subtotal:    $100
    Exception in thread "main" java.util.InputMismatchException
            at java.util.Scanner.throwFor(Scanner.java:864)
            at java.util.Scanner.next(Scanner.java:1485)
            at java.util.Scanner.nextDouble(Scanner.java:2413)
            at InvoiceApp.main(InvoiceApp.java:18)
    C:\murach\java\netbeans\book_apps\ch02_Invoice\nbproject\build-impl.xml:1026: The following error
    C:\murach\java\netbeans\book_apps\ch02_Invoice\nbproject\build-impl.xml:791: Java returned: 1
    BUILD FAILED (total time: 6 seconds)
```

Incorrect output produced by the Test Score application

```
Output - ch02_TestScore (run)  ×                                           —
    compile:
    run:
    Enter test scores that range from 0 to 100.
    To end the program, enter 999.


    Score count:   0
    Score total:   0
    Average score: NaN

    BUILD SUCCESSFUL (total time: 0 seconds)
```

Description

- A *syntax* or *compile-time error* occurs when a statement can't be compiled. Before you can test an application, you must fix the syntax errors.

- To *test* an application, you run it to make sure that it works properly no matter what combinations of valid and invalid data you enter. The goal of testing is to find the errors (or *bugs*) in the application.

- To *debug* an application, you find the causes of the bugs and fix them.

- One type of bug leads to a *runtime error* (also known as a *runtime exception*) that causes the program to end prematurely. This type of bug must be fixed before testing can continue.

- Even if an application runs to completion, the results may be incorrect due to *logic errors*. These bugs must also be fixed.

Debugging tips

- For a runtime error, go to the line in the source code that was running when the program crashed. In most IDEs, you can do that by clicking on the link to the line of source code. That should give you a strong indication of what caused the error.

- For a logical error, first figure out how the source code produced that output. Then, fix the code and test the application again.

Figure 2-19   How to test and debug an application

Perspective

The goal of this chapter has been to get you started with Java programming and to get you started fast. Now, if you understand how the Invoice and Test Score applications work, you've come a long way. You should also be able to write comparable programs of your own.

Keep in mind, though, that this chapter is just an introduction to Java programming. In the next few chapters, you'll learn more about data types, control statements, exceptions, testing, and debugging.

Summary

- *Statements* direct the operations of a program, and *comments* typically document what the statements do.

- A *class* stores Java code and may contain one or more *methods*.

- The *main method*, named main (), is a special type of method that's executed when you run the class that contains it.

- *Variables* are used to store data that changes, or *varies*, as a program runs.

- When you declare a variable, you must declare its data type. Two of the most common *data types* for numeric variables are the int and double types.

- You can use *assignment statements* to assign values to variables.

- A *string* is an object that's created from the String class that contains zero or more characters.

- You can use the plus sign to *join* a string with another string or a data type, and you can use assignment statements to *append* one string to another.

- To include special characters in strings, you can use *escape sequences*.

- The *Java API* uses *packages* to organize and store its classes. To make it easier to use classes that aren't in the java.lang package, you typically code an import statement for the class.

- You can use a *constructor* to create an *object* from a Java class. An object is an *instance* of the class. There may be more than one constructor for a class, and a constructor may require one or more *arguments*.

- You *call* a *method* from an object and you call a *static method* from a class. A method may require one or more arguments.

- You can use the methods of a Scanner object to read input from the *console*, and you can use the print() and println() methods of the System.out object to print output to the console.

- You can code *if statements* to control the logic of a program based on the true or false values that are returned by *Boolean expressions*.

- You can code *while statements* to repeat a series of statements until a Boolean expression becomes false.

- *Testing* is the process of finding the errors or bugs in an application. *Debugging* is the process of locating and fixing the bugs.

Before you do the exercises for this chapter

If you haven't done it already, you should install the JDK, Netbeans, and the source code for this book. For instructions on how to do this, you can refer to the appendixes for this book.

Exercise 2-1   Test the Invoice application

In this exercise, you'll test the Invoice application. This should give you a better idea of how this program works.

1. Open the project named ch02_ex1_Invoice. On a Windows system, this project should be in this directory:

   ```
   C:\murach\java\netbeans\ex_starts
   ```

2. Open the file named InvoiceApp.java. Review the code for this file and note that the IDE doesn't display any syntax errors, though it may display some hints or suggestions for improving your code.

3. Test this application with valid subtotal entries like 50, 150, 250, and 1000 so it's easy to see whether the calculations are correct.

4. Test the application with a subtotal value like 233.33. This should show that the application doesn't round the results to two decimal places. But that's OK for now. You'll learn how to do that in the next chapter.

5. Test the application with an invalid subtotal value like $1000. This time, the application should crash. Study the error message that's displayed and determine which line of source code in the InvoiceApp class was running when the error occurred. Then, jump to this line by clicking on the link to it. Again, that's OK for now. You'll learn how to prevent this crash in chapter 5.

6. Restart the application, enter a valid subtotal, and enter 20 when the program asks you whether you want to continue. What happens and why?

7. Restart the application and enter two values separated by whitespace (like 1000 20) before pressing the Enter key. What happens and why?

Exercise 2-2   Modify the Test Score application

In this exercise, you'll modify the Test Score application. This should give you a chance to write some code of your own.

1. Open the project named ch02_ex2_TestScore that's in the ex_starts directory shown in the previous exercise.

2. Test this application with valid data to see how it works. Then, test the application with invalid data. You should be able to crash the program at least once. Note that if you enter a test score like 125, the program ends, even though the instructions say that the program ends when you enter 999.

3. Open the file named TestScoreApp.java and modify the while statement so the program only ends when you enter 999. Then, test the program to see how this works.

4. . Modify the if statement so it displays an error message like "Invalid entry; not counted" if the user enters a score that's greater than 100 but isn't 999. Then, test this change.

5. Run the application again, enter 999 as the first score, and note what is displayed for the average score. Then, modify the code so it sets the initial value of average score to 0.0 and so it only calculates the average score if the value of the scoreCount variable is greater than zero. Test this change.

Exercise 2-3   Modify the Invoice application

In this exercise, you'll modify the Invoice application. When you're through with the modifications, a test run should look something like this:

```
Welcome to the Invoice Total Calculator

Enter subtotal:    100
Discount percent: 0.1
Discount amount:  10.0
Invoice total:    90.0

Continue? (y/n): y

Enter subtotal:    500
Discount percent: 0.25
Discount amount:  125.0
Invoice total:    375.0

Continue? (y/n): n

Number of invoices: 2
Average invoice:    232.5
Average discount:   67.5
```

1. Open the project named ch02_ex3_Invoice that's in the ex_starts directory. Then, open the file named InvoiceApp.java.

2. Modify the code so the application ends only when the user enters "n" or "N". As it is now, the application ends when the user enters anything other than "y" or "Y". To do this, you need to use a not operator (!) with the equalsIgnoreCase() method. Then, test this change.

3. Modify the code so it provides a discount of 25 percent when the subtotal is greater than or equal to 500. Then, test this change.

4. Modify the code so it displays the number of invoices, the average invoice amount, and the average discount amount when the user ends the program. Then, test this change.

5. Make sure that any comments in the application still match the application code. Change any comments that are no longer accurate.

Exercise 2-4   Use the Java API documentation

This exercise helps you use the Java API documentation to learn more about the Scanner, String, and Double classes. This should give you a better idea of how to use the documentation for the Java API.

1. Open a browser and display the Java API documentation as described in figure 2-10.

2. Click the java.util package in the upper left frame. Then, in the lower left frame, scroll down and click the Scanner class. This should display the documentation for the Scanner class in the right frame. Then, scroll through this documentation to get an idea of its scope.

3. Review the constructors for the Scanner class. The constructor that's presented in this chapter has just an InputStream object as its argument. When you code that argument, remember that System.in represents the InputStream object for the console.

4. Review the methods of the Scanner class with special attention to the next(), nextInt(), and nextDouble() methods. Note that there are three next() methods and two nextInt() methods. The ones used in this chapter have no arguments. Then, review the rest of the methods in the Scanner class. You'll learn how to use some of these methods in chapter 5.

5. View the documentation for the String class, which is in the java.lang package. Note that it offers a number of constructors. In this chapter, though, you learned the shortcut for creating String objects because that's the best way to do that. Then, review the methods for this class with special attention to the equals() and equalsIgnoreCase() methods.

6. View the documentation for the Double class, which is also in the java.lang package. Then, review the static parseDouble() and toString() methods that you'll learn how to use in the next chapter.

If you find the documentation difficult to follow, rest assured that you'll become comfortable with it before you finish this book. Once you learn how to create your own classes, constructors, and methods, it should make more sense.

3

How to work with the primitive data types

In chapter 2, you learned how to use two of the eight primitive data types as you declared and initialized variables and coded assignment statements that used simple arithmetic expressions. Now, you'll learn all of the details that you need for working with variables and data types at a professional level.

Basic skills for working with data

The next three figures review some of the skills presented in chapter 2 for working with data. In addition, these figures present some new skills that are related to this topic.

The eight primitive data types

Figure 3-1 shows the eight *primitive data types* provided by Java. You can use these eight data types to store numbers, characters, and true or false values.

In chapter 2, you learned how to use the int data type to store *integers* (whole numbers). However, Java provides three other data types for integers. For example, if a value is too big for the int type, you can use the long type. Conversely, if you only need to store small integer values and you want to save system resources, you can use the short and byte types.

In chapter 2, you also learned how to use the double data type for storing numbers with decimal places. However, if you want to save system resources, you can use the float data type. The values in both of these data types are stored as *floating-point numbers* that can hold very large and very small values, but with a limited number of *significant digits*. For instance, the double type has 16 significant digits. As a result, it supports numbers like 12,345,678,901,234.56 or 12,345,678.90123456 or 12.34567890123456. However, the float type only has 7 significant digits. However, it can still support very large and small numbers such as 1,234,567,000,000,000 and .0000000001234567. That's because in these numbers, the digits 1 through 7 are significant but the zeros are not.

To express the value of a floating-point number, you can use *scientific notation*. This lets you express very large and very small numbers in a sort of shorthand. To use this notation, you type the letter *e* or *E* followed by a power of 10. For instance, 3.65e+9 is equal to 3.65 times 10^9 (3,650,000,000). Similarly, 3.65e-9 is equal to 3.65 times 10^{-9} (.00000000365).

You can use the *char* type to store one character. Since Java uses the two-byte *Unicode character set*, it can store practically any character from any language around the world. As a result, you can use Java to create applications that read and print Greek or Chinese characters. In practice, though, you'll usually work with the characters that are stored in the older one-byte *ASCII character set*. These characters are the first 256 characters of the Unicode character set.

Last, you can use the boolean type to store a true or false value. This data type is typically used to represent a condition in a control statement that can be true or false.

The eight primitive data types

Type	Bytes	Use
byte	1	Very short integers from -128 to 127.
short	2	Short integers from -32,768 to 32,767.
int	4	Integers from -2,147,483,648 to 2,147,483,647.
long	8	Long integers from -9,223,372,036,854,775,808 to 9,223,372,036,854,775,807.
float	4	Single-precision, floating-point numbers from -3.4E38 to 3.4E38 with up to 7 significant digits.
double	8	Double-precision, floating-point numbers from -1.7E308 to 1.7E308 with up to 16 significant digits.
char	2	A single Unicode character that's stored in two bytes.
boolean	1	A *true* or *false* value.

Description

- *Integers* are whole numbers.

- *Floating-point numbers* provide for very large and very small numbers that require decimal positions, but with a limited number of *significant digits*. A *single-precision number* provides for numbers with up to 7 significant digits. A *double-precision number* provides for numbers with up to 16 significant digits.

- The *Unicode character set* provides for over 65,000 characters with two bytes used for each character. The *ASCII character set* provides characters for the English language. These characters are the first 256 characters of the Unicode character set.

- A *Boolean value* can be true or false. In Java, the boolean data type provides for Boolean values.

Technical notes

- To express the value of a floating-point number, you can use *scientific notation*. For example, 2.382E+5 means 2.382 times 10^5, which is a value of 238,200. Conversely, 3.25E-8 means 3.25 times 10^{-8}, which is a value of .0000000325. Java sometimes uses this notation to display the value of a floating-point number.

- Because of the way floating-point numbers are stored internally, they can't represent the exact value of the decimal places in some numbers. This can cause a rounding problem. Later in this chapter, you'll learn how to use the BigDecimal class to solve these rounding problems.

- By default, Java uses Intel 80-bit extended precision floating-point when it is available from the CPU. As a result, code that uses floating-point numbers may produce slightly different results on different systems.

Figure 3-1   The eight primitive data types

How to declare and initialize variables

In chapter 2, you learned how to *declare* and *initialize* a *variable*. Figure 3-2 reviews these skills, and it presents some new information. In particular, it shows how to declare and initialize some of the data types that weren't presented in chapter 2.

Although you usually declare and initialize a variable in one statement, it occasionally makes sense to do it in two. For instance, you may want to declare a variable at the start of a coding routine without giving it a starting value because its value won't be set until later on.

The one-statement examples in this figure show how to declare and initialize various types of variables. Here, the third and fourth examples show how to assign values to the float and long types. To do that, you can add a letter after the value. For a float type, you must add an *f* or *F* after the value. Otherwise, the code won't compile. For a long type, you can add an *L*. However, this isn't necessary for the code to compile. You can also use a lowercase *l*, but that letter can easily be mistaken for the number 1. As a result, it's generally considered a better practice to use an uppercase *L*.

The fifth and sixth statements show how to assign an integer value that has seven digits. Although these statements assign the same value, the second statement uses underscores to separate each group of three digits. Since you can't use commas in numeric literals, you'll want to use underscores whenever that improves the readability of your code. And you can use this technique with all types of numeric literals including double, float, and long values. However, since this feature was introduced with Java 7, you should only use it if you're sure your code will be run by Java 7 or later.

The seventh statement shows how you can use scientific notation as you assign a value to a variable. Then, the eighth example shows that you can assign a character to the char type by enclosing a character in single quotes. The ninth example shows that, because the characters in the Unicode character set map to integers, you can assign a character to the char type by supplying the integer for the character. And the tenth example shows how to initialize a variable named valid as a boolean type with a false value.

The last example shows that you can declare and initialize two or more variables in a single statement. Although you may occasionally want to do this, it's usually better to declare and initialize one variable per statement since it usually results in code that's easier to read and modify later.

The assignment operator

Operator	Name	Description
=	Assignment	Assigns a new value to the variable.

How to declare a variable and assign a value to it in two statements

Syntax

```
type variableName;
variableName = value;
```

Example

```
int counter;          // declaration statement
counter = 1;          // assignment statement
```

How to declare a variable and assign a value to it in one statement

Syntax

```
type variableName = value;
```

Examples

```
int counter = 1;                    // initialize an int variable
double price = 14.95;               // initialize a double variable
float interestRate = 8.125F;        // F indicates a floating-point value
long numberOfBytes = 20000L;        // L indicates a long integer
int population1 = 1734323;          // initialize an int variable
int population2 = 1_734_323;        // improve readability - Java 7 and later
double distance = 3.65e+9;          // scientific notation
char letter1 = 'A';                 // stored as a two-byte Unicode character
char letter2 = 65;                  // integer value for a Unicode character
boolean valid = false;              // where false is a keyword
int x = 0, y = 0;                   // initialize 2 variables with 1 statement
```

Description

- A *variable* stores a value that changes as an application executes. In other words, the value of a variable varies as an application executes.

- Before you can use a variable, you must *declare* its data type and its name.

- After you declare a variable, you can *assign* a value to the variable. To do that, you use the *assignment operator* (=).

- You can *initialize* a variable by declaring it and assigning a value to it. To do that, you can use two statements, but it's common to use one statement.

- To declare and initialize more than one variable for a single data type in a single statement, use commas to separate the assignments.

- To identify float values, you must type an *f* or *F* after the number.

- To identify long values, you can type an *l* or *L* after the number.

Naming conventions

- Start variable names with a lowercase letter and capitalize the first letter in all words after the first word. This naming convention is known as *camel case*.

- Try to use meaningful names that are easy to remember as you code.

Figure 3-2   How to declare variables and assign values to them

How to declare and initialize constants

In chapter 2, you learned that a variable stores a value that changes as an application executes. In other words, the value of a variable varies as an application executes. However, a *constant* stores a value that does not change as an application executes. In other words, the value of a constant remains constant as an application executes.

Most of the skills for declaring and initializing variables also apply to declaring and initializing constants. However, when you declare a constant, you begin the statement with the *final* keyword. As a result, constants are sometimes called *final variables*. In addition, it's a common coding convention to use all uppercase letters for the name of a constant and to separate the words in the name with an underscore as shown in figure 3-3.

How to declare and initialize a constant

Syntax

```
final type CONSTANT_NAME = value;
```

Examples

```
final int DAYS_IN_NOVEMBER = 30;
final float SALES_TAX = .075F;
final double LIGHT_YEAR_MILES = 5.879e+12;
```

Description

- A *constant* stores a value that does not change as an application executes. In other words, the value of a constant remains constant as an application executes.

- To declare a constant, you begin the declaration statement with the final keyword. After that, the skills for initializing variables also apply to constants.

- To make it easy to distinguish between variables and constants, most Java developers use camel case for variables and all caps for constants.

Naming conventions

- Capitalize all of the letters in constants and separate words with underscores.

- Try to use meaningful names that are easy to remember.

Figure 3-3 ·   How to declare and initialize constants

How to code arithmetic expressions

In chapter 2, you learned how to code simple *arithmetic expressions*. These expressions used the first four *arithmetic operators* shown in figure 3-4. Now, the next three figures show how to use more of the operators that Java provides for working with arithmetic expressions. These operators perform operations on the *operands* in the expression, which can be either literal values or variables.

How to use the binary operators

In figure 3-4, the first five operators work on two operands. As a result, they're referred to as *binary operators*. For example, when you use the subtraction operator (-), you subtract one operand from another.

The addition (+), subtraction (-), and multiplication (*) operators are self-explanatory. However, the division (/) and modulus (%) operators require some explanation.

If you're working with integer types, the division operator returns an integer value that represents the number of times the right operand fits into the left operand. Then, if necessary, you can use the modulus operator to return an integer value that represents the remainder (which is the amount that's left over after dividing the left operand by the right operand).

If you're working with floating-point types, the division operator returns a floating-point value. This value uses decimal places to indicate the result of the division. In most cases, that's what you want.

The arithmetic binary operators

Operator	Name	Description
+	Addition	Adds two operands.
–	Subtraction	Subtracts the right operand from the left operand.
*	Multiplication	Multiplies the right operand and the left operand.
/	Division	Divides the right operand into the left operand. If both operands are integers, then the result is an integer.
%	Modulus	Returns the value that is left over after dividing the right operand into the left operand.

Code that initializes two integer values

```
int x = 14;
int y = 8;
```

How to perform addition and subtraction

```
int result1 = x + y;        // result1 = 22
int result2 = x - y;        // result2 = 6
```

How to perform multiplication

```
int result3 = x * y;        // result3 = 112
```

How to perform integer division

```
int result4 = x / y;        // result4 = 1
int result5 = x % y;        // result5 = 6
```

Code that initializes two double values

```
double a = 8.5;
double b = 3.4;
```

How to perform decimal division

```
double result6 = a / b;     // result6 = 2.5
```

Description

- An *arithmetic expression* consists of *arithmetic operators* that operate on one or more numbers known as *operands*.

- *Binary operators* operate on two operands.

- An assignment statement can assign the value of an expression to a variable. Then, when Java executes the assignment statement, it determines the value of the expression and stores the result in the variable.

Figure 3-4   How to use the arithmetic binary operators

How to use the unary operators

Figure 3-5 shows four operators that work on one operand. As a result, they're referred to as *unary operators*. For example, you can code the increment operator (++) after an operand to increase the value of the operand by 1.

When you code an increment (++) or decrement (--) operator, you can *prefix* the operand by coding the operator before the variable. Then, the increment or decrement operation is performed before the rest of the statement is executed. Conversely, you can *postfix* the operand by coding the operator after the variable. Then, the increment or decrement operation isn't performed until after the statement is executed.

Often, an entire statement does nothing more than increment or decrement a variable as shown in the first two examples. Then, both the prefix and postfix forms yield the same result. However, if you use the increment and decrement operators as part of a larger statement, you can use the prefix and postfix forms of these operators to control when the operation is performed. This is shown by the third and fourth examples.

If necessary, you can code the negative sign operator (-) in front of an operand to reverse the value of the operand as shown in the fifth example. Although you can also code the positive sign operator (+) in front of an operand, it doesn't change the value of the operand. As a result, this unary operator is rarely used.

Since each char type is a Unicode character that maps to an integer, you can perform some integer operations on char types. For instance, the sixth example shows how you can use the increment operator to change the numeric value for a char variable from 67 to 68, which changes the character from *C* to *D*.

The arithmetic unary operators

Operator	Name	Description
++	Increment	Adds 1 to the operand (x = x + 1).
--	Decrement	Subtracts 1 from the operand (x = x - 1).
+	Positive sign	Indicates that the value is positive.
-	Negative sign	Changes a positive value to negative, and vice versa.

A typical statement that uses the increment operator

```
int i = 1;
i++;                          // after execution, i = 2
```

A typical statement that uses the decrement operator

```
int i = 10;
i--;                          // after execution, i = 9
```

How to postfix an increment operator

```
int x = 14;
int result = x++;             // after execution, x = 15, result = 14
```

How to prefix an increment operator

```
int x = 14;
int result = ++x;             // after execution, x = 15, result = 15
```

How to reverse the value of a number

```
int x = 14;
int result = -x;              // result = -14
```

How to perform an arithmetic operation on a character

```
char letter1 = 'C';           // letter1 = 'C'  Unicode integer is 67
char letter2 = ++letter1;     // letter2 = 'D'  Unicode integer is 68
```

Description

- *Unary operators* operate on just one operand.
- When you use an increment or decrement operator as a *postfix* to a variable, Java performs the increment or decrement operation after other operations.
- When you use an increment or decrement operator as a *prefix* to a variable, Java performs the increment or decrement operation before other operations.
- If you code an increment or decrement operation as a single statement, not as part of an expression, it doesn't matter whether the operator is prefixed or postfixed.

Figure 3-5   How to use the arithmetic unary operators

How to use the compound assignment operators

When coding assignment statements, it's common to code the same variable on both sides of the equals sign as shown by the first example in figure 3-6. That way, you can use the current value of the variable in an expression and update the variable by assigning the result of the expression to it.

Since it's common to write statements like this, the Java language provides the five *compound assignment operators* shown in this figure. Although these operators don't provide any new functionality, you can use them to write shorter code that doesn't require you to code the same variable on both sides of the equals sign. This is shown by the second example.

If, for example, you need to increment or decrement a variable by a value of 1, you can use a shortcut operator. For example:

```
month = month + 1;
```

can be coded with a shortcut operator as

```
month += 1;
```

which is equivalent to

```
month++;
```

Similarly, if you want to add the value of a variable named nextNumber to a summary field named sum, you can do it like this:

```
sum += nextNumber;
```

which is equivalent to

```
sum = sum + nextNumber;
```

The technique that you use is mostly a matter of preference because both techniques are easy to read and maintain.

The compound assignment operators

Operator	Name	Description
+=	Addition	Adds the operand to the starting value of the variable and assigns the result to the variable.
-=	Subtraction	Subtracts the operand from the starting value of the variable and assigns the result to the variable.
*=	Multiplication	Multiplies the operand by the starting value of the variable and assigns the result to the variable.
/=	Division	Divides the starting value of the variable by the operand and assigns the result to the variable. If the operand and the value of the variable are both integers, the result is an integer.
%=	Modulus	Derives the value that is left over after dividing the right operand by the value in the variable, and then assigns this value to the variable.

Statements that use the same variable on both sides of the equals sign

```
count = count + 1;          // count is increased by 1
count = count - 1;          // count is decreased by 1
total = total + 100.0;      // total is increased by 100.0
total = total - 100.0;      // total is decreased by 100.0
price = price * .8;         // price is multiplied by .8
sum = sum + nextNumber;     // sum is increased by the value of nextNumber
```

Statements that use the compound assignment operators

```
count += 1;                 // count is increased by 1
count -= 1;                 // count is decreased by 1
total += 100.0;             // total is increased by 100.0
total -= 100.0;             // total is decreased by 100.0
price *= .8;                // price is multipled by .8
sum += nextNumber;          // sum is increased by the value of nextNumber
```

Description

- Besides the assignment operator (=), Java provides for five *compound assignment operators*. These operators provide a shorthand way to code common assignment operations.

- The compound assignment operators are also referred to as the *augmented assignment operators*.

Figure 3-6   How to use the compound assignment operators

How to work with the order of precedence

Figure 3-7 gives more information about coding arithmetic expressions. In particular, it gives the *order of precedence* of the arithmetic operations. This means that all of the prefixed increment and decrement operations in an expression are done first, followed by all of the positive and negative operations, and so on. If there are two or more operations at the same order of precedence, the operations are done from left to right.

This sequence of operations doesn't always work the way you want it to. As a result, you sometimes need to override the sequence by using parentheses. Then, the expressions in the innermost sets of parentheses are done first, followed by the next sets of parentheses, and so on. Within the parentheses, though, the operations are done left to right by the order of precedence. In general, you should use parentheses to specify the sequence of operations whenever there's any doubt about it.

The first example shows why you sometimes need to use parentheses to specify the order of precedence. Here, the first expression that calculates price doesn't use parentheses. As a result, Java uses the default order of precedence and performs the multiplication operation before the subtraction operation, which gives an incorrect result. In contrast, the second expression that calculates price encloses the subtraction operation in parentheses. As a result, Java performs the subtraction operation before the multiplication operation, which gives a correct result.

The second example shows how you can use parentheses in a more complicated expression. Here, the first expression uses three sets of parentheses to calculate the current value of an investment account after a monthly investment amount is added to it, monthly interest is calculated, and the interest is added to it. If you have trouble following this, you can plug the initial values into the expression and evaluate it one set of parentheses at a time:

```
(5000 + 100) * (1 + (.12 / 12))
(5000 + 100) * (1 + .01)
5100 * 1.01
5151
```

If you have trouble creating an expression like this for a difficult calculation, you can often break the expression down into a series of statements as shown in the last four lines of code. Here, the first statement adds the monthly investment amount to the current value. The second statement calculates the monthly interest rate. The third statement calculates the monthly interest amount. And the fourth statement adds the interest to the current value. This takes away the need for parentheses. In addition, it makes the code easier to read and debug.

The order of precedence for arithmetic operations

1. Increment and decrement

2. Positive and negative

3. Multiplication, division, and remainder

4. Addition and subtraction

Code that calculates a discounted price

Using the default order of precedence

```
double discountPercent = .2;              // 20% discount
double price = 100;                       // $100 price
price = price * 1 - discountPercent;      // price = $99.8
```

Using parentheses to specify the order of precedence

```
price = price * (1 - discountPercent);    // price = $80
```

Code that calculates the current value of a monthly investment

```
double currentValue = 5000;         // current value of investment account
double monthlyInvestment = 100;     // amount added each month
double yearlyInterestRate = .12;    // yearly interest rate
```

Using parentheses to specify the order of precedence

```
currentValue = (currentValue + monthlyInvestment) *
               (1 + (yearlyInterestRate / 12));
```

Using separate statements to control the order of precedence

```
currentValue += monthlyInvestment;                        // add investment
double monthlyInterestRate = yearlyInterestRate / 12;
double monthlyInterest = currentValue * monthlyInterestRate;
currentValue += monthlyInterest;                          // add interest
```

Description

- Unless parentheses are used, the operations in an expression take place from left to right in the *order of precedence*.

- To specify the sequence of operations, you can use parentheses. Then, the operations in the innermost set of parentheses are done first, followed by the operations in the next set, and so on.

Figure 3-7   How to work with the order of precedence

How to work with casting

As you develop Java applications, you'll frequently need to convert data from one data type to another. To do that, you use a technique called *casting* as shown in figure 3-8.

Java provides for two types of casting. *Implicit casts* are performed automatically and can be used to convert data with a less precise type such as the float type to a more precise type such as the double type. Similarly, implicit casts can be used to convert data from a smaller type such as the int type to a larger type such as the long type. This is called a *widening conversion* because the new type is always wide enough to hold the original value. For instance, the first statement in this figure converts an integer value of 93 to a double value.

Java also performs an implicit cast on the values in an arithmetic expression if some of the values have more precise data types than other values as shown by the next three statements. Here, the variable named d is declared with the double type, and the variables named i and j are declared with the int type. Then, when these variables are used together in an expression, Java converts both i and j to double values when it evaluates this expression.

A *narrowing conversion* is one that casts data from a more precise data type to a less precise data type. With this type of conversion, the less precise data type may not be wide enough to hold the original value, which may result in the loss of some data. In that case, you must use an *explicit cast*.

To perform an explicit cast, you code the data type in parentheses before the variable that you want to convert. For instance, the first example that performs an explicit cast converts a double value of 93.75 to an int value of 93. Here, an explicit cast is required because Java won't perform an implicit cast for a narrowing conversion that may result in the loss of data. In this case, the conversion results in the loss of the decimal digits.

When you use explicit casting in an arithmetic expression, Java performs the casting before the arithmetic operations as shown by the last two examples of explicit casts. In the last example, Java casts two integer types to double types before the division is done so the result has decimal places if necessary. Without explicit casting, the expression would return an integer value that Java would then cast to a double.

When you code an explicit cast, an exception may occur at runtime if the JRE (Java runtime environment) isn't able to perform the cast. As a result, you should use an explicit cast only when you're sure that the JRE is able to perform the cast.

Although you typically cast between numeric data types, you can also cast between the int and char types as shown by the third example. That's because every char value corresponds to an int value that identifies it in the Unicode character set. Since there's no possible loss of data, you can implicitly cast between these data types. However, if you prefer, you can also code these casts explicitly.

If you use a compound assignment operator such as +=, an explicit cast is implied. This can result in the loss of data as shown in the fourth example. As a result, you should be careful when using the compound assignment operators and mixing data types.

How implicit casting works
Data types

byte→short→int→long→float→double

Examples

```
double grade = 93;                    // convert int to double

double d = 95.0;
int i = 86, j = 91;
double average = (d+i+j)/3;           // convert i and j to double values
                                      // average = 90.666666...
```

How to code an explicit cast
Syntax

```
(type) expression
```

Examples

```
int grade = (int) 93.75;              // convert double to int (grade = 93)

double d = 95.0;
int i = 86, j = 91;
int average = ((int)d+i+j)/3;         // convert d to int value (average = 90)
int remainder = ((int)d+i+j)%3;       // convert d to int value (remainer = 2)

double result = (double) i / (double) j;    // result has decimal places
```

How to cast between char and int types

```
char letterChar = 65;                 // convert int to char (letterChar = 'A')
char letterChar2 = (char) 65;         // this works too
int letterInt = 'A';                  // convert char to int (letterInt = 65)
int letterInt2 = (int) 'A';           // this works too
```

How the compound assignment operator can cause an explicit cast

```
int i = 4;
double d = 4.5;
i += d;                               // i = 8 (4.5 is cast to the int type)
```

Description

- If you assign a less precise data type to a more precise data type, or you assign a smaller data type to a larger data type, Java automatically performs the cast and makes the conversion. This can be referred to as an *implicit cast* or a *widening conversion*.

- When you code an arithmetic expression, Java implicitly casts the less precise data types to the most precise data type.

- To code an assignment statement that assigns a more precise data type to a less precise data type, you must use parentheses to specify the less precise data type. This can be referred to as an *explicit cast* or a *narrowing conversion*.

- When you code an explicit cast in an arithmetic expression, Java performs the cast before any arithmetic operations.

- Since each char value has a corresponding int value, you can implicitly or explicitly cast between these types.

Figure 3-8   How to work with casting

How to use the Java Shell to test code

If you're using JDK 9 or later, you can use the Java Shell, or JShell, to interactively test code as shown in figure 3-9. So, if you're confused by any of the examples presented in the previous figures, now is a good time to use the shell to test some of these examples! To do that, open the shell and start experimenting with the arithmetic operations.

In fact, you probably should take a break right now and do some experimenting, especially if you have any doubts about how the arithmetic operations work. For instance, test the use of each arithmetic operator. Test the use of each compound assignment operator. And test the results of floating-point operations. Along the way, you'll probably get some error messages, but that's all part of the learning process. Each one should give you a better understanding of how Java works.

The Java Shell after testing some code from the previous figures

```
[1]-> int x = 14
|   x ==> 14
[2]-> int y = 8
|   y ==> 8
[3]-> x + y
|   $1 ==> 22
[4]-> x / y
|   $2 ==> 1
[5]-> (double) x / y
|   $6 ==> 1.75
[6]-> x++
|   $8 ==> 14
[7]-> x
|   x ==> 15
[8]-> ++x
|   $9 ==> 16
[9]-> x
|   x ==> 16
[10]-> x += 20
|   $11 ==> 36
[11]-> 3 + 4 * 10
|   $15 ==> 43
[12]-> (3 + 4) * 10
|   $19 ==> 70
[13]-> X + 10
|   Error:
|   cannot find symbol
|     symbol:   variable X
|   X + 10
|   ^
[13]->
```

How to use the shell

- With NetBeans 9.0, you can start the Java Shell by selecting the Tools→Open Java Platform Shell command.

- To test a statement or expression, type it at the prompt and press the Enter key.

- When you enter a statement that declares a variable, the shell shows the name of the variable, followed by an arrow (==>), and the value of the variable.

- Any of the variables you create remain active for the rest of the session. As a result, you can use them later in the session.

- When you enter an expression, the shell automatically creates a variable that begins with $, and it stores the result of the expression in that variable.

- You can type the name of a variable at the prompt to view its value.

- If you enter code that causes an error, the shell displays the error.

Description

- The Java Shell, also called JShell, was introduced with JDK 9. It allows you to interactively test Java code.

Figure 3-9   How to use the Java Shell to test code

How to use Java classes to work with numbers

As you learned in chapter 2, Java provides hundreds of classes that include methods that you can use in your code. The next few figures present four classes that are designed to work with the numeric data types. In addition, they show how to use the BigDecimal class to fix rounding errors that sometimes occur with the floating-point types.

How to use the Integer and Double classes

Figure 3-10 shows how to use a few of the constructors and static methods that are provided by the Integer and Double classes. Since these classes can be used to create objects that wrap around the primitive types, they are sometimes referred to as *wrapper classes*. Wrapper classes also exist for the other six primitive data types.

The first group of statements in this figure shows how to create Integer and Double objects that can store int and double data types. This is useful when you want to provide an int or double data type as an argument to a method, but the method requires that the argument be an object, not a data type. You'll see how this works in a later chapter. Once you create an Integer or Double object, you can use any of the methods of these classes to work with the data it contains.

Note, however, that these classes also provide static methods that you can use without creating objects. For instance, the second group of statements in this figure shows how to use the static toString() method to convert a primitive type to a string. Here, the first statement converts the int variable named counter to a string and returns the value to a string variable named counterString. The second statement converts the double variable named price to a string and returns that value to the string variable named priceString.

Similarly, the third group of statements shows how to use the static parseXxx() methods to convert strings to primitive types. Here, the first statement uses the parseInt() method of the Integer class to convert a string to an int data type. The second statement uses the parseDouble() method of the Double class to convert a string to a double data type. Once these statements have been executed, you can use the quantity and price variables in arithmetic expressions.

But what happens if the string contains a non-numeric value like "ten" that can't be parsed to an int or double type? In that case, the parseInt() or parseDouble() method will cause a runtime error known as an exception. Using Java terminology, you can say that the method will *throw an exception*. In chapter 5, you'll learn how to *catch* the exceptions that are thrown by these methods.

Constructors for the Integer and Double classes

Constructor	Description
`Integer(int)`	Creates an Integer object from an int data type.
`Double(double)`	Creates a Double object from a double data type.

Two static methods of the Integer class

Method	Description
`parseInt(stringName)`	Attempts to convert the String object that's supplied as an argument to an int type. If successful, it returns the int value. If unsuccessful, it throws an exception.
`toString(intName)`	Converts the int value that's supplied as an argument to a String object and returns that String object.

Two static methods of the Double class

Method	Description
`parseDouble(stringName)`	Attempts to convert the String object that's supplied as an argument to a double type. If successful, it returns the double value. If unsuccessful, it throws an exception.
`toString(doubleName)`	Converts the double value that's supplied as an argument to a String object and returns that String object.

How to create Integer and Double objects

```
Integer quantityIntegerObject = new Integer(quantity);
Double priceDoubleObject = new Double(price);
```

How to use static methods to convert primitive types to String objects

```
String counterString = Integer.toString(counter);
String priceString = Double.toString(price);
```

How to use static methods to convert String objects to primitive types

```
int quantity = Integer.parseInt(quantityString);
double price = Double.parseDouble(priceString);
```

Description

- The Integer and Double classes are known as *wrapper classes* since they can be used to construct Integer and Double objects that contain (wrap around) int and double values. This can be useful when you need to pass an int or double value to a method that only accepts objects, not primitive data types.

- The Integer and Double classes also provide static methods that you can use for converting values from these data types to strings and vice versa.

- If the parseInt() and parseDouble() methods can't successfully parse the string, they will cause an error to occur. In Java terminology, this is known as *throwing an exception*. You'll learn how to handle or *catch* exceptions in chapter 5.

- Every primitive type has a wrapper class that works like the Integer and Double classes.

Figure 3-10   How to use the Integer and Double classes

How to use the Math class

The Math class provides a few dozen methods for working with numeric data types. Figure 3-11 presents some of the most useful ones.

The first example shows how to use the round() method. Here, the first statement rounds a double type to a long type, and the second statement rounds a float type to an int type. This works because the round() method only rounds to an integer value.

If you want to round to the specified number of decimal places, you can do that by multiplying the double or float value by a multiple of 10 and then dividing that value by the same multiple of 10. In this figure, for instance, the code shows how to round a value of 10.315 to 2 decimal places. To do that, the code multiplies the value by 100, rounds that value, and divides that value by 100. For this to work, you must cast the long value that's returned by the round() method to a double value. That way, Java uses decimal division, not integer division.

The second example shows how to use the pow() method to raise the first argument to the power of the second argument. This method returns a double value and accepts two double arguments. However, since Java automatically converts any arguments of a less precise numeric type to a double, the pow() method accepts all of the numeric types. In this example, the first statement is equal to 2^2, the second statement is equal to 2^3, and the third and fourth statements are equal to 5^2.

In general, the methods of the Math class work the way you would expect. However, you may need to cast numeric types to get the methods to work the way you want them to. For example, the pow() method returns a double type. So if you want to return an int type, you need to cast the double type to an int type as shown in the fourth example of the pow() method.

The third example shows how to use the sqrt() method to get the square root of a number. Then, the fourth example shows how to use the max() and min() methods to return the greater or lesser of two values. If you study these examples, you shouldn't have any trouble understanding how they work.

The fifth example shows how to use the random() method to generate random numbers. Since this method returns a random double value greater than or equal to 0.0 and less than 1.0, you can return any range of values by multiplying the random number by another number. In this example, the first statement returns a random double value greater than or equal to 0.0 and less than 100.0. Then, the second statement casts this double value to a long data type. If you want, you can use code like this to generate random values for an application.

If you have the right mathematical background, you shouldn't have any trouble using these or any of the other Math methods. For example, if you've taken a course in trigonometry, you should be able to understand the trigonometric methods that the Math class provides.

The Math class

```
java.lang.Math
```

Common static methods of the Math class

Method	Description
round(number)	Returns the closest long value to a double value or the closest int value to a float value. The result has no decimal places.
pow(number, power)	Returns a double value of a double argument (number) that is raised to the power of another double argument (power).
sqrt(number)	Returns a double value that's the square root of the double argument.
max(a, b)	Returns the greater of two float, double, int, or long arguments.
min(a, b)	Returns the lesser of two float, double, int, or long arguments.
random()	Returns a random double value greater than or equal to 0.0 and less than 1.0.

The round method

```
long result = Math.round(1.667);        // result is 2
int result = Math.round(1.49F);         // result is 1
```

How to round a double value to a specified number of decimal places

```
double x = 10.315;
x = (double) Math.round(x * 100) / 100;  // x is 10.32
x = (double) Math.round(x * 10) / 10;    // x is 10.3
```

The pow method

```
double result = Math.pow(2, 2);         // result is 4.0 (2*2)
double result = Math.pow(2, 3);         // result is 8.0 (2*2*2)
double result = Math.pow(5, 2);         // result is 25.0 (5 squared)
int result = (int) Math.pow(5, 2);      // result is 25 (5 squared)
```

The sqrt method

```
double result = Math.sqrt(20.25);       // result is 4.5
```

The max and min methods

```
int x = 67;
int y = 23;
int max = Math.max(x, y);               // max is 67
int min = Math.min(x, y);               // min is 23
```

The random method

```
double x = Math.random() * 100;   // result is a value >= 0.0 and < 100.0
long result = (long) x;           // converts the result from double to long
```

Description

- You can use the static methods of the Math class to perform common arithmetic operations.

- When a method requires one or more arguments, you code them between the parentheses, separating multiple arguments with commas.

- In some cases, you need to cast the result to the data type that you want.

Figure 3-11   How to use the Math class

How to use the NumberFormat class

When you use numeric values in a program, you often need to format them. For example, you may want to apply a standard currency format to a double value. To do that, you need to add a dollar sign and commas and to display just two decimal places. Similarly, you may want to display a double value in a standard percent format. To do that, you need to add a percent sign and move the decimal point two digits to the right.

To do this type of formatting, Java provides the NumberFormat class, which is summarized in figure 3-12. Since this class is part of the java.text package, you'll usually want to include an import statement for this class before you begin working with it.

Once you import this class, you can call one of its static methods to return a NumberFormat object. As you learned in chapter 2, you can call static methods directly from a class. In other words, you code the name of the class, followed by the dot operator, followed by the method. For instance, the first example calls the static getCurrencyInstance() method directly from the NumberFormat class.

Once you use a static method to return a NumberFormat object, you can call non-static methods from that object. To do that, you code the name of the object, followed by the dot operator, followed by the method. For instance, the first example calls the non-static format() method from the NumberFormat object named currency. This returns a string that consists of a dollar sign plus the value of the price variable with two decimal places. In this format, negative numbers are enclosed in parentheses.

The second example shows how to format numbers with the percent format. The main difference between the first and second examples is that you use the getPercentInstance() method to create a NumberFormat object that has the default percent format. Then, you can use the format() method of this object to format a number as a percent. In this format, negative numbers have a leading minus sign.

The third example shows how to format numbers with the number format, and how to set the number of decimal places for a NumberFormat object. Here, the format is changed from the default of three decimal places to just one decimal place. In this format, negative numbers also have a leading minus sign.

The fourth example shows how you can use one statement to create a NumberFormat object and use its format() method. Although this example accomplishes the same task as the second example, it doesn't create a variable for the NumberFormat object that you can use later in the program. As a result, you should only use code like this when you need to format just one number.

When you use the format() method of a NumberFormat object, the numbers are automatically rounded using a technique called *half-even*. This technique rounds up if the preceding digit is odd, but rounds down if the preceding digit is even. If, for example, the currency format is used for a value of 123.455, the formatted result is $123.46, which is what you would expect. But if the value is 123.445, the result is $123.44. Although this is okay for many applications, it can cause problems in others. You'll learn more about this later in this chapter.

The NumberFormat class

`java.text.NumberFormat`

Three static methods of the NumberFormat class

Method	Returns a NumberFormat object that ...
`getCurrencyInstance()`	Has the default currency format ($99,999.99).
`getPercentInstance()`	Has the default percent format (99%).
`getNumberInstance()`	Has the default number format (99,999.999).

Three methods of a NumberFormat object

Method	Description
`format(anyNumberType)`	Returns a String object that has the format specified by the NumberFormat object.
`setMinimumFractionDigits(int)`	Sets the minimum number of decimal places.
`setMaximumFractionDigits(int)`	Sets the maximum number of decimal places.

The currency format

```
double price = 11.575;
NumberFormat currency = NumberFormat.getCurrencyInstance();
String priceString = currency.format(price);        // returns $11.58
```

The percent format

```
double majority = .505;
NumberFormat percent = NumberFormat.getPercentInstance();
String majorityString = percent.format(majority);   // returns 50%
```

The number format with one decimal place

```
double miles = 15341.253;
NumberFormat number = NumberFormat.getNumberInstance();
number.setMaximumFractionDigits(1);
String milesString = number.format(miles);          // returns 15,341.3
```

Two NumberFormat methods that are coded in one statement

```
String majorityString = NumberFormat.getPercentInstance().format(majority);
```

Description

- You can use one of the three static methods of the NumberFormat class to create a NumberFormat object. Then, you can use the methods of that object to format one or more numbers.

- When you use the format() method, the result is automatically rounded by using a rounding technique called half-even. This means that the number is rounded up if the preceding digit is odd, but the extra decimal places are truncated if the preceding digit is even.

- Since the NumberFormat class is in the java.text package, you'll want to include an import statement when you use this class.

Figure 3-12   How to use the NumberFormat class

The Invoice application with formatting

To illustrate some of the skills you've just learned, figure 3-13 shows the console and code for an enhanced version of the Invoice application that was presented in chapter 2. This time, the application does a few more calculations and formats the results before displaying them, as shown at the top of this figure.

The shaded code in this figure identifies the primary changes to the Invoice application of the last chapter. First, two new values are calculated. Sales tax is calculated by multiplying the total before tax by the SALES_TAX_PCT constant that's declared and initialized at the beginning of the main() method. And the invoice total is calculated by adding the sales tax to the total before tax.

Second, this code calls the methods of the NumberFormat class to get currency and percent objects. Then, this code calls the format() methods of these objects to format the five values that have been calculated by this application. This shows how you can use one currency object to format two or more values. Each time the code calls the format() method, the format() method returns a string that this code adds to the message that's eventually displayed.

Although this application is now taking on a more professional look, it still has some shortcomings. First, it doesn't handle the exception that's thrown if the user doesn't enter a valid number. You'll learn how to fix that problem in chapter 5. Second, because of the way rounding works with the NumberFormat methods, the results may not always come out the way you want them to. You'll learn how to fix that in the next few figures.

The console with formatting

```
Enter subtotal:     150.50
Discount percent: 10%
Discount amount:  $15.05
Total before tax: $135.45
Sales tax:        $6.77
Invoice total:    $142.22

Continue? (y/n):
```

The code

```java
import java.util.Scanner;
import java.text.NumberFormat;

public class InvoiceApp {

    public static void main(String[] args) {
        final double SALES_TAX_PCT = .05;

        Scanner sc = new Scanner(System.in);
        String choice = "y";
        while (choice.equalsIgnoreCase("y")) {
            System.out.print("Enter subtotal:     ");
            double subtotal = sc.nextDouble();

            double discountPercent = 0.0;
            if (subtotal >= 100) {
                discountPercent = .1;
            } else {
                discountPercent = 0.0;
            }

            // calculate the results
            double discountAmount = subtotal * discountPercent;
            double totalBeforeTax = subtotal - discountAmount;
            double salesTax = totalBeforeTax * SALES_TAX_PCT;
            double total = totalBeforeTax + salesTax;

            // format and display the results
            NumberFormat currency = NumberFormat.getCurrencyInstance();
            NumberFormat percent = NumberFormat.getPercentInstance();
            String message =
                "Discount percent: " + percent.format(discountPercent) + "\n"
              + "Discount amount:  " + currency.format(discountAmount) + "\n"
              + "Total before tax: " + currency.format(totalBeforeTax) + "\n"
              + "Sales tax:        " + currency.format(salesTax) + "\n"
              + "Invoice total:    " + currency.format(total) + "\n";
            System.out.println(message);

            System.out.print("Continue? (y/n): ");
            choice = sc.next();
            System.out.println();
        }
    }
}
```

Figure 3-13   The Invoice application with formatting

How to debug a rounding error

The console at the top of figure 3-14 shows more output from the Invoice application in figure 3-13. Here, the results for a subtotal entry of 100.05 don't add up! If the discount amount is $10.00, the total before tax should be $90.05, but it's $90.04. What's causing this error, and how can we fix it?

To determine the cause, you can add debugging statements like the ones shown here. These statements display the unformatted results before the formatted results. For example, if you look at the unformatted results, you can begin to figure out what's causing the problem. To start, the discount amount is 10.005, which isn't a valid monetary amount. For most financial applications, this amount should be rounded up to 10.01. However, because of the way the NumberFormat class rounds the numbers, the discount amount value of 10.005 is rounded down to 10.00. Similarly, the rest of the numbers are not valid monetary amounts either, which could lead to more rounding problems.

Although an error like this may be acceptable in some applications, it is unacceptable in most business applications. And for those applications, you need to provide solutions that deliver the results that you want. Imagine getting an invoice that didn't add up!

One solution is to add code that rounds the results of each calculation to 2 decimal places. That way, the double types store valid monetary values. Then, you can use the NumberFormat class to format these numbers without worrying about it introducing a rounding error.

To implement this solution, you can add statements like the shaded statements shown in the second example. Here, the first shaded statement rounds the discountAmount value to 2 decimal places. Then, the second shaded statement rounds the salesTax value to 2 decimal places. It isn't necessary to round the totalBeforeTax or total variables since the code uses addition and subtraction to calculate these values. As a result, these calculations shouldn't introduce any new decimal places.

Although this solution is adequate for most applications, it uses the double data type, which is a floating-point number that's only designed to store approximate values. In addition, the round() method of the Math class doesn't give you much control over how the rounding works. So, if you need to be 100% sure that your decimal numbers are exact, or if you need more control over how those numbers are rounded, it's generally considered a best practice to use the BigDecimal class as described in the next few figures.

The console with a rounding error

```
Enter subtotal:      100.05
Discount percent: 10%
Discount amount:  $10.00
Total before tax: $90.04
Sales tax:        $4.50
Invoice total:    $94.55

Continue? (y/n):
```

Debugging statements that can be added to the code

```
String debugMessage = "\nUNFORMATTED RESULTS\n"
                    + "Discount percent: " + discountPercent + "\n"
                    + "Discount amount:  " + discountAmount + "\n"
                    + "Total before tax: " + totalBeforeTax + "\n"
                    + "Sales tax:        " + salesTax + "\n"
                    + "Invoice total:    " + total + "\n"
                    + "\nFORMATTED RESULTS";
System.out.println(debugMessage);
```

The console with debugging information

```
Enter subtotal:      100.05

UNFORMATTED RESULTS
Discount percent: 0.1
Discount amount:  10.005
Total before tax: 90.045
Sales tax:        4.50225
Invoice total:    94.54725

FORMATTED RESULTS
Discount percent: 10%
Discount amount:  $10.00
Total before tax: $90.04
Sales tax:        $4.50
Invoice total:    $94.55

Continue? (y/n):
```

Code that fixes the error by rounding the results to 2 decimal places

```
double discountAmount = subtotal * discountPercent;
discountAmount = (double) Math.round(discountAmount * 100) / 100;
double totalBeforeTax = subtotal - discountAmount;
double salesTax = totalBeforeTax * SALES_TAX_PCT;
salesTax = (double) Math.round(salesTax * 100) / 100;
double total = totalBeforeTax + salesTax;
```

Description

- To find the cause of a bug, you can add debugging statements to an application.
- To fix a rounding error, you can add statements that round the results of your calculations to the correct number of decimal places.

Figure 3-14   How to debug a rounding error

How to use the BigDecimal class

The BigDecimal class solves several problems that are associated with floating-point numbers of the double and float types. First, the BigDecimal class represents exact decimal numbers. Conversely, the double and float types represent approximate decimal numbers. Second, the BigDecimal class works with numbers that have more than 16 significant digits. Conversely, as you learned earlier in this chapter, the double type has a maximum of 16 significant digits, and the float type has a maximum of 7 significant digits. Third, if you need to round numbers, the BigDecimal class lets you specify several types of rounding. Conversely, the round() method of the Math class only provides for one type of rounding.

The constructors and methods

Figure 3-15 summarizes a few of the constructors that you can use with the BigDecimal class. These constructors accept an int, double, long, or string argument and create a BigDecimal object from it. Because floating-point numbers are limited to 16 significant digits and because these numbers don't always represent decimal numbers exactly, it's often best to create BigDecimal objects from strings rather than double values.

Once you create a BigDecimal object, you can use its methods to work with the data. In this figure, for example, the add(), subtract(), multiply(), and divide() methods let you perform those operations on the values stored in BigDecimal objects. The doubleValue() method lets you convert the value of a BigDecimal object to a double value. And the toString() method lets you convert the value of a BigDecimal object to a string.

This figure also includes the setScale() method, which lets you set the number of decimal places (*scale*) for the value in a BigDecimal object as well as the rounding mode. For example, you can use the setScale() method to return a number that's rounded to two decimal places like this:

```
salesTax = salesTax.setScale(2, RoundingMode.HALF_UP);
```

In this example, RoundingMode.HALF_UP is a value in the RoundingMode enumeration that's summarized in this figure. The scale and rounding mode arguments work the same for the divide() method.

Enumerations are similar to classes, and you'll learn more about them in chapter 10. For now, you can code the rounding mode as HALF_UP because it provides the type of rounding that is normal for business applications. However, you need to import the RoundingMode enumeration at the start of the application unless you want to qualify the rounding mode like this:

```
java.math.RoundingMode.HALF_UP
```

If you look at the API documentation for the BigDecimal class, you'll see that it provides several other methods and features that you may want to use.

The BigDecimal class

`java.math.BigDecimal`

Constructors of the BigDecimal class

Constructor	Description
`BigDecimal(String)`	Creates a new BigDecimal object with the specified String object. Because of the limitations of floating-point numbers, it's often best to create BigDecimal objects from strings.
`BigDecimal(int)`	Creates a new BigDecimal object with the specified int value.
`BigDecimal(double)`	Creates a new BigDecimal object with the specified double value.

Methods of the BigDecimal class

Method	Description
`add(value)`	Returns the value of this BigDecimal object after the specified BigDecimal value has been added to it.
`subtract(value)`	Returns the value of this BigDecimal object after the specified BigDecimal value has been subtracted from it.
`multiply(value)`	Returns the value of this BigDecimal object multiplied by the specified BigDecimal value.
`divide(value, scale, roundingMode)`	Returns the value of this BigDecimal object divided by the value of the specified BigDecimal object, sets the specified scale, and uses the specified rounding mode.
`setScale(scale, roundingMode)`	Sets the scale and rounding mode for the BigDecimal object.
`doubleValue()`	Converts the BigDecimal value to a double value.
`toString()`	Converts the BigDecimal value to a string.

The RoundingMode enumeration

`java.math.RoundingMode`

Two of the values in the RoundingMode enumeration

Value	Description
`HALF_UP`	Round towards the "nearest neighbor" unless both neighbors are equidistant, in which case round up.
`HALF_EVEN`	Round towards the "nearest neighbor" unless both neighbors are equidistant, in which case round toward the even neighbor.

Description

- The BigDecimal class provides a way to perform accurate decimal calculations in Java. It also provides a way to store numbers with more than 16 significant digits.

Figure 3-15   The constructors and methods of the BigDecimal class

Examples that work with the BigDecimal class

Figure 3-16 presents some examples that show how to work with the BigDecimal class. To start, you can code the statements that import the BigDecimal class and the RoundingMode enumeration as shown in the first example.

Once you've coded the import statements, you can use the constructors of the BigDecimal class to create the BigDecimal objects. Here, the second example creates two variables named subtotal and discountPercent from strings with the values "100.05" and ".1". Then, the third example creates a constant named SALES_TAX_PERCENT from a string with the value ".05". Since double values are approximate values, you should create BigDecimal objects from strings or integers whenever possible, not from double values.

The fourth example shows how to multiply two BigDecimal objects and round the result to 2 decimal places. Here, the first statement uses the multiply() method of one BigDecimal object and supplies the second BigDecimal object as the argument to that method. Then, the second statement uses the setScale() method to round the result to two decimal places, using the HALF_UP mode.

The fifth example works like the fourth, except that it uses a single statement to perform the multiplication and rounding operations. This is possible because the multiply() method returns a BigDecimal object. As a result, you can call the setScale() method directly from this object. This is known as *method chaining*, and it can result in code that's more concise and easier to maintain.

The sixth example shows how to use the add() and subtract() methods to add and subtract BigDecimal objects from each other. This works much like the multiply() method, except that you often don't need to round when you add and subtract.

The seventh example shows how to use the BigDecimal class to round a double value. This examples starts by creating a BigDecimal object from a double value in a variable named discountAmount. Then, it uses the setScale() method of that object to round the value to two decimal places using the HALF_UP mode. Finally, it uses the doubleValue() method to convert the BigDecimal value back to a double value. This works much like using the round() method of the Math class as shown earlier in this chapter. However, it lets you use any of the rounding modes that work with the setScale() method. In other words, it gives you more control over the rounding.

When working with BigDecimal objects, you may sometimes need to create one BigDecimal object from another BigDecimal object. However, you can't supply a BigDecimal object to the constructor of the BigDecimal class. Instead, you need to call the toString() method from the BigDecimal object to convert the BigDecimal object to a String object. Then, you can pass that String object as the argument of the constructor as shown by the eighth example.

How to import the classes for working with BigDecimal objects

```
import java.math.BigDecimal;
import java.math.RoundingMode;
```

How to create variables for BigDecimal numbers

```
BigDecimal subtotal = new BigDecimal("100.05");
BigDecimal discountPercent = new BigDecimal(".1");
```

How to create a constant for a BigDecimal number

```
final BigDecimal SALES_TAX_PCT = new BigDecimal(".05");
```

How to multiply and round BigDecimal numbers

```
BigDecimal discountAmount = subtotal.multiply(discountPercent);
discountAmount = discountAmount.setScale(2, RoundingMode.HALF_UP);
```

Another way to multiply and round BigDecimal numbers

```
BigDecimal discountAmount = subtotal.multiply(discountPercent)
                               .setScale(2, RoundingMode.HALF_UP);
```

How to add and subtract decimal numbers

```
BigDecimal totalBeforeTax = subtotal.subtract(discountAmount);
BigDecimal total = totalBeforeTax.add(salesTax);
```

How to use the BigDecimal class to round a double value

```
discountAmount = new BigDecimal(discountAmount)
        .setScale(2, RoundingMode.HALF_UP)
        .doubleValue();
```

How to create one BigDecimal object from another

```
BigDecimal subtotal2 = new BigDecimal(subtotal.toString());
```

Description

- If you need to make sure the decimal numbers you work with are exact, you can use BigDecimal objects. This also gives you complete control over rounding.

Figure 3-16   Examples that work with the BigDecimal class

The Invoice application with BigDecimal objects

Figure 3-17 shows an enhanced version of the Invoice application that uses BigDecimal objects. Here, the console shows that using BigDecimal objects solves the rounding error, so the application now works correctly.

The code for this application begins by importing the BigDecimal class and the RoundingMode enumeration. Then, inside the main() method, this code creates a constant named SALES_TAX_PCT that stores a sale tax percent of 5% in a BigDecimal object.

Within the while loop, the code starts by creating a BigDecimal object named subtotal from the subtotal string entered by the user. It also declares another BigDecimal object named discountPercent. Then, the subtotal variable is used in the condition on an if/else statement to determine the value of the discountPercent variable. Note, though, that the doubleValue() method must be used to convert the subtotal variable to a double value before it can be used in the comparison operation.

The rest of the code uses BigDecimal objects to store the numbers and perform the calculations. This code only rounds the discount amount and sales tax values because they're calculated using multiplication, which can result in extra decimal places. In contrast, the other numbers (total before tax and total) don't need to be rounded because they're calculated using subtraction and addition. Once this code finishes calculating and rounding the BigDecimal objects, it uses the NumberFormat objects to format the BigDecimal objects for display.

Is this a lot of work just to do simple business arithmetic? Relative to some other languages, you would have to say that it is. However, once you get comfortable working with the BigDecimal class, you should be able to solve floating-point and rounding errors with ease.

If the BigDecimal class solves all problems with decimal numbers, why isn't it the default way to work with decimal numbers? Unfortunately, using the BigDecimal class is extremely slow when compared to the double and float types. For most applications, this relative slowness isn't noticeable. However, it wouldn't be acceptable for games or scientific applications that need to make thousands of floating-point calculations per second.

The console after the rounding error has been fixed

```
Enter subtotal:     100.05
Discount percent: 10%
Discount amount:  $10.01
Total before tax: $90.04
Sales tax:        $4.50
Invoice total:    $94.54

Continue? (y/n):
```

The code

```java
import java.util.Scanner;
import java.text.NumberFormat;
import java.math.BigDecimal;
import java.math.RoundingMode;

public class InvoiceApp {

    public static void main(String[] args) {
        final BigDecimal SALES_TAX_PCT = new BigDecimal(".05");

        Scanner sc = new Scanner(System.in);
        String choice = "y";
        while (choice.equalsIgnoreCase("y")) {
            System.out.print("Enter subtotal:    ");
            String subtotalString = sc.next();

            // create the BigDecimal objects for subtotal and discount percent
            BigDecimal subtotal = new BigDecimal(subtotalString);
            BigDecimal discountPercent;
            if (subtotal.doubleValue() >= 100) {
                discountPercent = new BigDecimal(".1");
            } else {
                discountPercent = new BigDecimal("0.0");
            }

            // calculate the results
            BigDecimal discountAmount = subtotal.multiply(discountPercent)
                    .setScale(2, RoundingMode.HALF_UP);
            BigDecimal totalBeforeTax = subtotal.subtract(discountAmount);
            BigDecimal salesTax = SALES_TAX_PCT.multiply(totalBeforeTax)
                    .setScale(2, RoundingMode.HALF_UP);
            BigDecimal total = totalBeforeTax.add(salesTax);

            // the rest of the code for this class is the same as figure 3-13
```

Description

- This code uses BigDecimal objects to make sure that all decimal numbers are exact and that the results have been rounded correctly.

- Once the results have been calculated and rounded to two decimal places, this code uses the NumberFormat class to format the BigDecimal objects. Since the decimal numbers have already been rounded, this doesn't cause any rounding errors.

Figure 3-17   The Invoice application with BigDecimal objects

Perspective

If this chapter has succeeded, you should now be able to work with any of the primitive data types you need in your applications. In addition, you should be able to use the Integer, Double, Math, and NumberFormat classes whenever you need them. And you should be able to use the BigDecimal class to solve the problems that are associated with floating-point numbers such as rounding errors.

Summary

- Java provides eight *primitive data types* to store *integers*, *floating-point numbers*, *characters*, and *boolean values*.

- *Variables* store data that changes as an application runs. *Constants* store data that doesn't change as an application runs. You use *assignment statements* to assign values to variables.

- You can use *arithmetic operators* to form *arithmetic expressions*.

- *Binary operators* operate on two operands, and *unary operators* operate on just one operand.

- Besides the *assignment operator* (=), Java provides for five *compound assignment operators*. These operators provide a shorthand way to code common assignment operations.

- Unless parentheses are used, the operations in an expression take place from left to right in the *order of precedence*.

- Java can *implicitly cast* a less precise data type to a more precise data type. Java also lets you *explicitly cast* a more precise data type to a less precise data type.

- You can use the Java Shell that's available with NetBeans 9.0 to interactively test the results of a statement or expression or to view the value of a variable that's been declared during the session.

- You can use the constructors of the Double and Integer classes to create objects that wrap double and int values. As a result, these classes are known as *wrapper classes*. You can also use the static methods of these classes to convert strings to numbers and vice versa.

- You can use the static methods of the Math class to perform mathematical operations such as rounding numbers and calculating square roots.

- You can use the NumberFormat class to apply currency, percent, and number formats to any of the primitive numeric types.

- You can use the BigDecimal class to create BigDecimal objects that store exact decimal values that aren't limited to 16 significant digits. In addition, you can use the methods of these objects to perform operations such as addition, subtraction, multiplication, division, and rounding.

Exercise 3-1   Modify the Miles Per Gallon application

In this exercise, you'll modify an application that calculates miles per gallon based on the miles driven and gallons of gas entered by a user so it displays accurate results.

Test the application

1. Open the project named ch03_ex1_MPG that's in the ex_starts folder. Then, review the code for this project.

2. Run the application and test it with a range of values, noting that sometimes the miles per gallon number has several decimal places. Now, enter 400 miles and 15.8 gallons, and note that the miles per gallon value is 25.31645569620253.

Use the Math class for rounding

3. Use the round() method of the Math class to round the miles per gallon value to a whole number before displaying it. Remember that you may need to do an explicit cast to get the number to look the way you want it to. You should also import the Math class so your code is as simple as possible.

4. Run the application, enter 400 miles and 15.8 gallons, and compare the rounded miles per gallon value to the value in step 2 to see if it's correct.

5. Adjust the code that uses the round() method so it returns a miles per gallon value that's rounded to two decimal places. Then, run the application, enter 400 miles and 15.8 gallons, and compare the miles per gallon value to the value in step 2.

Use the NumberFormat class for rounding

6. Modify the application so it uses the NumberFormat class and the format() method to perform the rounding with the default of three decimal places. Be sure to import the NumberFormat class to make this easier to do. Then, run the application, enter 400 miles and 15.8 gallons, and compare the miles per gallon value to the value in step 2.

7. Adjust the code you added in step 6 so it rounds the miles per gallon value to two decimal places. Then, run the application, enter 400 miles and 15.8 gallons, and compare the miles per gallon value to the value in step 2.

Use the BigDecimal class for rounding and division

8. Modify the application so it uses the methods of the BigDecimal class to perform both the rounding and the division that calculates the miles per gallon value. Make sure to round the miles per gallon to two decimal places. Import the necessary classes to make this easy to do. Then, run the application, enter 400 miles and 15.8 gallons, and compare the miles per gallon value to the value in step 2.

9. Comment out any import statements that are no longer needed.

Exercise 3-2   Modify the Test Score application

In this exercise, you'll use some of the skills that you learned in this chapter to modify the Test Score application.

1. Open the project named ch03_ex2_TestScore that's in the ex_starts directory. Then, review the code for this project and run it until you understand how it works.

2. Use the ++ operator to increase the scoreCount variable, and use the += operator to increase the scoreTotal variable. Then, test this to make sure that it works.

3. As the user enters test scores, use the methods of the Math class to keep track of the minimum and maximum scores. When the user enters 999 to end the program, display these scores at the end of the other output data. Now, test these changes to make sure that they work. (This step can be challenging if you're new to programming, but you'll learn a lot by doing it.)

4. Use the NumberFormat class to round the average score to one decimal place before displaying it at the end of the program. Then, test this change. Note that the rounding method that's used doesn't matter in a program like this.

4

How to code control statements

In chapter 2, you learned how to code simple if/else statements and while loops to control the execution of your applications. Now, you'll learn more about coding these statements. In addition, you'll learn how to code some other control statements such as switch statements and for loops.

How to code Boolean expressions

A *Boolean expression* is an expression that evaluates to a *Boolean value* of true or false. Boolean expressions are used often in control statements like the ones described in this chapter. That's why this chapter begins by showing how to use the relational and logical operators to code Boolean expressions.

How to compare primitive data types

Figure 4-1 shows how to use the six *relational operators* to code a Boolean expression that compares operands that are primitive data types. In a Boolean expression, an operand can be a literal, a variable, an arithmetic expression, or a keyword such as true or false. Because you learned the basic skills for coding Boolean expressions in chapter 2, you shouldn't have any trouble understanding how they work.

The first three expressions in this figure use the equality operator (==) to check whether the two operands are equal. To use this operator, you must code two equals signs instead of one. That's because a single equals sign (=) is used for assignment statements. As a result, if you try to code a Boolean expression with a single equals sign, your code won't compile.

The fourth expression uses the inequality operator (!=) to check whether a variable is not equal to a numeric literal. Here, the expression evaluates to true if the variable named subtotal is not equal to zero.

The fifth and sixth expressions use the greater than operator (>) and the less than operator (<). Then, the seventh and eighth expressions use the greater than or equal operator (>=) and less than or equal operator (<=).

The last two expressions show that you don't need the == or != operator when you use a boolean variable in an expression. That's because, by definition, a boolean variable evaluates to a Boolean value. As a result, if you declare a boolean variable named isValid, then

```
isValid == true
```

is the same as

```
isValid
```

Although the first expression may be easier for a beginning programmer to understand, the second expression is commonly used by professional programmers.

When comparing numeric values, you usually compare values of the same data type. However, if you compare different types of numeric values, Java automatically casts the less precise numeric type to the more precise type. For example, if you compare an int type to a double type, Java casts the int type to the double type before performing the comparison.

Since floating-point numbers don't represent the exact value of a number, you shouldn't use the equality operator (==) to compare them for equality. Instead, you can use the greater than (>) and less than (<) operators to make sure two numbers fall within a range that's close enough to be considered equal.

Relational operators

Operator	Name	Description
==	Equality	Returns a true value if both operands are equal.
!=	Inequality	Returns a true value if the left and right operands are not equal.
>	Greater Than	Returns a true value if the left operand is greater than the right operand.
<	Less Than	Returns a true value if the left operand is less than the right operand.
>=	Greater Than Or Equal	Returns a true value if the left operand is greater than or equal to the right operand.
<=	Less Than Or Equal	Returns a true value if the left operand is less than or equal to the right operand.

Boolean expressions

```
discountPercent == 2.3     // equal to a numeric literal
letter == 'y'              // equal to a char literal
isValid == true            // equal to a true value

subtotal != 0              // not equal to a numeric literal

years > 0                  // greater than a numeric literal
i < months                 // less than a variable

subtotal >= 500            // greater than or equal to a numeric literal
quantity <= reorderPoint   // less than or equal to a variable

isValid                    // isValid is equal to true
!isValid                   // isValid is equal to false
```

Description

- You can use the relational operators to create a *Boolean expression* that compares two operands and returns a *Boolean value* that is either true or false.

- If you compare two numeric operands that are not of the same type, Java converts the less precise operand to the type of the more precise operand before comparing the operands.

- A variable of the boolean type stores a Boolean value of true or false.

- The floating-point types (double and float) don't always represent the exact value of a number. As a result, you shouldn't use the equals operator (==) to compare them for equality.

- String objects are reference types, not primitive types. As a result, you shouldn't use the equals operator (==) to compare them for equality. Instead, you should use the equals() or equalsIgnoreCase() method of the String class as described in chapter 2.

Figure 4-1   How to compare primitive data types

As you learned in chapter 2, a string is a reference type, not a primitive type. As a result, you shouldn't use the equals operator (==) to test two strings for equality. Instead, you should use the equals() or equalsIgnoreCase() method of the String class as described in chapter 2.

How to use the logical operators

Figure 4-2 shows how to use the *logical operators* to code a Boolean expression that consists of two or more Boolean expressions. For example, the first expression uses the && operator. As a result, it evaluates to true if both the first expression *and* the second expression evaluate to true. Conversely, the second expression uses the || operator. As a result, it evaluates to true if either the first expression *or* the second expression evaluate to true.

When you use the && and || operators, the second expression is only evaluated if necessary. Because of that, these operators are sometimes referred to as the *short-circuit operators*. To illustrate, suppose the value of subtotal in the first example is less than 250. Then, the first expression evaluates to false. That means that the entire expression returns a false value. As a result, Java doesn't evaluate the second expression, which is usually what you want.

You can also use multiple logical operators in the same expression as shown by the third example. Here, the && and || operators connect three expressions. As a result, the entire expression is true if the first *and* second expressions are true *or* the third expression is true.

When you code this type of expression, the expression is evaluated from left to right based on this order of precedence: arithmetic operations first, followed by relational operations, followed by logical operations. For logical operations, And operations are performed before Or operations. If you need to change this sequence or if there's any doubt about the order of precedence, you can use parentheses to clarify or control this evaluation sequence.

If necessary, you can use the ! operator to reverse the value of an expression. However, this can create code that's difficult to read. As a result, you should avoid using the ! operator whenever possible. For example, instead of coding

```
!(subtotal < 100)
```

you can code

```
subtotal >= 100
```

Both expressions perform the same task, but the second expression is easier to read.

Logical operators

Operator	Name	Description
&&	And	Returns a true value if both expressions are true. This operator only evaluates the second expression if necessary.
||	Or	Returns a true value if either expression is true. This operator only evaluates the second expression if necessary.
!	Not	Reverses the value of the expression.

Boolean expressions that use the logical operators

```
subtotal > 250 && subtotal < 500                // short-circuit AND
quantity <= 4 || quantity >= 12                 // short-circuit OR

(subtotal > 250 && subtotal < 500) || isValid   // 2 logical operators

!(counter++ >= years)                           // NOT
```

Description

- You can use the *logical operators* to create a Boolean expression that combines two or more Boolean expressions.

- Since the && and || operators only evaluate the second expression if necessary, they're sometimes referred to as *short-circuit operators*.

- By default, Not operations are performed first, followed by And operations, and then Or operations. These operations are performed after arithmetic operations and relational operations.

- You can use parentheses to change the sequence of operations. In addition, you can use parentheses to clarify the sequence of operations.

Figure 4-2   How to use the logical operators

How to code if/else and switch statements

In chapter 3, you were introduced to the basic skills for coding an if/else statement. Now, this topic reviews those skills and expands on them. In addition, it shows how to code the switch statement, which can be used instead of some types of if/else statements.

How to code if/else statements

Figure 4-3 reviews the use of the *if/else statement* (or just *if statement*). This is Java's implementation of the *selection structure*.

Whenever you code a set of braces in Java, you are explicitly defining a *block* of code that may contain one or more statements. Then, any variables declared within those braces have *block scope*. In other words, they can't be accessed outside of that block. As a result, if you want to access a variable outside of the block, you must declare it before the block.

The three examples in part 1 of this figure show how block scope works. In these examples, the variable named discountPercent is declared before the if/else statement. As a result, the blocks of code defined by the if/else statement can modify the value of this variable, and this variable is still available after the if/else statement finishes executing.

The first example shows an if/else statement that only contains an if clause. In this example, the statement that declares the discountPercent variable initializes it to a value of .05 (5%). Then, the if clause checks whether the subtotal is greater than or equal to 100. If it is, the discountPercent variable is set to a value of .1 (10%). Otherwise, the discountPercent variable is left at its default value of .05 (5%).

The second example shows an if/else statement that contains an if clause and an else clause. This performs the same task as the first example. However, it uses the else clause to set the value of the discountPercent variable.

The advantage of the second example is that the statements that set the value for the discountPercent variable are all coded at the same level. As a result, some programmers find it easier to read and understand this example. The disadvantage of this approach is that it requires three more lines of code. Since the first and second examples work equally well, you can choose the approach that you prefer.

The third example shows an if/else statement that contains multiple else if clauses. When coding a statement like this, it's important to remember that Java evaluates if/else statements from the top down. Once a clause evaluates to true, Java executes the statements for that clause and skips the rest of the if/else statement. As a result, it's most efficient to code the most likely conditions first and the least likely conditions last.

In the third example, for instance, the if clause contains the most likely condition (a subtotal greater than or equal to 100 and less than 200). For this to work, you must use a logical operator to connect two Boolean expressions.

The syntax of the if/else statement

```
if (booleanExpression) { statements }
[else if (booleanExpression) { statements }] ...
[else { statements }]
```

An if statement with only an if clause

```
double discountPercent = .05;
if (subtotal >= 100) {
    discountPercent = .1;
}
```

With an else clause

```
double discountPercent;
if (subtotal >= 100) {
    discountPercent = .1;
} else {
    discountPercent = .05;
}
```

With multiple else if clauses

```
double discountPercent;
if (subtotal >= 100 && subtotal < 200) {
    discountPercent = .1;
} else if (subtotal >= 200 && subtotal < 300) {
    discountPercent = .2;
} else if (subtotal >= 300) {
    discountPercent = .3;
} else {
    discountPercent = .05;
}
```

Description

- An *if/else statement*, or just *if statement*, always contains an if clause. In addition, it can contain one or more else if clauses and one else clause.

- A pair of braces defines a *block* of code. Any variables declared within a block have *block scope*. As a result, they can only be used within that block.

- Java evaluates if/else statements from the top down. Once a clause evaluates to true, Java skips the rest of the if/else statement. As a result, it's most efficient to code the most likely conditions first and the least likely conditions last.

Figure 4-3   How to code if/else statements (part 1 of 2)

If efficiency isn't your primary concern, you should code the conditions in a logical sequence. For example, you could start by coding a condition that checks for the highest subtotal and work your way down to the lowest subtotal. This would simplify the condition for each clause by removing the need for the logical operators. As always, the easier your code is to read and understand, the easier it is to test, debug, and maintain.

The first example in part 2 of this figure shows an if/else statement that contains multiple statements within each clause. Here, the first statement sets the variable named discountPercent, and the second statement sets the variable named shippingMethod. Since these clauses contain multiple statements, the braces are required.

If a clause only contains a single statement, the braces are optional. In that case, you can just end the clause with a semicolon as shown in the second and third examples. Here, the second example shows an if/else statement that uses two lines per clause. Then, the third example shows an if statement that uses one line. Some programmers prefer the second approach since it clearly shows that the clause should only contain a single statement.

However, it's generally considered a good coding style to use braces for all if/else statements. That's why the examples in part 1 of this figure use them. That way, you won't introduce bugs later if you add more statements and forget to add the braces.

When coding if statements, it's a common practice to code one if statement within another if statement. This is known as *nesting* if statements, and it's shown by the fourth example. When you nest if statements, it's a good practice to indent the nested statements and their clauses since this allows the programmer to easily identify where each nested statement begins and ends. In this figure, for example, Java only executes the nested statement if the customer type is "r". Otherwise, it executes the statements in the outer else clause.

An if statement with clauses that contain multiple statements

```
double discountPercent;
String shippingMethod = "";
if (subtotal >= 100) {
    discountPercent = .1;
    shippingMethod = "UPS";
} else {
    discountPercent = .05;
    shippingMethod = "USPS";
}
```

An if statement without braces

```
double discountPercent;
if (subtotal >= 100)
    discountPercent = .1;
else
    discountPercent = .05;
```

Another way to code an if statement without braces

```
double discountPercent;
if (subtotal >= 100) discountPercent = .1;
```

Nested if statements

```
double discountPercent;
if (customerType.equals("r")) {
    if (subtotal >= 100) {          // begin nested if
        discountPercent = .2;
    } else {
        discountPercent =.1;
    }                               // end nested if
} else {
    discountPercent = .4;
}
```

Description

- If a clause in an if/else statement contains just one statement, you don't have to enclose the statement in braces. You can just end the clause with a semicolon.

- It's generally considered a good coding style to use braces for all if/else statements. That way, you won't introduce bugs later if you add more statements and forget to add the braces.

- When necessary, you can *nest* one if statement within another.

Figure 4-3   How to code if/else statements (part 2 of 2)

How to code switch statements

Figure 4-4 shows how to work with the *switch statement*. This is the Java implementation of a control structure known as the *case structure*, which lets you code different actions for different cases. The switch statement can sometimes be used in place of an if/else statement.

Prior to Java 7, the switch statement could only be used with expressions that evaluate to an integer other than the long type. As a result, in early versions of Java, the switch statement had limited use. However, with Java 7 and later, the switch statement can also be used with expressions that evaluate to a string.

To code a switch statement, you start by coding the switch keyword followed by a switch expression that evaluates to one of the integer types other than long or to a string. After the switch expression, you can code one or more *case labels* that represent the possible values of the switch expression. Then, when the switch expression matches the value specified by the case label, the statements after the label are executed.

You can code the case labels in any sequence, but you should be sure to follow each label with a colon. Then, if the label contains one or more statements, you can code a *break statement* after them to jump to the end of the switch statement. Otherwise, the execution of the program *falls through* to the next case label and executes the statements in that label. The *default label* is an optional label that identifies the statements to execute if none of the case labels are executed.

The first example shows how to code a switch statement that sets the description for a product based on the value of an int variable named productID. Here, the first case label assigns a value of "Hammer" to the productDescription variable if productID is equal to 1. Then, the break statement exits the switch statement. Similarly, the second case label sets the product description to "Box of Nails" if productID is equal to 2 and then exits the switch statement. If productID is equal to something other than 1 or 2, the default case label is executed. Like the other two case labels, this one sets the value of the productDescription variable and then exits the switch statement.

The second example works like the first example, but the switch statement evaluates the value of a String variable named productCode. Here, the first case label assigns a value of "Hammer" to the productDescription variable if productCode is equal to "hm01". Since the switch statement is case-sensitive, this case label is only executed if the productCode variable stores a string with the exact same capitalization. For example, this case isn't executed if productCode is equal to "HM01". Similarly, the second case label sets the product description to "Box of Nails" if productCode is equal to "bn03".

The syntax of the switch statement

```
switch (switchExpression)  {
    case label1:
        statements
        break;
    [case label2:
        statements
        break;] ...
    [default:
        statements
        break;]
}
```

A switch statement that uses an int variable named productID

```
switch (productID) {
    case 1:
        productDescription = "Hammer";
        break;
    case 2:
        productDescription = "Box of Nails";
        break;
    default:
        productDescription = "Product not found";
        break;
}
```

A switch statement that uses a String variable named productCode

```
switch (productCode) {
    case "hm01":
        productDescription = "Hammer";
        break;
    case "bn03":
        productDescription = "Box of Nails";
        break;
    default:
        productDescription = "Product not found";
        break;
}
```

Description

- Prior to Java 7, the switch statement could only be used with an expression that evaluated to one of these integer types: char, byte, short, or int.

- Starting with Java 7, the switch statement can also be used with string expressions. Then, the switch statement uses the equals() method of the String object to compare the strings. As a result, the strings in switch statements are case-sensitive.

- The switch statement transfers control to the appropriate *case label*. If control isn't transferred to one of the case labels, the optional *default label* is executed.

Figure 4-4   How to code switch statements (part 1 of 2)

The example in part 2 of this figure shows how to code a switch statement that sets a day variable to "weekday" or "weekend" depending on the value of the integer in the variable named dayOfWeek. Here, the case labels for 1, 2, 3, and 4 don't contain any statements, so execution falls through to the case label for 5. As a result, day is set to "weekday" for any of those values. Similarly, whenever dayOfWeek equals 6 or 7, day is set to "weekend".

Although a break statement is coded at the end of the last case label in each of these examples, you should know that it isn't required. If you omit this break statement, program execution automatically falls through to the statement that follows the switch statement. However, it's generally considered a good programming practice to code a break statement at the end of the last case label. That way, if you add a new case label after the last case label, your switch statement still works correctly. Similarly, if you move the last case label so it occurs earlier in the switch statement, it still works correctly.

When you code switch statements, you can nest one statement within another. You can also nest if/else statements within switch statements and switch statements within if/else statements. Here again, you should try to code the statements with a logical structure that is relatively easy to understand. If necessary, you can also add comments that clarify the logic of your code.

A switch statement that falls through case labels

```
switch (dayOfWeek)  {
    case 1:
    case 2:
    case 3:
    case 4:
    case 5:
        day = "weekday";
        break;
    case 6:
    case 7:
        day = "weekend";
        break;
}
```

Description

- If a case label doesn't contain a break statement, code execution *falls through* to the next label. Otherwise, the break statement ends the switch statement.
- The case labels can be coded in any sequence.

Figure 4-4   How to code switch statements (part 2 of 2)

The Invoice application with a switch statement

To give you a better idea of how switch statements work, figure 4-5 presents an enhanced version of the Invoice application. This time, the console prompts the user for two entries: customer type and subtotal. Then, it uses a switch statement to determine what customer type the user entered, and it uses nested if/else statements to determine the discount for the customer based on the customer type.

If the user enters "r" or "R" for the customer type, the first if/else statement is executed. If the user enters "c" or "C", though, the second if/else statement is executed. In both cases, the discount percent is determined based on the value of the subtotal. If, for example, the customer type is "r" and the subtotal is less than 100, the discount percent is 0. Or, if the customer type is "c" and the subtotal is less than 250, the discount percent is .2.

In this example, the conditions in the nested if/else statements are coded in a logical order. For instance, the expressions in the if/else statement for customer types "r" and "R" go from a subtotal that's less than 100, to a subtotal that's greater than or equal to 100 but less than 250, to a subtotal that's greater than or equal to 250. That covers all of the possible subtotals from the smallest to the largest. Although you could code this statement in other ways, this sequence makes it easy to tell that all possibilities have been covered.

The console

```
The Invoice Total Calculator

Enter customer type (r/c): r
Enter subtotal:    100

INVOICE
Subtotal:          $100.00
Discount percent: 10%
Discount amount:   $10.00
Total before tax: $90.00
Sales tax:         $4.50
Invoice total:     $94.50

Continue? (y/n): n

Bye!
```

The switch statement and nested if/else statements that determine the discount percent

```
double discountPercent = 0;
switch(customerType) {
    case "r":
    case "R":
        if (subtotal < 100) {
            discountPercent = 0.0;
        } else if (subtotal >= 100 && subtotal < 250) {
            discountPercent = .1;
        } else if (subtotal >= 250) {
            discountPercent = .2;
        }
        break;
    case "c":
    case "C":
        if (subtotal < 250) {
            discountPercent = .2;
        } else if (subtotal >= 250) {
            discountPercent = .3;
        }
        break;
    default:
        discountPercent = .1;
        break;
}
```

Figure 4-5   The Invoice application with a switch statement

How to code loops

In chapter 3, you learned how to code while statements and while loops. Now, you'll review the coding for those loops and learn how to code two other Java statements that implement the *iteration structure*.

How to code while loops

Figure 4-6 shows how to use the while statement to code a *while loop*. When coding while loops, it's common to use a *counter variable* to execute the statements in the loop a certain number of times. For example, the first loop in this figure uses an int counter variable named i that's initialized to 1. Then, the last statement in the loop increments the counter variable with each iteration of the loop. As a result, the first statement in this loop is executed as long as the counter variable is less than or equal to 36. When working with counter variables, it is a common coding practice to name them with single letters like *i, j,* and *k.*

When you code loops, it's important to remember that the code within a loop has block scope. As a result, any variables that are declared within the loop can't be used outside of the loop. That's why the variables that are needed outside of the loops in this figure have been declared outside of the loop. In the first loop, for example, the variable named futureValue has been declared outside the loop. That way, you can use this variable after the loop has finished executing.

When you code loops, you usually want to avoid *infinite loops*. If, for example, you forget to code a statement that increments the counter variable, the loop never ends because its condition never becomes false. When this happens, you can stop the loop by clicking on the appropriate button in your IDE.

The syntax of the while loop

```
while (booleanExpression) {
    statements
}
```

A while loop that calculates a future value

```
int i = 1;
int months = 36;
while (i <= months) {
    futureValue = (futureValue + monthlyInvestment) *
                    (1 + monthlyInterestRate);
    i++;
}
```

Description

- In a *while loop*, the condition is tested before the loop is executed.

- A while loop executes the block of statements within the loop as long as its Boolean expression is true. If the expression is false when the loop starts, its code is never executed.

- If a loop requires more than one statement, you must enclose the statements in braces. This identifies the block of statements that are executed by the loop, and any variables or constants that are declared in that block have block scope.

- If a loop requires just one statement, you don't have to enclose the statement in braces. However, it's generally considered a good practice to use braces to identify the statements that are executed by the loop.

- If the condition for a loop never becomes false, the loop never ends. This is known as an *infinite loop*, and beginning programmers often code them accidentally. In NetBeans, you can cancel an infinite loop by clicking on the Stop button in the Output window.

Figure 4-6   How to code while loops

How to code do-while loops

Figure 4-7 shows how to code a *do-while loop*. The difference between a while loop and a do-while loop is that the Boolean expression is evaluated at the beginning of a while loop and at the end of a do-while loop. As a result, the statements in a while loop are executed zero or more times, but the statements in a do-while loop are always executed at least once.

Most of the time, you can use either of these two types of loops to accomplish the same task. For example, the first do-while loop in this figure performs the same calculation as the first while loop in the previous figure.

With a do-while loop, it's possible for a programmer to accidentally insert code between the loop and the while condition. This separates the while condition from the loop and can introduce a bug that's difficult to find and fix. As a result, it's generally considered a best practice to use while loops instead of do-while loops. In practice, do-while loops are rarely used.

The syntax of the do-while loop

```
do {
    statements
} while (booleanExpression);
```

A do-while loop that calculates a future value

```
int i = 1;
int months = 36;
do {
    futureValue = (futureValue + monthlyInvestment) *
                  (1 + monthlyInterestRate);
    i++;
} while (i <= months);
```

Description

- A *do-while loop* works like a while loop, except that the condition is tested after the loop is executed. Because of that, its code is always executed at least once.

- In general, while loops are preferred over do-while loops. In practice, while loops are commonly used and do-while loops are rarely used.

- One problem with a do-while loop is that it's possible for the while statement to get separated from the loop if a programmer inserts code between the loop and the while statement. This can introduce a bug that's difficult to find and fix.

Figure 4-7   How to code do-while loops

How to code for loops

Figure 4-8 shows how to use the for statement to code *for loops*. This type of loop is useful when you need to increment or decrement a counter that determines how many times the loop is executed.

To code a for loop, you start by coding the for keyword followed by three expressions enclosed in parentheses and separated by semicolons. The first expression is an initialization expression that specifies the starting value for the counter variable. This expression can also declare the counter variable, if necessary. The second expression is a Boolean expression that determines when the loop ends. And the third expression is an increment expression that determines how the counter is incremented or decremented each time the loop is executed.

The first example in this figure shows how to use these expressions. First, the initialization expression declares a counter variable named i that's of the int type and is initialized to a value of 0. Next, a Boolean expression specifies that the loop should be repeated as long as the counter variable is less than 20. Then, the increment expression increments the counter variable by 1 at the end of each loop. Since this loop stores the counter variable followed by a space in a string, this code stores the numbers 0 to 19 in a string variable with each number followed by a space.

The second example calculates the sum of 8, 6, 4, and 2. Here, the sum variable is declared before the loop so it's available outside of the loop. Within the parentheses of the for loop, the initialization expression initializes the counter variable to 8; the Boolean expression indicates that the loop repeats as long as the counter variable is greater than zero, and the increment expression uses an assignment operator to subtract 2 from the counter variable with each repetition of the loop. Within the loop, the value of the counter variable is added to the value that's already stored in the sum variable. As a result, the final value for the sum variable is 20.

The third example shows how to code a loop that calculates the future value for a series of monthly investments. Here, the loop executes one time for each month. If you compare this for loop with the while loop in figure 4-6, you can see how a for loop improves upon a while loop when a counter variable is required.

The fourth example performs the same task as the for loop that's shown in the first example. In this case, though, because this loop only contains a single statement, the braces for the loop are optional and have been omitted. This works the same as it does for the if/else statement. As with that statement, it's generally considered a good coding style to use braces. That's why the first three examples in this figure use them.

The syntax of the for loop

```
for (initializationExpression; booleanExpression; incrementExpression) {
    statements
}
```

A for loop that stores the numbers 0 through 19 in a string

```
String numbers = "";
for (int i = 0; i < 20; i++)  {
    numbers += i + " ";
}
```

The console after the string is printed to it

```
0 1 2 3 4 5 6 7 8 9 10 11 12 13 14 15 16 17 18 19
```

A for loop that adds the numbers 8, 6, 4, and 2

```
int sum = 0;
for (int i = 8; i > 0; i -= 2) {
    sum += i;
}
```

A for loop that calculates a future value

```
int months = 36;
for (int i = 1; i <= months; i++) {
    futureValue = (futureValue + monthlyInvestment) *
                  (1 + monthlyInterestRate);
}
```

A for loop without braces

```
String numbers = "";
for (int i = 0; i < 5; i++)
    numbers += i + " ";
```

Description

- A *for loop* is useful when you need to increment or decrement a counter that determines how many times the loop is executed.
- Within the parentheses of a for loop, you code an initialization expression that gives the starting value for the counter, a Boolean expression that determines when the loop ends, and an increment expression that increments or decrements the counter.
- The loop ends when the Boolean expression is false.
- If necessary, you can declare the counter variable before the for loop. Then, this variable is in scope after the loop finishes executing.

Figure 4-8   How to code for loops

The Future Value application

Now that you've learned the statements for coding loops, figure 4-9 presents a Future Value application that uses a for loop within a while loop. As the console for this application shows, the user starts by entering the values for the monthly investment, the yearly interest rate, and the number of years. Then, the application calculates and displays the future value.

If you look at the code for this application, you can see that it uses a while loop to determine when the program ends. Within this loop, the code starts by getting the three entries from the user. Next, it converts these entries to the same time unit, which is months. To do that, the number of years is multiplied by 12, and the yearly interest rate is divided by 12. Besides that, the yearly interest rate is divided by 100 so it works correctly in the calculation.

Once the code sets up those variables, the program enters a for loop that calculates the future value. When the loop finishes, the program formats and displays the future value and asks whether the user wants to continue.

Because this application doesn't validate the user's entries, it crashes if the user enters invalid data. However, you'll learn how to fix that in the next chapter. Otherwise, this application works the way you would want it to.

Because it can be hard to tell whether a loop is producing the correct results, it's sometimes helpful to add debugging statements within the loop while you're testing it. For instance, you could add this statement to the Future Value application as the last statement in the loop:

```
System.out.println("Month " + i + ": " + futureValue);
```

Then, the program prints one line to the console each time through the loop. This makes it easy for you to check that the calculation for each month is accurate. It also makes it easy for you to tell whether the loop was executed the correct number of times.

The console

```
The Future Value Calculator

Enter monthly investment:    100
Enter yearly interest rate: 3
Enter number of years:       3
Future value:               $3,771.46

Continue? (y/n):
```

The code

```java
import java.util.Scanner;
import java.text.NumberFormat;

public class FutureValueApp {

    public static void main(String[] args) {
        System.out.println("The Future Value Calculator\n");

        Scanner sc = new Scanner(System.in);
        String choice = "y";
        while (choice.equalsIgnoreCase("y")) {
            // get the input from the user
            System.out.print("Enter monthly investment:    ");
            double monthlyInvestment = sc.nextDouble();
            System.out.print("Enter yearly interest rate: ");
            double interestRate = sc.nextDouble();
            System.out.print("Enter number of years:       ");
            int years = sc.nextInt();

            // convert yearly values to monthly values
            double monthlyInterestRate = interestRate / 12 / 100;
            int months = years * 12;

            // use a for loop to calculate the future value
            double futureValue = 0.0;
            for (int i = 1; i <= months; i++) {
                futureValue = (futureValue + monthlyInvestment) *
                              (1 + monthlyInterestRate);
            }

            // format the result and display it to the user
            NumberFormat currency = NumberFormat.getCurrencyInstance();
            System.out.println("Future value:                "
                    + currency.format(futureValue));
            System.out.println();

            // see if the user wants to continue
            System.out.print("Continue? (y/n): ");
            choice = sc.next();
            System.out.println();
        }
        System.out.println("Bye!");
    }
}
```

Figure 4-9   The Future Value application

How to code nested loops

Like if and switch statements, you can also nest one loop within another loop. For example, figure 4-10 shows how to nest three loops within each other. To make it easy for other programmers to see that these loops are nested, this code indents each successive loop to clearly show how they're related.

The example in this figure uses three nested loops to display a table of future value calculations. In this table, the monthly investment is $100, the interest rate varies from 5.0% to 6.5%, and the number of years varies from 1 to 6. Before the nested loops, a for loop adds the header row to the table.

After that, the nested for loops display the table of future value calculations. First, the outermost for loop iterates through the years (1, 2, 3, 4, 5, and 6), adding one row for each year to the table. To do that, the code within this loop starts by adding the year to the row. Then, the next for loop iterates through the four interest rates (5%, 5.5%, 6%, and 6.5%). The code within this loop uses the innermost for loop to calculate the future value for each interest rate. Then, the code appends the result of each calculation to the row. When this loop finishes, the outermost loop appends the row to the table. After all three loops finish, the code prints the table to the console.

As you review this code, you might notice that spaces are used to align the data in the columns. Although it would be possible to use tab characters to align the columns, tab characters don't always work the way you want. As a result, if you want more precise control over the alignment of your data, you can use spaces as shown in this figure.

The console

```
Monthly investment: $100.00

Year       5.0%            5.5%            6.0%            6.5%
1      $1,233.00       $1,236.36       $1,239.72       $1,243.10
2      $2,529.09       $2,542.46       $2,555.91       $2,569.45
3      $3,891.48       $3,922.23       $3,953.28       $3,984.64
4      $5,323.58       $5,379.83       $5,436.83       $5,494.59
5      $6,828.94       $6,919.65       $7,011.89       $7,105.68
6      $8,411.33       $8,546.33       $8,684.09       $8,824.66
```

Nested loops that print a table of future values

```java
// get the currency and percent formatters
NumberFormat currency = NumberFormat.getCurrencyInstance();
NumberFormat percent = NumberFormat.getPercentInstance();
percent.setMinimumFractionDigits(1);

// set the monthly payment to 100 and display it to the user
int monthlyInvestment = 100;
System.out.println("Monthly investment: " +
        currency.format(monthlyInvestment) + "\n");

// create the header row and add it to the table
String table  = "";
String headerRow  = "Year        ";
for (double rate = 5.0; rate < 7.0; rate += .5) {
    headerRow += percent.format(rate/100) + "            ";
}
table += headerRow + "\n";

// loop through the years
for (int year = 1; year < 7; year++) {
    // add year to the start of the row
    String row = year + "      ";

    // loop through each interest rate
    for (double rate = 5.0; rate < 7.0; rate += .5) {
        int months = year * 12;
        double monthlyInterestRate = rate/12/100;

        // calculate the future value
        double futureValue = 0.0;
        for (int i = 1; i <= months; i++) {
            futureValue = (futureValue + monthlyInvestment) *
                        (1 + monthlyInterestRate);
        }

        // add the calculation to the row
        row += currency.format(futureValue) + "     ";
    }
    // add the row to the table
    table += row + "\n";
}
System.out.println(table);
```

Figure 4-10   How to code nested loops

How to code break and continue statements

The break and continue statements give you additional control over loops. The *break statement* breaks out of a loop by causing program execution to jump to the statement that follows the loop. This causes the loop to end. The *continue statement* continues a loop by causing execution to jump to the top of the loop. This causes the loop to reevaluate its Boolean condition.

How to code break statements

The first example in figure 4-11 shows how the break statement works. Here, the condition in the while loop is intentionally set to true. Because of that, the while loop won't end due to the condition becoming false. Note, however, that you can use a break statement in any loop to end the loop.

Within the loop, the first statement asks the user to enter a color. If the user enters a color, the code prints the color to the console. However, if the user enters "exit", this code executes the break statement. This causes execution to jump out of the current loop and execute the statement that follows the loop.

How to code continue statements

The second example in this figure shows how the continue statement works. This example uses a while loop that starts by getting an integer from a user. Then, it checks whether the integer is less than or equal to zero. If it is, this code displays a message that indicates that the number must be greater than zero. Then, it uses a continue statement to jump to the start of the while loop. This reevaluates the condition at the top of the loop. Since this condition still evaluates to true, this executes the first two statements in the loop, which prompt the user for a number again.

When working with nested loops, it's possible for the outer loop to have a *label* that allows the code in the inner loop to jump to the label. However, using labels with loops often yields code that's difficult to read and maintain. As a result, it's generally considered a best practice to avoid using labels with loops. That's why they're not shown in this figure.

A break statement that exits the loop

```
while (true) {
    System.out.print("Enter a color: ");
    String line = sc.nextLine();
    if (line.equalsIgnoreCase("exit")) {
        break;
    }
    System.out.println("You entered: " + line + "\n");
}
System.out.println("Bye!");
```

The console

```
Enter a color: blue
You entered: blue

Enter a color: exit
Bye!
```

A continue statement that jumps to the beginning of a loop

```
String choice = "y";
while (choice.equalsIgnoreCase("y")) {
    System.out.print("Enter a number: ");
    int number = sc.nextInt();
    if (number <= 0) {
        System.out.println("Number must be greater than 0. Try again.");
        continue;
    }
    System.out.println("You entered: " + number + "\n");

    System.out.print("Continue? (y/n): ");
    choice = sc.next();
    System.out.println();
}
System.out.println("Bye!");
```

The console

```
Enter a number: -100
Number must be greater than 0. Try again.
Enter a number: 100
You entered: 100

Continue? (y/n):
```

Description

- To jump to the end of the current loop, you can use the *break statement*.
- To skip the rest of the statements in the current loop and jump to the top of the current loop, you can use the *continue statement*.

Figure 4-11   How to code break and continue statements

The Guess the Number application

Figure 4-12 presents a Guess the Number application that uses the break and continue statements. In addition, this application uses the Math class to get a random number as described in the previous chapter.

To start, this application declares a constant named LIMIT that sets the highest number that the player can guess. Then, it displays a message that tells the user the range of numbers to guess from.

After displaying this message, the code gets a random number between 1 and 10. To do that, it uses the random() method of the Math class to return a random double value, and it multiplies that value by the LIMIT constant, which is 10. Then, it converts the double value to an int value and increments that value by 1.

After getting the random number, the code begins a while loop that allows the user to continue guessing until the right number is guessed. To do that, the condition on this loop is set to true. As you learned in the previous figure, that means that you must end the loop using a break statement.

Within the loop, the first two statements get the guess from the user. Then, this code checks whether the guess is less than 1 or greater than the LIMIT constant. If so, it displays an error message and executes a continue statement to continue at the top of the loop, which gets another guess from the user.

If the guess is within the specified range, this code checks whether the guess is higher or lower than the number. If it is, this code displays an appropriate message and increments the counter variable. However, if the guess is equal to the number, this code displays an appropriate message that includes the count of guesses, and it uses a break statement to break out of the loop. This jumps over the statement that increments the counter variable and out of the loop.

This program uses the constant named LIMIT to set the highest number that the user can guess because it makes it easier to modify the program later if you decide to change the highest number. In that case, you just need to change the value of the constant, which is used in three places in this code. If you didn't use this constant, you would need to change the limit in each of these three places.

Although this application uses break and continue statements, you should know that it could be coded without them. You'll get a chance to try this for yourself in one of the exercises at the end of this chapter.

The console

```
Guess the number!
I'm thinking of a number from 1 to 10

Your guess: 11
Invalid guess. Try again.
Your guess: 5
Too low.
Your guess: 7
You guessed it in 2 tries.

Bye!
```

The code

```java
import java.util.Scanner;

public class GuessNumberApp {

    public static void main(String[] args) {
        final int LIMIT = 10;

        System.out.println("Guess the number!");
        System.out.println("I'm thinking of a number from 1 to " + LIMIT);
        System.out.println();

        // get a random number between 1 and the limit
        double d = Math.random() * LIMIT; // d is >= 0.0 and < limit
        int number = (int) d;              // convert double to int
        number++;                          // int is >= 1 and <= limit

        Scanner sc = new Scanner(System.in);
        int count = 1;
        while (true) {
            System.out.print("Your guess: ");
            int guess = sc.nextInt();

            if (guess < 1 || guess > LIMIT) {
                System.out.println("Invalid guess. Try again.");
                continue;
            }

            if (guess < number) {
                System.out.println("Too low.");
            } else if (guess > number) {
                System.out.println("Too high.");
            } else {
                System.out.println("You guessed it in " +
                                count + " tries.\n");
                break;
            }
            count++;
        }
        System.out.println("Bye!");
    }
}
```

Figure 4-12   The Guess the Number application

Perspective

If this chapter has succeeded, you should now be able to use if/else, switch, while, and for statements. These are the Java statements that implement the selection, case, and iteration structures. You can use them to provide the logic of an application.

Summary

- You can use the *relational operators* to create *Boolean expressions* that compare primitive data types and return true or false values, and you can use the *logical operators* to connect two or more Boolean expressions.

- You can use *if/else statements* and *switch statements* to control the logic of an application, and you can *nest* these statements whenever necessary.

- You can use *while*, *do-while*, and *for loops* to repeatedly execute one or more statements until a Boolean expression evaluates to false, and you can nest these statements whenever necessary.

- You can use *break statements* to jump to the end of the current loop, and you can use *continue statements* to jump to the start of the current loop.

Exercise 4-1   Test the Future Value application

In this exercise, you'll test the Future Value application that's presented in this chapter.

1. Open the project named ch04_ex1_FutureValue that's stored in the ex_starts directory. Then, test it with valid data to see how it works.

2. To make sure that the results are correct, add a debugging statement within the for loop that calculates the future value. This statement should display the month and future value each time through the loop.

3. Test the program with simple entries like 100 for monthly investment, 12 for yearly interest (1 percent each month), and 1 for year. When the debugging data is displayed, check the results manually to make sure they're correct.

Exercise 4-2   Modify the Invoice application

In this exercise, you'll modify the switch statement and the nested if/else statements that are used to determine the discount percent for the Invoice application in figure 4-5. Then, you'll replace the switch statement with another if/else statement.

Open the project and change the switch and if/else statements

1. Open the project named ch04_ex2_Invoice that's stored in the ex_starts directory. Then, run the application to see how it works.

2. Change the code so customers of type "r" or "R" with a subtotal that is greater than or equal to $250 but less than $500 get a 25% discount, and those with a subtotal of $500 or more get a 30% discount. Then, test the application to make sure this works.

3. Change the code so customers of type "c" or "C" always get a 20% discount. Then, test the application to make sure this works.

4. Add another customer of type "t" or "T". Then, add code so customers of these types get a 40% discount for subtotals of less than $500, and a 50% discount for subtotals of $500 or more. Then, test the application.

5. Adjust the code so that no discount is provided for a customer type that isn't "r", "R", "c", "C", "t", or "T". Then, test the application.

Replace the switch statement with an if/else statement

6. Copy the switch statement and paste it above the original statement. Then, comment out the original statement.

7. Replace the copied switch statement with a nested if/else statement, making sure the user can enter the customer type in either upper or lower case. Test the application one more time to be sure it works.

Exercise 4-3   Modify the Guess the Number application

In this exercise, you'll modify the while loop in the Guess the Number application so it doesn't use the break or continue statements.

Open and run the project

1. Open the project named ch04_ex3_GuessNumber that's stored in the ex_starts folder. Then, run the application to see how it works.

Remove the break statement

2. Change the while loop so the Boolean expression checks that the values of the guess and number variables aren't equal. For this to work, you'll need to declare the guess variable outside the loop.

3. Move the statement that notifies the user of the correct guess so it executes after the while loop is finished.

4. Delete the else clause of the if/else statement. Since this means that the code that increments the counter variable will be executed even if the correct number is guessed, you should change that variable so it's initialized to 0 instead of 1.

5. Test the application to make sure it still works correctly.

Remove the continue statement

6. Combine the if statement that notifies the user of an invalid guess and the if/else statement that notifies the user of guesses that are too low or too high into a single if/else statement. Then, delete the continue statement from the if block.

7. Run and test the application. Note that invalid guesses are now included in the total guess count. To make the application to work the way it did before, you can decrement the counter variable for invalid guesses.

Exercise 4-4   Enhance the Future Value application

In this exercise, you'll modify the Future Value application so it displays a table of future values based on the data entered by the user.

```
Enter monthly investment: 100
Enter number of years:     5

Year    5.0%         5.5%         6.0%         6.5%
1       $1,233.00    $1,236.36    $1,239.72    $1,243.10
2       $2,529.09    $2,542.46    $2,555.91    $2,569.45
3       $3,891.48    $3,922.23    $3,953.28    $3,984.64
4       $5,323.58    $5,379.83    $5,436.83    $5,494.59
5       $6,828.94    $6,919.65    $7,011.89    $7,105.68

Continue? (y/n):
```

1. Open the project named ch04_ex4_FutureValue that's in the ex_starts folder.

2. Remove all the code inside the while loop, except for the code that gets the monthly investment amount and the number of years from the user and the code that asks if the user wants to continue.

3. Add code to the while loop that uses the NumberFormat class to create NumberFormat objects that can be used to format the interest rates and future values as shown above.

4. Code a for loop that displays the interest rates from 5.0% to 6.5%, at .5% increments. Use tabs ("\t") rather than spaces to align the rates.

5. Code nested for loops to calculate and display the future value for the investment amount at each interest rate and for the number of years entered by the user. Again, use tabs rather than spaces to align the data. Then, run and test the application.

5

How to code methods, handle exceptions, and validate data

In the last three chapters, you learned how to develop applications whose code is contained entirely within the static main() method. But you can also code your own static methods in addition to the main() method. This can help you break down the code for your applications into manageable parts that are reusable and easy to maintain. That's what you'll learn to do in the first part of this chapter.

Then, you'll learn the basic skills for catching and handling the exceptions that can occur when you get input from a user and perform calculations based on that input. This can prevent an application from crashing when the user enters data that the application can't handle. In addition, you'll learn how to validate input data to prevent exceptions from occurring in the first place. These are essential skills when you're developing professional applications.

How to code and call static methods

So far, you've learned how to code applications that consist of a single method, the static main() method that's executed automatically when you run a class. Now, you'll learn how to code and call other static methods. That's one way to divide the code for an application into manageable parts.

How to code static methods

Figure 5-1 shows how to code a *static method*. To start, you code an *access modifier* that indicates whether the method can be called from other classes (public) or just from the class that it's coded in (private). Next, you code the static keyword to identify the method as a static method.

After the static keyword, you code a return type that identifies the type of data that the method returns. The return type can be a primitive data type or a reference type like a String object. If the method doesn't return any data, you code the void keyword as shown by the first example.

After the return type, you code a method name that indicates what the method does. By convention, Java methods use camel case notation. In addition, it's common to start each method name with a verb followed by one or more nouns or adjectives, as in calculateFutureValue.

After the method name, you code a set of parentheses. Within the parentheses, you declare the *parameters* that are required by the method. If a method doesn't require any parameters, you can code an empty set of parentheses as shown by the first example. And if a method requires more than one parameter, you separate them with commas as shown by the second example. Later, when you call the method, you pass values to these parameters.

Next, you code a set of braces that contains the statements that the method executes. If the method returns a value, these statements must include a *return statement* that specifies the variable or object to return. This is illustrated by the calculateFutureValue() method in this figure.

When you code the method name and parameter list of a method, you form the *signature* of the method. As you might expect, each method must have a unique signature.

How to call static methods

Figure 5-1 also shows how to *call* a static method that's coded within the same class. This is just like calling a static method from a Java class, but you don't need to code the class name. Then, if the method includes parameters, you code the *arguments* that are passed to the parameters within parentheses, separating the arguments with commas. Otherwise, you code an empty set of parentheses.

If you pass arguments, the arguments must be in the same order as the parameters in the method. In addition, the arguments and parameters must have compatible data types. That means that an argument and parameter must have

The basic syntax for coding a static method

```
public|private static returnType methodName([parameterList]) {
    statements
}
```

A static method with no parameters and no return type

```
private static void printWelcomeMessage() {
    System.out.println("Hello New User");
}
```

A static method with three parameters that returns a double value

```
public static double calculateFutureValue(double monthlyInvestment,
        double monthlyInterestRate, int months) {
    double futureValue = 0.0;
    for (int i = 1; i <= months; i++) {
        futureValue = (futureValue + monthlyInvestment) *
                    (1 + monthlyInterestRate);
    }
    return futureValue;
}
```

The syntax for calling a static method that's in the same class

```
methodName([argumentList])
```

A call statement with no arguments

```
printWelcomeMessage();
```

A call statement that passes three arguments

```
double futureValue = calculateFutureValue(investment, rate, months);
```

Description

- To allow other classes to access a method, use the public *access modifier*. To prevent other classes from accessing a method, use the private modifier.

- To code a method that returns data, code a return type in the method declaration and code a *return statement* in the body of the method. The return statement ends the execution of the method and returns the specified value to the calling method.

- Within the parentheses of a method, you can code an optional *parameter list* that contains one or more *parameters* that consist of a data type and name. These are the values that must be passed to the method when it is called.

- The name of a method along with its parameter list form the *signature* of the method, which must be unique.

- When you call a method, the *arguments* in the *argument list* must be in the same order as the parameters in the parameter list defined by the method, and they must have compatible data types. However, the names of the arguments and the parameters don't need to be the same.

Figure 5-1   How to code and call static methods

the same data type, or the parameter must have a more precise data type than the argument so the argument can be implicitly cast to that type. To refresh your memory on implicit casting, you can refer back to chapter 3.

In practice, the terms *parameter* and *argument* are often used interchangeably. In this book, however, we'll use the term *parameter* to refer to the variables of a method declaration, and we'll use the term *argument* to refer to the variables that are passed to a method.

The Future Value application with a static method

To illustrate the use of a static method, figure 5-2 presents another version of the Future Value application. This time, the application uses a static method to calculate the future value. This method requires three arguments, and it includes the for loop that processes those arguments. When the loop finishes, the return statement returns the future value to the main() method.

To use the static method, the main() method prepares the three arguments so they're all in month units. Then, it calls the static method and passes the three arguments to it. This simplifies the main() method and illustrates how static methods can be used to divide a program into manageable parts.

In this case, the statement that calls the method passes arguments that have the same variable names as the parameters of the method. Although this isn't necessary, it makes the code easier to follow. However, it is necessary to pass the arguments in the same sequence as the parameters and for the arguments to have data types that are compatible with the data types of the parameters.

For this application, the calculateFutureValue() method works the same regardless of whether it's declared as public or private. Since this method might be useful to other classes, it's declared as public in this figure. On the other hand, the next figure shows an example of a method that's declared as private because it's only useful to the current class.

The Future Value application with a static method

```java
import java.util.Scanner;
import java.text.NumberFormat;

public class FutureValueApp {

    public static void main(String[] args) {
        System.out.println("Welcome to the Future Value Calculator\n");
        Scanner sc = new Scanner(System.in);
        String choice = "y";
        while (choice.equalsIgnoreCase("y")) {
            // get the input from the user
            System.out.print("Enter monthly investment:    ");
            double monthlyInvestment = sc.nextDouble();
            System.out.print("Enter yearly interest rate: ");
            double interestRate = sc.nextDouble();
            System.out.print("Enter number of years:      ");
            int years = sc.nextInt();

            // convert yearly values to monthly values
            double monthlyInterestRate = interestRate/12/100;
            int months = years * 12;

            // call the future value method
            double futureValue = calculateFutureValue(
                monthlyInvestment, monthlyInterestRate, months);

            // format and display the result
            NumberFormat currency = NumberFormat.getCurrencyInstance();
            System.out.println("Future value:               "
                            + currency.format(futureValue));
            System.out.println();

            // see if the user wants to continue
            System.out.print("Continue? (y/n): ");
            choice = sc.next();
            System.out.println();
        }
    }

    //  a static method that requires three arguments and returns a double
    public static double calculateFutureValue(double monthlyInvestment,
            double monthlyInterestRate, int months) {
        double futureValue = 0.0;
        for (int i = 1; i <= months; i++) {
            futureValue = (futureValue + monthlyInvestment) *
                        (1 + monthlyInterestRate);
        }
        return futureValue;
    }
}
```

Figure 5-2   The Future Value application with a static method

The Guess the Number application
with static methods

To further illustrate the use of static methods, figure 5-3 presents another version of the Guess the Number application from chapter 4. This time, the application uses two static methods in addition to the main() method to divide the code into more manageable parts.

To start, the displayWelcome() method prints a welcome message to the console. This method defines a single parameter named limit that specifies the highest number that the user can guess. Then, it prints a welcome message to the console that uses the limit parameter. Since this method is obviously only useful to the current class, it's declared as private.

Then, the getRandomInt() method gets a random integer from 1 to the parameter named limit. If you read the previous chapter, you should understand the code that gets the random number. The only difference here is that the method uses a return statement to return the random number to the calling code. Since this method might be useful to other classes, it's declared as public.

Finally, the main() method begins by declaring the LIMIT constant and setting it to a value of 10. Then, it calls the displayWelcome() method and passes it the LIMIT constant. Next, it calls the getRandomInt() method, passes it the LIMIT constant, and assigns the int value that's returned to the variable named number. After that, the code works the same as it did in chapter 4.

So, if this code works the same as the code in chapter 4, why bother breaking it into methods? One reason is that this approach can make your code easier to maintain and debug. That's because shorter methods are typically easier to understand and debug. A second reason is that this approach can make it possible to reuse your code. As a result, you don't have to repeat the same code in multiple places. A third reason is that it reduces the need for comments since the names of the methods should describe what the code does. For example, there's no need to include a comment that says, "get random integer" because that information is in the name of the getRandomInt() method.

For a short and simple application like this one, the benefits of using methods to organize your code are minimal. However, when you work with longer and more complex applications like the one presented at the end of this chapter, the benefits are significant.

The Guess the Number application with static methods

```java
import java.util.Scanner;

public class GuessNumberApp {

    private static void displayWelcome(int limit) {
        System.out.println("Guess the number!");
        System.out.println("I'm thinking of a number from 1 to " + limit);
        System.out.println();
    }

    public static int getRandomInt(int limit) {
        double d = Math.random() * limit;      // d is >= 0.0 and < limit
        int randomInt = (int) d;               // convert double to int
        randomInt++;                           // int is >= 1 and <= limit
        return randomInt;
    }

    public static void main(String[] args) {
        final int LIMIT = 10;

        displayWelcome(LIMIT);
        int number = getRandomInt(LIMIT);

        Scanner sc = new Scanner(System.in);
        int count = 1;
        while (true) {
            System.out.print("Your guess: ");
            int guess = sc.nextInt();

            if (guess < 1 || guess > LIMIT) {
                System.out.println("Invalid guess. Try again.");
                continue;
            }

            if (guess < number) {
                System.out.println("Too low.");
            } else if (guess > number) {
                System.out.println("Too high.");
            } else {
                System.out.println("You guessed it in " +
                                   count + " tries.\n");
                break;
            }
            count++;
        }
        System.out.println("Bye!");
    }
}
```

Figure 5-3   The Guess the Number application with static methods

How to handle exceptions

To prevent your applications from crashing, you can write code that handles exceptions when they occur. This is known as *exception handling*, and it plays an important role in most applications.

How exceptions work

When an application can't perform an operation, Java *throws* an *exception*. An exception is an object that's created from one of the classes in the Exception hierarchy, such as the ones shown in figure 5-4. Exception objects represent errors that have occurred, and they contain information about those errors. One of the most common causes of exceptions is invalid input data.

The Exception class that's at the top of the exception hierarchy defines the most general type of exception. The RuntimeException class is a *subclass* of the Exception class that defines a more specific type of exception. Similarly, the NoSuchElementException and IllegalArgumentException classes are subclasses of the RuntimeException class that define even more specific types of exceptions.

A well-coded application *catches* any exceptions that are thrown and handles them. Exception handling can be as simple as notifying users that they must enter valid data. Or, for more serious exceptions, it may involve notifying users that the application is being shut down, saving as much data as possible, cleaning up resources, and exiting the application as smoothly as possible.

When you're testing an application, it's common to encounter exceptions that haven't been handled. For a console application, this typically causes information about the exception to be displayed on the console. This information usually includes the name of the exception class, a brief message that describes the cause of the exception, and the *stack trace*. For example, this figure shows the information that's displayed when the user enters an invalid double value for the Invoice application.

The stack trace is a list of the methods that were called before the exception occurred. These methods are listed in the reverse order from the order in which they were called. In addition, each method includes a line number, which can help you find the statement that caused the exception in your source code. In this figure, for instance, the stack trace indicates that line 20 of the main() method of the InvoiceApp class threw an exception when it called the nextDouble() method of the Scanner class.

One common situation where you'll need to handle exceptions is when you convert string data to numeric data. If, for example, the nextInt() or nextDouble() method of the Scanner class can't convert the string the user enters to the correct data type, the method throws an InputMismatchException. Similarly, the parseDouble() and parseInt() methods of the Double and Integer classes throw a NumberFormatException when they can't convert a string to a double or int type.

The class for an exception is typically stored in the same package as the class that provides the methods that throw that type of exception. For instance, the

Some of the classes in the Exception hierarchy

```
Exception
    RuntimeException
        NoSuchElementException
            InputMismatchException
        IllegalArgumentException
            NumberFormatException
        ArithmeticException
        NullPointerException
```

The console after an InputMismatchException has been thrown

```
Enter subtotal:    $100
Exception in thread "main" java.util.InputMismatchException
    at java.util.Scanner.throwFor(Scanner.java:909)
    at java.util.Scanner.next(Scanner.java:1530)
    at java.util.Scanner.nextDouble(Scanner.java:2456)
    at InvoiceApp.main(InvoiceApp.java:20)
```

Four methods that might throw an exception

Class	Method	Throws
Scanner	nextInt()	InputMismatchException
Scanner	nextDouble()	InputMismatchException
Integer	parseInt(String)	NumberFormatException
Double	parseDouble(String)	NumberFormatException

Description

- An *exception* is an object that contains information about an error that has occurred. When an error occurs in a method, the method *throws* an exception.

- If an exception is thrown when you're testing a console application, some information about the exception, including its name and stack trace, is displayed at the console.

- A *stack trace* is a list of the methods that were called before the exception occurred. The list appears in reverse order, from the last method called to the first method called.

- All exceptions are *subclasses* of the Exception class. The Exception class represents the most general type of exception. Each successive layer of subclasses represents more specific exceptions.

- The class for an exception is usually stored in the same package as the class whose methods throw that type of exception. For instance, the InputMismatchException class is stored in the java.util package along with the Scanner class.

Figure 5-4   How exceptions work

Scanner class throws the InputMismatchException. As a result, this exception is stored in the same package as the Scanner class, the java.util package.

How to catch exceptions

Figure 5-5 shows how to use the *try/catch statement* to catch and handle exceptions. First, you code a try clause around one or more statements that may cause an exception. Then, you code a catch clause immediately after the try clause. This clause contains the block of statements that are executed if an exception is thrown by a statement in the try block. Since this block contains the code that handles the exception, it is known as an *exception handler*.

The second example in this figure shows how you could use a try/catch statement within the while loop of the Invoice application. Here, the try clause is coded around the nextDouble() method of the Scanner class, and a catch clause is coded for the InputMismatchException. Then, if the user enters a non-numeric value for the subtotal, the nextDouble() method throws an InputMismatchException and Java executes the code in the catch block. For this catch block to work, the code must import the class for that exception as shown in the first example.

In this case, the catch block starts by displaying an error message. Then, it calls the nextLine() method of the Scanner object to discard the entire line for the incorrectly entered value. That way, the scanner doesn't attempt to read this value the next time the nextDouble() method is called. This is necessary because the nextDouble() method isn't completed if an exception occurs. Finally, a continue statement jumps to the beginning of the loop, which causes the application to prompt the user to enter another subtotal.

When writing code like this, you might think that you could use the next() method to discard the string that the user enters. However, if the user enters two or more strings such as "$100 $300", the next() method only discards the first string ("$100"). Then, when the continue statement jumps to the top of the loop, the next call to the nextDouble() method attempts to read the second string ("$300"). Since that's not what you want, you'll typically use the nextLine() method instead of the next() method to discard all data entered by the user.

The catch block in this example is only executed if the InputMismatchException is thrown. Since this exception is the only exception that's likely to be thrown in the try block, this is the clearest way to catch this exception. However, if you wanted the catch clause to catch other exceptions as well, you could name an exception higher up in the Exception hierarchy. For example, if you wanted to catch all exceptions, you could code this catch clause:

```
catch (Exception e)
```

You'll learn more about how this works in chapter 16.

The syntax for a simple try/catch statement

```
try { statements }
catch (ExceptionClass exceptionName) { statements }
```

How to import the InputMismatchException class

```
import java.util.InputMismatchException;
```

A try/catch statement that catches an InputMismatchException

```
while (choice.equalsIgnoreCase("y")) {
    double subtotal = 0.0;
    try {
        System.out.print("Enter subtotal:    ");
        subtotal = sc.nextDouble();
    } catch (InputMismatchException e)  {
        System.out.println("Error! Invalid number. Try again.\n");
        sc.nextLine();    // discard all data entered by the user
        continue;         // jump to the top of the loop
    }
    .
    .
    .
}
```

Console output

```
Enter subtotal:    $100
Error! Invalid number. Try again.

Enter subtotal:
```

Description

- In a *try statement* (or *try/catch statement*), you code any statements that may throw an exception in a *try block*. Then, you can code a *catch block* that handles any exceptions that may occur in the try block.

- When an exception occurs, any remaining statements in the try block are skipped and the statements in the catch block are executed.

- Any variables or objects that are used in both the try and catch blocks must be declared before the try and catch blocks so both blocks can access them.

- If you use a catch block to catch a specific type of exception, you may need to import the exception class.

- You can use the nextLine() method to discard any data that the user enters on a line when that data isn't required by the application.

Figure 5-5   How to catch exceptions

The Future Value application with exception handling

Figure 5-6 presents an improved version of the Future Value application from figure 5-2. This version uses a try/catch statement that's coded within the while loop to catch any exceptions that might be thrown when data is retrieved from the user.

To start, this application begins with import statements that import the Scanner class and the InputMismatchException class from the java.util package. As a result, this application can use a Scanner object to get user input from the console, and it can catch the InputMismatchException object that may be thrown by the methods of the Scanner class.

To catch exceptions, all of the statements that get numeric input are coded within a try block. Then, if the user enters data with an invalid numeric format, the three statements in the catch block are executed. The first statement displays a message that indicates that the entry is not a valid number. Then, the second statement uses the nextLine() method to discard the entire line for the invalid entry. And finally, the continue statement jumps to the top of the while loop. That way, the code repeatedly prompts the user until the user enters valid data for all three values.

Although this technique works, it has two shortcomings. First, the user must start entering values from the beginning each time an exception is thrown even if some of the values are valid. Second, the application displays an error message that isn't as descriptive or helpful as it could be. Later in this chapter, you'll learn how to fix both of these shortcomings.

The Future Value application with exception handling

```java
import java.text.NumberFormat;
import java.util.Scanner;
import java.util.InputMismatchException;

public class FutureValueApp {

    public static void main(String[] args) {
        System.out.println("Welcome to the Future Value Calculator\n");
        Scanner sc = new Scanner(System.in);
        String choice = "y";
        while (choice.equalsIgnoreCase("y")) {
            double monthlyInvestment;
            double interestRate;
            int years;
            try {
                System.out.print("Enter monthly investment:   ");
                monthlyInvestment = sc.nextDouble();
                System.out.print("Enter yearly interest rate: ");
                interestRate = sc.nextDouble();
                System.out.print("Enter number of years:      ");
                years = sc.nextInt();
            } catch (InputMismatchException e) {
                System.out.println("Error! Invalid number. Try again.\n");
                sc.nextLine();    // discard the invalid number
                continue;         // jump to start of loop
            }

            // calculate future value
            double monthlyInterestRate = interestRate / 12 / 100;
            int months = years * 12;
            double futureValue = calculateFutureValue(
                    monthlyInvestment, monthlyInterestRate, months);

            // format and display the result
            NumberFormat currency = NumberFormat.getCurrencyInstance();
            System.out.println("Future value:               "
                    + currency.format(futureValue) + "\n");

            // see if the user wants to continue
            System.out.print("Continue? (y/n): ");
            choice = sc.next();
            System.out.println();
        }
    }

    private static double calculateFutureValue(double monthlyInvestment,
            double monthlyInterestRate, int months) {
        double futureValue = 0;
        for (int i = 1; i <= months; i++) {
            futureValue = (futureValue + monthlyInvestment) *
                        (1 + monthlyInterestRate);
        }
        return futureValue;
    }
}
```

Figure 5-6   The Future Value application with exception handling

How to validate data

Although you can use the try/catch statement to catch and handle an exception caused by invalid data, it's usually best to prevent exceptions from being thrown in the first place whenever that's possible. To do that, you can use a technique called *data validation*. Then, when an entry is invalid, the application displays an error message and gives the user another chance to enter valid data. This is repeated until all the entries are valid.

How to prevent exceptions from being thrown

Figure 5-7 presents four methods of the Scanner class that you can use to prevent exceptions from being thrown. For instance, the first example in this figure shows how to use the hasNextDouble() method to check whether the user has entered a string that can be converted to a double type. To do that, an if statement checks whether the hasNextDouble() method returns a true value. If it does, the code calls the nextDouble() method to get the value.

However, if the hasNextDouble() method returns a false value, it means the user has entered an invalid double value. In that case, the code displays an error message. Then, it calls the nextLine() method to discard the entire line that the user entered. Finally, it executes a continue statement to jump to the beginning of the loop that contains the if statement.

If you call the equals() or equalsIgnoreCase() method from a string that contains a null, Java throws an exception. Specifically, Java throws a NullPointerException. To prevent this exception from being thrown, you can use code like that in the second example. To start, this code checks the value of a variable named customerType. If it isn't null, the code that follows calls the equals() method. If it is null, no processing is performed. This type of code is often necessary when you call methods from objects that might be null.

Since code that checks user input without using exception handling runs faster than code that uses exception handling, you should avoid using exception handling to check user input whenever possible. In general, it's considered a good practice to use exception handling only when the situation is truly exceptional. For example, if you're unable to access an external resource such as a file or database, that's a truly exceptional situation. You'll learn about these types of exceptions later in this book. It's not exceptional that a user would accidentally enter a non-numeric value for a subtotal, though. As a result, you should use the methods of the Scanner class to prevent these types of exceptions whenever possible.

Methods of the Scanner class you can use to validate data

Method	Description
hasNext()	Returns true if the scanner contains another token.
hasNextInt()	Returns true if the scanner contains another token that can be converted to an int value.
hasNextDouble()	Returns true if the scanner contains another token that can be converted to a double value.
hasNextLine()	Returns true if the scanner contains another line.

Code that prevents an InputMismatchException

```
while (choice.equalsIgnoreCase("y")) {
    double subtotal = 0.0;
    System.out.print("Enter subtotal:     ");
    if (sc.hasNextDouble()) {
        subtotal = sc.nextDouble();
        sc.nextLine();      // discard any other data entered on the line
    } else {
        System.out.println("Error! Invalid number. Try again.\n");
        sc.nextLine();      // discard the entire line
        continue;           // jump to the top of the loop
    }
    .
    .
    .
}
```

Console output

```
Enter subtotal:     $100
Error! Invalid number. Try again.

Enter subtotal:
```

Code that prevents a NullPointerException

```
if (customerType != null) {
    if (customerType.equals("R"))
        discountPercent = .4;
}
```

Description

- The hasXxx() methods of the Scanner class let you check whether additional data is available at the console and whether that data can be converted to a specific data type. You can use these methods to prevent an exception from being thrown when one of the nextXxx() methods is called.

- When your code prevents an exception from being thrown, it runs faster than code that catches and then handles the exception.

Figure 5-7   How to prevent exceptions from being thrown

How to validate a single entry

When a user enters data, you may want to perform several types of data validation. In particular, it's common to perform the two types of data validation for numeric entries that are illustrated in figure 5-8.

First, if the application requires that the user enter a number at the prompt, you can check if the string that's entered by the user can be converted to a number. To do that, you can use one of the hasXxx() methods of the Scanner class. Second, if the application requires that the user enter a number within a specified range, you can use if/else statements to check that the number falls within that range. This is known as *range checking*.

To repeat this checking until an entry is valid, you can use a while loop like the one shown in this figure. This loop executes repeatedly until the user enters a valid double value within the specified range. Within this loop, the first if/else statement checks whether the user entered a valid double value. If so, the code retrieves that value and marks the data as valid. Otherwise, the else clause displays an error message.

After the if/else statement, this code uses the nextLine() method to discard any other data that the user might have entered on the line. This is necessary because it's possible that the user might have made an entry like this:

```
100 dollars
```

In that case, the hasDouble() method returns true. As a result, the nextDouble() method converts the first string of "100" to a double value, and the nextLine() method discards the second string of "dollars", which is what you want.

If the user enters a valid double value, the second if/else statement checks whether that value is in the specified range. To do that, it begins by checking if the value is less than or equal to 0 or greater than or equal to 10,000. If it is, an appropriate error message is displayed and the data is marked as invalid. This causes the loop to repeat.

Although this figure only shows how to check data that the user has entered at the console, the same principles apply to other types of applications. In section 4, for example, you'll see how these principles can be used to validate entries for an application that uses a graphical user interface (GUI).

Code that gets a valid double value within a specified range

```
Scanner sc = new Scanner(System.in);
double subtotal = 0.0;
boolean isValid = false;

while (!isValid) {
    // get a valid double value
    System.out.print("Enter subtotal:   ");
    if (sc.hasNextDouble()) {
        subtotal = sc.nextDouble();
        isValid = true;
    } else {
        System.out.println("Error! Invalid number. Try again.");
    }
    sc.nextLine();      // discard any other data entered on the line

    // check the range of the double value
    if (isValid && subtotal <= 0) {
        System.out.println("Error! Number must be greater than 0.");
        isValid = false;
    } else if (isValid && subtotal >= 10000) {
        System.out.println("Error! Number must be less than 10000.");
        isValid = false;
    }
}

System.out.println("Subtotal: " + subtotal);
```

Description

- When a user enters data, that data usually needs to be checked to make sure that it is valid. This is known as *data validation*.

- When an entry is invalid, the program needs to display an error message and give the user another chance to enter valid data. This needs to be repeated until the entry is valid. One way to code this type of validation routine is to use a while loop.

- Two common types of validity checking for a numeric entry are (1) to make sure that the entry has a valid numeric format, and (2) to make sure that the entry is within a valid range (known as *range checking*).

Figure 5-8   How to validate a single entry

How to code a method that validates an entry

Almost all professional applications require you to validate multiple entries. To do that, it often makes sense to store your validation code in methods like the ones shown in figure 5-9. These methods perform the same types of validation shown in the previous figure, but they work for any double entry instead of for a specific entry. As a result, you can use these methods instead of having to write validation code for each entry.

In this figure, the getDouble() method checks that the user enters a valid double value. This method accepts two parameters: a Scanner object and a String object that contains the text for the prompt. Then, this method displays the prompt to the user and, if the user enters a valid double value, uses the scanner to read that value. Finally, the return statement returns the value to the calling method.

The getDoubleWithinRange() method accepts four parameters. The first two parameters are the same as those used by the getDouble() method. The last two parameters contain doubles that specify the range of acceptable values. Within the while loop for this method, the first statement calls the getDouble() method and passes it the Scanner object and the prompt string. This gets a double value from the user. Then, the if/else statement checks whether the double value falls outside the specified range. If it does, the code displays an appropriate error message and the while loop continues to execute until the user enters a double value within the specified range. Otherwise, the code marks the data as valid. This ends the while loop and returns the valid value to the calling method.

The code at the bottom of this figure shows how to call these methods. The first statement creates the Scanner object that's needed by both methods. Then, the second statement calls the getDouble() method to get a valid double value for the subtotal. Finally, the third statement uses the getDoubleWithinRange() method to get a valid double value for a subtotal that is greater than 0 and less than 10,000. This shows that you can call the getDouble() method directly if you don't need to check the range. However, if you need to check the range, you can call the getDoubleWithinRange() method, which calls the getDouble() method for you.

Once you understand how the getDouble() and getDoubleWithinRange() methods work, you can code methods for other numeric types. For example, you can code the getInt() and getIntWithinRange() methods to work with the int type.

There are several advantages to using methods like these for validation. First, they make it possible to reuse your code. If, for example, your application needs to validate ten double values, you can call the getDoubleWithinRange() method ten times instead of repeating its code in ten different places in your application. Second, since you aren't repeating code in multiple locations, your code is easier to debug and maintain. In programming, this is known as the *Don't Repeat Yourself* (*DRY*) principle.

A method that gets a valid numeric format

```
public static double getDouble(Scanner sc, String prompt) {
    double d = 0;
    boolean isValid = false;
    while (!isValid) {
        System.out.print(prompt);
        if (sc.hasNextDouble()) {
            d = sc.nextDouble();
            isValid = true;
        } else {
            System.out.println("Error! Invalid number. Try again.");
        }
        sc.nextLine();    // discard any other data entered on the line
    }
    return d;
}
```

A method that checks for a valid numeric range

```
public static double getDoubleWithinRange(Scanner sc, String prompt,
        double min, double max) {
    double d = 0;
    boolean isValid = false;
    while (!isValid) {
        d = getDouble(sc, prompt);
        if (d <= min) {
            System.out.println(
                    "Error! Number must be greater than " + min + ".");
        } else if (d >= max) {
            System.out.println(
                    "Error! Number must be less than " + max + ".");
        } else {
            isValid = true;
        }
    }
    return d;
}
```

Code that uses these methods to return two valid double values

```
Scanner sc = new Scanner(System.in);
double subtotal1 = getDouble(sc, "Enter subtotal: ");
double subtotal2 = getDoubleWithinRange(sc, "Enter subtotal: ", 0, 10000);
```

Description

- Because most applications need to check more than one type of entry for validity, it often makes sense to create and use methods for data validation.

Figure 5-9   How to code a method that validates an entry

The Future Value application with data validation

Figure 5-6 presented a version of the Future Value application that used a try/catch statement to catch the most common exceptions that might be thrown. Now, figure 5-10 presents an improved version of this application that uses methods to validate the user entries. This code prevents the most common exceptions from being thrown, and it provides more descriptive messages to the user.

The console

Part 1 of figure 5-10 shows the console display when the user enters invalid data for the improved version of the Future Value application. Here, the error messages have been highlighted so you can see them more easily. For example, the first error message is displayed if the user doesn't enter a valid double value for the monthly investment. The second error message is displayed if the user enters a value that's out of range for the interest rate. And the third error message is displayed if the user doesn't enter a valid integer value for the years.

The Data Entry section in this figure uses descriptive error messages to identify the problem to the user, and it doesn't require that the user re-enter values that have already been successfully entered. In addition, it only uses the first value the user enters on a line, which is usually what you want. All other values are discarded.

After the user completes the Data Entry section, the Future Value application calculates the future value and displays it along with the user's entries in the Formatted Results section. This makes it easy to see what valid values the user entered, which is useful if the user has entered one or more invalid entries in the Data Entry section.

The console

```
Welcome to the Future Value Calculator

DATA ENTRY
Enter monthly investment: $100
Error! Invalid number. Try again.
Enter monthly investment: 100 dollars
Enter yearly interest rate: 120
Error! Number must be less than 30.0.
Enter yearly interest rate: 12.0
Enter number of years: one
Error! Invalid integer. Try again.
Enter number of years: 1

FORMATTED RESULTS
Monthly investment:     $100.00
Yearly interest rate:   12.0%
Number of years:        1
Future value:           $1,280.93

Continue? (y/n):
```

Description

- The Data Entry section gets input from the user and displays an appropriate error message if the user enters an invalid numeric format or a number that's outside the valid range.

- The Formatted Results section displays the data that was entered by the user along with the future value in a format that's easy to read.

Figure 5-10   The Future Value application with data validation (part 1 of 4)

The code

Parts 2 through 4 of figure 5-10 show the code for this version of the Future Value application. Part 2 shows the code for the main() method. Because this code is similar to code you've already seen, you shouldn't have any trouble understanding how it works. The biggest difference is that it uses methods named getDoubleWithinRange() and getIntWithinRange() to validate the data entered by the user. In this case, the monthly investment must be a double that's greater than 0 and less than 1000, the yearly interest rate must be a double that's greater than 0 and less than 30, and the number of years must be an int that's greater than 0 and less than 100. Since the code validates this data, you can be sure that the application can calculate the future value for any values within these ranges.

The getDouble() and getDoubleWithinRange() methods shown in part 3 of this figure are the ones presented in figure 5-9. As a result, if you have any trouble understanding how these methods work, you may want to review that figure. The getInt() and getIntWithinRange() methods in part 4 work like the getDouble() and getDoubleWithinRange() methods, except that they validate an int value instead of a double value. Note that all four of these methods, as well as the calculateFutureValue() method, might be useful to other classes. As a result, they are coded with the public access modifier.

As you review this code, notice how each method performs a specific task. For example, the getDouble() and getInt() methods prompt the user for an entry, validate the entry, and return the valid entry. Similarly, the calculateFutureValue() method performs a calculation and returns the result. This is a good design because it leads to code that's reusable and easy to maintain. For example, you can use the getDouble() and getInt() methods with any console application that gets double or int values from the user. If you want, you can copy these methods from one application to another. However, it's generally considered a better practice to store them in a class that's designed to be accessed by other classes. You'll learn how to do that in chapter 7.

The code   **Page 1**

```java
import java.text.NumberFormat;
import java.util.Scanner;

public class FutureValueApp {

    public static void main(String[] args) {
        System.out.println("Welcome to the Future Value Calculator\n");

        Scanner sc = new Scanner(System.in);
        String choice = "y";
        while (choice.equalsIgnoreCase("y")) {
            // get the input from the user
            System.out.println("DATA ENTRY");
            double monthlyInvestment = getDoubleWithinRange(sc,
                    "Enter monthly investment: ", 0, 1000);
            double interestRate = getDoubleWithinRange(sc,
                    "Enter yearly interest rate: ", 0, 30);
            int years = getIntWithinRange(sc,
                    "Enter number of years: ", 0, 100);
            System.out.println();

            // calculate the future value
            double monthlyInterestRate = interestRate / 12 / 100;
            int months = years * 12;
            double futureValue = calculateFutureValue(
                    monthlyInvestment, monthlyInterestRate, months);

            // get the currency and percent formatters
            NumberFormat c = NumberFormat.getCurrencyInstance();
            NumberFormat p = NumberFormat.getPercentInstance();
            p.setMinimumFractionDigits(1);

            // format the result as a single string
            String results
                = "Monthly investment:    " + c.format(monthlyInvestment) + "\n"
                + "Yearly interest rate: " + p.format(interestRate / 100) + "\n"
                + "Number of years:        " + years + "\n"
                + "Future value:           " + c.format(futureValue) + "\n";

            // print the results
            System.out.println("FORMATTED RESULTS");
            System.out.println(results);

            // see if the user wants to continue
            System.out.print("Continue? (y/n): ");
            choice = sc.next();
            sc.nextLine();  // discard any other data entered on the line
            System.out.println();
        }
    }
```

Figure 5-10   The Future Value application with data validation (part 2 of 4)

The code

```java
public static double getDoubleWithinRange(Scanner sc, String prompt,
        double min, double max) {
    double d = 0;
    boolean isValid = false;
    while (!isValid) {
        d = getDouble(sc, prompt);
        if (d <= min) {
            System.out.println(
                    "Error! Number must be greater than " + min + ".");
        } else if (d >= max) {
            System.out.println(
                    "Error! Number must be less than " + max + ".");
        } else {
            isValid = true;
        }
    }
    return d;
}

public static double getDouble(Scanner sc, String prompt) {
    double d = 0;
    boolean isValid = false;
    while (!isValid) {
        System.out.print(prompt);
        if (sc.hasNextDouble()) {
            d = sc.nextDouble();
            isValid = true;
        } else {
            System.out.println("Error! Invalid number. Try again.");
        }
        sc.nextLine();   // discard any other data entered on the line
    }
    return d;
}
```

Figure 5-10   The Future Value application with data validation (part 3 of 4)

The code   **Page 3**

```java
public static int getIntWithinRange(Scanner sc, String prompt,
        int min, int max) {
    int i = 0;
    boolean isValid = false;
    while (!isValid) {
        i = getInt(sc, prompt);
        if (i <= min) {
            System.out.println(
                    "Error! Number must be greater than " + min + ".");
        } else if (i >= max) {
            System.out.println(
                    "Error! Number must be less than " + max + ".");
        } else {
            isValid = true;
        }
    }
    return i;
}

public static int getInt(Scanner sc, String prompt) {
    int i = 0;
    boolean isValid = false;
    while (!isValid) {
        System.out.print(prompt);
        if (sc.hasNextInt()) {
            i = sc.nextInt();
            isValid = true;
        } else {
            System.out.println("Error! Invalid integer. Try again.");
        }
        sc.nextLine();   // discard any other data entered on the line
    }
    return i;
}

public static double calculateFutureValue(double monthlyInvestment,
        double monthlyInterestRate, int months) {
    double futureValue = 0;
    for (int i = 1; i <= months; i++) {
        futureValue
                = (futureValue + monthlyInvestment)
                * (1 + monthlyInterestRate);
    }
    return futureValue;
}
}
```

Figure 5-10   The Future Value application with data validation (part 4 of 4)

Perspective

Now that you've completed this chapter, you should be able to write console applications that are divided into multiple methods. You should also be able to validate the input data that's entered by the user and catch and handle any exceptions that occur. As a result, your applications should never crash. That, of course, is the way professional applications should work.

At this point, you've learned a complete subset of Java, and you know how to use some of the methods in a few of the classes in the Java API. But there's a lot more to Java programming than that. In particular, you need to learn how to create your own classes that have their own methods. That's the essence of object-oriented programming, and that's what you'll learn in the next section of this book.

Summary

- To code a *static method*, you code an access modifier, the static keyword, its return type, its name, and a *parameter* list. Then, to return a value, you code a *return statement* within the method.

- To call a static method that's in the same class, you code the method name followed by an *argument* list.

- An *exception* is an object that's created from the Exception class or one of its *subclasses*. This object contains information about an error that has occurred.

- The *stack trace* is a list of methods that were called before an exception occurred.

- You can code a *try/catch statement* to *catch* and handle any exceptions that are *thrown*. This is known as *exception handling*.

- *Data validation* refers to the process of checking input data to make sure that it's valid.

- *Range checking* refers to the process of checking an entry to make sure that it falls within a certain range of values.

Exercise 5-1   Add more static methods to the Future Value application

In this exercise, you'll add two more static methods to the Future Value application that you saw at the end of this chapter. When you're done, the main() method should be even easier to read and understand.

Open and test the project

1. Open the project named ch05_ex1_FutureValue in the ex_starts directory.

2. Review the FutureValueApp.java file, and notice how the code in the main() method calls the other methods in the file. Then, test the application to see how it works.

Add a method for displaying the results

3. Add a static method named printFormattedResults() anywhere in the file. This method should have private scope and a void return type, and it should accept the following parameters: a double named monthlyInvestment, a double named interestRate, an int named years, and a double named futureValue.

4. Move the code in the main() method that creates two NumberFormat objects, uses them to create a string, and then prints that string to the printFormattedFutureValueResults() method.

5. Add code to the main() method that calls the printFormattedResults() method and passes it the values entered by the user, along with the value in the futureValue variable. Then, test this enhancement to make sure the application still works properly.

Add a method for asking if the user wants to continue

6. Add another static method named askToContinue() anywhere in the file. This method should have public scope and a void return type, and it should accept a Scanner object named sc.

7. Move the code in the main() method that asks if the user wants to continue to the askToContinue() method. Then, adjust this code so it declares the choice variable as a String and so it returns the choice variable.

8. Add code to the main() method that passes the Scanner object to the askToContinue() method and stores the result in the choice variable. Then, test this enhancement to make sure the application still works properly.

Exercise 5-2   Add validation to the Guess the Number application

In this exercise, you'll add validation code to the Guess the Number application you saw in this chapter.

Open and test the project

1. Open the project named ch05_ex2_GuessNumber in the ex_starts directory. Then, test the application to see how it works.

2. As you test the application, enter an invalid number like "five" to see what happens when the application crashes.

Validate the number using a try/catch statement

3. Add a try/catch statement that catches the InputMismatchException after the statement in the while loop of the main() method that uses the nextInt() method to get the number entered by the user. For this to work, you'll need to import the InputMismatchException class.

4. Move the statement that uses the nextInt() method inside the try block. For this to work, you'll need to declare the guess variable before the try/catch statement so it can be used outside that statement.

5. Add code to the catch block that displays an error message, discards the invalid entry and any other entries on the line, and uses a continue statement to jump to the beginning of the while loop.

6. Test this enhancement by running the application and entering an invalid number.

Validate the number using data validation

7. Comment out the try/catch statement you just added, and replace it with an if/else statement.

8. Add code to the if block that uses the hasNextInt() method of the Scanner class to see if the value entered by the user is an int. If it is, use the nextInt() method to get that value and store it in the guess variable.

9. Add code to the else block that displays an error message, discards the invalid entry and any other entries on the line, and uses a continue statement to jump to the beginning of the while loop.

10. Test this enhancement by running the application and entering an invalid number.

Discard any extra entries when the first entry is valid

11. Run the application again and enter two or more valid numbers separated by a space. Press the Enter key and see what happens.

12. Modify the code so the application only accepts the first number the user enters. Then, test this enhancement.

6

How to test, debug, and deploy an application

As you develop a Java application, you need to test it to make sure that it performs as expected. Then, if you encounter any problems, you need to debug the application to locate the cause of the problems. Finally, when you're done testing and debugging an application, you need to deploy it so your users can run it.

Basic skills for testing and debugging

When you *test* an application, you run it to make sure that it works correctly. As you test the application, you try every possible combination of input data and user actions to be certain that the application works in every case. In other words, the goal of testing is to make an application fail.

When you *debug* an application, you fix the errors (*bugs*) that you discover during testing. Each time you fix a bug, you test again to make sure that the change you made didn't affect any other aspect of the application.

Typical test phases

When you test an application, you typically do so in phases. Figure 6-1 lists three common test phases.

In the first phase, you test the user interface. For a console application, that means you should make sure that the console displays the correct text and prompts the user for the correct data. For an application with a graphical user interface, that means you should visually check the controls, like the labels, text boxes, and buttons, to make sure they're displayed properly with the correct text. Then, you should make sure that all the keys and controls work correctly. For instance, you should test the Tab and Enter keys as well as the operation of check boxes and combo boxes.

In the second phase, you test the application with valid data. To start, you can enter data that you would expect a user to enter. Then, you should enter valid data that tests all of the limits of the application.

In the third phase, you try to make the application fail by testing every combination of invalid data and user action that you can think of. That should include random actions like pressing the Enter key or clicking the mouse at the wrong time.

The three types of errors

Three types of errors can occur as you test an application. These errors are described in figure 6-1.

Syntax errors, also called *compile-time errors*, prevent your application from compiling and running. This type of error is the easiest to find and fix. If you use an IDE like NetBeans or Eclipse, it automatically detects syntax errors as you type and gives you suggestions for how to fix them.

Unfortunately, some errors can't be detected until you run an application. These errors are known as *runtime errors*, and they throw *exceptions* that stop the execution of an application.

Even if an application runs without throwing exceptions, it may contain *logic errors* that prevent the application from working correctly. This type of error is often the most difficult to find and correct. For example, the Future Value application in this figure has a logic error. Can you tell what it is?

The Future Value application with a logic error

```
Welcome to the Future Value Calculator

DATA ENTRY
Enter monthly investment: 100
Enter yearly interest rate: 3
Enter number of years: 3

FORMATTED RESULTS
Monthly investment:        $100.00
Yearly interest rate:      3.0%
Number of years:           3
Future value:              $6,517.42

Continue? (y/n):
```

The goal of testing

- To find all errors before the application is put into production.

The goal of debugging

- To fix all errors before the application is put into production.

Three test phases

- Check the user interface to make sure that it works correctly.
- Test the application with valid input data to make sure the results are correct.
- Test the application with invalid data or unexpected user actions. Try everything you can think of to make the application fail.

The three types of errors that can occur

- *Syntax errors* violate the rules for how Java statements must be written. These errors, also called *compile-time errors*, are caught by the NetBeans IDE or the Java compiler before you run the application.
- *Runtime errors* don't violate the syntax rules, but they throw *exceptions* that stop the execution of the application.
- *Logic errors* are statements that don't cause syntax or runtime errors, but produce the wrong results. In the Future Value application shown above, the future value isn't correct, which is a logic error.

Description

- To *test* a Java application, you run it to make sure that it works properly no matter what combinations of valid or invalid data you enter.
- When you *debug* an application, you find and fix all of the errors (*bugs*) that you find when you test the application.

Figure 6-1   An introduction to testing and debugging

Common Java errors

Figure 6-2 presents some of the coding errors that are commonly made as you write a Java application. If you study this figure, you'll have a better idea of what to watch out for. And if you did the exercises for the first five chapters, you've probably experienced some of these errors already.

The code at the top of this figure is the start of the code for the static getDouble() method of the Future Value application, but with four errors introduced. The first error is that a data type has not been declared for the variable named d. Unlike some other languages, Java requires that you declare the data type for all variables.

The second error is a missing semicolon at the end of the statement that prints the prompt string to the console. As you know, Java requires a semicolon at the end of every statement unless the statement contains of a block of code that's enclosed in braces.

The third error is a missing closing parenthesis at the end of the condition for the if statement. Remember that every opening parenthesis, brace, or quotation mark must have a closing parenthesis, brace, or quotation mark.

The fourth error is that the statement that calls the nextDouble() method from the Scanner object named sc uses improper capitalization. For this statement, "NextDouble" should be "nextDouble" since Java is case-sensitive.

This figure also describes the problem that Java has with floating-point arithmetic. As you can see in the example near the bottom of this figure, floating-point arithmetic can produce strange results even with simple calculations. To prevent results like this, you can use BigDecimal numbers instead of floating-point numbers. Or, if you know the number of decimal places you want, you can round the number to the specified number of decimal places. Both of these techniques are described in chapter 3.

Code that contains syntax errors

```
public static double getDouble(Scanner sc, String prompt) {
    d = 0.0;                              // no data type declared
    while (true) {
        System.out.print(prompt)          // missing semicolon at end of statement
        if (sc.hasNextDouble() {          // missing closing parenthesis
            d = sc.NextDouble();          // improper capitalization
            sc.nextLine();
            return d;
        } else {
            System.out.println("Error! Invalid number. Try again.");
            sc.nextLine();
        }
    }
}
```

Common syntax errors

- Misspelling keywords.
- Forgetting to declare a data type for a variable.
- Forgetting an opening or closing parenthesis, bracket, brace, or comment character.
- Forgetting to code a semicolon at the end of a statement.
- Forgetting an opening or closing quotation mark.

Problems with identifiers

- Misspelling or incorrectly capitalizing an identifier.
- Using a reserved word, global property, or global method as an identifier.

Problems with values

- Not checking that a value is the right data type before processing it. For example, you expect a number to be entered, but the user enters a non-numeric value instead.
- Using one equals sign instead of two when testing numeric and Boolean values for equality.
- Using two equals signs instead of the equals() or equalsIgnoreCase() method to test two strings for equality.

A problem with floating-point numbers

- Using floating-point numbers that can lead to arithmetic errors. For example:

```
double d = 0.2 + 0.7    // d = 0.8999999999999999
```

You can prevent errors like this by using BigDecimal numbers or rounding, as described in chapter 3.

Figure 6-2   Common Java errors

A simple way to trace code execution

When you *trace* the execution of an application, you add statements to your code that display messages or variable values at key points in the code. You typically do this to help find the cause of a logic error.

If, for example, you can't figure out why the future value that's calculated by the Future Value application is incorrect, you can insert println statements into the code for the application as shown in figure 6-3. Here, the first println statement prints a message that indicates that the calculateFutureValue() method is starting. Then, the next three println statements print the values of monthlyInvestment, monthlyInterestRate, and months variables. Finally, the last println statement prints the value of the counter variable and the futureValue variable each time through the for loop. That should help you determine where the calculation is going wrong. Then, when you find and fix the problem, you can remove the println statements.

When you use this technique, you usually start by adding just a few println statements to the code. Then, if that doesn't help you solve the problem, you can add more. This works well for simple applications, but it creates extra work for you because you have to add statements to your code and remove them later.

In the next few figures, you'll learn how to use a tool known as a debugger to debug an application without having to add or remove statements. Since this is usually easier than adding and removing statements, you'll rarely need to use the technique shown in this figure. However, it can be useful in some cases.

Code that uses println statements to trace execution

```java
public static double calculateFutureValue(double monthlyInvestment,
        double monthlyInterestRate, int months) {
    System.out.println("starting calculateFutureValue method...");
    double futureValue = 0;
    System.out.println("monthlyInvestment: " + monthlyInvestment);
    System.out.println("monthlyInterestRate: " + monthlyInterestRate);
    System.out.println("months: " + months);
    for (int i = 1; i <= months; i++) {
        futureValue = (futureValue + monthlyInvestment) *
                        (1 + monthlyInterestRate);
        System.out.println("month " + i + " futureValue: " + futureValue);
    }
    return futureValue;
}
```

The data that's printed to the console

```
starting calculateFutureValue method...
monthlyInvestment: 100.0
monthlyInterestRate: 0.03
months: 36
month 1 futureValue: 103.0
month 2 futureValue: 209.09
month 3 futureValue: 318.3627
month 4 futureValue: 430.913581
month 5 futureValue: 546.84098843
...
...
```

Description

- A simple way to *trace* the execution of an application is to insert println statements at key points in the code that print messages to the console.

- The messages that are printed to the console can indicate what code is being executed, or they can display the values of variables.

- When you see an incorrect value displayed, there is a good chance that the application contains a logic error between the current println statement and the previous one.

Figure 6-3   A simple way to trace code execution

How to use NetBeans to debug an application

As you test applications, you will encounter errors that are commonly referred to as bugs. When that happens, you must find and fix those errors. This is known as *debugging*. Fortunately, NetBeans includes a powerful tool called a *debugger* that can help you find and fix these errors, and Eclipse includes a debugger that works similarly.

How to set and remove breakpoints

The first step in debugging an application is to determine the cause of the bug. To do that, it's often helpful to view the values of the variables at different points in the application's execution.

The easiest way to view the variable values as an application is executing is to set a *breakpoint* as shown in figure 6-4. To set a breakpoint, you click on the line number to the left of the line of code. Then, the breakpoint is marked by a red square. Later, when you run the application with the debugger, execution will stop just prior to the statement at the breakpoint. Then, you will be able to view the variables that are in scope at that point in the application. You'll learn more about that in the next figure.

When debugging, it's important to set the breakpoint before the line in the application that's causing the bug. Often, you can figure out where to set a breakpoint by reading the runtime exception that's displayed when your application crashes. Sometimes, though, you will have to experiment before finding a good location to set a breakpoint.

After you set the breakpoint, you need to run the application with the debugger. To do that, you can use the Debug Project button that's available from the toolbar (just to the right of the Run Project button). If you encounter any problems, try right-clicking on the .java file that contains the main() method and selecting the Debug File command to run the application with the debugger.

Note that once you set a breakpoint, it remains set until you remove it. That's true even if you close the project and exit from NetBeans. To remove a breakpoint, you can click on its icon.

A code editor window with a breakpoint

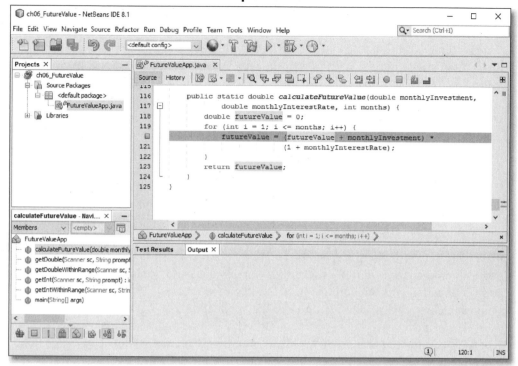

Description

- A *breakpoint* causes program execution to stop before the line that contains the breakpoint is executed.
- To set a breakpoint for a line, open the code editor for the class and click on the line number. The breakpoint is identified by a small red square that's placed to the left of the line of code.
- To remove a breakpoint, click on the breakpoint icon.
- You can set and remove breakpoints either before you start debugging or while you're debugging. In most cases, you'll set at least one breakpoint before you start debugging.
- To start debugging for a project, click the Debug Project button on the toolbar.
- You can also start debugging by right-clicking on a project and selecting the Debug command or by right-clicking on the file that contains the main() method you want to run and selecting the Debug File command.

Figure 6-4   How to set and remove breakpoints

How to step through code

When you run an application with the debugger and it encounters a breakpoint, execution stops just prior to the statement at the breakpoint. Once execution stops, a green arrow marks the next statement to be executed. In addition, NetBeans opens the Variables window shown in figure 6-5. This window shows the values of the variables that are in scope at the current point of execution.

NetBeans also displays the Debug toolbar while you're debugging. You can click the Step Over and Step Into buttons on this toolbar repeatedly to step through an application one statement at a time. Then, you can use the Variables window to observe exactly how and when the variable values change as the application executes. That can help you determine the cause of a bug.

As you step through an application, you can click the Step Over button if you want to execute a method without stepping into it. Or, you can use the Step Out button to step out of any method that you don't want to step through. When you want to continue normal execution, you can click the Continue button. Then, the application will run until the next breakpoint is reached. Or, you can use the Finish Debugger Session button to end the application's execution.

These are powerful debugging features that can help you find the cause of serious programming problems. Stepping through an application is also a good way to understand how the code in an existing application works. If, for example, you step through the loop in the calculateFutureValue() method, you'll get a better idea of how that loop works.

How to inspect variables

When you set breakpoints and step through code, the Variables window automatically displays the values of the variables that are in scope. In figure 6-5, the execution point is in the calculateFutureValue() method of the FutureValueApp class. Here, the Variables window shows the values of the three parameters that are passed to the method (monthlyInvestment, monthlyInterestRate, and months) and two local variables that are declared within the method (futureValue and i).

For numeric variables and strings, the value of the variable is shown in the Variables window. However, when an object such as one that's created from the Scanner class is displayed in the Variables window, it doesn't display the values of its variables automatically. Instead, it displays a plus sign to the left of the object name. Then, you can view the values for the object by clicking on that plus sign to expand it.

In the next chapter, you'll learn how to create objects from classes that you define. Then, if the code within one of these objects is executing, you'll see a variable named *this* in the Variables window. This is a keyword that's used to refer to the current object, and you can expand it to view the values of the variables that are defined by the object. That will make more sense when you start to learn about object-oriented programming in the next chapter.

A debugging session

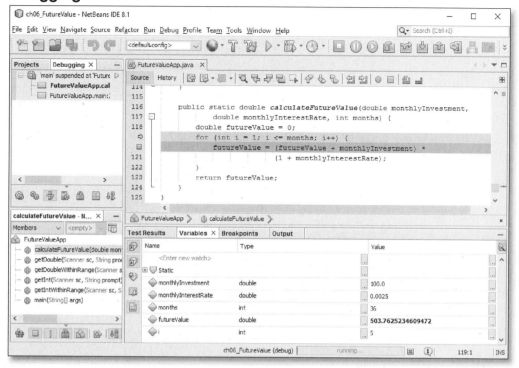

Some of the buttons on the Debug toolbar

Button	Keyboard shortcut	Description
Step Over	F8	Steps through the code one statement at a time, skipping over called methods.
Step Into	F7	Steps through the code one statement at a time, including statements in called methods.
Step Out	Ctrl+F7	Finishes executing the code in the current method and returns to the calling method.
Continue	F5	Continues execution until the next breakpoint.
Finish Debugger Session	Shift+F5	Ends the application's execution.

Description

- When a breakpoint is reached, program execution is stopped before the line is executed.
- The arrow in the bar at the left side of the code editor window shows the line that will be executed next.
- The Variables window shows the values of the variables that are in scope for the current method. This window is displayed by default when you start a debugging session. If you close it, you can open it again using the Window→Debugging→Variables command.
- If a variable in the Variables window refers to an object, you can view the values for that object by clicking the plus sign to the left of the object name to expand it.
- You can use the buttons on the Debug toolbar to control the execution of an application.

Figure 6-5   How to step through code and inspect variables

How to inspect the stack trace

When you're debugging, it's sometimes helpful to view the *stack trace*, which is a list of methods in the reverse order in which they were called. By default, NetBeans displays a stack trace in the Debugging window that's displayed in the group of windows to the left of the code editor. In addition, you can display a stack trace in the Call Stack window as described in figure 6-6.

In the Debugging window in this figure, you can see that code execution is on line 119 of the calculateFutureValue() method of the FutureValueApp class. You can also see that this method was called by line 25 of the main() method of the FutureValueApp class. At this point, you may want to display line 25 of the main() method to view the code that called the calculateFutureValue() method. To do that, you can double-click the main() method in the stack trace.

In this figure, both methods are stored in the same class. However, as you'll learn in the next few chapters, it's common for a method in one class to call a method in another class. In that case, double-clicking on a method in the stack trace displays the source code for the other class in the code editor. If you experiment with this, you'll find that it can help you locate the origin of a bug.

A debugging session with the Call Stack window displayed

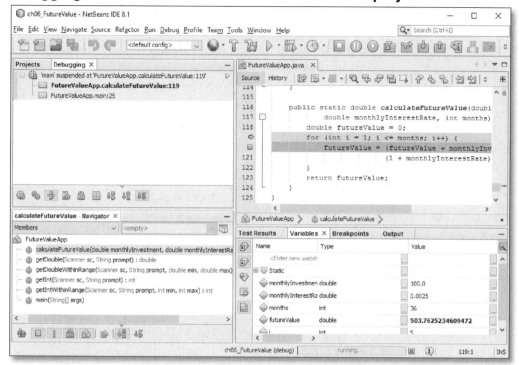

Description

- A *stack trace* is a list of the methods that have been called in the reverse order in which they were called.

- By default, NetBeans displays a stack trace in the Debugging window that's included in the group of windows at the left side of the IDE.

- If necessary, you can display a stack trace in the Call Stack window by selecting the Window→Debugging→Call Stack command. Then, this window appears below the code editor.

- To jump to a line of code in the code editor that's displayed in the stack trace, double-click on that line in the stack trace.

Figure 6-6   How to inspect the stack trace

How to deploy an application

This chapter finishes by describing three options for deploying a Java application. Then, it shows how to use the simplest of these options to deploy a GUI application or a console application.

An introduction to deployment

Figure 6-7 lists three options for deploying a Java application. Each of these options has its advantages and disadvantages.

The easiest way to deploy a Java application is to create an *executable* (*Java Archive*) *JAR file* that has all of the classes and resources needed by your application. Then, you can manually distribute this file to your users and show them how to run it.

Although this way of deploying an application is adequate for simple applications with just a few users, it doesn't provide a way to automatically install prerequisite files (such as the JRE that's needed to run Java applications), and it doesn't provide a way to automatically update the application. As a result, you'll only want to use this deployment option when you are prepared to help your users install the JRE and when you are willing to manually redistribute a new executable JAR file any time you have critical updates to your application. Still, when you're getting started, this is often an adequate way to deploy your applications. That's why the next few figures show how to create and deploy an executable JAR file.

The second way to deploy an application is known as *Java Web Start* (*JWS*). This type of deployment lets the user install and start a Java application by clicking on a link from a web page. This automates the process of installing the correct version of the JRE, and it can automatically update your application whenever you make an updated version available. Unfortunately, since Java Web Start allows users to download the application from the web, this option has some significant security restrictions that make it difficult to get this option to work correctly for all browsers on all platforms.

The third way to deploy an application is to use an *installer program* such as InstallAnywhere to create an install file for the application. Then, you can make this install file available to your users, and they can install your application just as they would install other professional applications. Although this is a huge advantage for a professional application, this technique also has several disadvantages. First, most installer programs are expensive commercial products. Second, most installer programs require more work to set up and configure. Third, most installer programs don't provide any way to automatically update the application after it has been installed.

Executable JAR file

An *executable JAR (Java Archive) file* stores all the classes and resources needed by your application. You can manually distribute this file to your users and show them how to run it.

Pros

- There are no significant security restrictions.

Cons

- The correct version of the JRE is *not* installed automatically, so you or your users must install it.
- The code is *not* automatically updated, so if the application changes, you must redistribute it.

Web Start

Java Web Start (JWS) allows users to download an application from the web, cache the application locally, and start it.

Pros

- The correct version of Java is automatically installed.
- The code is automatically updated.

Cons

- Security restrictions make it difficult to use.

Installer program

An *installer program* allows you to create an install file for every operating system that you want your application to run on. Then, users can use the install file for their operating system to install the application just as they would install any other application.

Pros

- The application installs and runs like a professional desktop application.
- The correct version of Java can be installed as part of the installation process.
- There are no significant security restrictions.

Cons

- The code is *not* automatically updated after the program is installed.
- Most installer programs are expensive commercial products.
- This approach requires more work to set up and configure.

Figure 6-7   An introduction to deployment

How to create an executable JAR file

You can use an executable JAR file to deploy an application just by making that file available to your users. Then, if the application is a GUI application, users can run the application by double-clicking on the JAR file. However, if the application is a console application, it usually makes sense to create a script file to run the application. Then, your users can double-click on the script file to run the console application.

Figure 6-8 describes how to create an executable JAR file with NetBeans. To do that, you simply clean and build the project. Then, NetBeans stores the JAR file that's created in the project's dist directory.

With NetBeans, you can review the options for the JAR file that's created for a project by displaying the Project Properties dialog box for the project and clicking on the Packaging category. This category shows the name and location of the JAR file, along with its properties. By default, the JAR file includes the .class files for the project, but does not include the .java files that contain the source code for the project. That makes sense because you typically don't want to make the source code available to users. The JAR file also contains any other files necessary to run the application, including any Java libraries that are needed by the application.

In addition to the class files and libraries, a JAR file always contains a *manifest file*. This file stores additional information about the files in the JAR file, including which .class file contains the main() method for the application.

Although it's possible to distribute the files for an application without storing them in a JAR file, it's almost always better to use a JAR file. This makes it easier to manage the files of the application. In addition, because JAR files use a compressed format, they take up considerably less disk space.

The properties for building a project

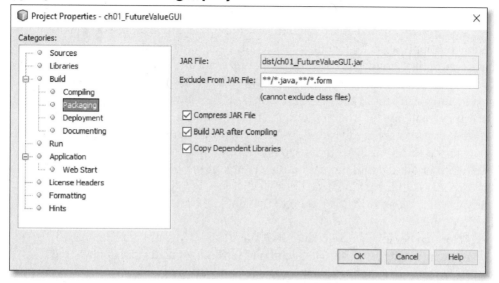

Description

- With NetBeans, you can create an executable JAR file in the project's dist directory by using the Run→Clean and Build Project command.

- An executable JAR file contains all of the files necessary to run the application, including any Java libraries that are needed by the application.

- An executable JAR file also contains a *manifest file* that stores information about the files that the JAR file contains, including which .class file contains the main() method for the application.

- Because a JAR file uses a compressed format, it can improve the download time for an application that's downloaded from the web.

Figure 6-8   How to create an executable JAR file

How to deploy the files for an application

Once you've created an executable JAR file for an application, you can deploy the application by making the JAR file available to your users. If you have appropriate privileges, you can do that by manually copying the file to their computers. Or, you can send the file to them as an email attachment. You can also include instructions for how to run the JAR file, how to install the JRE (if necessary), and tips for troubleshooting any problems they may encounter.

If a user's computer doesn't have the JRE installed, the user can install it by going to the Java website as indicated in figure 6-9. The user can also go to this website to install the minimum required version of the JRE. The exception is if the user's system is running Mac OS X. Then, the JRE is installed by default. If a newer version of the JRE is required, though, the user can install it as described in this figure.

After you deploy the executable JAR file to a user's computer that has a JRE, the user can run the JAR file. The technique for doing that depends on whether the file is for a GUI application or a console application.

How to run a GUI application

On most computers, the operating system associates the .jar extension with the Java Platform SE binary program that's included as part of the JRE. As a result, most users can run an executable JAR file for a GUI application by locating the file and double-clicking on it as described in figure 6-9. Then, the JRE should display the GUI for the application. For example, this figure shows the GUI for a Future Value application. However, if a user's operating system isn't attempting to use the Java binary program to run the executable JAR file, you may need to modify the user's system so it associates the .jar extension with Java.

How to deploy the files for an application

- Once you've created an executable JAR file for an application, you can deploy it by making the JAR file available to your users.

- The JRE has to be installed on the user's computer for the user to run an executable JAR file.

- To install the JRE on a system other than one running Mac OS X, the user can go to www.java.com.

- The JRE is installed on systems running Mac OS X by default. To install a newer version, the user can use the Software Update feature that's available from the Apple menu.

A GUI application running outside of an IDE

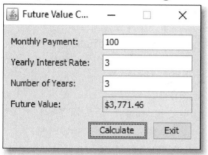

How to run an executable JAR file for a GUI application

- Locate the JAR file and then double-click on it.

- For this to work, the operating system must associate the .jar extension with the Java Platform SE binary program that's included as part of the JRE. As a result, if a user's operating system isn't attempting to use Java to run the executable JAR file, you may need to modify the user's system so it associates the .jar extension with Java.

Figure 6-9   How to deploy the files for an application and run a GUI application

How to run a console application

Figure 6-10 shows how to run an executable JAR file for a console application. Unfortunately, you can't do that by double-clicking on the file like you can for a GUI application. Instead, you need to work from the console for the operating system.

On a Windows system, for example, you can use the Start menu to start a Command Prompt window. Then, you can use the cd command to change to the directory that contains the JAR file. In this example, the JAR file has been deployed to the C:\murach\java\dist directory on the user's computer. Next, you can use the java command to run the executable JAR file. Although the details are slightly different, you can use a similar technique to run a console application on other operating systems such as Mac OS X or Linux.

To make it easier for users to run a console application, you can create a script file that starts the console and runs the application. In Windows, for example, you can create a batch (.bat) file that changes to the appropriate directory and executes the appropriate java command. Then, the user can start your application by double-clicking on the .bat file. On a Mac OS X or Linux system, you can create a bash (.sh) file that works similarly.

If you create a script file, you need to make both the script file and the JAR file available to your users. Then, your users can run the console application by double-clicking on the script file. For this to work, however, you need to store the JAR file in the directory that's specified by the script file. Otherwise, the script file won't be able to locate the JAR file.

In some cases, the operating system won't be able to find the java command. That's typically because the java command isn't in the system path. To fix this problem, you can specify an absolute path to the java command as shown in this figure. Or, you can modify the system's Path variable so it includes the bin directory for the JRE.

A console application running in the Windows command prompt

```
Command Prompt - java -jar ch01_FutureValueConsole.jar        —    □    ×

Microsoft Windows [Version 10.0.10586]
(c) 2015 Microsoft Corporation. All rights reserved.

C:\Users\Joel>cd \murach\java\dist

C:\murach\java\dist>java -jar ch01_FutureValueConsole.jar
Welcome to the Future Value Calculator

Enter monthly investment:    100
Enter yearly interest rate:  3
Enter number of years:       3
Future value:                $3,771.46

Continue? (y/n):
```

Syntax to run an executable JAR file

```
java -jar JarName.jar
```

A batch (.bat) file that runs a console application on Windows

```
:: Change to the directory that stores the JAR file
cd \murach\java\dist

:: Use the java command to run the JAR file
java -jar ch01_FutureValueConsole.jar
```

A bash (.sh) file that runs a console application on Mac OS X or Linux

```
#!/bin/bash

# Change to the directory that stores the JAR file
cd /murach/java/dist

#Use the java command to run the JAR file
java -jar ch01_FutureValueConsole.jar
```

Description

- To run an executable JAR file, the user starts a console and then uses the java command. This command is case-sensitive.

- For Windows, you can create a batch (.bat) file to start the console and execute the java command. For Mac OS X or Linux, you can create a bash (.sh) file.

- If a system can't find the java command, you can specify an absolute path to the command. For Windows, for example, the path will look like this:

  ```
  "C:\Program Files\Java\jre-9\bin"
  ```

  Or, you can modify the system's Path variable so it includes the bin directory for the JRE.

Figure 6-10   How to run a console application

Perspective

Now that you've completed this chapter, you should have the skills you need to test an application to identify any bugs it may contain. Then, you should be able to use the NetBeans debugger to determine the cause of those bugs.

You should know, however, that this debugger provides some additional features that you can use to test and debug your applications. After reading this chapter, you should be able to learn more about those features on your own. As you begin to develop more complex applications, you may also want to learn about unit testing, which is a way of creating tests for individual units of source code such as methods to make sure they work correctly.

Once you're sure that an application is free of bugs, you can deploy it to the computers where it will be used. In this chapter, you learned how to do that using a JAR file. At some point, though, you may want to learn more about the other two deployment options that were introduced here.

Summary

- To *test* an application, you run it to make sure that it works properly no matter what combinations of valid or invalid data you enter.

- When you *debug* an application, you find and fix all of the errors (*bugs*) that you find when you test the application.

- *Syntax errors* violate the rules for how Java statements must be written. These errors are detected by the NetBeans IDE or the Java compiler before you can run the application.

- *Runtime errors* occur as you run an application. These types of errors throw *exceptions* that stop the execution of the application.

- *Logic errors* don't cause the application to crash, but they prevent it from working correctly.

- A simple way to *trace* the execution of an application is to insert println statements at key points in the code.

- NetBeans includes a powerful tool known as a *debugger* that can help you find and fix errors.

- You can set a *breakpoint* on a line of code to stop code execution just before that line of code is executed. Then, you can step through the code and view the values of the variables as the code executes.

- A *stack trace* is a list of methods in the reverse order in which they were called.

- An *executable JAR (Java Archive) file* stores all classes and resources needed by your application. You can manually distribute this file to your users and show them how to run it.

- *Java Web Start* (*JWS*) allows users to download a Java GUI application from the web, cache the application locally, and start it.

- An *installer program* allows you to create an install file for every operating system that you want your application to run on.

- An executable JAR file contains a *manifest file* that stores information about the files that are stored within the JAR file, including the file that contains the main() method for the application.

Exercise 6-1   Test and debug the Invoice application

This exercise guides you through the process of using NetBeans to test and debug an application.

Test the Invoice application with invalid data

1. Open the ch06_ex1_Invoice project that's in the ex_starts directory. Then, test the Invoice application with an invalid subtotal like $1000 (enter the dollar sign too). This should cause the application to crash with a runtime error and to display an error message in the Output window.

2. Study the error message, and note the line number of the statement in the InvoiceApp class that caused the crash.

3. Click on the link to that line of code. This should open the InvoiceApp.java file in the code editor and highlight the line of code that caused the error. From this information, determine the cause of the problem and fix it.

Set a breakpoint and step through the application

4. Set a breakpoint on this line of code:

```
double discountPercent = 0.0;
```

   Then, click on the Debug Project button in the toolbar. This runs the project with the debugger on.

5. Click the Output tab to display the Output window and enter a value of 100 for the subtotal when prompted by the application. When you do, the application runs to the breakpoint and stops.

6. Click the Variables tab to display the Variables window and note that the choice, customerType, and subtotal variables have been assigned values.

7. Click the Step Into button in the toolbar repeatedly to step through the application one statement at a time. After each step, review the values in the Variables window to see how they have changed. Note how the application steps through the switch statement based on the customerType value and the if/else statements based on the subtotal value.

8. Click the Continue button in the toolbar to continue the execution of the application.

9. Display the Output window again. Then, enter "y" to continue and enter a value of 50 for the subtotal.

10. Display the Variables window again and inspect the values of the variables.

11. Click the Step Over button in the toolbar repeatedly to step through the application one statement at a time. After each step, review the values in the Variables window to see how they have changed.

12. When you're done inspecting the variables, click the Finish Debugger Session button to end the application. This should give you some idea of how useful the NetBeans debugging tools can be.

Exercise 6-2   Test and debug the Future Value application

In this exercise, you'll use NetBeans to find and fix syntax errors and a logic error in the Future Value application.

Use NetBeans to correct the syntax errors

1. Open the ch06_ex2_FutureValue project that's in the ex_starts directory, and then display the FutureValueApp.java file. Note that the getDouble() method in this file contains syntax errors.

2. Use NetBeans to find and fix the errors.

Use println statements to trace code execution

3. Scroll down to the calculateFutureValue() method, and add a println statement within the loop that prints the value of the month and the future value each time the loop is executed.

4. Run the application to see how the println statement works. Review the values that are displayed in the Output window, and notice that that the future value increases by too much each month.

5. Comment out the println statement so it no longer prints messages to the Output window.

Step through the application

6. In the main() method, set a breakpoint on the first of the three statements that calculate the future value.

7. Run the application and enter values when prompted. The application should stop at the breakpoint.

8. Experiment with the Step Into, Step Over, and Step Out buttons as you step through the code of the application. At each step, notice the values that are displayed in the Variables window and use them to find the logic error.

9. When you're done experimenting, click on the Finish Debugger Session button and remove the breakpoint.

10. Fix the logic error and then run the application again to be sure it produces correct results.

Exercise 6-3   Deploy the Future Value application

In this exercise, you'll deploy the console version of the Future Value application and then run it.

1. Open the project named ch06_ex3_FutureValue that's in the ex_starts directory. Then, run the application to see how it works.

2. Clean and build the project, and then find its JAR file in the project's dist directory.

3. Create a directory named fv that's in the murach/java/dist directory. Then, copy the JAR file into this directory.

4. Start a console and use the java command to run the JAR file.

5. Within the fv directory, create a script file to start the console and execute the JAR file. For Windows, create a .bat file. For Mac, create a .sh file.

6. Copy the fv directory to another computer and make sure you can run it on that computer. To get this to work, you may need to download the JRE from www.java.com, and you may need to modify the script file so it specifies the correct directory for the JAR file.

Exercise 6-4   Deploy a GUI version of the Future Value application

In this exercise, you'll deploy a GUI version of the Future Value application and then run it.

1. Open the project named ch06_ex4_FutureValueGUI that's in the ex_starts directory. Then, run the application and see how it works.

2. Clean and build the project, and then find its JAR file in the project's dist directory.

3. Double-click on the JAR file to run it.

4. Copy the JAR file to another computer and double-click on it to run it. To get this to work, you may need to download the JRE from www.java.com.

Section 2

Object-oriented programming

In the first section of this book, you learned how to use classes that are provided as part of the Java API. For instance, you learned how to use the Math class to perform common arithmetic operations, and you learned how to use the NumberFormat class to format numeric values. That's one part of object-oriented programming.

Besides the classes provided by the API, though, you can create your own classes. That's the other part of object-oriented programming, and that's what the four chapters in this section teach you to do. Specifically, chapter 7 presents the basic skills for creating and using your own classes. Chapter 8 presents the skills for using use inheritance, one of the most important features of object-oriented programming. Chapter 9 presents the skills for using interfaces. And chapter 10 presents some additional object-oriented skills.

Because each of the chapters in this section builds on the previous chapters, you should read these chapters in sequence. In addition, you should read all of the chapters in this section before going on to sections 3, 4, or 5. That's because many of the chapters in these sections rely on your knowledge of inheritance and interfaces.

7

How to define
and use classes

This chapter shows you how to create and use your own classes in Java applications. Here, you'll learn how to create classes that include regular fields and methods as well as classes that contain static fields and methods. In addition, you'll see two complete applications that use several user-defined classes.

When you complete this chapter, you'll start to see how creating your own classes can help simplify the development of an application. As a bonus, you'll have a better understanding of how the Java API works.

An introduction to classes

The topics that follow introduce you to the concepts that you need to know before you create your own classes. That includes how you'll use classes in a typical business application, how the fields and methods of a class can be encapsulated within the class, and how a class relates to its objects.

How classes can be used to structure an application

Figure 7-1 shows how you can use classes to simplify the design of a business application using a *multi-tiered architecture.* In a multi-tiered application, the classes that perform different functions of the application are separated into two or more layers, or tiers.

A *three-tiered* application architecture like the one shown in this figure consists of a presentation tier, a business tier, and a database tier. This is the most common architecture for structuring applications.

The classes in the *presentation tier* handle the details of the application's user interface. So far, all of the applications you've seen have been console applications. In these applications, most of the presentation tier is handled by the main() method, which may call methods of other classes. In section 4, though, you'll learn how to write Java applications that display a graphical user interface (GUI) that consists of multiple windows. In these applications, a separate class is usually created for each window displayed by the application.

The classes of the *database tier* are responsible for all of the database access that's required by the application. These classes typically include methods that connect to the database and retrieve, add, update, and delete information from the database. Then, the other tiers can call these methods to access the database, leaving the details of database access to the database classes. Although we refer to this tier as the database tier, it can also contain classes that work with data that's stored in files.

The *business tier* provides an interface between the database tier and the presentation tier. This tier often includes classes that correspond to business entities (for example, products and customers). It may also include classes that implement business rules, such as discount or credit policies. The classes in this tier are often referred to as *business classes*, and the objects that are created from these classes are often called *business objects.*

One advantage of developing applications with a multi-tier architecture is that you should be able to swap out one tier without having to modify the other tiers. For example, you should be able to swap out the presentation tier so it uses a GUI instead of the console without having to modify any classes in the business or database tiers.

A second advantage of developing applications with a tiered architecture is that it allows the work to be spread among members of a development team. For example, one group of developers might work on the database tier, another group on the business tier, and still another group on the presentation tier.

The architecture of a three-tiered application

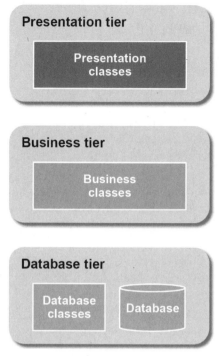

Description

- To simplify development and maintenance, many applications use a *three-tiered architecture* to separate the application's user interface, business rules, and database processing. Classes are used to implement the functions performed by each tier of the architecture.

- The classes in the *presentation tier* control the application's user interface. For a console application, the presentation tier typically consists of a class with a main() method and any other classes related to console input and output. For a GUI application, the user interface typically consists of one class for each window that makes up the GUI.

- The classes in the *database tier* handle all of the application's data processing.

- The classes in the *business tier* define the *business objects* and rules for the application. These classes act as an interface between the classes in the presentation and database tiers.

- The classes that make up each tier are often stored in packages that can be shared among applications. For more information, see chapter 10.

Figure 7-1   How classes can be used to structure an application

A third advantage is that it allows classes to be shared among applications. In particular, the classes that make up the database and business tiers can be stored in packages that can be used by more than one project. You'll learn how to work with packages in chapter 10.

How encapsulation works

Figure 7-2 shows a *class diagram* for a class named Product. This diagram uses *Unified Modeling Language* (*UML*), a modeling language that has become the industry standard for working with all object-oriented programming languages including Java.

In this class diagram, the class contains three *fields* and seven *methods*. Here, the minus sign (-) identifies fields and methods that are available only within the current class, while the plus sign (+) identifies fields and methods that are available to other classes.

In this case, all of the methods are available to other classes, but none of the fields are. However, the methods make the data stored by the fields available to other classes. For instance, the getCode() method returns the value stored in the code field, and the setCode() method assigns a new value to the code field.

This illustrates the concept of *encapsulation*, which is a fundamental concept of object-oriented programming. This means that the programmer can *hide*, or encapsulate, some fields and methods of a class, while *exposing* others. Since the fields (or data) of a class are typically encapsulated within a class, encapsulation is sometimes referred to as *data hiding*.

When you use a class, encapsulation lets you think of it as a black box that provides useful fields and methods. When you use the parseInt() method of the Integer class, for example, you don't know how the method converts a string to an integer, and you don't need to know. Similarly, if you use the getPrice() method of the Product class in this figure, you don't know how the method works, and you don't need to know.

This also means that you can change the code for a method within a class without affecting the classes that use the method. For instance, you can change the code for the getPrice() method without changing the classes that use that method. This makes it easier to upgrade or enhance an application because you only need to change the classes that need upgrading.

A class diagram for the Product class

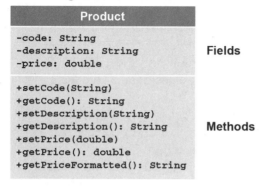

Fields

Methods

Description

- The *fields* of a class store the data of a class.

- The *methods* of a class define the tasks that a class can perform. Often, these methods provide a way to work with the fields of a class.

- *Encapsulation* is one of the fundamental concepts of object-oriented programming. This means that the class controls which of its fields and methods can be accessed by other classes. As a result, the fields in the class can be hidden from other classes, and the methods in a class can be modified or improved without changing the way that other classes use them.

UML diagramming notes

- *UML* (*Unified Modeling Language*) is the industry standard used to describe the classes and objects of an object-oriented application.

- The minus sign (-) in a UML *class diagram* marks the fields and methods that can't be accessed by other classes, while the plus sign (+) marks the fields and methods that can be accessed by other classes.

- For each field, the name is given, followed by a colon, followed by the data type.

- For each method, the name is given, followed by a set of parentheses. If a method requires parameters, the data type of each parameter is listed in the parentheses. Otherwise, the parentheses are left empty, and the data type of the value that's going to be returned is given after the colon.

Figure 7-2   How encapsulation works

The relationship between a class and its objects

Figure 7-3 uses UML diagrams to show the relationship between a class and its objects. In this figure, one class diagram and two *object diagrams* show how objects are created from a class. Here, the diagrams show only the fields, not the methods, of the class and its objects. In this case, two objects named product1 and product2 are created from the Product class.

Once an *instance* of a class is created, it has an *identity* and a *state*. An object's identity is its address in internal memory, which is always unique. An object's state refers to the values that are stored by the object. For example, the states of the two Product objects in this figure are determined by the three values that they hold. As a program executes, the state of an object may change, but the identity of the object won't.

The relationship between a class and its objects

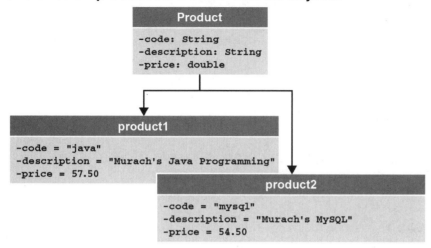

Description

- A *class* can be thought of as a template from which *objects* are made.
- An *object diagram* provides the name of the object and the values of the fields.
- Once an *instance* of a class is created, it has an *identity* (a unique address) and a *state* (the values that it holds). Although an object's state may change throughout a program, its identity never does.

Figure 7-3   The relationship between a class and its objects

How to work with a class that defines an object

Now that you've learned some of the basic concepts for using classes, you're ready to learn the basic skills for creating your own classes. To start, the next few figures show how to create a class named Product that you can use to store data about a product.

How to use NetBeans to create a new class

When you develop object-oriented applications, you'll frequently need to add new classes to your projects. To do that with NetBeans, you can use the New Java Class dialog box shown in figure 7-4. In this figure, for example, this dialog box is being used to create a class named Product.

Notice here that a package isn't specified for the class. Because of that, the class will be stored in the default package. Although it's typically a good idea to use packages to organize the classes in an application, this chapter and the next two chapters will focus on creating and using classes. Then, in chapter 10, you'll learn how to create and use packages.

When you complete the New Java Class dialog box, NetBeans creates a file that will store the Java code for the class. For the Product class in this figure, that file will be named Product.java. NetBeans also generates the starting code for the class as shown in this figure. Note that the name of the class matches the name of the file, which is required. In addition, the public *access modifier* is used so the class can be accessed from other classes.

The dialog box for creating a new Java class

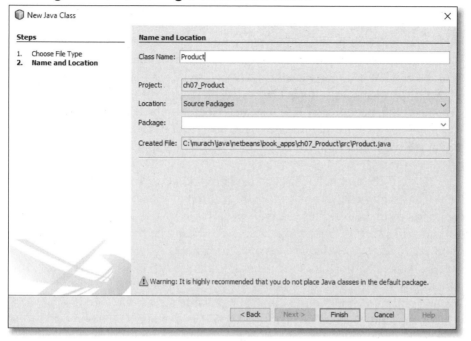

The code that's generated for the Product class

```
public class Product {
}
```

Description

- To create a new class, right-click on the package where you want to add the class, select the New→Java Class command, and respond to the resulting dialog box. At the least, you should enter a name for the class in the Class Name text box.

- Although this dialog box encourages you to select a package for the class, this isn't required. If you don't select a package for the class, NetBeans will store the class in the default package. To learn how to create and use packages, see chapter 10.

Figure 7-4   How to use NetBeans to create a new class

The Product class

Figure 7-5 presents the code for the Product class. This code implements the fields and methods of the class diagram in figure 7-2. In the next six pages, you'll learn the details of writing code like the code shown here. For now, I'll just present a preview of this code so you have a general idea of how it works.

The first three statements in this class are declarations for the fields of the class. The *fields* are the variables or constants that are available to the class and its objects. In this example, all three fields define *instance variables*, which store the data for the code, description, and price variables that apply to each Product object.

After the field declarations, this class declares the *constructor* of the Product class. This constructor creates an instance of the Product class and initializes its instance variables to their default values. As you'll see later in this chapter, you can also code constructors that accept parameters. Then, the constructor can use the parameter values to initialize the instance variables.

Next are the declarations for the methods of the Product class. In this class, the methods provide access to the values stored in the three fields. For each field, a *get method* returns the value stored in the field, while a *set method* assigns a new value to the field. Of these methods, the getPriceFormatted() method is the only method that does any work beyond getting or setting the value provided by the instance variable. This method applies the standard currency format to the price variable and returns the resulting string.

Although the Product class includes both a get and a set method for each field, you don't always have to code both of these methods for a field. In particular, it's common to code just a get method for a field so its value can be retrieved but not changed. This can be referred to as a *read-only field*. Although you can also code just a set method for a field, that's uncommon.

The private and public keywords determine which *members* of a class are available to other classes. Since all of the instance variables of the Product class use the private keyword, they are only available within that class. The constructor and the methods, however, use the public keyword. As a result, they are available to all classes. Keep in mind, though, that you can include both public and private instance variables and methods in any class.

By the way, this class follows the three coding rules that are required for a *JavaBean*. First, it includes a constructor that requires no arguments. Second, all of the instance variables are private. Third, it includes get and set methods for all instance variables that you want to be able to access. As you progress with Java, you'll find that there are many advantages to creating classes that are also JavaBeans. For example, if you develop JavaServer Pages (JSPs) for a web application, you can use special JSP tags to create a JavaBean and to access its get and set methods.

Now that you've seen the code for the Product class, you might want to consider how it uses encapsulation. First, the three fields are hidden from other classes because they're declared with the private keyword. In addition, all of the code contained within the constructor and methods is hidden. Because of that, you can change any of this code without having to change the other classes that use this class.

The Product class

```
import java.text.NumberFormat;

public class Product {

    // the instance variables
    private String code;
    private String description;
    private double price;

    // the constructor
    public Product() {
        code = "";
        description = "";
        price = 0;
    }

    // the set and get methods for the code variable
    public void setCode(String code) {
        this.code = code;
    }

    public String getCode() {
        return code;
    }

    // the set and get methods for the description variable
    public void setDescription(String description) {
        this.description = description;
    }

    public String getDescription() {
        return description;
    }

    // the set and get methods for the price variable
    public void setPrice(double price) {
        this.price = price;
    }

    public double getPrice() {
        return price;
    }

    // a custom get method for the price variable
    public String getPriceFormatted() {
        NumberFormat currency = NumberFormat.getCurrencyInstance();
        return currency.format(price);
    }
}
```

Figure 7-5   The Product class

How to code instance variables

Figure 7-6 shows how to code the instance variables that define the types of data that are used by the objects created from a class. When you declare an instance variable, you should use an access modifier to control its accessibility. If you use the private keyword, the instance variable can be used only within the class that defines it. In contrast, if you use the public keyword, the instance variable can be accessed by other classes. You can also use other access modifiers that give you finer control over the accessibility of your instance variables. You'll learn about those modifiers in the chapters that follow.

This figure shows four examples of declaring an instance variable. The first example declares a variable of the double type. The second one declares a variable of the int type. The third one declares a variable that's an object of the String class. And the last one declares an object from the Product class...the class that you're learning how to code right now.

Although instance variables work like regular variables, they must be declared within the class body, but not inside methods or constructors. That way, they'll be available throughout the entire class. In this book, all of the instance variables for a class are declared at the beginning of the class. However, when you read through code from other sources, you may find that the instance variables are declared at the end of the class or at other locations within the class.

The syntax for declaring instance variables

```
public|private primitiveType|ClassName variableName;
```

Examples

```
private double price;
private int quantity;
private String code;
private Product product;
```

Where you can declare instance variables

```
public class Product {

    // common to code instance variables here
    private String code;
    private String description;
    private double price;

    // the constructors and methods of the class
    public Product(){}
    public void setCode(String code){}
    public String getCode(){ return code; }
    public void setDescription(String description){}
    public String getDescription(){ return description; }
    public void setPrice(double price){}
    public double getPrice(){ return price; }
    public String getPriceFormatted(){ return formattedPrice; }

    // also possible to code instance variables here
    private int test;
}
```

Description

- An instance variable may be a primitive data type, an object created from a Java class such as the String class, or an object created from a user-defined class such as the Product class.

- To prevent other classes from accessing instance variables, use the private keyword to declare them as private.

- You can declare the instance variables for a class anywhere outside the constructors and methods of the class.

Figure 7-6   How to code instance variables

How to code constructors

Figure 7-7 shows how to code a constructor for a class. When you code one, it's a good coding practice to assign a value to all of the instance variables of the class as shown in the four examples. You can also include any additional statements that you want to execute within the constructor. For instance, the fourth example gets a Product object with the code that was passed to the constructor and then uses two get methods of the Product class to get the description and price for the product.

When you code a constructor, you must use the public access modifier and the same name, including capitalization, as the class name. Then, if you don't want to accept arguments, you must code an empty set of parentheses as shown in the first example. On the other hand, if you want to accept arguments, you code the parameters for the constructor as shown in the next three examples. When you code the parameters for a constructor, you must code a data type and a name for each parameter. For the data type, you can code a primitive data type or the class name for any class that defines an object.

The second example shows a constructor with three parameters. Here, the first parameter is a String object named code; the second parameter is a String object named description; and the third parameter is a double type named price. Then, the three statements within the constructor use these parameters to initialize the three instance variables of the class.

In this example, the names of the parameters are the same as the names of the instance variables. As a result, the constructor must distinguish between the two. To do that, it uses the *this* keyword to refer to the instance variables of the current object. You'll learn about other ways you can use this keyword later in this chapter.

The third example works the same as the second example, but it doesn't need to use the this keyword because the parameter names aren't the same as the names of the instance variables. In this case, though, the parameter names aren't very descriptive. As a result, the code in the second example is easier for other programmers to read than the code in the third example.

The fourth example shows a constructor with one parameter. Here, the first statement assigns the first parameter to the first instance variable of the class. Then, the second statement calls a method of a class named ProductDB to get a Product object for the specified code. Finally, the last two statements call methods of the Product object, and the values returned by these methods are assigned to the second and third instance variables.

When you code a constructor, the class name plus the number of parameters and the data type for each parameter form the *signature* of the constructor. You can code more than one constructor per class as long as each constructor has a unique signature. For example, the first two constructors shown in this figure have different signatures, so they could both be coded within the Product class. This is known as *overloading* a constructor.

If you don't code a constructor, Java will create a *default constructor* that doesn't accept any parameters and initializes all instance variables to null, zero, or false. If you code a constructor that accepts parameters, though, Java won't

The syntax for coding constructors

```
public ClassName([parameterList]) {
    // the statements of the constructor
}
```

A constructor that assigns default values

```
public Product() {
    code = "";
    description = "";
    price = 0.0;
}
```

A custom constructor with three parameters

```
public Product(String code, String description, double price) {
    this.code = code;
    this.description = description;
    this.price = price;
}
```

Another way to code the constructor shown above

```
public Product(String c, String d, double p) {
    code = c;
    description = d;
    price = p;
}
```

A constructor with one parameter

```
public Product(String code) {
    this.code = code;
    Product p = ProductDB.getProduct(code);
    description = p.getDescription();
    price = p.getPrice();
}
```

Description

- The constructor must use the same name and capitalization as the name of the class.

- If you don't code a constructor, Java will create a *default constructor* that initializes all numeric types to zero, all boolean types to false, and all objects to null.

- To code a constructor that has parameters, code a data type and name for each parameter within the parentheses that follow the class name.

- The name of the class combined with the parameter list forms the *signature* of the constructor. Although you can code more than one constructor per class, each constructor must have a unique signature.

- In the second and fourth examples above, the this keyword is used to refer to an instance variable of the current object.

Figure 7-7   How to code constructors

create this default constructor. So if you need a constructor like that, you'll need to code it explicitly. To avoid this confusion, it's a good practice to code all of your own constructors. That way, it's easy to see which constructors are available to a class, and it's easy to check the values that each constructor uses to initialize the instance variables.

How to code methods

Figure 7-8 shows how to code the methods of a class. To start, you code an access modifier. Most of the time, you can use the public keyword to declare the method so it can be used by other classes. However, you can also use the private keyword to hide the method from other classes.

After the access modifier, you code the return type for the method, which refers to the data type that the method returns. After the return type, you code the name of the method followed by a set of parentheses. Within the parentheses, you code the parameter list for the method. Last, you code the opening and closing braces that contain the statements of the method.

Since a method name should describe the action that the method performs, it's a common coding practice to start each method name with a verb. For example, methods that set the value of an instance variable usually begin with *set*. Conversely, methods that return the value of an instance variable usually begin with *get*. These types of methods are typically referred to as *accessors* because they let you access the values of the instance variables. Methods that perform other types of tasks also begin with verbs such as print, save, read, and write.

The first example shows how to code a method that doesn't accept any parameters or return any values. To do that, it uses the void keyword for the return type and it ends with a set of empty parentheses. When this method is called, it prints the instance variables of the Product object to the console, separating each instance variable with a pipe character (|).

The next three examples show how to code methods that return data. To do that, these methods specify a return type, and they include a return statement to return the appropriate variable. When coding a method like this, you must make sure that the return type that you specify matches the data type of the variable that you return. Otherwise, your code won't compile.

In the fourth example, the getPriceFormatted() method uses a NumberFormat object to apply standard currency formatting to the double variable named price. This also converts the double variable to a String object. Then, the return statement returns the String object to the calling method.

The fifth and sixth examples show two possible ways to code a set method. In the fifth example, the method accepts a parameter that has the same name as the instance variable. As a result, the assignment statement within this method uses the this keyword to identify the instance variable. In the sixth example, the parameter has a different name than the instance variable. As a result, the assignment statement doesn't need to use the this keyword. Since the parameter name for both examples are descriptive, both of these examples work equally well.

The syntax for coding a method

```
public|private returnType methodName([parameterList]) {
    // the statements of the method
}
```

A method that doesn't accept parameters or return data

```
public void printToConsole() {
    System.out.println(code + "|" + description +  "|" + price);
}
```

A get method that returns a string

```
public String getCode() {
    return code;
}
```

A get method that returns a double value

```
public double getPrice() {
    return price;
}
```

A custom get method

```
public String getPriceFormatted() {
    NumberFormat currency = NumberFormat.getCurrencyInstance();
    return currency.format(price);
}
```

A set method

```
public void setCode(String code) {
    this.code = code;
}
```

Another way to code a set method

```
public void setCode(String productCode) {
    code = productCode;
}
```

Description

- To allow other classes to access a method, use the public keyword. To prevent other classes from accessing a method, use the private keyword.

- To code a method that doesn't return data, use the void keyword for the return type. To code a method that returns data, code a return type in the method declaration and code a return statement in the body of the method.

- When you name a method, you should start each name with a verb. It's a common coding practice to use the verb *set* for methods that set the values of instance variables and to use the verb *get* for methods that return the values of instance variables. These methods are typically referred to as set and get *accessors*.

Figure 7-8   How to code methods

How to create an object from a class

Figure 7-9 shows how to create an object with one and with two statements. Most of the time, you'll use one statement to create an object. However, as you'll see later in this book, certain types of coding situations require you to create an object with two statements.

When you use two statements to create an object, the first statement declares the class and the name of the variable that the object will be assigned to. However, an instance of the object isn't actually created until the second statement is executed. This statement uses the new keyword to call the constructor for the object, which initializes the instance variables. Then, a reference to this object is assigned to the variable. At this point, you can use the variable to refer to the object.

When you pass arguments to the constructor of a class, you must make sure that the constructor will be able to accept the arguments. To do that, you must pass the right number of arguments, in the right sequence, and with data types that are compatible with the data types specified in the parameter list of the constructor. When a class contains more than one constructor, the constructor with parameters that match the arguments is the constructor that will be executed.

The two-statement example in this figure creates a new Product object without passing any arguments to the constructor of the Product class. The same task is accomplished by the first one-statement example. Then, the second and third examples show how to pass a single argument to the constructor of the Product class. Both of these statements pass a String object, but the second example passes a literal while the third example passes a variable that refers to a String object. The fourth example passes three arguments to the constructor.

How to create an object in two statements

Syntax

```
ClassName variableName;
variableName = new ClassName(argumentList);
```

Example with no arguments

```
Product product;
product = new Product();
```

How to create an object in one statement

Syntax

```
ClassName variableName = new ClassName(argumentList);
```

No arguments

```
Product product = new Product();
```

One literal argument

```
Product product = new Product("java");
```

One variable argument

```
Product product = new Product(productCode);
```

Three arguments

```
Product product = new Product(code, description, price);
```

Description

- To create an object, you use the new keyword to create a new instance of a class. Each time the new keyword creates an object, Java calls the constructor for the object, which initializes the instance variables for the object.

- After you create an object, you assign it to a variable. When you do, a reference to the object is stored in the variable. Then, you can use the variable to refer to the object.

- To pass arguments to the constructor, code the arguments between the parentheses that follow the class name. To pass more than one argument, separate the arguments with commas.

- When you pass arguments to the constructor, the arguments must be in the sequence called for by the constructor and they must have data types that are compatible with the data types of the parameters for the constructor.

Figure 7-9   How to create an object from a class

How to call the methods of an object

Figure 7-10 shows how to call the methods of an object. By now, you should be familiar with the basic syntax for calling a method, so this figure should just be review. To start, you type the object name followed by the dot operator and the method name. Then, if the method requires arguments, you code the argument list between the parentheses, separating multiple arguments with commas. Otherwise, you code an empty set of parentheses.

The first two examples show two ways to call methods that don't return any data. The first example doesn't pass an argument, while the second example passes an argument named productCode. In this case, the argument is a variable that represents a String object, but the argument could also be a literal value such as "java". Either way, you need to pass the right number of arguments, and the data types of those arguments must be compatible with the data types specified in the parameter list of the method.

The third and fourth examples show how to call a method that returns a value and assigns that value to a variable. In the third example, the getPrice() method doesn't have any arguments, but it does return a value. Then, that value is assigned to a double variable named price. In the fourth example, the getPriceFormatted() method passes a boolean variable as an argument that indicates whether a dollar sign should be included in the formatted value. This is a variation of the getPriceFormatted() method you saw back in figure 7-5. Like that method, this method returns a string that is then stored in a string variable.

The fifth example shows how to call a method within an expression. Here, the expression includes a call to the getCode() method, which returns a String object. Then, that String object is joined with three string literals, and the result is assigned to another String object.

How to call a method

Syntax
```
objectName.methodName(argumentList)
```

Passes no arguments and returns nothing
```
product.printToConsole();
```

Passes one argument and returns nothing
```
product.setCode(productCode);
```

Passes no arguments and returns a double value
```
double price = product.getPrice();
```

Passes an argument and returns a String object
```
String formattedPrice = product.getPriceFormatted(includeDollarSign);
```

A method call within an expression
```
String message = "Code: " + product.getCode() + "\n\n"
             + "Press Enter to continue or enter 'x' to exit:";
```

Description

- To call a method that doesn't accept arguments, type an empty set of parentheses after the method name.

- To call a method that accepts arguments, enter the arguments between the parentheses that follow the method name. Here, the data type of each argument must be compatible with the data type that's specified by the method's parameters.

- To code more than one argument, separate the arguments with commas.

- If a method returns a value, you can code an assignment statement to assign the return value to a variable. Here, the data type of the variable must be compatible with the data type of the return value.

Figure 7-10   How to call the methods of an object

How to use NetBeans to work with classes

Figure 7-11 shows how NetBeans can make it easier to work with classes. To start, after you enter the private fields for a class, you can use NetBeans to generate the get and set methods for those fields. To do that, you use the Encapsulate Fields dialog box shown in this figure.

As you can see, this dialog box lists all the private fields and lets you select what methods you want to generate for each field. It also lets you set several options that control how the methods are generated. When you use the Encapsulate Fields dialog box, the get and set methods for a field are formatted like this:

```
public String getCode() {
    return code;
}

public void setCode(String code) {
    this.code = code;
}
```

Once you've created a class, you can use the Navigator window shown in this figure to jump to any member of the class. To do that, just double-click on the member name. Although the usefulness of this feature isn't obvious for a simple class like the Product class, it can be helpful for classes with more members.

The NetBeans window for the Product application

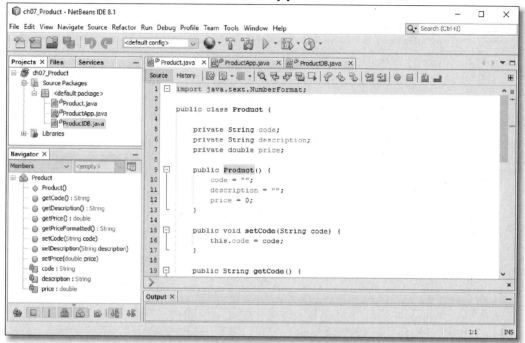

The dialog box for generating get and set methods

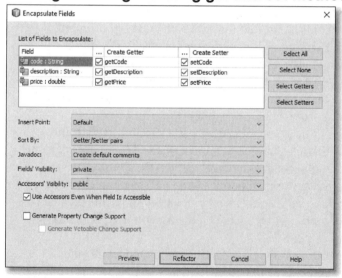

Description

- To generate get and set methods for one or more fields, select the Refactor→Encapsulate Fields command and respond to the resulting dialog box.

- The Navigator window lists all the members of the currently selected class. To display this window, use the Window→Navigator command. To jump to a member, double-click on it in the Navigator window.

Figure 7-11   How to use NetBeans to work with classes

How to code and use static fields and methods

In chapters 2 and 3, you learned how to call static methods from some of the classes in the Java API. In chapter 4, you learned how to code static methods in the same class as the main() method. Now, you'll learn how to code static fields and methods in your own classes and how to call them from other classes.

How to code static fields and methods

Figure 7-12 shows how to code *static fields* and *static methods*. While instance variables and regular methods belong to an object that's created from a class, static fields and static methods belong to the class itself. As a result, they're sometimes called *class fields* and *class methods*.

The top of this figure shows how to code static fields. In short, you use a syntax that's similar to the syntax for a regular variable or constant. However, you use the static keyword so the variable or constant belongs to the class, not the object. Then, you supply an initial value for the variable or constant. Typically, the static variables of a class are declared with private access, but the static constants of a class are declared with public access. That way, other classes can access and use these constants.

The first example shows how to code a class that contains one static field and a static method. The static field is a constant that stores the number of months per year. The static method is similar to the calculateFutureValue() method that you learned how to code in chapter 4. However, this method uses the static field named MONTHS_IN_YEAR, and it is coded in a separate class named FinancialCalculations. Note that since this class doesn't contain any non-static fields or methods, you don't need to code a constructor for this class.

The second example shows how you can add a static variable and a static method to the Product class. In this example, a static variable named objectCount counts the number of Product objects that are created from the Product class. This variable is declared as private so no other class can access it directly. Then, the constructor increments the static variable each time a new object is created from this class. Finally, the static getObjectCount() method returns the static objectCount variable.

When you code a class that mixes regular fields and methods with static fields and methods, it's a good practice to keep your fields and methods organized. To do that, you can group your fields and methods by type (instance or static; variable or constant) and by access modifier (private or public). To illustrate, the second example lists all instance variables in a group, followed by the single static variable. For small classes, grouping fields and methods like this isn't critical. However, as your classes get longer, grouping can make your code easier to read and maintain.

How to declare static fields

```
private static int numberOfObjects = 0;
private static double majorityPercent = .51;
public static final int DAYS_IN_JANUARY = 31;
public static final float EARTH_MASS_IN_KG = 5.972e24F;
```

A class that contains a static constant and a static method

```
public class FinancialCalculations {

    public static final int MONTHS_IN_YEAR = 12;

    public static double calculateFutureValue(double monthlyPayment,
        double yearlyInterestRate, int years) {
        int months = years * MONTHS_IN_YEAR;
        double monthlyInterestRate = yearlyInterestRate/MONTHS_IN_YEAR/100;
        double futureValue = 0;
        for (int i = 1; i <= months; i++)
            futureValue = (futureValue + monthlyPayment) *
                (1 + monthlyInterestRate);
        return futureValue;
    }
}
```

The Product class with a static variable and a static method

```
public class Product {

    private String code;
    private String description;
    private double price;

    private static int objectCount = 0;       // declare a static variable

    public Product() {
        code = "";
        description = "";
        price = 0;
        objectCount++;                         // update the static variable
    }

    public static int getObjectCount() {       // get the static variable
        return objectCount;
    }
    ...
}
```

Description

- You can use the static keyword to code *static fields* and *static methods*. Since static fields and static methods belong to the class, not to an object created from the class, they are sometimes called *class fields* and *class methods*.

- When you code a static method, you can only use static fields and fields that are defined in the method. You can't use instance variables in a static method because they belong to an instance of the class, not to the class as a whole.

Figure 7-12   How to code static fields and methods

How to call static fields and methods

Figure 7-13 shows how to call static fields and methods. As you would expect, you use the same syntax for calling static fields and methods from your own classes as you would for calling static fields and methods from the Java API.

To call a static field, you just code the class name, followed by the dot operator and the field name. To illustrate, the first statement calls the PI field from the Math class. This field returns a double value for *pi*, which is the ratio of the circumference of a circle to its diameter. Then, the second statement calls the MONTHS_IN_YEAR field from the FinancialCalculations class in the previous figure.

The third statement shows how to call an objectCount field from the Product class. If you declare this static field as public in the Product class, you can use code like this to directly get or set this int value, which represents the number of objects that have been created from the Product class. However, if you declare this static field as private as shown in the previous figure, you can only use static methods to get or set its value. And if you only declare a get method, the field is a read-only field.

To call a static method, you code the class name, followed by the dot operator, the name of the static method, and a pair of parentheses. Within the parentheses, you code the arguments required by the method (if any). To illustrate, the first statement in the static method examples calls the static getCurrencyInstance() method of the NumberFormat class. This method doesn't take any arguments, and it returns a NumberFormat object. The second statement calls the static parseInt() method of the Integer class. This method takes a string argument, converts it to an int value, and returns that value. And the third statement uses the static pow() method of the Math class to return the squared value of a variable named r.

The fourth statement calls the static calculateFutureValue() method from the FinancialCalculations class shown in the previous figure. This method accepts three arguments and returns the future value that's calculated based on the three arguments. Then, the fifth statement calls the static getObjectCount() method of the Product class. This method returns the value stored in the static objectCount field.

The last statement in this figure shows how you can use both a static field and a static method in an expression. Here, the value that's returned by the static pow() method of the Math class is multiplied by the static PI field of the Math class. Then, the result is assigned to a double variable named area.

Although the examples in this figure call static fields and methods from the classes that contain them, you can also call a static field or method from an object created from the class that contains it. For example, you can call the getObjectCount() method from a Product object named product like this:

```
int productCount = product.getObjectCount();
```

To make it clear that a field or method is static, however, we recommend that you always call it from the class.

The syntax for calling a static field or method

```
className.FINAL_FIELD_NAME
className.fieldName
className.methodName(argumentList)
```

How to call static fields

From the Java API

```
Math.PI
```

From a user-defined class

```
FinancialCalculations.MONTHS_IN_YEAR
Product.objectCount     // if objectCount is declared as public
```

How to call static methods

From the Java API

```
NumberFormat currency = NumberFormat.getCurrencyInstance();
int quantity = Integer.parseInt(inputQuantity);
double rSquared = Math.pow(r, 2);
```

From a user-defined class

```
double futureValue = FinancialCalculations.calculateFutureValue(
    monthlyPayment, yearlyInterestRate, years);
int productCount = Product.getObjectCount();
```

A statement that calls a static field and a static method

```
double area = Math.PI * Math.pow(r, 2);     // pi times r squared
```

Description

- To call a static field, type the name of the class, followed by the dot operator and the name of the static field.

- To call a static method, type the name of the class, followed by the dot operator, the name of the static method, and a set of parentheses. If the method requires arguments, code the arguments within the parentheses, separating multiple arguments with commas.

Figure 7-13   How to call static fields and methods

How to code a static initialization block

When it takes more than one statement to initialize a static field, you can use a *static initialization block* to initialize the field as shown in figure 7-14. To start, you just code the static keyword followed by braces. Then, you code the statements of the block within the braces. The statements in this block are executed when the class is loaded, which happens when you call one of the class constructors or static methods.

In the example in this figure, the ProductDB class contains a static initialization block that executes several statements that initialize the static Connection object. This object is used by some of the static methods in the class to connect to a database. Since a static initialization block runs as soon as any method of the class is called, this makes the Connection object available to the rest of the methods in the class.

For now, don't worry if you don't understand the code in the static block. The point is that it takes several statements to initialize the static Connection object. You'll learn more about these statements and how to connect to a database in chapter 20.

When to use static fields and methods

Now that you know how to code static fields and methods, you may wonder when to use them and when to use regular fields and methods. In general, when you need to create objects from a class, you should use regular fields and methods. That way, you can create several objects from a class, and each object has its own data in its own instance variables. Then, you can use the methods of each object to process that data.

In contrast, if you just need to perform a single task like a calculation, you can use a static method. Then, you pass the arguments that the method needs, and the method returns the result that you need without ever creating an object. As you progress through this book, you'll see many examples that will give you a better idea of when static fields and methods are appropriate.

The syntax for coding a static initialization block

```
public class className {
    // any field declarations
    static {
        // any initialization statements for static fields
    }
    // the rest of the code for the class
}
```

A class that uses a static initialization block

```
public class ProductDB {

    private static Connection connection;           // static variable

    // the static initialization block
    static {
        try {
            String url = "jdbc:mysql://localhost:3306/MurachDB";
            String user = "root";
            String password = "sesame";
            connection = DriverManager.getConnection(url, user, password);
        }
        catch (Exception e) {
            System.err.println("Error connecting to database.");
        }
    }

    // static methods that use the Connection object
    public static Product get(String code){...}
    public static boolean add(Product product){...}
    public static boolean update(Product product){...}
    public static boolean delete(String code){...}
}
```

Description

- To initialize the static variables of a class, you typically code the values in the declarations. If a variable can't be initialized in a single statement, however, you can code a *static initialization block*.

- When a class is loaded, Java initializes all static variables and constants of the class. Then, it executes all static initialization blocks in the order in which they appear. (A class is loaded when one of its constructors or static methods is called.)

Figure 7-14   How to code a static initialization block

The Product Viewer application

The next two figures present an object-oriented application that lets you view the data for the product with the specified code. This application uses the Product class you saw earlier in this chapter as well as the ProductDB class that's presented next.

The ProductDB class

Figure 7-15 presents a database class named ProductDB that provides the data processing required by the Product Viewer application. This class consists of a single static method named getProduct() that returns a Product object based on the product code that's passed to it.

The code within the getProduct() method starts by creating a Product object. If you look back to figure 7-5, you'll see that this causes the code and description fields to be set to empty strings and the price to be set to zero.

After the Product object is created, its setCode() method is called to assign the product code that was passed to the getProduct() method to the code field of this object. Next, the getProduct() method uses an if/else statement to determine what values are assigned to the description and price fields of the Product object depending on the value of the product code. Notice that the setDescription() and setPrice() methods of the Product object are used to set these values. Also notice that if the product code doesn't match any of the specified products, this method sets the description to "Unknown" and it leaves the price at its default value of zero. Finally, this method returns the Product object.

Because this class doesn't retrieve the data for a product from a file or database, it isn't realistic. However, it does simulate the processing that would be done by a class like this. In fact, you could use code like this to test the basic functions of an application before you add the code that works with a file or database. In chapter 15 of this book, you'll learn how to implement a class like this so it gets the required data from a file, and in chapter 21, you'll learn how to implement a class like this so it gets the required data from a database.

The ProductDB class

```
public class ProductDB  {

    public static Product getProduct(String productCode) {
        // create the Product object
        Product p = new Product();

        // fill the Product object with data
        p.setCode(productCode);
        if (productCode.equalsIgnoreCase("java")) {
            p.setDescription("Murach's Java Programming");
            p.setPrice(57.50);
        }
        else if (productCode.equalsIgnoreCase("jsp")) {
            p.setDescription("Murach's Java Servlets and JSP");
            p.setPrice(57.50);
        }
        else if (productCode.equalsIgnoreCase("mysql")) {
            p.setDescription("Murach's MySQL");
            p.setPrice(54.50);
        }
        else {
            p.setDescription("Unknown");
        }
        return p;
    }
}
```

Notes

- The ProductDB class provides the database layer that creates a Product object and gets the data for it from a file or database. In this case, though, the ProductDB class just simulates the processing that would be done by a database class.

- In a more realistic application, the database class would use the product code to retrieve the data for a product from a file or database and then fill the Product object with that data. It would also include methods for adding new products and for modifying and deleting existing products. You'll learn how to code classes like this in chapters 15 and 21.

Figure 7-15   The ProductDB class

The user interface and the ProductApp class

Figure 7-16 presents a ProductApp class that uses the ProductDB class and the Product object it creates. As you can tell from the console at the top of this figure, this application prompts the user for a product code. Then, it retrieves and displays the description and price of that product.

The ProductApp class shown here contains the main() method for the application, which means that this method is executed when the application starts. To make it easy to tell which class of an application contains the main() method, it's common to add a suffix to the class name. In this book, we use "App" as the suffix as you've seen in all the applications we've presented to this point.

The main() method in this class is similar to the other ones that you've seen. It uses a loop to retrieve and display the product data for each product code the user enters. The code that uses the Product and ProductDB classes in this loop is highlighted. The first statement calls the getProduct() method of the ProductDB class to create a Product object named product. Notice here that except for the capitalization, the object and class have the same name. That's possible because Java is a case-sensitive language.

Once the Product object is created and initialized, this program displays the product's description and price. To get that information, it calls the getDescription() and getPriceFormatted() methods of the Product object.

The console

```
Welcome to the Product Viewer

Enter product code: java

SELECTED PRODUCT
Description: Murach's Java Programming
Price:        $57.50

Continue? (y/n):
```

The ProductApp class

```java
import java.util.Scanner;

public class ProductApp {

    public static void main(String args[]) {
        // display a welcome message
        System.out.println("Welcome to the Product Viewer");
        System.out.println();

        // display 1 or more products
        Scanner sc = new Scanner(System.in);
        String choice = "y";
        while (choice.equalsIgnoreCase("y")) {
            // get the input from the user
            System.out.print("Enter product code: ");
            String productCode = sc.next();  // read the product code
            sc.nextLine();   // discard any other data entered on the line

            // get the Product object
            Product product = ProductDB.getProduct(productCode);

            // display the output
            System.out.println();
            System.out.println("SELECTED PRODUCT");
            System.out.println("Description: " + product.getDescription());
            System.out.println("Price:       " + product.getPriceFormatted());
            System.out.println();

            // see if the user wants to continue
            System.out.print("Continue? (y/n): ");
            choice = sc.nextLine();
            System.out.println();
        }
    }
}
```

Note

- This class contains the main() method that provides the entry point for the Product application. In this book, we've used the suffix "App" to identify this type of class.

Figure 7-16   The user interface and the ProductApp class

More skills for working with objects and methods

If you understand the Product Viewer application, you understand the basic concepts and skills for coding classes and methods. Now, this chapter presents some additional concepts and skills that you may need when you're working with classes and methods.

Reference types compared to primitive types

By now, you should know that a class such as the Product class defines a reference type. In addition, you should know that reference types such as the Product type work differently than primitive types such as the double and int types. That's because a primitive type stores a value, but a reference type refers to an object. Figure 7-17 summarizes a few important differences between reference types and primitive types.

The first example shows how assignment statements work. With primitive types, the assignment statement makes a copy of the double value. As a result, the third statement changes the double value that's stored in the variable named p2, but not the double value that's stored in the variable named p1.

With reference types, the assignment statement does *not* store a copy of the object. Instead, it causes both variables to refer to the same Product object. As a result, when the third statement uses the variable named p2 to change the double value that's stored in that Product object, this change is also reflected in the variable named p1. That's because both variables refer to the same Product object. As a result, if you have multiple variables that refer to the same object, you need to be careful about changing its data.

The second example shows how the parameters of a method work. This example uses a method named increasePrice() that increases the price by 10%. With a primitive type, the price parameter stores a copy of the double value. Then, the first statement increases the price parameter by 10%. However, this doesn't change the price in the calling code. As a result, the second statement returns the price to the calling code so it can access the new price.

With a reference type, the product parameter refers to the same Product object as the calling code. As a result, this method doesn't need to return the Product object to the calling code. Instead, its second statement can set the new price in the Product object. This changes the price in the calling code.

The third example shows the code that calls the methods in the second example. With a primitive type, the code that calls the increasePrice() method assigns the return value to the variable named price to change it. With a reference type, the code just calls the increasePrice() method. This increases the price that's stored in the product variable in this example.

Most of the time, you can write your code without thinking too much about the differences between reference types and primitive types. Occasionally, though, you do need to be aware of these differences. When you do, you can refer back to this figure to refresh your memory.

How assignment statements work

For primitive types

```
double p1 = 54.50;
double p2 = p1;                    // p1 and p2 store copies of 54.50
p2 = 57.50;                        // only changes p2
```

For reference types

```
Product p1 = new Product("mysql", "Murach's MySQL", 54.50);
Product p2 = p1;                   // p1 and p2 refer to the same object
p2.setPrice(57.50);               // changes p1 and p2
```

How parameters work

For primitive types

```
public static double increasePrice(double price) {
    // the price parameter is a copy of the double value
    price = price * 1.1;           // does not change price in calling code
    return price;                  // returns changed price to calling code
}
```

For reference types

```
public static void increasePrice(Product product) {
    // the product parameter refers to the Product object
    double price = product.getPrice() * 1.1;
    product.setPrice(price);       // changes price in calling code
}
```

How method calls work

For primitive types

```
double price = 54.50;
price = increasePrice(price);     // assignment necessary
```

For reference types

```
Product product = new Product();
product.setPrice(54.50);
increasePrice(product);           // assignment not necessary
```

Description

- A variable for a primitive type always stores its own copy of the primitive value. As a result, changing the value for one primitive type variable doesn't change the value of any other primitive type variables.

- A variable for a reference type stores a *reference* to the object. This allows multiple reference type variables to *refer* to the same object. As a result, changing the data for one object also changes the data for any other variables that refer to that object.

- When you code a method that has a primitive type parameter, the parameter gets its own copy of the value that's passed to the method. As a result, if the method changes the value of the parameter, that change doesn't affect any variables outside the method.

- When you code a method that has a reference type parameter, the parameter refers to the object that's passed to the method. As a result, if the method uses the parameter to change the data in the object, these changes are reflected by any other variables outside the method that refer to the same object.

Figure 7-17   Reference types compared to primitive types

How to overload methods

Figure 7-18 shows how to overload a method, which is similar to overloading a constructor. When you overload a method, you code two or more methods with the same name, but with unique combinations of parameters. In other words, you code methods with unique signatures.

For a method signature to be unique, the method must have a different number of parameters than the other methods with the same name, or at least one of the parameters must have a different data type. Note that the names of the parameters aren't part of the signature. So using different parameter names isn't enough to make the signatures unique. Also, the return type isn't part of the signature. As a result, you can't create two methods with the same name and parameters but different return types.

The purpose of overloading is to provide more than one way to invoke a given method. For example, this figure shows three versions of the printToConsole() method. The first one accepts a String parameter named sep that's used to separate the code, price, and description of a Product object. Then, it prints the resulting string to the console.

The second method doesn't accept a parameter that specifies the separator string. Instead, it separates the code, price, and description with the pipe character. To do that, it calls the first printToConsole() method and passes the pipe character to it. Although I could have just called the println() method to print the line, calling an overloaded method can often prevent code duplication.

The third method accepts a String parameter for the separator along with a boolean parameter that indicates whether to print a blank line after printing the data to the console. This method begins by passing the sep parameter to the first printToConsole() method. Then, it uses an if statement to determine whether to print a blank line.

When you refer to an overloaded method, the number of arguments you specify and their types determine which version of the method is executed. The three statements in this figure that call the printToConsole() method illustrate how this works. Because the first statement doesn't specify an argument, it causes the second version of the printToConsole() method to be executed. In contrast, the second statement specifies a String argument of four blank spaces and a boolean argument of true. As a result, it will cause the third version of the printToConsole() method to be executed. Finally, the third statement specifies a single String argument, which causes the first version of the printToConsole() method to be executed.

A method that accepts one argument

```
public void printToConsole(String sep) {
    System.out.println(code + sep + description + sep + price);
}
```

An overloaded method that provides a default value

```
public void printToConsole() {
    printToConsole("|");    // this calls the method in the first example
}
```

An overloaded method with two arguments

```
public void printToConsole(String sep, boolean printLineAfter) {
    printToConsole(sep);    // this calls the method in the first example
    if (printLineAfter)
        System.out.println();
}
```

Code that calls these methods

```
Product p = ProductDB.getProduct("java");
p.printToConsole();
p.printToConsole("     ", true);
p.printToConsole("     ");
```

The console

```
java|Murach's Java Programming 2|57.5
java     Murach's Java Programming  57.5

java     Murach's Java Programming  57.5
```

Description

- When you create two or more methods with the same name but with different parameter lists, the methods are overloaded. It's common to use overloaded methods to provide two or more versions of a method that work with different data types or that supply default values for omitted parameters.

Figure 7-18   How to overload methods

How to use the this keyword

In figures 7-7 and 7-8, you saw how to use the this keyword to refer to an instance variable from a constructor or a method. Now, figure 7-19 reviews this skill. In addition, it shows how to use the this keyword to call another constructor of the current class, to call methods of the current object, or to pass the current object to another method.

The first example shows how to use the this keyword to refer to instance variables. If the parameters of a constructor or method have the same names as the instance variables of the class, you need to use the this keyword to explicitly identify the instance variables. Of course, another approach would be to change the parameter names so they aren't the same as the instance variable names.

The second example shows how to call one constructor from another constructor in the same class. In this example, the constructor uses the this keyword to call the constructor in the first example that accepts three parameters, and it passes three arguments to it. This is an easy way to overload a constructor so it provides default data for missing parameters.

The third example shows how to call the getPrice() method of the current object. In this case, the this keyword isn't necessary because it would be added implicitly. However, it does make it clear that the getPrice() method is a method of the current object.

The fourth example shows how to use the this keyword to pass the current object to a method. In this example, a method named printCurrentObject() passes the current object to the println() method of the System.out object. If this printCurrentObject() method was added to the Product class shown in this chapter, you could call this method from a Product object to print that object to the console.

How to refer to instance variables of the current object

Syntax
```
this.variableName
```

A constructor that refers to three instance variables
```
public Product(String code, String description, double price) {
    this.code = code;
    this.description = description;
    this.price = price;
}
```

How to call a constructor of the current object

Syntax
```
this(argumentList);
```

A constructor that calls another constructor of the current object
```
public Product() {
    this("", "", 0.0);
}
```

How to call a method of the current object

Syntax
```
this.methodName(argumentList)
```

A method that calls another method of the current object
```
public String getPriceFormatted() {
    NumberFormat currency = NumberFormat.getCurrencyInstance();
    String priceFormatted = currency.format(this.getPrice());
    return priceFormatted;
}
```

How to pass the current object to a method

Syntax
```
methodName(this)
```

A method that passes the current object to another method
```
public void printCurrentObject() {
    System.out.println(this);
}
```

Description

- Java implicitly uses the this keyword for instance variables and methods. As a result, you don't need to explicitly code it unless a method parameter or a variable that's declared within a method has the same name as an instance variable. Then, you need to use the this keyword to identify the instance variable.

- If you use the this keyword to call one constructor from another constructor in the same class, the statement that uses the this keyword must be the first statement in the constructor.

Figure 7-19   How to use the this keyword

The Line Item application

The topics that follow present a Line Item application that calculates the total price for an invoice line item entered by the user. As you'll see, this application is more complex than the Product Viewer application you saw earlier in this chapter. As a result, it should give you a better feel for what you can do when you divide your applications into classes. It also illustrates how easy it is to use business and database classes in two or more applications.

The user interface

Figure 7-20 shows the console for the Line Item application. This application starts by prompting the user to enter a product code. Then, it prompts the user to enter a quantity for that product. Finally, it displays the data for the line item that's retrieved and calculated by the application.

The class diagram

Figure 7-20 also shows a class diagram for the classes used by the Line Item application. Here, the Product and ProductDB classes that you saw earlier are used again without any changes. Since you're already familiar with those classes, I'll focus on the other classes in this diagram.

The LineItem class defines two instance variables named product and quantity. Here, the product variable holds a Product object that stores the data for the product, and the quantity variable holds an int value for the quantity.

The LineItem class also defines six methods. The first four are the get and set methods that provide access to the instance variables. In contrast, the getTotal method returns a double value for the line item total. Similarly, the getTotalFormatted method returns a String object that represents the total after currency formatting has been applied. This works similarly to the getPriceFormatted method of the Product class.

The Console class contains methods that are similar to the generic methods for validating user input that you saw in chapter 5. It includes methods for validating string, integer, and double input. You'll see the details of how these methods work in a minute.

The arrows between the ProductDB and Product classes and the LineItem and Product classes indicate that one class uses another class. In this diagram, both the ProductDB and LineItem classes use the Product class. That's because the getProduct method of the ProductDB class returns a Product object, and the LineItem class declares an instance variable of the Product type. However, the Product class doesn't use either of the other classes. Instead, it only uses the String class and primitive types. As you'll see in a minute, all of the classes shown here, including the Console class, are also used by the class that contains the main() method for the Line Item application.

The console

```
Welcome to the Line Item Calculator

Enter product code: java
Enter quantity:     2

LINE ITEM
Code:          java
Description: Murach's Java Programming
Price:         $57.50
Quantity:     2
Total:         $115.00

Continue? (y/n):
```

The class diagram

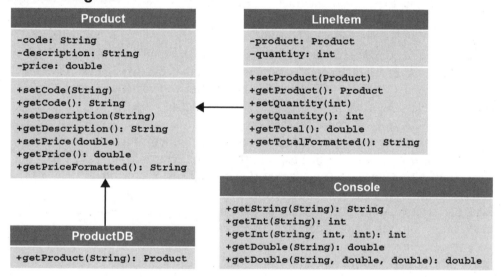

Description

- The Line Item application accepts a product code and quantity from the user, creates a line item using that information, and displays the result to the user.
- The Console class is used to get valid data from the console.
- The two instance variables of the LineItem class store a Product object and an int value for the quantity. The first four methods of the LineItem class access the values of these variables. The getTotal() method calculates the line item total. And the getTotalFormatted() method formats the total as a currency value.

Figure 7-20   The user interface and the class diagram for the Line Item application

The code for the classes

Figure 7-21 shows the code for the LineItemApp class. This class contains the main() method that gets the input from the user and displays the output to the user. To get the input, this method uses the static getString() and getInt() methods of the Console class to get a valid product code and quantity. Unlike the methods you saw in chapter 5, it's not necessary to pass a Scanner object to these methods. That's because, as you'll see in a minute, the Console class defines its own Scanner object.

After the main() method gets valid user entries, it calls the getProduct() method of the ProductDB class to get a Product object that corresponds to the product code that was entered by the user. Then, it creates a new LineItem object from the LineItem class, passing in the values for the Product object and the quantity. Finally, this application uses the get methods of the Product and LineItem objects to get the output that's displayed.

Since you've already seen the Product and ProductDB classes, you shouldn't have much trouble understanding how the code in the LineItemApp class works. To understand it completely, however, you need to understand the code for the Console and LineItem classes that's presented in the next two figures. As a result, you may want to refer back to this figure after you've had a chance to study these classes.

Figure 7-22 shows the code for the Console class. To start, it includes a static field for a Scanner object that can be used to get input from the user. Then, it contains five static methods that use this object: one getString() method, two overloaded getInt() methods, and two overloaded getDouble() methods.

The getString() method accepts a string that's used to prompt the user for input and returns a valid String value. This method uses the next method of the Scanner object to read the data that the user enters. Notice that, unlike the generic methods you saw in chapter 5 for validating numeric data, this method doesn't include code to prevent an InputMismatchException. That's because the next method stores the data that's retrieved from the console as a string, so an InputMismatchException isn't possible. After the next method, the nextLine() method is used to retrieve and discard any extra data the user may have entered at the console.

After the getString() method are two methods named getInt(). These methods work the same as the getInt() and getIntWithinRange() methods you saw in chapter 5. In this case, though, they have the same name so they are overloaded. Notice, however, that the second getInt() method still calls the first getInt() method to get a valid integer from the user. That way, this code doesn't have to be repeated in the second method.

Although they're not used by the Line Item application, the Console class also includes two methods named getDouble(). As you can see on page 2 of the code listing for this class, these methods provide the same functions as the getDouble() and getDoubleWithinRange() methods you saw in chapter 5, but this time they are overloaded methods. By including these methods, the Console class can be used by any application that requires the user to enter a double type.

The LineItemApp class

```
public class LineItemApp {

    public static void main(String args[]) {
        // display a welcome message
        System.out.println("Welcome to the Line Item Calculator");
        System.out.println();

        // create 1 or more line items
        String choice = "y";
        while (choice.equalsIgnoreCase("y")) {
            // get the input from the user
            String productCode = Console.getString("Enter product code: ");
            int quantity = Console.getInt("Enter quantity:    ", 0, 1000);

            // get the Product object
            Product product = ProductDB.getProduct(productCode);

            // create the LineItem object
            LineItem lineItem = new LineItem(product, quantity);

            // display the output
            System.out.println();
            System.out.println("LINE ITEM");
            System.out.println("Code:        " + product.getCode());
            System.out.println("Description: " + product.getDescription());
            System.out.println("Price:       " + product.getPriceFormatted());
            System.out.println("Quantity:    " + lineItem.getQuantity());
            System.out.println("Total:       "
                    + lineItem.getTotalFormatted() + "\n");

            // see if the user wants to continue
            choice = Console.getString("Continue? (y/n): ");
            System.out.println();
        }
    }
}
```

Description

- After the user enters a valid product code and quantity, the getProduct() method of the ProductDB class is called to get a Product object for the product with that code. Then, a new line item object is created with that product and quantity.

- The getCode(), getDescription(), and getPriceFormatted() methods of the Product object are used to get the code, description, and price fields so they can be displayed at the console. The getQuantity() and getTotalFormatted() methods of the LineItem class are used to get the quantity and total.

Figure 7-21   The code for the LineItemApp class

Figure 7-23 shows the LineItem class that defines a line item for an invoice. Like the Product class, the LineItem class defines a business object in the application's business tier. If you review the code for this object, you shouldn't have any trouble understanding how it works.

As you can see, this class contains two constructors. The first one initializes the instance variables to default values. Notice here that the product variable is initialized to a null. As a result, if you try to call a method from this variable before you assign an object to it, this class will throw a NullPointerException. To prevent this exception, you could initialize this variable to a new Product object. However, it's often a good idea to allow the class to throw an exception if it hasn't been initialized correctly.

The second constructor allows the user to supply the product and quantity for the line item. This accomplishes the same task as using the first constructor, the setProduct() method, and the setQuantity() method. As a result, it isn't necessary. However, it does make the class easier to use.

After the constructors, the next four methods provide get and set methods for the two instance variables. These methods access the corresponding instance variables.

The fifth method returns a double value for the line item total. To do that, this method calls the getPrice() method of the Product object to get the price of the product, multiplies the price by the quantity, and returns the result.

The sixth method returns a string object for the line item total after currency formatting has been applied to it. To do that, this method calls the getTotal() method to return a double value for the total. Then, it uses the NumberFormat class to apply currency formatting to this double value, and it returns the resulting String object.

The Console class

```java
import java.util.Scanner;

public class Console {

    private static Scanner sc = new Scanner(System.in);

    public static String getString(String prompt) {
        System.out.print(prompt);
        String s = sc.next();  // read user entry
        sc.nextLine();  // discard any other data entered on the line
        return s;
    }

    public static int getInt(String prompt) {
        int i = 0;
        boolean isValid = false;
        while (!isValid) {
            System.out.print(prompt);
            if (sc.hasNextInt()) {
                i = sc.nextInt();
                isValid = true;
            } else {
                System.out.println("Error! Invalid integer. Try again.");
            }
            sc.nextLine();  // discard any other data entered on the line
        }
        return i;
    }

    public static int getInt(String prompt, int min, int max) {
        int i = 0;
        boolean isValid = false;
        while (!isValid) {
            i = getInt(sc, prompt);
            if (i <= min) {
                System.out.println(
                        "Error! Number must be greater than " + min + ".");
            } else if (i >= max) {
                System.out.println(
                        "Error! Number must be less than " + max + ".");
            } else {
                isValid = true;
            }
        }
        return i;
    }
```

Figure 7-22   The code for the Console class (part 1 of 2)

The Console class

```java
public static double getDouble(String prompt) {
    double d = 0;
    boolean isValid = false;
    while (!isValid) {
        System.out.print(prompt);
        if (sc.hasNextDouble()) {
            d = sc.nextDouble();
            isValid = true;
        } else {
            System.out.println("Error! Invalid number. Try again.");
        }
        sc.nextLine();   // discard any other data entered on the line
    }
    return d;
}

public static double getDouble(String prompt, double min, double max) {
    double d = 0;
    boolean isValid = false;
    while (!isValid) {
        d = getDouble(sc, prompt);
        if (d <= min) {
            System.out.println(
                    "Error! Number must be greater than " + min + ".");
        } else if (d >= max) {
            System.out.println(
                    "Error! Number must be less than " + max + ".");
        } else {
            isValid = true;
        }
    }
    return d;
}
}
```

Description

- This class is part of the presentation layer for a console application. It can be called from the application's main method.

Figure 7-22   The code for the Console class (part 2 of 2)

The LineItem class

```java
import java.text.NumberFormat;

public class LineItem {

    private Product product;
    private int quantity;

    public LineItem() {
        this.product = null;
        this.quantity = 0;
    }

    public LineItem(Product product, int quantity) {
        this.product = product;
        this.quantity = quantity;
    }

    public void setProduct(Product product) {
        this.product = product;
    }

    public Product getProduct() {
        return product;
    }

    public void setQuantity(int quantity) {
        this.quantity = quantity;
    }

    public int getQuantity() {
        return quantity;
    }

    public double getTotal() {
        double total = product.getPrice() * quantity;
        return total;
    }

    public String getTotalFormatted() {
        NumberFormat currency = NumberFormat.getCurrencyInstance();
        return currency.format(this.getTotal());
    }
}
```

Figure 7-23   The code for the LineItem class

Perspective

Now that you've completed this chapter, you may be wondering why you should go to the extra effort of dividing an application into classes. The answer is twofold. First, dividing the code into classes makes it easier to use the classes in two or more applications. For example, any application that needs to work with product data can use the Product class. Second, using classes helps you separate the business logic and database processing of an application from the presentation elements. That can simplify the development of the application and make the application easier to maintain and enhance later on.

In this chapter, though, you've just learned the basic skills for creating and using classes. As you will soon see, there's a lot more to creating classes than what's presented here. And that's what the next three chapters are going to show you.

Summary

- In a *three-tiered architecture*, an application is separated into three layers, or *tiers*. The *presentation tier* consists of the user interface. The *database tier* consists of the database and the database classes that work with it. And the *business tier* provides an interface between the presentation tier and the database tier. Its classes are often referred to as *business classes*.

- The *Unified Modeling Language* (*UML*) is the standard modeling language for working with object-oriented applications. You can use UML *class diagrams* to identify the *fields* and *methods* of a class.

- *Encapsulation* lets you control which fields and methods within a class are *exposed* to other classes. When fields are encapsulated within a class, it's called *data hiding*.

- Multiple *objects* can be created from a single *class*. Each object can be referred to as an *instance* of the class.

- The data that makes up an object can be referred to as its *state*. Each object is a separate entity with its own state.

- A *field* is a variable or constant that's defined at the class level. An *instance variable* is a field that's allocated when an object is instantiated. Each object has a separate copy of each instance variable.

- You can use a *constructor* to create, or construct, an object from a class. To do that, you use the new keyword.

- When you code the methods of a class, you often code public *get* and *set* methods, called *accessors*, that provide access to the fields of the class.

- If you want to code a method or constructor that accepts arguments, you code a list of *parameters* between the parentheses for the constructor or method. For each parameter, you must include a data type and a name.

- When you use a class that contains only *static fields*, *static methods*, and *static initialization blocks*, you don't create an object from the class. Instead, you call these fields and methods directly from the class.

- When Java passes a *primitive type* to a method, it passes the value of the variable so the variable can't be changed directly. When Java passes an object (a *reference type*) to a method, the value it passes is a reference to the object so the method can change the values of the object's variables.

- The name of a method or constructor combined with the list of parameter types is known as the *signature* of the method or constructor. You can *overload* a method or constructor by coding different parameter lists for constructors or methods that have the same name.

- When coding a class, you can use the *this* keyword to refer to the current object.

Exercise 7-1   Modify the Product Viewer application

This exercise guides you through the process of testing and modifying the Product Viewer application that's presented in this chapter.

Review and test the project

1. Open the project named ch07_ex1_Product that's in the ex_starts folder. Then, open the Product, ProductDB, and ProductApp classes and review their code.

2. Run the project and test it with valid product codes like "java", "jsp", and "mysql" to make sure this application works correctly. Then, test it with an invalid code to see how that works.

Modify the ProductDB class

3. In the ProductDB class, modify the if/else statement so it includes another product.

4. Run the project and test it to make sure the new product code works. This shows that you can modify the code for a class without needing to modify the other classes that use it.

Add a constructor to the Product class

5. In the Product class, add a constructor that defines three parameters and uses them to set the values of the three instance variables.

6. In the ProductDB class, modify the code so it uses the new constructor to set the data in the Product object instead of using the setCode, setDescription, and setPrice methods. To do that, you can assign a new Product object to the Product variable within each if/else clause.

7. Run the project to make sure it still works correctly.

Add a method to the Product class

8. In the Product class, add a method named getPriceNumberFormat that returns the price with number formatting (not currency formatting). This method should return the number with 2 decimal places but no currency symbol.

9. In the ProductApp class, modify the code so it uses this method.

10. Run the project to make sure it still works correctly.

Modify the ProductDB class so it defines an object

11. In the ProductDB class, modify the getProduct method so it's a regular method instead of a static method.

12. In the ProductApp class, modify the code so it creates a ProductDB object named db. Then, use this object to call the getProduct method of the ProductDB class.

13. Run the project to make sure it still works correctly.

Exercise 7-2   Enhance the Future Value application

This exercise guides you through the process of modifying the Future Value application so it uses classes that provide static methods.

1. Open the project named ch07_ex2_FutureValue that's stored in the ex_starts directory. Then, review the code for the FutureValueApp class.

2. Start a new class named Console in the same package as the FutureValueApp class. Then, move the getDouble(), getDoubleWithinRange(), getInt(), and getIntWithinRange() methods from the FutureValueApp class to the Console class. For this to work, you will also need to add an import statement for the Scanner class to the Console class.

3. Change the name of the getDoubleWithinRange() method to getDouble(), and change the name of the getIntWithinRange() method to getInt(). This overloads the getDouble() and getInt() methods.

4. Modify the FutureValueApp class so it uses the methods in the Console class. Then, run the application to make sure it still works correctly.

5. Start a new class named FinancialCalculations in the same package as the other classes. Then, move the calculateFutureValue() method from the FutureValueApp class to the FinancialCalculations class, and make sure that the method is public.

6. Modify the FutureValueApp class so it uses the static calculateFutureValue() method that's stored in the FinancialCalculations class. Then, run the application to make sure that it still works properly.

Exercise 7-3   Use objects in the Area and Perimeter application

This exercise guides you through the process of converting an Area and Perimeter application from a procedural application to an object-oriented application.

Create and use an object

1. Open the project named ch07_ex3_AreaAndPerimeter that's stored in the ex_starts folder. Then, review the code for the AreaAndPerimeterApp class.

2. Create a class named Rectangle and store it in the same package as the AreaAndPerimeterApp class.

3. In the Rectangle class, add instance variables for length and width. Then, code the get and set methods for these instance variables. If possible, use your IDE to generate the get and set methods. With NetBeans, you can get started by selecting the Refactor→Encapsulate Fields command.

4. Add a constructor with no parameters that initializes the length and width to 0.

5. Add a get method that calculates the area of the rectangle and returns a double value for the result. If you want, you can copy the code that performs this calculation from the AreaAndPerimeterApp class.

6. Add a get method that returns the area as a String object with standard numeric formatting and a minimum of three decimal places. To make it easy to refer to the NumberFormat class, you should add an import statement for it.

7. Repeat the previous two steps for the perimeter.

8. Display the AreaAndPerimeterApp class. Then, add code that creates a Rectangle object and sets its length and width.

9. Modify the code that displays the calculations so it uses the methods of the Rectangle object to get the area and perimeter of the rectangle.

10. Remove any leftover code from the AreaAndPerimeterApp class that's unnecessary, including any unnecessary import statements.

11. Run the application and test it with valid data. It should calculate the area and perimeter for a rectangle.

Overload the constructor

12. Display the Rectangle class. Then, overload the constructor by adding a second constructor that accepts two parameters: length and width. This constructor should set the length and width of the rectangle to the values supplied by these parameters.

13. Display the AreaAndPerimeterApp class. Then, modify its code so it uses this constructor instead of the constructor with no parameters.

14. Run the application and test it to make sure it still works correctly.

8

How to work with inheritance

Inheritance is one of the key concepts of object-oriented programming. It lets you create a class that's based on another class. When used correctly, inheritance can reduce code duplication and simplify the overall design of an application.

An introduction to inheritance

Inheritance allows you to create a class that's based on another class. The next two figures introduce some of the basic concepts of inheritance.

How inheritance works

Figure 8-1 illustrates how inheritance works. When inheritance is used, a *subclass* inherits the fields and methods of a *superclass*. Then, when you create an object from the subclass, that subclass can use these fields and methods. The subclass can also provide its own fields and methods that *extend* the superclass, and it can *override* fields and methods of the superclass by providing new code for them.

The three classes presented in this figure show how this works. Here, the superclass is the Product class. This class has eight public methods. By now, you should already be familiar with the first seven methods. And the next two figures show how to work with the eighth method, the toString() method.

In this figure, the Product class has two subclasses: the Book and Software classes. These classes inherit the first eight methods from the Product class. Then, they both extend the Product class by providing two new methods. In particular, the Book class adds the setAuthor() and getAuthor() methods, and the Software class adds the setVersion() and getVersion() methods.

In this book, we'll primarily use superclass to refer to a class that another class inherits and subclass to refer to a class that inherits another class. However, a superclass can also be called a *base* or *parent class*, and a subclass can also be called a *derived* or *child class*.

Business classes for a Product Manager application

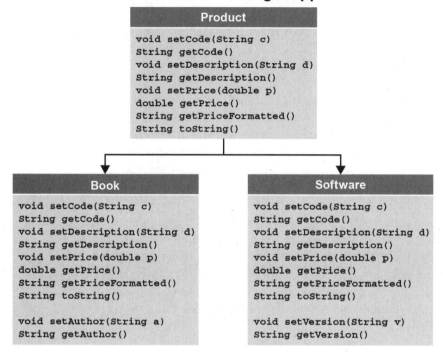

Description

- *Inheritance* lets you create a new class based on an existing class. Then, the new class *inherits* the fields and methods of the existing class.

- A class that inherits from an existing class is called a *derived class*, *child class,* or *subclass.*

- A class that another class inherits is called a *base class*, *parent class*, or *superclass.*

- A subclass can *extend* the superclass by adding new fields and methods to the superclass. It can also *override* a method from the superclass with its own version of the method.

Figure 8-1   How to use inheritance in your applications

How the Object class works

The Object class is the superclass for all Java classes. In other words, every class automatically inherits the Object class. As a result, the methods of the Object class are available from every object. Some of the most common methods of the Object class are summarized in figure 8-2. Since subclasses often override these methods, these methods may work differently from class to class. For example, you'll learn how to override the toString() method in the next figure.

Perhaps the most common method of the Object class is the toString() method. That's because the Java compiler implicitly calls this method when it needs a string representation of an object. For example, when you supply an object as the argument of the println() method, this method implicitly calls the toString() method of the object.

When you code a class, it's generally considered a good practice to override the toString() method of the Object class to provide more detailed information about the object. If possible, this information should be concise, informative, and easy for a person to read. Otherwise, the toString() method that's provided by the Object class returns the name of the class, followed by the @ symbol and a hexadecimal representation of the *hash code* of the object. In case you aren't familiar with hexadecimal, it is a numbering system with a base of 16. To represent the 16 values, Java uses the numbers 0-9 plus the letters a-f.

In contrast, the hashCode() method returns an int value that represents the hash code of the object in base 10. If necessary, other code can use the hash code of an object when storing or manipulating the object.

If you need to compare objects of a class for equality, you can override the equals() method of the class so it compares two objects to check whether their instance variables are equal as shown later in this chapter. Otherwise, the equals() method of the Object class returns true only if the two variables refer to the same object. In other words, it might return false, even if the two variables refer to objects that store the same data.

The Object class

```
java.lang.Object
```

Methods of the Object class

Method	Description
toString()	Returns a String object containing the class name, followed by the @ symbol and a hexadecimal representation of the hash code for this object. If that's not what you want, you can override this method as shown in the next figure.
equals(Object)	Returns true if this variable refers to the same object as the specified variable. Otherwise, it returns false, even if both variables refer to objects that contain the same data. If that's not what you want, you can override the equals() method as shown later in this chapter.
getClass()	Returns a Class object that represents the type of this object.
clone()	Returns a copy of this object as an Object object. Before you can use this method, the class must implement the Cloneable interface.
hashCode()	Returns an int value that represents the hash code for this object.

A typical value returned by a Product object's toString() method

```
murach.business.Product@15db9742
```

A typical value returned by a Product object's hashCode() method

```
366712642
```

Description

- The Object class in the java.lang package is the superclass for all classes. In other words, every class inherits the Object class or some other class that ultimately inherits the Object class. As a result, the methods defined by the Object class are available to all classes.

- When coding classes, it's recommended that you override the toString() method so it returns a string that's concise, informative, and easy for a person to read.

Figure 8-2   How the Object class works

Basic skills for working with inheritance

Now that you've been introduced to the basic concepts of inheritance, you're ready to learn the details for coding superclasses and subclasses. In addition, you'll learn how to work with one of the major features of inheritance, polymorphism.

How to create a superclass

Figure 8-3 shows how to create a class that can be used as a superclass for one or more subclasses. To do that, you define the fields, constructors, and methods of the class just as you would for any other class.

The table in this figure lists several *access modifiers* you can use to indicate whether members of a superclass are accessible to other classes. By now, you should be familiar with the private and public access modifiers. To review, you use the private keyword for any fields or methods that you want only to be available within the current class. In contrast, you use the public keyword for any fields or methods that you want to be available to all other classes.

Beyond that, you may occasionally want to use the protected keyword to code *protected members*. A protected member is a member that can be accessed within the defining class, any class in the same package, and any class that inherits the defining class, but not by any other class. This lets subclasses access certain parts of the superclass without exposing those parts to other classes. For example, the Product class in this figure includes a static field named count that has protected access. As a result, any subclass of the Product class can access this field, regardless of whether the subclass is in the same package as the Product class.

You can also code a field or method without an access modifier. Then, the classes in the same package are able to access the field or method, but classes in other packages aren't able to do that.

The Product class shown in this figure includes a toString() method that overrides the toString() method of the java.lang.Object class. This method returns the description for the product, which is a concise and easy-to-read representation of this object. As a result, any subclasses of this class can use this toString() method. Or, they can override the toString() method to provide their own code for that method.

When you override a method, it's generally considered a good practice to add an *annotation* to the method in the subclass to clearly indicate that the method in the subclass overrides the method in the superclass. An annotation is a standard way to provide information about your code that can be used by the compiler, the JRE, and other software development tools. In this figure, for example, an @Override annotation is coded above the toString() method.

Although this annotation isn't required, it's helpful for two reasons. First, the compiler can use this information to make sure that the toString() method correctly overrides the toString() method in the superclass. If it doesn't, the compiler can generate an error. Second, this makes it easy for other programmers to see that this method overrides a method in the superclass.

Access modifiers

Keyword	Description
`private`	Available within the current class.
`public`	Available to classes in all packages.
`protected`	Available to classes in the same package and to subclasses.
no keyword coded	Available to classes in the same package.

An annotation for overriding a method

```
@Override
// method declaration goes here
```

The code for the Product superclass

```java
import java.text.NumberFormat;

public class Product {

    private String code;
    private String description;
    private double price;
    protected static int count = 0;

    public Product() {
    }

    // get and set accessors for the code, description, and price
    // instance variables

    @Override
    public String toString() {
        return description;
    }

    public static int getCount()  {   // create public access for the
                                       // count variable
        return count;
    }
}
```

Description

- *Access modifiers* specify the accessibility of the members declared by a class.
- *Protected members* are accessible to the current class, to other classes in the same package, and to subclasses.
- An *annotation* is a standard way to provide information about your code. When you override a method, you can add the @Override annotation to the method.

Figure 8-3   How to create a superclass

How to create a subclass

Figure 8-4 shows how to create a subclass. To indicate that a class is a subclass, you follow the class name on the class declaration with the extends keyword and the name of the superclass that the subclass inherits. For example, the code for the Book class shown in this figure specifies that the Book class extends the Product class. In other words, the Book class is a subclass of the Product class.

After you declare the subclass, you can extend the functionality of the superclass by adding fields, constructors, and methods. In this figure, for example, the Book class adds a new instance variable and a new constructor. It also adds new setAuthor() and getAuthor() methods, and it overrides the toString() method defined by the Product class.

The constructor for the Book subclass starts by using the super keyword to call the default constructor of the Product class. This initializes the code, description, and price fields. Next, this constructor assigns a default value of an empty string to the author field. Finally, this constructor increments the count field. This constructor can access this field because the superclass declared it with protected access.

To override a method of the superclass, you just code a method with the same signature as the method in the superclass. In this case, the toString() method of the Book class overrides the toString() method of the Product class. This method accepts no parameters and returns a string. The code within this method uses the super keyword to call the toString() method of the Product class. This method returns a string representation of the Product object. Then, this code appends the author's name to this string. Finally, it returns the string. Note that the toString() method of the Book class is clearly marked with the @Override annotation.

The syntax for creating subclasses

To declare a subclass

```
public class SubclassName extends SuperClassName{}
```

To call a superclass constructor

```
super(argumentList)
```

To call a superclass method

```
super.methodName(argumentList)
```

The code for a Book subclass

```
public class Book extends Product {

    private String author;

    public Book() {
        super();  // call constructor of Product superclass
        author = "";
        count++;
    }

    public void setAuthor(String author) {
        this.author = author;
    }

    public String getAuthor() {
        return author;
    }

    @Override
    public String toString() {        // override the toString() method
        return super.toString() +     // call method of Product superclass
            " by " + author;
    }
}
```

Description

- You can directly access fields that have public or protected access in the superclass from the subclass.

- You can extend the superclass by adding new fields and methods to the subclass.

- You can override the public and protected methods in the superclass by coding methods in the subclass that have the same signatures as methods in the superclass. However, you can't override private methods in the superclass because they aren't available to the subclass.

- You use the super keyword to call a constructor or method of the superclass. If you call a constructor of the superclass, it must be the first statement in the constructor of the subclass.

Figure 8-4   How to create a subclass

How polymorphism works

Polymorphism is one of the most important features of object-oriented programming and inheritance. As figure 8-5 shows, polymorphism lets you treat objects of different types as if they were the same type by referring to a superclass that's common to both objects. For example, the Book class presented in figure 8-4 inherits the Product class. As a result, you can treat a Book object as if it is a Product object.

One benefit of polymorphism is that you can write generic code that's designed to work with a superclass. Then, you can use that code with instances of any class that's derived from the superclass. For example, suppose you have a method named getDiscountPercent() that accepts a Product object as a parameter. Because the Book and Software classes both inherit the Product class, the getDiscountPercent() method also works with Book and Software objects.

The examples in this figure show how polymorphism works. To start, the first three examples show the toString() methods for the Product, Book, and Software classes. The Book version of the toString() method adds the author's name to the end of the string that's returned by the toString() method of the Product class. Similarly, the Software version adds the version number to the end of the string that's returned by the toString() method of the Product class.

The fourth example shows how polymorphism works with these classes. This code begins by creating an instance of the Book class, assigning it to a variable named b, and assigning values to its instance variables. After that, it creates an instance of the Software class, assigns it to a variable named s, and assigns values to its instance variables.

Next, a variable named p of type Product is declared, and the Book object is assigned to it. Then, the toString() method of the Product class is called. When the JRE sees that the p variable refers to a Book object and that this object contains an overridden version of the toString() method, it calls the overridden version of this method.

This example finishes by doing the same thing with the Software object. First, this Software object is assigned to the Product variable. Then, the toString() method defined by the Product class is called, which causes the toString() method of the Software class to be executed.

The key to polymorphism is that the decision on what method to call is based on the inheritance hierarchy at runtime. This can be referred to as *late binding*. At compile time, the compiler simply recognizes that a method with the specified signature exists.

Three versions of the toString() method

The toString() method in the Product superclass

```java
public String toString() {
    return description;
}
```

The toString() method in the Book class

```java
public String toString() {
    return super.toString() + " by " + author;
}
```

The toString() method in the Software class

```java
public String toString() {
    return super.toString() + " " + version;
}
```

Code that uses the overridden methods

```java
Book b = new Book();
b.setCode("java");
b.setDescription("Murach's Java Programming");
b.setPrice(57.50);
b.setAuthor("Joel Murach");

Software s = new Software();
s.setCode("netbeans");
s.setDescription("NetBeans");
s.setPrice(0.00);
s.setVersion("8.2");

Product p;
p = b;
System.out.println(p.toString());  // calls toString from the Book class
p = s;
System.out.println(p.toString());  // calls toString from the Software class
```

Description

- *Polymorphism* is a feature of inheritance that lets you treat objects of different subclasses that are derived from the same superclass as if they had the type of the superclass. If, for example, Book is a subclass of Product, you can treat a Book object as if it were a Product object.

- If you access a method of a superclass object and the method is overridden in the subclasses of that class, polymorphism determines which method is executed based on the object's type. For example, if you call the toString() method of a Product object, the toString() method of the Book class is executed if the object is a Book object.

Figure 8-5   How polymorphism works

The Product application

Now that you've learned how to code superclasses and subclasses, the following topics present a version of the Product application that uses inheritance. This version of the application uses both the Book and Software classes. In addition, it uses a ProductDB class that can return two distinct types of products: books and software.

The console

Figure 8-6 shows the console for the Product application. This application works much like the Product application presented in chapter 7. However, there are three main differences. First, this application displays an additional piece of information about each product, which varies depending on whether the product is a book or software. In particular, it displays the author for a book and the version number for software. Second, this application displays a count of the total number of objects it has created. Third, if the user enters an invalid product code, the application displays an appropriate error message.

The console for the Product application

```
Welcome to the Product Viewer

Enter product code: java

Description: Murach's Java Programming by Joel Murach
Price:          $57.50

Product count: 1

Continue? (y/n): y

Enter product code: netbeans

Description: NetBeans 8.2
Price:          $0.00

Product count: 2

Continue? (y/n): y

Enter product code: xxxx

No product matches this product code.

Continue? (y/n):
```

Description

- This version of the Product application handles two types of products: books and software.

- If you enter the product code for a book, the information about the product includes the author.

- If you enter the product code for software, the information about the product includes the version number.

Figure 8-6   The console for the Product application

The Product, Book, and Software classes

Figures 8-7 and 8-8 show the code for the Product superclass and its two subclasses, Book and Software. Since most of the code for the Product and Book classes was presented earlier in this chapter, you shouldn't have much trouble understanding how they work.

In addition, the Software class works like the Book class. As a result, you shouldn't have much trouble understanding it either. After it extends the Product class, it declares a private instance variable named version. Next, it provides a constructor that has no parameters that creates a new Software object with default values. This constructor also increments the count variable defined by the Product class. Finally, the Software class provides setVersion(), getVersion(), and toString() methods.

The toString() method of the Software class overrides the toString() method of the Product class. However, it uses the super keyword to call the toString() method of the Product class, which returns a string for the description of the product. Then, it appends information about the software version to the end of this string.

The ProductDB class

Figure 8-9 shows the code for the getProduct() method of the ProductDB class, which returns the Book and Software objects used by the Product application. Here, the return type for the getProduct() method is a Product object. Since the Book and Software classes are subclasses of the Product class, this method can return both Book and Software objects.

Within the getProduct() method, the first statement declares a Product variable named p and assigns a null to it. Then, if the user doesn't enter a product code that matches a product, this null is returned.

If the product code that's passed to this method matches one of the valid book codes, a new Book object is created. Then, the instance variables for that object are set depending on the book code. Finally, that Book object is assigned to the Product variable.

If, on the other hand, the product code that's passed to this method matches the code for a software product, a new Software object is created and its instance variables are set. Then, that Software object is assigned to the Product variable.

The last statement in this method returns the Product variable to the calling method. Here, the Product variable can contain a Book object, a Software object, or a null. As a result, the calling method can check whether the product code is valid by checking whether the Product variable is null.

This chapter presents the ProductDB class as part of an application that shows how inheritance works. However, this class is not a realistic way to get an object and fill it with data, since adding any new data would require updating and recompiling the source code. Typically, the data for an object is stored in a database as shown later in this book. Then, a class such as the ProductDB class can read the data from the database and return one or more objects that contain this data.

The code for the Product class

```java
import java.text.NumberFormat;

public class Product  {

    private String code;
    private String description;
    private double price;
    protected static int count = 0;

    public Product() {}

    public void setCode(String code) {
        this.code = code;
    }

    public String getCode(){
        return code;
    }

    public void setDescription(String description) {
        this.description = description;
    }

    public String getDescription()  {
        return description;
    }

    public void setPrice(double price) {
        this.price = price;
    }

    public double getPrice() {
        return price;
    }

    public String getPriceFormatted() {
        NumberFormat currency = NumberFormat.getCurrencyInstance();
        return currency.format(price);
    }

    @Override
    public String toString() {
        return description;
    }

    public static int getCount() {
        return count;
    }
}
```

Figure 8-7   The code for the Product class

The code for the Book class

```
public class Book extends Product   {

    private String author;

    public Book() {
        super();
        author = "";
        count++;
    }

    public void setAuthor(String author) {
        this.author = author;
    }

    public String getAuthor() {
        return author;
    }

    @Override
    public String toString() {
        return super.toString() + " by " + author;
    }
}
```

The code for the Software class

```
public class Software extends Product {

    private String version;

    public Software()   {
        super();
        version = "";
        count++;
    }

    public void setVersion(String version) {
        this.version = version;
    }

    public String getVersion() {
        return version;
    }

    @Override
    public String toString() {
        return super.toString() + " " + version;
    }
}
```

Figure 8-8   The code for the Book and Software classes

The code for the ProductDB class

```java
public class ProductDB {

    public static Product getProduct(String productCode) {
        // In a more realistic application, this code would
        // get the data for the product from a file or database.
        // For now, this code just uses if/else statements
        // to return the correct product data.

        Product p = null;

        if (productCode.equalsIgnoreCase("java")
                || productCode.equalsIgnoreCase("jsp")
                || productCode.equalsIgnoreCase("mysql")) {
            Book b = new Book();
            if (productCode.equalsIgnoreCase("java")) {
                b.setCode(productCode);
                b.setDescription("Murach's Java Programming");
                b.setPrice(57.50);
                b.setAuthor("Joel Murach");
            } else if (productCode.equalsIgnoreCase("jsp")) {
                b.setCode(productCode);
                b.setDescription("Murach's Java Servlets and JSP");
                b.setPrice(57.50);
                b.setAuthor("Mike Urban");
            } else if (productCode.equalsIgnoreCase("mysql")) {
                b.setCode(productCode);
                b.setDescription("Murach's MySQL");
                b.setPrice(54.50);
                b.setAuthor("Joel Murach");
            }
            p = b; // set Product object equal to the Book object
        } else if (productCode.equalsIgnoreCase("netbeans")) {
            Software s = new Software();
            s.setCode("netbeans");
            s.setDescription("NetBeans");
            s.setPrice(0.00);
            s.setVersion("8.2");
            p = s; // set Product object equal to the Software object
        }
        return p;
    }
}
```

Figure 8-9   The code for the ProductDB class

The ProductApp class

Figure 8-10 shows the code for this version of the ProductApp class. This code is similar to the code for the ProductApp class presented in chapter 7. However, in this version of the application, the getProduct() method of the ProductDB class returns a null if the product code is invalid. Otherwise, it returns a Product variable that refers to a Book or Software object that corresponds to the product code.

Within the loop, this class uses an if/else statement to test whether the Product variable contains a null. If it does, this code displays an error message. Otherwise, it calls the toString() method of the object that the Product variable refers to. If the object is a book, this calls the toString() method of the Book class. If the object is software, it calls the toString() method of the Software class. In other words, this statement uses polymorphism to determine which method to call.

In this application, the product code that's entered by the user determines whether a Book object or a Software object is created. As a result, the application doesn't know at compile time which version of the toString() method to call. At runtime, however, the JRE determines what type of object the Product variable refers to, and it calls the appropriate method.

The code for the ProductApp class

```java
import java.util.Scanner;

public class ProductApp {

    public static void main(String args[]) {
        // display a welcome message
        System.out.println("Welcome to the Product Viewer");
        System.out.println();

        // perform 1 or more selections
        Scanner sc = new Scanner(System.in);
        String choice = "y";
        while (choice.equalsIgnoreCase("y")) {
            System.out.print("Enter product code: ");
            String productCode = sc.nextLine();  // read the product code

            // get the Product object
            Product p = ProductDB.getProduct(productCode);

            // display the output
            System.out.println();
            if (p != null) {
                System.out.println("Description: " + p.toString());
                System.out.println("Price:        " + p.getPriceFormatted());
            } else {
                System.out.println("No product matches this product code.");
            }

            System.out.println();
            System.out.println("Product count: " + Product.getCount() + "\n");

            // see if the user wants to continue
            System.out.print("Continue? (y/n): ");
            choice = sc.nextLine();
            System.out.println();
        }
    }
}
```

Figure 8-10   The code for the ProductApp class

More skills for working with inheritance

Now that you've learned the basic skills for working with inheritance and polymorphism, you're ready to learn some additional skills for working with inheritance. You might not need to use these skills often, but they provide useful information about how Java works, and they are necessary for some types of applications.

How to cast objects

One potentially confusing aspect of using inheritance is knowing when to cast inherited objects explicitly. The basic rule is that Java can implicitly cast a subclass to its superclass, but you must use explicit casting if you want to treat a superclass object as one of its subclasses.

The first example in figure 8-11 shows how this works. To start, the first group of statements creates a Book object, assigns this object to a Book variable named b, and assigns values to the object's instance variables.

The second group of statements shows how you can cast a subclass to its superclass without explicitly coding a cast. The first statement in this group casts the Book object to a Product variable named p. Since this cast goes up the inheritance hierarchy (from more data to less), you don't need to explicitly code the cast. Once you perform a cast like this, you can't call methods that are specific to the subclass. For example, once you cast a Book object to a Product object, you can't call the setAuthor() method of the Book object. However, you can call methods of the Product class such as the setDescription() method.

The third group of statements shows how to explicitly cast a superclass to a subclass. Since this cast goes down the inheritance hierarchy (from less data to more), you need to code the class name within parentheses in the assignment statement before you code the name of the object you're casting. Here, the first statement casts a Product object to a Book object. This works because the Product object is actually the Book object that was created in the first group of statements. This makes all methods of the Book object available again and doesn't cause any of the data in the original Book object to be lost.

The fourth group of statements shows a cast that causes a ClassCastException to be thrown. Here, the first statement creates a Product object. Then, the second statement attempts to cast this object to the Book type. Since the Product variable named p2 refers to an instance of the Product class, not an instance of the Book class, an exception is thrown when this statement is executed.

The second example shows how you can check an object's type. This code uses the instanceof operator to check whether the variable named p is an instance of the Book object. You can use code like this to avoid a ClassCastException like the one shown by the last statement in the first example.

Code that casts Product and Book objects

```
Book b = new Book();
b.setCode("java");
b.setDescription("Murach's Beginning Java");
b.setAuthor("Andrea Steelman");
b.setPrice(49.50);

Product p = b;              // cast Book object to a Product object
p.setDescription("Test");   // OK - method in Product class
//p.setAuthor("Test");      // not OK - method not in Product class

Book b2 = (Book) p;         // cast the Product object back to a Book object
b2.setAuthor("Test");       // OK - method in Book class

Product p2 = new Product();
Book b3 = (Book) p2;        // throws a ClassCastException because
                            // p2 is a Product object not a Book object
```

Code that checks an object's type

```
Product p = new Book();     // create a Book object
if (p instanceof Book) {
    System.out.println("This is a Book object");
}
```

The console

```
This is a Book object
```

Description

- Java can implicitly cast a subclass to a superclass. As a result, you can use a subclass whenever a reference to its superclass is called for. For example, you can specify a Book object whenever a Product object is expected because Book is a subclass of Product.

- You must explicitly cast a superclass object when a reference to one of its subclasses is required. For example, you must explicitly cast a Product object to Book if a Book object is expected. This only works if the Product object is a valid Book object. Otherwise, this throws a ClassCastException.

- Casting affects the methods that are available from an object. For example, if you store a Book object in a Product variable, you can't call the setAuthor() method because it's defined by the Book class, not the Product class.

- You can use the instanceof operator to check if an object is an instance of a particular class.

Figure 8-11   How to cast objects and check an object's type

How to compare objects

As you learned earlier in this chapter, the Object class includes an equals() method that you can use to determine if two variables refer to the same object. In most cases, that's not the behavior you want when comparing objects for equality. Instead, you'll want to compare two objects to find out if they contain the same data. To do that, you can override the equals() method. In fact, many classes in the API, such as the String class, override this method.

The first two examples in figure 8-12 show how the equals() method of the Object class works when the Product class doesn't override the equals() method. In the first example, the first two statements create two variables that refer to the same object. Since both variables point to the same object, the expression that uses the equals() method to compare these variables evaluates to true.

In the second example, though, the first two statements create two objects that contain the same data. However, since the two variables in this example don't refer to the same object, the expression that uses the equals() method to compare these variables evaluates to false. But that's usually not what you want.

The third example shows how to code an equals() method in the Product class that overrides the equals() method of the Object class. To start, this method uses the same signature as the equals() method of the Object class, which returns a boolean value and accepts a parameter of the Object type. Then, an if statement uses the instanceof operator to make sure that the passed object is an instance of the Product class. If so, it casts the Object parameter to a Product object. Then, an if statement compares the three instance variables stored in the Product object with the instance variables stored in the current object. If all instance variables are equal, this statement returns true. Otherwise, it returns false. As a result, both the first and second examples in this figure return a true value if the Product class contains this method.

The fourth example shows how to code an equals() method in the LineItem class you saw in the previous chapter. The code for this method works the same as the code for the equals() method of the Product class. However, because a LineItem object contains a Product object, the equals() method of the LineItem class uses the equals() method of the Product class. As a result, you must code an equals() method for the Product class for this method to work correctly.

How the equals() method of the Object class works

Both variables refer to the same object

```
Product product1 = new Product();
Product product2 = product1;
if (product1.equals(product2))              // expression returns true
```

Both variables refer to different objects that store the same data

```
Product product1 = new Product();
Product product2 = new Product();
if (product1.equals(product2))              // expression returns false
```

How to override the equals() method of the Object class

The equals() method of the Product class

```
@Override
public boolean equals(Object object) {
    if (object instanceof Product)  {
        Product product2 = (Product) object;
        if (code.equals(product2.getCode()) &&
            description.equals(product2.getDescription()) &&
            price == product2.getPrice()) {
                return true;
        }
    }
    return false;
}
```

The equals() method of the LineItem class

```
@Override
public boolean equals(Object object) {
    if (object instanceof LineItem) {
        LineItem li = (LineItem) object;
        if (product.equals(li.getProduct()) &&
            quantity == li.getQuantity()) {
                return true;
        }
    }
    return false;
}
```

Description

- To test if two objects variables refer to the same object, you can use the equals() method of the Object class.

- To test if two objects store the same data, you can override the equals() method in the subclass so it tests whether all instance variables in the two objects are equal.

- Many classes from the Java API (such as the String class) already override the equals() method to test for equality.

Figure 8-12   How to compare objects by overriding the equals() method

How to work with the abstract and final keywords

The last two figures in this chapter show how you can require or restrict the use of inheritance in the classes you create by using the abstract and final keywords.

How to work with the abstract keyword

An *abstract class* is a class that can't be instantiated. In other words, you can't create an object directly from an abstract class. Instead, you can code a class that inherits an abstract class, and you can create an object from that class.

Figure 8-13 shows how to work with abstract classes. To declare an abstract class, you include the abstract keyword in the class declaration as shown in the Product class at the top of this figure. Within an abstract class, you can use the abstract keyword to code *abstract methods*. For example, the Product class shown here includes an abstract method named getDisplayText() that returns a string. The declaration for this method includes the abstract keyword, it ends with a semicolon, and no method body is coded.

When you include abstract methods in an abstract class, you must override them in any class that inherits the abstract class. This is illustrated in the second example in this figure. Here, a class named Book that inherits the Product class overrides the abstract getDisplayText() method that's defined by that class.

When you work with an abstract class, you can still declare a variable of the abstract type. However, you can't use the new keyword to create an instance of the abstract type. For example, you can still declare a Product variable from the Product class in this figure. However, you can't use the new keyword to create a Product object to store in this variable. Instead, you must store a Book or Software object in the Product variable.

So, why you would use abstract classes? One common use is to implement most, but not all, of the functionality of a class as a convenience to the programmer. That way, the programmer must code only a few abstract methods that are specific to the subclass.

An abstract Product class

```
public abstract class Product {
    private String code;
    private String description;
    private double price;

    // regular constructors and methods for instance variables

    @Override
    public String toString() {
        return description;
    }

    public abstract String getDisplayText();  // an abstract method
}
```

A class that inherits the abstract Product class

```
public class Book extends Product {
    private String author;

    // regular constructor and methods for the Book class

    @Override
    public String getDisplayText()  {  // implement the abstract method
        return super.toString() + " by " + author;
    }
}
```

Description

- An *abstract class* is a class that can be inherited by other classes but that you can't use to create an object. To declare an abstract class, code the abstract keyword in the class declaration.

- An abstract class can contain fields, constructors, and methods just like other superclasses. In addition, an abstract class can contain abstract methods.

- To create an *abstract method*, you code the abstract keyword in the method declaration and you omit the method body. Abstract methods cannot have private access. However, they may have protected or default access (no access modifier).

- When a subclass inherits an abstract class, all abstract methods in the abstract class must be overridden in the subclass. Otherwise, the subclass must also be abstract.

- An abstract class doesn't have to contain abstract methods. However, any class that contains an abstract method must be declared as abstract.

Figure 8-13   How to work with the abstract keyword

How to work with the final keyword

Figure 8-14 shows how to use the final keyword to declare *final classes, final methods*, and *final parameters*. You can use this keyword whenever you want to make sure that no one can override or change your classes, methods, or parameters. When you declare a final class, other programmers won't be able to create a subclass from your class. When you declare a final method, other programmers won't be able to override that method. And when you declare a final parameter, other programmers won't be able to assign a new value to that parameter.

In early versions of Java, using final methods sometimes resulted in a significant performance gain. However, with modern versions of Java, the performance gain is almost nonexistent.

So, why would you want to use final classes, methods, or parameters? The main reason is because you may not want other programmers to be able to change the behavior of a method or a class. For example, you may need to make a method public so other programmers can use it. However, changing that method in a subclass might cause the method to not work properly. In that case, you can declare the method as final.

The first example shows how to declare a final class. This example declares the Book class that inherits the Product class as final. When you declare a final class like this, all methods in the class automatically become final methods.

The second example shows how to declare a final method. Since this method is in the Software class, which hasn't been declared as final, the class can still be inherited by other classes. However, any class that inherits the Software class won't be able to override the getVersion() method.

The third example shows how you can declare a final parameter when you're coding a method. In most cases, there's no reason to declare a parameter as final. However, in some rare cases, you may need to declare a parameter as final to guarantee that the parameter cannot change. In these cases, the compiler usually gives a warning that the variable must be final or effectively final. Then, you can add the final keyword to the declaration of the parameter.

In most cases, you'll declare an entire class as final rather than declaring specific methods as final. Because of that, you typically don't need to worry about whether individual methods of a class are final. However, if you encounter final methods, you should now understand how they work.

A final class

```
public final class Book extends Product {
    // all methods in the class are automatically final
}
```

A final method

```
public final String getVersion() {
    return version;
}
```

A final parameter

```
public void setVersion(final String version)  {

    // version = "new value"; // not allowed
    this.version = version;
}
```

Description

- To prevent a class from being inherited, you can create a *final class* by coding the final keyword in the class declaration.

- To prevent subclasses from overriding a method of a superclass, you can create a *final method* by coding the final keyword in the method declaration. In addition, all methods in a final class are automatically final methods.

- To prevent a method from assigning a new value to a parameter, you can code the final keyword in the parameter declaration to create a *final parameter*. Then, if a statement in the method tries to assign a new value to the parameter, the compiler reports an error.

Figure 8-14   How to work with the final keyword

Perspective

Conceptually, this is one of the most difficult chapters in this book. Although the basic idea of inheritance isn't that difficult to understand, the complications of polymorphism, overriding, and casting make inheritance a difficult topic. So if you find yourself a bit confused right now, don't be disheartened. It will become clearer as you actually use the techniques you've learned here and see them used in the Java API.

The good news is that you don't have to understand every nuance of how inheritance works to use it. In fact, since all classes automatically inherit the Object class, you've already been using inheritance without even knowing it. Now that you've completed this chapter, you should have a better understanding of how the Java API works. In addition, you should have a better idea of how you can use inheritance to improve the design of your own classes.

Summary

- *Inheritance* lets you create a new class based on an existing class. The existing class is called the *superclass*, *base class*, or *parent class*, and the new class is called the *subclass*, *derived class*, or *child class*.

- A subclass inherits all of the fields and methods of its superclass that aren't private. The subclass can *extend* the superclass by adding its own fields and methods, and it can *override* a method with a new version of the method.

- All classes inherit the java.lang.Object class. This class provides methods, such as the toString() and equals() methods, that are available to all classes.

- You can use *access modifiers* to limit the accessibility of the fields and methods declared by a class. *Protected members* can be accessed only by classes in the same package or by subclasses.

- An *annotation* is a standard way to provide information about your code to other software tools and developers. When you override a method, it's generally considered a good practice to add the @Override annotation to the method.

- In a subclass, you can use the super keyword to access the fields, constructors, and methods of the superclass.

- *Polymorphism* is a feature of inheritance that lets you treat subclasses as though they were their superclass.

- Java can implicitly cast a subclass type to its superclass type, but you must use explicit casting to cast a superclass type to a subclass type.

- You can use the instanceof operator to check if an object is an instance of a particular class.

- *Abstract classes* can be inherited by other classes but can't be used to create an object. Abstract classes can include *abstract methods*.

- If you extend an abstract class, you must implement all abstract methods. Otherwise, you must also declare your class as abstract.

- You can use the final keyword to declare *final classes*, *final methods*, and *final parameters*. No class can inherit a final class, no method can override a final method, and no statement can assign a new value to a final parameter.

Exercise 8-1   Use inheritance with the Product application

In this exercise, you'll modify the Product application shown in this chapter so it provides for an additional kind of product: a music album. When you enter the code for a music album, it should look like this:

```
Enter product code: sgtp

Description: Sgt. Peppers (The Beatles)
Price:       $14.99

Product count: 1
```

Create a new subclass named Album

1. Open the project named ch08_ex1_Product that's in the ex_starts folder. Then, review the code.

2. Create a new class named Album that inherits the Product class. This new class should store data about the artist of the album. In addition, its toString() method should append the name of the artist to the end of the string as shown above.

Modify the ProductDB class so it returns an Album object

3. Modify the ProductDB class so it creates at least one Album object.

4. Run the application to make sure that it works correctly.

Modify the protected variable

5. Open the Product class and delete the protected access modifier for the count variable. This restricts the availability of this variable even further, making it only available to the other classes in the current package.

6. Run the application to make sure that the count is maintained properly.

Exercise 8-2   Use the abstract and final keywords

In this exercise, you'll experiment with the abstract and final keywords to see how they work.

Use an abstract class with an abstract method

1. Open the project named ch08_ex2_Product that's in the ex_starts folder. Then, review the code.

2. Open the Product class. Then, add the abstract keyword to the class declaration.

3. In the Product class, add an abstract method named getDisplayText(). This method should accept no parameters, and it should return a String object.

4. Attempt to compile the application. This should display an error message that indicates that the Book and Software classes must override the getDisplayText() method.

5. Open the Book and Software classes. Then, add a getDisplayText() method to these classes that overrides the abstract getDisplayText() method of the Product class. One easy way to do that is to rename the toString() method to getDisplayText().

6. Open the ProductApp class. Then, modify it so it calls the getDisplayText() method of a product object instead of the toString() method.

7. Run the application to make sure it works correctly.

Use a final class

8. In the Book class, add the final keyword to its class declaration.

9. Create a new class named UsedBook that inherits the Book class. You don't need to include any code in the body of this class. This should display an error message that indicates that the Book class can't be inherited because it is final.

10. In the Book class, remove the final keyword from its class declaration.

11. Run the application to make sure it works correctly.

Use a final method

12. In the Book class, add the final keyword to the getDisplayText() method.

13. Add a getDisplayText() method to the UsedBook class to override the getDisplayText() method of the Book class. This method can return an empty string. This should display an error message that indicates that the getDisplayText() method can't be overridden because it is final.

14. In the Book class, remove the final keyword from the getDisplayText() method.

15. Run the application to make sure it works correctly.

Exercise 8-3   Code an equals() method

In this exercise, you'll add an equals() method to the Product and LineItem classes that you can use to compare the instance variables of two objects.

1. Open the project named ch08_ex3_EqualsTest in the ex_starts folder. This application creates and compares two Product objects and two LineItem objects using the equals() method. Review this code to see how it works.

2. Run the project. Since the equals() method isn't overridden in the Product or LineItem class, the output from this application should indicate that the comparisons are based on object references and not the data the objects contain like this:

```
The Product class is comparing references.
The LineItem class is comparing references.
```

3. Open the Product class, and add an equals() method as shown in this chapter. Then, run the project again. This time, the output should indicate that the products are being compared based on their data like this:

```
The Product class is comparing data.
The LineItem class is comparing references.
```

4. Repeat step 3 for the LineItem class. This time, the comparisons for both the products and line items should be based on their data like this:

```
The Product class is comparing data.
The LineItem class is comparing data.
```

9

How to define and use interfaces

Interfaces are similar to abstract classes. However, they have several advantages that make them easier to create and more flexible to use.

The Java API defines hundreds of interfaces, and many classes in the Java API use these interfaces. You can also use interfaces from the Java API in your own applications. In addition, you can create and use your own interfaces.

An introduction to interfaces

In some object-oriented programming languages, such as C++, a class can inherit more than one class. This is known as *multiple inheritance*. Although Java doesn't support multiple inheritance, it does support a special type of coding element known as an *interface*. An interface provides many of the advantages of multiple inheritance without some of the problems that are associated with it.

A simple interface

Figure 9-1 illustrates how you create and use an interface. Here, the first example shows the code for a simple interface named Printable. This code is similar to the code that defines a class and is stored in a file named Printable. java. However, the code for an interface uses the interface keyword instead of the class keyword. In addition, all of the methods in an interface are automatically public and abstract. As a result, you don't need to code the public or abstract keywords for the methods in an interface.

The second example shows a Product class that *implements* the Printable interface. To implement the Printable interface, the declaration for the Product class uses the implements keyword followed by the name of the interface. Then, the body of the Product class implements the print() method that's specified by the Printable interface.

The third example shows that a Product object that implements the Printable interface can be stored in a variable of the Printable type. In other words, an object created from the Product class shown in this figure is both a Product object and a Printable object. As a result, you can use this object anywhere a Printable object is expected as shown later in this chapter.

A Printable interface that defines an abstract print() method

```java
public interface Printable {
    void print();        // this method is automatically public and abstract
}
```

A Product class that implements the Printable interface

```java
import java.text.NumberFormat;

public class Product implements Printable {
    private String code;
    private String description;
    private double price;

    public Product(String code, String description, double price) {
        this.code = code;
        this.description = description;
        this.price = price;
    }

    // get and set methods for the fields

    public void print()        // implement the Printable interface
        System.out.println(description);
    }
}
```

Code that uses the print() method of the Product class

```java
Printable p = ProductDB.get("java");
p.print();
```

Resulting output

```
Murach's Java Programming
```

Description

- An *interface* can define one or more methods. These methods are automatically public and abstract. As a result, the interface only specifies the method signatures, not any code that implements the methods.

- A class that *implements* an interface can use any constants defined by the interface. In addition, it must provide an implementation for each abstract method defined by the interface. If it doesn't, the class must be declared as abstract.

Figure 9-1   A simple interface

Interfaces compared to abstract classes

So, how does an interface compare to an abstract class like the abstract class presented in the last chapter? Figure 9-2 shows the similarities and differences and lists some of the advantages of each.

Abstract classes and interfaces are similar in some ways. To start, with all versions of Java, both abstract classes and interfaces can define abstract methods and static constants. In addition, you can't create an object from an abstract class or an interface.

Abstract classes and interface also have some important differences. To start, with all versions of Java, an abstract class can also define and use other types of fields such as instance variables, and it can define regular methods and static methods. However, interfaces can't.

Java 8 introduced two new features that make interfaces more powerful. First, they can define *default methods*, which work much like regular methods in a class. Second, they can define static methods. As a result, with Java 8 and later, abstract classes have fewer advantages over interfaces. In addition, interfaces have always had one important advantage over abstract classes: a class can implement multiple interfaces, but it can only inherit one class.

To illustrate, suppose you want to create several types of products, such as books, software, and music albums, and you want each type of product to have a print() method that prints information about the product that's appropriate for the product type. You could implement this hierarchy using inheritance, with an abstract Product class at the top of the hierarchy and Book, Software, and Album classes that extend the Product class. Then, the Product class would provide features common to all products, such as a product code, description, and price. In addition, the Product class would declare an abstract print() method, and the Book, Software, and Album classes would provide their own implementations of this method.

The drawback of this approach is that there are undoubtedly other objects in the applications that use these classes that can be printed as well. For example, objects such as invoices and customers have information that can be printed. Obviously, these objects wouldn't inherit the abstract Product class, so they'd have to define their own print() methods.

In contrast, if you created a Printable interface like the one in this figure, it could be implemented by any class that represents an object that can be printed. One advantage of this is that it enforces consistency within the application by guaranteeing that any Printable object will be printed using a method named print(). Without the interface, some printable objects might use a method called print(), while others might use methods with names like display() or show().

More importantly, an interface defines a Java type, so any object that implements an interface is marked as that interface type. As a result, an object that's created from a Book class that extends the Product class and implements the Printable interface is not only an object of the Book type and of the Product type, but also an object of the Printable type. That means you can use the object, or any other object that implements the Printable interface, wherever a Printable type is called for. You'll see examples of this later in this chapter.

An abstract class compared to an interface

Abstract class
Variables
Constants
Static variables
Static constants
Methods
Static methods
Abstract methods

Interface
Static constants
Methods (new with Java 8)
Static methods (new with Java 8)
Abstract methods

A Printable interface

```
public interface Printable {
    void print();
}
```

A Printable abstract class

```
public abstract class Printable {
    public abstract void print();
}
```

Advantages of an abstract class

- An abstract class can use instance variables and constants as well as static variables and constants. Interfaces can only use static constants.

- An abstract class can define regular methods that contain code. Prior to Java 8, an interface couldn't define regular methods.

- An abstract class can define static methods. Prior to Java 8, an interface couldn't define static methods.

Advantages of an interface

- A class can only directly inherit one other class, but a class can implement multiple interfaces.

Description

- A *default method* of an interface works much like a regular (non-static) method of a class.

Figure 9-2   Interfaces compared to abstract classes

Basic skills for working with interfaces

Now that you have an idea of how interfaces work, you're ready to learn some basic skills for coding and implementing them. To get you started, the next five figures show how to work with interfaces using the features that were available prior to Java 8.

How to code an interface

Figure 9-3 shows how to code an interface. To start, you code the public keyword, followed by the interface keyword, followed by the name of the interface. When you name an interface, it's common to end the name with a suffix of "able" or "er". For example, the Java API uses names like Cloneable, Comparable, EventListener, ActionListener, and so on. Another common naming strategy is to prefix the name of an interface with "I". For example, some programmers use names such as IProduct.

The first example in this figure shows the code for the Printable interface. This interface contains a single abstract method named print that doesn't accept any arguments or return any data. As with all abstract methods, you don't code braces at the end of the method. Instead, you code a semicolon immediately after the parentheses.

The second example shows the code for an interface named ProductWriter. This interface contains three abstract methods: add(), update(), and delete(). All three of these methods accept a Product object as an argument and return a boolean value that indicates whether the operation was successful.

The third example shows how to code an interface that defines constants. In this case, an interface named DepartmentConstants defines three constants that map departments to integer values. You'll see how you can use constants like these in the next figure.

When you code an abstract method in an interface, you don't have to use the public and abstract keywords. That's because Java automatically supplies these keywords for all methods. Similarly, Java automatically supplies the public, static, and final keywords for constants. As a result, most programmers typically don't code these keywords in their interfaces. However, you can code these keywords if you think they help clarify the code.

The fourth example shows the code for an interface named Serializable. This interface is available from the java.io package of the Java API, and it's designed to let programmers identify objects that can be stored (serialized) and then later reconstructed (unserialized) for reuse. For example, you might use this interface if you want to transport an object over a network or save an object to disk. Since this interface contains no constants or methods, it is known as a *tagging interface*. To code a tagging interface, you code an interface that doesn't contain any constants or methods.

The syntax for declaring an interface

```
public interface InterfaceName {
    type CONSTANT_NAME = value;          // static constant
    returnType methodName([parameterList]);  // abstract method
}
```

An interface that defines one abstract method

```
public interface Printable {
    void print();
}
```

An interface that defines three abstract methods

```
public interface ProductWriter {
    boolean add(Product p);
    boolean update(Product p);
    boolean delete(Product p);
}
```

An interface that defines three static constants

```
public interface DepartmentConstants {
    int ADMIN = 1;
    int EDITORIAL = 2;
    int MARKETING = 3;
}
```

A tagging interface with no members

```
public interface Serializable {
}
```

Description

- Declaring an interface is similar to declaring a class except that you use the interface keyword instead of the class keyword.

- In an interface, all methods are automatically declared public and abstract.

- In an interface, all fields are automatically declared public, static, and final.

- When working with an interface, you can code the public, abstract, and final keywords. However, they're optional.

- An interface that doesn't contain any methods is known as a *tagging interface*. This type of interface is typically used to identify that an object is safe for a certain type of operation such as cloning or serializing.

Figure 9-3   How to code an interface

How to implement an interface

Figure 9-4 shows how to code a class that implements an interface. To do that, you code the implements keyword after the name of the class, followed by the names of one or more interfaces separated by commas. For example, this figure shows a class named Employee that implements both the Printable and DepartmentConstants interfaces.

A class that implements an interface must implement all of the abstract methods defined by that interface. For example, the Employee class implements the Printable interface. As a result, it must implement the print() method declared by that interface. If this method isn't implemented, the class must be declared as abstract, or it won't compile.

Notice here that the print() method is preceded by the @Override annotation. Although this isn't required, it makes it clear that this method overrides the abstract print() method of the interface. This works just like it does for an abstract method of a class.

When a class implements an interface, you can use any of the constants defined by that interface. To do that, you can code the name of the constant without any qualification as shown in this figure. Here, the Employee class implements the DepartmentConstants interface. As a result, this class can use the ADMIN, EDITORIAL, and MARKETING constants defined by that interface. In this example, the print() method includes an if/else statement that uses these constants to determine the department name to include in the output.

If you want, you can qualify the constant with the name of the interface. To do that, code the name of the interface, followed by the dot operator and the name of the constant. For example, you can qualify the ADMIN constant like this:

```
DepartmentConstants.ADMIN
```

Although this makes it clear where the constant is stored, it also takes more code. As a result, most programmers typically omit the interface name when referring to constants.

Even if a class doesn't implement an interface, you can still use any of the constants defined by that interface. However, in that case, you must qualify the constant with the name of the interface as shown above.

The syntax for implementing an interface

```
public class ClassName implements Interface1[, Interface2]...{}
```

A class that implements two interfaces

```java
public class Employee implements Printable, DepartmentConstants {

    private int department;
    private String firstName;
    private String lastName;

    public Employee(int department, String lastName, String firstName) {
        this.department = department;
        this.lastName = lastName;
        this.firstName = firstName;
    }

    @Override
    public void print() {
        String dept = "Unknown";
        if (department == ADMIN) {
            dept = "Administration";
        } else if (department == EDITORIAL) {
            dept = "Editorial";
        } else if (department == MARKETING) {
            dept = "Marketing";
        }

        System.out.println(firstName + " " + lastName + " (" + dept + ")");
    }
}
```

Description

- To declare a class that implements an interface, you use the implements keyword. Then, you provide an implementation for each method defined by the interface.

- If you forget to implement a method that's defined by an interface that you're implementing, the compiler will issue an error message.

- A class that implements an interface can use any constant defined by that interface.

Figure 9-4   How to implement an interface

How to inherit a class and implement an interface

Figure 9-5 shows how to code a class that inherits another class and implements an interface. In particular, this figure shows how the Book class that you learned about in the previous chapter can inherit the Product class and implement the Printable interface. To do that, the declaration for the Book class uses the extends keyword to indicate that it inherits the Product class. Then, it uses the implements keyword to indicate that it implements the Printable interface. Finally, the Book class implements the print() method specified by the Printable interface. As a result, an object created from the Book class can be used anywhere a Book, Product, or Printable object is required.

In figure 9-1, you saw a Product class that implements the Printable interface. If the Book class inherits this version of the Product class, it automatically implements the Printable interface, and it can use the print() method implemented by the Product class. If you want, however, you can include the implements keyword on the declaration for the Book class to clearly show that this class implements the Printable interface. In that case, though, you don't need to implement the print() method since it's already implemented in the Product class. However, if you want, you can override this method. In this figure, for example, the Book class overrides the print() method to provide code that's different than the code provided by the print() method of the Product class.

The syntax for inheriting a class and implementing an interface

```
public class SubclassName extends SuperclassName implements Interface1
    [, Interface2]...{}
```

A Book class that inherits Product and implements Printable

```
public class Book extends Product implements Printable {

    private String author;

    public Book(String code, String description, double price,
            String author) {
        super(code, description, price);
        this.author = author;
    }

    public void setAuthor(String author) {
        this.author = author;
    }

    public String getAuthor() {
        return author;
    }

    @Override
    public void print() {    // implement the Printable interface
        System.out.println(super.getDescription() + " by " + author);
    }
}
```

Description

- A class can inherit another class and also implement one or more interfaces.
- If a class inherits another class that implements an interface, the subclass automatically implements the interface. However, you can code the implements keyword in the subclass for clarity.
- If a class inherits another class that implements an interface, the subclass has access to any methods of the interface that are implemented by the superclass and can override those methods.

Figure 9-5   How to inherit a class and implement an interface

How to use an interface as a parameter

Figure 9-6 shows how to code a method that uses an interface as the type for one of its parameters. When you do that, the statement that calls the method can pass any object that implements the interface to the method. Then, the method can call any of the methods that are defined by the interface and implemented by the object. You can use this type of code to create a flexible design that provides for processing objects created from different classes.

The first example in this figure shows a method named printMultiple that accepts two parameters. The first parameter is an object that implements the Printable interface, and the second parameter is an integer value that specifies the number of times to print the first parameter. Since the first parameter specifies Printable as the type, the printMultiple() method doesn't know the type of the object. However, it does know that the object contains a print() method. As a result, the code in the body of the method can call the print() method.

In the second example, the code uses the printMultiple() method to print two copies of a Product object to the console. This works because the Product class implements the Printable interface. Here, the first statement creates the Product object and assigns it to a variable of the Product type. Then, the second statement uses the printMultiple() method to print two copies of the Product object.

The third example works like the second example. The only difference is that it declares the variable using an interface as the type. In other words, it declares the variable as being of the Printable type. Then, you can assign any object that implements the interface to the variable, and you can pass the variable to any method that accepts the interface as a parameter. This code yields the same result as the second example, but it clearly shows that the Product object implements the Printable interface.

The fourth example also works like the second example. However, it prints one copy of an Employee object to the console. This is another way of showing that the printMultiple() method accepts any object that implements the Printable interface.

A method that accepts a Printable object

```
private static void printMultiple(Printable p, int count) {
    for (int i = 0; i < count; i++) {
        p.print();
    }
}
```

Code that passes a Product object to the method

```
Product product = new Product("java", "Murach's Java Programming", 57.50);
printMultiple(product, 2);
```

Resulting output

```
Murach's Java Programming
Murach's Java Programming
```

Another way to pass a Product object to the method

```
Printable product = new Product("java", "Murach's Java Programming", 57.50);
printMultiple(product, 2);
```

Code that passes an Employee object to the method

```
Employee employee = new Employee(
        DepartmentConstants.EDITORIAL, "Murach", "Joel");
printMultiple(employee, 1);
```

Resulting output

```
Joel Murach (Editorial)
```

Description

- You can declare a parameter that's used by a method as an interface type. Then, you can pass any object that implements the interface to the parameter.

- You can also declare a variable as an interface type. Then, you can assign an instance of any object that implements the interface to the variable, and you can pass the variable as an argument to a method that accepts the interface type.

Figure 9-6   How to use an interface as a parameter

How to use inheritance with interfaces

Figure 9-7 shows how one interface can inherit other interfaces. To start, this figure presents three interfaces: ProductReader, ProductWriter, and ProductConstants. Then, it presents a ProductDAO interface that inherits the first three interfaces. This interface is named ProductDAO because it defines an object that provides data access for products. In other words, DAO stands for "Data Access Object."

When an interface inherits other interfaces, any class that implements that interface must implement all of the abstract methods declared by that interface and the inherited interfaces. For example, if a class implements the ProductDAO interface, it must implement all of the methods defined by the ProductReader and ProductWriter interfaces. If it doesn't, the class must be declared as abstract so that no objects can be created from it.

When a class implements an interface that inherits other interfaces, it can use any of the constants stored in the interface or any of its inherited interfaces. For example, any class that implements the ProductDAO interface can use any of the constants in the ProductConstants interface.

When a class implements an interface that inherits other interfaces, you can use an object created from that class anywhere any of the interfaces in the inheritance hierarchy are expected. If a class implements the ProductDAO interface, for example, an object created from that class can be passed to a method that accepts the ProductReader type as a parameter. Similarly, the object can be passed to a method that accepts the ProductWriter type as a parameter. That's because any class that implements the ProductDAO interface must also implement the ProductReader and ProductWriter interfaces.

Although you can pass an object created from the ProductDAO interface to a method that accepts the ProductReader or ProductWriter type, you should realize that the method can only use methods and constants of the specified type. For example, if a method accepts the ProductReader type, it can only use the get() and getAll() methods. Similarly, if a method accepts the ProductWriter type, it can only use the add(), update(), and delete() methods.

The syntax for declaring an interface that inherits other interfaces

```
public interface InterfaceName
    extends InterfaceName1[, InterfaceName2]... {
    // the constants and methods of the interface
}
```

A ProductReader interface

```
public interface ProductReader {
    Product get(String code);
    String getAll();
}
```

A ProductWriter interface

```
public interface ProductWriter {
    boolean add(Product p);
    boolean update(Product p);
    boolean delete(Product p);
}
```

A ProductConstants interface

```
public interface ProductConstants {
    int CODE_SIZE = 5;
    int DESCRIPTION_SIZE = 34;
    int PRICE_SIZE = 10;
}
```

A ProductDAO interface that inherits these three interfaces

```
public interface ProductDAO extends ProductReader, ProductWriter,
        ProductConstants {
    // all methods and constants are inherited
}
```

Description

- An interface can inherit one or more other interfaces by specifying the inherited interfaces in an extends clause.

- An interface can't inherit a class.

- A class that implements an interface must implement all abstract methods declared by the interface as well as all abstract methods declared by any inherited interfaces unless the class is defined as abstract.

- A class that implements an interface can use any of the constants declared in the interface as well as any constants declared by any inherited interfaces.

Figure 9-7   How to use inheritance with interfaces

How to use NetBeans to work with interfaces

Figure 9-8 shows how NetBeans can make it easier to work with interfaces. To start, you can create an interface using a technique similar to the one you use to create a class. Then, NetBeans generates the declaration for the interface, and you can enter the constants and methods for the interface.

When coding a class that implements an interface, you can automatically generate all the method declarations for the interface. To do that, you click the yellow light bulb icon that appears to the left of the class declaration when you enter the implements keyword followed by the name of an interface. This displays a menu that includes the "Implement all abstract methods" command as shown in this figure. Then, you can select this command to generate the method declarations for the interface. In this figure, for example, NetBeans generated the method declarations that implement the ProductDAO interface. This saves you time and eliminates coding errors.

In the generated code, each method contains a single statement that throws an exception that indicates that the method is not supported yet. At this point, you can delete this statement and write the code that implements the method. For more information about the statement that throws the exception, see chapter 16.

A class that implements the ProductDAO interface

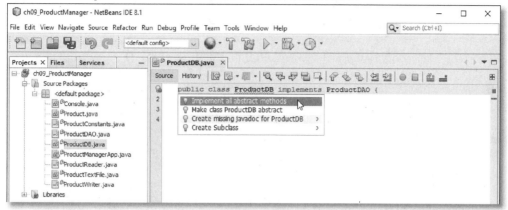

The code that's generated by NetBeans

```
public class ProductDB implements ProductDAO {

    @Override
    public Product get(String code) {
        throw new UnsupportedOperationException("Not supported yet.");
    }

    @Override
    public String getAll() {
        throw new UnsupportedOperationException("Not supported yet.");
    }

    @Override
    public boolean add(Product p) {
        throw new UnsupportedOperationException("Not supported yet.");
    }

    @Override
    public boolean update(Product p) {
        throw new UnsupportedOperationException("Not supported yet.");
    }

    @Override
    public boolean delete(Product p) {
        throw new UnsupportedOperationException("Not supported yet.");
    }
}
```

Description

- To add an interface to a project, right-click on the package you want to add the interface to, select the New→Java Interface command, and use the resulting dialog box to enter a name for the interface.

- When coding a class that implements an interface, you can automatically generate all the method declarations for the interface. To do that, create a new class as described in chapter 7, use the implements keyword to identify the interface, click on the light bulb icon in the left margin, and select the "Implement all abstract methods" command.

Figure 9-8   How to use NetBeans to work with interfaces

New features for working with interfaces

Now that you know how to work with interfaces using the features available prior to Java 8, you're ready to learn how to use the new features for interfaces available with Java 8 and later.

How to work with default methods

Prior to Java 8, interfaces could only contain abstract methods. This was a significant limitation and sometimes resulted in a lot of code duplication. For example, the print() method in the Printable interface may be virtually identical for most classes. However, using the techniques you've seen up until now, you'd still need to implement the print() method for every class that implements the Printable interface.

Fortunately, Java 8 provides a new feature that allows you to include regular (non-abstract) methods in interfaces. These methods are known as *default methods*. If a class implements an interface, it doesn't have to override the default methods of the interface. Instead, it can use these default methods. However, whenever necessary, a class can override a default method to change its functionality.

The first example in figure 9-9 shows an interface that declares a default method named print(). This method calls the toString() method from the object that implements the interface to get a String object that represents the object. Then, it prints that String object to the console.

The second example shows a class that implements this interface and uses the default print() method. Since this method is included in the interface, this class does not need to implement the print() method. Instead, it can use the functionality that's provided by the default method in the interface. This works as if the class had inherited the method from another class.

The third example shows a class that implements the interface in the first example and overrides the print() method. This allows the class to change the functionality that's provided by the default method. Again, this works as if the class had overridden a method in another class.

The syntax for declaring a default method (Java 8 and later)

```
default returnType methodName([parameterList]);
```

An interface that defines a default method

```
public interface Printable {
    default void print() {
        System.out.println(toString());
    }
}
```

A class that uses the default method

```
public class Product implements Printable {
    // This class doesn't override the print method.
    // As a result, it uses the print method defined by the interface.
}
```

A class that overrides the default method

```
public class Product implements Printable {
    @Override
    public void print() {
        System.out.println(getDescription() + "|" + getPriceFormatted());
    }
}
```

Description

- With Java 8 and later, you can add regular (non-abstract) methods to an interface. These methods are known as *default methods*.

- To add a regular method to an interface, you can begin the declaration for the method with the default keyword.

- When you code a class that implements an interface, you don't need to implement its default methods. Instead, you can use the default methods defined in the interface in your class. However, if you want to change the functionality of a default method, you can override it.

Figure 9-9   How to work with default methods

How to work with static methods

With Java 8 and later, you can also code static methods in interfaces. Since this works similarly to coding static methods in classes, you shouldn't have much trouble understanding how this works.

The first example in figure 9-10 shows an interface named Printer that includes a static print() method. This static method accepts a parameter of the Printable type. This method contains a single statement that calls the print() method of the Printable object.

The second example shows code that uses the Printer interface. To start, the first statement creates a Printable object named product. Then, the second statement passes this object to the static print() method of the Printer interface. As you can see, this works much like calling a static method from a class.

The syntax for declaring a static method (Java 8 and later)

```
static returnType methodName([parameterList]);
```

An interface that defines a static method

```
public interface Printer {
    static void print(Printable p) {
        p.print();
    }
}
```

Code that calls a static method from an interface

```
Printable product = new Product("java", "Murach's Java Programming", 57.50);
Printer.print(product);
```

Resulting output

```
Murach's Java Programming
```

Description

- With Java 8 and later, you can include static methods in interfaces.
- To call a static method from an interface, prefix the static method with the name of the interface.

Figure 9-10   How to work with static methods

The Product Viewer application

Now that you know the skills for creating and using interfaces, this chapter presents another version of the Product Viewer application that you saw in chapter 7. This version uses the ProductReader interface presented earlier in this chapter.

The console

Figure 9-11 shows the console for the Product Viewer application. From the user's perspective, this application works the same as earlier versions of the Product Viewer application. In short, it allows the user to enter a product code. Then, it displays the details of the product with the specified code.

The ProductReader interface

The ProductReader interface specifies the methods of the database layer for reading products: get() and getAll(). Here, the get() method returns a Product object for the specified code, and the getAll() method returns a string that represents the data for all products.

The ProductDB class

The ProductDB class in this figure is similar to the ProductDB class that you saw in chapter 7. However, this ProductDB class implements the ProductReader interface. To do that, it includes a regular get() method that implements the abstract get() method specified by the ProductReader interface. This method is like the getProduct() method you saw in chapter 7. The main difference is that the get() method isn't static. Because of that, any class that uses this method will have to create an instance of the ProductDB class.

In addition, this ProductDB class implements the abstract getAll() method specified by the ProductReader interface. To do that, it just throws an exception that indicates that the operation isn't supported yet. When you're developing classes that implement interfaces, it's common to start methods with code like this. Then, you can provide better implementations of these methods later as you develop the application. In this case, the Product Viewer application only needs the get() method, not the getAll() method. As a result, this version of the ProductDB class doesn't need to provide a better implementation of the getAll() method.

The console

```
Welcome to the Product Viewer

Enter product code: java

PRODUCT
Code:        java
Description: Murach's Java Programming
Price:       $57.50

Continue? (y/n):
```

The ProductReader interface

```java
public interface ProductReader {
    Product get(String code);
    String getAll();
}
```

The ProductDB class

```java
public class ProductDB implements ProductReader {

    public ProductDB() {}

    @Override
    public Product get(String productCode) {
        Product product = new Product();
        product.setCode(productCode);
        if (productCode.equalsIgnoreCase("java")) {
            product.setDescription("Murach's Java Programming");
            product.setPrice(57.50);
        } else if (productCode.equalsIgnoreCase("jsp")) {
            product.setDescription("Murach's Java Servlets and JSP");
            product.setPrice(57.50);
        } else if (productCode.equalsIgnoreCase("mysql")) {
            product.setDescription("Murach's MySQL");
            product.setPrice(54.50);
        } else {
            product.setDescription("Unknown");
        }
        return product;
    }

    @Override
    public String getAll() {
        throw new UnsupportedOperationException(
                "This method hasn't been implemented yet.");
    }
}
```

Figure 9-11   The console, ProductReader interface, and ProductDB class

The ProductApp class

Figure 9-12 shows the code for the ProductApp class. This code is similar to versions of the ProductApp class you've seen throughout this book. However, because the methods of the ProductDB class aren't static, it declares a ProductReader variable named reader and assigns a new ProductDB object to that variable. Then, it calls the get() method from the ProductReader object to get a Product object.

When you use an interface like this, you can minimize the connection between the presentation and database layers of the application. In this application, for example, the ProductApp class refers to the ProductDB class only when it creates an instance of that class. After that, it can use the reader variable to call methods of the ProductReader interface. Because of that, it would be easy to replace the ProductDB class with another class that implements the ProductReader interface.

The ProductApp class

```
import java.util.Scanner;

public class ProductApp {

    public static void main(String args[]) {
        // display a welcome message
        System.out.println("Welcome to the Product Viewer");
        System.out.println();

        // display 1 or more products
        Scanner sc = new Scanner(System.in);
        String choice = "y";
        while (choice.equalsIgnoreCase("y")) {
            // get input from user
            System.out.print("Enter product code: ");
            String productCode = sc.nextLine();

            // Use a ProductReader object to get the Product object
            ProductReader reader = new ProductDB();
            Product product = reader.get(productCode);

            // display the output
            String message = "\nPRODUCT\n" +
                "Code:        " + product.getCode() + "\n" +
                "Description: " + product.getDescription() + "\n" +
                "Price:       " + product.getPriceFormatted() + "\n";
            System.out.println(message);

            // see if the user wants to continue
            System.out.print("Continue? (y/n): ");
            choice = sc.nextLine();
            System.out.println();
        }
        System.out.println("Bye!");
    }
}
```

Figure 9-12   The ProductApp class

How to implement the Cloneable interface

Almost every package in the Java API includes one or more interfaces. To illustrate how you can use these interfaces in your own applications, this topic shows how to use the Cloneable interface.

The Cloneable interface is a general-purpose tagging interface in the java.lang package that lets you *clone* an object. That means that you create a new instance of the object that contains all the same data as the first object. To do that, you can call the clone() method of the Object class. But first, you must implement the Cloneable interface to tell the compiler that it's safe to use this method.

A Product class that implements the Cloneable interface

Figure 9-13 shows how to code a Product class that can be cloned. First, the Product class implements the Cloneable interface. This allows the Product class to call the clone() method of the Object class. However, the clone() method of the Object class has protected access. As a result, this method will only be available to subclasses and classes in the same package. To give public access to this method, the Product class overrides the clone() method of the Object class and gives it public access. Then, the clone() method of the Product class uses the super keyword to call the clone() method of the Object class. This clones the product, which is then returned to the calling method.

Because the clone() method of the Object class throws a CloneNotSupportedException, you must either throw or catch this exception when you override this method. In this example, you can see that the clone() method in the Product class throws this exception. You'll learn more about throwing exceptions in chapter 16.

The code that uses the clone() method of the Product class shows how the clone() method works. Here, the first group of statements creates a Product object and fills it with data. Then, the next statement uses the clone() method to make a copy of the Product object. Since the clone() method returns an Object type, this method casts the Object type to a Product type. At this point, the p1 and p2 variables both refer to their own copies of a Product object. As a result, you can change the price in one Product object without also changing the price in the other Product object.

By the way, it's a common mistake to try to clone an object using code like this:

```
Product p2 = p1;
```

However, this simply assigns the reference to an object that's stored in one variable to another variable. In other words, after executing this statement, both variables will refer to the same Product object. As a result, if you change the price in one variable, the price will also be changed in the other variable.

A Product class that implements the Cloneable interface

```java
public class Product implements Cloneable {
    private String code;
    private String description;
    private double price;

    // the code for the constructor and methods

    @Override
    public Object clone() throws CloneNotSupportedException {
        return super.clone();
    }
}
```

Code that uses the clone method of the Product class

```java
try {
    // create a new product
    Product p1 = new Product();
    p1.setCode("java");
    p1.setDescription("Murach's Java Programming");
    p1.setPrice(54.50);

    // clone the product
    Product p2 = (Product) p1.clone();

    // change a value in the cloned product
    p2.setPrice(57.50);

    // print the results
    System.out.println(p1);
    System.out.println(p2);
} catch (CloneNotSupportedException ex) {
    System.out.println(ex);
}
```

The result

```
Code:        java
Description: Murach's Java Programming
Price:       $54.50

Code:        java
Description: Murach's Java Programming
Price:       $57.50
```

Description

- You can use the clone method of the Object class to *clone* a user-defined class only if the user-defined class implements the Cloneable interface.
- Since the clone() method in the Object class has protected access, it is only available to subclasses and other classes in the same package. To make this method available to all classes, you can override the clone() method of the Object class with a clone() method that has public access.
- The clone() method returns an Object type.
- The clone() method of the Object class throws a CloneNotSupportedException.

Figure 9-13   A Product class that implements the Cloneable interface

A LineItem class that implements the Cloneable interface

The Product class that you saw in the previous figure contains only a primitive type (double) and two *immutable* objects (String). A String object is immutable because its value can't be changed. Instead, when you assign a new value to a string variable, the original String object is deleted and it's replaced with a new String object that contains the new value. To clone an object like this, you can simply call the clone() method of the Object class.

In contrast, if a class contains *mutable* objects (objects that can be changed), the clone() method of the Object class may not work properly. In that case, you'll need to override this method when you implement the Cloneable interface. Figure 9-14 shows how this works.

At the top of this figure, you can see a LineItem class that implements the Cloneable interface. Since this class contains an instance variable of a mutable object (a Product object), you must clone both the LineItem object and the Product object. So, the first statement in the clone() method clones the LineItem object by calling the clone() method of the Object class. Because this method returns an Object type, that object is cast to a LineItem so it can be stored in a LineItem variable. At this point, you have two LineItem objects, but they both point to the same Product object.

To clone the Product object, the second statement calls the clone() method of that object. Then, the object that's returned by that method is cast to a Product object and stored in a Product variable. The third statement assigns this object to the Product instance variable. At this point, each LineItem object points to its own copy of the Product object. As a result, this clone method will work properly for a LineItem object.

The code that uses the clone() method of the LineItem class shows how this works. This code starts by creating a Product object and filling it with data. Then, it creates a LineItem object, supplying the data for the line item to the constructor. Next, the clone() method of the LineItem object is called to clone the line item. To illustrate that both the line item and the product it contains have been cloned, the next two statements change the quantity of the second line item and the price of the product stored in that line item. Then, the last two statements print both LineItem objects to the console so you can see that the changes were applied only to the second line item and product.

A LineItem class that implements the Cloneable interface

```java
public class LineItem implements Cloneable {
    private Product product;
    private int quantity;
    private double total;

    // the code for the constructors and methods

    @Override
    public Object clone() throws CloneNotSupportedException {
        LineItem li = (LineItem) super.clone();
        Product p = (Product) product.clone();
        li.setProduct(p);
        return li;
    }
}
```

Code that uses the clone method of the LineItem class

```java
Product p1 = new Product();
p1.setCode("java");
p1.setDescription("Murach's Java Programming");
p1.setPrice(54.50);

LineItem li1 = new LineItem(p1, 3);

// clone the line item
LineItem li2 = (LineItem) li1.clone();

// change values in the cloned LineItem and its Product object
li2.setQuantity(2);
li2.getProduct().setPrice(57.50);

// print the results
System.out.println(li1);
System.out.println(li2);
```

The result

```
Code: java
Description: Murach's Java Programming
Price: $54.50
Quantity: 3
Total: $163.50

Code: java
Description: Murach's Java Programming
Price: $57.50
Quantity: 2
Total: $115.00
```

Description

- To clone an object that contains an instance variable for a *mutable object*, you need to override the clone() method and manually clone that object.

Figure 9-14   A LineItem class that implements the Cloneable interface

Perspective

In this chapter, you've learned how to use interfaces and how they can be used to improve the design of an application. That means that you should now be able to implement all types of classes that are commonly used in business applications. In the next chapter, though, you'll learn some additional object-oriented skills that will round out your knowledge of object-oriented programming.

Summary

- An *interface* is a special type of coding element that can contain static constants and abstract methods.

- With Java 8 and later, an interface can also contain regular methods, known as *default methods*, and static methods.

- A class can only inherit one other class, but it can *implement* more than one interface.

- To implement an interface, a class must implement all the abstract methods defined by the interface.

- An interface can inherit other interfaces. Then, the implementing class must also implement all the abstract methods of the inherited interfaces.

- An interface defines a Java type. As a result, you can use an object that's created from a class that implements an interface anywhere that interface is expected.

- A class does not have to implement default methods provided by the interface, but it can override them.

- When you *clone* an object, you make an identical copy of the object.

- Before you can use the clone() method of the Object class, you need to implement the Cloneable interface. Then, you can override the clone() method so it is public and so it works correctly with *mutable* objects.

Exercise 9-1   Create and work with interfaces

In this exercise, you'll create the DepartmentConstants interface presented in this chapter. In addition, you'll implement an interface named Displayable that's similar to the Printable interface presented in this chapter.

Create the interfaces

1. Open the project named ch09_ex1_DisplayableTest in the ex_starts folder. Then, review the code.

2. Note that this code includes an interface named Displayable that contains a single method named getDisplayText() that returns a String.

3. Open the DisplayableTestApp class. Then, note that it includes a method named display() that accepts a Displayable object as an argument.

4. Add an interface named DepartmentConstants that contains these three constants: ADMIN, EDITORIAL, and MARKETING.

Implement the interfaces

5. Open the Product class. Then, edit it so it implements the Displayable interface. To do that, add a getDisplayText() method that returns a description of the product.

6. Open the Employee class. Then, edit it so it implements the DepartmentConstants and Displayable interfaces. To do that, add a getDisplayText() method that uses the constants in the DepartmentConstants interface to include the department name and the employee's name in the string that it returns.

Use the classes that implement the interfaces

7. Open the DisplayableTestApp class. Then, modify the variable that stores the Employee object so it is of the Displayable type.

8. Add code that passes the Displayable object to the static display() method that's coded at the end of this class.

9. Run the application to make sure that it displays the employee information.

10. Repeat the previous three steps for a Product object. When you're done, the console should look like this:

```
Welcome to the Displayable Test application

John Smith (Editorial)
Murach's Java Programming
```

Use a default method

11. In the Employee and Product classes, rename the getDisplayText() methods to toString() methods so they override the toString() method of the Object class. This should prevent the classes from compiling and display an error message that indicates that the classes don't implement the getDisplayText() method.

12. In the Displayable interface, modify the getDisplayText() method so it's a default method. The code for this method should return the String object that's returned by the toString() method. This should allow the Employeee and Product classes to compile since they can now use the default method.

13. Run the application to make sure it works as before.

Exercise 9-2   Implement the Cloneable interface

In this exercise, you'll implement the Cloneable interface for the Product and LineItem classes.

1. Open the project named ch09_ex2_CloneableTest in the ex_starts directory. Display the ProductCloneApp class and review its code. Note that this class contains an error because the clone() method has protected access in the Object class and isn't available from the Product class. Also note that the clone() method is coded within the try block of a try/catch statement that catches the CloneNotSupportedException.

2. Implement the Cloneable interface for the Product class. When you do, the ProductCloneApp class should no longer display an error.

3. Run the ProductCloneApp class to make sure it works correctly. To do that, you can right-click on this class and select the Run File command.

4. Repeat steps 1 through 3 for the LineItemCloneApp and LineItem classes. When you implement the Cloneable interface for the LineItem class, be sure to provide for the mutable Product object that this class contains.

10

More object-oriented programming skills

In this chapter, you'll learn some more skills related to object-oriented programming. In particular, you'll learn how to work with packages and libraries, critical skills for any professional programmer. Then, you'll learn how to work with modules, the most import new feature of Java 9. Next, you'll learn how to generate API documentation for your classes that looks and works like the documentation for the Java API. Finally, you'll learn how to work with enumerations.

Most modern Java IDEs make it easier than ever to work with packages, libraries, modules, and documentation. This chapter shows how to use NetBeans to do that. However, the download for this book includes a PDF file that shows how to perform the same tasks using Eclipse.

How to work with packages

To make it easy for you to find and access classes, the Java API organizes its classes into *packages*. This allows you to import just the classes and packages that an application needs. Now, you'll learn how to organize your own classes into packages.

Packages provide two main advantages. First, when a project contains a large number of classes, packages can provide some logical structure to your application and make it easier to find the classes that you're looking for. Second, packages provide a way to avoid naming conflicts between classes. This is particularly important if you make your classes available to other programmers.

An introduction to packages

Figure 10-1 shows the directories and files of the Line Item application presented in chapter 7 after packages have been used to organize the classes in that application. Here, the ch10_LineItem\src directory contains the subdirectories that correspond with each package. Then, each subdirectory contains the classes for a package. For example, the murach\business directory that corresponds with the murach.business package stores the Product and LineItem classes that define the business objects for this application.

When you name a package, you can use any name you want. However, if you want to make sure that the name of your package is unique, it's considered a good practice to use your Internet domain name in reverse as the first level of the package name. For example, since our Internet domain name is murach.com, all packages created by our company would begin with com.murach.

Even if you don't follow this convention, you should avoid using a generic name that might be used by someone else. For example, a package name of business is too generic. However, murach.business is specific enough that it's unlikely to conflict with any other package names. For this book, I used murach as the first level of the package name to clearly identify the company that created these packages. Then, I used the second level to organize the packages within the first level.

Once you store a class in the correct directory, you must code a package statement at the beginning of the class. This statement consists of the package keyword followed by the name of the package. In this figure, for example, the LineItem, Product, and ProductDB classes each begins with a package statement that corresponds with the directory that contains the class. Although you can code comments before the package statement, that's not usually necessary.

If a class is stored in a package, it can't be accessed from classes in other packages without qualifying it with the package name. As a result, you typically import the class to make it easier to refer to. This works the same for the packages and classes that you create as it does for the classes of the Java API. In this figure, for example, the ProductDB class imports the Product class from the murach.business package. As a result, the ProductDB class can use the Product class without needing to qualify its name.

The directories and files for an application that uses packages

```
ch10_LineItem\src
    murach
        app
            LineItemApp.java
        business
            LineItem.java
            Product.java
        database
            ProductDB.java
        presentation
            Console.java
```

The LineItem class

```java
package murach.business;

import java.text.NumberFormat;

public class LineItem {...}
```

The Product class

```java
package murach.business;

import java.text.NumberFormat;

public class Product {...}
```

The ProductDB class

```java
package murach.database;

import murach.business.Product;

public class ProductDB {...}
```

Description

- A *package* can store one or more classes. A package can also store interfaces, although this chapter focuses on classes.

- Each package name corresponds with a directory that has the same name. The names you use should be unique to prevent conflicts with other packages.

- When you organize an application into packages, it's common to store all the classes in packages other than the default package. That includes the class that contains the main() method for the application.

- When you store a class in a package, the first statement of the class must be a package statement that specifies the name of the package.

- After the package statement, you can code the import statements for the class. These statements work the same for the packages and classes that you create as they do for the packages and classes of the Java API.

Figure 10-1   An introduction to packages

How to work with packages

When you work with packages, you need to make sure that the name of the package corresponds with the name of the directory for the package. If you have to do this manually, it can quickly become a tedious task. Fortunately, most IDEs handle this for you automatically.

With NetBeans, you can use the Projects window to navigate through the packages for the project. To do that, you can click on the plus and minus signs to the left of the packages to expand or collapse them. In figure 10-2, for example, the Projects window displays the four packages for the Line Item application that were described in the previous figure.

To get started with packages, you can add a new package to a project as described in this figure. As you do that, remember that package names correspond to the directories and subdirectories that store the source code for the packages. If these directories and subdirectories don't already exist, they're created when you create the packages.

Once you've created packages for your application, your IDE typically takes care of more of the details for you automatically. For example, NetBeans automatically adds the necessary package statement to any new class that you add to a package. In addition, if you rename a package, NetBeans automatically renames the corresponding directories and modifies the package statements for all classes in the package. Similarly, if you move a class from one package to another, NetBeans can modify the package statement for that class.

A NetBeans project that contains multiple packages

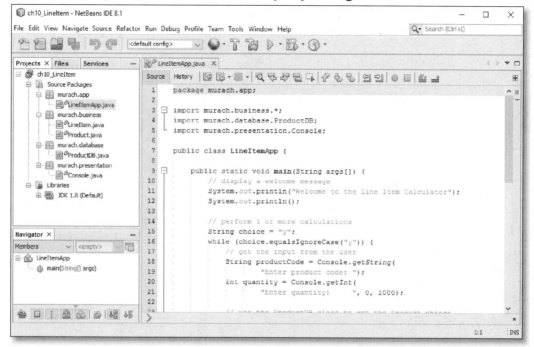

Description

- To navigate through existing packages, use the Projects window to expand or collapse the packages within a project.

- To add a new package to a project, right-click on the project name or the Source Packages folder in the Projects window, select the New→Java Package command, and enter the name of the package in the resulting dialog box. This creates a directory, if necessary, as well as a subdirectory within that directory.

- If you specify a package when you add a new class and that package doesn't already exist, it's automatically created for you.

- To remove a package from a project, right-click on the package and select the Delete command from the resulting menu. This deletes the directory for the package and all subdirectories and files within that directory.

- If you add a new class to a package, NetBeans automatically adds the necessary package statement to the class.

- To rename a package, use the Refactor→Rename command. Then, NetBeans automatically modifies the package statement.

- To move a class from one package to another, drag it in the Projects window. Then, click the Refactor button in the Move Class dialog box that's displayed so NetBeans modifies the package statement.

Figure 10-2   How to work with packages

How to work with libraries

If you want to make the packages of an application available to other applications, you can store them in a *library*. For example, you might want to use the classes in the murach.business, murach.database, and murach.presentation packages from the previous figure with other applications. To do that, you can typically use your IDE to create a library that stores these packages. For example, figure 10-3 shows how to use NetBeans to create this library.

To start, you create a project that contains just the packages and classes that you want to include in the library. One way to do that is to copy an existing project that contains the packages and classes you want and then delete any packages and classes from that project that you don't want to include in the library. To create the ch10_MurachLib project shown in this figure, for example, I copied the ch10_LineItem project shown in figure 10-2. Then, I renamed that project and deleted the murach.app package from it.

Another way to create a project for a library is to create a new Java Application project without a main class. Then, you can open another project that contains the packages and classes that you want to include in the library. Finally, you can copy those packages from the existing project and paste them into the new project.

After you create the project, you clean and compile it to create a *Java Archive (JAR) file* that contains the packages and classes for the library. This file is stored in the dist subdirectory of the project's root directory, and it has the same name as the project. In some cases, you may want to copy the JAR file to the project's src subdirectory. That prevents other developers from modifying the file, and it makes sure that the file is always moved with the project. Note that the JAR file doesn't include the source code (.java files) by default. Instead, it only includes the .class files, which is usually what you want.

This figure also shows how to use a library after you create it. To do that, you start by creating or opening the project that is going to use the library. Then, you add the JAR file for the library to the project's Libraries folder. In this figure, for example, the project named ch10_Product uses the library that's stored in the ch10_MurachLib.jar file. Finally, you add import statements for these packages to the classes that use them. The ProductApp class shown in this figure, for example, imports all the classes from all three packages that are available from the library.

When you create a library that you want other applications to use, you typically store it in a central location. In addition, you typically give the JAR file a name that identifies its contents somewhat. For example, you might give the ch10_MurachLib.jar file a name like murach.jar to show that it comes from Mike Murach & Associates (www.murach.com).

A NetBeans project that uses a library

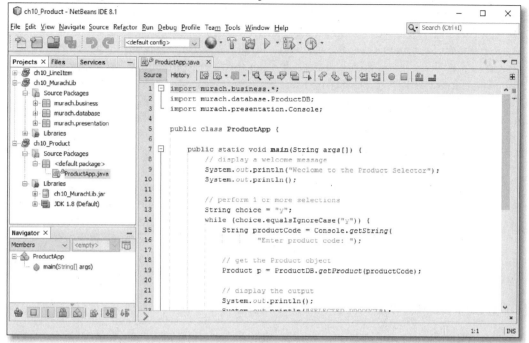

How to create a library

1. Create a project that contains just the packages and classes that you want to include in the library.

2. Right-click on the project and select the Clean and Build command to compile the project and remove any files that are no longer needed. Then, NetBeans automatically creates a JAR file for the project and stores it in the dist subdirectory for the project.

How to use a library

1. Create or open the project that is going to use the library.

2. Right-click on the Libraries directory and select the "Add JAR/Folder" command. Then, use the resulting dialog box to select the JAR file for the library.

3. Code the import statements for the packages and classes in the library that you want to use. Then, you can use the classes stored in those packages.

Description

*   A *library* can store one or more packages that each contains one or more classes.
*   When you create a library, the library is stored in a *Java Archive (JAR) file*.
*   After you create a library, you can make it available to other programmers by storing it in a central location.

Figure 10-3   How to work with libraries

How to work with modules

In software development, it's considered a best practice for code to be modular. That means that the software should be a collection of independent modules that communicate with each other through Application Programming Interfaces (APIs), often referred to as just interfaces. This has many benefits, including making it easier to develop, test, debug, and maintain the software.

Prior to JDK 9, developers could use the object-oriented features of Java that you've already learned about along with JAR files to provide some modularity. However, this fell short of a truly modular system. To fix this, JDK 9 added a module system that strengthens and enhances the way that Java provides modularity.

This module system also made it possible to divide the Java platform itself into a series of independent modules. JDK 9 accomplished that with a project known as *Project Jigsaw*. You'll learn about some of the advantages of the module system and Project Jigsaw in just a minute. But first, you should know more about what a module is.

An introduction to the module system

Figure 10-4 begins by briefly describing a Java *module*. First, a module is a project that has a name that uniquely identifies it. This is necessary because a JAR file doesn't provide a good mechanism for making sure that its name is unique. Second, a module explicitly declares its dependencies, which are the other modules that it requires to work correctly. This is necessary because the module system needs to know how modules are related. Third, a module explicitly declares which of its parts are accessible to other modules. This strengthens encapsulation by preventing developers from intentionally or accidentally using parts of the module that weren't designed to be used by other modules.

The new module system introduced in JDK 9 provides several advantages. To start, dividing the Java platform into modules makes it easier to scale an application for small devices. In addition, it improves the security and maintainability of the Java platform, it improves Java application performance, and it makes it easier to construct and maintain libraries and large applications. If you're developing applications that can benefit from any of these features, then, you should consider using the new module system. Otherwise, you should know that one option is to ignore the use of modules and continue to use the features that were available prior to JDK 9.

If you decide to use modules, you should know that the java.base module is automatically available to all modules. This module exports the essential packages of the Java platform. That includes cores packages such as java.lang and java.math, as shown in the excerpt of the source code for the java.base module. That also includes the module system itself, which is stored in the java.lang.module package.

The packages of the Java platform that aren't exported by the java.base module are exported by other modules that are available from the Java platform. For example, the java.sql module exports the java.sql package that's described in chapter 21.

A module...

- Has a name that uniquely identifies it.
- Explicitly declares the other modules that it depends on.
- Explicitly declares which of its public types are accessible to other modules.

Advantages of the new module system

- Makes the Java platform more easily scalable down to small devices.
- Improves the security and maintainability of the Java platform.
- Improves Java application performance.
- Makes it easier to construct and maintain libraries and large applications.

Code that defines the java.base module

```
module java.base {
    exports java.io;
    exports java.lang;
    exports java.lang.annotation;
    exports java.lang.invoke;
    exports java.lang.module;
    exports java.lang.ref;
    exports java.lang.reflect;
    exports java.math;
    exports java.net;
    ...
}
```

Description

- Prior to JDK 9, Java used its object-oriented features and JAR files to provide modularity. Although this was a good start, it didn't provide a truly modular system.
- With JDK 9 and later, Java provides a way to create and use modules. A *module* is an independent unit of code that has a unique name and clearly identifies all other modules that it requires and all public types that it exports.
- With JDK 9 and later, *Project Jigsaw* divides the Java platform into a set of independent modules. This is made possible by the new module system.
- The java.base module exports the essential packages of the Java platform and is automatically available to all modules.
- The packages of the Java platform that aren't exported by the java.base module are exported by other modules available from the Java platform. For example, the java.sql module exports the java.sql package that's described in chapter 21.

Figure 10-4   An introduction to the module system

How to create modules

Figure 10-5 shows the library you saw earlier in this chapter after it has been converted to a module. Here, the name of the project has been changed to ch10_MurachMod to indicate that the project is for a module, not a library. In addition, a module-info file has been added to the default directory. Typically, it's easy to use an IDE to add a module-info file to your project, and this figure shows how to use NetBeans to add one.

The module-info file shown in this figure accomplishes three tasks. First, it specifies a unique name of com.murach for the module. To make sure that it's unique, this name uses the standard convention of reversing the domain name for the company's website address. In this case, the code reverses murach.com. Of course, you could easily provide an even more unique name by appending more specifiers such as com.murach.lineitem.

Second, this module-info file specifies all dependencies for the module. To do that, it uses a requires statement to specify that the module requires the java.base module described in the previous figure. Note that because the java.base module is automatically available to all other modules, it isn't necessary to code this statement. In the next figure, though, you'll see some examples of when this statement is required.

Third, the module-info file specifies all packages that the module exports. To do that, it uses three exports statements to identify three packages. If you wanted to split this module into three smaller modules, you could create one module for each package.

A NetBeans project that defines a module

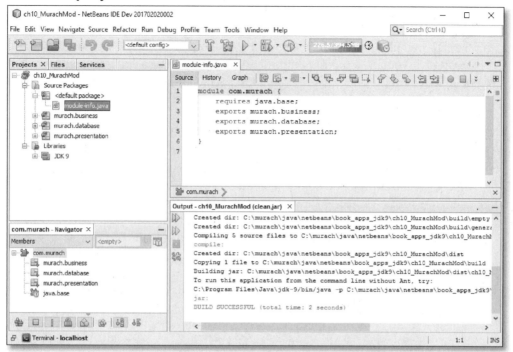

A module-info file for a module named com.murach

```
module com.murach {
    requires java.base;
    exports murach.business;
    exports murach.database;
    exports murach.presentation;
}
```

Description

- A module must contain a module-info.java file in its root (default) directory.

- With NetBeans, you can add a module-info file by right-clicking on the project name and selecting the New→Other command. Then, select Java→Java Module Info from the resulting dialog box.

- The module-info file should specify a unique name for the module immediately after the module keyword. This prevents naming conflicts with other modules.

- The module-info file must specify all other modules that the module requires. To do that, it can include one or more requires statements.

- The module-info file must specify all packages that the module exports. To do that, it can include one or more exports statements.

Figure 10-5   How to create modules

How to use modules

If you don't add a module-info file to a project, Java searches the classpath for the required libraries and loads them. This is how Java worked prior to JDK 9. However, if you add a module-info file to a project, the project uses the new module system to load the required modules. As mentioned earlier, this has many potential benefits, including improved security and performance.

Figure 10-6 shows a project that uses the module created in the previous figure. To start, the JAR file for the module has been added to the Libraries directory for the project. To do that, you can use the same technique you use to add a JAR file for a library.

In addition, this project includes a module-info file. This file specifies a unique name for the project. More importantly, it specifies that this project requires the com.murach module that was created in the previous figure. It also requires the java.base module, which is automatically available.

Finally, the LineItemApp file is stored in the murach.app directory. This is necessary because the module system doesn't allow you to store any classes in the default package. As a result, once you add a module-info file to a project, you need to move any files that are in the default package to a different package.

The last example in this figure shows a module-info file that would be appropriate for an application that uses a SQLite database such as the Product Manager application that you'll see in chapter 21. Here, the first statement specifies that the project requires the java.sql module. Then, the second statement specifies that the project requires the sqlite.jdbc module that's available from the library that's stored in the sqlite-jdbc JAR file. This library and the java.sql package are described in chapter 21.

A NetBeans project that uses a module

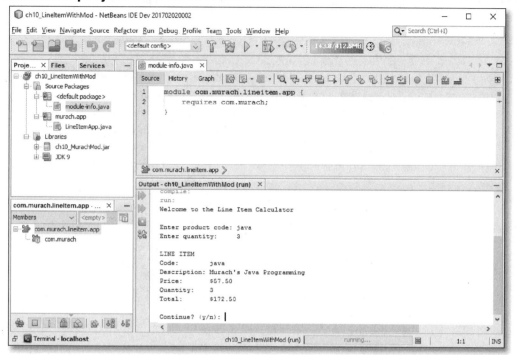

A module-info file that requires the com.murach module

```
module com.murach.lineitem.app {
    requires com.murach;
}
```

A module-info file that requires the java.sql and sqlite.jdbc modules

```
module com.murach.product.app {
    requires java.sql;
    requires sqlite.jdbc;
}
```

Description

- If you don't add a module-info file to a project, Java searches the classpath for the required libraries and loads them. This is how Java worked prior to JDK 9.
- If you add a module-info file to a project, the project uses the module system to load the required modules.
- The module-info file must specify the names of all modules that the project requires, except for the java.base module, which is automatically available to all applications.

Figure 10-6   How to use modules

How to use javadoc to document a package

If you develop classes that you intend to distribute to other programmers, you typically organize those classes into one or more packages as shown in the previous topics. In addition, you typically want to provide some documentation for your classes so other programmers can easily learn about the fields, constructors, and methods of those classes. Fortunately, the JDK includes a utility called javadoc that makes it easy to generate HTML-based documentation for your classes. This documentation looks and works like the documentation for the Java API.

How to add javadoc comments to a class

Figure 10-7 shows how to add simple *javadoc comments* to a class. A javadoc comment begins with /** and ends with */. For these comments to work correctly, they must be coded directly above the class, field, constructor, or method that they describe.

An IDE like NetBeans or Eclipse makes it easy to enter javadoc comments. To do that, you enter a slash followed by two asterisks (/**) on a blank line before the code for a class, field, constructor, or method. Then, when you press the Enter key, NetBeans generates the starting comment for the class or its member. That includes one line with a single asterisk where you can start entering the comment, followed by a line with the */ characters that end the comment. It can also include one or more of the javadoc tags you'll learn about in the next figure.

The Product class with javadoc comments

```java
package murach.business;

import java.text.NumberFormat;

/**
 * The Product class represents a product and is used by
 * the LineItem and ProductDB classes.
 */
public class Product   {

    private String code;
    private String description;
    private double price;

    /**
     * Creates a new Product with default values.
     */
    public Product() {
        code = "";
        description = "";
        price = 0;
    }

    /**
     * Sets the product code to the specified String.
     */
    public void setCode(String code) {
        this.code = code;
    }

    /**
     * Returns a String that represents the product code.
     */
    public String getCode() {
        return code;
    }

    ...
```

Description

- A *javadoc comment* begins with /** and ends with */. You can use javadoc comments to describe a class and its public and protected fields, constructors, and methods.

- A comment should be placed immediately above the class or member it describes. For a class, that means that the comment must be placed after any import statements.

- If you type a slash followed by two asterisks (/**) on a blank line before a method and press Enter, both NetBeans and Eclipse generate the rest of the javadoc comment. That may include some of the javadoc tags you'll learn about in the next figure.

Figure 10-7   How to add javadoc comments to a class

How to use HTML and javadoc tags in javadoc comments

To help format the information that's displayed in the documentation for a class, you can include HTML and javadoc tags in your javadoc comments as shown in figure 10-8. The *HTML tag* you're most likely to use is the <code> tag. You can use this tag to display text in a monospaced font. In this figure, for example, the javadoc comments use this tag to format the names of classes such as Product and String. If you want, you can also use this tag to format references to primitive types such as int and double.

The four *javadoc tags* shown here should be self-explanatory. You typically use the @author and @version tags in the class comment to document the author and current version of the class. By default, this information isn't displayed in the documentation that's generated. Although you can specify that you want to include this information when you generate the documentation, that's usually not necessary.

You use the @param tag to describe a parameter that's accepted by a constructor or public method. In this figure, for example, the code uses the @param tag to document the code parameter defined by the setCode() method. Similarly, if a method returns a value, you can use the @return tag to describe that value. In this figure, the code uses the @return tag to document the String that's returned by the getCode() method.

In addition to the tags shown here, you should realize that additional HTML and javadoc tags are available. For example, you can use the <i> tag to italicize text, and you can use the <b> tag to boldface text. To create a hyperlink, you can use the javadoc @see tag. For more information on this and other javadoc tags, see the online documentation for the javadoc utility.

Common HTML tag used to format javadoc comments

HTML tag	Description
`<code></code>`	Displays the text between these tags with a monospaced font.

Common javadoc tags

Javadoc tag	Description
`@author`	Identifies the author of the class. Not displayed by default.
`@version`	Describes the current version of the class. Not displayed by default.
`@param`	Describes a parameter of a constructor or method.
`@return`	Describes the value that's returned by a method.

The Product class with comments that use HTML and javadoc tags

```java
package murach.business;

import java.text.NumberFormat;

/**
 * The <code>Product</code> class represents a product and is used by the
 * <code>LineItem</code> class.
 * @author Joel Murach
 * @version 1.0.0
 */
public class Product {
    private String code;
    private String description;
    private double price;

    /**
     * Creates a <code>Product</code> with default values.
     */
    public Product() {
        code = "";
        description = "";
        price = 0;
    }

    /**
     * Sets the product code.
     * @param code a <code>String</code> for the product code
     */
    public void setCode(String code) {
        this.code = code;
    }

    /**
     * Gets the product code.
     * @return a <code>String</code> for the product code
     */
    public String getCode() {
        return code;
    }
    ...
```

Figure 10-8   How to use HTML and javadoc tags in javadoc comments

How to generate documentation

After you add javadoc comments to the classes of a project, you can use NetBeans to generate the documentation for those classes as described in figure 10-9. After it generates the documentation, NetBeans displays it in your default web browser as shown here. Then, you can review this documentation to be sure that it contains all the necessary information.

By default, NetBeans stores the documentation for a project in the dist\javadoc subdirectory of the project's root directory. This documentation consists of a number of files and subdirectories. Note that if you generate documentation for a project and the dist\javadoc directory already contains documentation, NetBeans overwrites the old files with the new ones, which is usually what you want.

How to view the documentation for a package

You can use a web browser to view the documentation for user-defined classes the same way that you view the documentation for the Java API. The main difference is that the index.html file for user-defined classes is stored somewhere on your hard drive. In figure 10-6, for example, the documentation is stored in this directory:

\book_apps\ch10_MurachLib\dist\javadoc

Here, I selected the murach.business package from the upper left frame. When I did that, the two classes in that package were listed in the lower left frame. Then, when I selected the Product class, the documentation for that class was displayed in the right frame.

The documentation for the Product class indicates that the Product class is in the murach.business package. It also includes a brief description of the Product class, which was generated from the javadoc comment for the class. Next, it provides a summary of the constructors and methods of the class that are available to other classes, along with the descriptions I provided. If this class contained public or protected fields, the documentation would also include a summary of those fields. Finally, the documentation includes details of all the fields, constructors, and methods in the summaries. This is where the documentation displays any information provided by the @param and @return tags.

Note that the documentation doesn't expose the code that is encapsulated within the class. As a result, the documentation makes it easy for other programmers to use your classes without knowing the details of how they're coded.

The API documentation that's generated for the Product class

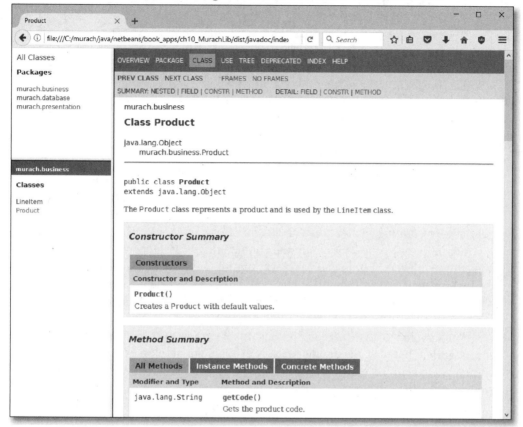

Description

- With NetBeans, you can generate and view the documentation for a project by right-clicking on the project in the Projects window and selecting the Generate Javadoc command. When you do, NetBeans generates the Java documentation for the project and displays it in the default web browser.

- By default, NetBeans stores the documentation for a project in a subdirectory named dist\javadoc that's subordinate to the project's root directory.

- If the project already contains documentation, NetBeans overwrites existing files without any warning.

- You can view the generated documentation by starting a web browser and navigating to the index.html file that's created in the dist\javadoc directory.

Figure 10-9   How to generate and view the documentation for a package

How to work with enumerations

An *enumeration* is a set of related constants that define a type. Enumerations were introduced with JDK 1.5. In chapter 3, you learned how to use the RoundingMode enumeration of the Java API to set the rounding mode for a BigDecimal object. Now, you'll learn how to create and use your own enumerations.

How to declare an enumeration

Figure 10-10 shows how to declare an enumeration. To do that, you code the public keyword, followed by the enum keyword and the name of the enumeration. Then, within the enumeration, you code the names of one or more constants, separating each name with a comma.

Internally, each constant within the enumeration is assigned an integer value beginning with zero. For instance, in the ShippingType enumeration shown in the first example in this figure, the UPS_NEXT_DAY constant has a value of zero, the UPS_SECOND_DAY constant has a value of one, and so on. In most cases, though, you won't use these integer values.

When coding your own enumerations, it's common to store them in a separate file. That way, the enumeration is available to all classes within the current package. If an enumeration is used by a single class, however, you can store it in the same file as that class.

How to use an enumeration

The next three examples in figure 10-10 show how you can use an enumeration. The second example shows that you can declare a variable as an enumeration type. Then, you can assign a constant in that enumeration to the variable. In this case, the UPS_SECOND_DAY constant is assigned to a ShippingType variable named secondDay.

The third example shows a getShippingAmount() method that accepts a ShippingType enumeration as a parameter. Then, the code within the method compares the constant that's passed to the method with two of the constants in the enumeration to determine the shipping amount.

The fourth example shows a statement that calls the getShippingAmount() method. This statement passes the UPS_SECOND_DAY constant of the ShippingType enumeration to the getShippingAmount() method.

The statement that's commented out in the fourth example illustrates that you can't use an integer, or any other type, in place of an enumeration even though the constants in the enumeration are assigned integer values. In other words, enumerations are *type-safe*. In contrast, if you didn't code the constants in an enumeration, you could use the constant name or its value wherever the constant is expected. This is one of several reasons that enumerations are generally preferred to constants.

The syntax for declaring an enumeration

```
public enum EnumerationName {
    CONSTANT_NAME1[,
    CONSTANT_NAME2]...
}
```

An enumeration that defines three shipping types

```
public enum ShippingType {
    UPS_NEXT_DAY,
    UPS_SECOND_DAY,
    UPS_GROUND
}
```

A statement that uses the enumeration and one of its constants

```
ShippingType secondDay = ShippingType.UPS_SECOND_DAY;
```

A method that uses the enumeration as a parameter type

```
public static double getShippingAmount(ShippingType st) {
    double shippingAmount = 2.99;
    if (st == ShippingType.UPS_NEXT_DAY)
        shippingAmount = 10.99;
    else if (st == ShippingType.UPS_SECOND_DAY)
        shippingAmount = 5.99;
    return shippingAmount;
}
```

A statement that calls the method

```
double shippingAmount = getShippingAmount(ShippingType.UPS_SECOND_DAY);
// double shippingAmount2 = getShippingAmount(1); // Wrong type, not allowed
```

Description

- An *enumeration* contains a set of related constants. The constants are defined with the int type and are assigned values from 0 to the number of constants in the enumeration minus 1.

- An enumeration defines a type. Because of that, you can't specify another type where an enumeration type is expected. That means that enumerations are *type-safe*.

- To add an enumeration to a project using NetBeans, right-click on the package where you want to add the enumeration and select the New→Other command. Then, select Java→Java Enum from the resulting dialog box.

Figure 10-10   How to declare and use enumerations

How to enhance an enumeration

Most of the time, the skills presented in figure 10-10 are the only ones you'll need for working with enumerations. You should know, however, that you can override methods that an enumeration inherits from the java.lang.Object and java.lang.Enum classes. You can also add your own methods. When you do that, you may want to use methods of the enumeration constants. Two of those methods are shown at the top of figure 10-11.

This figure also shows an enhanced version of the ShippingType enumeration. This enumeration includes a toString() method that overrides the toString() method of the Enum class. Without this method, the toString() method of the Enum class would return the name of the constant.

In this example, a semicolon is coded following the constants of the enumeration. This semicolon lets the compiler know that there are no more constants. Then, the toString() method uses a series of if/else statements to return an appropriate string for each constant in the enumeration. To do that, it begins by using the ordinal() method to return an int value for the constant. Then, it compares that value to integer values and returns a string that's appropriate for the current constant.

How to work with static imports

In addition to enumerations, JDK 1.5 introduced a new feature known as *static imports*. This feature lets you simplify references to the constants in an enumeration. Figure 10-11 shows how.

To use the static import feature, you begin by coding a static import statement. This statement is similar to a regular import statement, but you code the static keyword after the import keyword, and you typically use the wildcard character (*) to import all of the constants of an enumeration. In this figure, for example, the static import statement specifies that all of the constants in the ShippingType enumeration in the murach.business package should be imported. (This assumes that the ShippingType enumeration has been stored in the murach. business package described earlier in this chapter.)

Once you code a static import statement, you no longer need to code the name of the enumeration that contains the constants. For example, after you import the ShippingType enumeration, you no longer need to code the ShippingType qualifier when you refer to a constant in this enumeration. In this figure, for example, you can see a statement that refers to the UPS_GROUND constant of this enumeration.

In addition to using static imports to import enumerations, you can use them to import the static fields and methods of a class. For example, you could use a static import to import all the static fields and methods of the java.lang.Math class. Then, you could refer to those fields and methods without qualification.

Although you can save some typing by using static imports, they often result in code that's more difficult to read. That's because it may not be obvious where the constants, fields, and methods that an application refers to are stored. As a result, you should use static imports only when they don't cause confusion.

Two methods of an enumeration constant

Method	Description
name()	Returns a String for the enumeration constant's name.
ordinal()	Returns an int value that corresponds to the enumeration constant's position.

How to add a method to an enumeration

An enumeration that overrides the toString() method

```
public enum ShippingType {
    UPS_NEXT_DAY,
    UPS_SECOND_DAY,
    UPS_GROUND;

    @Override
    public String toString() {
        String s = "";
        if (this.ordinal() == 0)
            s = "UPS Next Day (1 business day)";
        else if (this.ordinal() == 1)
            s = "UPS Second Day (2 business days)";
        else if (this.ordinal() == 2)
            s = "UPS Ground (5 to 7 business days)";
        return s;
    }
}
```

Code that uses the toString() method

```
ShippingType ground = ShippingType.UPS_GROUND;
System.out.println("toString: " + ground.toString() + "\n");
```

Resulting output

```
toString: UPS Ground (5 to 7 business days)
```

How to work with static imports

How to code a static import statement

```
import static murach.business.ShippingType.*;
```

The code above when a static import is used

```
ShippingType ground = UPS_GROUND;
System.out.println("toString: " + ground.toString() + "\n");
```

Description

- All enumerations inherit the java.lang.Object and java.lang.Enum classes and can use or override the methods of those classes or add new methods.

- By default, the toString() method of an enumeration constant returns the same string as the name() method.

- You can use a *static import* to import all of the constants of an enumeration or all of the static fields and methods of a class.

Figure 10-11   How to enhance an enumeration and work with static imports

Perspective

Now that you've finished this chapter, you should be able to package and document your code so other programmers can use it. If necessary, you also should be able to use the module system that was introduced with JDK 9 to make this code more modular. In addition, you should be able to create and work with enumerations.

At this point, you have a solid foundation of object-oriented programming skills. Now, you're ready to learn how to use other parts of the Java API, such as the interfaces and classes for working with collections that are described in chapter 12. In addition, you have a solid foundation for learning how to develop GUI applications. Along the way, you'll learn two more object-oriented skills—working with inner classes and working with anonymous classes—that are commonly used when developing GUIs.

Summary

- You can use *packages* to organize the classes in your application. Then, you can use import statements to make the classes in those packages available to other classes.

- You can use a *library* that's stored in a *Java Archive (JAR) file* to make packages and classes available to other applications.

- JDK 9 added a module system that lets you divide applications into a collection of independent modules. A *module* is an independent unit of code that has a unique name and clearly identifies all other modules that it requires and all public types that it exports.

- *Project Jigsaw* uses the module system to divide the Java platform into a set of independent modules.

- You can use *javadoc comments* to document a class and its fields, constructors, and methods. Then, you can generate HTML-based documentation for your class.

- You can use an *enumeration* to define a set of related constants as a type. Then, you can use the constants in the enumeration anywhere the enumeration is allowed.

- You can use *static imports* to import the constants of an enumeration or the static fields and methods of a class. Then, you can refer to the constants, fields, and methods without qualification.

Exercise 10-1   Work with packages and libraries

This exercise guides you through the process of using packages to organize the classes of an application, and it gives you a chance to work with a library.

Review a project that uses packages

1. Open the project named ch10_ex1_LineItem that's in the ex_starts directory, and notice that this project is organized into packages.

2. Review the code for each of the classes, and note that the package statement for each class corresponds with the package directories that are shown in the Projects window.

3. Review the subdirectories and files of this directory:

   ex_starts\ch10_ex1_LineItem\src

   Note that these subdirectories and files correspond with the packages and classes for this project.

Work with packages

4. Add a new package named murach.test to the project.

5. Move the LineItemApp class from the murach.app package to the murach.test package. When the Move Class dialog box is displayed, click the Refactor button so that NetBeans automatically modifies the package statement for this class.

6. Delete the package named murach.app.

7. Rename the murach.database package to murach.db. Note that NetBeans automatically renames the directory that corresponds with this package and modifies the package statement for the class that's stored in this package.

8. Open the ProductDB class and comment out its import statement. If you're using NetBeans, this should cause syntax errors that indicate that the ProductDB class can't find the Product class. To fix this, uncomment the import statement.

9. Run the project to make sure it's working correctly.

Create a library

10. Use the Build command to compile the project. Then, look in the file system and note that the ch10_ex1_LineItem\dist subdirectory contains a JAR file named ch10_ex1_LineItem.jar.

11. Rename the JAR file to murach.jar.

Use a library

12. Copy the murach.jar file into the ch10_ex1_Product\src directory. Then, open the project named ch10_ex1_Product and review the code in the ProductApp class.

13. Delete the murach.business, murach.database, and murach.presentation packages, but not the murach.product package. If you're using NetBeans, this should cause syntax errors in the ProductApp class that indicate that the packages in the import statements and the Product, ProductDB, and Console classes can't be found.

14. Add the library that's stored in the murach.jar file to the project's Libraries folder. Note that the ProductApp class still can't find the ProductDB class.

15. Modify the import statement for the ProductDB class so it works correctly. Hint: You modified the name of this package earlier in this exercise.

16. Run this project to make sure it works correctly.

Exercise 10-2 Work with documentation

This exercise guides you through the process of using NetBeans to add javadoc comments to the Console class and to generate the API documentation for all the murach packages.

17. Open the project named ch10_ex2_LineItem that's stored in the ex_starts directory.

18. Open the Product class that's in the murach.business package. Then, view the javadoc comments that have been added to this class. Note that these comments don't include the @param or @return tags.

19. Open the LineItem class that's in the murach.business package. Note that a single javadoc comment has been added at the beginning of this class.

20. Open the Console class that's in the murach.presentation package. Then, add javadoc comments to this class and each of its methods. Make sure to include @param and @return tags for all of its methods.

21. Generate the documentation for the project. This should automatically open the documentation in a web browser.

22. View the documention for the LineItem class so you can see the documentation that's generated for a class by default.

23. View the documentation for the Product class. Note that the details for the methods don't include a description of the parameters or return values.

24. View the documentation for the Console class. Note that the details for the methods include the descriptions of the parameters and return values. Then, close your browser.

25. Navigate to the dist\javadoc directory for the project and view the files for this directory. Then, open the index.html page in your browser. Note that it displays the documentation for the project.

Exercise 10-3   Create and use an enumeration

In this exercise, you'll create an enumeration and then use it in a test application.

1. Open the project named ch10_ex3_Enumeration that's in the ex_starts directory.

2. Create an enumeration named CustomerType. This enumeration should contain constants that represent three types of customers: retail, trade, and college.

3. Open the CustomerTypeApp class. Then, add a method to this class that returns a discount percent (.10 for retail, .30 for trade, and .20 for college) depending on the CustomerType variable that's passed to it.

4. Add code to the main() method that declares a CustomerType variable, assigns one of the customer types to it, gets the discount percent for that customer type, and displays the discount percent. Run the application to be sure that it works correctly.

5. Add a statement to the main() method that displays the string returned by the toString() method of the customer type. Then, run the application again to see the result of this method.

6. Add a toString() method to the CustomerType enumeration. This method should return a string that contains "Retail customer," "Trade customer," or "College customer" depending on the customer type. Run the application one more time to view the results of the toString() method.

Section 3

More essential skills

This section is designed to add to the skills that you developed in sections 1 and 2 of this book. The chapters in this section are designed so you can read them in the sequence that you prefer. If, for example, you want to learn how to work with collections, you can skip to chapter 12. Or, if you want to learn more about working with strings, you can skip to chapter 13.

The only exception to this rule is that chapter 15 (How to work with file I/O) uses the skills for working with collections that are presented in chapter 12 and the skills for working with strings that are presented in chapter 13. As a result, you may want to read those chapters before you move on to chapter 15. Eventually, you'll want to read all of the chapters in this section because they all present essential skills that every Java programmer should have. This includes how to work with arrays, collections, generics, strings, dates, times, file I/O, and exceptions.

11

How to work with arrays

In this chapter, you'll learn how to work with arrays, which are important in many types of Java applications. For example, you can use a sales array to hold the sales amounts for each of the 12 months of the year. Then, you can use that array to perform calculations on those amounts. In this chapter, you'll learn the basic concepts and techniques for working with arrays.

Basic skills for working with arrays

In the topics that follow, you'll learn how to use an array to work with primitive types or objects. First, you'll learn how to create an array. Next, you'll learn how to assign values to an array. Then, you'll see some examples that show how to work with arrays.

How to create an array

An *array* is an object that contains one or more items called *elements*. Each element is a primitive type such as an int or a double or an object such as a String or a custom type. All of the elements in an array must be of the same type. Thus, an int array can contain only integers, and a double array can contain only doubles. Note, however, that an array can contain elements that are derived from the array's base type. As a result, if you declare an array of type Object, the array can contain any type of object because all Java classes are ultimately derived from the Object class.

The *length* (or *size*) of an array indicates the number of elements that it contains. In Java, arrays have a fixed length. So once you create an array, you can't change its length. If your application requires that you change the length of an array, you should consider using one of the collection classes described in chapter 12 instead of an array.

Figure 11-1 shows several ways to create an array. To start, you must declare a variable that will be used to refer to the array. Then, you instantiate an array object and assign it to the variable. You can use separate statements to declare the array variable and instantiate the array, or you can declare the variable and instantiate the array in a single statement.

Notice that when you declare the array variable, you use an empty set of brackets to indicate that the variable is an array. You can code these brackets after the variable name or after the array type. Most programmers prefer to code the empty brackets after the array type to indicate that the array is an array of a particular type, but either technique is acceptable.

When you instantiate an array, you use another set of brackets to indicate the number of elements in the array. If you know the size of the array at compile time, you can code the number of elements as a literal or as a constant of type int. If you won't know the size of the array until runtime, you can use a variable of type int to specify its size.

The first three examples show how to declare an array of double types. The first example simply declares an array variable without instantiating an array. The second example instantiates an array that holds four doubles and assigns it to the array variable declared in the first example. The third example combines these two statements into a single statement that both declares and instantiates the array.

The other group of examples in this figure shows other ways to create arrays. The first two examples in this group create arrays of String and Product objects. And the last two examples use a constant and a variable to provide the length for an array of String objects.

The syntax for declaring and instantiating an array

Two ways to declare an array
```
type[] arrayName;
type arrayName[];
```

How to instantiate an array
```
arrayName = new type[length];
```

How to declare and instantiate an array in one statement
```
type[] arrayName = new type[length];
```

Examples of array declarations

Code that declares an array of doubles
```
double[] prices;
```

Code that instantiates an array of doubles
```
prices = new double[4];
```

Code that declares and instantiates an array of doubles in one statement
```
double[] prices = new double[4];
```

Other examples

An array of String objects
```
String[] titles = new String[3];
```

An array of Product objects
```
Product[] products = new Product[5];
```

Code that uses a constant to specify the array length
```
final int TITLE_COUNT = 100;                // array size set at compile time
String[] titles = new String[TITLE_COUNT];
```

Code that uses a variable to specify the array length
```
Scanner sc = new Scanner(System.in);
int titleCount = sc.nextInt();              // array size not set until runtime
String[] titles = new String[titleCount];
```

Description

- An *array* can store more than one primitive type or object. An *element* is one of the items in an array.

- To create an array, you must declare a variable of the correct type and instantiate an array object that the variable refers to. You can declare and instantiate the array in separate statements, or you can combine the declaration and instantiation into a single statement.

- To declare an array variable, you code a set of empty brackets after the type or the variable name. Most programmers prefer coding the brackets after the array type.

- To instantiate an array, you use the new keyword and specify the *length*, or *size*, of the array in brackets following the array type. You can specify the length by coding a literal value or by using a constant or variable of type int.

- When you instantiate an array of primitive types, numeric types are set to zeros and boolean types to false. When you create an array of objects, they are set to nulls.

Figure 11-1   How to create an array

How to assign values to the elements of an array

Figure 11-2 shows how to assign values to the elements of an array. As the syntax at the top of this figure shows, you refer to an element in an array by coding the array name followed by an *index* in brackets. The index must be an int value starting at 0 and ending at one less than the size of the array. In other words, an index of 0 refers to the first element in the array, 1 refers to the second element, 2 refers to the third element, and so on.

The first three examples in this figure show how to assign values to the elements in an array by coding one statement per element. The first example creates an array of 4 double values, then assigns a literal value to each element. In this example, the first element holds the value 14.95, the second holds 12.95, the third holds 11.95, and the fourth holds 9.95. The second example creates an array that holds String objects and initializes the strings. And the third example creates an array that holds Product objects and initializes those objects.

If you specify an index that's outside of the range of the array, Java will throw an ArrayIndexOutOfBoundsException. For instance, the commented out line at the end of the first example in this figure refers to the element with index number 4. Because this array has only four elements, however, this statement would cause an ArrayIndexOutOfBoundsException. Although you can catch this exception, it's better to write your code so it avoids using indexes that are out of bounds. You'll see examples of code like that in the next figure.

The syntax and examples at the bottom of this figure show how to create an array and assign values to the elements of the array in one statement. Here, you declare the array variable as usual. Then, you use the special assignment syntax to assign the initial values. With this syntax, you simply list the values you want assigned to the array within braces following the equals sign. Then, the number of values you list within the braces determines the size of the array that's created. The last three examples show how to use this special syntax to create the same arrays that were created by the first three examples in this figure.

The syntax for referring to an element of an array

```
arrayName[index]
```

Examples that assign values by accessing each element

Code that assigns values to an array of double types

```
double[] prices = new double[4];
prices[0] = 14.95;
prices[1] = 12.95;
prices[2] = 11.95;
prices[3] = 9.95;
//prices[4] = 8.95;     // this would throw ArrayIndexOutOfBoundsException
```

Code that assigns values to an array of String types

```
String[] names = new String[3];
names[0] = "Ted Lewis";
names[1] = "Sue Jones";
names[2] = "Ray Thomas";
```

Code that assigns objects to an array of Product objects

```
Product[] products = new Product[2];
products[0] = new Product("java");
products[1] = new Product("jsps");
```

The syntax for creating an array and assigning values in one statement

```
type[] arrayName = {value1, value2, value3, ...};
```

Examples that create an array and assign values in one statement

```
double[] prices = {14.95, 12.95, 11.95, 9.95};
String[] names = {"Ted Lewis", "Sue Jones", "Ray Thomas"};
Product[] products = {new Product("java"), new Product("jsps")};
```

Description

- To refer to the elements in an array, you use an *index* that ranges from zero (the first element in the array) to one less than the number of elements in the array.

- If you specify an index that's less than zero or greater than the upper bound of the array, an ArrayIndexOutOfBoundsException will be thrown when the statement is executed.

- You can instantiate an array and provide initial values in a single statement by listing the values in braces. The number of values you provide determines the size of the array.

Figure 11-2   How to assign values to the elements of an array

How to use for loops with arrays

For loops are commonly used to process the elements in an array one at a time by incrementing an index variable. Figure 11-3 shows how to process an array using a for loop.

The syntax at the top of this figure shows how to use the length field to return the length of an array. Since length is a field rather than a method, you don't need to include parentheses after it. The length field returns an int value that represents the length of the array. You'll typically use this value in the Boolean expression of a for loop to stop the loop after the last element has been processed.

The first example in this figure shows how to create an array of 10 int values and fill it with the numbers 0 through 9. Here, an int variable named i is used in the for loop both to index the array and to assign a value to each element in the array. Since the same variable is used to index the array and assign the element values, the value that's stored within each element is equal to the index for the element.

The second example shows how you can use a for loop to print the contents of an array to the console. Here, an array of doubles named prices is created with initial values. Then, a for loop is used to access each element of the array. The single statement within the loop prints the value of each element in the array to the console as shown.

The third example shows how you can use a for loop to calculate the average of the prices array. This example assumes you've already created the prices array as shown in the previous example. Then, it uses a for loop to add the value of each array element to a variable named sum. When the for loop finishes, sum contains the total of all the prices in the array. Then, the average is calculated by dividing this total by the number of elements in the array.

The syntax for getting the length of an array

```
arrayName.length
```

Code that puts the numbers 0 through 9 in an array

```
int[] values = new int[10];
for (int i = 0; i < values.length; i++) {
   values[i] = i;
}
```

Code that prints an array of prices to the console

```
double[] prices = {14.95, 12.95, 11.95, 9.95};
for (int i = 0; i < prices.length; i++) {
   System.out.println(prices[i]);
}
```

The console output

```
14.95
12.95
11.95
9.95
```

Code that computes the average of the array of prices

```
double sum = 0.0;
for (int i = 0; i < prices.length; i++) {
   sum += prices[i];
}
double average = sum / prices.length;
```

Description

- You can use the length field of an array to determine how many elements are defined for the array.

- For loops are often used to process each element in an array.

Figure 11-3   How to use for loops with arrays

How to use enhanced for loops with arrays

In addition to the standard for loop, JDK 1.5 introduced an *enhanced for loop* that's designed especially for working with arrays and collections. The enhanced for loop is sometimes called a *foreach loop* because it's used to process each element in an array or collection. Figure 11-4 shows how this loop works.

As the syntax at the top of this figure shows, the enhanced for loop doesn't use separate expressions to initialize, test, and increment a counter variable like the for loop does. Instead, it declares a variable that will be used to refer to each element of the array. Then, within the loop, you can use this variable to access each array element.

To understand how this works, the first example in this figure shows how you can use an enhanced for loop to print the elements of an array of doubles. This example performs the same function as the second example in figure 11-3. In the enhanced for loop version, a variable named price is used to access each element in the prices array. Then, the statement within the for loop simply prints the price variable to the console. Notice that because the enhanced for loop keeps track of the current element automatically, no indexing is required.

The second example shows how to use an enhanced for loop to calculate the average value in the prices array. This example performs the same function as the third example in figure 11-3. Again, no indexing is required since the enhanced for loop automatically indexes the array.

The syntax of the enhanced for loop

```
for (type variableName : arrayName) {
    statements
}
```

Code that prints an array of prices to the console

```
double[] prices = {14.95, 12.95, 11.95, 9.95};
for (double price : prices) {
    System.out.println(price);
}
```

The console output

```
14.95
12.95
11.95
9.95
```

Code that computes the average of the array of prices

```
double sum = 0.0;
for (double price : prices) {
    sum += price;
}
double average = sum / prices.length;
```

Description

- Version 1.5 of the JDK introduced a new form of the for loop called an *enhanced for loop*. The enhanced for loop simplifies the code required to loop through arrays. The enhanced for loop is sometimes called a *foreach loop* because it lets you process each element of an array.

- Within the parentheses of an enhanced for loop, you declare a variable with the same type as the array followed by a colon and the name of the array.

- With each iteration of the loop, the variable that's declared by the for loop is assigned the value of the next element in the array.

Note

- You can also use enhanced for loops to work with collections. See chapter 12 for details.

Figure 11-4   How to use enhanced for loops with arrays

How to use the Arrays class

Now that you know the basic language skills for creating and using arrays, you're ready to learn how to use the Arrays class of the java.util package to perform some additional operations on arrays. This class contains static methods that you can use to fill, sort, search, copy, and compare arrays. Figure 11-5 presents three of these methods, and figure 11-6 presents two more.

When you work with these methods, you can supply any type of one-dimensional array as the array argument. Similarly, you can supply a primitive value or an object as the value argument. However, you must make sure that the value or object type matches the array type.

How to fill, sort, and search arrays

The first example in figure 11-5 shows how to use the fill() method to assign a value to all of the elements in an array. Here, the first statement creates an array of 5 int values. By default, this statement automatically initializes each element to 0. Then, the second statement uses the fill() method of the Arrays class to set all five elements to a value of 1.

The second example shows how to use the sort() method to sort an array of 10 int values. Here, the first statement creates an unsorted array of int values from 0 to 9. Then, the second statement uses the sort() method to sort these values. After that, this code uses an enhanced for loop to print the contents of the array to the console. This shows that the sort() method successfully sorted the array.

The third example shows how to use the binarySearch() method. This method searches for an element with a specific value and returns its index. However, before you can use this method, you must use the sort() method to sort the array. In this example, the first statement creates an array of unsorted strings. Then, the second statement uses the sort() method to sort this array. For strings, this sorts the array alphabetically from A to Z. In other words, it sorts the strings of this array like this: "java", "jsp", and "mysql". As a result, the binarySearch() method that's called in the third statement returns a value of 2, which means that the string is the third element of the array.

The Arrays class

```
java.util.Arrays
```

Some static methods of the Arrays class

Method	Description
fill(array, value)	Fills all elements of the specified array with the specified value.
sort(array)	Sorts the elements of an array into ascending order.
binarySearch(array, value)	Returns an int value for the index of the specified value in the specified array. Returns a negative number if the specified value is not found in the array. For this method to work correctly, the array must first be sorted by the sort() method.

How to fill an array

```
int[] quantities = new int[5];     // all elements are set to 0
Arrays.fill(quantities, 1);        // all elements are set to 1
```

How to sort an array

```
int[] numbers = {2,6,4,1,8,5,9,3,7,0};
Arrays.sort(numbers);
for (int number : numbers) {
    System.out.print(number + " ");
}
```

The console output

```
0 1 2 3 4 5 6 7 8 9
```

How to search an array

```
String[] productCodes = {"mysql", "jsp", "java"};
Arrays.sort(productCodes);
int index = Arrays.binarySearch(productCodes, "mysql");  // sets index to 2
```

Description

- All of these methods accept arrays of primitive data types and arrays of objects for the array argument, and they all accept primitive types and objects for the value argument.

- For the sort() method to work correctly with an array of objects created from a user-defined class, such as the Product class, the class must implement the Comparable interface as shown in figure 11-7. For more information about implementing interfaces, see chapter 9.

Figure 11-5   How to fill, sort, and search arrays

How to refer to, copy, and compare arrays

Like a string, an array is a *reference type*. As a result, it works differently than primitive types. To start, when you use the assignment operator (=) to assign an array to a variable, the variable doesn't store a copy of the array. Instead, it *refers* to the array object. As a result, it's possible for multiple variables to refer to the same array object.

The first example in figure 11-6 shows how this works. Here, the code creates two variables that refer to the same array. More specifically, the grades variable and the percentages variable both refer to the same array. Because of that, any change to the grades variable is reflected by the percentages variable and vice versa. In this example, for instance, the third statement sets percentages[1] to 70.2. As a result, this change is reflected by grades[1]. This is shown by the statement that prints grades[1]. Since the percentages and grades variables both refer to the same array, this statement prints the value 70.2.

If you want to create a copy of an array instead of another reference to the array, you can use the static copyOf() method to copy the elements of one array to another array. This is illustrated by the second example in this figure. When you use this method, each array variable points to its own copy of the array, and any changes that are made to one array aren't reflected in the other array.

In this example, the length argument is set to the length of the grades array. As a result, this example copies all of the elements of the grades array into the percentages array. However, if you specified a larger number for the length argument, the percentages array would be padded with extra elements with a default value of zero. Or, if you specified a smaller number for the length argument, the extra elements would be truncated from the percentages array.

The copyOf() method was introduced with Java 6. As a result it doesn't work with earlier versions of Java. If you need to use an earlier version of Java, you can create a copy of an array by using the arraycopy() method of the System class. This method is a little more difficult to use than the copyOf() method of the Arrays class. However, you should be able to figure out how to use it if you refer to the documentation for the Java API.

When you use the copyOf() method with an array of reference types, you need to know that it produces a *shallow copy*, not a *deep copy*. That means that it creates a new array with copies of the references to the objects in the original array. As a result, if you change a value in one of the objects from one array, the object in the other array also changes.

If you want to check whether two variables refer to the same array object, you can use the equality operator (==) as shown in the third example. However, this only checks whether the two variables refer to the same array object, not whether the two arrays store the same number of elements with the same values for each element. To do that, you need to use the equals() method of the Arrays class as shown in the fourth example. When you use this method with an array of reference types, you may need to override the equals() method for the reference type as described in chapter 8.

More static methods of the Arrays class

Method	Description
`copyOf(array, length)`	Copies the specified array, truncating or padding with default values as necessary so the copy has the specified length.
`copyOfRange(array, index1, index2)`	Copies the specified range of the specified array into a new array.
`equals(array1, array2)`	Returns true if both arrays are of the same type and all of the elements within the arrays are equal to each other.

How to create a reference to an array

```
double[] grades = {92.3, 88.0, 95.2, 90.5};
double[] percentages = grades;
percentages[1] = 70.2;                             // changes grades[1] too
System.out.println("grades[1]=" + grades[1]);      // prints 70.2
```

How to create a shallow copy of an array (Java 6 or later)

```
double[] grades = {92.3, 88.0, 95.2, 90.5};
double[] percentages = Arrays.copyOf(grades, grades.length);
percentages[1] = 70.2;                             // doesn't change grades[1]
System.out.println("grades[1]=" + grades[1]);      // prints 88.0
```

How to determine if two variables refer to the same array

```
if (grades == percentages) {
    System.out.println("Both variables refer to the same array.");
} else {
    System.out.println("Each variable refers to a different array.");
    System.out.println("However, these arrays may contain the same data.");
}
```

How to determine if two variables contain the same data

```
if (Arrays.equals(grades, percentages)) {
    System.out.println("Both variables contain the same data.");
} else {
    System.out.println("Both variables do not contain the same data.");
}
```

Description

- Like a string, an array is a *reference type*.

- To create a *reference* to an existing array, you can use the assignment operator (=) to assign a variable that points to an existing array to another variable. Then, both variables point to the same array.

- To check if two array variables refer to the same array, you can use the equality operator (==).

- The copyOf() method was introduced with Java 6. Prior to Java 6, you had to use the arraycopy() method of the System class to copy an array.

- When you copy an array, the new array must be the same type as the source array.

Figure 11-6   How to refer to, copy, and compare arrays

How to implement the Comparable interface

In chapter 9, you learned how to implement the Cloneable interface of the Java API so you can clone an object created from a class that you create. Another interface you may need to implement in the classes you create is the Comparable interface. When a class implements this interface, you can use the sort() method of the Arrays class to sort an array of objects created from the class. To implement this interface, you must provide an implementation of its compareTo() method. Figure 11-7 shows how you can do this for a simple Item class.

The code at the top of this figure shows how the Comparable interface is defined by the Java API. This interface provides a single method named compareTo() that accepts an Object as an argument. This method should return a negative number if the current object is less than the passed object, 0 if the two objects are equal, and a positive number if the current object is greater than the passed object.

The Item class in this figure begins by declaring two private instance variables named number and description, a constructor that accepts values for these fields, and methods that return the values of these fields. Then, it provides a compareTo() method that compares Item objects based on the values of the number fields. In other words, two items are considered equal if they have the same item number.

The compareTo() method begins by casting the object passed to it to an Item object. Then, it uses if statements to compare the item numbers and determine whether to return -1, 0, or 1. These values are used by the sort() method to determine if the current object is less than, equal to, or greater than the object it's being compared to.

The code example after the Item class shows how you can sort an array of Item objects. Here, an array of three Item objects is created. Then, the sort() method of the Arrays class is used to sort the array. Finally, an enhanced for loop is used to print the contents of the array. As you can see in the resulting output, the array is printed in item number sequence even though the array elements were created in a different sequence.

In this example, the objects are compared based on a numeric field. Because of that, you can use the greater than and less than operators to determine if one object is greater than or less than another. If you want to compare two objects based on a string field, however, you can't do that using these operators. Instead, you need to use the compareTo() or compareToIgnoreCase() method of the String class. You'll get a chance to use the compareToIgnoreCase() method in exercise 11-3.

The Comparable interface defined in the Java API

```
public interface Comparable {
    int compareTo(Object obj);
}
```

An Item class that implements the Comparable interface

```
public class Item implements Comparable {
    private int number;
    private String description;

    public Item(int number, String description) {
        this.number = number;
        this.description = description;
    }

    public int getNumber() { return number; }
    public String getDescription() { return description; }

    @Override
    public int compareTo(Object o) {
        Item i = (Item) o;
        if (this.getNumber() < i.getNumber()) {
            return -1;
        }
        if (this.getNumber() > i.getNumber()) {
            return 1;
        }
        return 0;
    }
}
```

Code that sorts an array of Item objects

```
Item[] items = new Item[3];
items[0] = new Item(102, "Duct Tape");
items[1] = new Item(103, "Bailing Wire");
items[2] = new Item(101, "Chewing Gum");
Arrays.sort(items);
for (Item i : items) {
    System.out.println(i.getNumber() + ": " + i.getDescription());
}
```

The console output

```
101: Chewing Gum
102: Duct Tape
103: Bailing Wire
```

Description

- To use the sort() method of the Arrays class with an array of objects created from a user-defined class, the class must implement the Comparable interface in a way that sorts the objects correctly.

- The compareTo() method should return -1 if the current object is less than the object that's passed it, 0 if the objects are equal, and 1 if the current object is greater than the object that's passed to it.

Figure 11-7   How to implement the Comparable interface

The Number Cruncher application

To show how some of the skills you've just learned can be applied, figure 11-8 presents the Number Cruncher application. This application creates an array of random integers and displays these random numbers along with some statistics that have been calculated about them.

To start, this code imports the Arrays class. Then, it declares a class named NumberCruncherApp that contains the code for the application. Within this class, the main() method begins by declaring an array of 11 integers. Then, it uses a for loop to assign a random number from 0 to 50 to each of the 11 elements in the array. This works because the random() method returns a number that's greater than or equal to 0 and less than 1, which means that multiplying the number by 51 always results in a number that's less than 51. Then, because the number is cast to an int type, the number will always be less than or equal to 50.

After the random numbers have been assigned, the code uses the sort() method of the Arrays class to sort the array so the random numbers are in sequence, and it uses an enhanced for loop to display the numbers in the array on the console. Then, it uses a similar enhanced for loop to calculate and display the total for all of the numbers in the array. Next, this code gets and displays the count of the numbers. To do that, this code uses the length field of the array.

After displaying the count of the numbers, this code calculates and displays the average. To do that, this code divides the total by the count. Since both of these numbers are integer values, this code casts the total value to the double type. That way, Java uses decimal division, not integer division. Then, this code uses the Math class to round the total to 1 decimal place as described in chapter 3.

After displaying the average, this code checks whether the count of numbers is an odd number. If it is, it gets the median value from the array, which is the value that half the values are below and half the values are above. To get the index for the median value, it divides the number of elements by 2. In this example, for instance, the array contains 11 elements, so the index for the element that contains the median value is 5. (Remember that integer division always returns an integer.) In this case, the values in the elements with indexes 0 through 4 are below the median, and the values in the elements with indexes 6 through 11 are above it. Of course, this only works correctly if the count of the numbers is odd, which is why this code is within the if statement.

The console

```
Numbers: 16 17 17 19 21 30 31 37 39 42 46
Total: 315
Count: 11
Average: 28.6
Median: 30
```

The code

```java
import java.util.Arrays;

public class NumberCruncherApp {

    public static void main(String[] args) {
        // create array of 11 random integers
        int[] numbers = new int[11];
        for (int i = 0; i < numbers.length; i++) {
            numbers[i] = (int) (Math.random() * 51);   // num is >= 0 and <= 50
        }

        // sort the array
        Arrays.sort(numbers);

        // display numbers
        String numbersString = "";
        for (int number : numbers) {
            numbersString += number + " ";
        }
        System.out.println("Numbers: " + numbersString);

        // calculate total and display
        int total = 0;
        for (int number : numbers) {
            total += number;
        }
        System.out.println("Total: " + total);

        // get count of numbers and display
        int count = numbers.length;
        System.out.println("Count: " + count);

        // calculate average and display
        double average = (double) total / count;
        average = (double) Math.round(average * 10) / 10;
        System.out.println("Average: " + average);

        // if count of numbers is odd
        if (count % 2 != 0) {
            int medianIndex = count / 2;
            int median = numbers[medianIndex];
            System.out.println("Median: " + median);
        }
    }
}
```

Figure 11-8   The Number Cruncher application

How to work with two-dimensional arrays

So far, this chapter has shown how to work with an array that uses one index to store a single set of elements. You can think of that as a *one-dimensional array*. Now, you'll learn how to work with *two-dimensional arrays* that use two indexes to store data. You can think of a two-dimensional array as a table made up of rows and columns where each element in the array is at the intersection of a row and column.

If you're familiar with array processing in other languages such as C++ or even Visual Basic, you may be surprised to discover that Java doesn't directly support two-dimensional arrays in the same way those languages do. Instead, Java implements a two-dimensional array as an *array of arrays* where each element of the first array is itself an array. Although the syntax is different, the effect is nearly the same.

How to work with rectangular arrays

Figure 11-9 shows how to create and use the simplest type of two-dimensional array, called a *rectangular array*. In a rectangular array, each row has the same number of columns. For example, a 5x10 array consists of an array of five elements, each of which is a 10-element array. If you think of this rectangular array as a table, the 5-element array represents the table's rows, and each 10-element array represents the columns for one of the rows.

The syntax and code at the top of this figure show how to create a rectangular array. As you can see, you specify two sets of empty brackets following the array type. Then, you specify the number of rows and columns when you instantiate the array. Thus, the code example shown here declares and instantiates a rectangular array with 3 rows, each with two columns.

To refer to an element in a rectangular array, you specify two index values in separate sets of brackets. The first value refers to the row index, and the second value refers to the column index. Thus, numbers[1][0] refers to row 2, column 1 of the numbers array.

You can also create a rectangular array and assign values to its elements using a single statement. To do that, you use the same shorthand notation you use for one-dimensional arrays. However, you code each element of the array as a separate array as shown in this figure. Here, the numbers array is assigned three elements, each of which is a two-element array with the values {1, 2}, {3, 4}, and {5, 6}.

The last example in this figure shows how to use nested for loops to process the elements of a rectangular array. Here, the outer for loop uses the variable i to index the rows of the array, and numbers.length is used to determine the number of rows in the array. Then, the inner for loop uses the variable j to index the columns, and numbers[i].length is used to determine the number of columns in each row.

How to create a rectangular array

The syntax for creating a rectangular array

```
type[][] arrayName = new type[rowCount][columnCount];
```

A statement that creates a 3x2 array

```
int[][] numbers = new int[3][2];
```

How to assign values to a rectangular array

The syntax for referring to an element of a rectangular array

```
arrayName[rowIndex][columnIndex]
```

The indexes for a 3x2 array

```
[0][0]          [0][1]
[1][0]          [1][1]
[2][0]          [2][1]
```

Code that assigns values to the array

```
numbers[0][0] = 1;
numbers[0][1] = 2;
numbers[1][0] = 3;
numbers[1][1] = 4;
numbers[2][0] = 5;
numbers[2][1] = 6;
```

Code that creates a 3x2 array and initializes it in one statement

```
int[][] numbers = { {1,2}, {3,4}, {5,6} };
```

How to use nested for loops to process a rectangular array

Code that processes a rectangular array with nested for loops

```
int[][] numbers = { {1,2}, {3,4}, {5,6} };
for (int i = 0; i < numbers.length; i++) {
    for (int j = 0; j < numbers[i].length; j++)
        System.out.print(numbers[i][j] + "  ");
    System.out.print("\n");
}
```

The console output

```
1   2
3   4
5   6
```

Description

- *Two-dimensional arrays* use two indexes and allow data to be stored in a table that consists of rows and columns. This can also be thought of as an *array of arrays* where each row is a separate array of columns.

- A *rectangular array* is a two-dimensional array whose rows all have the same number of columns.

- Although it's rarely necessary, you can extend this two-dimensional syntax to work with arrays that have more than two dimensions.

Figure 11-9   How to work with rectangular arrays

Although it's not shown in figure 11-9, you should realize that you can also use nested foreach loops to work with rectangular arrays. To do that, you declare an array variable in the outer for loop that you can use to refer to the rows in the array. Then, you declare a variable in the inner for loop that you can use to refer to the columns in each row. For example, figure 11-10 uses nested foreach loops to work with another type of two-dimensional array called a jagged array.

How to work with jagged arrays

A *jagged array* is a two-dimensional array in which the rows contain unequal numbers of columns. This is possible because each row of a two-dimensional array is actually a separate one-dimensional array, and Java doesn't require that each of these arrays be the same size. Figure 11-10 shows how to work with jagged arrays.

When you instantiate a jagged array, you specify the number of rows but not the number of columns. Then, you instantiate the array for each row separately, specifying as many columns as are necessary for that row. To illustrate, the first statement in the first example in this figure creates a jagged array named numbers that has 3 rows. Then, the next three statements create arrays of 10, 15, and 20 elements for the three rows of the numbers array.

The second example in this figure shows how you can initialize a jagged array using the shorthand notation. Here, a jagged array of strings is created with three rows. The first row contains three elements, the second row contains four elements, and the third row contains two elements.

In the third example, a jagged array of type int is created with four rows. Then, a for loop cycles through the rows and creates a different number of elements for each column array. The first time through the loop, i will be equal to 0 so the length of the array will be set to 1. The second time through the loop, i will be equal to 1 so the length of the array will be set to 2. And so on.

For each column array, another for loop is used to initialize the element values. This loop uses a variable named j to index the columns. A variable named number is used to assign a value to each column. This variable is incremented within this for loop. As a result, the first row will have one element with the value 0. The second row will have two elements with the values 1 and 2. The third row will have three elements with the values 3, 4, and 5. And so on.

The fourth example in this figure uses nested for loops to print the contents of the array created in the third example. Here, each row is printed on a separate line so you can clearly see the number of elements it contains.

The fifth example shows how you can use nested foreach loops to produce the same output. In this example, the outer for loop accesses each element in the pyramid array as an array of int values named row. Then the inner for loop accesses each element in the row array as an int value named col.

The syntax for creating a jagged array

```
type[][] arrayName = new type[rowCount][];
```

Code that creates a jagged array of integers

```
int[][] numbers = new int[3][];
numbers[0] = new int[10];
numbers[1] = new int[15];
numbers[2] = new int[20];
```

Code that creates and initializes a jagged array of strings

```
String[][] titles = {{"War and Peace", "Wuthering Heights", "1984"},
                     {"Casablanca", "Wizard of Oz", "Star Wars", "Birdy"},
                     {"Blue Suede Shoes", "Yellow Submarine"}};
```

Code that creates and initializes a jagged array of integers

```
int number = 0;
int[][] pyramid = new int[4][];
for (int i = 0; i < pyramid.length; i++) {
    pyramid[i] = new int[i+1];
    for (int j = 0; j < pyramid[i].length; j++)
        pyramid[i][j] = number++;
}
```

Code that prints the contents of the jagged array of integers

```
for (int i = 0; i < pyramid.length; i++) {
    for (int j = 0; j < pyramid[i].length; j++)
        System.out.print(pyramid[i][j] + " ");
    System.out.print("\n");
}
```

The console output

```
0
1 2
3 4 5
6 7 8 9
```

Code that uses foreach loops to print a jagged array

```
for (int[] row : pyramid) {
    for (int col : row)
        System.out.print(col + " ");
    System.out.print("\n");
}
```

Description

- A *jagged array* is a two-dimensional array whose rows have different numbers of columns. When you create a jagged array, you specify the number of rows in the array, but you leave the size of each column array unspecified and set it later.

Figure 11-10   How to work with jagged arrays

Perspective

Now that you've finished this chapter, you should know how to work with one-dimensional and two-dimensional arrays. Although you'll use arrays in many applications, they may not always provide the functionality you need. In that case, you can use a more advanced data structure called a collection. You'll learn how to work with collections in the next chapter.

Summary

- An *array* is a special type of object that can store more than one primitive data type or object. The *length* (or *size*) of an array is the number of *elements* that are stored in the array. The *index* is the number that is used to identify any element in the array.

- For loops are often used to process arrays. With JDK 1.5 and later, you can use an *enhanced for loop*, or *foreach loop*, to process each element of an array without using indexes.

- You can use the Arrays class to fill, compare, copy, sort, and search arrays. You can use an assignment statement to create a second *reference* to the same array.

- To provide for sorting a user-defined class, that class must implement the Comparable interface.

- A *one-dimensional array* provides for a single list or column of elements so just one index value is required to identify each element. In contrast, a *two-dimensional array*, or an *array of arrays*, can be used to organize data in a table that has rows and columns. As a result, two index values are required to identify each element.

- A two-dimensional array can be *rectangular,* in which case each row has the same number of columns, or *jagged,* in which case each row can have a different number of columns.

Exercise 11-1   Use one-dimensional arrays

In this exercise, you can get some practice using one-dimensional arrays. When you finish this exercise, it should display output that looks something like this:

```
Monthly Sales

Enter month number: 3
Sales for March: $1,784.59

Continue? (y/n): y

Enter month number: 9
Sales for September: $3,279.62

Continue? (y/n): n

Total sales: $30,693.01
```

1. Open the project named ch11_ex1_MonthSales in the ex_starts directory. Then, open the MonthSalesApp class.

2. Create a one-dimensional array named monthNames that contains 12 string values with the names of the months.

3. Create another one-dimensional array named monthSales that contains 12 double values with the sales for each month in month order. Use any values you like.

4. Add code that displays the name of the month and the sales for the month as shown above if the month number entered by the user is valid. Now, test this code.

5. Use a for loop to sum the values in the array when the while loop ends. Then, display that value as shown above. Test this enhancement.

6. Comment out the for loop you just added. Then, use an enhanced for loop to sum the values in the array. Test this change.

Exercise 11-2   Use a rectangular array

This exercise guides you through the process of adding a rectangular array to the Future Value application. This array will store the values for up to ten of the calculations that are performed. When the program ends, it will print a summary of those calculations that looks something like this:

```
Future Value Calculations

Inv/Mo. Rate   Years   Future Value
$100.00 8.0%   10      $18,416.57
$125.00 8.0%   10      $23,020.71
$150.00 8.0%   10      $27,624.85
```

1. Open the project named ch11_ex2_FutureValue in the ex_starts directory. Then, review the code and run the application to make sure it works correctly.

2. Declare variables at the beginning of the main() method for a row counter and a rectangular array of strings that provides for 10 rows and 4 columns.

3. After the code that calculates, formats, and displays the results for each calculation, add code that stores the formatted values as strings in the next row of the array. (Hint: You can use the toString() method of the Integer class to store the years value.)

4. Add code to display the elements in the array at the console when the user indicates that the program should end. The output should be formatted as shown above and should only include the rows that contain data. Then, test the program by making up to 10 future value calculations.

Exercise 11-3 Sort an array of user-defined objects

In this exercise, you'll modify a Customer class so it implements the Comparable interface. Then, you'll sort an array of objects created from this class. When you finish this exercise, it should display output that looks something like this:

```
anne@murach.com Anne Boehm
joel@murach.com Joel Murach
mike@murach.com Mike Murach
```

1. Open the project named ch11_ex3_SortedCustomers in the ex_starts directory. Then, review the code in the Customer and SortedCustomersApp classes.

2. Modify the declaration for the Customer class so it implements the Comparable interface. Then, start the declaration for the compareTo() method.

3. Add code to the compareTo() method that compares the email field of the current customer with the email field of another customer. Because the email field is a string, you'll need to use the compareToIgnoreCase() method of the String class to do that. This method compares the string it's executed on with the string that's passed to it as an argument. If the first string is less than the second string, this method returns a negative integer. If the first string is greater than the second string, it returns a positive integer. And if the two strings are equal, it returns 0.

4. Add code to the SortedCustomersApp class that creates an array of Customer objects that can hold 3 elements, and create and assign Customer objects to those elements. Be sure that the email values you assign to the objects aren't in alphabetical order. Sort the array.

5. Code a foreach loop that prints the email, firstName, and lastName fields of each Customer object on a separate line.

6. Test the program until you're sure it works correctly.

Exercise 11-4   Work with a deck of cards

In this exercise, you'll write an application that uses arrays and loops to work with a deck of cards. When you finish this exercise, it should display output that looks something like this:

```
DECK
|Ace of Spades|2 of Spades|3 of Spades|4 of Spades|...
SHUFFLED DECK
|8 of Clubs|Jack of Hearts|4 of Hearts|9 of Hearts|...
HAND OF 2 CARDS
|8 of Clubs|Jack of Hearts|
```

1. Open the project named ch11_ex4_CardDeck in the ex_starts directory. Then, open the CardDeckApp class. Note that this class provides methods for getting a deck of cards, which is an array of strings, as well as methods for displaying cards, shuffling the deck, and dealing cards.

2. Add code to the getDeck() method so it returns a standard deck of 52 cards. To do that, create one array of strings for the four suites (Spades, Hearts, Clubs, and Diamonds), and a second array of strings for the 13 ranks for each suit. Then, use nested loops to create a deck of 52 cards.

3. Add code to the displayCards() method so it prints all cards in the array that's passed to it. Separate each card with a pipe character. Test the application to be sure the code gets and displays the deck properly.

4. Add code to the shuffleDeck() method that shuffles the deck of cards. To do that, this method can loop through each card in the deck and swap the current card with another card that's randomly selected. Test the application to be sure that the cards are shuffled.

5. Add code to the dealCards() method that creates a hand of cards by dealing the specified number of cards from the cards array. Test the application to be sure that the cards are dealt properly. Note that this doesn't remove the cards from the deck. As a result, it only works correctly for the first hand. In the next chapter, you'll learn an easy way to solve this issue.

12

How to work with collections and generics

In this chapter, you'll learn how to work with collections. As you'll see, collections are similar to arrays but provide more advanced features. Along with collections, you'll learn how to use generics, a feature that was introduced with Java 1.5 that lets you specify the type of objects that can be stored in a collection.

An introduction to collections

Like an array, a *collection* is an object that can hold one or more elements. However, unlike arrays, collections aren't a part of the Java language itself. Instead, collections are classes that are available from the Java API.

A comparison of arrays and collections

Figure 12-1 presents a brief comparison of arrays and collections. This shows that you can use arrays or collections to store multiple elements of the specified type. In fact, some collection classes—most notably the ArrayList class—actually use an array internally to store elements. However, this is transparent to the programmer.

Although arrays and collections have some similarities, they also have many differences. One important difference is that arrays are fixed in size. That means that if you initially create an array with 100 elements and then need to add another element, you must create a new array large enough to hold 101 elements, copy the 100 elements from the first array to the new array, add the new element, and discard the old array.

In contrast, a collection automatically increases its size when necessary. Behind the scenes, a collection may copy elements between arrays, but this is transparent to the programmer. As a result, when you create a collection, you don't need to specify the maximum size of the collection. Instead, you add as many elements to the collection as you want. Then, if necessary, the collection expands automatically to hold the new elements.

A second difference between arrays and collections is that arrays can store primitive types such as int and double values, but collections must use wrapper classes to store primitive types. Fortunately, with Java 5 and later, collections automatically add and remove the wrapper classes whenever necessary using a feature known as *autoboxing*.

A third difference is that you typically use the methods of a collection to set and get the elements of a collection. Since you can't call methods from an array, you typically use its indexes to set and get its elements. The two code examples in this figure show how this works. Here, the first example uses indexes to set three values in an array, but the second example uses the add() method of the ArrayList class to set the elements in the collection. Then, both examples use an enhanced for loop to get the elements and print them to the console.

By the way, don't worry if you don't understand all of the code in the second example. You'll learn the details of working with the ArrayList class later in this chapter. This example is only meant to illustrate some of the differences between working with arrays and collections.

How arrays and collections are similar

- Both can store multiple elements of the same type.

How arrays and collections differ

- Arrays are fixed in size and require the programmer to increase the size if necessary. Collections automatically increase their size if necessary.

- Arrays can store primitive types without using wrapper classes. Collections must use wrapper classes to store primitive types.

- Arrays don't provide methods for operations such as adding, replacing, and removing elements. Collections often provide methods that perform these operations.

Code that uses an array

```
String[] codes = new String[3];
codes[0] = "java";
codes[1] = "jsp";
codes[2] = "mysql";
for (String s : codes) {
    System.out.println(s);
}
```

Code that uses a collection

```
ArrayList<String> codes = new ArrayList<>();
codes.add("java");
codes.add("jsp");
codes.add("mysql");
for (String s : codes) {
    System.out.println(s);
}
```

Description

- A *collection* is an object that can hold other objects. Collections are similar to arrays, but are more flexible to use.

- With Java 5 and later, collections use a feature known as *autoboxing* to automatically add and remove the wrapper classes for primitive types whenever necessary.

Figure 12-1   A comparison of arrays and collections

An overview of the Java collection framework

Figure 12-2 shows a simplified diagram of the Java *collection framework*. This framework consists of a hierarchy of interfaces and classes. Here, the boxes with darker shading (Collection, Set, List, and Map) represent interfaces that define the basic collection types, and the boxes with lighter shading (ArrayList, LinkedList, HashSet, HashMap, and TreeMap) represent classes that implement these interfaces.

The collection framework provides two main types of collections represented by two distinct class hierarchies. The first hierarchy begins with an interface named Collection. A *collection* is an object that can hold one or more objects. The Set and List interfaces inherit the Collection interface and define two distinct types of collections. A *set* is a collection of unique objects. In most cases, sets are also unordered. That means that sets don't retain information about the order of elements added to the set.

On the other hand, a *list* is an ordered collection of objects. A list always maintains some sort of order for the objects it contains. Depending on the type of list, the order might be the order in which the items were added to the list, or it might be a sorted order based on a key value. In addition, lists allow duplicate elements.

The second main type of collection is called a *map*, and it's defined by the Map interface. A map is similar to a collection, but its elements consist of *key-value pairs* where each value is associated with a unique key. Each key must be associated with one and only one value. For example, a map might be used to store Customer objects mapped to customer numbers. In that case, the customer numbers are the keys and the Customer objects are the values. Even though the Map interface doesn't inherit the Collection interface, the term *collection* is often used to refer to both collections and maps.

Although Java provides more than 30 classes that implement the List, Set, or Map interfaces, you don't need to know how to use them all. The second table in this figure lists five collection classes that are commonly used. However, to get started, you can begin by learning how to use the ArrayList class as shown in this chapter. This is the only collection that you need to be able to work with for all of the applications presented in this book. Once you learn how to use this class, you shouldn't have much trouble learning how to use other collection classes if the need arises. If necessary, you can learn more about the other collection classes by searching the Internet.

The ArrayList class is an implementation of the List interface. This class defines an *array list* that works much like a standard array. In fact, the ArrayList class uses an array internally to store the elements of the list. The ArrayList class provides efficient access to the elements in the list. However, inserting an element into the middle of a list can be inefficient because all of the elements after the insertion point must be moved to accommodate the inserted element.

The LinkedList class is another implementation of the List interface. This class uses a special structure called a *linked list* to store the list's elements. The LinkedList class provides an efficient way to insert elements into the middle of a list. However, a linked list is less efficient when accessing elements.

The collection framework

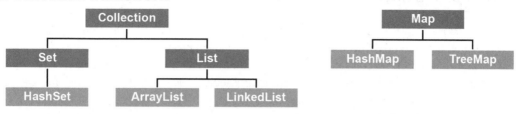

Collection interfaces

Interface	Description
Collection	Defines the basic methods available for all collections.
Set	Defines a collection that does not allow duplicate elements.
List	Defines a collection that maintains the sequence of elements in the list. It accesses elements by their integer index and typically allows duplicate elements.
Map	Defines a map. A map is similar to a set. However, it holds one or more key-value pairs instead of storing only values (elements). Each key-value pair consists of a key that uniquely identifies the value, and a value that stores the data.

Common collection classes

Class	Description
ArrayList	More efficient than a linked list for accessing individual elements randomly. However, less efficient than a linked list when inserting elements into the middle of the list.
LinkedList	Less efficient than an array list for accessing elements randomly. However, more efficient than an array list when inserting items into the middle of the list.
HashSet	Stores a set of unique elements. In other words, it does not allow duplicates elements.
HashMap	Stores key-value pairs where each key must be unique. In other words, it does not allow duplicate keys, but it does allow duplicate values.
TreeMap	Stores key-value pairs in a hierarchical data structure known as a *tree*. In addition, it automatically sequences elements by key.

Description

- The Java *collection framework* is interface based, which means that each class in the collection framework implements one of the interfaces defined by the framework.

- The collection framework consists of two class hierarchies: Collection and Map. A *collection* stores individual objects as elements. A *map* stores key-value pairs where you can use a key to retrieve a value.

Figure 12-2   The Java collection framework and classes

An introduction to generics

Prior to Java 5, the elements of a collection were defined as the Object type. As a result, you could store any type of object as an element in a collection. At first, this flexibility might seem like an advantage. But with it comes two disadvantages. First, there's no way to guarantee that objects of only a certain type are added to a collection. For example, you can't limit an ArrayList so it can hold only Product objects. Second, you must use casting whenever you retrieve an object from a collection. That's because an element can be any type of object. For example, to retrieve a Product object from a collection, you must cast the object to the Product type.

Java 5 introduced a new feature called *generics* that addresses these two problems. The generics feature lets you specify the element type for a collection. Then, Java can make sure that it only adds objects of the specified type to the collection. Conversely, Java can automatically cast any objects you retrieve from the collection to the correct type.

Figure 12-3 shows how the generics feature works. To specify a type when you declare a collection, you code the type in angle brackets immediately following the name of the collection class (such as ArrayList or LinkedList). To illustrate, the first example shows a statement that declares and instantiates an instance of an array list collection named codes that holds String objects. Here, <String> is specified following the ArrayList class name to indicate that the elements of the array list must be String objects.

The second and third examples are similar, but they create collections that can hold integers and Product objects. Here, the second example uses a *wrapper class* (the Integer class) instead of the primitive type (the int type). This allows the collection to store an array of integer values. That's necessary because it's illegal to declare a collection with a primitive type like this:

```
ArrayList<int> numbers = new ArrayList<int>();   // illegal!
```

In the first three examples, you can see that the type is coded twice: once to declare the collection and again on the constructor that creates an instance of the collection. If you're using Java 7 or later, though, you can omit the type from the brackets that follow the constructor as long as the compiler can infer the type from the context. The fourth example shows how this works. Here, the code accomplishes the same task as the first example but without duplicating the collection type. Since this feature results in shorter and simpler code, it's used throughout the rest of this chapter.

The syntax for specifying the type of elements in a collection

```
CollectionClass<Type> collectionName = new CollectionClass<Type>();
```

A statement that creates an array list of String objects

```
ArrayList<String> codes = new ArrayList<String>();
```

A statement that creates an array list of integers

```
ArrayList<Integer> numbers = new ArrayList<Integer>();
```

A statement that creates an array list of Product objects

```
ArrayList<Product> products = new ArrayList<Product>();
```

The syntax for using type inference with Java 7 or later

```
CollectionClass<Type> collectionName = new CollectionClass<>();
```

A statement that creates an array list of String objects

```
ArrayList<String> codes = new ArrayList<>();
```

Description

- *Generics* refers to a feature that lets you create typed collections. A *typed collection* is a collection that can hold objects of only a certain type. This feature was introduced with Java 5.

- To declare a variable that refers to a typed collection, you list the type in angle brackets (<>) following the name of the collection class.

- When you use a constructor for a typed collection, you can specify the type variable in angle brackets following the constructor name. The type variable can't be a primitive type such as int or double, but it can be a wrapper class such as Integer or Double. It can also be a user-defined class such as Product.

- Beginning with Java 7, you can omit the type from within the brackets that follow the constructor if the compiler can infer the type from the context. This empty set of brackets is known as the *diamond operator*.

- If you do not specify a type for a collection, the collection can hold any type of object. However, the Java compiler will issue warning messages whenever you access the collection to warn you that type checking can't be performed for the collection.

Figure 12-3   An introduction to generics

How to work with an array list

The ArrayList class is one of the most commonly used collections in Java. You can use this class to create a type of collection called an *array list*. An array list uses an array internally to store list elements. As a result, an array list is similar to an array in many ways. However, unlike an array, an array list automatically adjusts its size as you add elements to it. Because of that, you don't have to write any special code to make sure that you don't exceed the capacity of an array list.

How to create an array list

Figure 12-4 shows two constructors that you can use to create an array list. These constructors use a capital letter E to indicate that you must specify the type of element that you want to store in the collection within the angle brackets.

The first example in this figure creates an array list named codes that can store String objects. Since this code uses the default constructor for the ArrayList class, this example creates an array list that has an initial capacity of 10 elements. Then, if necessary, the array list automatically increases capacity to be able to store more elements.

Unfortunately, increasing the capacity of an array list is not an efficient operation, especially if the array list is large. First, the ArrayList class must create a new array of the expanded size. Then, the elements of the old array must be copied to the new array. Next, the new element must be added to the new array. Finally, the old array must be removed from memory.

As a result, if you know the number of elements that you're going to need to store, it's more efficient to create an array list that has an initial capacity that's slightly larger than the number of elements. To do that, you can use code like the code shown in the second example. This code creates an array list that has an initial capacity of 200 elements.

The last example in this figure shows that you can use a variable of the List type to refer to an ArrayList object. This works because the ArrayList class implements the List interface. In other words, an ArrayList object is also a List object. There are two advantages to declaring an array list as a List object. First, it requires less typing. Second, and more importantly, it reduces the connection between the code and the ArrayList list class because it only allows the code to use methods that are available from the List interface. As a result, if you later decide that you want to use a different type of object for the list, it's easy to change from the ArrayList class to another class that implements the List interface, such as the LinkedList class.

The ArrayList class

```
java.util.ArrayList
```

Common constructors of the ArrayList class

Constructor	Description
`ArrayList<E>()`	Creates an empty array list of the specified type with the default capacity of 10 elements.
`ArrayList<E>(intCapacity)`	Creates an empty array list of the specified type with the specified capacity.

Code that creates an array list of String objects

With the default starting capacity of 10 elements

```
ArrayList<String> codes = new ArrayList<>();
```

With a specified starting capacity of 200 elements

```
ArrayList<String> codes = new ArrayList<>(200);
```

Code that uses the List type to store an ArrayList object

```
List<Product> products = new ArrayList<>();
```

Description

- The ArrayList class uses an array internally to store the elements in the list.
- The capacity of an array list automatically increases whenever necessary.
- When you create an array list, you can use the default starting capacity of 10 elements, or you can specify the starting capacity.
- If you know the number of elements that your list needs to be able to store, you can improve the performance of the ArrayList class by specifying a starting capacity that's just over that number of elements.
- Since the ArrayList class implements the List interface, an ArrayList object is also a List object. As a result, you can use a variable of the List type to refer to an ArrayList object.

Figure 12-4   How to create an array list

How to add and get elements

The first example of figure 12-5 shows how to add elements to an array list. More specifically, it adds three String objects to the array list named codes. To do that, it uses the add() method of the ArrayList class. Here, the third statement specifies an index of 0. As a result, this statement adds the string ("java") as the first element in the array list. Then, the array list automatically moves the other strings in the list ("jsp" and "mysql") back by one index.

The second example gets an element from the array list named codes. More specifically, it gets the last element in the list. To do that, it calculates the index for the last element by subtracting a value of 1 from the size. Then, it uses this index to get the last element in the array list.

Although you may need to get one element from an array list, it's more common to need to process all elements of an array list. To do that, it's common to use an enhanced for loop as shown in the third example. This example prints each element in the array list to the console. However, if necessary, you could perform more complex processing on each element.

The fourth example shows another way to get and display the values in a collection. To do that, you specify the name of the collection in the println() method. This implicitly calls the collection's toString() method, which returns a string that lists the value of each element. Since this displays all elements on the same line and enclosed in brackets, this technique is useful only for small collections. However, this technique is often useful when developing and debugging applications.

Common methods of the ArrayList class

Method	Description
add(object)	Adds the specified object to the end of the list.
add(index, object)	Adds the specified object at the specified index position.
get(index)	Returns the object at the specified index position.
size()	Returns the number of elements in the list.

Code that adds three elements to an array list

```
codes.add("jsp");
codes.add("mysql");
codes.add(0, "java");
```

Code that gets the last element

```
int lastIndex = codes.size() - 1;
String lastCode = codes.get(lastIndex);     // "mysql"
```

Code that gets and displays each element of an array list

```
for (String code : codes) {
    System.out.println(code);
}
```

Resulting output

```
java
jsp
mysql
```

An easy way to display the contents of a collection

```
System.out.println(codes);
```

Resulting output

```
[java, jsp, mysql]
```

Description

- You can use the methods of the ArrayList class to add elements to an array list and to get elements from an array list.

Figure 12-5   How to add and get the elements of an array list

How to replace, remove, and search for elements

The first example in figure 12-6 shows how to replace an element in an array list. To do that, the first statement calls the set() method to replace the element that's stored at the index of 2 with "andr." In other words, it changes the third element of the array list to "andr".

The second example shows how to remove an element from an array list. To do that, this code calls the remove() method and specifies an index of 1. As a result, this code removes the second element from the array list and stores it in the String variable named code.

The output for this example shows that the second element ("jsp") was removed and all elements after it were shifted forward. For instance, the third element ("andr") is now the second element.

The third example shows how to search for an element in an array list. To do that, this code calls the contains() method and specifies the object that it's searching for. If this object exists, the code in this example prints a message to the console that indicates that the object exists. However, once you know an object exists in the array list, you can perform any type of processing on it.

More methods of the ArrayList class

Method	Description
`clear()`	Removes all elements from the list.
`contains(object)`	Returns true if the specified object is in the list.
`indexOf(object)`	Returns the index position of the specified object.
`isEmpty()`	Returns true if the list is empty.
`remove(index)`	Removes the object at the specified index position and returns that object.
`remove(object)`	Removes the specified object and returns a boolean value that indicates whether the operation was successful.
`set(index, object)`	Sets the element at the specified index to the specified object.
`toArray()`	Returns an array containing the elements of the list.

Code that replaces an element

```
codes.set(2, "andr");
System.out.println(codes);
```

Resulting output

```
[java, jsp, andr]
```

Code that removes an element

```
String code = codes.remove(1);    // removes "jsp"
System.out.println("'" + code + "' was removed.");
System.out.println(codes);
```

Resulting output

```
'jsp' was removed.
[java, andr]
```

Code that searches for an element

```
String searchCode = "andr";
if (codes.contains(searchCode)) {
    System.out.println("This list contains: '" + searchCode + "'");
}
```

Resulting output

```
This list contains: 'andr'
```

Description

- You can use the methods of the ArrayList class to replace, remove, and search the elements of an array list.

Figure 12-6   How to replace, remove, and search the elements of an array list

How to store primitive types in an array list

Figure 12-7 shows how to store primitive types such as int values in an array list. To do that, you can use a *wrapper class* to specify the type of element that can be stored by the array list.

In this figure, for instance, the first example creates an array list of Integer objects. Then, it adds the int values 1, 2, and 3 to the array list. This works because the compiler automatically converts the int values to Integer objects before it stores them in the array list.

Conversely, the second and third examples get int values from the array list, even though this list stores Integer objects. Again, that's possible because the compiler automatically converts the Integer objects to int values.

This feature is known as *autoboxing*, and it is available with Java 5 and later. Prior to Java 5, it was necessary to write extra code to store primitive types in their wrapper classes and to get them out of their wrapper classes. Fortunately, that's not necessary with recent versions of Java.

Code that stores primitive types in an array list

```
ArrayList<Integer> numbers = new ArrayList<>();
numbers.add(1);
numbers.add(2);
numbers.add(3);
System.out.println(numbers);
```

Resulting output

```
[1, 2, 3]
```

Code that gets a primitive type from an array list

```
int firstNumber = numbers.get(0);      // 1
```

An enhanced for loop that gets primitive types from an array list

```
for (int number : numbers) {
    System.out.println(number);
}
```

Resulting output

```
1
2
3
```

Description

- All primitive types have corresponding *wrapper classes*. For example, the Integer class is the wrapper class for the int type, the Double class is the wrapper class for the double type, and so on.

- To store a primitive type in a collection, you can specify its wrapper class as the type for the collection. Then, the compiler automatically converts the primitive value to its wrapper type when adding values to the collection. This feature is known as *autoboxing*.

- To get a primitive type from a collection, you don't need to do anything because the compiler automatically gets the primitive value from the wrapper class for you.

Figure 12-7   How to store primitive types in an array list

The Invoice application

Now that you know how to work with an array list, this chapter shows how to use an array list within the context of the Invoice application that's presented in the next few figures.

The console

Figure 12-8 presents the console for the Invoice application. This console works much like the Line Item application presented in earlier chapters. However, it accepts one or more line items for each invoice. Then, when the user finishes adding line items, the Invoice application displays each line item and the total for the invoice. To do that, it uses the Invoice class that's presented next.

The console

```
Welcome to the Invoice application

Enter product code: java
Enter quantity:     2
Another line item? (y/n): y

Enter product code: jsp
Enter quantity:     1
Another line item? (y/n): n

Description                     Price    Qty  Total
Murach's Java Programming       $57.50   2    $115.00
Murach's Java Servlets and JSP  $57.50   1    $57.50

Invoice total: $172.50
```

Description

- This application accepts one or more line items for an invoice from the user. After all the line items have been entered, the application displays the line items along with the total amount for the invoice.

- To enter a line item, the user enters a product code and quantity. To enter another line item, the user can enter "y". To complete the invoice, the user can enter "n".

Figure 12-8   The console for the Invoice application

The Invoice class

The Invoice class shown in figure 12-9 begins by defining one instance variable, a list of LineItem objects named lineItems that's implemented as an array list. This list stores the line items for the invoice. The default constructor for the Invoice class creates this list but doesn't add any line items to it. However, the addItem() method provides a way to add line items to the invoice. This method defines a LineItem object as a parameter. Then, it calls the add() method of the lineItems list and adds the LineItem object to the list.

The getLineItems() method provides a way to get the lineItems list. The return type for this method (List<LineItem>) uses generics to specify that the list can only store LineItem objects, which is what you want.

The getTotal() method uses an enhanced for loop to process each LineItem element in the lineItems list. Within this loop, the code calls the getTotal() method of the current line item, which simply returns the line item total. Then, it adds that total to the invoiceTotal variable. After this loop, the getTotal() method returns the invoiceTotal variable.

The getTotalFormatted() method formats the invoice total as a currency string. To do that, this method calls the getTotal() method of the invoice. That way, the getTotalFormatted() method doesn't duplicate any code in the getTotal() method.

The Invoice class

```java
package murach.business;

import java.text.NumberFormat;
import java.util.List;
import java.util.ArrayList;

public class Invoice {
    // the instance variable
    private List<LineItem> lineItems;

    // the constructor
    public Invoice() {
        lineItems = new ArrayList<>();
    }

    // a method that adds a line item
    public void addItem(LineItem lineItem) {
        lineItems.add(lineItem);
    }

    // the get accessor for the line item collection
    public List<LineItem> getLineItems() {
        return lineItems;
    }

    // a method that gets the invoice total
    public double getTotal() {
        double invoiceTotal = 0;
        for (LineItem lineItem : lineItems) {
            invoiceTotal += lineItem.getTotal();
        }
        return invoiceTotal;
    }

    // a method that returns the invoice total in currency format
    public String getTotalFormatted() {
        NumberFormat currency = NumberFormat.getCurrencyInstance();
        return currency.format(getTotal());
    }
}
```

Figure 12-9   The Invoice class

The InvoiceApp class

Figure 12-10 shows the code for the InvoiceApp class. This class contains a main() method that begins by declaring a variable that stores an Invoice object. Then, it passes this object to the other two static methods in this class.

The static getLineItems() method contains the code that prompts the user to enter the product code and quantity for each line item. To do that, it uses the Console class presented earlier in this book. Then, this method creates a new LineItem object from the user input and adds that object to the Invoice object.

The displayInvoice() method contains the code that displays the Invoice object after the user has finished entering line items. To do that, it uses an enhanced for loop to get each line item for the invoice. This loop starts by getting the product for the line item. Then, it formats and displays the data for the product and line item. Then, after all of the line items are displayed, the invoice total is displayed.

The InvoiceApp class

```java
package murach.ui;

import murach.db.ProductDB;
import murach.business.Invoice;
import murach.business.LineItem;
import murach.business.Product;

public class InvoiceApp {

    public static void main(String args[]) {
        System.out.println("Welcome to the Invoice application\n");
        Invoice invoice = new Invoice();
        getLineItems(invoice);
        displayInvoice(invoice);
    }

    public static void getLineItems(Invoice invoice) {
        String choice = "y";
        while (choice.equalsIgnoreCase("y")) {
            String productCode = Console.getString("Enter product code: ");
            int quantity = Console.getInt("Enter quantity:       ");

            Product product = ProductDB.getProduct(productCode);
            invoice.addItem(new LineItem(product, quantity));

            choice = Console.getString("Another line item? (y/n): ");
            System.out.println();
        }
    }

    public static void displayInvoice(Invoice invoice) {
        System.out.println("Code\tDescription\t\t\tPrice\tQty\tTotal");
        System.out.println("----\t-----------\t\t\t-----\t---\t-----");
        for (LineItem lineItem : invoice.getLineItems()) {
            Product product = lineItem.getProduct();
            String s = product.getCode()
                + "\t" + product.getDescription()
                + "\t" + product.getPriceFormatted()
                + "\t" + lineItem.getQuantity()
                + "\t" + lineItem.getTotalFormatted();
            System.out.println(s);
        }
        System.out.println("\n\t\t\t\t\tInvoice total:\t"
            + invoice.getTotalFormatted() + "\n");
    }
}
```

Figure 12-10   The InvoiceApp class

How to work with a linked list

The LinkedList class is similar to the ArrayList class, but it provides more features and uses a different technique to store its data. The topics that follow describe the LinkedList class and show some examples that illustrate how you can use this class.

How to create a linked list and add and get elements

Figure 12-11 shows how to use the constructor for the LinkedList class to create a *linked list*. This works just like the constructor for the ArrayList class, except that you can't specify an initial capacity for a linked list. For instance, the first example in this figure creates a linked list named codes that can store String objects.

After you create a linked list, you can add elements to it. You should realize, though, that unlike an array list, a linked list doesn't use an array to store its elements. Instead, the elements you add to a linked list are stored as separate objects. Each list element is stored along with pointers to the objects that precede it and follow it. As a result, the LinkedList class can use these pointers to navigate through the entire list.

Because the entries for a linked list aren't stored in an array, inserting an element into the middle of a linked list is more efficient than inserting an element into the middle of an array list. To insert an element into the middle of an array list, all of the elements that follow the insertion point must be moved down in the list. The more elements in the array list and the closer to the beginning of the array the insertion point is, the longer it takes to insert the element. In contrast, an element can be inserted into the middle of a linked list by simply adjusting the previous and next pointers for the elements that precede and follow the insertion point.

The second example illustrates how this works. Here, the first two statements use the add() method to add elements at index positions 0 and 1 (the end of the list). Then, the third add() method indicates that the element should be added at index position 1, moving the element that's currently in that position to index position 2. To do that, the next pointer for the first element and the previous pointer for what is now the third element are changed so they point to the new element.

This increased efficiency for inserting elements has a trade-off, however. Although a linked list can be updated more quickly than an array list, it can't be accessed as quickly. Because all of the elements in an array list are stored in adjacent memory locations, access to those elements is fast. In contrast, access to the elements in a linked list is relatively slow because the pointers for the elements must be used.

For example, suppose you use the get() method to access the 500th element in a linked list with more than 1,000 elements. To do that, the get() method begins by accessing the first element in the list to get the pointer to the second

The LinkedList class

```
java.util.LinkedList
```

A constructor for the LinkedList class

Constructor	Description
`LinkedList<E>()`	Creates an empty linked list using the specified type.

Common methods of the LinkedList class

Method	Description
`add(object)`	Adds the specified object to the end of the list.
`add(index, object)`	Adds the specified object at the specified index position.
`get(index)`	Returns the object at the specified index position.
`size()`	Returns the number of elements in the list.

Code that creates a linked list of String objects

```
LinkedList<String> codes = new LinkedList<>();
```

Code that adds three elements to the list

```
codes.add("mysql");
codes.add("jsp");
codes.add(1, "java");
System.out.println(codes);
```

Resulting output

```
[mysql, java, jsp]
```

Code that gets the last element of the linked list

```
int lastIndex = codes.size() - 1;
String lastCode = codes.get(lastIndex);     // "jsp"
```

Code that gets and displays each element of the linked list

```
for (String code : codes) {
    System.out.println(code);
}
```

Resulting output

```
mysql
java
jsp
```

Description

- A *linked list* is a collection that's similar to an array list. However, the LinkedList class doesn't use an array to store its elements. Instead, each element in the list contains pointers that are used to refer to adjacent elements.

- Like the ArrayList class, the LinkedList class implements the List interface. Because of that, you can use any of the methods of the List class to work with a linked list.

Figure 12-11   How to create a linked list and add and get elements

element. It then accesses the second element to get a pointer to the third element. This process continues until the 500ᵗʰ element has been retrieved. In other words, to access a particular element in a linked list, all of the elements that precede it must be accessed.

Actually, the get() method first checks to see if the element being retrieved is closer to the first or last element in the list. If the element is closer to the last element, the search for the element begins at the last element and proceeds backwards until the desired element is located. To retrieve the last element of a linked list as shown in the third example in figure 12-11, for instance, only that element needs to be retrieved.

The fourth example in figure 12-11 shows code that uses an enhanced for loop to process all of the elements in the linked list. Note that you could also process the list using a standard for loop with an index variable and the get() method. However, processing a linked list with an enhanced for loop is more efficient than processing it with a standard for loop. That's because the enhanced for loop is able to efficiently use the pointers stored with each list entry to access the next element in the list. For example, to move from the 100ᵗʰ element to the 101ˢᵗ element, the enhanced for loop simply uses the pointer to the next element. In contrast, the get() method must start at the beginning of the list each time an element is accessed.

How to replace, remove, and search for elements

Figure 12-12 presents some additional methods for working with linked lists. If you compare the examples that use these methods to the examples in figure 12-6 that use the methods of the ArrayList class, you'll see that they're identical. That's because all of these methods are members of either the Collection or List interface, which are implemented by both the ArrayList and LinkedList classes. In addition to these two interfaces, however, the LinkedList class also implements the Queue and Deque interfaces. You'll learn about some of the functionality provided by these two interfaces next.

More methods of the LinkedList class

Method	Description
`clear()`	Removes all elements from the list.
`contains(object)`	Returns true if the specified object is in the list.
`indexOf(object)`	Returns the index position of the specified object.
`isEmpty()`	Returns true if the list is empty.
`remove(index)`	Removes and returns the object at the specified index position.
`remove(object)`	Removes the specified object.
`set(index, object)`	Replaces the element at the specified index position with the specified object.
`toArray()`	Returns an array containing the elements of the list.

Code that replaces an element

```
codes.set(2, "andr");
System.out.println(codes);
```

Resulting output

```
[mysql, java, andr]
```

Code that removes an element

```
String code = codes.remove(1);    // removes "java"
System.out.println("'" + code + "' was removed.");
System.out.println(codes);
```

Resulting output

```
'java' was removed.
[mysql, andr]
```

Code that searches for an element

```
String searchCode = "andr";
if (codes.contains(searchCode)) {
    System.out.println("This list contains: '" + searchCode + "'");
}
```

Resulting output

```
This list contains: 'andr'
```

Figure 12-12   How to replace, remove, and search the elements of a linked list

How to use the methods of the Queue and Deque interfaces

Figure 12-13 presents some of the methods of the Queue and Deque interfaces that are implemented by the LinkedList class. To start, the addFirst() and addLast() methods let you add elements to the beginning and end of a list, as shown in the first example in this figure. You can use these methods instead of the add() methods that you saw in figure 12-11.

The next three methods let you remove elements from a list. The remove() and removeFirst() methods both remove and return the first element in the list. You might want to use removeFirst() to make it clear what element you're removing. The removeLast() method removes and returns the last element in the list. This is illustrated by the second example in this figure.

If you want to return but not remove the first or last element in a list, you can use the element(), getFirst(), or getLast() method. The element() and getFirst() methods return the first element in a list. Because the getFirst() method makes it clear what element is being retrieved, you'll typically use it instead of the element() method. The getLast() method returns the last element in a list and can be used in place of the size() and get() methods shown in figure 12-11.

All three of the remove methods as well as the element(), getFirst(), and getLast() methods throw a NoSuchElementException if the list is empty. In contrast, the poll() and peek() methods, which perform the same functions as the removeFirst() and getFirst() methods, return null if the list is empty. The poll() and peek() methods are traditionally used with queues, which you'll learn more about in the next figure.

The third example illustrates how the getFirst() and peek() methods differ. Here, after the first statement declares a variable named firstCode, the second statement uses the clear() method to remove all of the elements from the codes list. Then, the next two statements use the getFirst() and peek() methods to get the first element in the list. Because the list is empty, though, the getFirst() method throws a NoSuchElementException. In contrast, the peek() method returns null.

Another method that's traditionally used with queues is the offer() method. You can use this method in place of the addLast() method to add an object to the end of a list. Unlike the addLast() method, though, the offer() method returns a true or false value to indicate if the object was added successfully.

When you develop a Java application that calls for a list, you should carefully consider whether to implement the collection using the ArrayList class or the LinkedList class. This is especially important if the list will contain a large number of elements. The larger the list, the more important the performance trade-offs of using an array list or a linked list become. In many cases, though, you'll use a linked list simply because you need the additional features that the Queue and Deque interfaces provide.

Methods of the Queue and Deque interfaces implemented by the LinkedList class

Method	Description
addFirst(object)	Adds the specified object to the beginning of the list.
addLast(object)	Adds the specified object to the end of the list.
remove()	Removes and returns the first element from the list. Throws NoSuchElementException if the list is empty.
removeFirst()	Removes and returns the first element from the list. Throws NoSuchElementException if the list is empty.
removeLast()	Removes and returns the last element from the list. Throws NoSuchElementException if the list is empty.
element()	Returns but doesn't remove the first element in the list. Throws NoSuchElementException if the list is empty.
getFirst()	Returns the first element in the list. Throws NoSuchElementException if the list is empty.
getLast()	Returns the last element in the list. Throws NoSuchElementException if the list is empty.
poll()	Returns and removes the first element from the list. Returns null if the list is empty.
peek()	Returns but doesn't remove the first element in the list. Returns null if the list is empty.
offer(object)	Attempts to add the specified object to the end of the list. Returns true if the object was added. Returns false if the object is rejected.

Code that adds elements to the beginning and end of the list

```
codes.addFirst("java");
codes.addLast("jscr");
System.out.println(codes);
```

Resulting output

```
[java, mysql, andr, jscr]
```

Code that removes the last element of the list

```
String lastCode = codes.removeLast();
System.out.println(lastCode);
System.out.println(codes);
```

Resulting output

```
jscr
[java, mysql, andr]
```

Code that clears the list and then tries to get the first element

```
String firstCode;
codes.clear();
firstCode = codes.getFirst();    // throws NoSuchElementException
firstCode = codes.peek();        // returns null
```

Figure 12-13   How to use the methods of the Queue and Deque interfaces

A class that uses generics and a linked list to define a queue

A *queue* is a type of collection that lets you access elements on a *first-in, first-out* (*FIFO*) basis. This is similar to standing in a line, or queue. The first person to get in the queue is the first person to get out of the queue. Queues are used in many different types of data processing applications. For example, a company might use a queue to process invoices in the order they were received.

As figure 12-14 shows, a queue traditionally supports two basic operations: enqueue and dequeue. An *enqueue* operation adds an element to the end of the queue, and a *dequeue* operation retrieves the element that's at the front of the queue. In addition, a dequeue operation removes the element from the queue. As a result, all of the other elements in the queue move up one position in the queue.

The LinkedList class provides the basic operations you need to implement a queue. The addLast() method provides the enqueue operation, and the removeFirst() method provides the dequeue operation. Although the LinkedList class provides many other operations, you don't need them for a queue.

The first example shows a class that implements a simple queue. Here, the class creates a linked list as a private class variable. Then, it exposes three methods: enqueue(), dequeue(), and size(). The enqueue() method calls the addLast() method of the LinkedList class. The dequeue() method calls the removeFirst() method of the LinkedList class. And the size() method calls the size() method of the LinkedList class. When you use the Queue class, all other features of the LinkedList class are effectively hidden.

The declaration for the Queue class uses generics to include a type variable named E. This allows you to store any type of object in the queue. This class also uses the same type variable to specify the type of objects that the linked list can store, to specify the parameter type for the enqueue() method, and to specify the return type for the dequeue() method. As a result, if the user specifies Product for the queue type, the Queue class creates a linked list that can store Product objects. In addition, the enqueue() method accepts a Product object, and the dequeue() method returns a Product object.

The second example shows how this works. The code in this example starts by creating a queue that stores strings. Then, it calls the enqueue() method three times to add three entries to the queue. Next, it uses the println() method to display the number of entries in the queue. To do that, it calls the size() method of the queue. Finally, it uses a while loop to retrieve each entry using the dequeue() method and then print that entry. This loop executes as long as the size() method of the queue indicates that there is at least one more entry in the queue.

The main purpose of this figure is to show you how to use generics to create your own collection classes. However, the Java API includes many other classes for working with collections, including classes for working with queues. As a result, before creating your own collection classes, you should check whether the Java API already has a collection that provides the functionality you need. To do that, you can start by looking in the documentation for the java.util package. For example, this package contains the Queue interface and a list of known classes that implement the Queue interface.

Methods of a queue

Method	Description
enqueue(element)	Adds the specified element to the end of the queue.
dequeue()	Retrieves and removes an element from the front of the queue.
size()	Returns the number of elements in the queue.

Code for a class that uses generics to implement a queue

```java
import java.util.LinkedList;

public class Queue<E> {
    private LinkedList<E> list = new LinkedList<>();

    public void enqueue(E item) {
        list.addLast(item);
    }

    public E dequeue() {
        return list.removeFirst();
    }

    public int size() {
        return list.size();
    }
}
```

Code that uses the Queue class

```java
Queue<String> invoices = new Queue<>();
invoices.enqueue("Invoice 1");
invoices.enqueue("Invoice 2");
invoices.enqueue("Invoice 3");
System.out.println("The queue contains " + invoices.size() + " invoices");

while (invoices.size() > 0) {
    String invoice = invoices.dequeue();
    System.out.println("Processing: " + invoice);
}
System.out.println("The queue contains " + invoices.size() + " invoices");
```

Resulting output

```
The queue contains 3 invoices
Processing: Invoice 1
Processing: Invoice 2
Processing: Invoice 3
The queue contains 0 invoices
```

Description

- A *queue* is a *first-in, first-out (FIFO)* collection. To implement a simple queue, you can use generics and a linked list as shown above.

Figure 12-14   A class that uses generics and a linked list to define a queue

How to work with maps

The next two topics show you how to work with two classes that implement the Map interface: HashMap and TreeMap. These classes let you create collections in which objects can be accessed by using a key. The main difference between a *hash map* and a *tree map* is that the entries in a hash map are not stored in any particular sequence, while the entries in a tree map are automatically sorted by key.

The HashMap and TreeMap classes

Figure 12-15 presents the HashMap and TreeMap classes. Both of these classes implement the Map interface, which defines the basic behavior of a map. A *map* is a collection whose elements are pairs of keys and values. For example, you might use a map to store a collection of Product objects that can be accessed by a product code. In that case, the keys would be product codes and the values would be Product objects.

Unlike the other collections you've seen in this chapter, you specify two types when you declare a map. The first, identified as K in the figure, represents the type of the map's keys. The second, identified as V, is the type of the map's values. Often, the key is a simple type such as String or Integer and the value is a user-defined type such as Product or Customer.

Like other collections, you use the get() method to retrieve an object from a map. The get() method accepts a single parameter that represents the key value for the object you want to retrieve. Then, the get() method returns the value object that corresponds to the specified key. If the key isn't in the map, the get() method returns null.

Although it's unlikely, it's possible for a key to be in the map, but for the value associated with the key to be null. In that case, the get() method returns null. As a result, a null can mean that either the key isn't in the map, or the key is in the map but the value object associated with the key is null. To distinguish between these possibilities, you can use the containsKey() method. This method returns true if the key is in the map and false if it isn't.

Unlike other types of collections, maps don't have an add() method. Instead, the Map interface uses the put() method to add an element to a map. The put() method accepts two arguments that represent the key and value. If the key is already in the map, the put() method replaces the existing value.

Each element of a map implements the Map.Entry interface. Because of that, the elements of a map are typically referred to as *entries*. As this figure shows, the Map.Entry interface provides two methods that you can use to get the key and value for an entry: getKey() and getValue().

In case you're interested, a hash map and a tree map use different data structures to store their entries. A hash map uses a data structure called a *hash table*, and a tree map uses a structure called a *red-black tree*. The details of how these structures work are beyond the scope of this book. But if you're interested, you can search the Internet for more information.

The HashMap and TreeMap classes

```
java.util.HashMap
java.util.TreeMap
```

Common constructors

Constructor	Description
`HashMap<K,V>()`	Creates an empty HashMap using the specified types for the keys and values.
`TreeMap<K,V>()`	Creates an empty TreeMap using the specified types for the keys and values.

Common methods

Method	Description
`clear()`	Removes all entries from the map.
`containsKey(key)`	Returns true if the specified key is in the map.
`containsValue(value)`	Returns true if the specified value is in the map.
`entrySet()`	Returns a set of all the entries in the map as Map.Entry objects.
`get(key)`	Returns the value for the entry with the specified key. Returns null if the key isn't found.
`put(key, value)`	Adds an entry with the specified key and value, or replaces the value if an entry with the key already exists.
`remove(key)`	Removes the entry with the specified key.
`size()`	Returns the number of entries in the map.

Common methods of the Map.Entry interface

Method	Description
`getKey()`	Returns the key for the map entry.
`getValue()`	Returns the value for the map entry.

Description

- A *map* is a collection that contains values that are associated with keys. The two most commonly used classes that implement maps are HashMap and TreeMap.

- The main difference between a hash map and a tree map is that a tree map automatically maintains entries in order based on the key values. In contrast, a hash map doesn't maintain its entries in sorted order. If an application doesn't require that the entries be kept in order, a hash map is often more efficient than a tree map.

- Each entry of a map implements the Map.Entry interface in the java.util package. You can use the methods provided by this interface to get the key and value for an entry.

Note

- You can use a custom class for the key objects of a hash map. To do that, the class must override the hashCode() and equals() methods inherited from the Object class. For more information, see the Java documentation.

Figure 12-15   The HashMap and TreeMap classes

Code examples that work with maps

Figure 12-16 shows two code examples that work with maps. The only difference between these two examples is that the first one uses the HashMap class and the second one uses the TreeMap class. Other than that, the code for these two examples is identical. However, the two examples produce different output.

Both examples start by declaring and creating a map named books. This map stores book titles that are associated with codes. Because both the book titles and codes are strings, this statement specifies String for both the key and value type.

The next three statements use the put() method to add three entries to the map. Then, an enhanced for loop displays the entries in the map. In this loop, the object type is Map.Entry. Because of that, the entrySet() method is used to get all of the Map.Entry objects from the books map. Then, the statement within the loop can use the getKey() and getValue() methods of the Map.Entry interface to get the key and value for an entry. After this loop executes, the get() method gets the title of the book whose code is "java" and prints that title to the console.

The output for the first example shows that the books in the hash map aren't stored in key sequence. In addition, they aren't stored in the order they were added to the map. Instead, their positions in the collection are determined by a hashing function that converts the keys to indexes. In contrast, the output for the second example shows that the books in the tree map are stored in alphabetical sequence by key.

Code that uses a hash map

```
// create an empty hash map
Map<String,String> books = new HashMap<>();

// add three entries
books.put("jscr", "Murach's JavaScript and jQuery");
books.put("andr", "Murach's Android Programming");
books.put("java", "Murach's Java Programming");

// print the entries
for (Map.Entry book : books.entrySet()) {
    System.out.println(book.getKey() + ": " + book.getValue());
}

// print the entry whose key is "java"
System.out.println("\nCode java is " + books.get("java"));
```

Resulting output

```
java: Murach's Java Programming
andr: Murach's Android Programming
jscr: Murach's JavaScript and jQuery

Code java is Murach's Java Programming
```

Code that uses a tree map

```
// create an empty tree map
Map<String,String> books = new TreeMap<>();

// add three entries
books.put("jscr", "Murach's JavaScript and jQuery");
books.put("andr", "Murach's Android Programming");
books.put("java", "Murach's Java Programming");

// print the entries
for (Map.Entry book : books.entrySet()) {
    System.out.println(book.getKey() + ": " + book.getValue());
}

// print the entry whose key is "java"
System.out.println("\nCode java is " + books.get("java"));
```

Resulting output

```
andr: Murach's Android Programming
java: Murach's Java Programming
jscr: Murach's JavaScript and jQuery

Code java is Murach's Java Programming
```

Figure 12-16   Code examples that work with hash maps and tree maps

The Word Counter application

To show another use of a map, figure 12-17 shows the Word Counter application. This application counts the number of times a word occurs in a string of text. At first glance, this application might not seem very useful. However, you could enhance this application to analyze the word frequency for any kind of text, including large amounts of text that come from the web.

The main() method for this application starts by printing a welcome message and defining a string that contains some text. Then, the next three statements process the string by removing commas and periods and by converting all words to lowercase. Next, this code splits the text into an array of words. To accomplish these tasks, this code uses the replace(), toLowerCase(), and split() methods of the String class. You'll learn more about these methods in the next chapter. For now, you can just focus on how the resulting array is processed.

After getting the array of words, this code defines a tree map that contains a key that's a string and a value that's an integer. Then, this code loops through each word in the array. Within this loop, the first statement checks whether the map contains the word. If it does, the code gets the count for the word, increments it by 1, and updates the word with the new count. Otherwise, the code puts the word in the map with a count of 1.

After filling the map with the words and their counts, this code prints each entry in the map to the console. This code uses a colon and a space to separate the key (the word) and its value (the count). Since this code uses a tree map, the map is automatically sorted by key. In this case, that means that the words are sorted alphabetically, which is appropriate for this application.

The console

```
The Word Counter application

be: 2
is: 1
not: 1
or: 1
question: 1
that: 1
the: 1
to: 2
```

The code

```java
import java.util.Map;
import java.util.TreeMap;

public class WordCounterApp {

    public static void main(String[] args) {
        System.out.println("The Word Counter application\n");

        // define a string that contains text
        String text = "To be or not to be, that is the question.";

        // process the string
        text = text.replace(",", "");      // remove commas
        text = text.replace(".", "");      // remove periods
        text = text.toLowerCase();         // convert to lower case

        // split the string into an array
        String[] words = text.split(" ");

        // define a map and fill it with words and their counts
        Map<String,Integer> wordMap = new TreeMap<>();
        int count;
        for (String word : words) {
            if (wordMap.containsKey(word)) {      // word is in map
                count = wordMap.get(word);
                count++;
                wordMap.put(word, count);
            } else {                              // new word for map
                wordMap.put(word, 1);
            }
        }

        // print the entries
        for (Map.Entry entry : wordMap.entrySet()) {
            System.out.println(entry.getKey() + ": " + entry.getValue());
        }
    }
}
```

Figure 12-17   The Word Counter application

Perspective

Now that you've finished this chapter, you should know how to work with array lists and linked lists, the two most commonly used Java collections. In addition, you should know how to use hash maps and tree maps to work with collections that store key-value pairs.

However, the interfaces and classes for working with collections presented in this chapter only begin to scratch the surface of what's available from the Java API. Many other classes for working with collections are available, and each of these classes provides functionality that's useful in certain situations. As a result, if the collections presented in this chapter don't provide the functionality that your program requires, there's a good chance that the Java API includes a collection that does. To find the collection that you need and to learn how it works, you can start by looking in the documentation for the java. util package. Then, you can use many of the skills presented in this chapter to work with the collection.

Summary

- A *collection* is an object that's designed to store other objects.
- The *generics* feature, which became available with Java 1.5, lets you specify the type of elements a collection can store. This feature also lets you create *generic classes* that work with variable data types.
- The *diamond operator*, which became available with Java 1.7, allows you to code an empty set of brackets (<>) in the constructor of a typed collection instead of having to code the type within those brackets.
- A *list* is a collection of objects that maintains the sequence of elements.
- You can use the ArrayList and LinkedList classes to create lists. An *array list* uses an array internally to store its data. A *linked list* uses a data structure with next and previous pointers.
- A *map* is a collection that contains key-value pairs.
- You can use the HashMap and TreeMap classes to create maps. A *tree map* maintains its entries in key sequence and a *hash map* does not.

Exercise 12-1   Use an array list

This exercise has you modify the Card Deck application of exercise 11-4 so it uses array lists instead of arrays for the deck of cards and the hands.

```
DECK
|Ace of Spades|2 of Spades|3 of Spades|4 of Spades|…
SHUFFLED DECK
|King of Hearts|Jack of Clubs|King of Diamonds|9 of Hearts|…
FOUR HANDS OF 2 CARDS
|King of Hearts|King of Diamonds|
|Jack of Clubs|3 of Spades|
|9 of Hearts|5 of Hearts|
|8 of Clubs|Jack of Hearts|
CARDS LEFT IN DECK: 44
```

Open the project and add the required import statement

1. Open the project named ch12_ex1_CardDeck in the ex_starts directory. Then, review the code for this application and run it to refresh your memory on how it works.

2. Add an import statement to the CardDeckApp file that makes the ArrayList class available.

Modify the application to use array lists

3. Modify the declaration for the getDeck() method so it returns an array list of strings instead of an array of strings. Then, modify the code in this method so it stores the cards in an array list instead of an array. When you declare the array list, set its capacity to 52 since that's the maximum number of cards.

4. Modify the statement in the main() method that calls the getDeck() method so it stores the deck in an array list instead of an array.

5. Modify the displayCards() method so it accepts an array list instead of an array. Since the code for this method uses an enhanced for loop, no additional changes are needed.

6. Modify the shuffleDeck() method so it accepts an array list instead of an array. Then, modify the code for this method so it uses the array list.

7. Modify the dealCards() method so it accepts and returns an array list instead of an array. Then, modify the code for this method so it gets and removes the specified number of cards from the deck and adds them to the hand.

8. Delete the import statement for the Arrays class since it's no longer needed. Then, modify the statement in the main() method that calls the dealCards() method so it stores the hand in an array list instead of an array. Test the application to be sure it works like it did before.

Display the number of cards left in the deck and deal multiple hands

9.   To be sure that dealt cards are removed from the deck, add a statement that displays the number of cards left in the deck. Then, test this change.

10. Add code to the main() method that deals and displays four hands instead of a single hand. To do that, you can use a loop. Be sure that the statement that displays the number of cards left in the deck is coded outside the loop. Test the application again.

Exercise 12-2   Use a linked list

This exercise will guide you through the process of adding a linked list to the Future Value application. This linked list will store the values for each calculation that is performed. When the program ends, it will print a summary of those calculations in reverse order so it looks something like this:

```
Future Value Calculations

Inv/Mo.    Rate   Years   Future Value
$150.00    8.0%   10      $27,624.85
$125.00    8.0%   10      $23,020.71
$100.00    8.0%   10      $18,416.57
```

1.   Open the project named ch12_ex2_FutureValue that's stored in the ex_starts directory. Then, review the code for this application and run it to make sure it works correctly.

2.   Declare a variable at the beginning of the main() method for a linked list that stores strings.

3.   After the code that calculates, formats, and displays the results for each calculation, add code that formats a string with the results of the calculation and then stores the string in the linked list.

4.   Add code to display the elements in the linked list at the console when the user indicates that the program should end. This code should retrieve the elements of the linked list in reverse order. To do that, you'll need to use methods of the LinkedList class. Then, test the program by making at least three future value calculations.

Exercise 12-3   Create a stack

In this exercise, you'll create a class named Stack that uses a linked list to implement a *stack*, which is a collection that lets you access entries on a *last-in, first-out* (*LIFO*) basis. Then, you'll add code to another class that uses the Stack class. The Stack class should implement these methods:

Method	Description
`push(element)`	Adds an element to the top of the stack.
`pop()`	Returns the element at the top of the stack and removes it.
`peek()`	Returns the element at the top of the stack but does not remove it.
`size()`	Returns the number of elements in the stack.

Create the Stack class

1. Open the project named ch12_ex3_Stack that's in the ex_starts directory.

2. Create a new class named Stack that specifies a type variable that provides for generics.

3. Declare a linked list that will hold the elements in the stack. Then, use the linked list to implement the methods shown above.

Add code that uses the Stack class

4. Open the StackApp class. Then, declare a generic stack at the beginning of the main() method that will store String objects.

5. Add code to the main() method that uses the push() method to add at least three items to the stack. After each item is added, display its value at the console (you'll need to use a string literal to do this). Then, use the size() method to return the number of items in the stack and display that value.

6. Use the peek() method to return the first item and display that item, and use the size() method to return the number of items again and display that value.

7. Use the pop() method to return each item, displaying it as it's returned, and display the number of items one more time.

8. Run the project. If it works correctly, your output should look something like this:

```
Push: Apples
Push: Oranges
Push: Bananas
The stack contains 3 items

Peek: Bananas
The stack contains 3 items

Pop: Bananas
Pop: Oranges
Pop: Apples
The stack contains 0 items
```

13

How to work with strings

In section 1 of this book, you learned some basic skills for working with strings. In this chapter, you'll learn more about working with strings. Because you'll use strings in many of the applications that you develop, you should know how to use all of the skills presented in this chapter.

How to work with the String class

In chapter 2, you learned how to create and join strings. In addition, you learned how to use two methods of the String class to compare strings. Now, you'll review those skills, and you'll learn some new skills for working with strings.

How to create strings

The first example in figure 13-1 shows how to create and initialize string variables. The first statement creates a string variable named productCode and assigns an empty string ("") to it. The second statement creates a string variable named title and assigns a string literal of "Murach's Java Programming" to it. And the third statement creates a string variable named bookTitle and assigns the string variable named title to it. As a result, both of these variables refer to the same String object.

How to join strings

The second and third examples show how to *join* strings. This is also known as *concatenating* strings. To do that, you can use the + operator to join string variables and string literals. In the second example, for instance, the second statement creates a string variable named message that refers to a string of "Hi, Bob".

When you join or append other data types to a string variable, Java automatically converts the other data types so they can be used as part of the string. In the third example, for instance, the second statement joins a string literal of "Years: " with an int value of 3 and assigns the result to a string variable named message. As a result, this string variable refers to a string of "Years: 3".

How to append data to a string

The fourth and fifth examples show how to append data to a string. This works the same as joining strings except that it adds the new data to the end of the string.

In the fourth example, for instance, the first statement declares a string variable that refers to a first name. Then, the second statement appends a space to that variable, and the third statement appends a last name. Here, the name variable is coded on both sides of the equals sign, and the + operator joins the new string literal to this variable.

The fifth example works the same as the fourth example. However, it uses the += operator to append the data. As a result, it isn't necessary to code the name variable on both sides of the equals sign. Since this is easy to read and requires less code than the previous example, it's more commonly used.

The String class

```
java.lang.String;
```

How to declare and initialize string variables

```
String productCode = "";                            // refers to an empty string
String title = "Murach's Java Programming";        // refers to a string literal
String bookTitle = title;  // refers to the same object as another variable
```

How to join strings

```
String name = "Bob";                     // name is "Bob"
String message = "Hi, " + name;          // message is "Hi, Bob"
```

How to join a string and a number

```
int years = 3;
String message = "Years: " + years;      // message is "Years: 3"
```

How to append one string to another

```
String name = "Bob";                     // name is "Bob"
name = name + " ";                       // name is "Bob "
name = name + "Smith";                   // name is "Bob Smith"
```

A more common way to append one string to another

```
String name = "Bob";                     // name is "Bob"
name += " ";                             // name is "Bob "
name += "Smith";                         // name is "Bob Smith"
```

Description

- You can initialize a string variable by assigning a string literal or another variable that refers to a String object.

- To *join* (or *concatenate*) one string with another string or another data type, you can use the + operator.

- To *append* a string or another data type to a string, you can use the += operator.

- When you join or append other data types to a String object, Java automatically converts the other data types to String objects so they can be used as part of the string.

Figure 13-1   How to create, join, and append strings

How to compare strings

In chapter 3, you learned how to use the equals() and equalsIgnoreCase() methods of the String class to compare strings. Now, figure 13-2 reviews those methods and introduces you to more methods that you can use to compare strings.

All of the methods in this figure return a Boolean value of true or false. For example, the equals() method compares strings and returns a true value if the strings are equal and have the same capitalization. Similarly, the startsWith() method checks whether a string starts with a certain combination of characters and returns a true value if it does.

The first example shows a common mistake that beginners often make when comparing strings. Here, the code uses the equality operator (==) that's used for comparing primitive types to compare strings. But, this doesn't check whether two strings are equal. Instead, it checks whether they refer to the same String object. However, it's possible that two string variables may refer to different String objects and still have the same combination of characters. As a result, this isn't a reliable way to check for equality.

The second example shows how to use the equals() method to compare strings. This checks whether two string variables store the same characters with the same capitalization. As a result, it's a reliable way to check for equality.

As you learned in chapter 3, if you don't care about capitalization, you can use the equalsIgnoreCase() method to check two strings for equality. This method works the same as the equals() method, but it isn't case-sensitive.

The third example shows how to use the equals() method to check for an empty string. To do that, you just supply an empty string as the argument of the equals() method. Here, the if statement checks whether the string variable named productCode refers to an empty string. If so, it prints a message to the console.

The fourth example shows how to use the isEmpty() method that was introduced with Java 6 to check for an empty string. This example works like the equals() method in the previous example. However, some programmers consider the isEmtpy() method easier to read.

The fifth example shows how to use the startsWith() method. Here, the if statement checks whether the string variable named productDescription starts with a string of "Murach". If so, it prints a message to the console.

The sixth example shows how to use the endsWith() method. Here, the if statement checks whether the string variable named productDescription ends with a string of "Programming". If so, it prints a message to the console.

Methods for comparing strings

Method	Description
equals(String)	Returns a true value if the specified string is equal to the current string. This comparison is case-sensitive.
equalsIgnoreCase(String)	Returns a true value if the specified string is equal to the current string. This comparison is *not* case-sensitive.
isEmpty()	Returns a true value if this string contains an empty string. This method was introduced with Java 6.
startsWith(String)	Returns a true value if this string starts with the specified string.
endsWith(String)	Returns a true value if this string ends with the specified string.

A common mistake when testing for equality

```
if (productCode == "java") {
    System.out.println("This does not test for equality.");
}
```

How to use the equals() method to test for equality

```
if (productCode.equals("java")) {
    System.out.println("This tests for equality.");
}
```

How to use the equals() method to check for an empty string

```
if (productCode.equals("")) {
    System.out.println("You must enter a product code.");
}
```

How to use the isEmpty() method (Java 6 and later)

```
if (productCode.isEmpty()) {
    System.out.println("You must enter a product code.");
}
```

How to use the startsWith() method

```
if (productDescription.startsWith("Murach")) {
    System.out.println("This book is a Murach book.");
}
```

How to use the endsWith() method

```
if (productDescription.endsWith("Programming")) {
    System.out.println("This book is about programming.");
}
```

Description

- The String class provides methods that you can use to compare strings.

- The equality operator (==) checks whether two strings refer to the same String object. It's possible for two strings to contain the same characters, but to refer to different String objects. As a result, you should not use this operator to check whether two strings contain the same characters.

Figure 13-2   How to compare strings

How to work with string indexes

Figure 13-3 begins by listing some methods that you can use to work with the indexes of a String object. Here, the indexOf() and lastIndexOf() methods return a value that represents an *index* within a string. When you work with indexes, you need to remember that the first index is 0, not 1. As a result, the index for the first character is 0, the index for the second character is 1, the index for the third character is 2, and so on.

The first example shows how to use the length() method. Here, the length() method is called from a string variable named productCode that refers to a string of "java". As a result, the length() method returns a value of 4.

The second example shows how to use the length() method to check for an empty string. To do that, the if statement checks whether the string variable named productCode has a length of 0.

The third example shows how to use the indexOf() method. Here, the first call to the indexOf() method returns an index for the first occurrence of the space character in the specified string. Then, the second call to the indexOf() method returns an index for the second occurrence of the space character in the specified string. To do that, this code adds a value of 1 to the index for the first space and starts searching at that index. As a result, this code finds the second occurrence of the space character instead of finding the first occurrence again.

The fourth example shows how to use the lastIndexOf() method. This works like the third example. However, it begins searching from the end of the string and works toward the beginning of the string. To do that, this code subtracts a value of 1 from the index for the first space that's found.

The fifth example shows another way to use the indexOf() method. Here, the indexOf() method searches the string for a value of "Van". This shows that you can use the indexOf() method to search for a string of characters. In addition, it shows that the index that's returned is for the first character in this string. In other words, this code returns an int value of 7 because that's the index for where "Van" begins in this string.

The sixth example shows how to use the charAt() method. This code gets the first three characters in the specified string variable and stores them in variables of the char type. This shows how indexes work. In addition, it shows that a string contains a sequence of char values. Because of that, you can loop through all of the characters in a string as shown in the seventh example.

When using methods that require an index, you must be careful to supply a valid index. If you supply an index argument that doesn't exist in the String object, the method will throw a StringIndexOutOfBoundsException. This is a mistake that's often made by beginning programmers. Fortunately, you can prevent this exception by making sure that you use indexes that are greater than or equal to 0 and less than the length of the String object. In the seventh example, for instance, the loop begins at an index of 0 and stops at an index of one less than the length of the String object for the itemNumber variable.

Methods for working with string indexes

Method	Description
`length()`	Returns an int value for the number of characters in this string.
`indexOf(String)`	Returns an int value for the index of the first occurrence of the specified string in this string. If the string isn't found, this method returns -1.
`indexOf(String, startIndex)`	Returns an int value for the index of the first occurrence of the specified string starting at the specified index. If the string isn't found, this method returns -1.
`lastIndexOf(String)`	Returns an int value for the index of the last occurrence of the specified string in this string.
`lastIndexOf(String, startIndex)`	Returns an int value for the index of the last occurrence of the specified string in this string starting at the specified index.
`charAt(index)`	Returns the char value at the specified index.

How to get the length of a string

```
String productCode = "java";
int length = productCode.length();            // length is 4
```

How to use the length() method to check for an empty string

```
if (productCode.length() == 0) { ... }
```

Code that gets the index values for the two spaces

```
String name = "Martin Van Buren";
int index1 = name.indexOf(" ");               // index1 is 6
int index2 = name.indexOf(" ", index1+1);     // index2 is 10
```

Another way to get the index values for the two spaces

```
String name = "Martin Van Buren";
int index1 = name.lastIndexOf(" ");           // index1 is 10
int index2 = name.lastIndexOf(" ", index1-1); // index2 is 6
```

Code that gets the index of a string

```
String name = "Martin Van Buren";
int index = name.indexOf("Van");              // index is 7
```

Code that gets the character at the specified index

```
String name = "Martin Van Buren";
char char1 = name.charAt(0);                  // char1 is 'M'
char char2 = name.charAt(1);                  // char2 is 'a'
char char3 = name.charAt(2);                  // char3 is 'r'
```

Code that uses an index in a for loop

```
String itemNumber = "RT-123";
for (int i = 0; i < itemNumber.length(); i++) { ... }
```

Description

- You can use an *index* to refer to each character within a string where 0 is the first character, 1 is the second character, and so on.

Figure 13-3   How to work with string indexes

How to modify strings

Figure 13-4 begins by listing some methods that you can use to modify strings. The first four methods return another String object that occurs within the current String object. This String object that's returned is known as a *substring*. The fifth method returns an array of String objects.

The first example shows how to use the trim() method to remove any spaces from the beginning and end of a String object. As a result, after this code executes, the string variable named choice refers to a string literal of "y".

The second example shows how to use the substring() method to parse the first name and last name from a string for a full name. Here, the first statement sets the string to a string literal that includes a first and last name. Then, the second statement uses the indexOf() method to get the index of the first space in the string, which is the space between the first and last names. Next, the third statement uses the substring() method to set the first name variable equal to the string that begins at the first character of the string and ends at the first space character in the string. Finally, the fourth statement uses the substring() method to set the last name variable equal to the string that begins one index after the index for the space and continues to the end of the string.

The third example shows how to add dashes to a Visa credit card number. To do that, this example creates four strings, one for each four-digit part of the credit card number. To do that, it uses the substring() method to return four String objects from the String object for the credit card number. Then, the last statement joins the four parts of the credit card number, adding dashes at the appropriate locations in the string.

The fourth example shows how to replace one character in a string with another character. To do that, it uses the replace() method. Here, this method is used to replace the dashes in a phone number with periods.

You can also use the replace() method to remove a character from a string. To do that, you replace the character with an empty string. This is illustrated by the fifth example, which removes the dashes from a credit card number.

The last example shows how to use the split() method to split the characters in a name into an array of String objects. In this case, the first name, middle initial, and last name are separated from each other by a space. Because of that, the split() method uses a space as the delimiter. After this method is executed, the array contains three elements with the three parts of the name as shown here.

Although the delimiter for the split() method is typically a single character or an escape sequence such as "\t" for tabs or "\n" for returns, it can be any *regular expression*. A regular expression is a complicated expression that can contain wildcards and other special characters. To learn more about regular expressions, you can search the web for "java regular expression".

Methods for modifying strings

Method	Description
`trim()`	Returns a String object with any spaces removed from the beginning and end of this string.
`substring(startIndex)`	Returns a String object that starts at the specified index and goes to the end of this string.
`substring(startIndex, endIndex)`	Returns a String object that starts at the specified start index and goes to, but doesn't include, the end index.
`replace(oldChar, newChar)`	Returns a String object that results from replacing all instances of the specified old char value with the specified new char value.
`split(delimiter)`	Returns an array of String objects that were separated in the original string by the specified delimiter.

Code that removes spaces from the start and end of a string

```
String choice = "  y  ";
choice = choice.trim();                           // choice is "y"
```

Code that parses a first name and last name from a string

```
String name = "Mike Murach";
int index = name.indexOf(" ");            // index is 4
String firstName = name.substring(0, index);    // firstName is "Mike"
String lastName = name.substring(index + 1);    // lastName is "Murach"
```

Code that adds dashes to a credit card number

```
String ccNumber = "4012888888881881";
String part1 = ccNumber.substring(0,4);
String part2 = ccNumber.substring(4,8);
String part3 = ccNumber.substring(8,12);
String part4 = ccNumber.substring(12,16);
ccNumber = part1 + "-" + part2 + "-" + part3 + "-" + part4;
```

Code that changes the separator character in a phone number

```
String phoneNumber = "977-555-1212";
phoneNumber = phoneNumber.replace("-", ".");
```

Code that removes dashes from a credit card number

```
String ccNumber = "4012-8888-8888-1881";
ccNumber = ccNumber.replace("-", "");
```

Code that stores the parts of a name in an array

```
String name = "Michael R Murach";
String[] nameParts = name.split(" ");
String firstName = nameParts[0];          // firstName is "Michael"
String middleInitial = nameParts[1];      // middleInitial is "R"
String lastName = nameParts[2];           // lastName is "Murach"
```

Figure 13-4   How to modify strings

How to work with the StringBuilder class

When you make changes to the String object that a string variable refers to, you should know that Java creates a new String object and assigns it to the existing string variable. That's because String objects are *immutable*, which means that they have a fixed length and can't be edited. As you can imagine, then, making changes to the value of a string variable can be inefficient.

If you want more flexibility when working with strings, you can use the StringBuilder class. When you use this class, you create strings that are *mutable*. Then, you can edit the characters that are stored in the StringBuilder object without creating a new StringBuilder object. For example, you can append characters to the end of the string, insert characters into the middle of the string, or delete characters from the string. This makes it easier to write code that works with strings, and it can improve the efficiency of your code.

The StringBuilder class was introduced with Java 5. It's designed to be a more efficient replacement for the StringBuffer class that was used prior to Java 5. Because the API for the StringBuffer class is identical to the API for the StringBuilder class, you can easily switch between the two classes. However, the StringBuilder class is not thread-safe. As a result, if you need your code to be thread-safe, you should use the StringBuffer class.

How to create a StringBuilder object

Figure 13-5 shows three constructors and three methods of the StringBuilder class. The first constructor creates an empty StringBuilder object with an initial capacity of 16 characters. Then, if you add more than 16 characters to this StringBuilder object, Java automatically increases the capacity. You'll see how that works in just a minute.

Whenever possible, you should set the capacity to an appropriate value by using the second or third constructor. Otherwise, Java has to allocate memory each time the capacity is exceeded, and that can cause your code to run less efficiently. On the other hand, if you set a large capacity and use a small percentage of it, you waste memory.

How to append data to a string

Once you create a StringBuilder object, you can use the methods of the StringBuilder class to work with the object. For instance, the first example shows how to use the append() method of the StringBuilder class. Here, the first statement creates an empty StringBuilder object with the default capacity of 16 characters. Then, the next four statements use the append() method to add 16 characters to the string. As a result, the length of the string is 16 and the capacity of the StringBuilder object is 16.

The StringBuilder class

```
java.lang.StringBuilder;
```

Constructors of the StringBuilder class

Constructor	Description
StringBuilder()	Creates an empty StringBuilder object with an initial capacity of 16 characters.
StringBuilder(capacity)	Creates an empty StringBuilder object with an initial capacity of the specified number of characters.
StringBuilder(String)	Creates a StringBuilder object that contains the specified string plus an additional capacity of 16 characters.

Some starting methods of the StringBuilder class

Methods	Description
append(data)	Adds a string for the specified primitive type or object to the end of the string.
capacity()	Returns an int value for the capacity of this StringBuilder object.
length()	Returns an int value for the number of characters in this StringBuilder object.

Code that creates a credit card number

```
StringBuilder ccNumber = new StringBuilder();
ccNumber.append("4012");
ccNumber.append("8888");
ccNumber.append("8888");
ccNumber.append("1881");
```

Code that shows how capacity automatically increases

```
StringBuilder name = new StringBuilder(8);     // capacity is 8
name.append("Raymond R. Thomas");
int length = name.length();          // length is 17
int capacity2 = name.capacity();     // capacity2 is 18 (2 * capacity1 + 2)
```

Description

- String objects are *immutable*. As a result, they can't grow or shrink.
- StringBuilder objects are *mutable*, which means you can modify the characters in the string. The capacity of a StringBuilder object is automatically increased if necessary.
- The StringBuilder class was introduced with Java 5. It's designed to replace the older StringBuffer class.
- The StringBuffer class has identical constructors and methods as the StringBuilder class. As a result, you can use it to accomplish the same tasks.
- The StringBuffer class isn't as efficient as the StringBuilder class, but it is thread-safe. As a result, you can use it instead of the StringBuilder class whenever you need to make sure your code is thread-safe.

Figure 13-5   How to create a StringBuilder object and append data to it

As you learned earlier in this chapter, you can accomplish the same task by using the String class and the += operator. If you do that, however, Java must create a new String object for each statement. In contrast, when you use the append() method of the StringBuilder class, Java doesn't create a new StringBuilder object. Instead, it increases the length of the StringBuilder object. If necessary, it also increases the capacity of the StringBuilder object. As a result, the StringBuilder object usually works more efficiently than the String object.

The second example in figure 13-5 shows how a StringBuilder object automatically increases its capacity as the length of the string increases. Here, the first statement creates an empty StringBuilder object with a capacity of 8 characters. Then, the second statement appends a string of 17 characters to the empty string. Since this exceeds the capacity of the StringBuilder object, Java automatically increases the capacity by doubling the current capacity and adding 2. As a result, this code increases the capacity from 8 to 18 characters.

In this example, the new length is less than two times the current capacity plus 2. But what if the new length is more than that? In that case, Java will increase the capacity so it's the same as the length. If you appended a 25-character string in this example, for instance, the new capacity would be 25.

How to modify strings

Figure 13-6 shows some more methods of the StringBuilder class. Some of these methods provide functionality that isn't available from the String class. For example, you can use the methods of the StringBuilder class to insert, replace, or delete strings or characters. However, the StringBuilder class also provides methods like charAt() and substring() that work the same as the methods of the String class. As a result, you shouldn't have any trouble using these methods.

The first example adds dashes to the Visa credit card number string created in the previous figure. Here, the first statement uses the insert() method to insert a dash after the first four characters. This pushes the remaining numbers back one index. Then, the second statement uses the insert() method to insert a dash after the ninth character in the string, which was the eighth character in the original string. This pushes the remaining eight numbers in the string back one index. And so on. Note that this task is easier to accomplish with a mutable StringBuilder object than it was with an immutable String object.

The second example shows how to remove dashes from a credit card number. Here, a loop cycles through each character, using the charAt() method to check if the current character is a dash. If it is, the deleteCharAt() method deletes that character. Since this causes all characters to the right of the dash to move forward one index, the next statement decrements the counter. That way, the loop doesn't skip any characters. Although this task is more difficult to accomplish with a mutable StringBuilder object than it was with an immutable String object, it's usually more efficient to use a StringBuilder object.

The third example shows how to use the substring() method of the StringBuilder class to separate the four parts of a credit card number. This shows that the substring() method works the same for the String class as it does for the StringBuilder class.

More methods of the StringBuilder class

Methods	Description
insert(index, data)	Inserts a string for the specified primitive type or object at the specified index pushing the rest of the string back.
replace(startIndex, endIndex, String)	Replaces the characters from the start index to, but not including, the end index with the specified string.
delete(startIndex, endIndex)	Removes the substring from the start index to, but not including, the end index. This moves the rest of the string forward.
deleteCharAt(index)	Removes the character at the specified index.
setCharAt(index, character)	Replaces the character at the specified index with the specified character.
charAt(index)	Returns a char value for the character at the specified index.
substring(index)	Returns a String object for the characters starting at the specified index to the end of the string.
substring(startIndex, endIndex)	Returns a String object for the characters from the start index to, but not including, the end index.
toString()	Returns a String object for the string that's stored in the StringBuilder object.

Code that adds dashes to a credit card number

```
ccNumber.insert(4, "-");
ccNumber.insert(9, "-");
ccNumber.insert(14, "-");
```

Code that removes dashes from a credit card number

```
for(int i = 0; i < ccNumber.length(); i++) {
    if (ccNumber.charAt(i) == '-') {
        ccNumber.deleteCharAt(i);
        i--;
    }
}
```

Code that parses a credit card number

```
String part1 = ccNumber.substring(0,4);
String part2 = ccNumber.substring(4,8);
String part3 = ccNumber.substring(8, 12);
String part4 = ccNumber.substring(12);
```

Description

- The StringBuilder class provides many of the same methods as the String class. In addition, it contains some methods that make it easier to modify strings.

Figure 13-6   How to modify a StringBuilder object

The Product Lister application

This chapter finishes by presenting a Product Lister application that allows the user to print a list of one or more products. This application shows some of the skills presented in this chapter within the context of an application. In addition, this application uses a StringUtil class that contains a static method that makes it easier to work with strings.

The user interface

Figure 13-7 begins by showing the console for this application. Here, the user starts by entering the product code for the first product and "y" to continue entering product codes. Then, the user enters a second product code and "n" to stop entering product codes. At this point, the application displays the list of products.

The list shown here consists of three columns. At the top of the list is a header row that displays the names of the columns. This row is followed by another row that acts as a separator between the header row and the remaining rows in the list. Then, the remaining rows display the code, description, and price for each product in the list.

The StringUtil class

This figure also shows the StringUtil class. This class contains a single static method named pad(). You can use this method to add spaces to the end of the string until it is a specified length. This is known as *padding* a string.

The pad() method accepts two parameters. The first parameter is the String object that you want to pad. The second is the length that you want the String to be.

Within the method, an if/else statement begins by checking whether the length of the String parameter is less than the length parameter. If it is, this code adds spaces to the string until it's the specified length and then returns that string. Otherwise, this code truncates the string and returns it. Either way, the String object that's returned has a length that's equal to the length parameter.

Within the if clause, the first statement creates a StringBuilder object that starts with the String parameter. To do that, this code passes the String parameter to the constructor of the StringBuilder class. Then, this code uses a while loop to append spaces to the StringBuilder object until the length of this object is equal to the length parameter. Finally, it converts the StringBuilder object to a String object and returns that object.

The console

```
Welcome to the Product Lister

Enter product code: java
Another product? (y/n): y

Enter product code: mysql
Another product? (y/n): n

Code        Description                       Price
=========  ===============================  =========
java        Murach's Java Programming          $57.50
mysql       Murach's MySQL                     $54.50
```

The StringUtil class

```java
package murach.ui;

public class StringUtil {

    public static String pad(String s, int length) {
        if (s.length() < length) {
            // append spaces until the string is the specified length
            StringBuilder sb = new StringBuilder(s);
            while (sb.length() < length) {
                sb.append(" ");
            }
            return sb.toString();
        } else {
            // truncate the string to the specified length
            return s.substring(0, length);
        }
    }
}
```

Figure 13-7   The Product Lister application (part 1 of 2)

The ProductListerApp class

Part 2 of figure 13-7 shows the code for the ProductListerApp class of the Product Lister application. This code begins by declaring three constants that specify the width in characters for the code, description, and price columns.

After declaring the constants, this code creates a StringBuilder object for the list. Then, it appends the header row to this string. To do that, it uses the static pad() method of the StringUtil class to append spaces to each column heading so it's the correct width.

After setting up the header row, this code uses a while loop to allow the user to enter product codes. Within this loop, the first statement gets the product code from the user. To do that, it uses the static getString() method of the Console class. Then, it gets a Product object for the specified code. To do that, it uses the static getProduct() method of the ProductDB class.

After getting the Product object for the specified code, this code appends a row for the product to the list. To do that, it uses the static pad() method of the StringUtil class.

The three constants defined at the beginning of this method are used in three places. First, they are used to specify the width of the three columns in the header row. Second, they are used to specify the width of the three columns that create a separator between the header row and the rest of the rows. Third, they are used to specify the width of the three columns for the data for each product.

As a result, if you want to change the width of a column, you only need to change the value of the constant. For example, if you want to make the description column 50 characters wide, you just need to change the value of the constant named DESC_WIDTH to 50.

The ProductListerApp class

```java
package murach.ui;

import murach.db.ProductDB;
import murach.business.Product;

public class ProductListerApp {

    public static void main(String args[]) {
        System.out.println("Welcome to the Product Lister\n");

        final int CODE_WIDTH = 10;
        final int DESC_WIDTH = 34;
        final int PRICE_WIDTH = 10;

        // set up display string
        StringBuilder list = new StringBuilder();
        list.append(StringUtil.pad("Code", CODE_WIDTH));
        list.append(StringUtil.pad("Description", DESC_WIDTH));
        list.append(StringUtil.pad("Price", PRICE_WIDTH));
        list.append("\n");

        list.append(
            StringUtil.pad("=========", CODE_WIDTH));
        list.append(
            StringUtil.pad("=================================", DESC_WIDTH));
        list.append(
            StringUtil.pad("=========", PRICE_WIDTH));
        list.append("\n");

        // perform 1 or more calculations
        String choice = "y";
        while (choice.equalsIgnoreCase("y")) {
            // get the input from the user
            String productCode = Console.getString("Enter product code: ");

            Product product = ProductDB.getProduct(productCode);

            list.append(
                StringUtil.pad(product.getCode(), CODE_WIDTH));
            list.append(
                StringUtil.pad(product.getDescription(), DESC_WIDTH));
            list.append(
                StringUtil.pad(product.getPriceFormatted(), PRICE_WIDTH));
            list.append("\n");

            // see if the user wants to continue
            choice = Console.getString("Another product? (y/n): ");
            System.out.println();
        }
        System.out.println(list);
    }
}
```

Figure 13-7   The Product Lister application (part 2 of 2)

Perspective

Now that you've finished this chapter, you should be able to use the String and StringBuilder classes to work with strings. These skills are fundamental to developing Java applications. Keep in mind that this chapter has only covered some of the most useful methods of these classes. As a result, if you want to learn about the other methods of these classes, you can look them up in the documentation for the Java API.

Summary

- You can use methods of the String class to compare all or part of a string, locate a string within another string, and return parts of a string.

- When working with strings, you often need to use an *index* to refer to the characters that make up the string. In a string, the first character has an index of 0, the second character has an index of 1, and so on.

- String objects are *immutable*. As a result, when you add, delete, or modify individual characters in a string, Java creates a new String object and assigns it to the same string variable.

- StringBuilder objects are *mutable*. As a result, you can use the methods of the StringBuilder class to append, insert, delete, or replace characters in a StringBuilder object.

- StringBuilder objects are more efficient than String objects, especially if you need to modify the string that you're working with.

Exercise 13-1   Parse a name

In this exercise, you'll write an application that parses full names into first and last name or first, middle, and last name, depending on whether the user enters a string consisting of two or three words. The output for the application should look something like this:

```
Enter a name: Joel Murach

First name:  Joel
Last name:   Murach
```

Or this:

```
Enter a name: Joel Ray Murach

First name:  Joel
Middle name: Ray
Last name:   Murach
```

1. Open the project named ch13_ex1_NameParser that's in the ex_starts folder. Then, review the code in the NameParserApp class.

2. Add code that separates the name into two or three strings depending on whether the user entered a name with two words or three.

3. Display each word of the name on a separate line.

4. If the user enters fewer than two words or more than three words, display an error message. For simplicity, you can assume that each part of a name consists of a single word.

5. Make sure the application works even if the user enters one or more spaces before or after the name.

6. Test the application to make sure it works correctly.

Exercise 13-2   Improve the Future Value application

In this exercise, you'll improve the Future Value application by allowing the user to enter dollar signs ($) and percent signs (%) when they enter numbers for monetary and percent values like this:

```
Welcome to the Future Value Calculator

Enter monthly investment:    $100
Enter yearly interest rate: 3%
Enter number of years:       3
Future value:                $3,771.46
```

1. Open the project named ch13_ex2_FutureValue that's in the ex_starts folder. Then, open the FutureValueApp and Console classes and review the code.

2. Open the Console class and modify the getDouble() method so it removes any dollar ($) or percent (%) signs from the string that's entered by the user.

3. Run the application and test it to make sure it works correctly. You should be able to enter dollar signs and percent signs.

14

How to work with dates and times

In this chapter, you'll learn how to work with dates and times, which are necessary for many types of Java applications. To start, this chapter introduces you to the date/time API that was available prior to Java 8 as well as the new date/time API that's available with Java 8 and later.

Oracle recommends the new date/time API for new development. As a result, this chapter only shows how to use the new date/time API. However, if you need to use the older date/time API, you can learn more about it by searching the Internet or by consulting an older book such as the 4th edition of this book.

An introduction to date/time APIs

Figure 14-1 summarizes the two date/time APIs that are available with Java 8. The first was available prior to Java 8 and is included with Java 8 and later for backwards compatibility. The second is a new and improved date/time API that was added to Java 8. Oracle recommends this date/time API for new development.

The date/time API prior to Java 8

If you need your application to work with older versions of Java, you can use the Date, Calendar, and GregorianCalendar classes of the java.util package to work with dates and times. These classes are available to all modern versions of Java. To format these dates and times, you can use the DateFormat or SimpleDateFormat classes of the java.text package. These classes are also available to all modern versions of Java.

However, these classes have some design flaws. To start, they are not thread-safe. In addition, most programmers consider the design of these classes to be unintuitive. For example, in the Date class, years start at 1900, months start at 1, and days start at 0. Finally, these classes don't make it easy to localize your application for parts of the world that don't use the Gregorian calendar. For example, when using these classes, it isn't easy to write code that supports the Lunar calendar.

The date/time API for Java 8 and later

To fix these problems, Java 8 introduced a new date/time API. All of the classes and enumerations for this new API are stored in the java.time package.

This API is thread-safe because all of its classes are immutable. In other words, the methods of these objects always return a new object instead of modifying the existing one. In addition, most programmers consider the design to be more intuitive than the old API. Finally, the new API supports separate calendars, which makes it easier to localize your application for parts of the world that don't use the Gregorian calendar.

The date/time API prior to Java 8

Package	Description
`java.util`	An older package that contains the Date, Calendar, and GregorianCalendar classes. Prior to Java 8, programmers commonly used these classes to work with dates and times.
`java.text`	An older package that contains the DateFormat and SimpleDateFormat classes. Prior to Java 8, programmers used these classes to format dates and times.

Pros

- Works with older versions of Java.

Cons

- Not thread-safe.
- Not intuitive.
- Not easy to localize for parts of the world that don't use the Gregorian calendar.

The date/time API with Java 8 and later

Package	Description
`java.time`	A newer package that contains the LocalDate, LocalTime, LocalDateTime, and DateTimeFormatter classes as well as the Month and DayOfWeek enumerations. With Java 8 and later, you can use these classes and enumerations to work with dates and times.

Pros

- Thread-safe.
- Intuitive.
- Easier to localize for parts of the world that don't use the Gregorian calendar.

Cons

- Doesn't work with versions of Java prior to Java 8.

Description

- Java 8 introduces a new date/time API that fixes some of the problems with the old date/time API that was used prior to Java 8.

Figure 14-1   A summary of Java date/time APIs

How to use the new date/time API

The rest of this chapter shows how to use the new date/time API that was introduced with Java 8. As a result, this code only works with Java 8 and later. For new development, this is usually fine. However, if you need your application to work with older versions of Java, or if you need to modify code for an old application, you may want to use the old date/time API.

How to create date and time objects

With the new date and time API, you typically begin by using one of these three classes: LocalDate, LocalTime, or LocalDateTime. As the name implies, the LocalDate class stores a date but not the time. Conversely, the LocalTime class stores the time but not the date. And the LocalDateTime class stores both the date and time.

All three of these classes work from the observer's perspective. In other words, they use time zone and location information from the system the application is running on and work with the local date and time.

Figure 14-2 shows how you can create date and time objects using these classes. All of these classes use static methods that return dates and times.

The now() method works the same for all three classes. It returns the current local time, date, or date and time. In this figure, for example, the first statement returns the current local date, the second returns the current local time, and the third returns the current local date and time.

The of() method takes different parameters depending on whether it's called from the LocalDate, LocalTime, or LocalDateTime class. To create a LocalDate object, you can call the of() method from the LocalDate class and pass it the year, month, and day as parameters. To specify the month, you can use the constants from JANUARY through DECEMBER that are available from the Month enumeration. Or, you can specify an int value for the month where January is 1, February is 2, and so on.

To create a LocalTime object, you can call the of() method from the LocalTime class and pass it integer values for the hours, minutes, seconds, and nanoseconds. These parameters are in 24-hour format. This means they start at 00:00, which is midnight, and go to 23:59, which is 11:59 PM. Of these parameters, the hours and minutes are required. However, you can specify seconds and nanoseconds if you need to as shown in this figure.

To create a LocalDateTime object, you can call the of() method of the LocalDateTime class and pass it values for the year, month, day, hour, minute, second, and nanosecond. This works like a combination of the LocalDate and LocalTime classes.

The parse() method allows you to create a date, time, or date/time from a string. For a LocalDate object, you specify the date in this format: YYYY-MM-DD. For a LocalTime object, you specify the time in this format: HH:MM:SS.NNNNNNNNN. Here, the seconds and nanoseconds are optional. For a LocalDateTime object, you separate the strings for the date and time with a T. This indicates the start of the time part of the string.

The java.time package

Class	Description
LocalDate	A class for working with dates but not times.
LocalTime	A class for working with times but not dates.
LocalDateTime	A class for working with dates and times.

Enumeration	Description
Month	An enumeration that contains the months in the year (JANUARY through DECEMBER).
DayOfWeek	An enumeration that contains the days of the week (MONDAY through SUNDAY).

Static methods of the LocalDate, LocalTime, and LocalDateTime classes

Method	Description
now()	Returns an appropriate object for the current local date, time, or date/time.
of(parameters)	Return an appropriate object for the specified date, time, or date/time parameters.
	For a date, you can specify the year, month, and day parameters.
	For a time, you can specify the hour, minute, second, and nanosecond parameters. The second and nanosecond are optional and default to 0.
	For a date/time, you can specify all of the parameters.
parse(string)	Returns an appropriate object for the specified string.
	For a date, you specify a string in the form YYYY-MM-DD.
	For a time, you specify a string in the form HH:MM:SS.NNNNNNNNN. The seconds and nanoseconds are optional and default to 0.
	For a date/time, the date and time are separated by a "T".

Code that creates date/time objects

```
LocalDate currentDate = LocalDate.now();
LocalTime currentTime = LocalTime.now();
LocalDateTime currentDateTime = LocalDateTime.now();

LocalDate halloween1 = LocalDate.of(2017, Month.OCTOBER, 31);
LocalDate halloween2 = LocalDate.of(2017, 10, 31);
LocalTime startTime1 = LocalTime.of(14, 32);                // minutes
LocalTime startTime2 = LocalTime.of(14, 32, 45);            // seconds
LocalTime startTime3 = LocalTime.of(14, 32, 45, 123456789); // nanoseconds
LocalDateTime startDateTime1 = LocalDateTime.of(2017, 10, 31, 14, 32);

LocalDate halloween3 = LocalDate.parse("2017-10-31");
LocalTime startTime4 = LocalTime.parse("02:32:45");
LocalDateTime startDateTime2 =
        LocalDateTime.parse("2017-10-31T02:32:45.123456789");
```

Description

- These classes represent the local date and time from the observer's perspective.
- The LocalDateTime class is a combination of the LocalDate and LocalTime classes.

Figure 14-2   How to create LocalDate, LocalTime, and LocalDateTime objects

If any of the values are out of range, these methods typically throw a DateTimeException. For example, if you specify a day of 32, these methods throw this exception since no month has 32 days. Similarly, if you specify 25 hours or 61 seconds, these methods throw this exception.

All three of these classes have more static methods for creating dates and times, but the ones presented in figure 14-2 are the most common. For more information on any of the available methods, you can refer to the API documentation for these classes.

How to get date and time parts

Figure 14-3 shows several methods you can use to access the various parts of a date and time. The getMonth() and getMonthValue() methods return the same information, but in different formats. For example, if the date is set to October 31, 2017, the getMonth() method returns the OCTOBER constant of the Month enumeration. On the other hand, the getMonthValue() method returns an int value of 10. This value corresponds with the OCTOBER constant of the Month enumeration.

The toString() method of the Month enumeration returns the name of the constant in all caps. As a result, if you print a constant of the Month enumeration to the console, it displays the name of the month in all caps.

The LocalDateTime class supports all of the methods shown in this figure. However, the LocalDate class only supports the methods for getting date parts, and the LocalTime class only supports the methods for getting time parts. This is logical since it doesn't make sense to call the getHour() method on a LocalDate object because that object doesn't store the time. Similarly, it doesn't make sense to call the getYear() method on a LocalTime object because that object doesn't store the date.

Unlike most classes, these get methods do not have corresponding set methods. That's because, as mentioned previously, the objects of these classes are immutable. In other words, you can't change them once they have been constructed.

Methods for getting parts of date and time objects

Method	Description
getYear()	Returns the current year as an integer.
getMonth()	Returns the current month as a Month object.
getMonthValue()	Returns the current month as an integer between 1 and 12.
getDayOfMonth()	Returns the current day of the month as an integer.
getDayOfYear()	Returns the current day of the year as an integer.
getDayOfWeek()	Returns the current day of the week as a DayOfWeek object.
getHour()	Returns the current hour of the day as an integer in 24-hour format.
getMinute()	Returns the current minute of the hour as an integer.
getSecond()	Returns the current second of the minute as an integer.
getNano()	Returns the current nanosecond of the second as an integer.

Code that gets the parts of a LocalDateTime object

```
// Assume a current date/time of October 31, 2017 14:32:45.898000000

int year = currentDateTime.getYear();                         // 2017
Month month = currentDateTime.getMonth();                     // OCTOBER
int monthValue = currentDateTime.getMonthValue();             // 10
int day = currentDateTime.getDayOfMonth();                    // 31

int dayOfYear = currentDateTime.getDayOfYear();               // 304
DayOfWeek dayOfWeek = currentDateTime.getDayOfWeek();         // TUESDAY

int hour = currentDateTime.getHour();                         // 14
int minute = currentDateTime.getMinute();                     // 32
int second = currentDateTime.getSecond();                     // 45
int nano = currentDateTime.getNano();                         // 898000000
```

Description

- The LocalDateTime class supports all of the get methods.
- The LocalDate class only supports the get methods relevant to getting dates.
- The LocalTime class only supports the get methods relevant to getting times.
- LocalDate, LocalTime, and LocalDateTime objects are immutable. As a result, these get methods do not have corresponding set methods.

Figure 14-3   How to get date and time parts

How to compare dates and times

Figure 14-4 shows several ways that you can compare dates and times. To determine whether a date or time is before another date or time, you can use the isBefore() method. In this figure, for instance, the first example checks if the current date is before October 31, 2017. If so, it prints an appropriate message to the console.

To do that, this code compares two LocalDate objects. However, you could use similar techniques with two LocalDateTime objects or two LocalTime objects. When you compare date/time objects, you can only compare objects of the same type. For example, you can't compare a date to a time.

Conversely, you can use the isAfter() method to determine whether a date or time object is after another date or time. In this figure, for instance, the second example checks if the current time is after 15:30, which is 3:30PM. If so, it prints an appropriate message to the console. To do that, this code compares two LocalTime objects.

In most cases, you only need to use the isBefore() or isAfter() methods to compare dates. However, in some cases, you may need to use the compareTo() method to determine whether a date/time is before, after, or equal to another date/time. This works because the compareTo() method returns a negative value if a date/time is before another date/time, a positive value if a date/time object is after another date/time object, and 0 if the two date/time objects are equal. In this figure, for instance, the third example checks whether the current date is before, after, or equal to October 31, 2017.

Methods for comparing dates and times

Method	Description
isBefore(dateTime)	Returns true if the date or time is before the other specified date or time. Otherwise, this method returns false.
isAfter(dateTime)	Returns true if date or time is after the other specified date or time. Otherwise, this method returns false.
compareTo(dateTime)	Returns a negative value if the date or time is before the specified date or time, a positive value if the date or time is after the specified date or time, and 0 if the date or time is equal to the specified date or time.

Code that uses the isBefore() method

```
LocalDate currentDate = LocalDate.now();
LocalDate halloween = LocalDate.of(2017, Month.OCTOBER, 31);
if (currentDate.isBefore(halloween)) {
    System.out.println("Current date is before Halloween.");
}
```

Code that uses the isAfter() method

```
LocalTime currentTime = LocalTime.now();
LocalTime startTime = LocalTime.of(15, 30);
if (currentTime.isAfter(startTime)) {
    System.out.println("Current time is after start time.");
}
```

Code that uses the compareTo() method

```
LocalDate currentDate = LocalDate.now();
LocalDate halloween = LocalDate.of(2017, Month.OCTOBER, 31);
if (currentDate.compareTo(halloween) < 0) {
    System.out.println("Current date is BEFORE Halloween.");
} else if (currentDate.compareTo(halloween) > 0) {
    System.out.println("Current date is AFTER Halloween.");
} else if (currentDate.compareTo(halloween) == 0) {
    System.out.println("Current date is Halloween.");
}
```

Description

- You can use these methods to compare LocalTime, LocalDate, and LocalDateTime objects.

Figure 14-4   How to compare dates and times

How to adjust dates and times

Sometimes, you might need to create a new date time object by adjusting an existing date/time object. To do this, you can use the methods shown in figure 14-5. These methods can be referred to as *adjusters* because they adjust parts of a date/time object.

In the first example, for instance, the first statement creates a LocalDate object that's set to October 20, 2017. Then, the second statement creates a new LocalDate object that's set to October 31, 2017. To do that, this statement calls the withDayofMonth() method on the first LocalDate object to change the day of the month from 20 to 31.

As usual, the LocalDateTime class supports all of these methods. However, the LocalDate and LocalTime classes only support the methods that are relevant to them. For example, the LocalTime class doesn't support the withMonth() method.

When you use these methods, you should be aware of some potential inconsistent behaviors. To start, if you call a method and pass it an invalid value, the method typically throws a DateTimeException. For instance, the second example calls the withDayOfMonth() method and passes it a value of 29. However, in this case, the month is February, and the year is 2017, which is not a leap year. As a result, February 2017 only has 28 days. So, this code throws a DateTimeException. This is what most programmers would expect.

However, what happens if you set the date to October 31, 2017 and then call the withMonth() method to set the month to February as shown in the third example? This time, the class quietly adjusts the day to the last day of February. In other words, it sets the day to February 28. This might not be what most programmers would expect. As you develop applications, it's important to keep this in mind. If you don't, it could cause bugs in your application.

Methods for adjusting dates and times

Method	Description
`withDayOfMonth(day)`	Returns a new object based on the original with the day of month changed to day.
`withDayOfYear(dayOfYear)`	Returns a new object based on the original with the month and day set to dayOfYear (1 to 365).
`withMonth(month)`	Returns a new object based on the original with the month changed to month.
`withYear(year)`	Returns a new object based on the original with the year changed to year.
`withHour(hour)`	Returns a new object based on the original with the hour changed to hour.
`withMinute(minute)`	Returns a new object based on the original with the minute changed to minute.

An example that changes the day of the month

```
LocalDate date = LocalDate.of(2017, 10, 20);
LocalDate newDate = date.withDayOfMonth(31);
```

An example that throws an exception due to an invalid day of month

```
LocalDateTime dateTime1 = LocalDateTime.parse("2017-02-28T15:30");
LocalDateTime newDateTime1 = dateTime.withDayOfMonth(29);
// Throws a DateTimeException because 2017 is not a leap year.
// As a result, February only has 28 days
```

An example that quietly changes the day of month

```
LocalDateTime dateTime2 = LocalDateTime.parse("2017-10-31T15:30");
LocalDateTime newDateTime2 = dateTime.withMonth(2);
// Does not throw an exception, but quietly changes the day to 28
// because there are only 28 days in February 2017.
```

Description

- To adjust a date/time object, you can use the with methods, which are referred to as *adjusters*.
- These methods create a new object from the existing date/time object. In other words, they don't alter the existing date/time object.
- The LocalDateTime class supports all of the methods in the table.
- The LocalDate class only supports the methods relevant to dates.
- The LocalTime class only supports the methods relevant to times.
- These methods can throw a DateTimeException for arguments that are out of range.
- The withMonth() method may change the day if the current day stored in the object is out of range for the new month.

Figure 14-5   How to adjust dates and times

How to add or subtract a period of time

Figure 14-6 shows how to create new date and time objects by adding or subtracting a specified time period from an existing date or time. One way to do that is to use the plus() or minus() methods. These methods take two parameters. The second parameter uses a constant in the ChronoUnit enumeration to specify the unit of time. The first parameter specifies the number of units.

The first example shows how these methods work. Here, the first statement adds three weeks to the current date by using the plus() method and the ChronoUnit.WEEKS constant. Similarly, the second statement subtracts one day from the current date using the minus() method and the ChronoUnit. DAYS constant. Both of these statements create a new LocalDateTime object. In contrast, the third statement creates a new LocalTime object by using the plus() method and the ChronoUnit.HOURS constant to add 12 hours to the current time.

All of the ChronoUnit constants shown in this figure also have shortcut methods. For example, you can use the plusWeeks() and minusWeeks() methods shown in this figure to adjust the date by the specified number of weeks. Similarly, you can use the plusHours() or minusHours() methods to adjust a time by the specified number of hours. The second example shows how to use some of these methods to accomplish the same thing as the first example.

The third example in this figure shows how you can use method chaining when adjusting dates and times. Here, the code creates a new LocalDateTime object that is three weeks and three hours after the current date and time.

As you may have guessed, the LocalDate class doesn't support the ChronoUnit constants or shortcut methods that work with times. Conversely, the LocalTime class doesn't support the ChronoUnit constants or shortcut methods that work with dates.

A common mistake among new programmers is to assume that these methods change the date or time stored in the existing objects. However, like all of the methods in the new date/time API, these methods return new objects and don't change the existing objects.

This figure only lists the most commonly used ChronoUnit constants. Although there are others, you probably won't need them unless you need to deal with very small or large units of time.

How to get the time between two dates

Figure 14-6 also shows how to get the time between two dates. To do that, you can use the until() method of the LocalDateTime or LocalDate class or the between() method of the ChronoUnit enumeration. Both of these methods return a long value that indicates the number of units that you specify between the two dates. Although it's not shown here, you can also use these methods to calculate the time between two date/time or time objects.

The last example in figure 14-6 illustrates how these methods work. Here, the first statement uses the until() method to calculate the number of days between the current date and a due date. The second statement performs the same calculation, but it uses the between() method.

Methods for adding or subtracting time

Method	Description
plus(long, chronoUnit)	Returns a new date/time object after adding the specified amount of time.
minus(long, chronoUnit)	Returns a new date/time object after subtracting the specified amount of time.

Common constants of the ChronoUnit enumeration (java.time.temporal)

YEARS	MONTHS	WEEKS	DAYS	HOURS	MINUTES	SECONDS

Code that modifies the current date/time

```
LocalDateTime newDateTime = currentDateTime.plus(3, ChronoUnit.WEEKS);
LocalDateTime newDateTime = currentDateTime.minus(1, ChronoUnit.DAYS);
LocalTime newTime = currentTime.plus(12, ChronoUnit.HOURS);
```

Shortcut methods for adding or subtracting weeks

Method	Description
plusWeeks(long)	Returns a new object after adding the specified number of weeks.
minusWeeks(long)	Returns a new object after subtracting the specified number of weeks.

Shortcut methods for the previous three statements

```
LocalDateTime newDateTime = currentDateTime.plusWeeks(3);
LocalDateTime newDateTime = currentDateTime.minusDays(1);
LocalTime newTime = currentTime.plusHours(12);
```

Code that uses method chaining

```
LocalDateTime newDateTime = currentDateTime.plusWeeks(3).plusHours(3);
```

Methods for calculating the time between two dates

Method	Description
until(dateTime, chronoUnit)	Returns the amount of time until the specified date/time.
between(dateTime, dateTime)	Returns the amount of time between two date/time objects.

Code that gets the number of days between two date objects

```
long numDays = currentDate.until(dueDate, ChronoUnit.DAYS);
long numDays = ChronoUnit.DAYS.between(currentDate, dueDate);
```

Description

- To adjust the date or time forward or backward, you can use the plus() and minus() methods with the ChronoUnit enumeration to specify a period of time. However, it's usually easier to use the shortcut methods such as plusWeeks() or minusWeeks().

- Shortcut methods exist for all of the ChronoUnit constants shown in this figure.

- The LocalDateTime class supports all of the methods and ChronoUnit constants. The LocalDate and LocalTime classes only support the methods and constants that are relevant to them.

- All of the plus and minus methods return new objects of the same type. In other words, they do not alter the existing objects.

Figure 14-6   How to add or subtract a period of time and get the time between two dates

How to format dates and times

If necessary, you could format dates and times by using the get methods presented earlier to build a string containing the date and time formatted the way you want. However, this approach has one major disadvantage: It doesn't account for local formatting preferences. Fortunately, the new date/time API includes a DateTimeFormatter class that accounts for local formatting preferences.

Figure 14-7 shows several static methods you can call on the DateTimeFormatter class to get different format styles for dates and times. These formatters automatically present the date in a format that's appropriate for the current locale. So, depending on your locale, the format might look different than the format shown in this figure.

For example, suppose you have a LocalDate object set to October 31, 2017, and you use the SHORT format style to format it. In the United States, it's customary to start a date with the month, followed by the day. As a result, in the United States this formats the date as:

`10/31/17`

However, in many European countries, it is customary to start a date with the day, followed by the month. As a result, in those countries, the same formatter formats the date as:

`31/10/17`

The same is true with the time formatter. For example, suppose you have a LocalTime object set to 14:30, and you use the SHORT format style to format it. In the United States, the 12-hour AM/PM clock is the norm. As a result, in the United States, this formats the time as:

`2:30 PM`

However, in countries that use a 24-hour clock, this formats the time as:

`14:30`

The FormatStyle enumeration provides for four format styles: SHORT, MEDIUM, LONG, and FULL. Dates support all four of these format styles. However, times only support the SHORT and MEDIUM styles. As a result, if you want to use the same format style for both the date and time as shown in the first example, you must use the SHORT or MEDIUM styles. Otherwise, the compiler throws a DateTimeException. If you want, though, you can specify one format style for the date and another style for the time as shown in the second example.

Although several other formatters are available, they are beyond the scope of this chapter. Also, if you can't find a formatter that does what you need, you can write your own. For more information on how to do this, see the API documentation for the DateTimeFormatter class.

A class and an enumeration for formatting dates and times

```
java.time.format.DateTimeFormatter
java.time.format.FormatStyle
```

Common static methods of the DateTimeFormatter class

Method	Description
`ofLocalizedDate(dateStyle)`	Returns a DateTimeFormatter object for the date, but not the time.
`ofLocalizedTime(timeStyle)`	Returns a DateTimeFormatter object for the time, but not the date.
`ofLocalizedDateTime(dateTimeStyle)`	Returns a DateTimeFormatter object for the date and time.
`ofLocalizedDateTime(dateStyle, timeStyle)`	Returns a DateTimeFormatter object for the date and time, but with a different formatting style used for each.

A common method of the DateTimeFormatter class

Method	Description
`format(dateTime)`	Returns a String object for the formatted date/time.

Constants of the FormatStyle enumeration

Constant	Date example	Time example
`FormatStyle.SHORT`	10/31/17	6:30 PM
`FormatStyle.MEDIUM`	Oct 31, 2017	6:30:00 PM
`FormatStyle.LONG`	October 31, 2017	DateTimeException
`FormatStyle.FULL`	Tuesday, October 31, 2017	DateTimeException

Code that uses the same style to format both the date and time

```
DateTimeFormatter dtf = DateTimeFormatter.ofLocalizedDateTime(
        FormatStyle.MEDIUM);
String currentDateTimeFormatted = dtf.format(currentDateTime);
```

Code that uses separate styles for the date and time

```
DateTimeFormatter dtf = DateTimeFormatter.ofLocalizedDateTime(
        FormatStyle.LONG, FormatStyle.SHORT);
String currentDateTimeFormatted = dtf.format(currentDateTime);
```

Description

- You can use the ofLocalized methods to format a date and time for the locale of the system that the application is running on.

- You can use the FormatStyle constants to specify the format style for the date and time.

- If you attempt to use the LONG or FULL style to format a time, the compiler throws a DateTimeException.

- If none of the formats included with the API meets your needs, you can write your own custom formatters.

Figure 14-7   How to format dates and times

An Invoice class that includes an invoice date

Figure 14-8 shows how to add a date to the Invoice class that was presented in the previous chapter. To start, this class declares a LocalDateTime instance variable to store the invoice date. As a result, the invoice date includes both a date and a time.

The constructor for this class sets the invoice date to the current date and time. To do that, it uses the now() method of the LocalDateTime class.

If you don't want to store the time, you can use a LocalDate object to store the date. In this figure, for example, you could use a LocalDate object to store the invoice date. However, it's entirely possible that you may also want to know what time an invoice was created. As a result, it usually makes sense to store the extra data as shown by the class in this figure.

This class includes three methods that provide access to the invoice date. First, the setInvoiceDate() method allows you to set the invoice date. For example, if you get the data for an Invoice object from a database, you can use this method to set the invoice date. Second, the getInvoiceDate() method returns the invoice date as a LocalDateTime object.

Third, the getInvoiceDateFormatted() method returns a String object for the invoice date after the code has applied formatting to the LocalDateTime object for the invoice date. Within this method, the first statement creates a formatter for the date only that uses the SHORT format style. Then, the second statement uses this formatter to format the invoice date and return the resulting String object. As a result, this method only displays the date the invoice was created, even though the Invoice object also stores the time the invoice was created. If that's not what you want, you can add more methods to this class that get the date and time in other formats.

An Invoice class that includes a date

```java
package murach.business;

import java.text.NumberFormat;
import java.time.LocalDateTime;
import java.time.format.DateTimeFormatter;
import java.time.format.FormatStyle;
import java.util.ArrayList;

public class Invoice {

    private ArrayList<LineItem> lineItems;
    private LocalDateTime invoiceDate;

    public Invoice() {
        lineItems = new ArrayList<>();
        invoiceDate = LocalDateTime.now();
    }

    public void addItem(LineItem lineItem) {
        lineItems.add(lineItem);
    }

    public ArrayList<LineItem> getLineItems() {
        return lineItems;
    }

    public double getTotal() {
        double invoiceTotal = 0;
        for (LineItem lineItem : lineItems) {
            invoiceTotal += lineItem.getTotal();
        }
        return invoiceTotal;
    }

    public String getTotalFormatted() {
        NumberFormat currency = NumberFormat.getCurrencyInstance();
        return currency.format(getTotal());
    }

    public void setInvoiceDate(LocalDateTime invoiceDate) {
        this.invoiceDate = invoiceDate;
    }

    public LocalDateTime getInvoiceDate() {
        return invoiceDate;
    }

    public String getInvoiceDateFormatted() {
        DateTimeFormatter dtf = DateTimeFormatter.ofLocalizedDate(
                FormatStyle.SHORT);
        return dtf.format(invoiceDate);
    }
}
```

Figure 14-8   An Invoice class that includes an invoice date

Perspective

Now that you've finished this chapter, you should understand some of the differences between the old date/time API that was available prior to Java 8 and the new date/time API that's available with Java 8 and later. In addition, you should be able to use the classes provided by the new date/time API to work with dates and times.

Summary

- Prior to Java 8, it was common to use classes in the java.util and java.text packages to work with and format dates and times.

- With Java 8 or later, you can use the java.time package to work with and format dates and times. Unlike the java.util and java.text packages, this package is thread-safe, intuitive, and easier to use with calendars other than the Gregorian calendar.

- You can use the LocalDate, LocalTime, and LocalDateTime classes and the Month, DayOfWeek, and ChronoUnit enumerations to create and work with dates and times.

- You can use the DateTimeFormatter class and the FormatStyle enumeration to format dates and times.

Exercise 14-1   Add a due date to the Invoice application

For this exercise, you'll modify the Invoice class that's shown at the end of this chapter so it contains methods that return a due date, calculated as 30 days after the invoice date.

1. Open the project named ch14_ex1_Invoice that's in the ex_starts folder. Then, review the code in the Invoice and InvoiceApp classes.

2. In the Invoice class, modify the getInvoiceDateFormatted() method so it returns the due date using the MEDIUM format style.

3. In the Invoice class, add a method named getDueDate(). This method should calculate and return a LocalDateTime object that's 30 days after the invoice date.

4. In the Invoice class, add a method named getDueDateFormatted(). This method should return the due date using the MEDIUM format style.

5. In the InvoiceApp class, modify the displayInvoice() method so it displays the invoice date and the due date before it displays the line items like this:

```
Invoice date:     Apr 1, 2017
Invoice due date: May 1, 2017

Description                    Price    Qty   Total
Murach's Java Programming      $57.50    2    $115.00

Invoice total: $115.00
```

6. Run the application to make sure it works correctly.

Exercise 14-2   Calculate the user's age

In this exercise, you'll write an application that gets the user's date of birth, calculates the user's age in years, and displays the user's age. When you're done, the console should look something like this:

```
Welcome to the Age Calculator

Enter your date of birth (YYYY-MM-DD): 1968-02-04

Your date of birth is Feb 4, 1968
The current date is Apr 11, 2017
Your age is 49
```

1. Open the project named ch14_ex2_AgeCalculator that's in the ex_starts folder. Then, review the code in the AgeCalculatorApp class.

2. Add code to this class that gets the current date and stores it in a LocalDate object.

3. Add code that parses the string entered by the user to create a LocalDate object.

4. Add code to format and print the user's date of birth.

5. Add code to format and print the current date.

6. Add code to calculate and print the user's age in years.

7. Run the application and test it to make sure it works correctly for a date in the correct format.

8. Run the application and test it with a date in an invalid format such as "Feb 4, 1968". This should cause an exception to occur.

9. Run the application again, enter a date of birth that's after the current date, and notice that the age is displayed as a negative number. To fix this, validate the date to be sure it isn't after the current date. If it is, display an error message. Run the application one more time to test this change.

15

How to work with file I/O

In this chapter, you'll learn how to work with file input and output, or file I/O, for two types of files: text files and binary files. Although binary files are required for some applications, text files are preferred whenever possible because they are more portable and less platform dependent. That's why this chapter presents the skills for working with text files first.

When you work with files, you often need to use collections as described in chapter 12 and strings as described in chapter 13. In addition, this chapter shows how to implement an interface similar to the one presented in chapter 9 that provides for data access. As a result, you may want to review those chapters as you progress through this chapter.

Introduction to directories and files

Prior to Java 7, it was common to use the File class from the java.io package to perform some basic operations on directories and files. However, this class has many limitations. That's why Java 7 introduced the java.nio.file package (also known as NIO.2). This package provides an improved way to access the default file system. As a result, it's generally considered a best practice to use the classes and interfaces of this package to work with directories and files.

A package for working with directories and files

Figure 15-1 begins by presenting the static get() method of the Paths class in the java.nio.file package. You can pass one or more strings to this method to return a Path object that represents a path to a directory or a file. A Path object includes *name elements* that represent the directories and file in the path. For example, the path

```
c:\murach\java\files\products.txt
```

includes name elements for three directories and one file. In addition, it includes the root component "c:".

Once you have a Path object, you can use the methods of the Path interface to get information about the path. For example, you can use the getName() method to get a Path object for the name element at the specified index. The index refers to the position of the name element in the path, where the first element is at index 0.

You can also use the static methods of the Files class to get information about a path. For example, you can use the first four methods to check whether a path exists and whether you can read from or write to a path. Similarly, you can use the next two methods to test whether the path refers to a directory or a file. Then, if the path refers to a file, you can use the size() method to return the number of bytes in the file.

To display the contents of a directory, you can use the newDirectoryStream() method with a Path object. This method returns a DirectoryStream<Path> object. Then, you can use this object to loop through all of the subdirectories and files within that directory. You'll see an example of how this works in the next figure.

You can use the last four methods of the Files class to create and delete directories and files. If these methods aren't able to create or delete a file or directory, they throw exceptions that should give you a good idea of why they failed. For example, if you attempt to create a file that already exists, you will get a FileAlreadyExistsException. Similarly, if you attempt to delete a directory that contains files, you will get a DirectoryNotEmptyException. To handle these exceptions, you can use a try statement as you'll see later in this chapter.

As you review these methods, you should know that they're only some of the most commonly used methods of the java.nio.file package. So, if you need to perform other file-handling tasks, you can consult the Java API documentation for this package.

A package for working with directories and files
`java.nio.file`

A static method of the Paths class

Method	Description
`get(String[, String]...)`	Returns a Path object for the string or series of strings that specify the path.

Methods of the Path interface

Method	Description
`getFileName()`	Returns a Path object for the name of the file or directory.
`getName(int)`	Returns a Path object for the element at the specified index.
`getNameCount()`	Returns an int value for the number of name elements in the path.
`getParent()`	Returns a Path object for the parent path if one exists. Returns a null value if a parent does not exist.
`getRoot()`	Returns a Path object for the root component of the path. Returns a null value if a root does not exist.
`toAbsolutePath()`	Returns a Path object for the absolute path to the file or directory.
`toFile()`	Returns a File object for the path.

Static methods of the Files class

Method	Description
`exists(Path)`	Returns a true value if the path exists.
`notExists(Path)`	Returns a true value if the path does not exist.
`isReadable(Path)`	Returns a true value if the path exists and is readable.
`isWritable(Path)`	Returns a true value if the path exists and is writable.
`isDirectory(Path)`	Returns a true value if the path exists and refers to a directory.
`isRegularFile(Path)`	Returns a true value if the path exists and refers to a regular file.
`size(Path)`	Returns a long value for the number of bytes in the file.
`newDirectoryStream(Path)`	Returns a DirectoryStream<Path> object that you can use to loop through all files and subdirectories of the directory.
`createFile(Path)`	Creates a new file for the specified Path object if one doesn't already exist. Returns a Path object for the file.
`createDirectory(Path)`	Creates a new directory for the specified Path object if the directory doesn't already exist and all parent directories do exist. Returns a Path object for the directory.
`createDirectories(Path)`	Creates a new directory represented by the specified Path object including any necessary but non-existent parent directories. Returns a Path object for the directory.
`delete(Path)`	Deletes the file or directory represented by the Path object. A directory can only be deleted if it's empty.

Description
- You can use a Path object to work with a directory or file.

Figure 15-1   A package for working with directories and files

Code examples that work with directories and files

The first example in figure 15-2 shows how to create a new directory. To do this, the first statement creates a string that refers to a directory. In this case, the directory is murach\java\files on the C drive. Then, the second statement uses the Paths class to get a Path object for this directory. Finally, an if statement checks whether this directory already exists. If not, this code calls the static createDirectories() method of the Files class to create the directory and any necessary parent directories.

The second example shows how to create a new file. To do this, the first statement creates a string that contains the name of the file. Then, the second statement gets a Path object that refers to the directory and file. In this case, the file is named products.txt and the directory is c:\murach\java\files. If the file doesn't already exist, the last statement calls the static createFile() method of the Files class to create the file.

As you review this example, note that the get() method of the Paths class includes two arguments: one for the directory and one for the file. When you code the get() method like this, it joins the arguments and separates them with a separator character. In most cases, the separator character is the same as the character that's used to separate the name elements in the arguments. In this case, the separator character is a front slash.

In addition, note that the Path object contains an *absolute path name*. In other words, this example specifies the entire path and file name for the file. However, if you want to create a Path object that refers to a file that's in the same directory as the application, you can use a *relative path name*. To do that, you just specify the name of the file.

The third example shows how to get information about the Path object created in the second example. The output below this example shows the result of the three statements. First, the getFileName() method returns the name of the file. Then, the toAbsolutePath() method returns a Path object for the full path. Finally, the static isWritable() method of the Files class returns a true value to show that the file is not read-only, which is the default.

The fourth example shows how to list the names of the files in a directory. To start, an if statement checks whether the path exists and whether it is a directory. If both are true, this code prints the name of the directory to the console. Then, the static newDirectoryStream() method of the Files class returns a DirectoryStream<Path> object. Finally, this code loops through all of the Path objects in this stream, checks if the Path object is a file, and prints the file name to the console if it is.

If you're used to working with Windows, you may be surprised to find that you use a front slash instead of a backslash to separate the parts of a path. That's because Java uses the backslash to identify escape characters. This makes it cumbersome to use backslashes when specifying paths. However, using a front slash works equally well for both Windows and other operating systems such as Linux. The output for these examples shows that the Java API automatically converts the front slash to a backslash when necessary.

Code that creates a directory if it doesn't already exist

```
String dirString = "c:/murach/java/files";
Path dirPath = Paths.get(dirString);
if (Files.notExists(dirPath)) {
    Files.createDirectories(dirPath);
}
```

Code that creates a file if it doesn't already exist

```
String fileString = "products.txt";
Path filePath = Paths.get(dirString, fileString);
if (Files.notExists(filePath)) {
    Files.createFile(filePath);
}
```

Code that displays information about a file

```
System.out.println("File name:      " + filePath.getFileName());
System.out.println("Absolute path:  " + filePath.toAbsolutePath());
System.out.println("Is writable:    " + Files.isWritable(filePath));
```

Resulting output

```
File name:      products.txt
Absolute path:  c:\murach\java\files\products.txt
Is writable:    true
```

Code that displays the files in a directory

```
if (Files.exists(dirPath) && Files.isDirectory(dirPath)) {
    System.out.println("Directory: " + dirPath.toAbsolutePath());
    System.out.println("Files: ");
    DirectoryStream<Path> dirStream = Files.newDirectoryStream(dirPath);
    for (Path p: dirStream) {
        if (Files.isRegularFile(p))
            System.out.println("      " + p.getFileName());
    }
}
```

Description

- Java SE 7 introduced the java.nio.file package (also known as NIO.2). This package provides an improved way to access the default file system and is designed to replace the functionality that was available from the java.io.File class.

- The java.nio.file package provides support for many features that aren't provided by the java.io.File class.

- When coding paths, you can use a front slash to separate directory names. This works equally well for Windows and other operating systems.

- To identify the name and location of a file, you can use an *absolute path name* to specify the entire path for a file. You can also use a *relative path name* to specify the path of the file relative to the directory that contains the class that identifies the path.

Figure 15-2   Code examples that work with directories and files

Introduction to file I/O

This topic introduces the types of files and streams that you can use for file input and output, or *file I/O*. Then, it presents an example that introduces the code that's needed to perform input and output operations on a file. Finally, it shows how to handle the exceptions that occur most frequently when you perform input and output operations.

How files and streams work

Figure 15-3 presents the two types of files and the two types of streams that you use when you perform I/O operations. To start, a *text file* stores its data as *Unicode* characters on disk. Often, this type of file uses delimiters like tabs and new line characters to separate the fields and records. In this figure, for example, the text file uses tabs to separate fields and new line characters to separate records. Other types of text files include XML and HTML files. These types of files use special tags to structure their data.

In contrast, a *binary file* does not store all of its data as characters. As a result, a text editor can't display all of the data in this file as characters that are easily read by humans. In this figure, for example, when the text editor displays the binary file, some characters look like gibberish. Also, since the records in a binary file don't end with new line characters, all records are displayed on a single line by a text editor. Other types of binary files include image, audio, video, and application files.

To handle I/O operations, Java uses *streams*. You can think of a stream as the flow of data from one location to another. For instance, an *output stream* can flow from the internal memory of an application to a disk file, and an *input stream* can flow from a disk file to internal memory. When you work with a text file, you use a *character stream*. When you work with a binary file, you use a *binary stream*.

Although this chapter shows how to use streams with disk files, Java also uses streams with other types of devices. For instance, you can use an output stream to send data to the console or to a network connection. In fact, the System.out object is the standard output stream for writing data to the console. Similarly, you can use an input stream to read data from a source like a keyboard or a network connection. In fact, the System.in object that's used by the Scanner class is the standard input stream for reading data from the keyboard.

When you save a text or binary file, you can use any extension for the file name. In this book, we have used *txt* as the extension for all text files and *bin* for all binary files. For instance, the text file in this figure is named products.txt, and the binary file is named products.bin.

A text file that's opened by a text editor

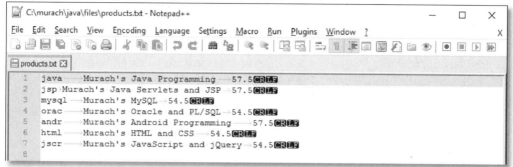

A binary file that's opened by a text editor

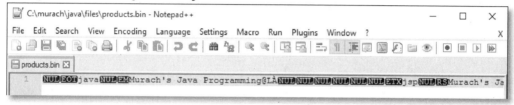

Two types of files

File	Description
Text	A file that contains characters. The fields and records in this type of file are often delimited by special characters like tab and new line characters.
Binary	A file that may contain characters as well as other non-character data types that can't be read by a text editor.

Two types of streams

Stream	Description
Character	Used to transfer text data to or from an I/O device.
Binary	Used to transfer binary data to or from an I/O device.

Description

- An *input file* is a file that is read by a program; an *output file* is a file that is written by a program. Input and output operations are often referred to as *I/O operations* or *file I/O*.

- A *stream* is the flow of data from one location to another. To write data to a file from internal storage, you use an *output stream*. To read from a file into internal storage, you use an *input stream*.

- To read and write *text files*, you use *character streams*. To read and write *binary files*, you use *binary streams*.

- Streams are not only used with disk devices, but also with input devices like keyboards and network connections and output devices like PC monitors and network connections.

Figure 15-3   How files and streams work

A file I/O example

To give you an overview of file I/O, figure 15-4 shows how to read from and write to a text file. To start, the first example shows how to import two packages for working with file I/O. Because most of the classes for working with file I/O are stored in the java.io package, any class that works with file I/O typically imports all of the classes in this package. In addition, the import statement for the java.nio.file package makes it easy to work with the classes (Paths and Files) and interfaces (Path) described earlier in this chapter.

The second example shows how to create a File object that refers to a file named products.txt. To start, the first statement creates a Path object that refers to the file. Since no directory is specified for the file, the Path object refers to a file that's stored in the working directory, which is usually the directory the application was started from. Then, the second statement calls the toFile() method of the Path object to convert it to a File object. This is necessary because many of the classes in the file.io package are designed to work with a File object and don't work directly with a Path object.

The third example shows how to write data to a file. To start, you create an output stream. To create a stream that has all the functionality that you need, you can *layer* two or more objects into a single stream. In this example, the code creates an output stream from the PrinterWriter, BufferedWriter, and FileWriter objects.

The BufferedWriter object adds a block of internal memory known as a *buffer* to the stream. This causes the data in the stream to be stored in a buffer before it is written to the output device. Then, when the buffer is full or the stream is closed, all of the data in the buffer is *flushed* to the disk file in a single I/O operation. Similarly, when you use a buffer for input, a full buffer of data is read in a single I/O operation.

The benefit of buffering is that it reduces the number of I/O operations that are done by a disk device. For each I/O operation, the disk has to rotate to the starting disk location. Since this rotation is extremely slow relative to internal operations, buffering dramatically improves the performance of I/O operations. That's why you should use buffers for all but the most trivial disk operations.

After creating the output stream, this code uses the println() method of the output stream to write the data to a file. Then, it calls the close() method of the stream. This flushes any data that's in the buffer to the file and frees any system resources associated with the output stream.

The fourth example reads the data that was written by the third example. To start, it creates a buffered input stream for the file. Then, the next two statements read the first line of that file and print that line to the console. Finally, this code closes the input stream, which flushes the buffer and frees all system resources associated with the input stream.

Because this figure is only intended to give you an idea of how file I/O works, you shouldn't worry if you don't understand it completely. As you progress through this chapter, you'll learn about all of the classes and methods shown here in more detail. Also, you should know that this code won't compile unless you handle the exceptions that it throws as described in the next figure.

Import all necessary packages

```
import java.io.*;
import java.nio.file.*;
```

Get a Path object for the file

```
Path productsPath = Paths.get("products.txt");
File productsFile = productsPath.toFile();
```

Write data to the file

```
// open an output stream
PrintWriter out = new PrintWriter(
                new BufferedWriter(
                new FileWriter(productsFile)));

// write data to the stream
out.println("java\tMurach's Java Programming\t57.50");

// close the output stream and free system resources
out.close();
```

Read data from the file

```
// open an input stream
BufferedReader in = new BufferedReader(
                new FileReader(productsFile));

// read data from the stream and print it to the console
String line = in.readLine();
System.out.println(line);

// close the input stream and free system resources
in.close();
```

Resulting output

```
java    Murach's Java Programming       57.50
```

Description

- The java.io package contains dozens of classes that can be used to work with different types of streams that have different functionality.

- To get the functionality you need for a stream, you often need to combine, or *layer*, two or more streams. You'll learn more about how this works as you progress through this chapter.

- To make disk processing more efficient, you can use a *buffered stream* that adds a block of internal memory called a *buffer* to the stream.

- When working with buffers, you often need to *flush* the buffer. This sends all data in the buffer to the I/O device. One way to do that is to use a try-with-resources statement to automatically close the I/O stream after you use it. See figure 15-5 for details.

Figure 15-4   A file I/O example

How to work with I/O exceptions

If you've read chapter 5, you should be familiar with a simple try statement that you can use to catch and handle exceptions. Now, figure 15-5 shows how to handle the most common exceptions that are thrown by I/O operations.

To start, this figure summarizes three exceptions that are commonly thrown by classes that perform file I/O operations. To start, the IOException class is the most general type of I/O exception, and it's inherited by the other two exception classes, which are for more specific I/O exceptions. In particular, an EOFException is thrown when a program attempts to read beyond the end of a file (EOF), and a FileNotFoundException is thrown when a program attempts to open a file that can't be found.

When you work with I/O exceptions, you need to know that the IOException class and all of its subclasses are known as *checked exceptions* because the compiler checks to make sure that you have handled these exceptions. As a result, you must write code that handles these exceptions before you can compile your code.

The example in this figure starts by showing how to prevent a FileNotFoundException. To do that, this code gets a Path object for a file. Then, it uses the exists() method of the Files class to check if a file exists for that path. If so, the code within the if block executes. Otherwise, the code in the else block prints a message to the console that indicates that the file doesn't exist.

Within the if block, the first statement converts the Path object to a File object. Then, a *try-with-resources* statement creates an input stream for the file. This is a special type of try statement that you can use to initialize an object that uses system resources. Then, when this statement is done executing, it automatically closes the object and releases any system resources that it's using. This is true even if an error occurs, and it makes working with file I/O operations easier and safer than it was prior to Java 7.

Within the try block, the first statement starts by reading the first record in the file. Then, it uses a while loop to display the current record and read the next record. This continues as long as the string that's returned isn't null. If the string is null, it indicates that the end of the file has been reached and the loop ends. This prevents the EOFException from occurring.

To handle any other I/O exceptions that might occur as the file is read, the try-with-resources statement includes a catch clause that catches the IOException. Within the catch block, the code prints the exception object to the console. This displays some information about the exception, including the exception's class name and a brief description of the exception if one is available.

A subset of the IOException hierarchy

```
IOException
    EOFException
    FileNotFoundException
```

Common I/O exceptions

Exception	Description
IOException	Thrown when an error occurs in I/O processing.
EOFException	Thrown when a program attempts to read beyond the end of a file.
FileNotFoundException	Thrown when a program attempts to open a file that doesn't exist.

The syntax for a simple try-with-resources statement

```
try (resourceInitializationStatement) { statements }
catch (ExceptionType exceptionObject) { statements }
```

Code that handles I/O exceptions

```
Path productsPath = Paths.get("products.txt");
if (Files.exists(productsPath)) {        // prevent the FileNotFoundException
    File productsFile = productsPath.toFile();
    try (BufferedReader in = new BufferedReader(
                        new FileReader(productsFile))) {
        String line = in.readLine();
        while(line != null) {             // prevent the EOFException
            System.out.println(line);
            line = in.readLine();
        }
    } catch (IOException e) {              // catch the IOException
        System.out.println(e);            // print the exception to the console
    }
} else {
    System.out.println(productsPath.toAbsolutePath() + " doesn't exist");
}
```

Description

- The IOException class and all of its subclasses define *checked exceptions*. The compiler checks these exceptions to make sure that you have handled them. As a result, you must handle these exceptions before you can compile your code.

- When you create objects from the classes in the java.io package, you must make sure to release the system resources that they use when you're done with them.

- The *try-with-resources* statement is a special type of try statement that you can use to initialize an object that uses system resources. This statement automatically closes the object and releases its resources when it's done executing.

- The try-with-resources statement was introduced with Java 7. As of Java 7, most of the classes in the Java API that use system resources have been retrofitted to work with the try-with-resources statement.

- In the catch block, you can print the exception to the console. This displays the exception's class name and a brief description of the exception, if one is available.

Figure 15-5   How to work with I/O exceptions

How to work with text files

When working with text files, you need to layer two or more classes to create a stream of characters for input or output. You'll learn how to do that in the topics that follow. In addition, you'll learn how to use the methods of these classes to work with text files. Then, you'll see a complete class that you can use to store Product objects in a text file.

How to connect a character output stream to a file

Before you can write to a text file, you need to create an output stream of characters, and you need to connect that stream to the file. To do that, you must layer two or more of the classes in the Writer hierarchy as shown in figure 15-6. Then, you use the methods of the PrintWriter class to write data to the output stream, you use the BufferedWriter class to create a buffer for the output stream, and you use the FileWriter class to connect the stream to a file.

Although it's typically a good coding practice to use a buffer, the first example in this figure shows how to connect to a file without using a buffer. Here, the first statement creates a FileWriter object by passing a String object for a path name to the constructor of the FileWriter class. Alternately, this statement could pass a File object for a file to this constructor. Either way, the second statement creates a PrintWriter object by passing the FileWriter object to the constructor of the PrintWriter class.

The second example shows a more concise way to code the first example. Here, you don't assign the FileWriter object to a named variable. Instead, you create the FileWriter object within the constructor of the PrintWriter class. You can align these nested constructor calls any way you like. In this example, the whole statement is coded on one line, but it's often easier to read if each constructor call is coded on a separate line as shown in the next three examples.

The third example shows how to include a buffer in the output stream. To do that, you use a BufferedWriter object in addition to a FileWriter and PrintWriter object.

The fourth example shows how to append data to an existing file. To do that, you set the second argument of the FileWriter constructor to true. If you don't code a value for this argument, the existing data in the file is overwritten.

By default, the data in an output stream is flushed from the buffer to the disk when the buffer is full. However, if you set the second argument of the PrintWriter constructor to true, the *autoflush feature* is turned on. Then, the buffer is flushed each time the println() method is executed. Because this can be inefficient, you won't typically include this argument.

The constructors in this figure should help you understand how to layer output streams. Here, the PrintWriter constructor accepts any class derived from the Writer class. As a result, you can supply a BufferedWriter object or a FileWriter object as an argument of this constructor. Similarly, since the BufferedWriter constructor also accepts any Writer object, you can supply a FileWriter object as an argument of this constructor.

A subset of the Writer hierarchy

```
Writer <<abstract>>
    BufferedWriter
    PrintWriter
    OutputStreamWriter
        FileWriter
```

Classes used to connect a character output stream to a file

PrintWriter   contains the methods for writing data to a text stream

   →**BufferedWriter**   creates a buffer for the stream

      →**FileWriter**   connects the stream to a file

Constructors of these classes

Constructor	Throws
PrintWriter(Writer[, booleanFlush])	None
BufferedWriter(Writer)	None
FileWriter(File[, booleanAppend])	IOException
FileWriter(StringPathName[, booleanAppend])	IOException

How to connect without a buffer (not recommended)

```
FileWriter fileWriter = new FileWriter("products.txt");
PrintWriter out = new PrintWriter(fileWriter);
```

A more concise way to code the previous example

```
PrintWriter out = new PrintWriter(new FileWriter("products.txt"));
```

How to connect to a file with a buffer

```
PrintWriter out = new PrintWriter(
            new BufferedWriter(
            new FileWriter("products.txt")));
```

How to connect for an append operation

```
PrintWriter out = new PrintWriter(
            new BufferedWriter(
            new FileWriter("products.txt", true)));
```

How to connect with the autoflush feature turned on

```
PrintWriter out = new PrintWriter(
            new BufferedWriter(
            new FileWriter("products.txt")), true);
```

Description

- The Writer class is an abstract class that's inherited by all classes in the Writer hierarchy.

- If the output file doesn't exist when the FileWriter object is created, it's created automatically. If it does exist, it's overwritten by default. If that's not what you want, you can specify true for the second argument of the constructor to append data to the file.

- If you specify true for the second argument of the PrintWriter constructor, the *autoflush feature* flushes the buffer each time the println() method is called.

Figure 15-6   How to connect a character output stream to a file

How to write to a text file

Figure 15-7 shows how to write to a text file. To do that, you use the print() and println() methods to write data to the file. These methods work like the print() and println() methods of the System.out object, but they write data to the output stream instead of writing data to the console.

Typically, you use a try-with-resources statement to create a stream as shown earlier in this chapter. Then, the stream is automatically closed and flushed when the try-with-resources statement ends. As a result, you typically don't need to call the close() or flush() methods. However, if you don't use a try-with-resources statement, you can use the close() method to manually close the output stream. This flushes the buffer and frees any system resources that are being used by the output stream. Or, if you want to keep the output stream open, you can use the flush() method to flush all the data in the stream to the file.

Either way, you need to catch or throw the IOException that can be thrown by these methods. For now, you can use a try-with-resources statement to catch the IOException as shown in this chapter. In the next chapter, you can learn how to throw an exception.

The first example in this figure shows how to append a string and an object to a text file named log.txt. To start, the code creates a FileWriter object that can append data to the file. If no file named log.txt exists in the current directory, this statement creates the file. Then, the print() method prints a string, and the println() method prints a LocalDateTime object that represents the current date and time. This works because Java automatically calls the toString() method of the LocalDateTime object, which converts the LocalDateTime object to a string.

For this code to work, you must import the LocalDateTime class from the java.time package. To do that, you can include this import statement at the top of the class:

```
import java.time.LocalDateTime;
```

The second example in this figure shows how to write the data that's stored in a Product object to a *delimited text file*. In this type of file, one type of *delimiter* is used to separate the *fields* (or *columns*) that are written to the file, and another type of delimiter is used to separate the *records* (or *rows*). In this example, the tab character (\t) is used as the delimiter for the fields, and the new line character is used as the delimiter for the records. That way, the code, description, and price for one product are stored in the same record separated by tabs. Then, the new line character ends the data for that product, and the data for the next product can be stored in the next record.

Common methods of the PrintWriter class

Method	Throws	Description
print(argument)	None	Writes the character representation of the argument type to the file.
println(argument)	None	Writes the character representation of the argument type to the file followed by the new line character. If the autoflush feature is turned on, this also flushes the buffer.
flush()	IOException	Flushes any data that's in the buffer to the file.
close()	IOException	Flushes any data that's in the buffer to the file and closes the stream.

Code that appends a string and an object to a text file

```
// open an output stream for appending to the text file
PrintWriter out = new PrintWriter(
                new BufferedWriter(
                new FileWriter("log.txt", true)));

// write a string and an object to the file
out.print("This application was run on ");
LocalDateTime currentDateTime = LocalDateTime.now();
out.println(currentDateTime);

// flush data to the file and close the output stream
out.close();
```

Code that writes a Product object to a delimited text file

```
// open an output stream for overwriting a text file
PrintWriter out = new PrintWriter(
                new BufferedWriter(
                new FileWriter(productsFile)));

// write the Product object to the file
out.print(product.getCode() + "\t");
out.print(product.getDescription() + "\t");
out.println(product.getPrice());

// flush data to the file and close the output stream
out.close();
```

Description

- To write a character representation of a data type to an output stream, you use the print() and println() methods of the PrintWriter class. If you supply an object as an argument, these methods will call the toString method of the object.

- To create a *delimited text file*, you delimit the *records* in the file with one *delimiter*, such as a new line character, and you delimit the *fields* of each record with another delimiter, such as a tab character.

- To flush all data to the file, you can use a try-with-resources statement to automatically close the stream when you're done using it. You can also use the flush() or close() methods of the stream to manually flush all data to the file.

Figure 15-7   How to write to a text file

How to connect a character input stream to a file

Before you can read characters from a text file, you must connect the character input stream to the file. Figure 15-8 shows how to do that with a buffer and a File object. To do that, you supply a FileReader object as the argument of the constructor of the BufferedReader class. This creates a stream that uses a buffer and has methods that you can use to read data.

If you look at the constructors for the BufferedReader and FileReader classes, you can see why this code works. Since the constructor for the BufferedReader object accepts any object in the Reader hierarchy, it can accept a FileReader object that connects the stream to a file. However, the BufferedReader object can also accept an InputStreamReader object, which can be used to connect the character input stream to the keyboard or to a network connection rather than to a file.

A subset of the Reader hierarchy

```
Reader <<abstract>>
    BufferedReader
    InputStreamReader
        FileReader
```

Classes used to connect to a file with a buffer

BufferedReader   contains the methods for reading data from the stream

→**FileReader**   connects the stream to a file

Constructors of these classes

Constructor	Throws
BufferedReader(Reader)	None
FileReader(File)	FileNotFoundException
FileReader(StringPathName)	FileNotFoundException

How to connect a character input stream to a file

```
BufferedReader in = new BufferedReader(
                    new FileReader("products.txt"));
```

Description

- The Reader class is an abstract class that's inherited by all classes in the Reader hierarchy. All classes in the java.io package that end with Reader are members of the Reader hierarchy.

- Although you can read files with the FileReader class alone, the BufferedReader class improves efficiency and provides better methods for reading character input streams.

Figure 15-8   How to connect a character input stream to a file

How to read from a text file

The two examples in figure 15-9 show how to read the two text files that are written by the examples in figure 15-7. In the first example, the first statement uses the readLine() method to read the first record in the log file. Then, a while loop prints the current record to the console and reads the next record. When the readLine() method attempts to read past the end of the file, it returns a null, which causes the while loop to end. Then, this code calls the close() method to close the input stream, which flushes the buffer.

The second example shows how to read a record from the products file. To do that, it uses the readLine() method. Then, because this file is a delimited text file, it parses the string into its individual fields. To do that, it uses the split() method of the String class to split the string into an array. In this example, the tab character is supplied as the argument of the split() method since this is the delimiter for the fields in the record.

This example continues by creating a Product object from the data in the fields array. Since the product code and description are strings, the fields that contain these values can be passed directly to the constructor of the Product object. However, the price field must be converted from a String object to a double value. To do that, this example uses the parseDouble() method of the Double class.

After the Product object is created, it's printed at the console. Finally, the close() method of the BufferedReader class is called to flush the buffer and free any system resources.

Common methods of the BufferedReader class

Method	Throws	Description
readLine()	IOException	Reads a line of text and returns it as a string.
close()	IOException	Closes the input stream and flushes the buffer.

Code that reads the records in a text file

```
// read the records of the file
String line = in.readLine();
while(line != null) {
    System.out.println(line);
    line = in.readLine();
}

// close the input stream
in.close();
```

Sample output

```
This application was run on 2017-04-28T12:06:55.084
This application was run on 2017-04-28T12:07:28.041
```

Code that reads a Product object from a delimited text file

```
// read the next line of the file
String line = in.readLine();

// parse the line into its fields
String[] fields = line.split("\t");
String code = fields[0];
String description = fields[1];
String price = fields[2];

// create a Product object from the data in the fields
Product p = new Product(code, description, Double.parseDouble(price));

// print the Product object
System.out.println(p);

// close the input stream
in.close();
```

Sample output

```
Code:        java
Description: Murach's Java Programming
Price:       $57.50
```

Figure 15-9   How to read from a text file

Two interfaces for data access

In chapter 9, you saw a ProductDAO interface that defines I/O methods and constants for a *data access object* (*DAO*). Now, figure 15-10 presents a similar interface that you can use to access data. Unlike the interface in chapter 9, this interface doesn't inherit other interfaces. Instead, it defines all of the methods that it requires.

There are two main differences between this interface and the one in chapter 9. First, it doesn't include the constants that specify the display size of the fields of a Product object. Second, the getAll() method returns a List<Product> object instead of a String object.

The ProductDAO interface defines five methods that you can use to read and write Product objects to a file or database. To start, this interface defines two methods that you can use to read Product objects from a file or database. Here, the get() method returns a single Product object for the product with the specified product code. Then, the getAll() method returns a List object that contains all Product objects in the file or database.

Next, this interface defines three methods that you can use to write product data to a file or database. Each of these methods accepts a Product object and returns a boolean value that indicates whether or not the operation was successful.

The problem with the ProductDAO interface is that it only works for one type of object, the Product object. Fortunately, Java's generics feature makes it possible to rewrite this interface so it works for multiple types of objects. To do that, you can use a DAO interface like the one shown in this figure.

When you implement the DAO interface, you specify the type of object you want to work with in the class declaration. If, for example, you declare that the class implements the DAO<Product> interface, the class must implement methods just like the ones in the ProductDAO interface. However, if you declare that the class implements the DAO<Customer> interface, the class would work for a Customer object, not a Product object.

The ProductDAO interface

```
package murach.db;

import java.util.List;
import murach.business.Product;

public interface ProductDAO {
    Product get(String code);
    List<Product> getAll();
    boolean add(Product p);
    boolean update(Product p);
    boolean delete(Product p);
}
```

A class that implements this interface

```
public class ProductTextFile implements ProductDAO {
    public Product get(String code) {}
    public List<Product> getAll() {}
    public boolean add(Product p) {}
    public boolean update(Product p) {}
    public boolean delete(Product p) {}
}
```

The DAO interface

```
package murach.db;

import java.util.List;

public interface DAO<T> {
    T get(String code);
    List<T> getAll();
    boolean add(T t);
    boolean update(T t);
    boolean delete(T t);
}
```

A class that implements this interface

```
public class ProductTextFile implements DAO<Product> {
    public Product get(String code) {}
    public List<Product> getAll() {}
    public boolean add(Product p) {}
    public boolean update(Product p) {}
    public boolean delete(Product p) {}
}
```

Description

- Both interfaces in this figure define an object for data access, or a *data access object* (*DAO*).

- The first interface only works with Product objects, but the second interface uses generics so it can work with multiple types of objects.

Figure 15-10   Two interfaces for data access

A class that works with a text file

Figure 15-11 shows a class named ProductTextFile that can be used to read and write products to a text file. This class implements the DAO<Product> interface shown in figure 15-10. As a result, it implements all five public methods of this interface. In addition, it includes a private method named saveAll() that's used by some of these methods.

To start, this class defines three instance variables and a constant. Here, the List object stores a list of Product objects for the products in the file, the Path object defines the path to the file, and the File object connects the input and output streams to the file. Then, the FIELD_SEP constant defines the character that's used to separate the fields in the products file.

The constructor for the ProductTextFile class initializes the instance variables. To do that, it creates a Path object for a file named products.txt that's stored in the working directory, which is usually the root directory for the application. Then, the constructor uses the toFile() method of the Path object to convert the Path object to a File object. Finally, it calls the getAll() method to get the list of all products.

The getAll() method returns a list of Product objects for all products stored in the file. This method starts by checking whether the products list has been created. If so, it returns that list. This increases efficiency by reading the file only when necessary.

If the list of Products hasn't been created, this code creates an empty ArrayList of Product objects. Then, it checks if the products file exists. If so, it uses a try-with-resources statement to create a buffered input stream.

To create the Product objects, this method starts by reading the first line from the products file into a string variable. Then, it uses a while loop to process the lines in the file until the end of the file is reached. As you learned earlier in this chapter, you can test for an end-of-file condition by checking whether the string that's returned by the readLine() method is null.

Within the while loop, the first statement uses the FIELD_SEP constant to split the line into its three fields (code, description, and price). Then, this loop creates a Product object from the values in these fields and adds the Product object to the array list. Finally, this loop reads the next line in the file.

If an IOException is thrown somewhere in the getAll() method, this method returns a null. That way, any method that calls the getAll() method can test whether it executed successfully by checking whether it returns a null. Whether or not an exception is thrown, the try-with-resources statement automatically closes the input stream.

In this class, all of the catch clauses, including the one in the getAll() method, print the exception to the console. This is useful when you're testing and debugging a program, but it might not be appropriate when you put a program into production. As a result, before putting a class like this into a production environment, you might want to change the way that exceptions are handled. For example, you might want to write the exception to a log file. Or, you might want to throw a custom exception that indicates that a data access error has occurred. For more information on how to do that, see the next chapter.

The ProductTextFile class

```java
package murach.db;

import java.io.*;
import java.nio.file.*;
import java.util.*;

import murach.business.Product;

public class ProductTextFile implements DAO<Product> {
    private List<Product> products = null;
    private Path productsPath = null;
    private File productsFile = null;
    private final String FIELD_SEP = "\t";

    public ProductTextFile() {
        productsPath = Paths.get("products.txt");
        productsFile = productsPath.toFile();
        products = this.getAll();
    }

    @Override
    public List<Product> getAll() {
        // if the products file has already been read, don't read it again
        if (products != null) {
            return products;
        }

        products = new ArrayList<>();
        if (Files.exists(productsPath)) {
            try (BufferedReader in = new BufferedReader(
                                  new FileReader(productsFile))) {

                // read products from file into array list
                String line = in.readLine();
                while (line != null) {
                    String[] fields = line.split(FIELD_SEP);
                    String code = fields[0];
                    String description = fields[1];
                    String price = fields[2];

                    Product p = new Product(
                            code, description, Double.parseDouble(price));
                    products.add(p);

                    line = in.readLine();
                }
            } catch (IOException e) {
                System.out.println(e);
                return null;
            }
        } else {
            System.out.println(
                    productsPath.toAbsolutePath() + "doesn't exist.");
            return null;
        }
        return products;
    }
```

Figure 15-11   A class that works with a text file (part 1 of 2)

The get() method returns a Product object for a product that matches the specified product code. To search for the product, this method loops through each product in the products list until it finds one with the specified product code. Then, it returns that product. If no product is found with the specified code, this method returns a null.

The saveAll() method writes all of the Product objects to the file. If this operation is successful, it returns a true value. If an IOException is thrown, this method returns a false value to indicate that the save operation wasn't successful.

The saveAll() method starts by creating a buffered output stream that connects to the products file. Then, this method uses a loop to write each product in the list of products to the file. To do that, it uses the FIELD_SEP constant to separate each field in a product record, and it uses the println() method to insert a new line character at the end of each product record.

The add() method starts by adding the product to the product list. Then, it calls the saveAll() method to save the modified list to the products file. That way, the list of products and the file contain the same data. Note that the add() method returns the boolean value that's returned by the saveAll() method. That way, if the saveAll() method returns a true value, the add() method also returns a true value.

The delete() method works similarly. It starts by removing the product from the list. Then, it calls the saveAll() method to save the list of products to the products file, and it returns the boolean value that's returned by that method.

The update() method works a little differently. This method updates the data for an existing product with the data in a new product. To start, this method uses the get() method to get the old Product object with the same product code as the new Product object. Then, it gets the index for the old product, and it removes that product from the list of products. Next, it inserts the new product into the list where the old product used to be. Finally, it calls the saveAll() method to save the list of products to the products file, and it returns a value that indicates whether the save operation was successful.

As you review this code, you should realize that this class won't work correctly for multiple users. For example, suppose that both user A and user B read the products file, and user A modifies that file. Then, suppose user B also modifies the file. At this point, user B's changes overwrite user A's changes. This is known as a *concurrency problem*.

One way to reduce concurrency problems would be to read the data from the file each time the getAll(), get(), add(), update(), and delete() methods are called. That way, the data is more likely to be current. However, this would be inefficient, particularly if the file contained thousands of records. That's why developers typically use databases to store data that's going to be accessed by multiple users.

The ProductTextFile class

```java
        @Override
        public Product get(String code) {
            for (Product p : products) {
                if (p.getCode().equals(code)) {
                    return p;
                }
            }
            return null;
        }

        private boolean saveAll() {
            try (PrintWriter out = new PrintWriter(
                                new BufferedWriter(
                                new FileWriter(productsFile)))) {

                // write all products in the list to the file
                for (Product p : products) {
                    out.print(p.getCode() + FIELD_SEP);
                    out.print(p.getDescription() + FIELD_SEP);
                    out.println(p.getPrice());
                }
                return true;
            } catch (IOException e) {
                System.out.println(e);
                return false;
            }
        }

        @Override
        public boolean add(Product p) {
            products.add(p);
            return this.saveAll();
        }

        @Override
        public boolean delete(Product p) {
            products.remove(p);
            return this.saveAll();
        }

        @Override
        public boolean update(Product newProduct) {
            // get the old product and remove it
            Product oldProduct = this.get(newProduct.getCode());
            int i = products.indexOf(oldProduct);
            products.remove(i);

            // add the updated product
            products.add(i, newProduct);

            return this.saveAll();
        }
    }
```

Figure 15-11   A class that works with a text file (part 2 of 2)

The Product Manager application

Now that you know how to code a data access class, this chapter presents a Product Manager application that uses a data access class. More specifically, it uses the ProductTextFile class described in the previous figure to work with the product data that's stored in a text file. In addition, it uses the Product, Console, and StringUtil classes described earlier in this book.

The console

Figure 15-12 shows the console for the Product Manager application. When it starts, this application displays a welcome message and a menu of commands. Then, it prompts the user to enter one of those commands. In this figure, for example, the user started by entering the list command. This displayed a list of the products that are stored in the text file.

After displaying the products, the user used the add command to add a new product to the text file. Then, the user used the del command to delete that product. Finally, the user entered the exit command to end the application.

The ProductManagerApp class

Figure 15-13 shows the code for the ProductManagerApp class. This class contains the main() method that's executed when the application starts. To start, this method displays a welcome message. Then, it calls the displayMenu() method to display the menu of commands for working with this application. After that, the main() method enters a loop that continues until the user enters the exit command.

Within this loop, the first statement prompts the user for a command. If the user enters "list", this code calls the displayAllProducts() method shown in part 2 of this figure. This method displays a list of products. To do that, it calls the getAll() method of the ProductTextFile class to get a list of Product objects. Then, it loops through these Product objects and builds a string that displays them. To do that, this code uses the StringUtil class presented earlier in this book to align the fields with the specified number of spaces.

If the user enters "add", this code calls the addProduct() method shown in part 2 to add a product to the text file. To do that, this method creates a Product object from the data that's entered by the user and passes this object to the add() method of the ProductTextFile class.

If the user enters "del" or "delete", this code calls the deleteProduct() method shown in part 2 to delete the product with the specified code from the text file. To do that, this method calls the get() method of the ProductTextFile class to get a Product object that corresponds with the specified code. Then, it calls the delete() method of the ProductTextFile class to delete this product from the text file.

The console

```
Welcome to the Product Manager

COMMAND MENU
list      - List all products
add       - Add a product
del       - Delete a product
help      - Show this menu
exit      - Exit this application

Enter a command: list

PRODUCT LIST
java      Murach's Java Programming              $57.50
jsp       Murach's Java Servlets and JSP         $57.50
mysql     Murach's MySQL                         $54.50
orac      Murach's Oracle and PL/SQL             $54.50
andr      Murach's Android Programming           $57.50
html      Murach's HTML and CSS                  $54.50
jscr      Murach's JavaScript and jQuery         $54.50

Enter a command: add

Enter product code: c++
Enter product description: Murach's C++ Programming
Enter price: 57.50

Murach's C++ Programming has been added.

Enter a command: del

Enter product code to delete: c++

Murach's C++ Programming has been deleted.

Enter a command: exit

Bye.
```

Description

- This application allows you to manage the products that are stored in a text file. When it starts, it displays a list of commands that you can use. Then, it prompts you to enter one of these commands.

Figure 15-12   The console for the Product Manager application

The ProductManagerApp class

```java
package murach.ui;

import murach.business.Product;
import murach.db.ProductTextFile;
import murach.db.DAO;

import java.util.List;

public class ProductManagerApp {
    private static DAO<Product> productFile = new ProductTextFile();

    public static void main(String args[]) {
        System.out.println("Welcome to the Product Manager\n");
        displayMenu();

        // perform 1 or more actions
        String action = "";
        while (!action.equalsIgnoreCase("exit")) {
            // get the input from the user
            action = Console.getString("Enter a command: ");
            System.out.println();

            if (action.equalsIgnoreCase("list")) {
                displayAllProducts();
            } else if (action.equalsIgnoreCase("add")) {
                addProduct();
            } else if (action.equalsIgnoreCase("del") ||
                        action.equalsIgnoreCase("delete")) {
                deleteProduct();
            } else if (action.equalsIgnoreCase("help") ||
                        action.equalsIgnoreCase("menu")) {
                displayMenu();
            } else if (action.equalsIgnoreCase("exit")) {
                System.out.println("Bye.\n");
            } else {
                System.out.println("Error! Not a valid command.\n");
            }
        }
    }

    public static void displayMenu() {
        System.out.println("COMMAND MENU");
        System.out.println("list    - List all products");
        System.out.println("add     - Add a product");
        System.out.println("del     - Delete a product");
        System.out.println("help    - Show this menu");
        System.out.println("exit    - Exit this application\n");
    }
```

Figure 15-13   The ProductManagerApp class (part 1 of 2)

The ProductManagerApp class

```java
public static void displayAllProducts() {
    System.out.println("PRODUCT LIST");

    List<Product> products = productFile.getAll();
    StringBuilder sb = new StringBuilder();
    for (Product p : products) {
        sb.append(StringUtils.padWithSpaces(
                p.getCode(), 8));
        sb.append(StringUtils.padWithSpaces(
                p.getDescription(), 40));
        sb.append(
                p.getPriceFormatted());
        sb.append("\n");
    }
    System.out.println(sb.toString());
}

public static void addProduct() {
    String code = Console.getString("Enter product code: ");
    String description = Console.getLine("Enter product description: ");
    double price = Console.getDouble("Enter price: ");

    Product product = new Product();
    product.setCode(code);
    product.setDescription(description);
    product.setPrice(price);
    productFile.add(product);

    System.out.println(description + " has been added.\n");
}

public static void deleteProduct() {
    String code = Console.getString("Enter product code to delete: ");

    Product p = productFile.get(code);
    if (p != null) {
        productFile.delete(p);
        System.out.println(p.getDescription()
                + " has been deleted.\n");
    } else {
        System.out.println("No product matches that code.\n");
    }
}
}
```

Figure 15-13   The ProductManagerApp class (part 2 of 2)

How to work with binary files

To connect a binary stream to a binary file, you use a technique that's similar to the technique you use to connect a character stream to a text file. However, the methods you use to read and write binary data are different from the methods you use to read and write character data. In the topics that follow, you'll learn how to work with the data that's stored in a binary file.

How to connect a binary output stream to a file

To create a binary output stream that's connected to a file, you can layer three streams in the OutputStream hierarchy as shown in figure 15-14. Here, both examples use a string to refer to a binary file named products.bin. However, these examples could also use a File object. This works just like it does for a text file.

Both examples create a buffered stream and connect to the specified binary file. In the first example, the code creates an output stream that creates the file if it doesn't exist or deletes all the data in the file if it does exist. Then, the second example shows how you can append data to the end of a file. To do that, you set the second argument of the FileOutputStream constructor to true.

The constructors shown in this figure should help you understand how to layer binary output streams. Here, you can see that the DataOutputStream constructor accepts an object created from any class in the OutputStream hierarchy. As a result, you can supply a BufferedOutputStream object as an argument of this constructor. Similarly, since the BufferedOutputStream constructor also accepts any OutputStream object, you can supply a FileOutputStream object as an argument of this constructor. Then, to create a FileOutputStream object, you can supply a File object or a String object that refers to a binary file.

A subset of the OutputStream hierarchy

```
OutputStream <<abstract>>
    FileOutputStream
    FilterOutputStream
        BufferedOutputStream
        DataOutputStream <<implements DataOutput interface>>
```

Classes used to connect a binary output stream to a file

DataOutputStream	writes data to the stream
→**BufferedOutputStream**	creates a buffer for the stream
→**FileOutputStream**	connects the stream to a file

Constructors of these classes

Constructor	Throws
DataOutputStream(OutputStream)	None
BufferedOutputStream(OutputStream)	None
FileOutputStream(File[, booleanAppend])	FileNotFoundException
FileOutputStream(StringPathName[, booleanAppend])	FileNotFoundException

How to connect to a file with a buffer

```
DataOutputStream out = new DataOutputStream(
                       new BufferedOutputStream(
                       new FileOutputStream("products.bin")));
```

How to connect for an append operation

```
DataOutputStream out = new DataOutputStream(
                       new BufferedOutputStream(
                       new FileOutputStream("products.bin", true)));
```

Description

- The OutputStream class is an abstract class that's inherited by all of the classes in the OutputStream hierarchy.

- All classes in the java.io and java.util.zip packages that end with OutputStream are members of the OutputStream hierarchy.

- If the output file doesn't exist when the FileOutputStream object is created, it's created automatically. If it does exist, it's overwritten by default. If that's not what you want, you can specify true for the second argument of the constructor to append data to the file.

Figure 15-14   How to connect a binary output stream to a file

How to write to a binary file

If you look back at figure 15-14, you can see that the DataOutputStream class implements the DataOutput interface. As a result, you can call any of the methods of the DataOutput interface from an output stream that includes a DataOutputStream object. Figure 15-15 summarizes some of the methods available from this interface.

You can use the methods in this figure to write primitive data types and strings to a binary output stream. For example, you can use the writeInt() method to write an int value. Similarly, you can use the writeUTF() method to write a string.

When you use the writeUTF() method, it starts by writing a two-byte number that indicates the length of the string. Then, it writes the *UTF (Universal Text Format)* representation of the string. Although this usually writes each ASCII character as one byte, it may write some Unicode characters as two or three bytes.

This figure also summarizes the size(), flush(), and close() methods of the DataOutputStream class. You can use these methods if you need to check the number of bytes that have been written to the stream, or if you need to flush data from the buffer. As always, you should use the close() method to close the stream when you're done working with it. Of course, if you use a try-with-resources statement to open the stream, that statement automatically closes the stream when it's done executing.

The example in this figure shows how to write the data that's stored in a Product object to a binary file. To start, the code uses the writeUTF() method to write the product's code and description, which are String objects. Then, the code uses the writeDouble() method to write the product's price to the file. Finally, the last statement closes the output stream, which flushes all data to the file and releases any resources being used by the stream object.

Most of the methods presented in this figure throw an IOException. As a result, you must either catch or throw this exception when you use these methods. Otherwise, your code won't compile. For now, you can use a try-with-resources statement to catch these exceptions as shown in this chapter. In the next chapter, you'll learn how to throw these exceptions.

Common methods of the DataOutput interface

Method	Throws	Description
writeBoolean(boolean)	IOException	Writes a boolean value to the output stream.
writeInt(int)	IOException	Writes an int value to the output stream.
writeDouble(double)	IOException	Writes a double value to the output stream.
writeChar(int)	IOException	Writes a char value to the output stream.
writeUTF(String)	IOException	Writes a UTF representation of the string to the output stream.

Methods of the DataOutputStream class

Method	Throws	Description
size()	None	Returns an int for the number of bytes written to this stream.
flush()	IOException	Flushes any data that's in the buffer to the file.
close()	IOException	Flushes any data that's in the buffer to the file and closes the stream.

Code that writes data to a binary file

```
// write a Product object to the file
out.writeUTF(product.getCode());
out.writeUTF(product.getDescription());
out.writeDouble(product.getPrice());

// flush data to the file and close the output stream
out.close();
```

Description

- Since the DataOutputStream class implements the DataOutput interface, you can call any of the methods shown above from a DataOutputStream object.

- The writeUTF() method writes a two-byte number that indicates the number of bytes in the string. Then, it writes the characters using the *Universal Text Format* (*UTF*).

Figure 15-15   How to write to a binary file

How to connect a binary input stream to a file

To create a binary input stream, you can layer three streams from the InputStream hierarchy as shown in figure 15-16. The example in this figure shows how you do that. Here, a String object identifies the binary file. Alternately, this example could use a File object.

The constructors of the classes shown here explain how you can layer these streams. For example, the DataInputStream and BufferedInputStream constructors accept an InputStream object. As a result, you can use an object created from any class in the InputStream hierarchy as an argument for these constructors. So, the DataInputStream constructor can accept a BufferedInputStream object, the BufferedInputStream constructor can accept a FileInputStream object, and the FileInputStream constructor can accept a String object or a File object.

In the InputStream hierarchy, the DataInputStream implements the DataInput interface. As a result, you can call any methods of this interface from an input stream that includes a DataInputStream object as shown in the next figure.

A subset of the InputStream hierarchy

```
InputStream <<abstract>>
    FileInputStream
    FilterInputStream
        BufferedInputStream
        DataInputStream <<implements DataInput interface>>
```

Classes used to connect a binary input stream to a file

DataInputStream	reads data from the stream
→**BufferedInputStream**	creates a buffer for the stream
→**FileInputStream**	connects the stream to the file

Constructors of these classes

Constructor	Throws
DataInputStream(InputStream)	None
BufferedInputStream(InputStream)	None
FileInputStream(File)	FileNotFoundException
FileInputStream(StringPathName)	FileNotFoundException

How to connect a binary input stream to a file

```
DataInputStream in = new DataInputStream(
                     new BufferedInputStream(
                     new FileInputStream("products.bin")));
```

Description

- The InputStream class is an abstract class that's inherited by all of the classes in the InputStream hierarchy. To learn more about the InputStream hierarchy, check the documentation for the Java API.

- All classes in the java.io and java.util.zip packages that end with InputStream are members of the InputStream hierarchy.

Figure 15-16   How to connect a binary input stream to a file

How to read from a binary file

Figure 15-17 starts by summarizing some of the most common methods of the DataInput interface that's implemented by the DataInputStream class. You can use the first four methods in this figure to read primitive data types from a binary input stream. For example, you can use the readInt() method to read an int value from a binary input stream. You can use the readUTF() method to read binary data that's stored in the Universal Text Format described earlier in this chapter. Usually, that means that you'll use the readUTF() method to read data that was written with the writeUTF() method.

When working with a binary input stream, you can also use some methods from the DataInputStream class. In particular, you can use the available() method to return the number of bytes in the input stream that haven't been read, and you can use the close() method to close the input stream and release any of its resources.

The example in this figure shows how to read the data for Product objects from a binary file. To start, the while loop uses the available() method to determine when the end of the file has been reached. Then, the first two statements in the while loop use the readUTF() method to read the product's code and description. This should work if these fields were written using the writeUTF() method as shown in figure 15-15. Then, the third statement uses the readDouble() method to read the product's price. Again, this should work if the product's price was written using the writeDouble() method.

Once the three fields have been read, the fourth statement uses the fields to create a Product object. Unlike the example that reads from a text file, this example doesn't convert the price from a string to a double value. That's because the price was written and read as a double value. Finally, after the loop finishes, the last statement uses the close() method to close the file. As always, if you use a try-with-resources statement to initialize the stream, you don't need to explicitly call this method.

A class that works with a binary file

Parts 1 and 2 of figure 15-18 show a class named ProductBinaryFile that can be used to read and write products to a binary file. Like the ProductTextFile class presented earlier in this chapter, this class implements the DAO<Product> inter- face shown in figure 15-10. As a result, it includes the same five public methods, and these methods work similarly. In fact, the get(), add(), update(), and delete() methods are exactly the same.

However, you should notice two differences between these classes. To start, there's no need for a FIELD_SEP constant since a binary file doesn't use delim- iters to separate fields. As a result, the getAll() and saveAll() methods don't use delimiters when reading and writing fields. In addition, the saveAll() method writes the price to the binary file as a double value. As a result, the getAll() method can read that double value from the file. In other words, there's no need to convert a double value to a string and back when you use a binary file.

Common methods of the DataInput interface

Method	Throws	Description
readBoolean()	EOFException	Reads 1 byte and returns a boolean value.
readInt()	EOFException	Reads 4 bytes and returns an int value.
readDouble()	EOFException	Reads 8 bytes and returns a double value.
readChar()	EOFException	Reads 2 bytes and returns a char value.
readUTF()	EOFException	Reads and returns the string encoded with UTF.

Common methods of the DataInputStream class

Method	Throws	Description
available()	IOException	Returns the number of bytes remaining in the file.
close()	IOException	Closes the stream.

Code that reads Product objects from a binary file

```
while (in.available() > 0) {
    // read product data from a file
    String code = in.readUTF();
    String description = in.readUTF();
    double price = in.readDouble();

    // create the Product object from its data
    Product p = new Product(code, description, price);
}

// close the input stream
in.close();
```

Description

- Since the DataInputStream class implements the DataInput interface, you can call any of the methods shown above from an object of this class.
- The readUTF() method reads characters that were written with the Universal Text Format.

Figure 15-17   How to read from a binary file

The ProductBinaryFile class

```java
package murach.db;

import java.io.*;
import java.nio.file.*;
import java.util.*;

import murach.business.Product;

public final class ProductBinaryFile implements DAO<Product> {
    private List<Product> products = null;
    private Path productsPath = null;
    private File productsFile = null;

    public ProductBinaryFile() {
        productsPath = Paths.get("products.bin");
        productsFile = productsPath.toFile();
        products = this.getAll();
    }

    @Override
    public List<Product> getAll() {
        // if the products file has already been read, don't read it again
        if (products != null) {
            return products;
        }

        products = new ArrayList<>();
        if (Files.exists(productsPath)) {
            try (DataInputStream in = new DataInputStream(
                                      new BufferedInputStream(
                                      new FileInputStream(productsFile)))) {

                // read products from file into array list
                while (in.available() > 0) {
                    // read product data from a file
                    String code = in.readUTF();
                    String description = in.readUTF();
                    double price = in.readDouble();

                    Product p = new Product(code, description, price);
                    products.add(p);
                }
            } catch (IOException e) {
                System.out.println(e);
                return null;
            }
        } else {
            System.out.println(
                    productsPath.toAbsolutePath() + " doesn't exist.");
            return null;
        }
        return products;
    }
```

Figure 15-18   A class that works with a binary file (part 1 of 2)

The ProductBinaryFile class   **Page 2**

```java
@Override
public Product get(String code) {
    for (Product p : products) {
        if (p.getCode().equals(code)) {
            return p;
        }
    }
    return null;
}

private boolean saveAll() {
    try (DataOutputStream out = new DataOutputStream(
                                new BufferedOutputStream(
                                new FileOutputStream(productsFile)))) {

        // write all products in the list to the file
        for (Product p : products) {
            out.writeUTF(p.getCode());
            out.writeUTF(p.getDescription());
            out.writeDouble(p.getPrice());
        }
        return true;
    } catch (IOException e) {
        System.out.println(e);
        return false;
    }
}

@Override
public boolean add(Product p) {
    products.add(p);
    return this.saveAll();
}

@Override
public boolean delete(Product p) {
    products.remove(p);
    return this.saveAll();
}

@Override
public boolean update(Product newProduct) {
    // get the old product and remove it
    Product oldProduct = this.get(newProduct.getCode());
    int i = products.indexOf(oldProduct);
    products.remove(i);

    // add the updated product
    products.add(i, newProduct);

    return this.saveAll();
}
}
```

Figure 15-18   A class that works with a binary file (part 2 of 2)

Perspective

Now that you've seen how to work with text and binary files, you might want to take a moment to consider the advantages and disadvantages of each. For example, since you don't need to convert int and double values to strings and back, binary files make it easier to work with numbers. However, text files are more portable because they make it easier to share data with other programs. For example, the data in a text file can be viewed in a text editor or a web browser. As a result, they're easier for other people to read and understand.

As you work with files, remember that they are only one option for storing data. Another option is to store data in a database. Because databases provide sophisticated features for organizing and managing data, they're used for most serious applications. You'll learn how to work with databases in chapters 20 and 21.

Summary

- To identify a file when you create a File object, you can use an *absolute path name* or a *relative path name*.

- The java.nio.file package provides classes and interfaces that you can use to check whether a file or directory exists, to get information about a path, to create or delete directories and files, and to create a File object.

- A *text file* stores data as characters. A *binary file* stores data in a binary format.

- In a *delimited text file*, *delimiters* are used to separate the *fields* and *records* of the file.

- You use *character streams* to read and write text files and *binary streams* to read and write binary files. To get the functionality you need, you can *layer* two or more streams.

- A *buffer* is a block of memory that is used to store the data in a stream before it is written to or after it is read from an I/O device. When an output buffer is full, its data is *flushed* to the I/O device.

- When you work with I/O operations, you'll need to catch or throw three types of checked exceptions: IOException, FileNotFoundException, and EOFException.

- You can use the classes in the Writer and Reader hierarchies to work with a text file.

- You can use the classes in the OutputStream and InputStream hierarchies to work with a binary file.

Exercise 15-1   Work with a text file

In this exercise, you'll add code to a Customer Manager application for reading and writing data from a text file named customers.txt. Each record in this file contains three fields with the customer's first name, last name, and email. The fields are separated by a tab character, and the records are separated by a new line character.

1.   Open the project named ch15_ex1_CustomerManager that's in the ex_starts directory.

2.   Open the Customer class and review its code.

3.   Open the CustomerTextFile class, and notice the three class variables that declare a list of Customer objects, a Path object for the file, and a File object for the file. Add code to the constructor that initializes these variables.

4.   Add code to the getAll() method that loads the customer list variable with the Customer objects that are created from the data in the customers.txt file. Be sure to check that this file exists, and if it does, use a try-with-resources statement to open the input stream. If an IOException occurs when the input stream is opened, print the exception to the console and return a null to the calling method.

5.   Add code to the saveAll() method that writes the data in each Customer object in the customer list to a record in the customer file. Be sure to delimit the fields and records with the appropriate character. If an IOException occurs when the output stream is opened, print the exception to the console and return false to the calling method.

6.   Run the application. Then, test the list, add, and delete commands to be sure they work correctly.

7.   Find the customers.txt file and open it in a text editor. The text editor should be able to display the data in this file in a way that you can easily read.

Exercise 15-2   Work with a binary file

In this exercise, you'll enhance the Product Manager application so it can use a binary file.

1.   Open the project named ch15_ex2_ProductManager that's in the ex_starts directory.

2.   Rename the ProductTextFile class to ProductBinaryFile.

3.   Modify the code for the ProductBinaryFile class so it uses binary data in a file named products.bin. Be sure to store the product code and description using UTF.

4.   Run the application and test the list command. This should print a message that indicates that the products.bin file doesn't exist, and it should throw a NullPointerException that causes the application to crash.

5. Add code to the constructor of the class that creates the products.bin file if it doesn't already exist.

6. Run the application. When you start it, it should display a message that indicates that the application is creating the products.bin file.

7. Test the list and add commands. Since the products.bin file is empty, the application shouldn't display any products at first. However, you should be able to use the add command to add products to the file.

8. Continue to experiment with the application. You should be able to add and delete products. Make sure to leave at least 1 product record in the file.

9. Find the products.bin file and open it in a text editor. Note that you can't read some of the data in this file.

Exercise 15-3   Improve the handling of null values

In this exercise, you'll improve the way that exceptions are handled by the ProductManagerApp and ProductTextFile classes.

1. Open the project named ch15_ex3_ProductManager that's in the ex_starts directory.

2. Open the ProductTextFile class and comment out both statements in the getAll()method that print the exceptions to the console.

3. Open the ProductManagerApp class, and modify the displayAllProducts() method so it displays an appropriate error message if the getAll() method returns a null.

4. Find the products.txt file that's in the root directory of the application and change its name to products_bak.txt.

5. Run the application and test the list command to make sure it works properly if the getAll() method returns a null value.

6. When you're sure this works correctly, change the name of the text file back to products.txt.

16

How to work with exceptions

In chapter 5, you learned how to use a simple try statement to catch exceptions. Then, in chapter 15, you learned how to use a try-with-resources statement to catch I/O exceptions. In this chapter, you'll review some of those skills, and you'll learn the rest of what you need to know to develop professional applications that handle all types of exceptions.

An introduction to exceptions

All applications can encounter errors when they run. For example, a user may enter data that's not appropriate, or a file that your application needs may get moved or deleted. These types of errors may cause a poorly-coded application to crash and cause the user to lose data. In contrast, when an error occurs in a well-coded application, the application notifies the user and attempts to recover from the error. If it can't recover, it saves as much data as possible, cleans up resources, and exits the application as smoothly as possible.

In the old days of programming, handling errors was difficult because programming languages didn't provide an easy way to check for errors. Even worse, they didn't provide an easy way to communicate those errors to other parts of the application that might need to know about them. To address this problem, most modern programming languages, including Java, support an error handling mechanism known as *exceptions*. Exceptions allow you to write robust code that can handle errors more easily and reliably. Before you learn how to handle errors, though, you need to learn about the exception hierarchy and the exception handling mechanism.

The exception hierarchy

In Java, an *exception* is an object that's created from the Exception class or one of its subclasses. An exception represents an error that has occurred, and it contains information about the error. All exception classes are derived from the Throwable class as shown by the diagram in figure 16-1.

As this diagram shows, two classes directly inherit the Throwable class: Error and Exception. The classes that inherit the Error class represent internal errors that you usually can't do anything about, such as problems with the Java runtime environment. As a result, you can ignore these errors most of the time (or in some cases, file a bug report with the JVM vendor). In contrast, you need to handle most of the exceptions that are derived from the Exception class.

The classes in the Exception hierarchy are divided into two categories: (1) exceptions that are derived from the RuntimeException class and (2) all other exceptions. The exceptions that are derived from the RuntimeException class are called *unchecked exceptions* because the compiler doesn't check them and force you to explicitly handle them. On the other hand, the compiler checks all other exceptions derived from the Exception class and forces you to explicitly handle them. As a result, these exceptions are known as *checked exceptions*.

Unchecked exceptions often occur because of coding errors. For example, if an application attempts to access an array with an invalid index, Java throws an exception that indicates that the array index is out of bounds. If you're careful when you write your code, you can usually prevent these types of exceptions from being thrown.

Checked exceptions, on the other hand, usually occur due to circumstances that are beyond the programmer's control, such as a missing file or a bad network connection. Although you can't avoid these exceptions, you can write code that handles them when they occur.

The Throwable hierarchy

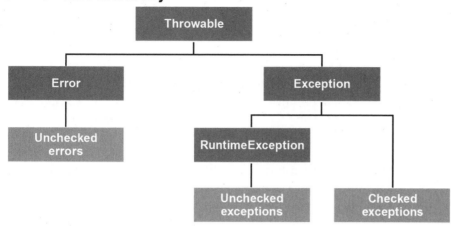

Common checked exceptions

```
ClassNotFoundException
IOException
    EOFException
    FileNotFoundException
```

Common unchecked exceptions

```
ArithmeticException
IllegalArgumentException
    NumberFormatException
IndexOutOfBoundsException
    ArrayIndexOutOfBoundsException
    StringIndexOutOfBoundsException
NoSuchElementException
    InputMismatchException
NullPointerException
```

Description

- An *exception* is an object of the Exception class or any of its subclasses. It represents a condition that prevents a method from successfully completing.

- The Exception class is derived from a class named Throwable. Two types of exceptions are derived from the Exception class: checked exceptions and unchecked exceptions.

- *Checked exceptions* are checked by the compiler. As a result, you must write code that handles all checked exceptions before you can compile your code.

- *Unchecked exceptions* are not checked by the compiler, but they can occur at runtime. It's generally considered a good practice to write code that handles unchecked exceptions. If an unchecked exception occurs and isn't handled by your code, your application terminates.

- Like the Exception class, the Error class is also derived from the Throwable class. However, the Error class identifies internal errors that are rare and can't usually be recovered from. As a result, you can usually ignore the Error class.

Figure 16-1   The exception hierarchy

How exceptions are propagated

Figure 16-2 shows how the exception handling mechanism works in Java. To start, when a method encounters a problem that can't be solved within that method, it *throws* an exception. Most of the time, exceptions are thrown by methods from classes in the Java API. Then, any method that calls a method that throws a checked exception must either throw the exception again or catch it and handle it. The code that catches and handles the exception is known as the *exception handler*. You'll learn the details of throwing, catching, and handling exceptions in this chapter.

Once a method throws an exception, the runtime system begins looking for the appropriate exception handler. To do this, it searches through the execution *stack trace,* also called the *call stack*. The stack trace is the list of methods that have been called in the reverse order that they were called. In this diagram, for example, the stack trace when the code in methodD() executes is: methodD(), methodC(), methodB(), and methodA().

This figure shows how methodA() calls methodB(), which calls methodC(), which calls methodD(). Here, methodD() may throw an exception. If it does, methodD() throws the exception up to methodC(), which throws it to methodB(), which throws it to methodA(), which catches it in a catch clause.

If you throw a checked exception all the way out of the application by coding a throws clause on each method in the call stack, including the main() method, the application crashes when the exception occurs. Then, Java displays information about the exception at the console.

Note that unchecked exceptions work the same way, except that you don't have to explicitly list unchecked exceptions in the throws clause of a method declaration. For example, suppose the try statement in methodA() also included a catch clause for a runtime exception such as the ArithmethicException. Then, if the code in methodD() throws an ArithmeticException, the exception propagates up through methodC() and methodB() and is handled by the exception handler in methodA(), even though none of the method declarations include a throws clause for the ArithmeticException.

How Java propagates exceptions

```
MethodA() {
    try {
        MethodB();
    } catch(ExceptionOne e) {
        // handle exception here
    }
}


MethodB() throws ExceptionOne {
    MethodC();
}


MethodC() throws ExceptionOne {
    MethodD();
}


MethodD() throws ExceptionOne {
    throw new ExceptionOne();
}
```

Two ways to handle checked exceptions

- Throw the exception to the calling method
- Catch the exception and handle it

Description

- When a method encounters a condition it can't handle, that method should throw an exception. This allows users of the method to handle the exception in a way that's appropriate for their applications. Many methods in the Java API throw exceptions.

- When a method calls another method that throws a checked exception, the method must either throw the exception to its caller or catch the exception and handle it directly. Code that catches an exception is known as an *exception handler*.

- When an exception occurs, the runtime system looks for the appropriate exception handler. To do that, it looks through the *stack trace*, or *call stack*, which lists the methods that have been called until it finds a method that catches the exception.

Figure 16-2   How exceptions are propagated

How to catch exceptions

In the figures that follow, you'll learn everything you need to know about catching exceptions. This reviews some information that's been covered earlier in this book and expands on that information.

How to use the try statement

Figure 16-3 starts by showing the complete syntax for coding a try statement that catches exceptions. This syntax shows that a *try statement* begins with a *try block* that's coded around any statements that may throw an exception. The try block is followed by a *catch block* for each type of exception that may be thrown in the try block.

When you add catch blocks, you should be sure to code them in sequence from the most specific class in the Throwable hierarchy to the least specific class. For example, the FileNotFoundException inherits IOException, so FileNotFoundException must be coded before IOException. Otherwise, the code won't compile. For exceptions that are at the same level in the exception hierarchy, such as FileNotFoundException and EOFException, the order doesn't matter.

After the catch blocks, you can code a *finally block* to free any system resources that are used by the try statement. For example, you might close files or release database connections in a finally block. The finally block is optional, but if you code it, it is always executed. This is true whether or not an exception has been thrown, and it's true even if a return statement has been executed.

The code example shows a method named readFirstLine() that contains a try statement that includes two catch blocks and a finally block. This method accepts a string that specifies the path to a file, and it returns a string for the first line of the file. Within the body of the method, the first statement initializes a variable that can store a BufferedReader object. This object lets you read data from a file in an efficient way.

Within the try block, the first statement creates a BufferedReader object by passing it a new FileReader object for the file at the specified path. If the file doesn't exist, this constructor throws a FileNotFoundException, and code execution jumps into the first catch block. However, if the file exists, the second statement calls the readLine() method of the BufferedReader object to read the first line of the file. If this method isn't able to read the first line, it throws an IOException and code execution jumps into the second catch block. Otherwise, the return statement in the try block returns a String object for the first line to the calling method.

Both catch blocks work similarly. To start, the first statement prints a message to the console that briefly describes the error. Then, the second statement returns a null to the calling method. This return value is appropriate since the method was unable to read the first line of the file.

Within the finally block, the code attempts to close the BufferedReader object by calling its close() method. Unfortunately, if the code in the try block doesn't execute successfully, the BufferedReader object may be null. As a result,

The syntax of the try statement

```
try { statements }
[catch (MostSpecificExceptionType e) { statements }] ...
[catch (LeastSpecificExceptionType e) { statements }]
[finally { statements }]
```

A method that catches two types of exceptions and uses a finally clause

```java
public static String readFirstLine(String path) {
    BufferedReader in = null;
    try {
        in = new BufferedReader(
            new FileReader(path));       // may throw FileNotFoundException
        String line = in.readLine();     // may throw IOException
        return line;
    } catch (FileNotFoundException e) {
        System.out.println("File not found.");
        return null;
    } catch(IOException e) {
        System.out.println("I/O error occurred.");
        return null;
    } finally {
        try {
            if (in != null) {
                in.close();              // may throw IOException
            }
        } catch (IOException e) {
            System.out.println("Unable to close file.");
        }
    }
}
```

Description

- You can code a *try block* around any statements that may throw an exception.

- You can code one *catch block* for each type of exception that may be thrown in the try block. You should code the catch clauses in sequence from the most specific class in the Throwable hierarchy to the least specific class.

- You can code a *finally block* to free any system resources that are used by objects created in the try block. The code in the finally block is always executed.

Figure 16-3   How to use the try statement

this code checks that this object is not null before it calls its close() method. In addition, the close() method may throw an IOException, so you need to code a try statement within the finally block that catches this exception.

When you code try statements, it's often tempting to create empty catch clauses for checked exceptions just to get your code to compile. However, this can make debugging difficult because if an exception is thrown, you never find out about it. Instead, your code doesn't work correctly and gives no indication of what went wrong. Furthermore, it's easy to forget to code the exception handler later. In that case, the exception never gets handled. Instead, the empty catch clause catches the exception and ignores it. This is sometimes called *swallowing an exception*, or *eating an exception*, and it's rarely an acceptable coding practice.

How to use the try-with-resources statement

Prior to Java 7, you had to use a finally block to release system resources as you saw in the previous figure. That required including additional exception handling code in case the code in the finally block threw exceptions. Unfortunately, the length of this exception handling code can make it difficult to read and maintain your code.

That's why Java 7 introduced the *try-with-resources* statement that's described in figure 16-4. This is a special type of try statement that declares and instantiates one or more objects that use system resources and automatically closes those objects and releases the resources after the try statement finishes executing. This allows you to write less error handling code and to focus on the logic of your code. For example, the readFirstLine() method in this figure accomplishes the same task as the method in the previous figure, but without the unwieldy finally clause. As a result, the code is easier to read and maintain.

To use the try-with-resources statement, you begin by coding a set of parentheses after the try keyword but before the braces for the try block. Then, within the parentheses, you can code one or more statements that declare and instantiate objects that use system resources. In this figure, for example, the statement that creates the BufferedReader object is coded within these parentheses. To create multiple objects, you just separate the statements that declare and instantiate them with a semicolon.

Note that you can only use the try-with-resources statement with objects that implement the java.lang.AutoCloseable interface. However, as of Java 7, most of the classes in the Java API that work with system resources have been retrofitted to implement this interface. That includes all of the classes for working with files and databases that are described in this book.

The syntax of the try-with-resources statement

```
try (statement[;statement] ...) { statements }
[catch (MostSpecificExceptionType e) { statements }] ...
[catch (LeastSpecificExceptionType e) { statements }]
```

A method that catches two types of exceptions and automatically closes the specified resource

```
public static String readFirstLine(String path) {
    try (BufferedReader in = new BufferedReader(
                            new FileReader(path))) {
        String line = in.readLine();
        return line;
    } catch (FileNotFoundException e) {
        System.out.println("File not found.");
        return null;
    } catch (IOException e) {
        System.out.println("I/O error occurred.");
        return null;
    }
}
```

Description

- The *try-with-resources* statement is a special type of try statement that declares and instantiates one or more objects that use system resources and automatically closes those objects and releases the resources after the try statement finishes executing.

- The try-with-resources statement was introduced with Java 7.

- Any object that implements the java.lang.AutoCloseable interface can be created using the try-with-resources statement.

- As of Java 7, most of the classes in the Java API that use system resources have been retrofitted to implement the AutoCloseable interface.

- If an object doesn't implement the AutoClosable interface and you attempt to use a try-with-resources statement with it, your code won't compile.

Figure 16-4   How to use the try-with-resources statement

How to use the methods of an exception

Figure 16-5 shows how to use the methods of an exception to get more information about the exception. Since the Throwable class provides these methods, they are available to all exception objects.

The first example uses the first three methods in the table to print increasing amounts of information about an exception. In this case, the catch block catches an IOException object and assigns it to a variable named e. Within the catch block, the first statement uses the getMessage() method to get the exception's message, and it prints this message to the console. Then, the second statement uses the toString() method to get the exception's class and message, and it prints this data to the console. Next, the third statement uses the printStackTrace() method to print the exception's class, message, and stack trace to the console.

When you write code that handles exceptions, you need to decide how much information is the right amount to display. For example, in some cases, you only want to use the getMessage() method to display the exception's message. However, not all exceptions include messages. Because of that, it's often helpful to use the toString() method to display the exception's class name and message. Other times, you may want to use the printStackTrace() method to display a complete stack trace for the exception. This can help you debug your applications when you're testing them. However, it's generally considered a good practice to remove the printStackTrace() method from production applications or replace it with a better way of logging exceptions.

In the first example, the statements in the catch block use the System.err object to print data to the standard error output stream. This works the same as using the System.out object to print data to the standard output stream. In NetBeans, for example, both of these objects print data to the Output window. However, the error output stream is displayed in red, which is consistent with how NetBeans displays exceptions. As a result, it's common to use the error output stream for displaying information about exceptions. You can also direct the standard output stream to one source (such as the console) and the standard error output stream to another source (such as a log file).

If you don't supply an argument for the printStackTrace() method, it prints its data to the error output stream (System.err). However, if you want to print this data to another output stream such as the standard output stream (System.out), you can specify that output stream as an argument of the method. In this figure, for example, all of the statements in the second example print data to the standard output stream.

Four methods available from all exceptions

Method	Description
getMessage()	Returns the exception's message, if one is available.
toString()	Returns the exception's class name and message, if one is available.
printStackTrace()	Prints the exception's class name, message, and stack trace to the standard error output stream (System.err).
printStackTrace(outputStream)	Prints the exception's class name, message, and stack trace to the specified output stream.

How to print exception data to the error output stream

```
catch(IOException e) {
    System.err.println(e.getMessage() + "\n");
    System.err.println(e.toString() + "\n");
    e.printStackTrace();
    return null;
}
```

Resulting output for a FileNotFoundException

```
c:\murach\java\produx.txt (The system cannot find the file
specified)

java.io.FileNotFoundException: c:\murach\java\produx.txt
(The system cannot find the file specified)

java.io.FileNotFoundException: c:\murach\java\produx.txt
(The system cannot find the file specified)
  at java.io.FileInputStream.open(Native Method)
  at java.io.FileInputStream.<init>(FileInputStream.java:131)
  at java.io.FileInputStream.<init>(FileInputStream.java:87)
  at java.io.FileReader.<init>(FileReader.java:58)
  at ProductApp.readFirstLine(ProductApp.java:70)
  at ProductApp.main(ProductApp.java:10)
```

How to print exception data to the standard output stream

```
catch(IOException e) {
    System.out.println(e.getMessage() + "\n");
    System.out.println(e.toString() + "\n");
    e.printStackTrace(System.out);
    return null;
}
```

Description

- The Throwable class provides methods that are available to all exceptions.
- The System.err object works like the System.out object, but it prints data to the standard error stream instead of the standard output stream.
- It's generally considered a good practice to remove the printStackTrace() method from production applications or replace it with a better way of logging exceptions.

Figure 16-5   How to use the methods of an exception

How to use a multi-catch block

Figure 16-6 shows how to use the *multi-catch block* feature that was introduced with Java 7. This feature allows you to use a single catch block for multiple exceptions that are at the same level in the inheritance hierarchy. To do that, you separate the exceptions with a pipe character (|) as shown in the syntax at the top of this figure.

To illustrate how the multi-catch block works, the first example in this figure shows how you would catch both the FileNotFoundException and the EOFException prior to Java 7. Here, a separate catch clause is coded for each exception. Because these exceptions are at the same level in the inheritance hierarchy, though, and because the code in the catch blocks for these exceptions is identical, you can catch them in a multi-catch block as shown in the second example.

On a related note, both FileNotFoundException and EOFException are subclasses of IOException. As a result, if you want to execute the same code for all three exceptions, you only need to code a catch block for the IOException like this:

```
try (BufferedReader in = new BufferedReader(
                         new FileReader(path))) {
    String line = in.readLine();        // may throw IOException
    return line;
} catch(IOException e) {
    System.err.println(e.toString());
    return null;
}
```

In this case, the same code is executed for IOException and all of its subclasses, including the FileNotFoundException and EOFException. Although this technique doesn't provide as much flexibility as the multi-catch block feature, it's commonly used and works for all versions of Java.

The syntax of the multi-catch block

```
catch (ExceptionType | ExceptionType [| ExceptionType]... e) { statements }
```

A method that does not use a multi-catch block

```java
public static String readFirstLine(String path) {
    try (BufferedReader in = new BufferedReader(
                            new FileReader(path))) {
        String line = in.readLine();      // may throw IOException
        return line;
    } catch (FileNotFoundException e) {
        System.err.println(e.toString());
        return null;
    } catch (EOFException e) {
        System.err.println(e.toString());
        return null;
    } catch(IOException e) {
        e.printStackTrace();
        return null;
    }
}
```

A method that uses a multi-catch block

```java
public static String readFirstLine(String path) {
    try (BufferedReader in = new BufferedReader(
                            new FileReader(path))) {
        String line = in.readLine();      // may throw IOException
        return line;
    } catch (FileNotFoundException | EOFException e) {
        System.err.println(e.toString());
        return null;
    } catch(IOException e) {
        e.printStackTrace();
        return null;
    }
}
```

Description

- The *multi-catch block* allows you to use a single catch block for multiple exceptions that are at the same level in the inheritance hierarchy.

- The multi-catch block was introduced with Java 7.

Figure 16-6   How to use a multi-catch block

How to throw exceptions

Now that you know how to catch exceptions, you're ready to learn how to throw them, which is another important part of exception handling. To do that, you can use the throws clause and the throw statement.

How to use the throws clause

When you call a method from the Java API that throws a checked exception, you must either catch the exception as described earlier in this chapter or throw it. If you can't handle the exception properly in the method that you're coding, you can code a throws clause on the method declaration as shown in figure 16-7. This throws the exception up to the calling method, which can handle it with a try statement or throw it again. Eventually, the exception should propagate up to a level where it can be handled properly.

The first example shows a readFirstLine() method that's similar to the other readFirstLine() methods that you've seen in this chapter. However, this method throws the exception instead of catching it. Here, the first statement in this method calls the constructor of the FileReader class, which may throw a FileNotFoundException. Then, the next statement calls the readLine() method of the BufferedReader object, which may throw an IOException. Since the FileNotFoundException class inherits the IOException class, this method can throw both types of exceptions by using a throws clause to throw an IOException.

If the first example throws a FileNotFoundException, that exception is implicitly cast to an IOException. As a result, the calling method can catch or throw either exception. That's true even though the throws clause of the readLine() method doesn't explicitly throw the FileNotFoundException.

The second example shows how to explicitly throw both exceptions. To do that, you use commas to separate the exceptions in the throws clause. The advantage of this approach is that it clearly identifies all exceptions that can be thrown by the method. The disadvantage of this approach is that it requires more code for the same functionality that's provided by the first example.

This figure also shows an example of an error message that the compiler generates if you don't catch or throw a checked exception. More specifically, the compiler generates an error message like this if you call the readLine() method and don't catch or throw the IOException.

At this point, you may be wondering when you should throw an exception and when you should handle an exception. In general, you should throw exceptions early and catch them late. In other words, if you are at a low level in your application where you aren't able to handle the exception, you should throw it. Then, the exception propagates up to a higher level where you can catch the exception and handle it in a way that makes sense for your application. For example, you can ask the user how to handle the exception. You can display a user-friendly error message. Or, if necessary, you can save data, close resources, and exit the application as gracefully as possible.

The syntax for the declaration of a method that throws exceptions

```
modifiers returnType methodName([parameterList]) throws exceptionList {}
```

A method that throws an IOException

```
public static String readFirstLine(String path) throws IOException {
    BufferedReader in = new BufferedReader(
                        new FileReader(path));
    String line = in.readLine();
    return line;
}
```

A method that throws two exceptions

```
public static String readFirstLine(String path)
        throws FileNotFoundException, IOException {
    BufferedReader in = new BufferedReader(
                        new FileReader(path));
    String line = in.readLine();
    return line;
}
```

Compiler error if you don't catch or throw a checked exception

```
error: unreported exception IOException; must be caught or declared to
be thrown
```

Description

- Any method that calls a method that throws a checked exception must either catch the exception or throw the exception. Otherwise, the application won't compile.

- To throw a checked exception, you code a throws clause in the method declaration. The throws clause must name each checked exception that's thrown up to the calling method. If you list multiple exceptions, you separate exceptions with a comma.

- Although you can specify unchecked exceptions in the throws clause, the compiler doesn't force you to handle unchecked exceptions.

Figure 16-7   How to use the throws clause

How to use the throw statement

When you're coding a method, you may sometimes need to throw an exception. For example, you may need to throw an exception when a method encounters a problem that prevents it from completing its task, such as when the method is passed unacceptable argument values. You may also need to throw an exception to test an exception handler. Finally, you may need to throw an exception when you want to catch an exception, perform some processing, and then throw the exception again so it can be handled by the calling method.

Figure 16-8 shows how to throw an exception. To do that, you code a throw statement that throws an object of an exception class. To do that, you usually use the new keyword to create an object from the exception class. Since all exception classes inherit the Throwable class, you can use either of the constructors shown in this figure to create an exception. If you use the first constructor, no message is assigned to the exception. If you use the second constructor, the message you specify is assigned to the exception.

The first example in this figure shows a method named calculateFuture-Value() that accepts three parameters and throws an IllegalArgumentException if any of these parameters are less than or equal to zero. In general, it's a good coding practice for any public method to throw an IllegalArgumentException if the method is passed any parameters that have unacceptable values.

The second example shows how you might throw an exception to test an exception handler. This technique is useful for exceptions that are difficult to force otherwise. For example, you can easily test a handler for FileNotFoundException by providing a file name that doesn't exist. But testing a handler for IOException can be difficult. Sometimes, the easiest way is to explicitly throw the exception at the point you would expect it to occur.

When you throw an exception for testing, the throw statement must be the last statement of the try clause, or it must be coded within an if statement. Otherwise, the code won't compile, and the compiler will display a message that indicates that the code contains unreachable statements. In the second example, because a statement is coded after the throw statement, the throw statement is coded within an if statement. Notice that this if statement is coded so its condition is always true, so the exception is always thrown. However, this if statement allows the code to compile.

The third example shows code that rethrows an exception after processing it. Here, the exception handler prints an error message that indicates an exception has occurred. Then, it rethrows the exception so the calling method can handle it. To do that, the throw statement throws the IOException object named e that was declared in the catch clause.

The syntax of the throw statement

```
throw throwableObject;
```

Common constructors of the Throwable class

Constructor	Description
Throwable()	Creates a new exception with a null message.
Throwable(message)	Creates a new exception with the specified message.

A method that throws an unchecked exception

```
public double calculateFutureValue(double monthlyPayment,
        double monthlyInterestRate, int months) {
    if (monthlyPayment <= 0) {
        throw new IllegalArgumentException("Monthly payment must be > 0");
    }
    if (monthlyInterestRate <= 0) {
        throw new IllegalArgumentException("Interest rate must be > 0");
    }
    if (months <= 0) {
        throw new IllegalArgumentException("Months must be > 0");
    }

    // code to calculate and return future value goes here
}
```

Code that throws an IOException for testing purposes

```
try {
    // code that reads the first line of a file

    if (true) {
        throw new IOException("I/O exception test");
    }
    return firstLine;
} catch (IOException e) {
    // code to handle IOException goes here
}
```

Code that rethrows an exception

```
try {
    // code that throws IOException goes here
} catch (IOException e) {
    System.out.println("IOException thrown in readFirstLine() method.");
    throw e;
}
```

Description

- You use the throw statement to throw an exception. You can throw any object that's created from a subclass of the Throwable class.

- You can use the constructors of the Throwable class to create a new exception. Then, you can throw that exception. To throw an existing exception, you must first catch it.

Figure 16-8   How to use the throw statement

How to work with custom exceptions

Although the Java API contains a wide range of exceptions, you may encounter a situation where none of those exceptions describes your exception accurately. In other cases, you may want to wrap an exception with a different exception in order to make code more flexible. In either case, you can code a class that defines a custom exception as described in the following topics. Then, you can throw your exception just as you would throw any other exception.

How to create a custom exception class

Figure 16-9 shows how to create a custom exception class. To do that, you inherit the Exception class or one of its subclasses to create a checked exception. To illustrate, the first example in this figure shows an exception class named DAOException that inherits the Exception class. As a result, DAOException is a checked exception. However, you can also code a class that defines an unchecked exception by inheriting the RuntimeException class or one of its subclasses.

By convention, all exception classes should have a default constructor that doesn't accept any arguments and another constructor that accepts a string argument. As a result, if you code these constructors for your exception classes, they will behave like the rest of the exception classes in the Java API. The first example shows how to code these two constructors. Here, the second constructor uses the super keyword to call the constructor of the Exception class and passes the message parameter to it.

The second example shows code that throws the custom DAOException. This example defines a method named getProduct(), which calls a method named readProduct() to retrieve a Product object for a specified product code. The readProduct() method throws an IOException, which is caught by the catch clause. The catch clause then throws a DAOException.

The third example shows code that catches the custom exception. Here, the getProduct() method is called in a try statement and the DAOException is caught by the catch clause. In the exception handler for the DAOException, an error message is displayed at the console.

At first glance, it might seem that the custom exception defined by these examples isn't necessary. After all, couldn't the getProduct() method simply throw an IOException if an IO error occurs? Although it could, that would result in a poor design because it would expose too many details of the getProduct() method's operation. An IOException can occur only when file I/O operations are used. As a result, throwing IOException would reveal that the getProduct() method uses file I/O to access the product data.

What if the application is changed so the product data is kept in a database instead of a file? In that case, the getProduct() method would throw some type of database exception instead of an IOException. Then, any methods that call the getProduct() method would have to be changed to handle the new exception. By creating a custom DAOException for the getProduct() method, you can hide the details of how the getProduct() method works from methods that call it. So even if the application is changed to use a database, the getProduct() method can still throw a DAOException if an error occurs while retrieving a product object.

Code for the DAOException class

```
public class DAOException extends Exception {
    public DAOException() {}

    public DAOException(String message) {
        super(message);
    }
}
```

A method that throws the DAOException

```
public static Product getProduct(String productCode) throws DAOException {
    try {
        Product p = readProduct(productCode);    // may throw IOException
        return p;
    } catch (IOException e) {
        throw new DAOException(
            "An error occurred while reading the product.");
    }
}
```

Code that catches the DAOException

```
try {
    Product p = getProduct("1234");
} catch (DAOException e) {
    System.out.println(e.getMessage());
}
```

Resulting output

```
An error occurred while reading the product.
```

When to define your own exceptions

- When a method requires an exception that isn't provided by any of Java's exception types.
- When using a built-in Java exception would inappropriately expose details of a method's operation.

Description

- To define a checked exception, inherit the Exception class or any of its subclasses.
- To define an unchecked exception, inherit the RuntimeException class or any of its subclasses.
- By convention, each exception class should contain a default constructor that doesn't accept any arguments and another constructor that accepts a string argument.

Figure 16-9   How to create a custom exception class

How to use exception chaining

You'll often throw custom exceptions in response to other exceptions that occur. For example, in the previous figure, DAOException was thrown in response to IOException. Unfortunately, information about the underlying error that led to the DAOException is lost. And that information might prove invaluable to determining what caused the DAOException to occur.

Figure 16-10 shows how you can throw a custom exception without losing the details of the original exception that was thrown. This feature is called *exception chaining* because it lets you chain exceptions together. Whenever you create a custom exception type, it's a good practice to use exception chaining to avoid losing valuable debugging information.

To use exception chaining, you use an exception constructor that lets you specify an exception object as the cause for the new exception you're creating. In the first example, for instance, the DAOException class lets you specify a cause via the constructor. Here, the second constructor accepts a Throwable object as a parameter. Then, it passes this parameter on to the Exception constructor.

The second example shows code that throws a DAOException in response to an IOException. Here, the IOException object is passed to the DAOException constructor as an argument. That way, all of the information contained in the original IOException is saved as part of the DAOException object.

The third example shows code that catches a DAOException and displays information about the exception. Here, an error message is displayed that indicates that a DAOException has occurred, that the DAOException was caused by a FileNotFoundException, and it includes the message that's stored in the FileNotFoundException. In most cases, that should be all the information you need to determine the cause of this exception.

A constructor of the Throwable class for exception chaining

Constructor	Description
Throwable(cause)	Creates a new exception with the specified exception object as its cause.

A custom exception class that uses exception chaining

```java
public class DAOException extends Exception {
    public DAOException() {}

    public DAOException(Exception cause) {
        super(cause);
    }
}
```

Code that throws a DAOException with chaining

```java
catch (IOException e) {
    throw new DAOException(e);
}
```

Code that catches a DAOException

```java
catch (DAOException e) {
    System.err.println(e);
}
```

Resulting output

```
DAOException: java.io.FileNotFoundException:
c:\murach\produx.txt (The system cannot find the file specified)
```

Description

- *Exception chaining* lets you maintain exception information for exceptions that are caught when new exceptions are thrown. Exception chaining uses the cause field, which represents the original exception that caused the current exception to be thrown.

Figure 16-10   How to use exception chaining

An interface that uses custom exceptions

Figure 16-11 shows an enhanced version of the DAO interface that was presented in the previous chapter. In this figure, all five methods of the interface throw a DAOException. As a result, when programmers implement this interface and encounter data access exceptions, they can wrap those exceptions in a DAOException and throw them to the calling code. Then, the calling code can handle those exceptions in a way that's appropriate for that level of the application.

A class that uses custom exceptions

Parts 1 and 2 of figure 16-12 show a ProductTextFile class that implements the DAO interface for the Product type. Most of this code is the same as the ProductTextFile shown in the previous chapter. However, all of the methods throw the DAOException class. In addition, the catch blocks in the getAll() and saveAll() methods wrap the IOException in a DAOException and throw it to the calling code.

As a result, the code in the presentation layer can catch and handle these exceptions, which is usually what you want. That way, the user interface can display a user-friendly message that an error occurred while accessing the data, and it can take an appropriate action. For example, if the getAll() method throws a DAOException, a programmer could handle it like this:

```
try {
    file = new ProductTextFile();
} catch (DAOException e) {
    System.out.println("Error reading product data.");
    System.out.println(e.getMessage());
    System.out.println("Exiting application.\n");
    return;
}
```

Here, the first statement in the catch clause displays a user-friendly message. The second statement displays the error message, which might be helpful in fixing the error. The third statement tells the user that the application is exiting. And the fourth statement is a return statement that ends the current method.

If this code is in the main() method, a return statement exits the application. However, if you need to exit the application from another method, you can call the exit() method of the System class like this:

```
System.exit(0);
```

This method accepts an argument of an int value. By convention, an int value of 0 indicates that the program exited normally, and a nonzero value indicates that the program did not exit normally.

An interface that uses a custom exception

```
package murach.db;

import java.util.List;

public interface DAO<T> {
    T get(String code) throws DAOException;
    List<T> getAll() throws DAOException;
    boolean add(T t) throws DAOException;
    boolean update(T t) throws DAOException;
    boolean delete(T t) throws DAOException;
}
```

Description

- When programmers implement the methods of the DAO interface, they will most likely encounter data access exceptions. For example, if they're using a file to store the data, they may encounter the IOException described in the previous chapter. Or, if they're using a database to store the data, they may encounter the SQLException described in chapter 20.

- The methods of the DAO interface throw a DAOException. That makes this interface more flexible because it doesn't tightly couple the interface to a specific exception type.

Figure 16-11   An interface that uses custom exceptions

A class that uses custom exceptions

```java
package murach.db;

import java.io.*;
import java.nio.file.*;
import java.util.*;

import murach.business.Product;

public final class ProductTextFile implements DAO<Product> {
    private List<Product> products = null;
    private Path productsPath = null;
    private File productsFile = null;
    private final String FIELD_SEP = "\t";

    public ProductTextFile() throws DAOException {
        productsPath = Paths.get("products.txt");
        productsFile = productsPath.toFile();
        products = this.getAll();
    }

    @Override
    public List<Product> getAll() throws DAOException {
        // if the products file has already been read, don't read it again
        if (products != null) {
            return products;
        }

        products = new ArrayList<>();
        try (BufferedReader in = new BufferedReader(
                            new FileReader(productsFile))) {

            // read products from file into array list
            String line = in.readLine();
            while (line != null) {
                String[] columns = line.split(FIELD_SEP);
                String code = columns[0];
                String description = columns[1];
                String price = columns[2];

                Product p = new Product(
                        code, description, Double.parseDouble(price));
                products.add(p);

                line = in.readLine();
            }
        } catch (IOException e) {
            throw new DAOException(e);
        }
        return products;
    }
```

Figure 16-12   A class that uses custom exceptions (part 1 of 2)

A class that uses custom exceptions

```java
    @Override
    public Product get(String code) throws DAOException {
        for (Product p : products) {
            if (p.getCode().equals(code)) {
                return p;
            }
        }
        return null;
    }

    @Override
    public boolean add(Product p) throws DAOException {
        products.add(p);
        return this.saveAll();
    }

    @Override
    public boolean delete(Product p) throws DAOException {
        products.remove(p);
        return this.saveAll();
    }

    @Override
    public boolean update(Product newProduct) throws DAOException {
        // get the old product and remove it
        Product oldProduct = this.get(newProduct.getCode());
        int i = products.indexOf(oldProduct);
        products.remove(i);

        // add the updated product
        products.add(i, newProduct);

        return this.saveAll();
    }

    private boolean saveAll() throws DAOException {
        try (PrintWriter out = new PrintWriter(
                            new BufferedWriter(
                            new FileWriter(productsFile)))) {

            // write all products in the array list
            // to the file
            for (Product p : products) {
                out.print(p.getCode() + FIELD_SEP);
                out.print(p.getDescription() + FIELD_SEP);
                out.println(p.getPrice());
            }
            return true;
        } catch (IOException e) {
            throw new DAOException(e);
        }
    }
}
```

Figure 16-12   A class that uses custom exceptions (part 2 of 2)

Perspective

In this chapter, you learned the most important techniques for handling exceptions in Java. Exceptions can help you write more robust, error-free code by allowing an error to be propagated up the call stack to a high-level method that can handle it better than the low-level method where the error occurred. For example, a getAll() method that retrieves a list of Product objects probably has no idea what should be done if an error occurs. So, this low-level method should throw an exception that can be handled by a higher-level method. Then, this higher-level method can write the exception to a log file, display an error message, save data, or even exit the application.

Summary

- In Java, an *exception* is an object that's created from a class that's derived from the Exception class or one of its subclasses. When an exception occurs, a well-coded application notifies its users of the exception and minimizes any disruptions or data loss that may result from the exception.

- Exceptions derived from the RuntimeException class and its subclasses are *unchecked exceptions* because they aren't checked by the compiler. All other exceptions are *checked exceptions*.

- Any method that calls a method that *throws* a checked exception must either throw the exception by coding a throws clause or *catch* it by coding *try/catch/finally blocks* as an *exception handler*.

- The *try-with-resources* statement is a special type of try statement that declares and instantiates one or more objects that use system resources and automatically closes the objects and releases the resources after the try statement finishes executing.

- The *multi-catch block* allows you to use a single catch block for multiple exceptions that are at the same level in the inheritance hierarchy.

- When coding your own methods, if you encounter a potential error that can't be handled within that method, you can code a *throw statement* that throws the exception to another method. If you can't find an appropriate exception class in the Java API, you can code a custom exception class.

- You can create custom exception classes to represent exceptions your methods might throw. This is often useful to hide the details of how a method is implemented.

- When you create custom exceptions, you can use *exception chaining* to save information about the cause of an exception.

Exercise 16-1   Throw and catch exceptions

In this exercise, you'll experiment with ways to throw and catch exceptions.

1. Open the project named ch16_ex1_ExceptionTester in the ex_starts folder. Then, open the ExceptionTesterApp class and review its code. Run this class to get a feel for how it works.

2. Add code to method3() that throws an unchecked exception by attempting to divide an integer by zero. Compile and run the application and note where the exception is thrown.

3. Delete the code you just added to method3(). Then, add a statement to this method like the one in figure 16-7 that creates an object from the BufferedReader class, but use the string "products.ran" in place of the path variable. The constructor for this class throws a checked exception named FileNotFoundException. Note the error message that indicates that you haven't handled the exception. If this error message isn't shown, compile the class to display the error message.

4. Add throws clauses to all of the methods including the main() method. Then, run the application to see how a checked exception can propagate all the way out of an application.

5. Add the code necessary to handle the FileNotFoundException in method1(). To do that, you'll need to remove the throws clauses from the main() method and method1(), and you'll need to add a try statement to method1() that catches the exception. The catch block should display an appropriate error message. Run the application to make sure the exception handler works.

Exercise 16-2   Release system resources

In this exercise, you'll get a chance to use try and try-with-resources statements to release the system resources used by an object.

1. Open the project named ch16_ex2_ResourcesTester in the ex_starts folder. Then, open the ResourcesTesterApp class. Note that the main() method calls two other methods that open a BufferedReader object but don't close it.

2. Modify the method named readLineWithResources() so it uses a try-with-resources statement to close the BufferedReader object. Run the application to make sure it works correctly. If it does, the try-with-resources statement is working correctly too.

3. Modify the method named readLineWithFinally() so it uses a finally block to close the BufferedReader object. To do that, you'll need to declare this object outside the try block. Add statements to the finally block that print information to the console to indicate whether the file was closed (this is typical for normal operations), never opened (which happens if the file can't be found), or unable to close (which happens only in rare cases).

4. Run the application to make sure the finally clause works as expected. To test what happens if the file is never opened, you can change the name of the file to cause a FileNotFoundException. To test what happens if the close() method doesn't work, you can throw an IOException just before the statement that closes the resource.

Exercise 16-3   Create a custom class

In this exercise, you'll experiment with custom classes and chained exceptions.

1. Open the project named ch16_ex3_CustomTester in the ex_starts folder. Then, create a custom checked exception class named TestException that contains two constructors: one that accepts no parameters and one that accepts a message.

2. Open the CustomTesterApp class. Then, add a statement to method3() that throws a TestException without a message. Add the code necessary to catch this exception in method2(). The catch block should print a message of your choice at the console. Run the application to make sure it works correctly.

3. Modify your solution so a custom message of your choice is passed to the TestException and is then displayed in the catch block. Run the application to make sure the custom message is displayed correctly.

4. Add another constructor to the TestException class that accepts a Throwable object as a parameter.

5. Add a try statement to method3() of the Main class. The try block should throw an IOException, and the catch block should throw a TestException, passing the IOException to its constructor.

6. Modify the catch block in method2() that catches the TestException so it prints a message that gives information about the exception and its underlying cause. Run the application to make sure it works correctly.

Section 4

GUI programming

So far in this book, all of the applications have been *console applications*. Of course, most modern applications use *graphical user interfaces* (*GUIs*). If you want to use Java to develop a GUI, you can choose from several APIs including AWT, SWT, Swing, and JavaFX.

Of these APIs, JavaFX is the newest and has the most advanced features for creating GUIs. That's why chapter 17 shows how to use JavaFX to code a GUI that contains several controls.

Although JavaFX is the newest Java API for creating GUIs, Swing is the most widely-used. That's why chapter 18 shows how to use Swing to code a GUI that contains several controls and why chapter 19 shows how to add more Swing controls to a GUI.

In this section, chapters 17 and 18 are independent modules. As a result, if you don't want to learn JavaFX, you can skip directly to chapter 18 to learn about Swing. However, you should read chapter 18 before moving on to chapter 19.

All of the chapters in this section show you how to write the Java code for a GUI by hand. This approach forces you to have a thorough understanding of how this code works, which is essential if you need to maintain existing GUI code, especially if that code was written by hand. In addition, this approach helps solidify your understanding of the Java language by showing a practical use of several features of the Java language, including inheritance, anonymous classes, and lambda expressions.

17

How to get started with JavaFX

In this chapter, you'll learn the basics of developing GUI applications with JavaFX. This is the newest API for developing GUI applications with Java, and it's more consistent and easier to use than the older Swing API. In addition, it provides many features that aren't available from Swing.

An introduction to GUI programming

Before you start learning how to code GUIs, you need to understand some basic concepts and terms related to GUIs.

A GUI that displays ten controls

Figure 17-1 starts by showing the graphical user interface for the Future Value application that's presented in this chapter. Here, the GUI *window*, also known as a *form*, contains ten *controls*: four *labels*, four *text fields* (also called *text boxes*), and two *buttons*. Here, the fourth text field has been modified so it can display output but it can't accept input from the user. Its appearance is the same as the other text fields, however.

By default, JavaFX controls look and act the same on any platform. However, these controls look and act slightly different than the controls that are native to a particular platform. For example, the user interface shown in this figure looks slightly different than the native Windows 10 user interface where it was displayed. Although JavaFX provides classes that let programmers change the *look and feel* of a user interface, the default look and feel is appropriate for most applications. As a result, that's the look and feel that this book uses for all of its JavaFX applications.

A summary of GUI APIs

If you want to use Java to develop a GUI, you can choose from several APIs, which are often called *toolkits*. This figure shows the most common ones, but there are others.

AWT (*Abstract Window Toolkit*) was the first GUI toolkit for Java. AWT allows you to create native operating system *components* (also known as *controls* or *widgets*). However, this approach has several limitations and is not recommended for modern application development.

To address the shortcomings of AWT, Java 2 included a toolkit named *Swing*. Swing is built on top of AWT, but it creates its own components instead of using the ones provided by the operating system. In its early days, Swing was slow. In addition, the early Swing components didn't look good, and they didn't look like native components. Today, Swing applications perform much better, and modern themes can make them look like native applications.

To compete with early versions of Swing, IBM created *SWT* (*Standard Widget Toolkit*). Like AWT, SWT uses native controls, which improves its speed. However, it's not as powerful as Swing without the addition of more libraries. As a result, Swing became more widely used than SWT.

JavaFX is the newest framework for developing GUIs. This API is designed to replace the aging Swing API for developing desktop applications. In addition, it's designed to make it easier to create *rich Internet applications* (*RIAs*), which are web applications that have many of the characteristics of desktop applications.

A GUI that displays 10 controls

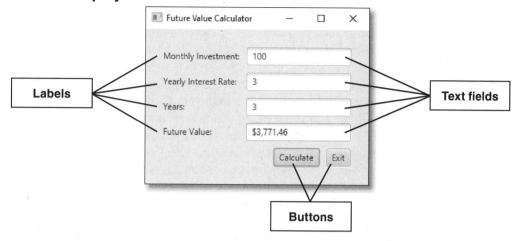

Common GUI APIs for Java

Library	Description
AWT	Abstract Window Toolkit. This is the oldest Java GUI library. It uses the native controls from the operating system. This library is not recommended for modern application development due to problems with cross-platform portability.
Swing	Created to replace AWT and fix the cross-platform portability problems. Swing controls are not native, but can use themes to look identical to native controls.
SWT	Standard Widget Toolkit. This library was created by IBM to fix performance problems and the non-native look and feel of earlier versions of Swing. This library uses native controls. However, it's not as powerful as Swing without adding more libraries.
JavaFX	Designed to replace the aging Swing library for developing GUIs for desktop applications and to make it easier to develop rich Internet applications (RIAs), which are web applications that have many of the characteristics of a desktop application.

Description

- When creating GUIs, you typically use a *window* to display *controls* such as *labels*, *text fields*, and *buttons*.

- A window is also known as a *form*, controls are also known as *components* or *widgets*, and a text field is also known as a *text box*.

- When creating GUIs with Java, you have several possible libraries that you can use. Of these libraries, JavaFX is the newest. However, Swing is the most widely used.

Figure 17-1   An introduction to GUI programming

The inheritance hierarchy for JavaFX nodes

Figure 17-2 presents a simplified inheritance hierarchy for GUI programming with JavaFX. Although the Java API contains an overwhelming number of classes for GUI programming, this chapter presents a basic set that you can use to start developing GUI applications with JavaFX. Once you understand how to use these classes, it should be easier to learn how to use the rest of them.

This inheritance hierarchy shows some of the classes that define controls such as the Label, TextField, and Button classes. In addition, it shows some of the classes that define *layout managers* such as the GridPane, FlowPane, BorderPane, HBox, and VBox classes. These layout managers are used to lay out the controls on the GUI.

All JavaFX controls and layout managers inherit the abstract Node and Parent classes. Then, controls inherit the abstract Control class, and layout managers inherit the Region and Pane classes. As a result, the methods defined by the Node and Parent classes are available to all controls and layout managers. Similarly, the methods defined by the Control class are available to all controls, and the methods defined by the Region and Pane classes are available to all layout managers.

The inheritance hierarchy for JavaFX nodes

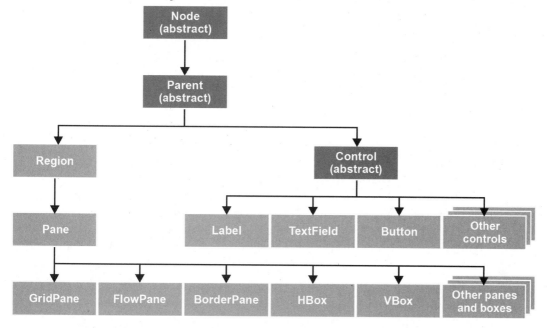

A summary of layout managers

Manager	Description
GridPane	Lays out controls in a grid.
FlowPane	Lays out controls by flowing them from left to right, or right to left, similar to words on a page.
BorderPane	Lays out controls by providing five areas that can each hold one control. The five areas are north, south, east, west, and center.
HBox	Lays out controls in a horizontal row of cells.
VBox	Lays out controls in a vertical column of cells.

Description

- A *layout manager* lays out the controls on the GUI.
- All JavaFX controls and layout managers inherit the abstract Node and Parent classes.
- All JavaFX controls inherit the abstract Control class.
- All JavaFX layout managers inherit the Region and Pane classes.

Figure 17-2   The inheritance hierarchy for JavaFX nodes

How to create a GUI that accepts user input

When you develop a GUI with JavaFX, you typically begin by displaying a main window for the application. Then, you add layout managers that contain controls such as labels and text fields. Next, you adjust the window and controls so the application looks the way you want it to.

To get started with JavaFX, you can use your IDE to create a file for a class that defines the GUI. Then, you can add code to this class that defines the GUI as shown in the figures that follow. However, if you're using NetBeans, you can create a new project that generates some of this code for you. To do that, select the New Project command from the File menu, select JavaFX from the Categories pane, and select JavaFX Application from the Projects pane. When you finish creating the project, you can use the generated code as the starting point for your own application.

How to create and display a window

In JavaFX, the user interface is defined in terms of a *stage* and a *scene*. The stage is the top-level JavaFX container, and the scene is the container for all content.

Figure 17-3 shows the code that creates the main window for the Future Value application. This code starts by importing the classes it needs from several javafx packages. Then, it declares a class named FutureValueApplication that extends the Application class from the javafx.application package. This is a common practice, since it allows you to store all the code that defines this application within a single class.

The FutureValueApplication class begins by overriding the start() method of the Application class. This method is the main entry point for all JavaFX applications. The start() method accepts a Stage object that's defined by the javafx.stage package and created by the operating system when an application starts. You can use this object to access the main window.

Within the start() method, the first statement uses the setTitle() method of the Stage object to set the title of the window. This is the text that displays in the upper left corner of the window. In this figure, the code sets the title of the window to "Future Value Calculator".

The second statement in this method creates a new GridPane object so the controls can be laid out in a grid. Then, the third statement creates a new Scene object and passes the GridPane object to it. This sets the GridPane object as the root pane for this scene.

The constructor of the Scene class also accepts two more arguments that set the width and height of the window in pixels. If you don't include these arguments, the window is sized to fit its content.

The last two statements in the start() method set the scene and display the stage. To do that, the code uses the setScene() method of the Stage object to

Constructors of the GridPane and Scene classes

Constructor	Description
`GridPane()`	Creates a GridPane object.
`Scene(Parent, width, height)`	Creates a Scene object with the specified height and width that contains the specified Parent object.

Methods of the Stage class

Method	Description
`setTitle()`	Sets the title for the Stage object.
`setScene(Scene)`	Adds the specified scene to the stage.
`show()`	Displays the window defined by the stage.

A class that creates and displays an empty window

```java
import javafx.application.Application;
import javafx.scene.Scene;
import javafx.scene.layout.GridPane;
import javafx.stage.Stage;

public class FutureValueApplication extends Application {
    @Override
    public void start(Stage primaryStage) {
        // set stage title
        primaryStage.setTitle("Future Value Calculator");

        // create grid, create scene, and add grid to scene
        GridPane grid = new GridPane();
        Scene scene = new Scene(grid, 300, 100);

        // set scene and display stage
        primaryStage.setScene(scene);
        primaryStage.show();
    }

    public static void main(String[] args) {
        // start the application by calling its static launch() method
        launch(args);
    }
}
```

The resulting window

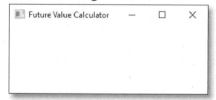

Description

- To define the main window for an application, code a class that inherits the Application class in the javafx.application package and override its start() method.

- The start() method receives a Stage object that represents the main window, known as the *stage*. Then, you can create a *scene* with a *pane* that contains other panes or controls.

Figure 17-3   How to create and display a window

add the scene to the stage. Then, this code calls the show() method of the Stage object to make the stage visible.

After the start() method, figure 17-3 shows the main() method for the application. This method calls the static launch() method of the Application class. The launch() method causes the start() method to be executed so the GUI is displayed.

How to work with labels

Most applications use one or more *labels* to display text that identifies the other controls in the GUI. In JavaFX, you use the Label class to create a label.

Figure 17-4 shows the package that you need to work with controls like Label controls. This is the same package that you'll need for other controls like the TextField and Button controls presented later in this chapter.

The first table in this figure presents two constructors and a method for the Label class. The first constructor creates a label without setting its text. If you use this constructor, you'll need to use the setText() method to set the text of the label. For example, you might want to do that if you use labels to display error messages. Otherwise, you can use the second constructor, which accepts a String argument that sets the text of the label.

The second table in this figure summarizes the add() method of the GridPane class. This method accepts three arguments. The first argument is a control, such as a Label object. The second and third arguments are integer values that specify column and row indexes. This determines where the control is displayed within the grid. Both the column and the row indexes start at zero. As a result, a column index of zero is the first column in the grid, and a row index of zero is the first row in the grid.

The code examples show how this works. In the first example, the first statement creates a Label control and sets its text to "Monthly Investment". Then, the second statement adds the label to the first column of the first row in the grid.

The second example shows how to create a label and add it to a grid in a single statement. This code works by calling the Label constructor from within the add() method. In this example, the code doesn't create a variable that refers to the Label object. This is a common way of adding a label to a grid if you don't need to call any methods of the Label class later.

The last example shows four labels that are added to a grid, and the window below it shows how the GUI displays these labels. This shows that, by default, there isn't any space between labels or between the grid and the window.

Although the labels in this figure display text, a label can also display an image. For example, you can use a label to display an icon that identifies a text field or to display a photograph of a product. For more information, see the JavaFX API documentation.

The package for controls

```
javafx.scene.control
```

Common constructors and a method of the Label class

Constructor	Description
`Label()`	Creates a Label object.
`Label(String)`	Creates a Label object and sets the text displayed by the label to the specified string.

Method	Description
`setText(String)`	Sets the text displayed by the label to the specified string.

A method of the GridPane class for adding controls

Method	Description
`add(control, colIndex, rowIndex)`	Adds the specified control to the grid pane at the specified column and row indexes.

How to create a Label object and add it to a grid

```
Label investmentLabel = new Label("Monthly Investment:");
grid.add(investmentLabel, 0, 0);
```

A common way of adding a label to a grid

```
grid.add(new Label("Monthly Investment:"), 0, 0);
```

Code that adds four labels to a grid

```
grid.add(new Label("Monthly Investment:"), 0, 0);      // col 1, row 1
grid.add(new Label("Yearly Interest Rate:"), 0, 1);    // col 1, row 2
grid.add(new Label("Years:"), 0, 2);                   // col 1, row 3
grid.add(new Label("Future Value:"), 0, 3);            // col 1, row 4
```

The resulting window

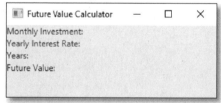

Description

- A Label control defines a *label*, which is a non-editable control that typically displays text that identifies other controls such as text fields.

- If you know that you won't need to call any methods from a Label object, it's a common practice to call the constructor of the Label class from within the add() method of a GridPane object. When you use this technique, no variable is created to refer to the Label object.

- A Label object can also display an image. However, that's not covered in this book.

Figure 17-4   How to work with labels

How to set alignment and padding

By default, a GridPane object doesn't provide any space, or *padding*, between controls or between the grid and the edges of the window. That's why the labels displayed in the previous figure don't have any space between them. And that's why there's no space between the labels and the edge of the window.

Figure 17-5 presents some methods of the GridPane class that you can use to improve the layout of your application. The setAlignment() method accepts one of the values of the Pos enumeration to determine the position of the grid in the scene. The default alignment of a GridPane object is TOP_LEFT, which means the grid is aligned in the top left of the scene that contains it.

The setPadding() method sets the padding around the grid. It accepts an Insets object whose constructor accepts four parameters that allow you to specify the top, left, bottom, and right padding in pixels. If you think of a clock, these values are in a counterclockwise direction, starting at the top of the clock.

The setVgap() and setHgap() methods set the space between the columns and rows in the grid. These methods both accept an int that specifies the space in pixels.

The code example in this figure shows how to set the alignment and padding for a GridPane object. Here, the grid is aligned at the top center of the scene, there are 25 pixels of padding around the grid, and there are 10 pixels of vertical space between the labels. (Although this code also specifies that there's 10 pixels of horizontal space between columns, it's not used here because the grid contains a single column.) The window below the code example shows how this looks. As you can see, these changes provide a noticeable improvement over the appearance of the window in the previous figure.

The package for working with alignment and padding

```
javafx.geometry
```

Common methods of the GridPane class for alignment and padding

Method	Description
setAlignment(Pos)	Sets the alignment of the grid using a constant of the Pos enumeration.
setPadding(Insets)	Sets the padding around the grid to the amount of space specified by the Insets object.
setHgap(int)	Sets the width of the horizontal gap between the columns in the grid.
setVgap(int)	Sets the height of the vertical gap between the rows in the grid.

Common constructor of the Insets class

Constructor	Description
Insets(top, left, bottom, right)	Specifies the top, left, bottom, and right padding in pixels.

Constants of the Pos enumeration

TOP_LEFT	TOP_CENTER	TOP_RIGHT
BASELINE_LEFT	BASELINE_CENTER	BASELINE_RIGHT
CENTER_LEFT	CENTER	CENTER_RIGHT
BOTTOM_LEFT	BOTTOM_CENTER	BOTTOM_RIGHT

Code that sets the alignment and padding for a grid

```
GridPane grid = new GridPane();
grid.setAlignment(Pos.TOP_CENTER);
grid.setPadding(new Insets(25, 25, 25, 25));
grid.setHgap(10);
grid.setVgap(10);
```

The resulting window

Description

- You can use methods of the GridPane class to set the alignment of the grid, set the padding around the grid, and set the space between the rows and columns in the grid.

- If you forget the order of the parameters for the constructor of the Insets class, it may help to remember that they start at the top and go counterclockwise.

Figure 17-5   How to set alignment and padding

How to work with text fields

Most applications use one or more *text fields*, also known as *text boxes*, to allow the user to enter data. The TextField class defines a text field that allows the user to enter or edit text and can also be used to display text to the user. Figure 17-6 summarizes the most common constructor and some of the methods of the TextField class.

The constructor creates a text field that doesn't contain any text. Then, if the uses enters text in the field, you get that text using the getText() method. Conversely, if you want to set the text in the field, you use the setText() method.

By default, a text field is editable. As a result, the user can enter text into it or edit the text that's already in it. However, if you want to create a read-only text field, you can pass a false value to its setEditable() method. Then, the user can't enter text into it.

So, why wouldn't you use a label if you want to display text that the user can't edit? One reason is that the user can select and copy text from a read-only text field. This is useful if you want to display some text that users can copy to the clipboard and paste somewhere else, but you don't want them to be able to edit the text that's displayed by the field. For example, you might want to allow the user to copy and paste an error message into an email to help the programmer debug a problem.

The setDisable() method works similarly to the setEditable() method. However, it also grays out the text box and doesn't allow selecting or copying text from the field. This is useful if you want to prevent users from entering data into a text field until after they've completed other steps.

The examples in this figure show how to create and work with text fields. Here, the first example creates a text field named investmentField, and the second example uses the getText() method to get the value from that text field and assign it to a String variable. Conversely, the third example uses the setText() method to set the value of the text field to the String value "100".

The final example shows how to add TextField controls to a grid. This works like the code you saw in figure 17-4 for adding Label controls to a grid. To start, you create the TextField control. Then, you call the add() method of the GridPane class and pass it the control and the column and row indexes that determine where the control will be displayed in the grid.

This figure also shows how these fields appear in a window when the application displays the GUI. Here, the fourth text field looks the same as the first three. However, the fourth field is read-only, so users can't change the text that it displays.

As you learned in figure 17-4, you could also create these text fields in one line by calling the TextField constructor from within the add() method. However, you almost always need to get or set the text that's stored in the field at some point in the application. As a result, you'll typically create a variable that refers to the TextField object so you can use this variable to work with the text field later.

Common constructor and methods of the TextField class

Constructor	Description
`TextField()`	Creates a TextField object.
Method	**Description**
`getText()`	Gets the text contained by the text field.
`setText(String)`	Sets the text displayed by the text field.
`setEditable(boolean)`	Determines whether the user can edit the text or not.
`setDisable(boolean)`	Determines whether the text field is enabled. If set to true, the text field is disabled and grayed out.

How to create a text field

```
TextField investmentField = new TextField();
```

How to get text from a field

```
String monthlyInvestment = investmentField.getText();
```

How to set text in a field

```
investmentField.setText("100");
```

Code that adds four text fields to a grid

```
TextField investmentField = new TextField();
grid.add(investmentField, 1, 0);              // col 2, row 1

TextField interestRateField = new TextField();
grid.add(interestRateField, 1, 1);            // col 2, row 2

TextField yearsField = new TextField();
grid.add(yearsField, 1, 2);                   // col 2, row 3

TextField futureValueField = new TextField();
futureValueField.setEditable(false);
grid.add(futureValueField, 1, 3);             // col 2, row 4
```

The resulting window

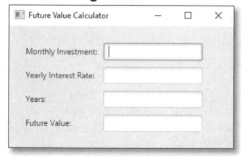

Description

- A TextField control defines a *text field* that displays text to the user and allows the user to enter text. This type of control is also known as a *text box*.

Figure 17-6   How to work with text fields

How to set column widths

When you add content to the columns of a grid, the GridPane layout manager sets the width of those columns to accommodate the content. By default, it makes each column wide enough to accommodate its widest content. In most cases, this is what you want.

However, there are times when the default approach can cause layout problems in your application. For example, if you have a column that contains labels that display error messages, the column is collapsed when there are no error messages. But when one or more error messages are displayed, the width of the column changes, which causes the width of all the other columns to change too if the width of the window is set. This can make the fields in your application jump around in response to user input.

To fix this, you can use the ColumnConstraints class to specify the width of a column in a GridPane as shown in figure 17-7. Here, the first table summarizes some of the constructors of the ColumnConstraints class. The first constructor creates a ColumnConstraints object with no width set. The second constructor creates a ColumnConstraints object with the width set. And the third constructor lets you specify a range of widths for the column rather than a single value. That way, if the size of the window changes, the column only collapses or expands to the specified minimum or maximum widths.

The second table summarizes some of the methods of the ColumnConstraints class. You can use the first three methods to set the minimum, maximum, and preferred widths of a column. You can also use the fourth method, setPercentWidth(), to specify the width as a percentage of the grid that contains it. That way, your application will maintain a consistent look when it's resized.

To work with the ColumnConstraints class, you use the getColumnConstraints() method of the grid to get the collection of column constraints. Then, you create one ColumnConstraints object for each column, and you add those objects to the column constraints collection. The code below the tables in this figure shows two ways to do that.

The first example uses a loop to add a constraint object for each column in the grid. Here, the loop runs twice, so it works for two columns. However, you could easily modify this loop to work for any number of columns.

Within the loop, the first statement creates a ColumnConstraints object that sets the width of the column to 150 pixels. Then, the second statement adds that object to the grid. To do that, it calls the add() method of the collection that's returned by the getColumnConstraints() method of the grid. This technique is useful if you want to make all the columns in a grid the same width.

The second example doesn't use a loop. Instead, the first four statements create two ColumnConstraints objects. The first constraint object sets the width of the column to 60% of the grid, and the second one sets the width to 40%. Then, this code adds both objects to the grid by calling the addAll() method of the collection that's returned by the grid's getColumnConstraints() method. This technique is useful if you need to specify different constraints for different columns in a grid.

The package for working with column widths

```
javafx.scene.layout
```

Common constructors of the ColumnConstraints class

Constructor	Description
`ColumnConstraints()`	Creates a ColumnConstraints object with no width set.
`ColumnConstraints(width)`	Creates a ColumnConstraints object with the width of the column set in pixels.
`ColumnConstraints(minWidth, prefWidth, maxWidth)`	Creates a ColumnConstraints object with the minimum width, preferred width, and maximum width of the column set.

Common methods of the ColumnConstraints class

Method	Description
`setMinWidth(minWidth)`	Sets the minimum width of the column in pixels.
`setMaxWidth(maxWidth)`	Sets the maximum width of the column in pixels.
`setPrefWidth(prefWidth)`	Sets the preferred width of the column in pixels.
`setPercentWidth(percentWidth)`	Sets the width of the column as a percentage of the grid's available width.

A method of the GridPane class for getting column constraints

Method	Description
`getColumnConstraints()`	Gets a list of column constraints. The first item in the list contains the constraints for the first column, the second item contains the constraints for the second column, and so on.

Code that uses a loop to add the same constraint for each column

```
for (int i = 0; i < 2; i++) {
    ColumnConstraints col = new ColumnConstraints(150);
    grid.getColumnConstraints().add(col);
}
```

Code that adds a different constraint for each column

```
ColumnConstraints col1 = new ColumnConstraints();
col1.setPercentWidth(60);
ColumnConstraints col2 = new ColumnConstraints();
col2.setPercentWidth(40);
grid.getColumnConstraints().addAll(col1, col2);
```

Description

- When you add content to the columns of a grid, the GridPane layout manager sets the width of those columns to accommodate it. This is adequate for most applications.

- If you need to set the column widths, you can create column constraints and add them to the list of column constraints that's stored in the grid.

Figure 17-7   How to set column widths

How to create a GUI that handles events

At this point, you've learned how to create a GUI application that lets a user enter data. However, you haven't learned how to process that data. In the topics that follow, you'll learn how to add buttons to your application, and you'll learn how to handle the events that occur when the user clicks those buttons. This event handling can include code that gets data from the user and displays data to the user.

How to work with buttons and boxes

Most applications use one or more *button* controls to allow users to submit the data they've entered. The first table in figure 17-8 summarizes a constructor and a method of the Button class. This shows that you can use the constructor to set the text that's displayed on the button, and you can use the setText() method to change the text if you need to do that.

When working with buttons, it's common to store a row of buttons within a pane such as the HBox pane described in this figure. Then, it's common to add this pane to the root pane. This allows you to align and pad the buttons differently than the other controls on the page.

The second table in this figure summarizes a constructor and two methods of the HBox class. The constructor allows you to set the padding that separates the controls in the pane, and the getChildren() method returns a collection of all the controls that the HBox contains. Then, you can use the add() method of that collection to add a control. Like the GridPane class, the HBox class also has a setAlignment() method that allows you to align the controls within the box.

The third table in this figure summarizes another add() method of the GridPane class. This add() method accepts the control as well as the column and row indexes like before. In addition, it accepts integer values for the number of columns and rows the control should span.

The example in this figure shows how this works. To start, this code creates two buttons and assigns them to variables named calculateButton and exitButton. Then, it creates a new HBox object that will separate any controls it contains by 10 pixels.

After that, the code adds the buttons to the HBox object. To do that, it calls the getChildren() method to get the collection of child controls. Then, it uses the add() method of that collection to add the buttons. Next, it aligns the buttons in the bottom right of the HBox object.

Finally, the code adds the HBox object to the fifth row of the root grid for the application. Note that the add() method specifies that the HBox object is in the first column of the grid. But it also specifies that the HBox object should span two columns. This, along with the alignment setting of the HBox object, is what causes the buttons to display all the way to the right of the grid.

Common constructor and method of the Button class

Constructor/Method	Description
`Button(String)`	Creates a Button object and sets the text displayed by the button.
`setText(String)`	Sets the text displayed by the button.

Common constructor and methods of the HBox class

Constructor/Method	Description
`HBox(space)`	Creates a horizontal box that separates the controls it contains with the specified amount of space in pixels.
`getChildren()`	Gets the collection of controls that the box contains.
`setAlignment(Pos)`	Sets the alignment of the box using a constant of the Pos enumeration.

Another method of the GridPane class for adding controls

Method	Description
`add(control, colIndex, rowIndex, colSpan, rowSpan)`	Adds the specified control to the grid at the specified column and row indexes, spanning the specified number of columns and rows.

Code that adds a box of two buttons to the fifth row of a grid

```
// create two buttons
Button calculateButton = new Button("Calculate");
Button exitButton = new Button("Exit");

// create a horizontal box and add the buttons to it
HBox buttonBox = new HBox(10);
buttonBox.getChildren().add(calculateButton);
buttonBox.getChildren().add(exitButton);
buttonBox.setAlignment(Pos.BOTTOM_RIGHT);

// add the box to row 5, spanning 2 columns and 1 row
grid.add(buttonBox, 0, 4, 2, 1);
```

The resulting window

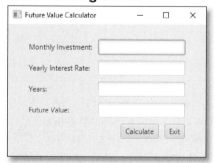

Description

- Users can click on a *button* to perform tasks such as processing the data that was entered.
- When working with buttons, it's common to store a row of buttons in an HBox object.

Figure 17-8   How to work with buttons and boxes

How to handle action events

Each time the user interacts with a GUI, an *event* occurs. For example, when the user clicks on a button, an event is fired notifying your code that the button was clicked. An event is also fired each time the user presses a key on the keyboard or moves the mouse.

If you want to respond to an event, you need to register an *event handler* for the event. To do that, you use the setOnAction() method of a control to identify the event handler object that handles the event. The examples in figure 17-9 illustrate how this works.

To start, you should know that an event handler must implement the EventHandler interface. This is a generic interface that can be used with any type of event object. This interface contains a single method named handle() that is executed when the specified event occurs.

The examples in this figure show how to respond to the user clicking on a button. In that case, an ActionEvent object is created and passed to the event handler. As a result, ActionEvent is coded as the type on the EventHandler interface. Note that an ActionEvent object contains information about the event that occurred. However, you don't need to use that information in simple cases like this.

Prior to Java 8, it was common to handle an action event by using an *inner class* as shown in the first example. Although you can't tell here, this class is coded within the start() method of the FutureValueApplication class. It implements the EventHandler interface, which has a method named handle() that receives the ActionEvent object. Then, this method just changes the title of the window. However, it could contain more complex code such as code that updates a database.

To register the event handler with the button, the last statement calls the setOnAction() method of the button and passes an object of the inner class to it. Then, when the button is clicked, the handle() method of the object is executed.

Prior to Java 8, it was even more common to handle an ActionEvent by using an *anonymous inner class*, as shown in the second example. Here, an anonymous class is coded within the parentheses of the setOnAction() method. This class is created from the EventHandler interface, and it includes a method named handle() that executes when the button is clicked. However, no name is provided for the class, which is why it's called an anonymous class.

With Java 8 and later, you can use a *lambda expression* instead of an anonymous class as shown in the third example. In this case, the lambda expression is more concise and easier to understand than the anonymous inner class. For now, you can think of a lambda expression as an anonymous method that provides the parameters and code for the method, but no name. Then, if you want to learn more about lambda expressions, you can read chapter 22.

Now that you know how to handle the event that occurs when a user clicks a button, you should know that you can handle other events using similar techniques. For more information on how to do that, you can refer to the JavaFX API documentation.

The package for working with events

```
javafx.event
```

A common method of most controls

Method	Description
`setOnAction(EventHandler<EventType>)`	Registers an event handler for a control such as a button so it can handle action events such as clicking on a button.

Three ways to add an event handler to a button

With an inner class (prior to Java 8)

```java
class CalculateButtonEventHandler implements EventHandler<ActionEvent> {
    @Override
    public void handle(ActionEvent event) {
        primaryStage.setTitle("Click!");
    }
}
calculateButton.setOnAction(new CalculateButtonEventHandler());
```

With an anonymous class (prior to Java 8)

```java
calculateButton.setOnAction(new EventHandler<ActionEvent>(){
    @Override
    public void handle(ActionEvent event) {
        primaryStage.setTitle("Click!");
    }
});
```

With a lambda expression (Java 8 and later)

```java
calculateButton.setOnAction(event -> {
    primaryStage.setTitle("Click!");
});
```

Description

- An *event* occurs when a user interacts with the GUI.

- To execute some code when an event occurs, you register an *event handler* for a control by calling its setOnAction() method. This method accepts an EventHandler object that contains the code that's executed when an event occurs.

- To create an event handler using an *inner class*, you code a class within the main class that implements the EventHandler<> interface. Then, you override the handle() method of that interface so it includes the code that's executed when the event occurs.

- To create an event handler using an *anonymous class*, you create an object from the EventHandler<> interface. Then, within the braces that define this object, you supply the code that implements the handle() method of the interface.

- You can also pass a *lambda expression* to the setOnAction() method. The lambda expression consists of the variable name for the event object, followed by the *lambda operator* (`->`) and the code that implements the EventHandler<> interface.

- Prior to Java 8, it was common to write inner classes or anonymous inner classes to handle events. With Java 8 or later, you can use lambda expressions, which are cleaner and more concise.

Figure 17-9   How to handle action events

The Future Value application

Figure 17-10 shows a Future Value application that puts the skills presented so far in this chapter into the context of a complete application.

The user interface

To start, this figure shows the GUI for the application. This GUI lets the user calculate the future value of a series of monthly investments. To start, the user enters appropriate numbers into the first three text fields. Then, the user clicks the Calculate button. Or, the user can press the Tab key to move the focus to the Calculate button and then press the spacebar. Either way, the application displays the future value in the fourth text field.

The code

This figure also shows the code for the FutureValueApplication class. To start, this class imports the FinancialCalculations class that's in the murach. business package. In addition, it imports the NumberFormat class from the Java API and several classes from the JavaFX API. After the import statements, the declaration for the class shows that the FutureValueApplication class inherits the Application class.

Within the body of the FutureValueApplication class, the code begins by declaring four private instance variables for the text fields. These variables are declared at the class level so the event handler for the Calculate button can access them.

After declaring the private instance variables, this code overrides the start() method of the Application class. This method accepts a Stage object that represents the main window. Within the start() method, the code sets the title of the main window and creates a new GridPane object. Then, it sets the alignment and padding of this GridPane. Next, it creates a new Scene object and passes the GridPane object to it. This sets the GridPane as the root element of the scene. Since this code doesn't specify the width and height of the Scene, the scene is just wide and tall enough to store the grid, which is appropriate for this application.

After setting up the grid, this code adds a series of Label and TextField objects to the grid. This code doesn't create variable names for the labels because it doesn't need to access the labels again. On the other hand, it assigns the text fields to the private instance variables because it needs to access the text fields later.

This code adds the label and text field for the Monthly Investment to the first and second columns of the first row. In the same way, this code adds the Yearly Interest Rate label and text field to the second row, and it adds the Years label and text field to the third row. Each of these text fields accepts an entry from the user.

The GUI

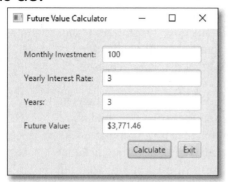

The FutureValueApplication class

```java
package murach.ui;

import murach.business.FinancialCalculations;
import java.text.NumberFormat;

import javafx.application.Application;
import javafx.geometry.Insets;
import javafx.geometry.Pos;
import javafx.scene.Scene;
import javafx.scene.control.Button;
import javafx.scene.control.Label;
import javafx.scene.control.TextField;
import javafx.scene.layout.GridPane;
import javafx.scene.layout.HBox;
import javafx.stage.Stage;

public class FutureValueApplication extends Application {
    private TextField investmentField;
    private TextField interestRateField;
    private TextField yearsField;
    private TextField futureValueField;

    @Override
    public void start(Stage primaryStage) {
        primaryStage.setTitle("Future Value Calculator");

        GridPane grid = new GridPane();
        grid.setAlignment(Pos.TOP_CENTER);
        grid.setPadding(new Insets(25, 25, 25, 25));
        grid.setHgap(10);
        grid.setVgap(10);

        Scene scene = new Scene(grid);

        grid.add(new Label("Monthly Investment:"), 0, 0);
        investmentField = new TextField();
        grid.add(investmentField, 1, 0);

        grid.add(new Label("Yearly Interest Rate:"), 0, 1);
        interestRateField = new TextField();
        grid.add(interestRateField, 1, 1);
```

Figure 17-10   The Future Value application (part 1 of 2)

This code adds the Future Value label and text field to the first and second columns of the fourth row. Unlike the previous text fields, though, this code calls the setEditable() method and passes it a value of false. As a result, users can copy and paste the text from this field, but they can't enter or change the text. In other words, this code creates a read-only field that displays the result of the future value calculation.

After adding the Future Value text field, this code creates two buttons and assigns them to variables. Each button calls the setOnAction() method and passes it a lambda expression that sets the event handler for that button. As a result, clicking the Calculate button executes the calculateButtonClicked() method that's shown after the start() method. Similarly, clicking the Exit button executes the exitButtonClicked() method.

Note that the lambda expressions shown here use a syntax that's slightly simpler than the lambda expression you saw in figure 17-9. Specifically, the code that's executed when an event occurs isn't enclosed in braces. As you'll learn in chapter 22, you can omit these braces if the lambda expression executes a single statement.

After creating the two buttons, this code creates an HBox object to hold the buttons. Then, it adds the buttons to its collection of controls, sets the alignment and padding of the HBox object, and adds the HBox object to the fifth row of the grid. In this case, the HBox object is added to the first column, but it spans two columns.

The last two statements in the start() method set the scene and show the stage. To do that, it passes the Scene object to the setScene() method of the Stage object. Then, it calls the show() method of the Stage object to make the window visible.

The calculateButtonClicked() method is the event handler for the action event of the Calculate button. To start, this event handler gets the string that the user entered into the first text field on the form by calling the getText() method of that control. Then, it converts this string to a double value named investment. After that, this method performs similar processing for the next two text fields to get the interest rate and number of years. Then, this method calls the calculateFutureValue() method of the FinancialCalculations class to calculate the future value. Finally, this code uses the NumberFormat class to apply currency formatting to the future value, and it uses the setText() method of the read-only text field to display the formatted value.

For this simple example, the calculateButtonClicked() method doesn't validate the data that's entered by the user. As a result, if the user enters an invalid value such as "xx", the application prints an error message to the console. To prevent this, you can validate the data that's entered by the user as shown later in this chapter.

The exitButtonClicked() method is the event handler for the action event of the Exit button. This method executes a single statement that exits the application with a status code of 0. By convention, a status code of 0 indicates that the application ended normally.

The last method for this application is the main() method. This method calls the launch() method of the Application class, which calls the start() method of the Application class that displays the GUI for the application.

The FutureValueApplication class (continued)

```java
        grid.add(new Label("Years:"), 0, 2);
        yearsField = new TextField();
        grid.add(yearsField, 1, 2);

        grid.add(new Label("Future Value:"), 0, 3);
        futureValueField = new TextField();
        futureValueField.setEditable(false);
        grid.add(futureValueField, 1, 3);

        Button calculateButton = new Button("Calculate");
        calculateButton.setOnAction(event -> calculateButtonClicked());

        Button exitButton = new Button("Exit");
        exitButton.setOnAction(event -> exitButtonClicked());

        HBox buttonBox = new HBox(10);
        buttonBox.getChildren().add(calculateButton);
        buttonBox.getChildren().add(exitButton);
        buttonBox.setAlignment(Pos.BOTTOM_RIGHT);
        grid.add(buttonBox, 0, 4, 2, 1);

        primaryStage.setScene(scene);
        primaryStage.show();
    }

    private void calculateButtonClicked() {
        // get data from text fields
        double investment = Double.parseDouble(investmentField.getText());
        double rate = Double.parseDouble(interestRateField.getText());
        int years = Integer.parseInt(yearsField.getText());

        // calculate future value
        double futureValue = FinancialCalculations.calculateFutureValue(
                investment, rate, years);

        // set data in read-only text field
        NumberFormat currency = NumberFormat.getCurrencyInstance();
        futureValueField.setText(currency.format(futureValue));
    }

    private void exitButtonClicked() {
        System.exit(0);    // 0 indicates a normal exit
    }

    public static void main(String[] args) {
        launch(args);
    }
}
```

Figure 17-10   The Future Value application (part 2 of 2)

How to validate user input

In chapter 5, you learned how to validate the input data for console applications. In the topics that follow, you'll see that you can use similar techniques to validate the input data for JavaFX applications.

How to display an error message in a dialog box

When you validate data in a JavaFX application, you need to be able to display an error message to inform the user that an invalid entry has been detected. One way to do that is to display the error message in a separate dialog box like the one shown in figure 17-11. To display a dialog box like this, you use the Alert class described in this figure.

The table in this figure summarizes a constructor and four methods of the Alert class. The constructor creates a dialog box with the appropriate image and values for the type of alert that's specified. The type is specified by passing a constant of the AlertType enumeration to the constructor.

The first three methods in the table accept a string and then display that string at various locations in the dialog box. For example, the setTitle() method displays the string in the upper left corner of the dialog box. The setHeaderText() method displays the string in the upper part of the dialog box below the title. And the setContentText() method displays the string in the lower part of the dialog box below the title and the header.

You use the last method in the table, showAndWait(), to display the dialog box. When you call this method, the user must respond to the dialog box before continuing. For example, the user can respond by clicking the OK button.

The code example in this figure shows how to display a simple error message in a dialog box. To start, the first statement creates a new Alert object with an alert type of ERROR. A dialog box of this type has an image of a red "X" in it. Then, the next three statements set the title, header, and content of the dialog box. Finally, the last statement displays the dialog box.

The class for working with dialog boxes

```
javafx.scene.control.Alert
```

Common constructors and methods of the Alert class

Constructor	Description
`Alert(AlertType)`	Creates a dialog box with an appropriate image and default values for the type specified by the AlertType constant.

Method	Description
`setTitle(String)`	Sets the title of the dialog box.
`setHeaderText(String)`	Sets the text that's displayed in the top part of the dialog box.
`setContentText(String)`	Sets the text that's displayed in the bottom part of the dialog box.
`showAndWait()`	Displays the dialog box and waits for the user to respond.

The five constants of the AlertType enumeration

```
ERROR
WARNING
CONFIRMATION
INFORMATION
NONE
```

Code that displays a dialog box with an error message

```
Alert alert = new Alert(Alert.AlertType.ERROR);
alert.setTitle("Error");
alert.setHeaderText("Invalid Entry");
alert.setContentText("Monthly Investment is a required field.");
alert.showAndWait();
```

The resulting dialog box

Description

- You can use the Alert class to display dialog boxes with error messages for data validation.

Figure 17-11   How to display an error message in a dialog box

How to validate the data entered into a text field

Figure 17-12 shows two techniques you can use to validate the data the user enters into a text field. The first example checks that the user has entered data into the field. To do that, it uses the getText() method to get the text the user entered as a string. Then, it uses the isEmpty() method of the string to check whether the string is empty. If it is, the code displays an error message in a dialog box.

After the user responds to the dialog box, this code executes a return statement to exit the method. This prevents the rest of the code in the method from being executed, which is often what you want for invalid data.

The second example shows how to check whether the user entered a numeric value. Here, the try clause uses the parseDouble() method of the Double class to parse the text entered by the user to a double value. Then, if a NumberFormatException occurs, the catch block displays an error message in a dialog box and exits the method after the user responds to the dialog box.

Code that checks if an entry has been made

```java
private void calculateButtonClicked() {
    if (investmentField.getText().isEmpty()) {
        Alert alert = new Alert(Alert.AlertType.ERROR);
        alert.setHeaderText("Invalid Entry!");
        alert.setContentText("Monthly Investment is a required field");
        alert.showAndWait();
        return;
    }

    // the rest of the code for the method
}
```

Code that checks if an entry is a valid number

```java
private void calculateButtonClicked() {
    double investment;
    try {
        investment = Double.parseDouble(investmentField.getText());
    } catch (NumberFormatException e) {
        Alert alert = new Alert(Alert.AlertType.ERROR);
        alert.setHeaderText("Invalid Entry!");
        alert.setContentText("Monthly Investment must be a valid number.");
        alert.showAndWait();
        return;
    }

    // the rest of the code for the method
}
```

Description

- Like console applications, GUI applications should validate all data entered by the user before processing the data.

- When an entry is invalid, the application can display an error message and give the user another chance to enter valid data.

- To test whether a value has been entered into a text field, you can use the getText() method of the text field to get a string that contains the text the user entered. Then, you can check whether the string is empty by using its isEmpty() method.

- To test whether a text field contains valid numeric data, you can code the statement that converts the data in a try block and use a catch block to catch a NumberFormatException.

Figure 17-12   How to validate the data entered into a text field

The Validation class

Figure 17-13 shows a class named Validation that you can use to validate the data entered into a text field. Like the Console class that was presented in chapter 7, this class uses methods to perform common validation functions. Unlike the Console class, the Validation class doesn't use static methods. As a result, you must create a Validation object before you can use the methods in this class. That makes it easier to use the methods if the name of the object variable is shorter than the class name, and it makes it easier to change the class that's used for validation if that need arises.

This class starts by defining a private instance variable named lineEnd that stores a string that's added to the end of each validation message. Then, this method defines two constructors that you can use to set the lineEnd variable. The first constructor sets the lineEnd variable to a string that contains a single new line character, and the second constructor sets the lineEnd variable to the string that's passed to it.

All three of the public methods return a string that indicates whether the specified string passed the validation test. In addition, all three of these methods define two string parameters. The first parameter specifies the text from the control that's being validated, and the second parameter specifies a name for the control to be used in the error message. Then, if the string passes the validation test, the method returns an empty validation message. This indicates that the string passed the validation test. Otherwise, the method returns a validation message followed by the lineEnd variable. This indicates that the string did not pass the validation test.

The isPresent() method determines whether the string value contains one or more characters. To do that, this code uses the isEmpty() method to check whether the string is empty. The isDouble() method determines whether the string value can be converted to a valid double value. Like the code in the second example in the previous figure, the parseDouble() method in this example is coded with a try statement that catches a NumberFormatException. Finally, the isInteger() method determines whether the string value can be converted to a valid int value. The code in this method is similar to the code for the isDouble() method. Of course, you can easily extend this class to perform other types of tests, such as checking whether a number is within a valid range.

As you review the Validation class, note that it doesn't refer to the controls in the GUI directly. Instead, it refers to the strings that the user enters into the controls. This is known as being *loosely coupled*, and it allows this class to work with different types of controls. For example, you can use this class to validate the string that's stored in a text field as shown in the next figure. However, you can also use this class to validate strings in other controls, including controls from other GUI APIs such as the Swing API described in the next chapter.

Similarly, the loose coupling allows you to decide how to display the validation messages. For example, you can use this class to display all validation messages in a dialog box as described in the next figure. However, you can also use this class to display validation messages in one or more labels on the GUI. To get that to work correctly, you might need to specify a different value for the lineEnd variable. For example, you might need to specify an empty string.

The code for the FXValidator class

```java
package murach.business;

public class Validation {

    private String lineEnd;

    public Validation() {
        this.lineEnd = "\n";
    }

    public Validation(String lineEnd) {
        this.lineEnd = lineEnd;
    }

    public String isPresent(String value, String name) {
        String msg = "";
        if (value.isEmpty()) {
            msg = name + " is required." + lineEnd;
        }
        return msg;
    }

    public String isDouble(String value, String name) {
        String msg = "";
        try {
            Double.parseDouble(value);
        } catch (NumberFormatException e) {
            msg = name + " must be a valid number." + lineEnd;
        }
        return msg;
    }

    public String isInteger(String value, String name) {
        String msg = "";
        try {
            Integer.parseInt(value);
        } catch (NumberFormatException e) {
            msg = name + " must be an integer." + lineEnd;
        }
        return msg;
    }
}
```

Figure 17-13   The Validation class

How to validate multiple entries

Figure 17-14 shows how you can use the Validation class presented in the previous figure in an event handler such as the calculateButtonClicked() method. To start, this code creates a Validation object named v. Then, it creates a variable named errorMsg to store the strings that are returned by calls to the methods of the Validation object.

After setting up the two variables, this method calls the isDouble() method from the Validation object and passes it the string that's stored in the Monthly Investment field. Then, it appends the result to the errorMsg variable. So, if the text in the Monthly Investment field can be converted to a double value, this code appends an empty string to the errorMsg variable. Otherwise, it appends a validation message for the Monthly Investment field to the errorMsg variable.

The next two calls to the methods of the Validation class work similarly. Here, the code uses the isDouble() method a second time to get an appropriate validation message for the Yearly Interest Rate field, and it uses the isInteger() method to get an appropriate validation message for the Years field.

After performing the validation tests, this code checks the errorMsg variable to see if it's empty. If it is, all fields passed the validation checks. As a result, this code can calculate the future value and display it in the GUI. However, if the errorMsg variable contains one or more validation messages, the application displays those messages in a dialog box like the one shown in this figure. Then, after the user clicks on the OK button, the dialog box is closed and the user can attempt to enter valid data. This process continues until the user enters valid data into all three text fields.

A validation dialog box that displays three error messages

Code that validates multiple entries

```
private void calculateButtonClicked() {
    Validation v = new Validation();
    String errorMsg = "";
    errorMsg += v.isDouble(investmentField.getText(),
            "Monthly Investment");
    errorMsg += v.isDouble(interestRateField.getText(),
            "Yearly Interest Rate");
    errorMsg += v.isInteger(yearsField.getText(),
            "Years");

    if (errorMsg.isEmpty()) {
        double investment = Double.parseDouble(
                investmentField.getText());
        double rate = Double.parseDouble(
                interestRateField.getText());
        int years = Integer.parseInt(
                yearsField.getText());

        double futureValue = FinancialCalculations.calculateFutureValue(
                investment, rate, years);

        NumberFormat currency = NumberFormat.getCurrencyInstance();
        futureValueField.setText(currency.format(futureValue));
    } else {
        Alert alert = new Alert(Alert.AlertType.ERROR);
        alert.setHeaderText("Invalid Data");
        alert.setContentText(errorMsg);
        alert.showAndWait();
    }
}
```

Description

- You can use the Validation class in the previous figure to validate multiple entries. If you want, you can display the error message that's returned by this class in a dialog box.

Figure 17-14   How to validate multiple entries

How to get started with FXML

The Future Value application presented earlier in this chapter contains over thirty lines of Java code that define the layout for the GUI. This code is mixed in with the code that provides the functionality for the GUI, which makes the code harder to read and maintain. To define the layout for the GUI separately, you can use a markup language known as FXML. Because FXML is based on XML, I'll start by presenting the basic skills for coding XML documents. Then, I'll present the basic skills for coding an FXML application.

An introduction to XML

XML (*Extensible Markup Language*) provides a standard way to structure data by using *tags* that identify each data element. Figure 17-15 shows a simple *XML document* that contains data for three products, each with a code, description, and price. Here, each tag begins with the < character and ends with the > character. As a result, each of the first four lines in the XML document in this figure contains a complete XML tag. In contrast, the fifth line contains two tags, <Description> and </Description>, with a text value in between.

The first tag in any XML document is an *XML declaration* that identifies the document as an XML document and indicates which XML version the document conforms to. An XML document can also contain comments. These are tags that begin with <!-- and end with --> and can contain any text you want.

Elements are the building blocks of XML. Each element in an XML document represents a single data item and is identified by a *start tag* that marks the beginning of the element and an *end tag* that marks the end of the element and repeats the name, prefixed by a slash. For example, <Description> and </Description> are the start tag and end tag for an element named Description.

A complete element consists of the element's start tag, its end tag, and the *content* between the tags. For example, <Description>Murach's Java Programming</Description> indicates that the content of the Description element is *Murach's Java Programming*.

Besides text, elements can contain other elements, known as *child elements*. This lets you add structure to a *parent element*. For example, a parent product element can have child elements that provide details about each product, such as the product's description and price.

The highest-level parent element in an XML document is known as the *root element*, and an XML document can have only one root element. In this example, the root element is Products.

Attributes are a concise way to provide data for XML elements. In the products XML document, for example, each Product element has a code attribute that provides an identifying code for the product. Thus, <Product code="java"> contains an attribute named code whose value is *java*.

Unlike other markup languages such as HTML, XML doesn't provide a pre-defined set of element or attribute names. Instead, you create your own element names to describe the contents of each element. Similarly, you create attributes as you need them, using names that describe the content of the attributes.

The products.xml document

```
<?xml version="1.0" encoding="utf-8" ?>
<!--Product data-->
<Products>
  <Product code="java">
    <Description>Murach's Java Programming</Description>
    <Price>57.50</Price>
  </Product>
  <Product code="jsp">
    <Description>Murach's Java Servlets and JSP</Description>
    <Price>57.50</Price>
  </Product>
  <Product code="mysql">
    <Description>Murach's MySQL</Description>
    <Price>54.50</Price>
  </Product>
</Products>
```

Description

- *XML*, which stands for *Extensible Markup Language*, is a method of structuring data using special *tags*. Each XML tag begins with < and ends with >.

- The *XML document* in this figure contains data for three products. Each product has an attribute named code and elements named Description and Price.

- An *element* is a unit of XML data that begins with a *start tag* and ends with an *end tag*. The start tag provides the name of the element and contains any attributes assigned to the element. The end tag repeats the name, prefixed with a slash (/). You can use any name you want for an XML element.

- Anything between an element's start and end tags is called the element's *content*. If an element doesn't contain content, you can close the tag for that element by coding a forward slash at the end of the opening tag.

- Elements can contain text or other elements. An element that's contained within another element is known as a *child element*. The element that contains a child element is known as the child's *parent element*.

- The highest-level parent element in an XML document is known as the *root element*. An XML document can have only one root element.

- You can include one or more *attributes* in the start tag for an element. An attribute typically consists of an attribute name, an equals sign, and a string value in quotes.

- If an element has more than one attribute, the order in which the attributes appear doesn't matter, but the attributes must be separated by one or more spaces.

- The first line in an XML document is an *XML declaration* that indicates which version of the XML standard is being used for the document. In addition, the declaration usually identifies the standard character set that's being used.

- You can use the <!-- and --> tags to include comments in an XML document.

Figure 17-15   An XML document

How to code an FXML application

Figure 17-16 presents the basic skills for coding an FXML application. To start, it shows three files that can store the code for an FXML application. Here, the file with the .fxml extension contains the FXML elements that define the GUI. The Java file whose name ends with "Controller" contains the event handlers that work with the controls defined by the FXML file. And the Java file whose name ends with "Application" starts the application and creates the Java objects that are declared by the FXML file.

The first set of examples in this figure shows how to code some of the elements that define the GUI. Because FXML is based on XML, you code them using a similar technique. The main difference is that you must use specific names for the elements and attributes in FXML. In these examples, for instance, you can see the definitions for a GridPane, Label, TextField, and Button element, along with the attributes that define them. You can also see a tag that imports classes that are used by the GUI. Notice that this type of tag begins and ends with a question mark.

The benefit of using a markup language like FXML is that it's *declarative*. This means that the language can just declare the controls without having to actually create them. As a result, the code is more concise, easier to read, and easier to maintain.

The second example in this figure shows code from the controller class for an FXML application. Here, the @FXML annotation allows the controller to access controls defined in the FXML file and supply event handlers for those controls. For example, the text field named investmentField refers to the TextField element in the FXML file with an fx:id attribute of "investmentField". Similarly, the calculateButtonClicked() method supplies the event handler for the button in the FXML file whose onAction attribute is set to "#calculateButtonClicked". Notice that the value of this attribute starts with a hashtag (#).

The third example shows how to load the objects defined by the FXML file. To do that, you use the static load() method of the FXMLLoader class in the start() method of the application class. This method accepts a URL for the FXML file that's retrieved using the getClass() and getResource() methods. The result is stored in a Parent object, which represents the hierarchy of the objects in the FXML file. After this object is created, you can use it to create the scene for the application, as you'll see later in this chapter.

How to create the files for an FXML application

By now, you shouldn't have any problem using your IDE to create the Java classes described in this figure. And with a little experimentation, you should also be able to create the FXML file. If you're using NetBeans, you can create all of these files at once by creating a new project for a Java FXML application. To do that, select the New Project button from the File menu, select JavaFX from the Categories pane, and select Java FXML Application from the Projects pane. Then, when you finish creating the project, NetBeans creates a simple working application that you can use as the starting point for your own application.

Three files for an application that uses FXML

File	Description
Name.**fxml**	The FXML file that defines the layout and controls for the GUI.
Name**Controller.java**	The Java class that provides the event handlers for the FXML file.
Name**Application.java**	The Java class that creates the controls defined in the FXML file and starts the application.

How to code the FXML file

How to code a GridPane element as the root element

```
<GridPane xmlns:fx="http://javafx.com/fxml"
          fx:controller="murach.ui.FutureValueController"
          alignment="TOP_CENTER" hgap="10" vgap="10">...</GridPane>
```

How to code Label and TextField elements

```
<Label text="Monthly Investment:"
    GridPane.columnIndex="0" GridPane.rowIndex="0"/>
<TextField fx:id="investmentField"
    GridPane.columnIndex="1" GridPane.rowIndex="0" />
```

How to define Button elements

```
<Button text="Calculate" onAction="#calculateButtonClicked"/>
```

How to import a class used by an FXML file

```
<?import javafx.scene.layout.*?>
```

How to access controls and supply event handlers in the controller class

```
@FXML private TextField investmentField;

@FXML
protected void calculateButtonClicked() {...}
```

How to load the objects defined by the FXML file in the application class

```
Parent root = FXMLLoader.load(getClass().getResource("FutureValue.fxml"));
Scene scene = new Scene(root);
```

Description

- FXML is an XML-based markup language that provides a way to separate the code that defines the layout of the GUI from the code that provides the functionality for the GUI. This makes an application easier to develop and maintain.

- The root element includes an xmlns:fx attribute to identify the XML namespace and an fx:controller attribute to identify the controller class.

- You can use the fx:id attribute to assign a unique name to a control.

- You can use the onAction attribute of a button to identify the method in the controller class that handles the event that occurs when the user clicks the button.

- You use the @FXML annotation in the controller class to mark fields and event handler methods that are used by the FXML file.

- Within the start() method of the application class, you call the load() method of the FXMLLoader class to load the Java objects defined by the FXML file into a Parent object. Then, you create a Scene object from the Parent object.

Figure 17-16   How to get started with FXML

The Future Value application with FXML

The next two figures present the code for a Future Value application that uses FXML. To the user, this application works exactly like the Future Value application presented earlier in this chapter. However, this application is easier for a programmer to develop and maintain because it uses FXML to define the GUI and a controller class to provide the event handlers for the GUI.

The FXML file

Figure 17-17 shows the FXML file that defines the Future Value GUI. Here, the three tags after the XML declaration import the classes needed by the application. Of these tags, the first two use an asterisk to import all classes for JavaFX layout managers and controls. However, the third statement imports a single class, the Insets class that's in the javafx.geometry package.

The root element for this file is the GridPane element. In addition to identifying the namespace and the controller class for the application, the alignment attribute for this element aligns the grid at the top center of the window. The hgap attribute sets the horizontal space between the rows in the grid, and the vgap attribute sets the vertical space between the columns.

The remaining elements are coded within the GridPane element. To start, the padding element sets the padding around the grid. To do that, the padding element uses an Insets element that contains top, left, bottom, and right attributes.

Next are the elements for the labels and text fields for the GUI. Here, each Label and TextField element has GridPane.columnIndex and GridPane.rowIndex attributes that indicate where the control is displayed. In addition, each Label element has a text attribute that specifies the text that it displays, and each TextField element has an fx:id attribute that specifies a name that uniquely identifies that text field. This attribute allows the controller to access this element.

Finally, the GridPane element contains an HBox element with two Button elements. The HBox element includes spacing and alignment attributes to set the space between the buttons in the HBox object and the alignment of the HBox object within the grid. It also includes GridPane.columnIndex and GridPane. rowIndex attributes to indicate where the pane should be displayed. And it includes GridPane.columnSpan and GridPane.rowSpan attributes to indicate that the pane spans two columns and one row.

Each Button element includes a text attribute that specifies the text that's displayed on the control. In addition, each button includes an onAction attribute that specifies the event handler that's executed when the button is clicked. You'll see the code for these event handlers in a minute. For now, just realize that you have to precede the name of the event handler with a hashtag (#).

Now that you've seen the FXML file for this application, you might want to compare it to the Java code in figure 17-10 that defines the GUI. If you do, you should see some similarities between the elements and attributes in the FXML file and the constructors and methods in the Java code. So once you learn how to use Java code to develop a GUI, you shouldn't have much trouble using FXML.

The FXML file

```xml
<?xml version="1.0" encoding="UTF-8"?>

<?import javafx.scene.layout.*?>
<?import javafx.scene.control.*?>
<?import javafx.geometry.Insets?>

<GridPane xmlns:fx="http://javafx.com/fxml"
          fx:controller="murach.ui.FutureValueController"
          alignment="TOP_CENTER" hgap="10" vgap="10">
    <padding>
        <Insets top="25" left="25" bottom="25" right="25"/>
    </padding>

    <!-- Monthly investment -->
    <Label text="Monthly Investment:"
        GridPane.columnIndex="0" GridPane.rowIndex="0"/>
    <TextField fx:id="investmentField"
        GridPane.columnIndex="1" GridPane.rowIndex="0" />

    <!-- Yearly interest rate -->
    <Label text="Yearly Interest Rate:"
        GridPane.columnIndex="0" GridPane.rowIndex="1"/>
    <TextField fx:id="interestRateField"
        GridPane.columnIndex="1" GridPane.rowIndex="1"/>

    <!-- number of years -->
    <Label text="Years:"
        GridPane.columnIndex="0" GridPane.rowIndex="2"/>
    <TextField fx:id="yearsField"
        GridPane.columnIndex="1" GridPane.rowIndex="2"/>

    <!-- Future value -->
    <Label text="Future Value:"
        GridPane.columnIndex="0" GridPane.rowIndex="3"/>
    <TextField fx:id="futureValueField" editable="false"
            GridPane.columnIndex="1" GridPane.rowIndex="3"/>

    <!-- Buttons -->
    <HBox spacing="10" alignment="bottom_right"
        GridPane.columnIndex="0" GridPane.rowIndex="4"
        GridPane.columnSpan="2" GridPane.rowSpan="1" >
        <Button text="Calculate" onAction="#calculateButtonClicked"/>
        <Button text="Exit" onAction="#exitButtonClicked"/>
    </HBox>

</GridPane>
```

Figure 17-17   The FXML file for the Future Value application

The controller class

Figure 17-18 shows the controller class for the Future Value application. This class starts by importing some classes, including the JavaFX classes it needs. Then, it declares the class. Note that the package for this class (murach.ui) and the name of this class (FutureValueController) match the package and name that's specified by the fx:controller attribute of the GridPane element you saw in the previous figure. That's how the FXML file identifies the controller it uses.

Within the controller class, the first four statements declare private TextField instance variables. These variables have names that match the names specified by the fx:id attributes of the TextField elements in the FXML file. In addition, these fields are marked with the @FXML annotation. As a result, when the application starts, it creates the TextField objects defined by the FXML file and assigns those objects to these variables.

Next, this class defines two event handler methods that have the same names as the values of the onAction attributes of the Button elements in the FXML file. Like the private instance variables, these methods are marked with the @FXML annotation. As a result, Java executes these methods when the user clicks the corresponding buttons.

The code for these event handlers is the same as the code shown earlier in this chapter. To save space, this figure doesn't show the code for the calculateButtonClicked() method. However, this code uses the first three TextField variables to get input from the user, and it uses the fourth TextField variable to display the future value to the user.

The application class

This figure also shows the class that defines and starts the Future Value application. This class starts by importing some classes it needs, including the FXMLLoader class that's used to create the Java objects from the FXML file.

Within the start() method, the first statement uses the static load() method of the FXMLLoader object to load the Java objects from the FXML file. This creates a hierarchy of the objects declared in the FXML file, and it connects those objects to the controller file. Then, the rest of this code sets those objects as the scene and displays that scene on the stage.

The controller class

```
package murach.ui;

import java.text.NumberFormat;
import javafx.fxml.FXML;
import javafx.scene.control.TextField;
import murach.business.FinancialCalculations;

public class FutureValueController {
    @FXML private TextField investmentField;
    @FXML private TextField interestRateField;
    @FXML private TextField yearsField;
    @FXML private TextField futureValueField;

    @FXML
    protected void calculateButtonClicked() {
        // same event handling code as shown in figure 17-10
    }

    @FXML
    protected void exitButtonClicked() {
        System.exit(0);    // 0 indicates a normal exit
    }
}
```

The application class

```
package murach.ui;

import javafx.application.Application;
import javafx.fxml.FXMLLoader;
import javafx.scene.Parent;
import javafx.scene.Scene;
import javafx.stage.Stage;

public class FutureValueApplication extends Application {

    @Override
    public void start(Stage stage) throws Exception {
        Parent root = FXMLLoader.load(getClass().getResource(
                "FutureValue.fxml"));
        Scene scene = new Scene(root);
        stage.setScene(scene);
        stage.setTitle("Future Value Calculator");
        stage.show();
    }

    public static void main(String[] args) {
        launch(args);
    }
}
```

Figure 17-18   The Java classes for the Future Value application

Perspective

In this chapter, you learned how to use the JavaFX API to build a GUI version of the Future Value application. This application uses some of the most common controls that are available from the JavaFX API, including labels, text fields, and buttons. In the next chapter, you'll learn how to use the Swing API to build the same application.

In addition, this chapter showed the basic skills for using FXML to define the layout for the GUI while still using Java to handle the events that occur when the user interacts with the application. This has the advantage of separating the code that defines the layout of the application from the code that defines its functionality. Once you get used to writing FXML, you might find that you prefer using it to define the appearance of a GUI.

Now that you know how to write this kind of code by hand, you might want to try using a graphical tool to define the layout for a JavaFX GUI by dragging and dropping controls onto a form. For example, you might want to try using the Scene Builder plugin that's available for both NetBeans and Eclipse. Keep in mind, though, that there are some downsides to using a graphical tool. First, you don't have as much control over the code because it's generated for you. Second, when you use a graphical tool, the FXML that's generated by the tool is often hard for developers to read and maintain. As a result, if the tool ever becomes obsolete, it may become difficult to maintain your code.

Summary

- A *graphical user interface,* or *GUI,* makes it easier for users to interact with an application. You can use several libraries to create a GUI, including AWT, Swing, SWT, and JavaFX.

- With JavaFX, the main window is knows as a *stage,* and the container that holds all the content is knows as a *scene.* Each scene has a root element, which is usually one of the layout manager controls.

- You use the GridPane layout manager to lay out controls in a grid. You use the Insets class to set the padding for a grid and the ColumnConstraints class to set the width of the columns in a grid.

- You use the Label class to create *labels* that identify other controls.

- You use the TextField class to create *text fields,* also known as *text boxes,* that allow a user to enter data.

- You use the Button class to create *buttons* that the user can click. It's common to add a row of buttons to a pane such as an HBox.

- You use the setOnAction() method of a control to register an *event handler* that's executed when an *event* occurs on a control, such as the user clicking a button.

- An event handler is an object that's created from the EventHandler class. This class includes a handle() method that must be overridden so it contains the code that's executed when the event occurs.

- You can use the Alert class to display messages to the user in dialog boxes.

- *XML (Extensible Markup Language)* provides a way to structure data by using *tags* to identify each data element.

- An *element* in an XML document can contain a *start tag*, *content*, and an *end tag*. An element can also contain other elements, and a start tag can contain *attributes*.

- FXML is an XML-based markup language that you can use to define the GUI for a JavaFX application.

Exercise 17-1   Create a JavaFX application

In this exercise, you'll code a JavaFX application that calculates the miles per gallon of a trip. When you're done, the application should look like this:

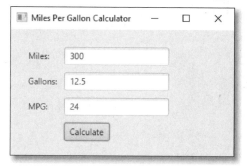

Open the project and review the code

1. Open the project named ch17_ex1_MPGFX in the ex_starts directory. This project contains some starting code for a new JavaFX application.

2. Review the code in the MPGApplication.java file, and notice that it includes a number of import statements needed by JavaFX. Also notice that the MPGApplication class inherits the Application class and overrides its start() method. In addition, the main() method calls the launch() method of the Application class to start the application.

3. Run the project and click the button in the GUI to see that a "Hello World" message is displayed. Then, close the application by clicking the "X" in the upper right corner.

Add the code for the layout

4. Modify the code for the start() method so it uses a GridPane instead of a StackPane. Then, add the three labels and three text fields before the button as shown above, and modify the text for the button. Be sure to include the column and row index for each control, and make the third text field read-only.

5. Run the project to see how it looks. Then, close the application.

6. Align the GridPane at the top center of the scene. In addition, add 25 pixels of padding between the grid and the edges of the window, and add 10 pixels of space between the rows and columns in the grid.

7. Run the project again to see how these changes affect the layout. Then, close the application.

Handle the events that occur when the user clicks the buttons

8. Find the event handler for the button and notice that it uses an anonymous class. Change the handle() method for this class so it gets the values from the miles and gallons text fields, calculates the miles per gallon, and then displays it in the read-only text field.

9. Run the project and test it with valid data. When you're done, close the application.

Exercise 17-2   Work with an FXML application

In this exercise, you'll make modifications to another version of the MPG application that uses FXML to define its GUI. When you're done, the application should look like this:

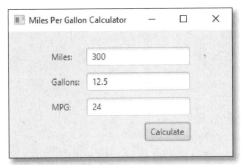

Open the project and review the code

1. Open the project named c17_ex2_MPGFXML in the ex_starts directory. Review the code in the FXML file to see that the root element is a GridPane.

2. Open the application class. Then, run the project to see that there's no space between the grid and the scene that contains it and there's not enough space between the controls. Close the application by clicking on the "X" in the upper right corner.

3. Change the grid so it's centered in the window and so the spacing between the rows and columns in the grid is 10 pixels. Then, run the project to see how this looks.

4. Perform a calculation, and then click in the MPG text field to see that you can change the text for that field. Then, change the MPG text field so it's a read-only field.

5. Add the button to an HBox element that will display the button at the bottom right of the HBox object. For this to work, the HBox object will need to span both columns. Run the project one more time to make sure this works.

18

How to get started with Swing

In the previous chapter, you learned the basics of developing a graphical user interface (GUI) with JavaFX. In this chapter, you'll learn the basics of developing a GUI with Swing. Although Swing is older than JavaFX, it's more widely-used than JavaFX. As a result, in the real world, you are most likely to encounter Swing, especially if you need to maintain legacy applications.

An introduction to GUI programming

The first two figures in this chapter present some terminology and concepts that are helpful to understand before you begin writing GUIs. If you read the previous chapter, you should already be familiar with most of this terminology and many of these concepts. Of course, there are a few differences between Swing and JavaFX.

A user interface with ten controls

Figure 18-1 presents the graphical user interface for the Future Value Calculator application that's presented in this chapter. In this figure, the GUI window, also known as a *form*, contains ten controls: four *labels*, four *text fields* (also called *text boxes*), and two *buttons*. Here, the fourth text field has been modified so it can display output but it can't accept input from the user.

A summary of GUI APIs

If you want to use Java to develop a GUI, you can choose from several APIs, which are often called *toolkits*. This figure shows the most common ones, though there are others available as well.

AWT (*Abstract Window Toolkit*) was the first GUI toolkit for Java. AWT allows you to create native operating system *components* (also known as *controls* or *widgets*). However, this approach has several limitations and is not recommended for modern application development.

To address the shortcomings of AWT, Java 2 included a toolkit named *Swing*. Swing is built on top of AWT, but creates its own components instead of using the ones provided by the operating system. In its early days, Swing was slow and inefficient. In addition, the early Swing components didn't look good and they didn't look like native components. Today, Swing performs much better, and, modern themes provided with Java can make Swing applications look like native applications.

To compete with early versions of Swing, IBM created *SWT* (*Standard Widget Toolkit*). Like AWT, SWT uses native components, which improves its speed. However, it's not as powerful as Swing without the addition of more libraries. As a result, Swing became more widely used.

JavaFX is the newest framework for developing GUIs. This API is designed to replace the aging Swing API for developing desktop applications. In addition, it's designed to make it easier to create *rich Internet applications* (*RIAs*), which are web applications that have many of the characteristics of desktop applications.

A Swing GUI that displays 10 controls

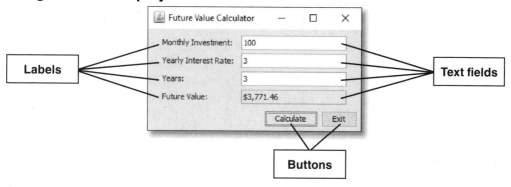

Common GUI libraries for Java

Library	Description
AWT	Abstract Window Toolkit. This is the oldest Java GUI library. It uses the native controls from the operating system. This library is not recommended for modern application development due to problems with cross-platform portability.
Swing	Created to replace AWT and fix the cross-platform portability problems. Swing controls are not native, but they can use themes to look like native controls. Most modern Java GUIs are written using Swing.
SWT	Standard Widget Toolkit. This library was created by IBM to fix performance problems and the non-native look and feel of earlier versions of Swing. This library uses native controls. However, it's not as powerful as Swing without adding more libraries.
JavaFX	Designed to replace the aging Swing library for developing GUIs for desktop applications and to make it easier to develop rich Internet applications (RIAs), which are web applications that have many of the characteristics of a desktop application.

Description

- When creating GUIs, you typically use a *window* to display *controls* such as *labels*, *text fields*, and *buttons*.

- A window is also known as a *form*, controls are also known as *components* or *widgets*, and a text field is also known as a *text box*.

- When creating GUIs with Java, you have several possible libraries that you can use. Of these libraries, JavaFX is the newest. However, Swing is the most widely used.

Figure 18-1   An introduction to GUI programming

The inheritance hierarchy for Swing components

Like all Java APIs, Swing is an object-oriented API, and the Swing classes exist in a hierarchy. Figure 18-2 shows a partial diagram of this hierarchy, along with some of its most common classes.

As mentioned in the previous figure, Swing builds on the older AWT framework. As a result, all Swing components ultimately inherit the abstract AWT Component and Container classes. In this diagram, all Swing classes begin with the letter J (for Java). This distinguishes them from AWT components with the same name. For example, Frame is an AWT component, and JFrame is a Swing component.

As this diagram shows, most Swing components inherit from the JComponent class. As a result, any method that accepts a JComponent object as a parameter accepts most Swing components. In this diagram, the exception is a JFrame component. This component inherits the Frame class, which inherits the Window class. Typically, an application uses a JFrame component to define its main window.

A *container* is a type of component that can hold other components. The diagram in this figure shows that all Swing components inherit from the Container class. As a result, all Swing components can act as a container to hold other components. That means it's possible for a JButton component to hold another JButton component. However, it's more common to use a container component such as a JFrame component to hold other components. Later in this chapter and in the next chapter, you'll learn about some other container components including the JPanel and JScrollPane components.

As a general rule, you should not mix AWT and Swing components. This typically results in bugs and display problems. For example, you should not put a JButton component inside a Frame object. Instead, you should put a JButton component inside a JFrame object.

The Swing inheritance hierarchy

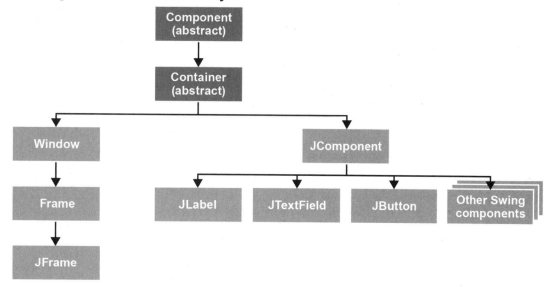

The package for most AWT classes
```
java.awt
```

The package for most Swing classes
```
javax.swing
```

A summary of these classes

Class	Description
Component	An abstract AWT class that defines any object that can be displayed. For instance, frames, panels, buttons, labels, and text fields are derived from this class.
Container	An abstract AWT class that defines any component that can contain other components.
Window	The AWT class that defines a window without a title bar or border.
Frame	The AWT class that defines a window with a title bar and border.
JFrame	The Swing class that defines a window with a title bar and border.
JComponent	A base class for Swing components such as JPanel, JButton, JLabel, and JTextField.
JPanel	The Swing class that defines a panel, which is used to hold other components.
JButton	The Swing class that defines a button.
JLabel	The Swing class that defines a label.
JTextField	The Swing class that defines a text field.

Description

- The Swing library is built upon the AWT library. In other words, Swing classes often inherit AWT classes.

- Most Swing classes begin with the letter J (for Java).

Figure 18-2   The inheritance hierarchy for Swing components

How to create a GUI that handles events

When you develop a GUI with Swing, you typically begin by displaying a *frame* that acts as the main window for the application. Then, you add components such as labels, text boxes, and buttons to the frame. Finally, you handle the events that occur when the user interacts with these components.

How to display a frame

A JFrame component has a border and contains all of the normal window controls for your operating system such as minimize, maximize, and close buttons. Figure 18-3 shows an example of an empty JFrame component along with the code that displays it. This shows what a frame looks like when displayed on Windows 10, but it would look appropriate for Mac OS or Linux if it was displayed on those operating systems.

To create a frame, you typically code a class that inherits the JFrame class. In this figure, for example, the code declares a class named FutureValueFrame that extends the JFrame class. This is a common practice since it allows you to store all the code that defines a frame within a single class.

The constructor of this class calls a method named initComponents() that initializes the frame and its components. To do that, it sets the title, size, and location of the frame. In addition, it sets the default close operation so the application exits if the user closes the window.

To set the title of the frame, you can call the setTitle() method and pass it the title of the frame.

To set the size of the frame, you can call the setSize() method. This method takes two integers that represent the width and height in pixels. In this figure, for example, the frame is set to a width of 400 pixels and a height of 100 pixels. You can also size a frame by calling the pack() method as described later in this chapter. This method takes no parameters and sizes the frame just large enough to hold all of the components it contains. If you don't set the size of the frame, you can't see any of the components it contains.

To set the location of the frame, you can pass a true value to the setLocationByPlatform() method. Then, the operating system determines the location of the frame, which is usually what you want.

To exit the application when the user clicks on the close button of a frame, you can call the setDefaultCloseOperation() method and pass it the EXIT_ON_CLOSE field of the JFrame class. If you don't do this and the user clicks the close button, the frame closes but the application continues running. That's because, by default, the close button only closes the frame, but doesn't end the application. Finally, to display the frame, you can call the setVisible() method and pass it a true value.

So far in this book, all of the applications have run on a single *thread* that's known as the *main thread*. This thread typically ends when the main() method

Common methods of the JFrame class

Method	Description
`setTitle(String)`	Sets the title of the frame to the specified string.
`setSize(width, height)`	Sets the size of the frame to the specified width and height.
`pack()`	Sizes the frame so it's just large enough to hold its components.
`setLocationByPlatform(boolean)`	If set to true, the operating system sets the location of the frame.
`setDefaultCloseOperation(operation)`	Set to the EXIT_ON_CLOSE field of the JFrame class to exit the application when the user clicks the close button of the frame.
`setVisible(boolean)`	Determines whether the frame is visible.

A class that creates and displays a frame

```java
import javax.swing.JFrame;

public class FutureValueFrame extends JFrame {

    public FutureValueFrame() {
        initComponents();
    }

    private void initComponents() {
        setTitle("Future Value Calculator");
        setSize(400, 100);
        setDefaultCloseOperation(JFrame.EXIT_ON_CLOSE);
        setLocationByPlatform(true);

        // other components go here

        setVisible(true);
    }

    public static void main(String args[]) {
        java.awt.EventQueue.invokeLater(new Runnable() {
            @Override
            public void run() {
                JFrame frame = new FutureValueFrame();
            }
        });
    }
}
```

The frame displayed by this class

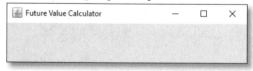

Description

- In Swing, a *frame* typically defines the main window of an application.

- Any code that runs in response to a Swing event runs on a special thread called the *event dispatch thread* or *EDT*.

Figure 18-3   How to work with frames

for the application ends. However, any code that runs in response to a Swing event runs on a special thread called the *event dispatch thread* or *EDT*. That way, the EDT continues running even after the code in the main() method finishes executing.

To make sure that the EDT works correctly, it's considered a best practice to add the code that displays the GUI to the event queue as shown by the main() method in figure 18-3. For now, you can code this method exactly as shown, changing the name of the class that defines the frame as necessary. Most IDEs generate code like this when you add a JFrame class to your project. In short, it creates a thread that displays the GUI. Then, it uses the static invokeLater() method of the EventQueue class to add this thread to the queue of events that are processed by the EDT. For more information about threads, please see chapter 23.

If you're using Java 8 or later, you can code such a main() method more concisely by using a lambda expression like this:

```
public static void main(String args[]) {
    java.awt.EventQueue.invokeLater(() -> {
        JFrame frame = new FutureValueFrame1();
    });
}
```

For more information about lambda expressions, please see chapter 22.

How to set the look and feel

Swing allows you to set the *look and feel* of its components. By default, Swing components use the Metal look and feel as shown by the window at the top of figure 18-4. This causes the Swing components to look and act the same on any operating system. However, these components look and act slightly differently than the components that are native to a particular operating system. In addition, the look and feel of the components on the window might not compliment the look and feel of the title bar. That's because the look and feel of the title bar depends on the operating system, even if you're using the Metal look and feel.

Before you display a frame, you can set the look and feel as shown in this figure. To do that, you can use the UIManager class that's available from the javax.swing package as shown in this figure. Here, the code sets the look and feel for the Swing components to the current operating system. As result, this application looks like a Windows application on the Windows operating system, a Mac application on the Mac operating system, and a Linux application on the Linux operating system.

The Metal look and feel on Windows 10

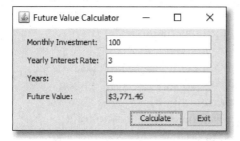

Code that sets the look and feel the same as the current operating system

```
try {
    UIManager.setLookAndFeel(
        UIManager.getSystemLookAndFeelClassName());
} catch (ClassNotFoundException | InstantiationException |
        IllegalAccessException | UnsupportedLookAndFeelException e) {
    System.out.println(e);
}
```

The Windows 10 look and feel

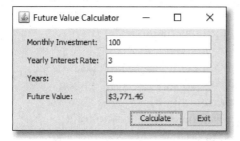

Description

- By default, Swing components use the Metal look and feel, which causes them to look and act the same on any operating system. The exception is the title bar for the frame, whose look and feel depends on the operating system.

- To set the look and feel to the default for the operating system, you call the setLookAndFeel() method of the UIManager class inside the try block of a try/catch statement.

Figure 18-4   How to set the look and feel

How to work with panels

Usually, the easiest way to build a GUI application is to use an invisible container known as a *panel* to group components. To do that with Swing, you can use the JPanel class. Then, you can add one or more panels to the frame.

Figure 18-5 shows an example of how to add a panel to a frame. To start, it creates a JPanel component named panel. Then, it calls the add() method of the frame that contains this code to add the panel to the frame. Since a panel is invisible, this doesn't display anything on the frame. To do that, you need to add one or more components to the panel.

How to work with buttons

The second example in figure 18-5 adds two buttons to the panel. To do that, it creates two buttons from the JButton class. Then, it uses the add() method of the panel to add the buttons to the panel.

To set the text that's displayed by a button, you can use the constructor of the JButton class that accepts the string to be displayed. Or, you can create the JButton component without passing a string and then call its setText() method. In this figure, the text for both buttons is set by the constructor of the JButton class.

The JButton class also provides some other commonly used methods. For example, you can use the setEnabled() method to disable a button and gray it out. If you want to disable an OK button until the user has filled in the required data, for instance, you can use this method. If you want to set a tooltip for a button, you can use the setToolTipText() method to do that. Then, the text you specify is displayed when the user hovers the mouse over an item for about one second.

A common method of the JFrame and JPanel classes

Method	Description
add(Component)	Adds the specified component to the frame or panel.

Common constructor and methods of the JButton class

Constructor	Description
JButton(String)	Creates a button and sets the text it displays.

Method	Description
setText(String)	Sets the text displayed by the button.
setEnabled(boolean)	Determines whether the button is enabled or disabled and grayed out.
setToolTipText(String)	Sets the text for the tooltip. If the user hovers the mouse over the button for about one second, the tooltip is displayed.

Code that adds a panel to a frame

```
JPanel panel = new JPanel();
add(panel);
```

Code that adds two buttons to a panel

```
JButton calculateButton = new JButton("Calculate");
JButton exitButton = new JButton("Exit");
panel.add(calculateButton);
panel.add(exitButton);
```

Two buttons in a panel

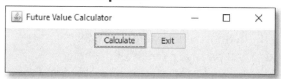

Description

- A *panel* is an invisible container that's used to group other components.
- To create a panel, you can create a JPanel object. Then, you can add it to a frame.
- To create a button, you can create a JButton object. Then, you can add it to a frame or a panel.
- You should add all of the panels and components to the frame before calling its setVisible() method. Otherwise, the user interface may flicker when it's first displayed.

Figure 18-5   How to work with panels and buttons

How to handle action events

The buttons displayed by the code in the previous figure don't do anything when you click on them. That's because there is nothing to handle the *event* that's generated by a button when it's clicked.

Each time the user interacts with your GUI, an event is fired. For example, when the user clicks on a button, an event is fired notifying your code that the button was clicked. An event is also fired each time the user presses a key on the keyboard or moves the mouse.

If you want to respond to an event, you need to register an *action listener*, or *event listener*, for the event. To do that, you use the addActionListener() method of the button to identify the object that handles the event, called an *event handler*. The event handler class must implement the ActionListener interface. This interface contains a single method named actionPerformed() that is executed when the specified event occurs.

The examples in figure 18-6 show how to respond to the user clicking on a button. In that case, an ActionEvent object is created and passed to the actionPerformed() method of the event handler. This ActionEvent object contains information about the event. However, in simple cases like this, you don't need that information. Instead, you just need to know that the button fired an ActionEvent.

Prior to Java 8, you could handle an action event by coding an *inner class* as shown in the first example. Although you can't tell here, the ExitButtonActionListener class is coded within the FutureValueFrame class. It implements the ActionListener interface, which has a method named actionPerformed() that receives the ActionEvent object. Then, this method contains a single statement that exits the application normally. Of course, this method could contain more complex code such as code that makes a calculation or updates a database.

To register the action listener with the button, the last statement calls the addActionListener() method of the button and passes an object of the inner class to it. Then, when the button is clicked, the actionPerformed() method is executed.

Prior to Java 8, the most common way to handle an ActionEvent was to use an *anonymous inner class*, as shown in the second example. Here, an anonymous class is coded within the parentheses of the addActionListener() method. This class is created from the ActionListener interface, and it includes a method named actionPerformed() that executes when the button is clicked. However, no name is provided for the class, which is why it's called an anonymous class.

With Java 8 and later, you can use a *lambda expression* instead of an anonymous class, as shown in the third example. In this case, the lambda expression is more concise and easier to understand than the anonymous inner class. For now, you can think of a lambda expression as an anonymous method that provides the parameters and code for the method, but no name. Then, if you want to learn more about lambda expressions, you can read chapter 22.

Now that you know how to handle the event that occurs when a user clicks a button, you should know that you can handle other events using similar techniques. You'll learn more about that in the next chapter.

The package that contains the events

```
java.awt.event
```

A common method of most components

Method	Description
`addActionListener(ActionEvent)`	Adds an event listener to a component such as a button so it can listen for and respond to events such as click events.

Three ways to add an action listener to a button

With an inner class (prior to Java 8)

```java
class ExitButtonActionListener implements ActionListener {
    @Override
    public void actionPerformed(ActionEvent e) {
        System.exit(0);    // exit the application normally
    }
}
exitButton.addActionListener(new ExitButtonActionListener());
```

With an anonymous class (prior to Java 8)

```java
exitButton.addActionListener(new ActionListener() {
    @Override
    public void actionPerformed(ActionEvent e) {
        System.exit(0);
    }
});
```

With a lambda expression (Java 8 and later)

```java
exitButton.addActionListener(e -> {
    System.exit(0);
});
```

Description

- To make a button do something when clicked, you add an *action listener* by calling its addActionListener() method.

- The addActionListener() method accepts an ActionListener object that includes an actionPerformed() method that accepts an ActionEvent object. Within the actionPerformed() method, you write the code that's executed when the button is clicked.

- An *inner class* is a class that's coded within another class.

- An *anonymous class* is an inner class that doesn't have a name. You can code the braces for an anonymous class immediately after the parentheses that create an object from the interface. Within the braces, you can supply the code that implements the interface.

- You can pass a *lambda expression* to the addActionListener() method. To code a lambda expression, you code the variable name for the ActionEvent object, followed by the *lambda operator* (->) and the code for the method.

- Prior to Java 8, it was common to use inner classes or anonymous inner classes to provide the code for an action listener. However, with Java 8 or later, you can use a lambda expression, which is cleaner and more concise.

Figure 18-6   How to handle action events

How to work with labels

Most applications use one or more *labels* to display text that identifies other controls. In figure 18-1, for example, the window contains four labels that label the four text fields. Now, figure 18-7 shows how to work with those labels.

The first example uses two statements to create a label and add it to a panel. Here, the first statement uses the constructor of the JLabel class to create a label and set its text to "Monthly Investment:". Then, the second statement adds the label to the panel.

The second example shows how to create a label and add it to a panel in a single statement. Here, the code doesn't create a variable that refers to the JLabel object. This is a common way of adding a label to a container if you don't need to call any methods of the JLabel class later.

The third example shows how to add four labels to a panel. Here, you can see that a panel displays these labels from left to right by default. Later in this chapter, you'll learn how to control the display of labels and other controls.

The fourth example shows how to use the setText() method of a label to change the text that's displayed by the label. Here, the label is named errorLabel, and the code sets its text to "Monthly Investment is a required entry." This is a common way to display error messages in the main window of a GUI.

Although the labels in this figure display text, a label can also display an icon or an image. However, using labels to display icons and images isn't covered in this book.

Common constructors and a method of the JLabel class

Constructor	Description
`JLabel()`	Creates a JLabel object.
`JLabel(String)`	Creates a JLabel object and sets the text displayed by the label to the specified string.

Method	Description
`setText(String)`	Sets the text displayed by the label to the specified string.

How to create a JLabel object and add it to a container

```
JLabel investmentLabel = new JLabel("Monthly Investment:");
panel.add(investmentLabel)
```

A common way of adding a JLabel to a container

```
panel.add(new JLabel("Monthly Investment:"));
```

Code that adds four labels to a panel

```
panel.add(new JLabel("Monthly Investment:"));
panel.add(new JLabel("Yearly Interest Rate:"));
panel.add(new JLabel("Years:"));
panel.add(new JLabel("Future Value:"));
```

The resulting window

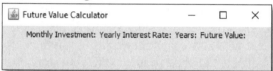

Code that changes the text that's displayed on a label

```
errorLabel.setText("Monthly Investment is a required entry.");
```

Description

- A JLabel component defines a *label*, which is a non-editable component that typically displays text that identifies other components such as text fields.
- If you know that you won't need to call any methods from a JLabel object, it's a common practice to call the constructor of the JLabel class from within an add() method. When you use this technique, no variable is created to refer to the JLabel object.
- A JLabel object can also display an image. However, that's not covered in this book.

Figure 18-7   How to work with labels

How to work with text fields

Most applications use one or more *text fields*, also known as *text boxes*, to allow the user to enter data. The JTextField class defines a text field that allows the user to enter or edit text. In addition, a programmer can use a text field to display text to the user.

Figure 18-8 summarizes some of the most common constructors and methods of the JTextField class. Then, it presents some examples that use these constructors and methods.

The first example creates a new text field named investmentField that's approximately 20 characters wide. This means that the width of the text field depends on the font size for the text field. Another way to do this is to use the first constructor in this figure to create a text field without specifying the number of columns it contains. Then, you can use the setColumns() method to set the number of columns.

Unfortunately, setting the size of a text field by setting the number of columns doesn't always work correctly. Another way to set the size of a text field—or any other component—is to use the setPreferredSize() and setMinimumSize() methods, which set the width in pixels. These methods have their problems too, though. But they can be used to fix a common problem that occurs when laying out components in a grid. You'll see this technique later in this chapter.

The second and third examples show how to get and set the text that's stored in a text field. Here, the second example uses the getText() method of the text field to get the string that's stored in a text field and assign it to a String variable. Conversely, the third example uses the setText() method of the text field to store the specified string in a text field.

By default, a text field is editable. As a result, the user can enter text into it or edit the text that's already in it. However, if you want to create a read-only text field, you can pass a false value to its setEditable() method as shown in the fourth example. Then, the user can't enter text into the field and can only read the text that's displayed by the field.

So, why wouldn't you use a label if you want to display text that users can't edit? One reason is that users can select and copy text from a read-only text field. This is useful if you want to display some text to users that they can copy to the clipboard and paste somewhere else, but you don't want them to be able to edit the text. For example, you might want to allow users to copy and paste an exception stack trace into an email to help the programmer debug a problem.

The setEnabled() method works similarly to the setEditable() method as shown in the fifth example. However, it also grays out the text in the field and doesn't allow selecting or copying text from the field. This is useful if you want to prevent users from entering data into a text field until after they have completed other steps.

Common constructors and methods of the JTextField class

Constructor	Description
JTextField()	Creates a text field.
JTextField(int)	Creates a text field with the specified number of columns (characters).

Method	Description
getText(String)	Gets the text contained by the text field.
setText(String)	Sets the text displayed by the text field.
setColumns(int)	Sets the width of the text field to the specified number of columns (characters). Many layout managers ignore this setting.
setEditable(boolean)	Determines whether the user can edit the text or not.
setEnabled(boolean)	Determines whether the text field is enabled. If set to false, the text field is disabled and grayed out so the user can't change the text in it.

How to create a text box for approximately 20 characters

```
JTextField investmentField = new JTextField(20);
```

How to get text from a text box

```
String investment = investmentField.getText();
```

How to set text in a text box

```
futureValueField.setText("$3,771.46");
```

How to create a read-only text box

```
futureValueField.setEditable(false);
```

How to disable a text box

```
futureValueField.setEnabled(false);
```

Code that adds two labels and two text fields

```
panel.add(new JLabel("Monthly Investment:"));
JTextField investmentField = new JTextField(20);
panel.add(investmentField);

panel.add(new JLabel("Years:"));
JTextField yearsField = new JTextField(10);
panel.add(yearsField);
```

The resulting window

Description

- A JTextField component defines a *text field* that displays text to the user and allows the user to enter text. This type of component is also known as a *text box*.

Figure 18-8   How to work with text fields

How to work with layout managers

In the old days of GUI design, it was common to place non-resizable components wherever you wanted them. This type of layout is known as fixed width layout. Although fixed width layout is quick and easy, it causes several problems. For example, if the window is resized, the components inside it don't resize with it, which means it's possible for components to disappear outside the boundaries of the window. Furthermore, if the user's operating system uses a different font size, it's possible for components to end up on top of each other or hidden underneath other components. To address this problem, most modern GUI APIs, including Swing, use a concept known as *layout managers* as described in the topics that follow.

A summary of layout managers

Java provides several built-in layout managers such as the ones summarized in figure 18-9. Some are easy to use, but are not flexible. Others are harder to use, but are flexible and can produce complex layouts. Still others are intended primarily for use by GUI tools that generate GUI code for programmers rather than for use by programmers who are coding by hand. In addition, several third-party layout managers are available for free that might be easier to use for some tasks.

This chapter shows how to use three of the most common layout managers included with Java: FlowLayout, BorderLayout, and GridBagLayout. The Future Value application presented in this chapter uses all three of these layout managers.

By default, a JFrame component uses the BorderLayout manager, and a JPanel component uses the FlowLayout manager. If the default layout manager provided by a container doesn't suit your needs, you can change it to a different one by calling the container's setLayout() method as shown by the example in this figure. This code changes the layout manager of the frame from its default of BorderLayout to FlowLayout instead.

The package that contains the layout managers

```
java.awt
```

A summary of layout managers

Manager	Description
BorderLayout	Lays out components by providing five areas that can each hold one component. The five areas are north, south, east, west, and center.
FlowLayout	Lays out components by flowing them from left to right, or right to left, similar to words on a page.
GridBagLayout	Lays out components in a rectangular grid of cells. Can be used to create more complex and flexible layouts than some of the other layout managers.
GridLayout	Lays out components in a rectangular grid of cells where each cell is the same size.
CardLayout	Lays out components on a card where only one card is visible at a time. This layout is rarely used, but can be useful for creating wizard dialogs that guide the user through a step-by-step procedure.
BoxLayout	Lays out components in a horizontal or vertical row of cells. This layout is rarely used, but it can be useful for producing rows of buttons.

A common method of most container components

Method	Description
setLayout(layout)	Sets the layout to the specified layout manager.

How to change a container's layout manager

```
JFrame frame = new JFrame();
frame.setLayout(new FlowLayout());
```

Description

- A *layout manager* determines how your components are placed in the container and how they behave if the container is resized or if the font size changes.
- By default, a JFrame uses the BorderLayout manager.
- By default, a JPanel uses the FlowLayout manager.

Figure 18-9   A summary of layout managers

How to use the FlowLayout manager

Of the three layout managers presented in this book, the FlowLayout manager is the easiest to use. It adds components in a row and aligns the components according to the alignment parameter. By default, the FlowLayout manager centers components. However, it's also possible to specify left or right alignment.

The first example in figure 18-10 calls a panel's setLayout() method and passes it a new instance of the FlowLayout manager with its alignment set to left. As a result, this code changes the alignment of the layout from its default of center to left.

After setting the layout manager, this code adds four buttons to the panel. As a result, the layout manager arranges these buttons from left to right in the same order that the code added them to the panel.

If there isn't enough space in the container to hold all of the components, FlowLayout wraps the components to the next row. This is similar to how a word processor wraps text when it reaches the right margin. Once again, the layout manager arranges the components according to the specified alignment.

A common constructor of the FlowLayout class

Constructor	Description
`FlowLayout(alignment)`	Sets the horizontal alignment of this manager. To set this alignment, you can specify the LEFT, RIGHT, or CENTER constant of the FlowLayout class.

How to set the layout for a container

```
panel.setLayout(new FlowLayout(FlowLayout.LEFT));
```

Code that adds four buttons to a panel

```
panel.add(new JButton("Add"));
panel.add(new JButton("Edit"));
panel.add(new JButton("Delete"));
panel.add(new JButton("Cancel"));
```

The FlowLayout when all components fit on one line

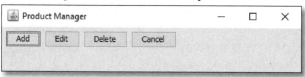

The FlowLayout when components wrap to the next line

Description

- If the components don't fit on one line, the FlowLayout manager wraps the components to a new line.

- The FlowLayout manager can align components to the left, right, or center. The default is center.

Figure 18-10   How to work with the FlowLayout manager

How to use the BorderLayout manager

The BorderLayout manager has five areas: north, south, east, west, and center. Each of these areas can hold a single component.

Figure 18-11 shows a frame that uses the BorderLayout manager to display one button in each of the five areas. Since BorderLayout is the default layout manager for a frame, the example in this figure doesn't set the layout manager. Instead, it adds a new button to the north area of the frame by calling the add() method of the frame. To do that, it passes the component as the first argument and the area as the second argument. Here, the component is a new JButton component that says "North", and the BorderLayout.NORTH constant specifies the north area. This causes the layout manager to size this component horizontally to fill the entire width of the frame and vertically to its preferred height, which is the height of a button.

In a similar fashion, this code adds a new button to the south area of the frame. Like the north area, the layout manager sizes the component horizontally to fill the entire width of the frame and vertically to its preferred height.

After adding a button to the north and sound areas, this code adds a button to the east and west areas. In this case, the layout manager sizes these components to fill all of the vertical space between the north and south areas. In addition, it sizes these components to their preferred width, which is the width of a button.

Finally, the code adds a button to the center area of the frame. In this case, the layout manager sizes this component both vertically and horizontally to fill any remaining space not used by the components in the other areas.

If you resize this window, the layout manager adjusts the size of the components in each area. The north and south components resize horizontally to fill the new space, but their height remains the same. The east and west components resize vertically to fill the new space, but their width remains the same. And the center component resizes to fill any remaining space.

If you don't provide a component for one or more of the areas in the BorderLayout, that area has a size of zero. For example, if you remove the button from the east area, the east area has a size of 0. As a result, the component in the center expands to the right edge of the frame.

The BorderLayout manager is often used to lay out the main window of an application. For example, suppose you were writing an email client. You might use the north area as a toolbar, the west area to hold a list of folders, the center area to hold the list of emails, and the south area to hold a status bar. In this case, you might not use the east area.

When working with the BorderLayout manager, it's important to remember that each area can only hold one component. As a result, if you want to add multiple components, you need to group those buttons into a panel before you add them. For example, if you want to add a toolbar with multiple buttons, you need to group those buttons into a panel (probably using FlowLayout for that panel) and then add the panel to the north area of the BorderLayout.

A common method of the BorderLayout class

Method	Description
add(component, area)	Adds the specified component to the specified area. To set the area, you can specify the NORTH, SOUTH, EAST, WEST, or CENTER constant of the BorderLayout class.

Code that adds a button to each area of a BorderLayout

```
add(new JButton("North"), BorderLayout.NORTH);
add(new JButton("South"), BorderLayout.SOUTH);
add(new JButton("East"), BorderLayout.EAST);
add(new JButton("West"), BorderLayout.WEST);
add(new JButton("Center"), BorderLayout.CENTER);
```

The resulting BorderLayout

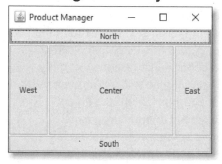

Description

- A BorderLayout has five areas: NORTH, SOUTH, EAST, WEST, and CENTER.
- The default area is CENTER. As a result, if you don't specify the area, the component is added to the center.
- The NORTH and SOUTH areas get their preferred height, which usually means they are tall enough to hold whatever is placed in them. The widths of these areas are set to the width of the frame, and the widths expand or contract as the width of the window changes.
- The WEST and EAST areas get their preferred width, which usually means they are wide enough to hold whatever is placed in them. The heights of these areas are set to the height of the frame, and the heights expand or contract as the height of the window changes.
- The CENTER area gets whatever space is left over, and the height and width expand or contract as the window is resized.
- Each area of a BorderLayout can only hold one component. If you need to add multiple components to an area, you can add them to a panel and then add the panel to the area.

Figure 18-11   How to work with the BorderLayout manager

How to use the GridBagLayout manager

The GridBagLayout manager is more complicated than the layout managers described in the previous figures. However, it's also more powerful and more flexible. With the GridBagLayout manager, you can lay out components in a grid of rows and columns.

Figure 18-12 shows how to use a GridBagConstraints object to control the layout of components inside a container that uses the GridBagLayout manager. This figure starts by showing some fields of the GridBagConstraints class.

To start, the gridx and gridy fields control the position on the grid where the component is placed. In this figure, for example, both the gridx and gridy fields are set to a value of 0 for the "Monthly Investment:" label. As a result, the layout manager places this label in the cell at the top left corner of the grid.

The first text field has a gridx value of 1 and a gridy value of 0. As a result, the layout manager places this text field in the cell that's at the intersection of the second column and the first row. The second text field has a gridx value of 1 and a gridy value of 1. As a result, the layout manager places this label in the cell at the intersection of the second row and the second column. And so on.

The anchor field controls where the layout manager places the component within the cell if the cell is larger than the component. By default, the layout manager places the component in the center of the cell. However, you can specify an anchor value of LINE_START to align the component with the left side of the cell. Or, you can use an anchor value of LINE_END to align the component with the right side of the cell. In this figure, for example, all of the labels and text fields, except for the last label, have an anchor field that's set to the LINE_START value.

Although LINE_START and LINE_END are two of the most common values for the anchor field, many other possible values exist. To view a complete list, see the API documentation for the anchor field.

The LINE_START and LINE_END values are relatively new to Java. Prior to their introduction, developers commonly used the WEST and EAST values instead. However, for new development, it's recommended that you use the newer LINE_START and LINE_END values because they're easier to understand.

The gridwidth and gridheight fields determine how many cells the component takes up. As a result, setting the gridwidth field to 2 causes a component to take up two horizontal cells rather than one. In this figure, for example, the fourth label takes up two horizontal cells rather than one.

The code example begins by using the setLayout() method to set the layout manager for the panel to the GridBagLayout manager. Then, this code creates a new GridBagConstraints object. In practice, it's common to use the variable named c for this, so that's what this code does.

After creating the GridBagConstraints object, this code sets the anchor field to LINE_START. Then, it sets the gridx and gridy fields of the GridBagConstraints object for each component, and it adds each component to the panel. To do that, it passes the component as the first argument and the GridBagConstraints object as the second argument.

Fields of the GridBagConstraints class for controlling layout

Field	Description
`gridx, gridy`	Sets the x and y coordinates of the component in the grid where 0, 0 is the top left cell of the grid.
`anchor`	Sets where the component is displayed if the component is smaller than the cell that is its display area. The most commonly used are LINE_START and LINE_END. In older versions of Java, these were called WEST and EAST.
`gridwidth, gridheight`	Sets the number of horizontal and vertical cells that the component occupies.

Code that uses a GridBagConstraints object to control layout

```
panel.setLayout(new GridBagLayout());

GridBagConstraints c = new GridBagConstraints();
c.anchor = GridBagConstraints.LINE_START;

c.gridx = 0; c.gridy = 0;
panel.add(new JLabel("Monthly Investment:"), c);

c.gridx = 1; c.gridy = 0;
panel.add(investmentField, c);

c.gridx = 0; c.gridy = 1;
panel.add(new JLabel("Yearly Interest Rate:"), c);

c.gridx = 1; c.gridy = 1;
panel.add(interestRateField, c);

c.gridx = 0; c.gridy = 2;
panel.add(new JLabel("Years:"), c);

c.gridx = 1; c.gridy = 2;
panel.add(yearsField, c);

c.gridx = 0; c.gridy = 3;
c.gridwidth = 2;
c.anchor = GridBagConstraints.LINE_END;
panel.add(new JLabel ("This right-aligned label spans both columns."), c);
```

The resulting grid

Description

- You can reuse the same GridBagConstraints object for multiple components. However, you must reset any values you don't want to use in the next component.

Figure 18-12   How to work with the GridBagLayout manager

In addition to the gridx and gridy fields, this code resets the anchor field and sets the gridwidth component before adding the last component. That way, the component takes up both columns and is aligned at the right rather than the left.

When you reuse a GridBagConstraints object like this, it's easy to view and edit the coordinates and alignment of each component. However, if you forget to reset values, you may end up accidentally reusing the values that were set for a previous component, which may cause strange layout behavior. As a result, you need to make sure to set all values correctly for each component. Alternatively, you can create a new GridBagConstraint object for each component.

How to add padding to a GridBagLayout

By default, a GridBagConstraints object doesn't provide any space, or *padding*, between the components in the grid or between components and the edge of the container. That's why the components displayed in the previous figure don't have any padding between them. And that's why there's no padding between the components and the edge of the container.

To make this layout more visually appealing, you can use the insets field of the GridBagConstraints object to apply some padding as shown in figure 18-13. This field uses an Insets object to determine the amount of padding around a component. Here, the four parameters of the Insets object are the top, left, bottom, and right padding in pixels. If you think of a clock, these values are in a counterclockwise direction, starting at the top of the clock.

In this figure, the insets field of the GridBagConstraints object is set to an Insets object that specifies 5 pixels of padding for the top, left, and right of the component and no padding for the bottom of the component. However, the last component uses an Insets object that specifies 5 pixels of padding for all four sides. As a result, the last component doesn't touch the bottom of the window.

When working with an Insets object, there are two important things to remember. First, unlike a GridBagConstraints object, you can't change the values of an Insets object and then reuse it. If you do, it causes your layout to behave strangely. Second, if you set 5 pixels of top spacing and 5 pixels of bottom spacing, the spacing between components is actually 10 pixels. In other words, the layout uses five pixels of space at the bottom of one component and five pixels of space at the top of the component in the next row for a total of 10 pixels. The same thing is true with left and right spacing.

Most of the time, you only need to use the insets field of the GridBagConstraints object to specify external padding. However, if you need to specify internal padding, you can use the ipadx and ipady fields shown in this figure. These fields determine how much padding is placed inside the component. For example, if you set the ipadx and ipady values of a JButton component to 10, the layout displays 10 pixels of padding between the text of the JButton component and the edges of the button.

Fields of the GridBagConstraints class for controlling padding

Field	Description
`insets`	Uses an Insets object to specify how much external padding should be applied to the components within the grid.
`ipadx, ipady`	Sets how much internal padding to add to the width and height of the component. The value applies to both sides.

The constructor of the Insets class

Constructor	Description
`Insets(top, left, bottom, right)`	Specifies the top, left, bottom, and right padding in pixels.

Code that uses an Insets object to add padding to a GridBagConstraints object

```
GridBagConstraints c = new GridBagConstraints();
c.anchor = GridBagConstraints.LINE_START;
c.insets = new Insets(5, 5, 0, 5);

// the code that adds the first three labels and text boxes

c.gridx = 0; c.gridy = 3;
c.gridwidth = 2;
c.anchor = GridBagConstraints.LINE_END;
c.insets = new Insets(5, 5, 5, 5);
panel.add(new JLabel ("This label spans both columns."), c);
```

The resulting grid

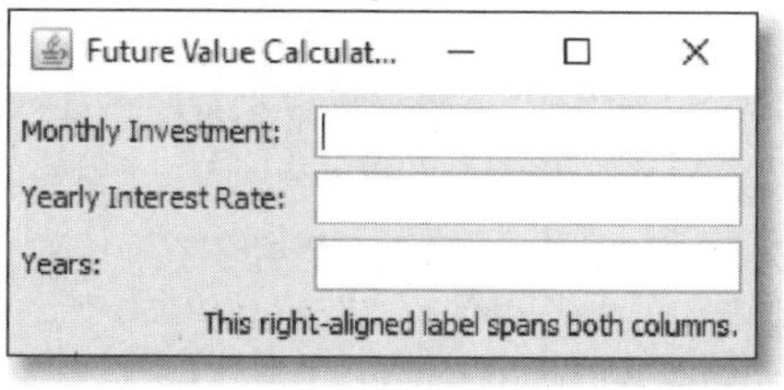

Description

- If you forget the order of the parameters for the constructor of the Insets class, it may help to remember that they start at the top and go counterclockwise.

Figure 18-13   How to add padding to a GridBagLayout

How to solve a common problem with the GridBagLayout

Figure 18-14 demonstrates a common problem with the GridBagLayout and shows how to avoid it. To start, this figure shows the same window shown in the previous figure after a user resizes it by shrinking its horizontal width slightly. This causes all of the text fields to collapse. What's going on here?

Basically, if the container isn't wide enough to display the component at its specified size, the GridBagLayout manager assigns the minimum size to the component instead. By default, a component has a minimum size of 0. As a result, this causes the width of the text fields to completely collapse.

One common way to solve this problem is to use the setPreferredSize() and setMinimumSize() methods on the text fields to set the preferred and minimum sizes to the same value as shown in this figure. Here, the first statement creates a new Dimension object that's 100 pixels wide and 20 pixels tall. Then, the next six statements set the preferred and minimum sizes of three text fields to that Dimension object.

If you run this code now and shrink the width of the window, the text fields don't collapse. However, the labels begin to collapse as the GridBagLayout manager tries to give the text fields their minimum size and still stay within the window. If you continue to press the issue by shrinking the window even further, the edges of the text fields eventually disappear outside the window.

Because the labels start collapsing, you might say that we solved one problem, but created another. In some ways, that's true. And this shows that the GridBagLayout manager is complex and often requires a lot of tweaking to get a layout to behave exactly as intended.

For the Future Value application, the user is unlikely to need to resize this window. As a result, the solution described in this figure is probably adequate.

Another possible solution to this problem is to prevent users from resizing the window. To do that, you can call the setResizable() method of the window and pass it a value of false. Again, for the Future Value application, this solution is acceptable. However, you should use this technique with caution as most users expect to be able to resize a window, especially if it helps the window fit better on their display.

There is a third possible solution that's more elegant but also more difficult to code. This solution involves using the weightx, weighty, and fill fields of the GridBagConstraints object to control how the components are resized when the user resizes a window. The weightx and weighty fields control how to distribute any extra horizontal or vertical space among the components. This allows you to specify a percentage for each component. In addition, the fill field determines whether the component resizes if the container is resized. A component can be set to resize either horizontally, vertically, both, or not at all. For more information on using this technique, see the API documentation for the GridBagConstraints class.

A common problem that occurs after horizontal resizing

A constructor of the Dimension class

Constructor	Description
Dimension(width, height)	Specifies the width and height of a component in pixels.

Two methods you can use to fix this problem

Method	Description
setMinimumSize(Dimension)	Specifies the minimum width and height of a component.
setPreferredSize(Dimension)	Specifies the preferred width and height of a component.

Code that sets the preferred and maximum sizes

```
Dimension dim = new Dimension(100, 20);
investmentField.setPreferredSize(dim);
investmentField.setMinimumSize(dim);
interestRateField.setPreferredSize(dim);
interestRateField.setMinimumSize(dim);
yearsField.setPreferredSize(dim);
yearsField.setMinimumSize(dim);
```

The improved example after horizontal resizing

```
┌─────────────────────────────────────┐
│ 🍵 Future V...   —    □    ✕         │
├─────────────────────────────────────┤
│ Monthly Investment: [│            ] │
│ Yearly Interest Rate: [           ] │
│ Years:              [             ] │
│ This right-aligned label spans both columns. │
└─────────────────────────────────────┘
```

Three ways to fix this problem

1. Use the window's setResizable() method to prevent the user from resizing the window. However, you should use this technique sparingly since users often expect to be able to resize a window.

2. Use the component's setPreferredSize() and setMinimumSize() methods. This isn't a perfect solution, but it's acceptable for most applications.

3. Use the weightx, weighty, and fill fields of the GridBagConstraints class to control how the components are resized. This technique can yield the best results, but it also requires the most work.

Description

- When a window is resized horizontally, components (especially text fields) can sometimes collapse to a size of zero. This is a common problem.

Figure 18-14   How to solve a common problem with the GridBagLayout

The Future Value application

In chapter 4, you were introduced to a console version of the Future Value application. Now, you're ready to see the code for a GUI version of the Future Value application that uses Swing.

The user interface

When the Future Value application starts, it displays a Future Value Calculator window like the one shown in part 1 of figure 18-15. At this point, the user can enter the monthly payment, yearly interest rate, and number of years. Then, the user can click on the Calculate button. Or, the user can press the Tab key to move the focus to the Calculate button and then press the Enter key or the spacebar. This performs the calculation and displays the result in the Future Value field.

The code

Figure 18-15 also shows the code for a simple version of the FutureValueFrame class. To start, the package statement stores the class in the package named murach.ui. Then, it imports all of the AWT and Swing classes needed by the application, as well as the NumberFormat class and the FinancialCalculations class from the murach.business package.

After the import statements, the declaration for the class shows that the FutureValueFrame class inherits the JFrame class. The body of the FutureValueFrame class begins by declaring four text fields. It's necessary to declare these text fields here so all methods of the class, including the event handlers, can access them.

The constructor for this class calls the initComponents() method to initialize the frame and its controls. To start, it sets the look and feel for the frame so it's the same as the current operating system. Then, it sets the title, default close operation, and location of the frame.

The Future Value Calculator form

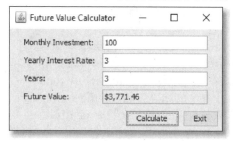

The FutureValueFrame class

```
package murach.ui;

import java.awt.BorderLayout;
import java.awt.Dimension;
import java.awt.FlowLayout;
import java.awt.GridBagConstraints;
import java.awt.GridBagLayout;
import java.awt.Insets;
import java.text.NumberFormat;
import javax.swing.JButton;
import javax.swing.JFrame;
import javax.swing.JLabel;
import javax.swing.JPanel;
import javax.swing.JTextField;
import javax.swing.UIManager;
import javax.swing.UnsupportedLookAndFeelException;

import murach.business.FinancialCalculations;

public class FutureValueFrame extends JFrame {

    private JTextField investmentField;
    private JTextField interestRateField;
    private JTextField yearsField;
    private JTextField futureValueField;

    public FutureValueFrame() {
        initComponents();
    }

    private void initComponents() {
        try {
            UIManager.setLookAndFeel(
                    UIManager.getSystemLookAndFeelClassName());
        } catch (ClassNotFoundException | InstantiationException |
                IllegalAccessException | UnsupportedLookAndFeelException e) {
            System.out.println(e);
        }

        setTitle("Future Value Calculator");
        setDefaultCloseOperation(JFrame.EXIT_ON_CLOSE);
        setLocationByPlatform(true);
```

Figure 18-15   The Future Value application (part 1 of 3)

Part 2 of this figure begins by creating the four text fields. Then, it modifies the fourth text field so the user can't edit its text, and it sets the preferred size and minimum size for these text fields.

After setting up the text fields, this code creates the Calculate and Exit buttons and adds an action listener to each one. To add these action listeners, this code uses lambda expressions. First, it uses a lambda expression to specify that the calculateButtonClicked() method shown in part 3 of this figure is the action listener for the Calculate button. Then, it uses a lambda expression to specify that the exitButtonClicked() method shown in part 3 of this figure is the action listener for the Exit button. Of course, you can only use lambda expressions to connect event handlers with Java 8 and later. If this application needed to work with Java 7 and earlier, it could use an anonymous inner class instead.

After creating the two buttons, it creates a panel to contain these buttons. Then, it sets the layout manager for this panel to a right-aligned FlowLayout, and it adds both buttons to the panel.

After creating the panel for the buttons, this code creates another JPanel to store the labels and text boxes for this GUI. Then, it sets the layout manager for this panel to the GridBagLayout manager, and it adds all of the labels and text fields to the grid. To do that, it uses the getConstraints() method that's shown in part 3 of this figure. This method makes it easier to get the GridBagConstaints object for each component.

After creating the button panel and the main panel, this code adds the main panel to the center of the BorderLayout, and it adds the button panel to the south of the BorderLayout. Then, it sets the size of the frame and makes it visible. This should display the GUI to the user, and the GUI should listen for events that it can handle.

The FutureValueFrame class (continued)

```java
        investmentField = new JTextField();
        interestRateField = new JTextField();
        yearsField = new JTextField();
        futureValueField = new JTextField();

        futureValueField.setEditable(false);

        Dimension dim = new Dimension(150, 20);
        investmentField.setPreferredSize(dim);
        interestRateField.setPreferredSize(dim);
        yearsField.setPreferredSize(dim);
        futureValueField.setPreferredSize(dim);
        investmentField.setMinimumSize(dim);
        interestRateField.setMinimumSize(dim);
        yearsField.setMinimumSize(dim);
        futureValueField.setMinimumSize(dim);

        JButton calculateButton = new JButton("Calculate");
        JButton exitButton = new JButton("Exit");

        calculateButton.addActionListener(e -> calculateButtonClicked());
        exitButton.addActionListener(e -> exitButtonClicked());

        // button panel
        JPanel buttonPanel = new JPanel();
        buttonPanel.setLayout(new FlowLayout(FlowLayout.RIGHT));
        buttonPanel.add(calculateButton);
        buttonPanel.add(exitButton);

        // main panel
        JPanel panel = new JPanel();
        panel.setLayout(new GridBagLayout());
        panel.add(new JLabel("Monthly Investment:"), getConstraints(0, 0));
        panel.add(investmentField, getConstraints(1, 0));
        panel.add(new JLabel("Yearly Interest Rate:"), getConstraints(0, 1));
        panel.add(interestRateField, getConstraints(1, 1));
        panel.add(new JLabel("Years:"), getConstraints(0, 2));
        panel.add(yearsField, getConstraints(1, 2));
        panel.add(new JLabel("Future Value:"), getConstraints(0, 3));
        panel.add(futureValueField, getConstraints(1, 3));

        add(panel, BorderLayout.CENTER);
        add(buttonPanel, BorderLayout.SOUTH);

        setSize(new Dimension(320, 180));
        setVisible(true);
    }
```

Figure 18-15   The Future Value application (part 2 of 3)

Part 3 of this figure begins by defining the getConstraints() method. This method returns a GridBagConstraints object. To do that, it starts by creating a GridBagConstraints object and setting values for alignment and padding. Then, it sets the x and y coordinates to the values that are passed to the method.

The calculateButtonClicked() method is the event handler for the action event of the Calculate button. In other words, it's executed when the Calculate button is clicked. To start, this method gets the string that the user entered into the first text field by calling the getText() method of that control. Then, it converts this string to a double value named investment. After that, this method performs similar processing for the next two text fields to get the interest rate and number of years. Next, this method calls the calculateFutureValue() method of the FinancialCalculations class to calculate and return the future value. Finally, it uses the NumberFormat class to format the future value, and it uses the setText() method of the future value field to display the formatted value in the fourth text field.

For this simple example, the calculateButtonClicked() event handler doesn't validate the data that's entered by the user. As a result, if the user enters an invalid value such as "xx", the application prints a stack trace to the console. To prevent this, you can validate the data that's entered by the user as shown in the next few figures.

The exitButtonClicked() method is the event handler for the action event of the Exit button. In other words, it's executed when the Exit button is clicked. This method executes a single statement that exits the application with a status code of 0. By convention, a status code of 0 indicates that the application ended normally.

The main() method contains the code that creates a thread that creates the FutureValueFrame object and adds it to the event queue that's used by the event dispatcher thread (EDT). Here, the code uses a lambda expression to do that. However, if this application needed to run on Java 7 or earlier, this lambda expression could be changed to an anonymous inner class as shown earlier in this chapter.

The FutureValueFrame class (continued)

```
// helper method for getting a GridBagConstraints object
private GridBagConstraints getConstraints(int x, int y) {
    GridBagConstraints c = new GridBagConstraints();
    c.anchor = GridBagConstraints.LINE_START;
    c.insets = new Insets(5, 5, 0, 5);
    c.gridx = x;
    c.gridy = y;
    return c;
}

private void calculateButtonClicked() {
    double investment = Double.parseDouble(investmentField.getText());
    double interestRate = Double.parseDouble(interestRateField.getText());
    int years = Integer.parseInt(yearsField.getText());

    double futureValue = FinancialCalculations.calculateFutureValue(
            investment, interestRate, years);

    NumberFormat currency = NumberFormat.getCurrencyInstance();
    futureValueField.setText(currency.format(futureValue));
}

private void exitButtonClicked() {
    System.exit(0);
}

public static void main(String args[]) {
    java.awt.EventQueue.invokeLater(() -> {
        JFrame frame = new FutureValueFrame();
    });
}
}
```

Figure 18-15   The Future Value application (part 3 of 3)

How to validate Swing input data

In chapter 5, you learned how to validate input data for console applications. Then, in chapter 7, you saw an example of a Console class that uses static methods to help validate data for console applications. In the topics that follow, you'll see that you can use similar techniques to validate the input data for Swing applications.

How to display a dialog box

When you validate data in a Swing application, you need to be able to display an error message to inform the user that an invalid entry has been detected. One easy way to do that is to display the error message in a separate dialog box as shown at the top of figure 18-16. To display a dialog box like this, you use the showMessageDialog() method of the JOptionPane class as described in this figure.

The four parameters accepted by this method are the parent component that determines the location of the dialog box, the message displayed in the dialog box, the title of the dialog box, and the message type, which determines the icon that's displayed in the dialog box. The parent component can be the control that's being validated or the frame that contains the control. It can also be null, in which case the dialog box is centered on the screen.

The code example in this figure shows how to display a simple error message. To start, the first statement defines a string for the message to display in the dialog box, and the second statement defines a string for the title of the dialog box. Then, the third statement calls the showMessageDialog() method. Here, the parent component argument is set to the this keyword. As a result, this code displays the dialog box in the center of the current frame. For this to work correctly, this code must be coded within a class such as the FutureValueFrame class that defines a Swing component. Finally, the message type argument is set to the ERROR_MESSAGE field of the JOptionPane class. This causes the dialog box to display an error icon.

An error message displayed in a JOptionPane dialog box

The showMessageDialog() method of the JOptionPane class

Syntax

```
showMessageDialog(parentComponent, messageString,
                  titleString, messageType)
```

Parameters

Parameter	Description
parent	An object representing the component that's the parent of the dialog box. If you specify null, the dialog box will appear in the center of the screen.
message	A string representing the message to be displayed in the dialog box.
title	A string representing the title of the dialog box.
messageType	An int that indicates the type of icon that will be used for the dialog box. You can use the fields of the JOptionPane class for this argument.

Fields used for the message type parameter

Field	Description
ERROR_MESSAGE	An error icon.
WARNING_MESSAGE	A warning icon.
INFORMATION_MESSAGE	An information icon.
QUESTION_MESSAGE	A question icon.
PLAIN_MESSAGE	No icon.

Code that displays the dialog box shown above

```
String message = "Monthly Investment is a required field.\n"
                 + "Please re-enter.";
String title = "Invalid Entry";
JOptionPane.showMessageDialog(this,
    message, title, JOptionPane.ERROR_MESSAGE);
```

Description

- The showMessageDialog() method is a static method of the JOptionPane class that is commonly used to display dialog boxes with error messages for data validation.
- To close a dialog box, the user can click the OK button or the close button in its title bar.
- You can also use the JOptionPane class to accept input from the user. For more information, see the API documentation for this class.

Figure 18-16   How to display a dialog box

How to validate the data entered into a text field

Figure 18-17 shows two techniques you can use to validate the data the user enters into a text field. The first code example checks that the user has entered data into the field. To do that, it uses the getText() method to get the text the user entered as a string. Then, it uses the isEmpty() method to check if the string is empty. If so, it uses the showMessageDialog() method to display an error message in a dialog box. Then, it calls the text field's requestFocusInWindow() method to attempt to move the focus to the text field after the user closes the dialog box. Finally, this example executes a return statement to exit the method. This prevents the rest of the code in the method from being executed, which is what you want for invalid data.

The second example shows how to check that the user entered a numeric value. Here, the try block uses the parseDouble() method of the Double class to parse the text entered by the user to a double value. Then, if a NumberFormatException occurs, the catch block catches the exception, displays an error message, moves the focus to the text field, and exits the method.

Code that checks if an entry has been made

```
private void calculateButtonClicked() {
    if (investmentField.getText().isEmpty()) {
        String message = "Monthly Investment is a required field.";
        String title = "Invalid Entry";
        JOptionPane.showMessageDialog(this, message,
            title, JOptionPane.ERROR_MESSAGE);
        investmentField.requestFocusInWindow();
        return;
    }

    // the rest of the code for the method
}
```

Code that checks if an entry is a valid number

```
private void calculateButtonClicked() {
    double investment;
    try {
        investment = Double.parseDouble(investmentField.getText());
    } catch (NumberFormatException e) {
        String message = "Monthly Investment must be a valid number.";
        String title = "Invalid Entry";
        JOptionPane.showMessageDialog(this, message,
            title, JOptionPane.ERROR_MESSAGE);
        investmentField.requestFocusInWindow();
        return;
    }

    // the rest of the code for the method
}
```

Description

- Like console applications, GUI applications should validate all data entered by the user before processing the data.

- When an entry is invalid, the application can display an error message and give the user another chance to enter valid data.

- To test whether a value has been entered into a text field, you can use the getText() method of the text field to get a string that contains the text the user entered. Then, you can check whether the string is empty by using its isEmpty() method.

- To test whether a text field contains valid numeric data, you can code the statement that converts the data in a try block and use a catch block to catch a NumberFormatException.

Figure 18-17   How to validate the data entered into a text field

The Validation class

Figure 18-18 shows a class named Validation that you can use to validate the data entered into a text component. Like the Console class that was presented in chapter 7, this class uses methods to perform common validation functions. Unlike the Console class, the Validation class doesn't use static methods. As a result, you must create a Validation object before you can use the methods in this class. That makes it easier to use the methods if the name of the object variable is shorter than the class name, and it makes it easier to change the class that's used for validation if that need arises.

This class starts by defining a private instance variable named lineEnd that stores a string that's added to the end of each validation message. Then, this method defines two constructors that you can use to set the lineEnd variable. The first constructor sets the lineEnd variable to a string that contains a single new line character, and the second constructor sets the lineEnd variable to the string that's passed to it.

All three of the public methods return a string that indicates whether the specified string passed the validation test. In addition, all three of these methods define two string parameters. The first parameter specifies the text from the control that's being validated, and the second parameter specifies a name for the control to be used in the error message. Then, if the string passes the validation test, the method returns an empty validation message. This indicates that the string passed the validation test. Otherwise, the method returns a validation message followed by the lineEnd variable. This indicates that the string did not pass the validation test.

The isPresent() method determines whether the string value contains one or more characters. To do that, this code uses the isEmpty() method to check whether the string is empty. The isDouble() method determines whether the string value can be converted to a valid double value. Like the code in the second example in the previous figure, the parseDouble() method in this example is coded with a try statement that catches a NumberFormatException. Finally, the isInteger() method determines whether the string value can be converted to a valid int value. The code in this method is similar to the code for the isDouble() method. Of course, you can easily extend this class to perform other types of tests, such as checking whether a number is within a valid range.

As you review the Validation class, note that it doesn't refer to the controls in the GUI directly. Instead, it refers to the strings that the user enters into the controls. This is known as being *loosely coupled*, and it allows this class to work with different types of controls. For example, you can use this class to validate the string that's stored in a text field as shown in the next figure. However, you can also use this class to validate strings in other controls, including controls from other GUI APIs such as the JavaFX API described in the previous chapter.

Similarly, the loose coupling allows you to decide how to display the validation messages. For example, you can use this class to display all validation messages in a dialog box as described in the next figure. However, you can also use this class to display validation messages in one or more labels on the GUI. To get that to work correctly, you might need to specify a different value for the lineEnd variable. For example, you might need to specify an empty string.

The code for the Validation class

```java
package murach.business;

public class Validation {

    private String lineEnd;

    public Validation() {
        this.lineEnd = "\n";
    }

    public Validation(String lineEnd) {
        this.lineEnd = lineEnd;
    }

    public String isPresent(String value, String name) {
        String msg = "";
        if (value.isEmpty()) {
            msg = name + " is required." + lineEnd;
        }
        return msg;
    }

    public String isDouble(String value, String name) {
        String msg = "";
        try {
            Double.parseDouble(value);
        } catch (NumberFormatException e) {
            msg = name + " must be a valid number." + lineEnd;
        }
        return msg;
    }

    public String isInteger(String value, String name) {
        String msg = "";
        try {
            Integer.parseInt(value);
        } catch (NumberFormatException e) {
            msg = name + " must be an integer." + lineEnd;
        }
        return msg;
    }
}
```

Figure 18-18   The Validation class

How to validate multiple entries

Figure 18-19 shows how you can use the SwingValidator class presented in the previous figure in an event handler such as the calculateButtonClicked() method. To start, this code creates a SwingValidator object named sv. To do that, this code uses the this keyword to pass the current object (the FutureValueFrame object) to the constructor of the SwingValidator class.

After creating the SwingValidator object, this code uses an if statement to call the methods of the SwingValidator class to perform the validation tests for each control. To do that, this code uses a compound conditional expression. Here, the validation tests are combined using the && (And) operator. That way, this compound expression returns a true value only if each of the separate calls to the SwingValidator methods returns a true value. If any of the SwingValidator calls returns a false value, the expression returns a false value.

If the user enters invalid data, the application displays a dialog box with an appropriate message. For example, the application might display one of the three dialog boxes shown in this figure. Then, after the user clicks on the OK button, the application moves the focus to the text field that contains the invalid data. This process continues until the user enters valid data into all three text fields.

Because of the way the SwingValidator class is designed, it's important to use the short-circuit And operator (**&&**) to connect the calls to the SwingValidator class. That way, the code only displays a dialog box for the first validation test that fails. If you used the *bitwise And operator* (**&**) instead, Java would evaluate each expression even if the previous expression evaluated to false. This would display one dialog box for each validation test that fails, which isn't what you want.

A validation dialog box that displays three error messages

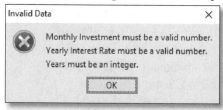

Code that validates multiple entries

```
private void calculateButtonClicked() {
    SwingValidator sv = new SwingValidator(this);
    if (sv.isPresent(investmentField, "Monthly Investment") &&
        sv.isDouble(investmentField, "Monthly Investment") &&
        sv.isPresent(interestRateField, "Yearly Interest Rate") &&
        sv.isDouble(interestRateField, "Yearly Interest Rate") &&
        sv.isPresent(yearsField, "Years") &&
        sv.isInteger(yearsField, "Years")) {

        double investment = Double.parseDouble(
                investmentField.getText());
        double interestRate = Double.parseDouble(
                interestRateField.getText());
        int years = Integer.parseInt(
                yearsField.getText());
        double futureValue = FinancialCalculations.calculateFutureValue(
                investment, interestRate, years);

        NumberFormat currency = NumberFormat.getCurrencyInstance();
        futureValueField.setText(currency.format(futureValue));
    }
}
```

Description

- You can use the SwingValidator class in the previous figure to validate multiple entries.

Figure 18-19   How to validate multiple entries

Perspective

In this chapter, you learned some essential skills for developing a GUI with Swing, the most widely used GUI API for Java. In particular, you learned how to create the main window of an application. You learned how to work with panels, buttons, labels, and text fields. You learned how to handle the events that occur when buttons are clicked. You learned how to work with the three most common layout managers. And you learned how to work with built-in dialog boxes.

In addition to buttons, labels, and text fields, Swing provides a number of other controls that you're likely to use in many of your applications. You'll learn how to work with some of these controls in the next chapter.

Summary

- *Swing* is the most widely used Java API for creating GUIs. It is based upon an older Java API for creating GUIs that's known as the *Abstract Window Toolkit (AWT)*. To differentiate between AWT and Swing, most Swing classes begin with the letter J.

- In Swing, the window that contains a GUI is called a *frame*. Within a frame, you add *components* such as *labels*, *text fields*, and *buttons*.

- A window is also known as a *form*, components are also known as *controls* or *widgets*, and text fields are also known as *text boxes*.

- A *panel* component is an invisible component that you can use to group other components.

- A component that can contain other components is called a *container*. Two commonly used containers are frames and panels.

- Swing provides a pluggable *look and feel* that you can change.

- To handle the *event* that occurs when the user clicks a JButton component, you can use the addActionListener() method to add an *action listener* to the button. Since an action listener contains the code that handles the event, it's also known as an *event handler*.

- Any code that runs in response to a Swing event runs on a special thread called the *event dispatch thread* or *EDT*.

- Prior to Java 8, it was common to use *inner classes* or *anonymous inner classes* to provide the code for an action listener. However, with Java 8 or later, you can use a *lambda expression*, which is cleaner and more concise.

- A *layout manager* lays out the components in a container and controls how they respond to events such as resizing the window.

- The BorderLayout, FlowLayout, and GridBagLayout managers are three of the most commonly used layout managers.

- You can use the methods of the JOptionPane class to display a dialog box.

Exercise 18-1   Modify an existing GUI

In this exercise, you'll modify the GUI for the Future Value Calculator that's described in this chapter.

1. Open the project named ch18_ex1_FutureValue that's in the ex_starts folder. Then, review the code and make sure you understand how it works.

2. Run the application and test the GUI.

3. Modify the code so the fourth text field is disabled instead of being not editable.

4. Run the application and test the GUI again. This should work similarly, but the text in the fourth text field should be grayed out.

5. Run the application and resize the GUI so it's taller and wider. Note how this separates the buttons from the labels and text boxes.

6. Modify the code so the button panel is displayed as the fifth row in the GridBagLayout. To do that, have the button panel span two columns in the grid. In addition, change the alignment for this column so the buttons are aligned on its right side.

7. Run the application and test the GUI. Resize it so it's taller and wider. Now, the buttons should always be displayed just below the labels and text boxes.

Exercise 18-2   Develop a new GUI

In this exercise, you'll create a GUI application that calculates the area and perimeter of a rectangle based on its length and width. When you're done, the application should look like this:

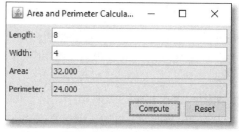

Review the existing code for the application

1. Open the project named ch18_ex2_AreaAndPerimeter that's in the ex_starts folder.

2. Open the Rectangle class in the murach.business package and review its fields and methods.

3. Open the AreaAndPerimeterFrame class in the murach.ui package and examine the existing code. Note that:

    -   This class extends the JFrame class.

    -   This class has a constructor that calls the initComponents() method.

    -   This class contains several methods such as the initComponents() method that haven't been implemented or that require additional code.

- This class contains a getConstraints() method that works like the getConstraints() method in the Future Value application shown in this chapter.

- This class contains a main() method that creates the frame, which causes the frame to be displayed.

4. Run the application. This should display a frame that doesn't contain any components. Then, resize the frame to make it larger so you can see its title.

Add the components to the frame

5. Add instance variables for the four text fields and two buttons.

6. Add code to the initComponents() method that initializes the frame and its components. This method should:

- Create the four text fields.

- Modify the text fields for the area and perimeter so the user can't edit them.

- Set the minimum and preferred dimension for all four fields.

- Create the two buttons.

- Create a panel that uses the GridBagLayout manager. Then, add the four labels and text fields to this panel. To do that, you can use the getConstraints() method. Finally, add this panel to the center of the frame.

- Create a panel that uses the FlowLayout manager with right alignment. Then, add the two buttons to this panel. Finally, add this panel to the bottom of the frame.

- Pack the frame to set its size.

7. Run the application. This should display a frame that looks like the frame shown above. However, if you click on one of the buttons, it should not perform an action.

Handle the events that occur when the user clicks the buttons

8. Add action listeners to both of the buttons. These action listeners should call the computeButtonClicked() and resetButtonClicked() methods.

9. Implement the computeButtonClicked() method.

- If the user enters an invalid length or width, this method should use a dialog box to display a user-friendly error message. Then, the user can try again. To do that, you can use the SwingValidator class.

- If the user enters a valid length and width, this method should calculate the area and perimeter and set the corresponding text fields. To do that, you can use the Rectangle class.

10. Implement the resetButtonClicked() method. This method should set all four text fields to empty strings.

19

More Swing controls

In the last chapter, you learned how to use Swing to code a graphical user interface that uses three of the most common controls: labels, text fields, and buttons. Now, you'll learn how to use some other common controls. This should help round out your understanding of GUI programming.

More skills for working with controls

This section shows how to work with five Swing controls: text areas, check boxes, radio buttons, combo boxes, and lists. In addition, it shows how to add a scroll pane to a control such as a text area or list box, and it shows how to add a title and a border to a panel.

How to work with text areas

A *text area* is similar to a text field, except that it lets you accept more than one line of input from the user. In fact, both the JTextField class and the JTextArea class extend the JTextComponent class, which provides many of the basic functions for both classes. For example, the getText() and setText() methods are defined by the JTextComponent class, so they're available to both text fields and text areas.

Figure 19-1 shows you how to use the JTextArea class to create a text area. When you create a text area, you specify the number of rows and columns you want it to contain. Then, you can use the setLineWrap() and setWrapStyleWord() methods to determine how the text wraps from one line to the next. By default, the text doesn't wrap at all. As a result, the user must press the Enter key to start a new line of text. If you want the text to wrap automatically, you must call the setLineWrap() method and supply a true value as the argument. In addition, wrapped lines are split wherever the line reaches the end of text area, even if that's in the middle of a word. To make sure that the text is wrapped between words, you must also call the setWrapStyleWord() method and supply a true value as the argument.

The first example in this figure shows how to declare a private instance variable for a text area. This allows the code in the event handlers for the class to access the text area.

The second example shows how to add a text area to a panel. Here, the first statement creates a text area with 6 rows and 30 columns and assigns to it the variable. The second and third statements set the wrapping for the text area. The fourth statement sets some default text for the text area. The fifth statement adds scroll bars to the text area if they're needed to view all of its text. And, finally, the last statement adds the text area to a panel on the GUI.

The third example shows how to retrieve the text that's displayed in a text area as a string. To do that, you use the getText() method just as you do for text fields. For example, you might want to use this code in the event handler that's executed when the user clicks on the Save button in this GUI.

How to add scroll bars

In the second example, the fifth statement adds the text area to a *scroll pane*. A scroll pane is a control that provides scroll bars for the control that it contains. As a result, if a text area contains more lines than can be displayed in the specified number of rows, the scroll pane displays a vertical scroll bar that

A frame with a text area that has a scroll bar

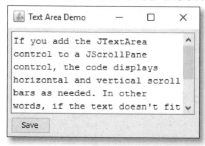

Common constructor and methods of the JTextArea class

Constructor/Method	Description
`JTextArea(rows, columns)`	Creates an empty text area with the specified number of rows and columns.
`setLineWrap(boolean)`	If set to true, this method causes the lines to wrap if they don't fit horizontally.
`setWrapStyleWord(boolean)`	If set to true and line wrapping is turned on, this method wraps lines between words.
`getText()`	Returns the text in the text area as a String.
`setText(String)`	Sets the text in the text area to the specified string.
`append(String)`	Appends the specified string to the text in the text area.

A common constructor of the JScrollPane class

Constructor	Description
`JScrollPane(Component)`	Creates a scroll pane that displays the specified component, along with vertical and horizontal scrollbars as needed.

Code that declares a private instance variable for the text area

```
private JTextArea commentTextArea;
```

Code that creates a text area and adds it to a scroll pane

```
commentTextArea = new JTextArea(6, 30);
commentTextArea.setLineWrap(true);
commentTextArea.setWrapStyleWord(true);
commentTextArea.setText("Enter your comment here");
JScrollPane commentScroll = new JScrollPane(commentTextArea);
panel.add(commentScroll);
```

Code that gets the text in a text area

```
String comments = commentTextArea.getText();
```

Description

- In contrast to a text field, a *text area* can be used to enter and display more than one line of text.

- A *scroll pane* can provide scroll bars for any control and is commonly used with text areas and lists.

Figure 19-1   How to work with text areas and add scroll bars

allows the user to scroll up or down as shown in this figure. Similarly, if a text area contains more characters than can be displayed in the specified number of columns, the scroll pane displays a horizontal scroll bar that allows the user to scroll left or right. By default, the scroll pane only displays a vertical or horizontal scroll bar if that scroll bar is needed, which is usually what you want. However, you can change how this works by using the methods of the JScrollPane class to set the horizontal or vertical scroll bar policy.

How to work with check boxes

Figure 19-2 shows how to use a *check box*. Here, if the box is checked, the Address text area is enabled so the user can enter a mailing address. Otherwise, the Address text area is disabled.

To create a check box, you can use the constructor of the JCheckBox class shown in this figure. Then, you can use the methods of this class to work with the check box.

The first example in this figure shows how to declare a private instance variable for a check box. This allows the code in the event handlers for the class to access the check box.

The second example shows how to add a check box to a panel. Here, the first statement creates the check box. The second statement selects the check box, which displays the check mark in the box. The third statement adds an action listener to the check box. To do that, it uses a lambda expression, but it could also use an anonymous inner class as described in the previous chapter. And the fourth statement adds the check box to a panel.

The third code example shows the code for the action listener method that's executed when the check box is selected or deselected. Within this method, an if statement checks whether the check box is checked. If it is, the code enables the text area so the user can enter an address. Otherwise, the code disables the text area.

You only need to add an action listener to a check box if you want the application to immediately respond when the user clicks the check box. In many cases, this isn't necessary. Instead, you just need to check the status of the check box when the user triggers some other event on the form, such as clicking on a button.

A frame with a check box

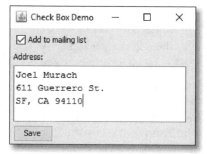

Common constructor and methods of the JCheckBox class

Constructor/Method	Description
`JCheckBox(String)`	Creates an unselected check box with a label that contains the specified string.
`isSelected()`	Returns a true value if the check box is selected.
`setSelected(boolean)`	Checks or unchecks the check box.

Code that declares a private instance variable for a check box

```
private JCheckBox mailingCheckBox;
```

Code that creates the check box and adds an action listener

```
mailingCheckBox = new JCheckBox("Add to mailing list");
mailingCheckBox.setSelected(true);
mailingCheckBox.addActionListener(e -> mailingCheckBoxChanged());
panel.add(mailingCheckBox);
```

A method that implements an action listener for the check box

```
private void mailingCheckBoxChanged() {
    if (mailingCheckBox.isSelected()) {
        addressTextArea.setEnabled(true);
    } else {
        addressTextArea.setEnabled(false);
    }
}
```

Description

- A *check box* lets the user choose to turn an option on or off.
- To select or deselect a check box, the user can click on the check box or move the focus to the check box and then press the spacebar.

Figure 19-2 How to work with check boxes

How to work with radio buttons

Figure 19-3 shows how to use *radio buttons*. When you work with radio buttons, you typically put them in a *button group*. Then, the user can select only one button from the group. In this figure, for example, the user can select one of three shipping methods: USPS, UPS, or FedEx.

The constructor and methods of the JRadioButton class work similarly to the constructor and methods of the JCheckBox class. As a result, you shouldn't have much trouble understanding them. In addition, this figure shows the constructor and method of the ButtonGroup class that you need to create a button group and add radio buttons to it. Notice that you can add any object that inherits the AbstractButton class to a button group. That includes radio buttons as well as check boxes and menu items that contain radio buttons and check boxes.

The first example shows how to declare three radio buttons as private instance variables of a class. To save vertical space, this example uses a single statement to declare all three radio buttons by separating them with commas.

The second example shows how to create the three radio buttons shown in this figure and add them to a button group. Here, the first three statements create radio buttons with the appropriate labels. Then, the fourth statement selects the USPS radio button.

The next four statements in this example create a button group using the ButtonGroup class and add the buttons to that group. This creates a logical grouping of radio buttons. As a result, when the user clicks one of the radio buttons in the group, the clicked radio button is selected and the rest of the radio buttons are deselected.

The last three statements add the radio buttons to a panel so they'll be displayed on the GUI. Although you might think that you could add the group that contains the radio buttons to the panel, that's not the case. That's because a ButtonGroup object simply defines a logical grouping of buttons.

The third example shows how to determine which of the three radio buttons is selected. To do that, it uses an if/else statement that tests the isSelected() method of each button. Then, it assigns an appropriate string value to the shipVia variable.

If necessary, you can add an action listener to a radio button just as you can with a check box or a regular button. In fact, the Payment application that's presented at the end of this chapter adds an action listener to both of its radio buttons.

A frame with three radio buttons

Common constructor and methods of the JRadioButton class

Constructor/Method	Description
`JRadioButton(String)`	Creates an unselected radio button with the specified text.
`isSelected()`	Returns a true value if the radio button is selected.
`setSelected(boolean)`	Selects or deselects the radio button.

Common constructor and method of the ButtonGroup class

Constructor/Method	Description
`ButtonGroup()`	Creates a button group used to hold a group of buttons.
`add(AbstractButton)`	Adds the specified button to the group.

Code that declares three radio buttons as private instance variables

```
private JRadioButton uspsRadioButton, upsRadioButton, fedexRadioButton;
```

Code that creates the three radio buttons and adds them to a button group

```
uspsRadioButton = new JRadioButton("USPS");
upsRadioButton = new JRadioButton("UPS");
fedexRadioButton = new JRadioButton("FedEx");
uspsRadioButton.setSelected(true);

ButtonGroup shipViaGroup = new ButtonGroup();
shipViaGroup.add(uspsRadioButton);
shipViaGroup.add(upsRadioButton);
shipViaGroup.add(fedexRadioButton);

panel.add(uspsRadioButton);
panel.add(upsRadioButton);
panel.add(fedexRadioButton);
```

Code that determines which radio button is selected

```
String shipVia = "";
if (uspsRadioButton.isSelected()) {
    shipVia = "USPS";
} else if (upsRadioButton.isSelected()) {
    shipVia = "UPS";
} else if (fedexRadioButton.isSelected()) {
    shipVia = "Federal Express";
}
```

Description

- *Radio buttons* let the user choose one option from among several options.
- You must add each radio button in a set of options to a ButtonGroup object. Selecting one radio button in a group automatically deselects all other radio buttons in the same button group.

Figure 19-3   How to work with radio buttons

How to add a border and title

Figure 19-4 shows how to add a *border* to a component. Although adding borders is an esthetic consideration that doesn't affect functionality, borders are important for two reasons. First, they let you visually group related components. This is especially important for radio buttons. Second, they let you add a *title*. In this figure, for example, the frame contains a panel with the three radio buttons from the previous figure. This panel has a border with a title of "Carrier".

You might expect that you could create a border for a component by simply calling a method to set the border style. Unfortunately, it isn't that simple. First, you must create a Border object with the style settings that you want to use. To do that, you can call one of the static methods of the BorderFactory class. This figure shows two of the most common methods for creating Border objects. The first creates a simple line border without a title, and the second creates a line border with a title. After you create the Border object, you can pass it to the setBorder() method of the component.

The code example in this figure shows how to create a panel that has a border and a title, and it shows how to add the three radio buttons created in the last figure to this panel. Here, the first statement creates a panel named shipViaPanel. The second statement uses the setBorder() method to set the border of the panel to the Border object that's returned by the createTitledBorder() method. The next three statements add the three radio buttons to the shipViaPanel. And the last statement adds the shipViaPanel to the main panel for the frame.

Radio buttons in a panel that has a title and a border

Static methods of the BorderFactory class

Method	Description
`createLineBorder()`	Creates a line border.
`createTitledBorder(`String`)`	Creates a line border with the specified title.

A method of the JComponent class

Method	Description
`setBorder(`Border`)`	Sets the border style for a component.

Code that creates a panel that has a title and a border

```
JPanel shipViaPanel = new JPanel();
shipViaPanel.setBorder(BorderFactory.createTitledBorder("Carrier"));
shipViaPanel.add(uspsRadioButton);
shipViaPanel.add(upsRadioButton);
shipViaPanel.add(fedexRadioButton);
panel.add(shipViaPanel);
```

Description

- *Borders* are used to visually group controls such as radio buttons or to enhance the appearance of controls. A border can include a *title*.

- It's common to add a border to a panel, which is a component that groups other components.

- Because a border only groups controls visually, you must still use a ButtonGroup object to group radio buttons logically.

Figure 19-4   How to add a border and title

How to work with combo boxes

Figure 19-5 shows how to create a *combo box*. A combo box is a control that lets the user choose from one of several options in a drop-down list. To display the drop-down list, the user can click on the arrow at the right side of the combo box. Then, the user can click on an item to select it. Depending on how the combo box is configured, the user may also be able to type data directly into the box. In effect, a combo box is a combination of a text field and a drop-down list.

To create a combo box, you can use the first constructor shown in this figure. Then, you can use the addItem method to add items to the combo box. Alternately, you can use the second constructor shown in this figure to create a combo box from an array of items. Either way, you can use the rest of the methods shown in this figure to work with the items in the combo box.

The first example in this figure declares a private instance variable for a combo box. The next two examples use this instance variable.

The second example shows how to create the combo box and fill it with items. Here, the first statement defines an array that contains the strings for three carriers. The second statement uses a constructor to create a combo box with one item for each element in the array. After that, the code adds an action listener to the combo box that's executed when the selected item in the combo box is changed. Finally, this code adds the combo box to the main panel of the GUI.

In most cases, that's all you need to do to create a combo box. However, you may also want to use the setSelectedIndex() method to change the item that's selected when the list is first displayed. By default, the first item in the list is selected, which is usually what you want.

The third example shows the method that's executed every time the user selects a new item from the combo box. Within this event handler, the first statement uses the getSelectedIndex() method to retrieve the index of the selected product. Then, the second statement uses the getSelectedItem() method to get the selected item from the combo box.

The fourth example in this figure shows another way to create a combo box and fill it with items. Here, the first statement creates an empty combo box and assigns it to a variable named yearsComboBox. Then, the for statement that follows uses the addItem method to add the integers 1 through 20 to the combo box. Finally, the last statement selects the third item in the list.

Although the combo boxes presented in this figure contain String and int objects, the addItem() method lets you add any type of object. For example, you could add Product objects to a combo box. In that case, the combo box would call each product's toString() method to get the text to display for the object.

By default, combo boxes aren't editable, so the user can't change the value that's displayed in the text field part of the combo box. Although that's usually what you want, you can use the setEditable() method to make the combo box editable. Then, the user can type the text of an item into the text field part of the combo box instead of selecting an item from the list. If you do this, keep in mind that the user might enter invalid data. As a result, you'll have to add some data validation code to prevent invalid entries.

A frame with a combo box

Common constructors and methods of the JComboBox class

Constructor/Method	Description
`JComboBox()`	Creates an empty combo box.
`JComboBox(Object[])`	Creates a combo box with the objects stored in the specified array.
`getSelectedItem()`	Returns an Object type for the selected item.
`getSelectedIndex()`	Returns an int value for the index of the selected item.
`setSelectedIndex(int)`	Selects the item at the specified index.
`getItemCount()`	Returns the number of items stored in the combo box.
`addItem(Object)`	Adds the specified item to the combo box.
`removeItemAt(int)`	Removes the item at the specified index from the combo box.
`removeItem(Object)`	Removes the specified item from the combo box.

Code that declares a private instance variable for a combo box

```
private JComboBox carrierComboBox;
```

Code that creates a combo box and fills it with items

```
String[] carriers = {"USPS", "UPS", "FedEx"};
carrierComboBox = new JComboBox(carriers);
carrierComboBox.addActionListener(event -> carrierComboBoxItemChanged());
panel.add(carrierComboBox);
```

Code that gets the selected item

```
private void carrierComboBoxItemChanged() {
    int shipViaIndex = carrierComboBox.getSelectedIndex();
    String shipVia = (String) carrierComboBox.getSelectedItem();
}
```

Another way to create a combo box and fill it with items

```
yearsComboBox = new JComboBox();
for (int year = 1; year < 21; year++) {
    yearsComboBox.addItem(year);
}
yearsComboBox.setSelectedIndex(2);
```

Description

- A *combo box* lets the user choose one of several items from a drop-down list.

Figure 19-5   How to work with combo boxes

How to work with lists

Figure 19-6 shows how to create a *list*, which allows the user to select zero or more elements. For example, the first frame at the top of this figure includes a list that displays three shipping carriers. Here, all of the carriers can be displayed in the list at once, so no vertical scroll bar is needed to allow the user to scroll through the entries. However, as with a text area, it's common to store a list within a scroll pane so scroll bars appear when necessary.

Unlike a combo box, a list allows a user to select more than one element by default. For example, the second frame at the top of this figure shows a list box with two elements selected. To select multiple elements, the user can hold down the Ctrl key while clicking on the elements. Or, the user can select one element and then hold down the Shift key and click on another element to select a range of elements that includes the first element through second element. To select another range of elements, the user can hold down the Ctrl key and select the first element in the range and then hold down the Ctrl and Shift keys and select the last element in the range.

If you need to, you can use the setSelectionMode() method to change the types of selections a user can make. For example, you can set this property so the user is limited to making a single selection as shown by the Payment application presented later in this chapter. Or, you can set this property so the user can select a single interval of consecutive elements. To do that, you use the fields in the ListSelectionModel interface.

The first example declares a private instance variable for the list. This variable is used by the next two examples.

The second example shows how to create a list and add it to a scroll pane. Here, the first statement defines an array of String objects for shipping carriers. The second statement creates a list with one element for each element of the array. The third statement selects the first element in the list. If you don't select an element in the list, no elements are selected by default. The fourth statement adds the list to a scroll pane. The fifth statement sets the preferred size of the scroll pane. And the sixth statement adds the scroll pane to a panel on the GUI.

The third example shows how to access the element or elements that have been selected by the user. Here, the getSelectedValuesList() method retrieves a list of selected values. At this point, you could use a loop to process these values. If necessary, you could use the getSelectedIndices() method to return the indexes of the selected elements. Similarly, for a list box that only allows a single selection, you can use the getSelectedIndex() or getSelectedValue() methods to get the selected index or value.

A frame that includes a list

A list with multiple elements selected

Common constructor and methods of the JList class

Constructor/Method	Description
`JList(Object[])`	Creates a list that contains the objects in the specified array.
`setSelectionMode(mode)`	Sets the selection mode to one of the fields in the ListSelectionModel interface.
`setSelectedIndex(int)`	Selects the element at the specified index.
`getSelectedValue()`	Returns the selected element as an Object type.
`getSelectedIndex()`	Returns an int value for the index of the selected element.
`getSelectedValuesList()`	Returns a List<> type that contains the selected elements.
`getSelectedIndices()`	Returns an array of int values for the indexes of the selected elements.

Fields of the ListSelectionModel interface

Field	Description
`SINGLE_SELECTION`	Allows just one selection.
`SINGLE_INTERVAL_SELECTION`	Allows a single interval of selections.
`MULTIPLE_INTERVAL_SELECTION`	Allows multiple intervals of selections. This is the default.

Code that declares an instance variable for a list

```
private JList carrierList;
```

Code that creates the list and adds it to a scroll pane

```
String[] carriers = {"USPS", "UPS", "FedEx"};
carrierList = new JList(carriers);
carrierList.setSelectedIndex(0);
JScrollPane carrierScrollPane = new JScrollPane(carrierList);
carrierScrollPane.setPreferredSize(new Dimension(150, 30));
panel.add(carrierScrollPane);
```

Code that gets the selected elements from the list

```
List<String> carriers = carrierList.getSelectedValuesList();
```

Description

- A *list* allows the user to select zero or more elements from a list of elements.

Figure 19-6   How to work with lists

How to work with list models

When you create a list, it uses a *list model* to store the elements in the list. When you create a list from an array as shown in the previous figure, the list model is read-only. As a result, once you create the list, you can't modify it by adding or removing elements.

If you need to be able to modify the elements of a list, you can create a list model for the list as shown in figure 19-7. Then, you can use the methods of the list model to add and remove elements from the list. A list model can be any object that implements the ListModel interface, but for most lists, you can create an object from the DefaultListModel class. This class works similarly to most of the collection classes in the Java API, so you shouldn't have much trouble using it.

To illustrate how this works, this figure shows a frame that includes a list and a Remove button. Although this list looks like the ones you saw in the previous figure, it uses a list model that's created from the DefaultListModel class. Because of that, you can remove the selected elements when the user clicks the Remove button.

The first example in this figure declares private instance variables for a list and its model. These instance variables are used by the next two examples. Notice that the list model can store String objects, which is appropriate for this example.

The second example shows how to create the model and the list. First, it defines an array of strings for a grocery list. Instead of passing this array to the JList constructor, however, it creates a DefaultListModel object and uses a loop to add each element of the array to the model. Then, this code creates the list and uses the setModel() method to set the model in the list.

The third example shows the event handler for the Remove button. Within this method, the first statement uses the getSelectedIndices() method of the list to get the selected indexes. Then, it loops through those indexes and uses the removeElementAt() method of the list model to remove each element from the model. This also removes the element from the list that's displayed on the GUI.

If you wanted to let the user add elements to this list, you could add a text field and an Add button to the frame shown in this figure. Then, in the event handler for the Add button, you could use the addElement() method to get the string from the text field and add it to the list model. This would also add the string to the list that's displayed on the GUI.

A list that allows its elements to be modified

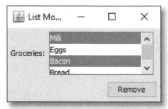

Another constructor and method of the JList class

Constructor/Method	Description
`JList()`	Creates a list that doesn't contain any elements.
`setModel(listModel)`	Sets the model for the list. One easy way to create this model is to use the DefaultListModel class.

Common constructor and methods of the DefaultListModel class

Constructor/Method	Description
`DefaultListModel()<E>`	Creates a default list model for the specified element type.
`contains(E)`	Returns a true value if the list contains the specified element.
`addElement(E)`	Adds the specified element to the list.
`removeElementAt(int)`	Removes the element at the specified position.
`clear()`	Removes all elements from the list.
`size()`	Returns the number of elements in the list.

Code that declares instance variables for a list and its model

```
private JList groceryList;
private DefaultListModel<String> groceryModel;
```

Code that sets up the model and the list

```
String[] groceries = {"Milk", "Eggs", "Bacon", "Bread"};
groceryModel = new DefaultListModel<>();
for (String item : groceries) {
    groceryModel.addElement(item);
}
groceryList = new JList();
groceryList.setModel(groceryModel);
```

Code that removes selected elements from the list

```
private void removeButtonClicked() {
    int[] selectedIndices = groceryList.getSelectedIndices();
    for (int index : selectedIndices) {
        groceryModel.removeElementAt(index);
    }
}
```

Description

- To modify the contents of a list using code, you can create a *list model* that defines the data displayed by the list. Then, you can use the list model to add or remove elements.

Figure 19-7   How to work with list models

The Payment application

Now that you understand how to work with different types of controls, you're ready to see a Payment application that uses some of these controls.

The user interface

Figure 19-8 shows the user interface for the Payment application. Here, the user can enter the data for a credit card by selecting the "Credit card" radio button and then using the other controls to enter the credit card data. Then, when the user clicks the Accept button, the application displays the credit card data in a dialog box.

Alternatively, the user can send a bill to the customer by selecting the "Bill customer" radio button. This disables the controls for entering credit card data. Then, the user can click the Accept button to display a message that indicates that the customer will be billed.

The user interface for the Payment application

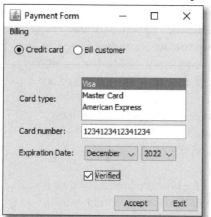
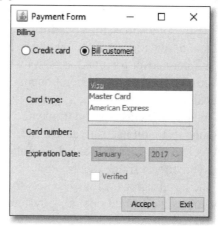

Typical dialog boxes displayed by the application

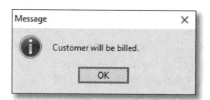

Description

- The Payment application uses some of the controls shown in this chapter to allow the user to enter information regarding a payment.

- To enter a credit card payment, the user selects the "Credit card" radio button, selects a card type from the list, enters a card number in the text field, and selects an expiration month and year from the combo boxes. If the credit card has been verified, the user can also select the check box. When the user clicks the Accept button, the application displays the credit card data that was entered in a dialog box.

- To send a bill to the customer, the user selects the "Bill customer" radio button. This disables the controls for entering credit card data. If the user clicks the Accept button, the application displays a dialog box with a message that indicates that the customer will be billed.

- To exit the application, the user clicks the Exit button.

Figure 19-8   The user interface for the Payment application

The code

Figure 19-9 shows the code for the frame that defines the GUI for the Payment application. This frame uses all of the controls that were presented in this chapter except for a text area. As a result, you can study this code to see how the various types of Swing components work together within the context of an application.

To start, the class for the frame declares instance variables for all of the components that it needs to access in the event handlers. That includes the radio buttons, the list, the text field, the combo boxes, and the check box that are displayed on this frame.

The constructor for the class sets the look and feel for the application so it's the same as the current operating system. Then, it calls the initComponents() method.

The initComponents() method begins by setting up the frame's title, location, and default close operation. Then, it sets up the radio buttons that are used for billing. To start, it creates a group for these buttons. Then, it creates the buttons, adds them to the button group, selects the first button, and adds an action listener to both radio buttons. This action listener calls the billingRadioButtonClicked() method shown on page 3 of this figure if the user selects one of these radio buttons.

After setting up the two radio buttons for billing, this code creates a panel to store these radio buttons. This panel has a border and a title of "Billing", and it uses FlowLayout with left alignment. Finally, this code adds the radio buttons to the panel.

The code for the Payment application   Page 1

```java
package murach.ui;

import javax.swing.*;
import java.awt.*;
import java.time.LocalDate;

public class PaymentFrame extends JFrame {
    private JRadioButton creditCardRadioButton;
    private JRadioButton billCustomerRadioButton;
    private JList cardTypeList;
    private JTextField cardNumberTextField;
    private JComboBox monthComboBox;
    private JComboBox yearComboBox;
    private JCheckBox verifiedCheckBox;

    public PaymentFrame() {
        try {
            UIManager.setLookAndFeel(
                    UIManager.getSystemLookAndFeelClassName());
        } catch (ClassNotFoundException | InstantiationException |
                IllegalAccessException | UnsupportedLookAndFeelException e) {
            System.out.println(e);
        }
        initComponents();
    }

    private void initComponents() {
        // set up frame
        setTitle("Payment Form");
        setLocationByPlatform(true);
        setDefaultCloseOperation(WindowConstants.EXIT_ON_CLOSE);

        // set up Billing components
        ButtonGroup billingGroup = new ButtonGroup();
        creditCardRadioButton = new JRadioButton("Credit card");
        billCustomerRadioButton = new JRadioButton("Bill customer");
        billingGroup.add(creditCardRadioButton);
        billingGroup.add(billCustomerRadioButton);
        creditCardRadioButton.setSelected(true);
        creditCardRadioButton.addActionListener(
                event -> billingRadioButtonClicked());
        billCustomerRadioButton.addActionListener(
                event -> billingRadioButtonClicked());

        // set up Billing panel
        JPanel billingPanel = new JPanel();
        billingPanel.setBorder(BorderFactory.createTitledBorder("Billing"));
        billingPanel.setLayout(new FlowLayout(FlowLayout.LEFT));
        billingPanel.add(creditCardRadioButton);
        billingPanel.add(billCustomerRadioButton);
```

Figure 19-9   The code for the Payment application (part 1 of 4)

Page 2 of this figure starts by setting up the list that allows the user to select a credit card type. This code creates a list that contains each item in the array of card types. It sets the selection mode so the user can only select one item at a time. And it adds the list to a scroll pane so that scroll bars are displayed if necessary.

Next, this code sets up the text field for the credit card number. This code uses a Dimension object like you saw in the last chapter to set the preferred and minimum sizes of the text field.

After setting up the text field, this code sets up combo boxes for the expiration month and year. To set up the combo box for the expiration month, this code creates a combo box that contains each item in an array of months. However, the code that creates the combo box for the expiration year begins by getting the current year. Then, it uses a for loop to add the current year and the next seven years to the combo box. Finally, this code creates a panel and adds both combo boxes to it.

Next, this code creates a check box that indicates whether the credit card has been verified. Note that this code doesn't call the setSelected() method. Because of that, this check box is unchecked when it's first displayed.

After setting up the check box, this code creates a panel that uses a grid to display the card type, card number, and expiration date controls. In addition, it adds labels to clearly identify what each control does. To set the column and row indexes for each control, this code uses the getConstraints() method that's shown on page 3.

The code for the Payment application   **Page 2**

```
// set up Card Type list
String[] cardTypes = {"Visa", "Master Card", "American Express"};
cardTypeList = new JList(cardTypes);
cardTypeList.setSelectionMode(ListSelectionModel.SINGLE_SELECTION);
JScrollPane cardTypeScrollPane = new JScrollPane(cardTypeList);
cardTypeScrollPane.setPreferredSize(new Dimension(150, 60));

// set up Card Number text field
cardNumberTextField = new JTextField();
Dimension dim = new Dimension(150, 20);
cardNumberTextField.setPreferredSize(dim);
cardNumberTextField.setMinimumSize(dim);

// set up Expiration month combo
String[] months = {"January", "February", "March", "April",
                   "May", "June", "July", "August",
                   "September", "October", "November", "December"};
monthComboBox = new JComboBox(months);

// set up Expiration year combo
LocalDate currentDate = LocalDate.now();
int startYear = currentDate.getYear();
int endYear = startYear + 8;
yearComboBox = new JComboBox();
for (int i = startYear; i < endYear; i++) {
    yearComboBox.addItem(Integer.toString(i));
}

// set up Expiration Date panel
JPanel expirationDatePanel = new JPanel();
expirationDatePanel.setLayout(new FlowLayout(FlowLayout.LEFT));
expirationDatePanel.add(monthComboBox);
expirationDatePanel.add(yearComboBox);

// set up Verified check box
verifiedCheckBox = new JCheckBox();
verifiedCheckBox.setText("Verified");

// set up the grid panel
JPanel gridPanel = new JPanel();
gridPanel.setLayout(new GridBagLayout());

gridPanel.add(new JLabel("Card type:"), getConstraints(0, 0));
gridPanel.add(cardTypeScrollPane, getConstraints(1, 0));
gridPanel.add(new JLabel("Card number:"), getConstraints(0, 1));
gridPanel.add(cardNumberTextField, getConstraints(1, 1));
gridPanel.add(new JLabel("Expiration Date:"), getConstraints(0, 2));
gridPanel.add(expirationDatePanel, getConstraints(1, 2));
gridPanel.add(verifiedCheckBox, getConstraints(1, 3));
```

Figure 19-9   The code for the Payment application (part 2 of 4)

Page 3 of this code begins by creating the Accept and Exit buttons. In addition, it adds an action listener to both of these buttons. As a result, if the user clicks on the Accept button, the action listener calls the acceptButtonClicked() method shown on page 4 of this figure. Similarly, if the user clicks on the Exit button, the action listener calls the exitButtonClicked() method. Finally, this code creates a panel and adds these buttons to it. This panel uses a FlowLayout with right alignment.

After creating the button panel, this code adds the three panels to three areas of the BorderLayout that's available from the frame. More specifically, it adds the panel that contains the radio buttons to the NORTH area, it adds the grid panel to the CENTER area, and it adds the panel that contains the buttons to the SOUTH area.

The last statement in the initComponents() method uses the pack() method to set the size of the frame to accommodate all of its components. This method is placed here because it must be called after all the components have been added to the frame for it to work properly.

The getConstraints() method is used to position components within the grid panel, as you saw in page 2 of this code. This works like the getConstraints() method that was used by the Future Value application that you saw in the last chapter. As a result, you can refer back to that chapter if you need to refresh your memory on how this works.

The billingRadioButtonClicked() method is the event handler that's executed if either of the radio buttons are clicked. Within this method, the first statement checks whether the credit card radio button is selected. If so, this code passes a true value to the enableCreditCardControls() method to enable the controls for entering the credit card data. Otherwise, this code disables the credit card controls.

The code for the Payment application

```java
        // set up Accept and Exit buttons
        JButton acceptButton = new JButton("Accept");
        acceptButton.addActionListener(event -> acceptButtonClicked());
        JButton exitButton = new JButton("Exit");
        exitButton.addActionListener(event -> exitButtonClicked());

        // set up button panel
        JPanel buttonPanel = new JPanel();
        buttonPanel.setLayout(new FlowLayout(FlowLayout.RIGHT));
        buttonPanel.add(acceptButton);
        buttonPanel.add(exitButton);

        // add billing panel to NORTH
        add(billingPanel, BorderLayout.NORTH);

        // add grid bag panel to CENTER
        add(gridPanel, BorderLayout.CENTER);

        // add button panel to SOUTH
        add(buttonPanel, BorderLayout.SOUTH);

        pack();
    }

    // Helper method to return GridBagConstraints objects
    private GridBagConstraints getConstraints(int x, int y) {
        GridBagConstraints c = new GridBagConstraints();
        c.anchor = GridBagConstraints.LINE_START;
        c.insets = new Insets(5, 5, 0, 5);
        c.gridx = x;
        c.gridy = y;
        return c;
    }

    private void billingRadioButtonClicked() {
        if (creditCardRadioButton.isSelected()) {
            enableCreditCardControls(true);
        } else if (billCustomerRadioButton.isSelected()) {
            enableCreditCardControls(false);
        }
    }

    private void enableCreditCardControls(boolean enable) {
        cardTypeList.setEnabled(enable);
        cardNumberTextField.setEnabled(enable);
        monthComboBox.setEnabled(enable);
        yearComboBox.setEnabled(enable);
        verifiedCheckBox.setEnabled(enable);
    }
```

Figure 19-9   The code for the Payment application (part 3 of 4)

Page 4 begins by showing the acceptButtonClicked() method. This method is the event handler that's executed if the user clicks the Accept button. Within this method, the first statement defines a variable that stores the message that's displayed. Then, this code gets the data entered by the user and formats it in a message. To do that, this code uses some of the methods described in this chapter. For example, it uses the getSelectedValue() method of the list box. This works because this list box only allows the user to select a single element. Similarly, it uses the getSelectedItem() method of the two combo boxes to get the selected expiration date. Since these methods return an Object type, this code casts the return values to String types.

After storing the appropriate message in the variable, this code displays the message in a dialog box. Then, it sets all of the controls to their default state. To do that, this code uses some of the methods described in this chapter. In particular, it uses the setSelectedIndex() method of the list and combo boxes to select the first item in those controls. In addition, it passes a false value to the setSelected() method of the check box to deselect that check box.

The code for the Payment application

```java
    private void acceptButtonClicked() {
        String message;
        if (creditCardRadioButton.isSelected()) {
            message = "Bill " + (String) cardTypeList.getSelectedValue()
                    + "\nNumber: " + cardNumberTextField.getText()
                    + "\nExpiration date: "
                    + (String) monthComboBox.getSelectedItem()
                    + ", " + (String) yearComboBox.getSelectedItem();
            if (verifiedCheckBox.isSelected()) {
                message += "\nCard has been verified.";
            } else {
                message += "\nCard has not been verified.";
            }
        } else {
            message = "Customer will be billed.";
        }

        // display message
        JOptionPane.showMessageDialog(this, message);

        // reset controls
        cardTypeList.setSelectedIndex(0);
        cardNumberTextField.setText("");
        monthComboBox.setSelectedIndex(0);
        yearComboBox.setSelectedIndex(0);
        verifiedCheckBox.setSelected(false);
    }

    private void exitButtonClicked() {
        System.exit(0);
    }

    public static void main(String args[]) {
        java.awt.EventQueue.invokeLater(() -> {
            new PaymentFrame().setVisible(true);
        });
    }
}
```

Figure 19-9   The code for the Payment application (part 4 of 4)

Perspective

In this chapter, you learned how to work with some new components. If you understand the Payment application that's presented at the end of this chapter, you've come a long way. Once you master the data access skills that are presented in the next section, you'll have a solid set of skills for developing Java applications at a professional level.

Summary

- A *text area* lets the user enter one or more lines of text. You can use many of the same techniques to work with text fields and text areas.
- A *scroll pane* can provide scroll bars for controls such as text areas and lists.
- *Radio buttons* let the user select one option from a group of options in a *button group*.
- When working with radio buttons and other related controls, you can visually group them by adding them to a panel that has a *border*.
- A *check box* lets the user select or deselect a single option.
- A *combo box* lets a user select one item from a drop-down list of items.
- A *list* lets a user select one or more elements from a list of elements.
- A list uses a *list model* to store the elements of the list.

Exercise 19-1   Modify the Future Value application

For this exercise, you'll modify the Future Value application presented in chapter 18 so it uses a combo box and a list. When you're done, the user interface should look something like this:

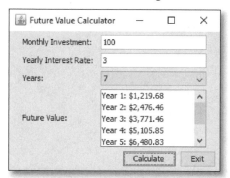

1. Open the project named ch19_ex1_FutureValue in the ex_starts directory. Then, review the design and code for the form.

2. Replace the Number of Years text field with a combo box. Then, code a method that fills this combo box with the values 1 through 20, and call this method from the constructor for the frame. Make any other necessary changes to provide for the combo box. Test the project to be sure it works correctly.

3. Replace the Future Value text field with a list that displays five rows and uses a vertical scroll bar but no horizontal scroll bar.

4. Modify the calculateButtonClicked() event handler so that instead of calculating a single value, it calculates the future value for each year up to the year selected via the combo box and adds a string showing the calculation for each year to the list.

5. Test the project to be sure it works correctly.

Exercise 19-2   Create a Pizza Calculator application

For this exercise, you'll develop an application that calculates the price of a pizza based on its size and toppings. The user interface for this application should look something like this:

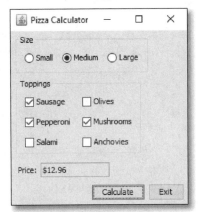

1. Open the project named ch19_ex2_PizzaOrder in the ex_starts directory. This project contains an empty frame and a couple of helper methods.

2. Add the controls and code necessary to implement this application. When the user selects a size and toppings for the pizza and clicks the Calculate button, the application should calculate the price of the pizza and display that price in the text field. To calculate the price of the pizza, add the price of the selected toppings to the base price of the pizza:

Item	Price
Small pizza	$6.99
Medium pizza	$8.99
Large pizza	$10.99
Sausage	$1.49
Pepperoni	$1.49
Salami	$1.49
Olives	$0.99
Mushrooms	$0.99
Anchovies	$0.99

3. Test the project to be sure it works correctly.

Section 5

Database programming

Most Java applications in the real world store their data in a database. In most cases, this provides many advantages over storing the data in a file as described in chapter 15. That's why the two chapters in this section present the essential database skills that you need for developing Java applications.

To start, chapter 20 presents some basic database concepts and skills for using SQL (Structured Query Language) to retrieve and modify the data in a database. Then, chapter 21 shows how to use JDBC (Java Database Connectivity) to write Java code that executes these SQL statements. To illustrate, these chapters use a SQLite database because it's a great way to get started with database programming. However, most of the skills for working with a SQLite database also apply to other popular databases such as Oracle, SQL Server, and MySQL.

20

An introduction to databases with SQLite

In chapter 15, you learned how to work with programs that store data in files. In the real world, though, most programs store data in databases. That's because storing data in a database provides many advantages over storing data in a file.

To start, this chapter teaches you some basic concepts for working with a relational database. Then, it shows you how to use SQL to work with a database. These skills apply to most databases including MySQL, Oracle, SQL Server, and SQLite databases. To finish, this chapter shows you some specific skills for working with a SQLite database.

SQLite is an embedded database that requires no configuration. And yet, it implements much of the SQL standard that applies to all databases. In addition, it's popular and used extensively, especially in Android programming. As a result, SQLite is a great way to get started with databases.

How a relational database is organized

In 1970, Dr. E. F. Codd developed a model for a new type of *database* called a *relational database*. This type of database eliminated some of the problems that were associated with earlier types of databases like hierarchical databases. By using the relational model, you can reduce data redundancy, which saves disk storage and leads to more efficient data retrieval. You can also view and manipulate data in a way that is both intuitive and efficient.

How a table is organized

A relational database stores data in *tables*. Each table contains *rows* and *columns* as shown in figure 20-1. In practice, rows and columns are often referred to by the traditional terms, *records* and *fields*. That's why this book uses these terms interchangeably.

In a relational database, a table has one column that's defined as the *primary key*. The primary key uniquely identifies each row in a table. That way, as you'll see in the next figure, the rows in one table can easily be related to the rows in another table. In the Products table shown here, the ProductCode column is the primary key.

The software that manages a relational database is called the *database management system* (*DBMS*) or *relational database management system* (*RDBMS*). The DBMS provides features that let you design the database. After that, the DBMS manages all changes to the data that's stored in the database. Four popular database management systems are Oracle, Microsoft's SQL Server, MySQL, and SQLite.

How the columns in a table are defined

This figure also shows how a DBMS defines the columns in a table. In particular, it shows how the DBMS defines a name and data type for each column. This is required by all relational databases. In this figure, the ProductCode and Description columns are defined with the VARCHAR data type. This data type maps to the String type in Java and allows the column to store a variable number of characters. Here, the ProductCode column can store a maximum of 10 characters, and the Description column can store a maximum of 40 characters. In contrast, the Price column is defined with the DOUBLE data type. This data type maps to the double type in Java.

In addition, most modern relational databases let you set other properties for each column in the database such as whether the column can store a *null value* to indicate that the value of the column is not known. In this figure, all of the columns specify NOT NULL to indicate that they don't allow null values. As a result, an application must provide a value for the column when it tries to add a row to the database.

The Products table

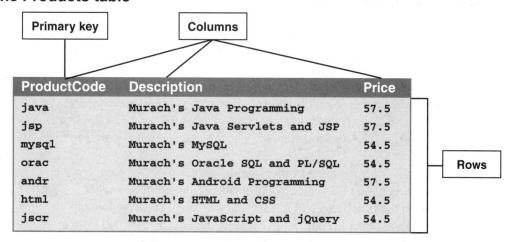

The design of the Products table

Column name	Data type	Allow Null?
ProductCode	VARCHAR(10)	NOT NULL
Description	VARCHAR(40)	NOT NULL
Price	DOUBLE	NOT NULL

Description

- A *relational database* uses *tables* to store and manipulate data. Each table contains one or more *rows*, or *records*, that contain the data for a single entity. Each row contains one or more *columns*, or *fields*, with each column representing a single item of data.

- Most tables contain a *primary key* that uniquely identifies each row in the table.

- The software that manages a relational database is called a *database management system* (*DBMS*). Four popular database management systems today are Oracle, Microsoft's SQL Server, MySQL, and SQLite.

- A database management system requires a name and data type for each column in a table. Depending on the data type, the column definition can include other properties such as the column's size.

- Each column definition also indicates whether or not the column can contain *null values*. A null value indicates that the value of the column is not known.

Figure 20-1   How a table is organized and defined

How tables are related

Figure 20-2 shows how a relational database uses the values in the primary key column to relate one table to another. Here, the ProductCode column in the LineItems table contains a value that identifies one row in the Products table. In other words, the ProductCode column in the LineItems table points to a primary key in another table. As a result, it's called a *foreign key*. In a large database, it's common for a table to have several foreign keys. In this figure, for example, the InvoiceID column of the LineItems table is also a foreign key that points to the Invoices table.

In this figure, each row in the Products table relates to one or more rows in the LineItems table. As a result, the Products table has a *one-to-many relationship* with the LineItems table. Although a one-to-many relationship is the most common type of relationship between tables, you can also have a *one-to-one relationship* or a *many-to-many relationship*. However, a one-to-one relationship between two tables is rare since the data can be stored in a single table. In contrast, a many-to-many relationship between two tables is typically implemented by using a third table that has a one-to-many relationship with both of the original tables.

Incidentally, the primary key in the LineItems table is the LineItemID column. It is automatically generated by the DBMS when a new row is added to the database. This type of primary key is often appropriate for tables like Invoice and Customer tables.

The relationship between the Products and LineItems tables

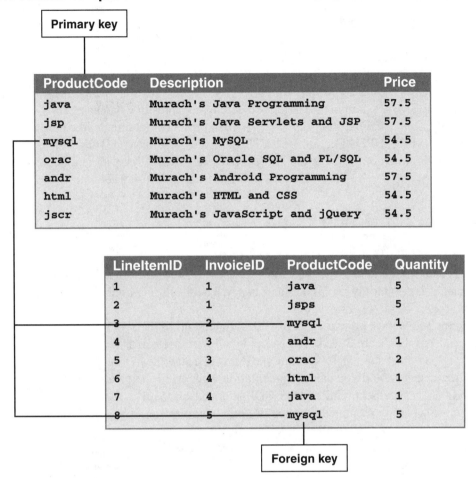

Description

- The tables in a relational database are related to each other through their key columns. For example, the Products and LineItems tables are related to each other through the ProductCode column. In the LineItems table, the ProductCode column is called a *foreign key* because it identifies a related row in another table.

- Three types of relationships can exist between tables. The most common type is a *one-to-many relationship* as illustrated above. However, two tables can also have a *one-to-one relationship* or a *many-to-many relationship*.

Figure 20-2   How tables are related

How to use SQL to work with a database

Structured Query Language (SQL) is a standard language that you can use to communicate with any modern DBMS. This language can be divided into two parts. The *Data Definition Language (DDL)* provides statements like the CREATE TABLE statement that let you define the tables in a database. In contrast, the *Data Manipulation Language (DML)* provides statements like the SELECT, INSERT, UPDATE, and DELETE statements that let you work with the data that's stored in those tables. These are the statements that programmers use every day, and they're the statements you'll learn how to use next.

How to query a single table

The *SELECT statement* is the most commonly used *SQL statement*. It retrieves data from one or more tables in a database. When you run a SELECT statement, it is commonly referred to as a *query*. The result of a query is a table known as a *result set*, or *result table*.

Figure 20-3 shows how to use a SELECT statement. In the syntax summary, the capitalized words are SQL keywords and the lowercase words represent the items that you must supply. To separate the items in a statement, you can use one or more spaces, and you can use indentation whenever it helps improve the readability of a statement. Unlike Java, SQL is not case-sensitive. As a result, you can use whatever capitalization you prefer when referring to SQL keywords. In this chapter, we capitalize all SQL keywords to make it easy to tell the difference between these keywords and other parts of the SQL language such as column names. In practice, though, many programmers use lowercase for SQL keywords when writing SQL statements.

The first example in this figure retrieves all columns and rows from the Products table. To do that, the SELECT clause uses an asterisk (*) to specify that all columns should be retrieved, and the FROM clause specifies the Products table. Since this example doesn't include a WHERE clause or an ORDER BY clause, it retrieves all rows from the Products table in no particular order.

The second example shows how to retrieve selected columns and rows from the Products table. Here, the SELECT clause identifies two columns, and the FROM clause identifies the table. Then, the WHERE clause limits the number of rows that are retrieved by specifying that the statement should only retrieve rows where the value in the Price column is greater than 55. Last, the ORDER BY clause indicates that the retrieved rows should be sorted in ascending order (from A to Z) by the Description column. However, if you wanted to switch the sort order, you could use the DESC keyword instead of the ASC keyword.

As you might guess, queries can have a significant effect on the performance of a database application. The more columns and rows that a query retrieves, the more traffic the network has to bear. As a result, when you design queries, you should try to keep the number of columns and rows to a minimum.

SELECT syntax for selecting from one table

```
SELECT column-1 [, column-2] ...
FROM table-1
[WHERE selection-criteria]
[ORDER BY column-1 [ASC|DESC] [, column-2 [ASC|DESC]] ...]
```

A SELECT statement that retrieves all columns and rows

```
SELECT *
FROM Products
```

The result set defined by the SELECT statement

ProductCode	Description	Price
java	Murach's Java Programming	57.5
jsp	Murach's Java Servlets and JSP	57.5
mysql	Murach's MySQL	54.5
orac	Murach's Oracle SQL and PL/SQL	54.5
andr	Murach's Android Programming	57.5
html	Murach's HTML and CSS	54.5
jscr	Murach's JavaScript and jQuery	54.5

A SELECT statement that gets selected columns and rows

```
SELECT Description, Price
FROM Products
WHERE Price > 55
ORDER BY Description ASC
```

The result set defined by the SELECT statement

Description	Price
Murach's Android Programming	57.5
Murach's Java Programming	57.5
Murach's Java Servlets and JSP	57.5

Description

- The SELECT statement is used to perform a *query* that retrieves rows and columns from a database.

- The *result set* (or *result table*) is the set of rows that are retrieved by a query.

- To select all of the columns in a table, you can code an asterisk (*) instead of coding column names.

- For efficiency, you should code your queries so the result set has as few rows and columns as possible.

Figure 20-3   How to query a single table

How to join data from two or more tables

Figure 20-4 shows how to use the SELECT statement to retrieve data from two tables. Since the data from the two tables is joined together into a single result set, this is known as a *join*. In this figure, for example, both SELECT statements join data from the Products and LineItems tables.

An *inner join* is the most common type of join. When you use an inner join, which is sometimes called an *equi-join*, the DBMS joins the two tables by matching the data in the specified columns. In this figure, for example, the first SELECT statement joins the Products and LineItems tables if the value of the ProductCode column is the same in both the Products table and the LineItems table. Inner joins are so common that they are the default type of join. That's why coding the INNER keyword before the JOIN keyword is optional.

In both SELECT statements shown in this figure, the SELECT clause creates the last column, the Total column, by multiplying the Price and Quantity columns. In other words, the Total column doesn't exist in a database table. Instead, the DBMS calculates this column and includes it in the result set. Because of that, this type of column is called a *calculated column*. When you code a calculated column, you typically use the AS keyword to specify an *alias* for the column as shown in this figure. This provides a user-friendly name for the column in the result set.

It's common for multiple tables to use the same column name. For example, the Products and LineItems tables both have a column named ProductCode. Then, when you join the two tables, you must qualify the name of the column with the name of the table or the SELECT statement won't work.

One way to qualify a column name is to code the entire table name before the column name as shown in the first SELECT statement. Here, the ProductCode column is qualified each time it appears in the statement. This approach is easy to read and understand. However, it can be tedious, especially if the table names are long.

Another way to qualify column names is to use the FROM clause to assign an alias to each table as shown in the second SELECT statement. This statement assigns an alias of p to the Products table and an alias of li to the LineItems table. Then, it uses these aliases to qualify the ProductCode column in the rest of the query. This approach generally works better for long SELECT statements, especially if it's necessary to qualify a large number of column names.

Although this figure only shows how to join data from two tables, you can extend this syntax to join data from additional tables. If, for example, you want to create a result set that includes data from three tables named Customers, Invoices, and LineItems, you could code the FROM clause like this:

```
FROM Customers c
    INNER JOIN Invoices i
        ON c.CustomerID = i.CustomerID
    INNER JOIN LineItems li
        ON i.InvoiceID = li.InvoiceID
```

Then, you could include any of the columns from the three tables in the column list of the SELECT statement.

SELECT syntax for joining two tables

```
SELECT column-1 [, column-2] ...
FROM table-1
    [INNER] JOIN table-2
    ON table-1.column-1 = table-2.column-2
[WHERE selection-criteria]
[ORDER BY column-1 [ASC|DESC] [, column-2 [ASC|DESC]] ...]
```

A SELECT statement that doesn't use table aliases

```
SELECT InvoiceID, Products.ProductCode, Price, Quantity,
       Price * Quantity AS Total
FROM Products
    JOIN LineItems
    ON Products.ProductCode = LineItems.ProductCode
WHERE InvoiceID = 1
```

A SELECT statement that uses table aliases

```
SELECT InvoiceID, p.ProductCode, Price, Quantity,
       Price * Quantity AS Total
FROM Products AS p
    JOIN LineItems AS li
    ON p.ProductCode = li.ProductCode
WHERE InvoiceID = 1
```

The result set defined by the SELECT statement

InvoiceID	ProductCode	Price	Quantity	Total
1	java	57.5	5	287.5
1	jsp	57.5	5	287.5

The syntax for coding a column alias

```
column-name-or-expression [AS] new-column-name
```

The syntax for coding a table alias

```
table-name [AS] new-table-name
```

How to work with aliases

- You can use an *alias* to provide a new name for a table or a column. When creating aliases, the AS keyword is optional, but it improves readability.

- If you use arithmetic operators to create a *calculated column*, you typically want to use a column alias to provide a user-friendly name for that column.

- If two tables use the same column name, you must qualify the name of the column by prefixing it with the name of the table or its alias.

Description

- A *join* lets you combine data from two or more tables into a single result set.

- An *inner join*, or *equi-join*, retrieves rows from both tables only if their related columns match.

Figure 20-4   How to join data from two or more tables

How to add, update, and delete data in a table

Figure 20-5 shows how to use the INSERT, UPDATE, and DELETE statements to add, update, and delete one or more rows in a database. To start, you can use the INSERT statement to add one row to a database. To do that, the first INSERT statement supplies the names of the columns that are going to receive values in the new row, followed by the values for those columns. When you insert a row, you can specify the list of column names if you don't want to specify every column or if you want to specify the columns in a different sequence than they occur in the table. However, if you are going to specify all column names in the same sequence as they occur in the table, you can omit the column list as shown by the second example.

Although you typically use the INSERT statement to add a single row, you can use the UPDATE statement to update a single row or multiple rows. In the first UPDATE example, the UPDATE statement updates the Description and Price columns in a single row where ProductCode is equal to "java". In the second example, the Price column is updated to 57.95 in all of the rows where Price is equal to 57.50.

Similarly, you can use the DELETE statement to delete a single row or multiple rows. Here, the first example deletes the row from the Products table where the ProductCode column equals "cppp". Since each row contains a unique value in the ProductCode column, this deletes a single row. However, in the second example, many rows in the Invoices table may have a ProductPrice column that's greater than 55. As a result, this statement deletes all of those products.

In the third example, the DELETE statement doesn't include a WHERE clause. As a result, it deletes all rows in the table. Although this is often useful when you're setting up and testing a database, you typically want to make sure to include a WHERE clause for your DELETE statements once the database has been set up correctly.

When coding literal values for strings, you must enclose them in single quotes. However, when coding literal values for numbers, enclosing them in single quotes is optional. In this figure, for instance, you could enclose the numeric values for the Price column in single quotes, and the SQL statements would still execute successfully.

If you want to include a single quote within a string, you can escape the single quote with another single quote. In other words, you can code two single quotes. In this figure, for instance, the string value for each Description column uses two single quotes to start the string with *Murach's*. If you attempted to use one single quote instead of two, the SQL statement would not execute successfully. Instead, it would return an error message indicating a SQL syntax error.

How to add rows

INSERT syntax for adding a single row

```
INSERT INTO table-name [(column-list)]
VALUES (value-list)
```

A statement that adds a row with a column list

```
INSERT INTO Products (ProductCode, Description, Price)
VALUES ('cppp', 'Murach''s C++ Programming', 59.50)
```

A statement that adds a row without a column list

```
INSERT INTO Products
VALUES ('cppp', 'Murach''s C++ Programming', 59.50)
```

How to update rows

UPDATE syntax

```
UPDATE table-name
SET expression-1 [, expression-2] ...
[WHERE selection-criteria]
```

A statement that updates a single row

```
UPDATE Products
SET Description = 'Murach''s Java Programming (5th Ed.)',
    Price = 59.50
WHERE ProductCode = 'java'
```

A statement that updates multiple rows

```
UPDATE Products
SET Price = 57.95
WHERE Price = 57.50
```

How to delete rows

DELETE syntax

```
DELETE FROM table-name
[WHERE selection-criteria]
```

A statement that deletes a single row

```
DELETE FROM Products WHERE ProductCode = 'cppp'
```

A statement that deletes multiple rows

```
DELETE FROM Products WHERE ProductPrice > 55
```

A statement that deletes all rows

```
DELETE FROM Products
```

Description

- When coding literal values for strings, you must enclose them in single quotes. However, when coding literal values for numbers, enclosing them in single quotes is optional.

- If you want to include a single quote in a string, you can escape the single quote with another single quote. In other words, you can code two single quotes.

Figure 20-5   How to add, update, and delete data in a table

How to use SQLite Manager

SQLite is a popular open-source relational database that can be embedded into programs. Many software products use SQLite, including the Firefox web browser. To work with a SQLite database, you can use a Firefox add-on called *SQLite Manager*. If you haven't already installed it, you can do it by following the directions in the appendix for your operating system.

An introduction to SQLite

Figure 20-6 describes the SQLite database. This database is a relational database management system (RDBMS) that implements most, but not all, of the SQL standard. SQLite is a lightweight programming library. You can add this library to a Java project, and it doesn't require any configuration or database administration.

When you create a SQLite database, that database is stored in a single file on a device. For example, a database file named products.sqlite stores the data for the Products and LineItems tables described in this chapter.

SQLite is a popular choice as an embedded database. It is used today by several web browsers and operating systems, including the Android operating system. One of the reasons that SQLite is used so widely is because it is open-source. As a result, it's free for most purposes.

If you're familiar with other database management systems such as MySQL or Oracle, you shouldn't have much trouble learning to work with SQLite. However, SQLite is different than other database systems in a few ways.

First, SQLite does not run in a server process that's accessed by client applications, which run in separate processes. Instead, it's embedded as part of the client application and runs in the same process.

Second, SQLite only supports these three data types: TEXT, INTEGER, and REAL. These data types correspond with these three Java data types: String, long, and double. As a result, other Java data types such as date/time and Boolean values must be converted into one of the SQLite types before saving them in the database. For example, a LocalDate type can be converted to a TEXT type before it's stored in the database. Then, when it's retrieved from the database, it can be converted from a TEXT type to a LocalDate type.

Third, SQLite is weakly-typed. In other words, a column in a SQLite database does not reject a value of an incorrect data type. For example, if you define a database column to accept the INTEGER type, you could still store a string value in this column and the database would not reject that value. Usually, this isn't a problem as the code for the application shouldn't attempt to store a string in an INTEGER column. However, you should be aware of this as it means that the code for your application must make sure to insert values of the correct type in each column.

SQLite is...

- **A RDBMS.** SQLite is a *relational database management system* (*RDBMS*).
- **Standards-compliant.** SQLite implements most of the SQL standard.
- **Embedded.** Unlike most database management systems, SQLite does not run in a server process that's accessed by client applications, which run in separate processes. Instead, it's embedded as part of the client application and runs in the same process.
- **Zero-configuration.** SQLite does not require any configuration or database administration.
- **Lightweight.** The SQLite programming library is small.
- **Popular.** SQLite is a popular choice as an embedded database and is used extensively for Android programming.
- **Open-source.** The source code for SQLite is in the public domain.

Data types supported by SQLite

SQLite data type	Java data type
TEXT	String
INTEGER	long
REAL	double

Description

- SQLite only supports three data types (String, long, and double). As a result, the code for the application must convert other Java data types such as date/time and Boolean values into one of the SQLite types before saving them in the database.
- SQLite is weakly-typed. In other words, a column in a SQLite database does not reject a value of an incorrect data type. As a result, the code for the application must make sure to insert values of the correct type.

Figure 20-6   An introduction to SQLite

How to connect to a SQLite database

Figure 20-7 begins by showing how to use SQLite Manager to connect to a database and view one of its tables. First, you start Firefox. Then, you start SQLite Manager.

Once you start SQLite Manager, you can connect to the database you want to work with by selecting Database→Connect Database from its menus. Then, you use the resulting dialog box to navigate to the file for the SQLite database. In this figure, SQLite Manager has opened a connection to the SQLite database named products.sqlite that's included as part of the download for this book.

How to work with a SQLite database

Once you connect to the database, you can view its tables by clicking the Browse & Search tab in SQLite Manager's main panel. Then, in the left panel, you can expand the Tables node and click the table you want to view. This displays the table in the main panel, along with all of its rows and columns. In this figure, SQLite Manager shows the Products table and its data.

As you view a table, you can click on a row to select it, and you can use the buttons at the top of the table to add, edit, or delete rows. In this figure, the first row is selected. As a result, you could click the Edit button to edit its data, or you could click the Delete button to delete the row.

Since the Products table doesn't start with an INTEGER column that uniquely identifies each row, SQLite Manager automatically generates a column named rowid and displays it as the first column of the table. However, this column isn't actually part of the Products table. Conversely, since the LineItems table starts with an INTEGER column that uniquely identifies each row, SQLite Manager doesn't generate the rowid column for this table.

After you expand the Tables node, you can work with a table by right-clicking on it (Ctrl-clicking on Mac) and selecting a command from the resulting menu. For example, you could select the Rename command to rename the table, or you could select the Delete command to delete the table.

SQLite Manager after using the Browse & Search tab to view a table

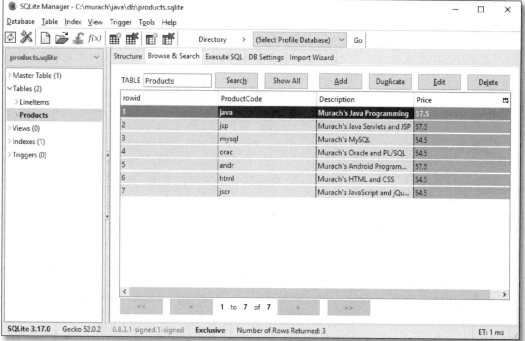

How to connect to a SQLite database and view a table

1. Start Firefox.
2. Start SQLite Manager. To do that, you can press Alt+T (Option+T on Mac) to access the Tools menu. Then, you can select the SQLite Manager item.
3. Select Database→Connect Database from SQLite Manager's menus. Then, use the resulting dialog box to select the SQLite database you want to open. The database for this chapter is located here:

   ```
   \murach\java\db\products.sqlite
   ```
4. In the main panel, click the Browse & Search tab.
5. In the left panel, expand the Tables node and click the table you want to view.

Description

- To install the Firefox browser and the SQLite Manager, use the instructions in the appendix for your operating system.

- As you view a table, you can click on a row to select it, and you can use the buttons at the top of the table to add, edit, or delete rows.

- After you expand the Tables node, you can right-click (Ctrl-click on Mac) on a table's name. Then, you can use the resulting menu to copy, rename, or delete the table.

Figure 20-7   How to use SQLite Manager to work with a database

How to execute SQL statements

After you use SQLite Manager to connect to a database, you can use it to execute SQL statements against that database. This can help you test your SQL statements before you use them in your Java code, and it can help you debug SQL statements that aren't working correctly.

Figure 20-8 shows how to use SQLite Manager to execute a SQL statement. To start, you click on the Execute SQL tab. Then, you enter a SQL statement and click the Run SQL button. When you do, SQLite Manager displays the result set just below the Run SQL button. In this example, SQLite Manager has executed a SELECT statement successfully and displayed a result set. However, if the SQL statement isn't valid, SQLite Manager displays an error message that can help you find and fix the problem.

Of course, the INSERT, UPDATE, or DELETE statements don't retrieve a result set. So, for those statements, SQLite Manager doesn't display a result set. However, it still executes the statement, which updates the data in the database. Or, if the statement causes an error to occur, it doesn't update the data. Instead, it displays an error message that indicates why it wasn't able to update the data.

To make it easy to identify the keywords in a SQL statement, the examples in this book capitalize the keywords. You should realize, however, that this capitalization is optional. So, if you want to use lowercase letters in the keywords when you type them into SQLite Manager, you can do that.

The Execute SQL tab after a SQL statement has been executed

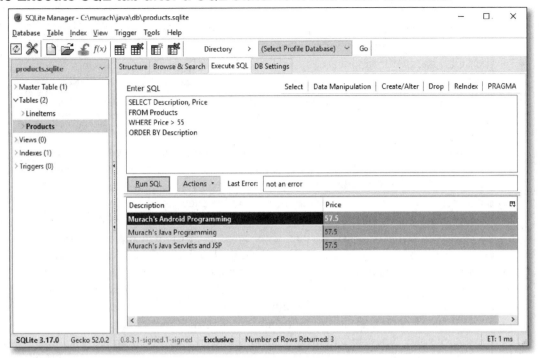

Description

- To execute a SQL statement, click the Execute SQL tab. Then, enter the SQL statement and click the Run SQL button.
- To sort the columns in the result set, click on the column name.

Figure 20-8   How to use SQLite Manager to execute SQL statements

How to create a SQLite database

Now that you know how to work with an existing SQLite database, you're ready to learn how to create a SQLite database. To do that, you typically store the SQL statements that create the database in a file known as a *script*. For example, figure 20-9 shows a script that contains the SQL statements that create the tables described in this chapter and insert data into them. When you code multiple SQL statements in a script, you must end each SQL statement with a semicolon as shown in this figure.

The two DROP TABLE statements at the beginning of this script delete the Products and LineItems tables if they exist. This deletes the definition for the table as well as all of the data that's stored in the table. Without these statements, the script would return an error message if the Products and LineItems tables already exist.

The two CREATE TABLE statements define the Products and LineItems tables. Here, the first CREATE TABLE statement creates a Products table that has three columns named ProductCode, Description, and Price with appropriate data types. In addition, it defines the ProductCode column as its primary key. As a result, this column must contain a unique value. Then, the second CREATE TABLE statement creates a LineItems table that defines four columns with appropriate data types. In addition, it defines the LineItemID column as its primary key, and it defines the ProductCode column as a foreign key that relates this table to the Products table.

After defining the two tables, this script includes INSERT statements that add some starting data to these tables. This figure doesn't show all of these statements, but the complete script is available from the download for this book if you'd like to view them.

Once you have a SQL script for creating your database, you can create it by following the procedure shown at the bottom of this figure. To start, you use SQLite Manager to create the database file. This automatically connects to the database file. Then, you use SQLite Manager's Import command to run the script that creates the database. If the script runs successfully, SQLite Manager creates the database. Otherwise, it displays an error message, and you can debug your script.

Instead of using a script to create the tables for a database, you can use the menus and resulting dialog boxes that are available from SQLite Manager. When you're done, you can use SQLite Manager's Export command to generate a SQL script for the database. Then, you can use this script to recreate the database later if you need to.

A script that creates a SQLite database

```
DROP TABLE IF EXISTS Products;
DROP TABLE IF EXISTS LineItems;

-- Create the tables
CREATE TABLE Products (
    ProductCode TEXT      PRIMARY KEY     NOT NULL,
    Description TEXT                      NOT NULL,
    Price       REAL                      NOT NULL
);

CREATE TABLE LineItems (
    LineItemID  INTEGER PRIMARY KEY       NOT NULL,
    InvoiceID   INTEGER                   NOT NULL,
    ProductCode TEXT                      NOT NULL,
    Quantity    INTEGER                   NOT NULL,
    FOREIGN KEY(ProductCode) REFERENCES Products(ProductCode)
);


-- Populate the Products table
INSERT INTO Products VALUES
('java', 'Murach''s Java Programming', 57.50);

INSERT INTO Products VALUES
('jsp', 'Murach''s Java Servlets and JSP', 57.50);

INSERT INTO Products VALUES
('mysql', 'Murach''s MySQL', 54.50);

...

-- Populate the LineItems table
INSERT INTO LineItems VALUES
(1, 1, 'java', 5);

INSERT INTO LineItems VALUES
(2, 1, 'jsp', 5);

INSERT INTO LineItems VALUES
(3, 2, 'mysql', 1);

...
```

How to create a SQLite database

1. Start SQLite Manager.

2. Select the Database→New Database command, and use the resulting dialog boxes to create the database file. When you finish, SQLite Manager connects to the database.

3. Select the Database→Import command to display the Import Wizard table. Then, click on the Select button and use the resulting dialog box to select the file for the script that creates the database.

4. Click the OK button to confirm the operation.

Figure 20-9   How to use SQLite Manager to create a SQLite database

Perspective

The goal of this chapter is to prepare you for developing programs that use a database. To do that, this chapter has introduced you to the SELECT, INSERT, UPDATE, and DELETE statements that you'll use in most database programs. This chapter has also shown you how to use SQLite Manager to execute these SQL statements. Now, if you understand the SQL statements presented in this chapter, you're ready to learn how to use Java to work with a SQLite database as shown in the next chapter.

You should know, however, that there's a lot more to learn about database programming. In contrast to SQLite databases, for example, MySQL, Oracle, and SQL Server are designed to run on a server and be accessed by remote clients. They also offer more features and functionality than SQLite.

Summary

- A *relational database* uses tables to store data. Each table contains one or more *rows*, or *records*, while each row contains one or more *columns*, or *fields*.

- A *primary key* is used to identify each row in a table. A *foreign key* is a key in one table that is used to relate rows to another table.

- Each database is managed by a *database management system* (*DBMS*) that supports the use of the *Structured Query Language* (*SQL*).

- The SELECT statement retrieves data from one or more tables into a *result set*.

- To retrieve data from two or more tables, a SELECT statement *joins* the data based on the data in related fields. An *inner join* retrieves a result set that includes data only if the related fields match.

- The INSERT, UPDATE, and DELETE statements add, update, and delete the data in a database. These statements don't retrieve a result set.

- A file that contains SQL statements is known as a *script*. Within a script, you must separate each SQL statement with a semicolon.

Exercise 20-1   Review a SQLite database and test some SQL statements

This exercise gives you a chance to use SQLite Manager to review the SQLite database that contains the Products and LineItems tables presented in this chapter. In addition, it lets you test some SQL statements presented in this chapter.

Use SQLite Manager to connect to the database

1. If you haven't already installed the Firefox browser and the SQLite Manager add-on, do that now. For instructions, please see the appendix for your operating system.

2. Start Firefox. Then, start SQLite Manager.

3. Use SQLite Manager to connect to the database named products.sqlite that's in this directory:

   ```
   murach/java/db
   ```

Review the tables in the database

4. In the left panel, expand the Tables node. Then, click the Products table. If necessary, click the Browse & Search tab. This should display the data for the Products table.

5. In the left panel, click the LineItems table. This should display the data for that table.

Run SQL statements against the database

6. In the main panel, click the Execute SQL tab. Then, enter a query that selects all columns from the Products table where the product's code is java, and click the Run SQL button to execute this statement. This should display a result set that has one row.

7. Modify the query so it selects a product that has a code of jscr. Then, run this query and view the result set.

8. Modify the query so it only retrieves the Description and Price columns. Then, run this query and view the result set.

9. Modify the query so it retrieves the Description and Price columns for all products and sorts the result set by price in descending order.

10. Enter an INSERT statement that inserts a new row into the Products table. Then, run this SQL statement. This shouldn't display a result set, but it should add a new row to the Products table.

11. Use the Browse & Search tab to view the new row.

12. Use the Execute SQL tab to run a DELETE statement that deletes the new row.

13. Use the Browse & Search tab to make sure the row was deleted.

14. Continue to experiment until you're sure that you understand the SQL statements that are presented in this chapter.

21

How to use JDBC to work with a database

This chapter shows how to use Java to work with a database. In particular, it shows the JDBC skills needed to create the classes for the database tier of an application. Most of the examples in this chapter show how to work with the SQLite database presented in the previous chapter. However, you can use most of the skills presented in this chapter to work with any kind of database including MySQL, Oracle, and SQL Server databases.

An introduction to database drivers

To write Java code that works with a database, you can use *JDBC*, which is sometimes referred to as *Java Database Connectivity*. The core JDBC API is stored in the java.sql package, which comes as part of Java SE.

Before you can use JDBC to work with a database, you must make a *database driver* available to your application. A database driver implements the interfaces stored in the java.sql package for a particular database. This allows JDBC to work with a database. For example, a database driver for SQLite implements the JDBC interfaces for a SQLite database.

Four types of JDBC database drivers

Figure 21-1 lists the four types of JDBC database drivers that you can use. Then, it shows how to download a database driver and make it available to your application. For most applications, you'll want to use a type-4 driver. The other three driver types are generally considered less preferable, with the type-1 driver being the least preferable. As a result, you'll only want to use these drivers if a type-4 driver isn't available for the database that you're using.

How to download a database driver

For a SQLite database, you can download a type-4 driver from the URL shown in this figure. For other types of databases, you can usually download a type-4 driver from the website for that database. The documentation for these drivers typically shows how to install and configure the driver.

To use the database driver in an application, you can add the JAR file that contains the database driver to the application's classpath. The easiest way to do that is to use your IDE to add the JAR file for the database driver to your project as shown in the next figure.

The package that contains the JDBC interfaces and classes

`java.sql`

The four types of JDBC database drivers

Type 1   A *JDBC-ODBC bridge driver* converts JDBC calls into ODBC calls that access the DBMS protocol. For this data access method, an ODBC driver must be installed on the client machine. A JDBC-ODBC bridge driver was included as part of the JDK prior to Java 8 but is not included or supported with Java 8 and later.

Type 2   A *native protocol partly Java driver* converts JDBC calls into the native DBMS protocol. Since this conversion takes place on the client, the database client library must be installed on the client machine.

Type 3   A *net protocol all Java driver* converts JDBC calls into a net protocol that's independent of any native DBMS protocol. Then, middleware software running on a server converts the net protocol to the native DBMS protocol. Since this conversion takes place on the server side, the database client library isn't required on the client machine.

Type 4   A *native protocol all Java driver* converts JDBC calls into the native DBMS protocol. Since this conversion takes place on the server, the database client library isn't required on the client machine.

A URL that provides a download of a JDBC database driver for SQLite

`https://bitbucket.org/xerial/sqlite-jdbc/downloads/`

How to download a database driver

- For SQLite databases, you can download a type-4 JDBC driver from the website shown above. However, a version of this driver is included with the download for this book, so you only need to download a new database driver if you want to use a different version.

- For other databases, you can usually download a type-4 JDBC driver from the database's website.

- The Connector/J driver for MySQL databases is included with NetBeans. As a result, if you're using NetBeans, you don't need to download this driver.

How to make a database driver available to an application

- Before you can use a database driver, you must make it available to your application. The easiest way to do this is to use your IDE to add the JAR file for the driver to your project as shown in the next figure.

Figure 21-1   An introduction to database drivers

How to add a database driver to a project

To work with a database from a project, you have to add the database driver to the project. In most cases, a database driver is stored in a JAR file. As a result, you can typically add a database driver to a project by adding the JAR file that contains the driver. Figure 21-2 shows how to do that in NetBeans.

Here, a JAR file named sqlite-jdbc.jar has been added to the Libraries folder. This file contains all the classes necessary to work with a SQLite database. Once you add this JAR file to a project, any classes in the project can use the database driver to work with the database.

If you're using NetBeans and you want to work with a MySQL database, you should know that the Connector/J driver for MySQL databases is included with NetBeans. As a result, you don't need to download this driver. Instead, you can add the driver to the project by right-clicking on the Libraries folder, selecting the Add Library command, and using the resulting dialog box to select the MySQL JDBC Driver library.

A project after a JDBC database driver for SQLite has been added

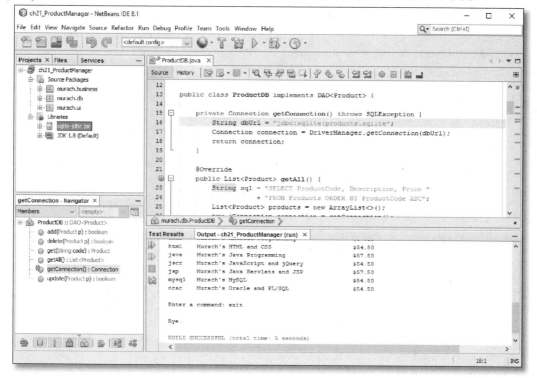

Description

- A database driver is a class that's typically stored in a JAR file.

- To add a database driver to a NetBeans project, right-click on the Libraries folder for the project, select the Add JAR/Folder command, and use the resulting dialog box to select the JAR file that contains the driver.

- After you add the JAR file that contains a database driver to a project, the JRE can find and run the class for the driver.

- To remove a database driver from a project, right-click on the JAR file that contains the driver and select the Remove command.

- To add the MySQL JDBC driver to a NetBeans project, right-click on the Libraries folder, select the Add Library command, and use the resulting dialog box to select the MySQL JDBC Driver library.

Figure 21-2   How to add a database driver to a project

How to work with a database

Now that you know how to add a database driver to the project, you're ready to write Java code that uses JDBC to work with a database.

How to connect to a database

Before you can access or modify the data in a database, you must connect to the database as shown in figure 21-3. To start, this figure shows the syntax for a database URL. Then, the first example shows a method that gets a connection to a SQLite database. Within this method, the first statement defines the database URL. This URL consists of the API (jdbc), the subprotocol (sqlite), and the name of the database file (products.sqlite). Since this database URL doesn't specify a path for the database file, this code looks for the database file in the working directory, which is usually the root directory for the application.

After defining the database URL, the first example uses the static getConnection() method of the DriverManager class to return a Connection object. Since SQLite doesn't require a password, this method only requires one argument, the database URL. Also, since this code may throw a SQLException, the getConnection() method shown in this example throws a SQLException, so it can be handled by the calling code.

The second example shows a database URL that specifies a path for the database file named products.sqlite. To do that, it uses front slashes (/) to specify the /murach/java/db directory.

The third example shows how to get a connection to a MySQL database that's running on a server. To start, the first statement defines a database URL that consists of the API (jdbc), the subprotocol (mysql), the host machine (localhost), the port for the database server (3306), and the name of the database (products). The second and third statements define a username and password for connecting to the database. And the fourth statement uses the static getConnection() method of the DriverManager class to return a Connection object using the database URL, username, and password.

In practice, connecting to the database is often frustrating because it's hard to figure out the correct URL, username, and password. So if your colleagues have already made a connection to the database that you need to use, you can start by asking them for this information. Otherwise, you can contact the database administrator.

The first and third examples use a feature of JDBC 4.0 and later called *automatic driver loading*. This feature loads the database driver automatically based on the database URL. However, if you're working with an older version of JDBC, you need to explicitly load the database driver before you call the getConnection() method. To do that, you can use the static forName() method of the Class class as shown by the fourth example. Even with JDBC 4.0 and later, for some databases, you may get a message that says, "No suitable driver found." In that case, you may be able to solve the problem by adding code that explicitly loads the driver.

Database URL syntax

```
jdbc:subprotocolName:databaseURL
```

A method that connects to a SQLite database in the working directory

```
private Connection getConnection() throws SQLException {
    String dbUrl = "jdbc:sqlite:products.sqlite";
    Connection connection = DriverManager.getConnection(dbUrl);
    return connection;
}
```

A database URL for a SQLite database that's in the specified directory

```
String dbUrl = "jdbc:sqlite:/murach/java/db/products.sqlite";
```

A method that connects to a MySQL database that's running on a server

```
private Connection getConnection() throws SQLException {
    String dbURL = "jdbc:mysql://localhost:3306/products";
    String username = "admin_user";
    String password = "sesame";
    Connection connection = DriverManager.getConnection(
        dbURL, username, password);
    return connection;
}
```

How to load a database driver prior to JDBC 4.0

```
try {
    Class.forName("org.sqlite.JDBC");
} catch(ClassNotFoundException e) {
    System.err.println(e);
}
```

Description

- Before you can get or modify the data in a database, you need to connect to it. To do that, you use the static getConnection() method of the DriverManager class to return a Connection object.

- When you use the getConnection() method of the DriverManager class, you must supply a URL for the database. In addition, you usually supply a username and a password, although you might not for an embedded database. This method throws a SQLException.

- Although the database URL is different for each driver, the documentation for the driver should explain how to create a database URL for that driver.

- With JDBC 4.0 and later, the database driver is loaded automatically. This feature is known as *automatic driver loading*.

- Prior to JDBC 4.0, you had to use the static forName() method of the Class class to load the driver. This method throws a ClassNotFoundException.

Figure 21-3   How to connect to a database

How to return a result set and move the cursor through it

Once you connect to a database, you're ready to retrieve data from it as shown in figure 21-4. Here, the first two examples show how to use Statement objects to create a *result set*. Then, the next two examples show how to move the *cursor* through the result set.

Both of the result sets in this figure are read-only, forward-only result sets. This means that you can only move the cursor forward through the result set, and that you can only read the rows in the result set. In other words, you can't scroll through the result set forwards and backwards, and you can't update the rows in the result set. Although JDBC supports other types of result sets that are scrollable and updatable, these features require some additional overhead, they aren't supported by SQLite, and they aren't necessary for most applications.

The first example calls the createStatement() method from a Connection object to return a Statement object. Then, it calls the executeQuery() method from the Statement object to execute the specified SELECT statement. This returns a ResultSet object named product that contains the result set for the SELECT statement. In this case, the SELECT statement only retrieves a single row (the row that has the specified product code). So, the ResultSet object contains the data for a single product.

The second example works like the first example. However, it returns all of the rows and columns for the Products table and puts this data in a ResultSet object named products. You can use this object to display all products.

The third example shows how to use the next() method of the ResultSet object to move the cursor to the first row of the result set that's created by the first example. When you create a result set, the cursor is positioned before the first row in the result set. As a result, the first call to the next() method attempts to move the cursor to the first row in the result set. If the row exists, the cursor moves to that row and the next() method returns a true value. In that case, you can retrieve values from the row as shown in the next figure. Otherwise, the next() method returns a false value. In that case, there's no data to process. Either way, when you're done with the result set, you should call its close() method to release the resources that it's using.

The fourth example shows how to use the next() method to loop through all of the rows in the result set that's created in the second example. Here, the while loop calls the next() method. Then, if the next row exists, the next() method moves the cursor to the row and returns a true value. As a result, the code within the while loop is executed. Otherwise, the next() method returns a false value and the while loop ends.

Since all of the methods described in this figure throw a SQLException, you either need to throw or catch this exception when you're working with these methods. The ProductDB class presented later in this chapter shows how this works.

Two methods of a ResultSet object

Method	Description
`next()`	Moves the cursor to the next row in the result set. If the next row exists, this method returns a true value. Otherwise, it returns a false value.
`close()`	Releases the resources that are being used by the result set.

How to create a result set that contains one row

```
Statement statement = connection.createStatement();
ResultSet product = statement.executeQuery(
    "SELECT * FROM Product " +
    "WHERE ProductCode = 'java'");
```

How to create a result set that contains multiple rows

```
Statement statement = connection.createStatement();
ResultSet products = statement.executeQuery(
    "SELECT * FROM Product");
```

How to move the cursor to the first row in the result set

```
boolean productExists = product.next();
if (productExists) {
    // statements that process the row
}
product.close();
```

How to loop through a result set

```
while (products.next()) {
    // statements that process each row
}
products.close();
```

Description

- To return a *result set*, you use the createStatement() method of a Connection object to create a Statement object. Then, you use the executeQuery() method of the Statement object to execute a SELECT statement that returns a ResultSet object.

- By default, the createStatement() method creates a forward-only, read-only result set. This means that you can only move the *cursor* through the result set from the first row to the last and that you can't update the result set. Although you can pass arguments to the createStatement() method that create other types of result sets, the default is appropriate for most applications.

- When a result set is created, the cursor is positioned before the first row. Then, you can use the next() method of the ResultSet object to move the cursor to the next row, which is the first row.

- All of the methods presented in this figure throw a SQLException. As a result, any code that uses these methods needs to catch or throw this exception.

Figure 21-4   How to return a result set and move the cursor through it

How to get data from a result set

When the cursor is positioned on the row that you want to get data from, you can use the methods in figure 21-5 to get that data. To start, this figure summarizes the getString(), getDouble(), and getInt() methods of the ResultSet object that you can use to return String objects as well as double and int values.

Each of these methods accepts two types of arguments. First, these methods accept an int value that specifies the index number of the column in the result set, where 1 is the first column, 2 is the second column, and so on. Second, these methods accept a String object that specifies the name of the column in the result set. Although using indexes requires less typing, using column names typically leads to code that's easier to read and maintain.

The first example shows how to use column indexes to return data from a result set named products. Here, the first and second statements use the getString() method to return the code and description, and the third statement uses the getDouble() method to return the list price. Since these methods use the column index, the first column in the result set must contain the product code, the second column must contain the product description, and so on.

The second example shows how to use column names to return data from the products result set. Since this code uses the column names, the order of the columns in the result set doesn't matter. However, the column names must exist in the result set or the method throws a SQLException that indicates that the column wasn't found.

The third example shows how you can use the get methods to create a Product object. Here, a single statement creates a new Product object from the data that's retrieved from the ResultSet object. Since objects are often created from data that's stored in a database, code like this is commonly used when you use the JDBC API.

Although the methods shown in this figure are commonly used, the ResultSet interface provides get methods for other types of data too. If you check the documentation for this interface, you'll see that it provides get methods for all of the primitive types as well as for other types of data such as the Date, Time, and Timestamp classes that are a part of the java.sql package.

Methods of a ResultSet object that return data from a result set

Method	Description
getString(columnIndex)	Returns a String object from the specified column number.
getString(columnName)	Returns a String object from the specified column name.
getDouble(columnIndex)	Returns a double value from the specified column number.
getDouble(columnName)	Returns a double value from the specified column name.
getInt(columnIndex)	Returns an int value from the specified column number.
getInt(columnName)	Returns an int value from the specified column name.

Code that uses indexes to return columns from the products result set

```
String code = products.getString(1);
String description = products.getString(2);
double price = products.getDouble(3);
```

Code that uses names to return the same columns

```
String code = products.getString("ProductCode");
String description = products.getString("Description");
double price = products.getDouble("Price");
```

Code that creates a Product object from the products result set

```
Product p = new Product(products.getString("ProductCode"),
                        products.getString("Description"),
                        products.getDouble("Price"));
```

Description

- The get methods of a ResultSet object can be used to return all eight primitive types. For example, the getLong() method returns the long type.

- The get methods of a ResultSet object can also be used to return some objects such as dates and times. For example, the getDate(), getTime(), and getTimestamp() methods return objects of the Date, Time, and Timestamp classes of the java.sql package.

- The get methods accept an argument that specifies the number or name of the column in the result set. The column numbers begin with 1.

Figure 21-5   How to get data from a result set

How to insert, update, and delete data

Figure 21-6 shows how to use JDBC to modify the data in a database. To do that, you can use the executeUpdate() method of a Statement object to execute SQL statements that add, update, and delete data.

When you work with the executeUpdate() method, you just pass a SQL statement to the database. In these examples, the code adds, updates, and deletes a product in the Products table. To do that, the code combines data from a Product object with the appropriate SQL statement. For the UPDATE and DELETE statements, the SQL statement uses the product's code in the WHERE clause to select a single product.

Unfortunately, if you build a SQL statement from user input and use a method of the Statement object to execute that SQL statement, you are susceptible to a security vulnerability known as a SQL injection attack. A *SQL injection attack* allows a hacker to execute SQL statements against your database to read sensitive data or to delete or modify data. For the Product Manager application, for instance, the user might be able to execute a DROP TABLE statement by entering the following code:

```
test'); DROP TABLE Products; --
```

Here, the first semicolon ends the first SQL statement. Then, the database might execute the second SQL statement, which deletes the entire Products table. To prevent most types of SQL injection attacks, you can use a prepared statement as described in the next figure.

In addition, if you build a SQL statement from user input and the user enters a string that includes a single quote such as "Murach's Java Programming", the executeUpdate() method throws an exception that indicates that the SQL statement has a syntax error. That's because you must escape a single quote with another single quote for the SQL statement to execute successfully. Fortunately, you can easily prevent this syntax error by using prepared statements as described in the next figure. Then, the prepared statement automatically escapes the single quote and the executeUpdate() method executes successfully.

How to use the executeUpdate() method to modify data

How to add a row

```
String query =
    "INSERT INTO Products (ProductCode, Description, Price) " +
    "VALUES ('" + product.getCode() + "', " +
            "'" + product.getDescription() + "', " +
            "'" + product.getPrice() + "')";
Statement statement = connection.createStatement();
int rowCount = statement.executeUpdate(query);
```

How to update a row

```
String query = "UPDATE Products SET " +
               "    Description = '" + product.getDescription() + "', " +
               "    Price = '" + product.getPrice() + "' " +
               "WHERE ProductCode = '" + product.getCode() + "'";
Statement statement = connection.createStatement();
int rowCount = statement.executeUpdate(query);
```

How to delete a row

```
String query = "DELETE FROM Products " +
               "WHERE ProductCode = '" + product.getCode() + "'";
Statement statement = connection.createStatement();
int rowCount = statement.executeUpdate(query);
```

Description

- The executeUpdate() method returns an int value that identifies the number of rows that were affected by the SQL statement.

Warnings

- If you build a SQL statement from user input and use a method of the Statement object to execute that SQL statement, you may be susceptible to a security vulnerability known as a SQL injection attack.

- A *SQL injection attack* allows a hacker to bypass authentication or to execute SQL statements against your database that can read sensitive data, modify data, or delete data.

- To prevent most types of SQL injection attacks, you can use prepared statements as described in the next figure.

- If you build a SQL statement from user input and a string includes a single quote, the executeUpdate() method throws a SQLException.

- To prevent the SQLException that's thrown when a string includes a single quote, you can use prepared statements as described in the next figure.

Figure 21-6   How to insert, update, and delete data

How to work with prepared statements

Figure 21-7 shows how to use a prepared SQL statement to return a result set or to modify data. When you use a *prepared statement*, you include placeholders in the statement for parameters whose values will vary. Then, before you execute the statement, you set the values of those parameters.

Prepared statements provide several benefits. First, because the database can cache and reuse prepared statements, they execute faster than regular statements. Second, because prepared statements prevent most types of SQL injection attacks, they are more secure. Third, because prepared statements automatically escape single quotes, they prevent errors when processing strings that contain single quotes. Because of these benefits, it's generally considered a best practice to use prepared statements whenever possible.

The first example uses a prepared statement to create a result set that contains a single product. Here, the first statement uses a question mark (**?**) to identify the parameter for the SELECT statement, which is the product code. The second statement uses the prepareStatement() method of the Connection object to return a PreparedStatement object for the specified SQL statement. The third statement uses the setString() method of the PreparedStatement object to set a value for the parameter. And the fourth statement uses the executeQuery() method of the PreparedStatement object to return a ResultSet object.

The second example shows how to use a prepared statement to execute an INSERT statement that requires three parameters. Here, the first statement uses three question marks to identify the three parameters of the INSERT statement. The second statement creates the PreparedStatement object for that statement. The third, fourth, and fifth statements set the three parameters in the order that they appear in the INSERT statement. And the sixth statement uses the executeUpdate() method of the PreparedStatement object to execute the INSERT statement.

The third and fourth examples show how to update and delete rows with prepared statements. This works similarly to the second example.

In this figure, the type of SQL statement that you're using determines whether you use the executeQuery() method or the executeUpdate() method. If you're using a SELECT statement to return a result set, you use the executeQuery() method. However, if you're using an INSERT, UPDATE, or DELETE statement, you use the executeUpdate() method. In other words, this works the same for a PreparedStatement object as it does for a Statement object.

How to use a prepared statement

To return a result set

```
String sql = "SELECT * FROM Products "
           + "WHERE ProductCode = ?";
PreparedStatement ps = connection.prepareStatement(sql);
ps.setString(1, productCode);
ResultSet product = ps.executeQuery();
```

To insert a row

```
String sql = "INSERT INTO Products (ProductCode, Description, Price) "
           + "VALUES (?, ?, ?)";
PreparedStatement ps = connection.prepareStatement(sql);
ps.setString(1, product.getCode());
ps.setString(2, product.getDescription());
ps.setDouble(3, product.getPrice());
int rowCount = ps.executeUpdate();
```

To modify a row

```
String sql = "UPDATE Products SET "
           + "    Description = ?, "
           + "    Price = ?"
           + "WHERE ProductCode = ?";
PreparedStatement ps = connection.prepareStatement(sql);
ps.setString(1, product.getDescription());
ps.setDouble(2, product.getPrice());
ps.setString(3, product.getCode());
int rowCount = ps.executeUpdate();
```

To delete a row

```
String sql = "DELETE FROM Products "
           + "WHERE ProductCode = ?";
PreparedStatement ps = connection.prepareStatement(sql);
ps.setString(1, product.getCode());
int rowCount = ps.executeUpdate();
```

Description

- When you use *prepared statements* in your Java applications, the database server only has to check the syntax and prepare an execution plan once for each SQL statement. This improves the efficiency of the database operations. In addition, it prevents most types of SQL injection attacks and automatically escapes single quotes within strings.

- To specify a parameter for a prepared statement, type a question mark (?) in the SQL statement.

- To supply values for the parameters in a prepared statement, use the set methods of the PreparedStatement interface. For a complete list of set methods, look up the PreparedStatement interface of the java.sql package in the Java API documentation.

- To execute a SELECT statement, use the executeQuery() method. This returns a ResultSet object.

- To execute an INSERT, UPDATE, or DELETE statement, use the executeUpdate() method. This returns a count of the number of rows modified by the statement.

Figure 21-7   How to work with prepared statements

A class for working with databases

Now that you know how to use JDBC to work with a database, you're ready to learn how to code a class that allows you to map business objects to a table in a database. In particular, you're ready to learn how to map Product objects to the Products table described in the previous chapter.

The DAO interface

Figure 21-8 presents the DAO interface that was originally presented in chapter 15. This interface uses generics so it can work with any type of business object. In chapter 15, you learned how to use file I/O to map Product objects to a file. Now, you'll learn how to use JDBC to map Product objects to a table in a database.

The ProductDB class

Figure 21-8 also presents the code for the ProductDB class. This class works with the data in the Products table of a database. To start, this class declares that it implements the DAO<Product> interface.

Within this class, the getConnection() method is a private method that's used by the other methods of this class. This method returns a Connection object. To do that, the first statement defines the URL for a SQLite database that's stored in the products.sqlite file in the working directory, which is usually the root directory of the application. Then, the second statement uses the DriverManager class to get a Connection object. If the second statement executes successfully, the third statement returns the Connection object. Otherwise, this method throws a SQLException that can be handled by the calling code.

The DAO interface

```
package murach.db;

import java.util.List;

public interface DAO<T> {
    T get(String code);
    List<T> getAll();
    boolean add(T t);
    boolean update(T t);
    boolean delete(T t);
}
```

The ProductDB class

```
package murach.db;

import murach.business.Product;

import java.sql.Connection;
import java.sql.DriverManager;
import java.sql.PreparedStatement;
import java.sql.ResultSet;
import java.sql.SQLException;
import java.util.ArrayList;
import java.util.List;

public class ProductDB implements DAO<Product> {

    private Connection getConnection() throws SQLException {
        String dbUrl = "jdbc:sqlite:products.sqlite";
        Connection connection = DriverManager.getConnection(dbUrl);
        return connection;
    }
```

Figure 21-8   The DAO interface and the ProductDB class (part 1 of 3)

The getAll() method returns a List object that contains all of the Product objects that are stored in the Products table of the database. Here, the first statement creates a string that contains a SQL statement that selects all columns from the Products table and sorts them in ascending order by the ProductCode column. Then, the second statement creates an ArrayList object for storing Product objects.

After creating the array list, this code uses a try-with-resources statement to create the Connection, PreparedStatement, and ResultSet objects that are needed by this method. That way, these objects are automatically closed when the try block ends. Within the try block, a while loop reads each row in the result set. Within the loop, the first two statements use the getString() method to return strings for the ProductCode and Description columns, and the third statement uses the getDouble() method to return a double value for the Price column. Then, this loop creates the Product object, stores the data in it, and adds it to the list of products array list.

If this code executes successfully, the getAll() method returns the products array list. However, if a SQLException is thrown anywhere in the try block, the catch block prints the exception to the console and returns a null value. That way, the calling code can check for a null value and handle it appropriately.

The get() method returns a Product object for a product that matches the specified product code. To do that, it uses a prepared SQL statement to return a result set. Then, it calls the next() method of the result set to attempt to move the cursor to the first row in the result set. If successful, this method continues by reading the columns from the row, creating a Product object from this data, closing the result set, and returning the Product object.

Unlike the getAll() method, the result set used by the get() method can't be created in the same try-with-resources statement that creates the prepared statement. That's because the value of the parameter in the prepared statement must be set before the result set can be opened.

If no product row contains a product code that matches the specified code, this method closes the result set and returns a null to indicate that the product couldn't be found. In addition, if a SQLException is thrown anywhere in this method, this method prints the exception to the console and returns a null value. That way, the code that calls the get() method can check whether it returned a null value and take appropriate action.

As you review the get() method, note that if the try block throws a SQLException, the result set isn't explicitly closed. In most cases, that's not a problem because the result set is automatically closed when the prepared statement that was used to create the result set is closed. If you wanted to close the result set explicitly, though, you could do that by adding a finally clause to the try statement.

The ProductDB class (continued)

```java
@Override
public List<Product> getAll() {
    String sql = "SELECT ProductCode, Description, Price "
                + "FROM Products ORDER BY ProductCode ASC";
    List<Product> products = new ArrayList<>();
    try (Connection connection = getConnection();
         PreparedStatement ps = connection.prepareStatement(sql);
         ResultSet rs = ps.executeQuery()) {
        while (rs.next()) {
            String code = rs.getString("ProductCode");
            String description = rs.getString("Description");
            double price = rs.getDouble("Price");

            Product p = new Product(code, description, price);
            products.add(p);
        }
        return products;
    } catch (SQLException e) {
        System.err.println(e);
        return null;
    }
}

@Override
public Product get(String code) {
    String sql = "SELECT ProductCode, Description, Price "
                + "FROM Products "
                + "WHERE ProductCode = ?";
    try (Connection connection = getConnection();
         PreparedStatement ps = connection.prepareStatement(sql)) {
        ResultSet rs = ps.executeQuery();
        if (rs.next()) {
            String description = rs.getString("Description");
            double price = rs.getDouble("Price");
            Product p = new Product(code, description, price);
            rs.close();
            return p;
        } else {
            rs.close();
            return null;
        }
    } catch (SQLException e) {
        System.err.println(e);
        return null;
    }
}
```

Figure 21-8   The DAO interface and the ProductDB class (part 2 of 3)

The add() method begins by creating a prepared SQL statement that provides three parameters that can be used to insert values into three columns of the Products table. Then, it sets the three parameters to the values stored in the Product object that's passed to it. Next, it calls the executeUpdate() method of the prepared statement. Finally, it returns a true value. If a SQLException is thrown anywhere in this method, this code prints the exception to the console and returns a false value. That way, the code that calls the get() method can check whether it returned a true or false value and take appropriate action.

The deleteProduct() method uses a prepared SQL statement to delete the product row that has the same product code as the Product object that's passed to it. Like the add() method, the delete() method returns a false value if it isn't able to execute successfully.

The update() method uses a prepared SQL statement to update an existing product in the Products table with the data that's stored in the Product object that's passed to it. Like the add() and delete() methods, this method returns a false value if it isn't able to execute successfully.

The code for this class only uses methods from JDBC 1.0. That's because this is still the most common way to use JDBC to work with databases. The disadvantage of this technique is that you must understand SQL. However, SQL is easy to learn, and most programmers who work with databases already know how to use it. In fact, some programmers prefer using SQL so they have direct control over the SQL statements that are sent to the database.

Each public method in this class opens a connection, does its processing, and automatically closes the connection. The advantage of this approach is that all the resources used by the Connection object are freed as soon as the connection is no longer needed. This is helpful if your application is used by a large number of users and the number of open database connections is an issue. The disadvantage of this approach is that opening a database connection can be a relatively time-consuming process. Because of that, this may have a negative impact on the performance of your application. However, it's acceptable for most applications.

Also, if you need to improve performance, you can look into using a connection pool. Then, the database class can get a connection from the pool when it needs one and return it to the pool when it's done with its processing.

None of the public methods in this class throw exceptions. Instead, these methods use a try statement to catch the exceptions that might be thrown. Then, the catch block prints the exception to the console and returns a value that indicates that the operation was not successful. One advantage of this approach is that the calling code doesn't need to handle these exceptions. One disadvantage is that it mixes the database layer and the presentation layer since it prints the exception to the console.

Another option for handling exceptions would be to have the catch block throw the SQLException to the calling method. That way, the calling method can throw or handle this exception. Ultimately, this should lead to the exception being handled at a level that's appropriate for the application, often by having the user interface display an appropriate user-friendly message to the user. Chapter 16 shows how to use this approach with file I/O, but you can modify it so it works with databases.

The ProductDB class (continued)

```java
@Override
public boolean add(Product p) {
    String sql = "INSERT INTO Products (ProductCode, Description, Price) "
            + "VALUES (?, ?, ?)";
    try (Connection connection = getConnection();
        PreparedStatement ps = connection.prepareStatement(sql)) {
        ps.setString(2, p.getDescription());
        ps.setDouble(3, p.getPrice());
        ps.executeUpdate();
        return true;
    } catch (SQLException e) {
        System.err.println(e);
        return false;
    }
}

@Override
public boolean delete(Product p) {
    String sql = "DELETE FROM Products "
            + "WHERE ProductCode = ?";
    try (Connection connection = getConnection();
        PreparedStatement ps = connection.prepareStatement(sql)) {
        ps.setString(1, p.getCode());
        ps.executeUpdate();
        return true;
    } catch (SQLException e) {
        System.err.println(e);
        return false;
    }
}

@Override
public boolean update(Product p) {
    String sql = "UPDATE Products SET "
            + "  Description = ?, "
            + "  Price = ? "
            + "WHERE ProductCode = ?";
    try (Connection connection = getConnection();
        PreparedStatement ps = connection.prepareStatement(sql)) {
        ps.setString(1, p.getDescription());
        ps.setDouble(2, p.getPrice());
        ps.setString(3, p.getCode());
        ps.executeUpdate();
        return true;
    } catch (SQLException e) {
        System.err.println(e);
        return false;
    }
}
}
```

Figure 21-8   The DAO interface and the ProductDB class (part 3 of 3)

Code that uses the ProductDB class

Figure 21-9 shows some code that uses the ProductDB class. You can use code like this in the user interface for a console application. For example, you can use code like this if you want to modify the Product Manager application presented in chapter 15 so it uses the ProductDB class instead of the ProductTextFile class. In fact, that should be easy since both of these data access classes implement the DAO interface.

The ProductDB class is stored in the murach.db package. As a result, if you're calling the code shown in this figure from a different package, you need to include an import statement for this class as shown in the first example. In addition, you need to include an import statement for the Product class that's stored in the murach.business package.

The second example shows how to create a ProductDB object that can be used by the rest of the code in this figure. To do that, you just call the constructor of the object. Typically, you call code like this when the application starts. In addition, you may want to store this object as a field of the class so it's available to all methods.

The third example shows how to get all products. To do that, you begin by declaring a List<Product> object to store the products. Then, you call the getAll() method from the ProductDB object to get the list of Product objects. If the getAll() method returns a null value, this code prints a user-friendly message to the console to indicate that something went wrong. In addition, the catch block of the getAll() method prints the exception to the console. This should provide more detailed technical information that may help a programmer or administrator resolve the problem.

The fourth example shows how to get a single product. This works much like the third example. However, it uses the get() method of the ProductDB object to get a Product object with the specified code. This code assumes that the variable named code stores a product code. In this case, the catch block of the get() method only prints an exception to the console if a SQLException occurs, not if the SQL statement doesn't return a row.

The fifth example shows how to add a product. This works much like the previous two examples. However, it uses the add() method of the ProductDB object to add a Product object to the database. If successful, this code prints a message to the console to indicate that it worked. Otherwise, it prints a message that indicates that it wasn't able to add the product. This code assumes that the variable named product stores a Product object.

The sixth example shows how to delete a product. This works much like the fifth example. However, it uses the ProductDB object to delete a row in the database. Like the fifth example, this example assumes that the product variable stores a Product object.

How to import the business and database classes

```
import murach.db.ProductDB;
import murach.business.Product;
```

How to create a ProductDB object

```
ProductDB productDB = new ProductDB();
```

How to get all products

```
List<Product> products = productDB.getAll();
if (products == null) {
    System.out.println("Error! Unable to get products");
}
```

How to get a product with the specified product code

```
Product product = productDB.get(code);
if (product == null) {
    System.out.println("Error! Unable to get product for code: " + code);
}
```

How to add a product

```
boolean success = productDB.add(product);
if (success) {
    System.out.println(product.getDescription() + " was added.\n");
} else {
    System.out.println("Error! Unable to add product.\n");
}
```

How to delete a product

```
boolean success = productDB.delete(product);
if (success) {
    System.out.println(product.getDescription() + " was deleted.\n");
} else {
    System.out.println("Error! Unable to delete product.\n");
}
```

Description

- You can use the methods of the ProductDB class to map Product objects to the rows of the Products table.

Figure 21-9   Code that uses the ProductDB class

Perspective

Now that you've finished this chapter, you should understand how to use JDBC to store data in a database and to retrieve data from a database. Although there's much more to learn about working with databases, those are the essential skills. To enhance your database skills, you can learn more about using database management systems like MySQL or Oracle. In addition, you can learn more about using SQL to work with the database that you're using.

You should also understand that the JDBC API requires the developer to write a significant amount of low-level code. This provides a good conceptual background if you are new to Java and databases. In addition, many legacy applications use JDBC. As a result, you may need to use it when working on old applications.

However, for new development, you might prefer to use another data access API such as JPA (Java Persistence API). This API handles much of the object to database mapping automatically. As a result, it doesn't require the developer to write as much code, and the code that the developer does need to write is often easier to maintain.

Summary

- With JDBC 4.0 (Java 6) and later, the *database driver* that's used to connect the application to a database is usually loaded automatically. This is known as *automatic driver loading*.

- A Java application can use one of four driver types to access a database. It's considered a best practice to use a type-4 driver if one is available for that database.

- To return a *result set*, you use the executeQuery() method of a Statement or PreparedStatement object to execute a SELECT statement.

- Once you have a result set, you can use the next() method to move the *cursor* through it. Then, you can get data from the row that the cursor is on.

- To execute statements that modify the data in a database, you can use the executeUpdate() methods of a Statement or PreparedStatement object to execute an INSERT, UPDATE, or DELETE statement.

- A *SQL injection attack* allows a hacker to bypass authentication or to execute SQL statements against your database that can read sensitive data, modify data, or delete data.

- You can use *prepared statements* to supply parameters to SQL statements. Since prepared statements provide better performance and security than regular statements, you should use them whenever possible.

Exercise 21-1   Work with JDBC

In this exercise, you'll write JDBC code that works with the SQLite database named products.sqlite that was described in the previous chapter.

Review the code and test the application

1. Open the project named ch21_ex1_DBTester that's in the ex_starts folder.

2. Expand the Libraries folder for this project and note that it includes a JAR file for the SQLite database driver. If it doesn't include this driver, add the SQLite driver that's in the java/db directory of the download for this book.

3. Open the DBTester class and review its code. Note that it connects to the database named products.sqlite that's in the application's root directory.

4. Run the project. It should print all of the rows in the Products table to the console three times with some additional messages.

Write and test code that uses JDBC

5. Write the code for the printFirstProduct() method. This method should print the first product in the list of products to the console. Use column names to retrieve the column values.

6. Run this application to make sure it's working correctly.

7. Write the code for the printProductByCode() method. This method should print the product with the specified code to the console. Use a prepared statement to create the result set, and use indexes to retrieve the column values.

8. Run this application to make sure it's working correctly.

9. Write the code for the insertProduct() method. This method should add the product to the database and print that product to the console.

10. Run this application to make sure it's working correctly. If you run this application multiple times, it should display an error message that indicates that the product can't be added because of a duplicate key.

11. Write the code for the deleteProduct() method. This method should delete the product that was added by the insertProduct() method.

12. Run this application to make sure it's working correctly. You should be able to run this application multiple times without it displaying any error messages.

Exercise 21-2 Modify the Product Manager application

In this exercise, you'll modify a Product Manager application that works with the SQLite database named products.sqlite that was described in the previous chapter.

Review the code and test the application

1. Open the project named ch21_ex2_ProductManager that's in the ex_starts folder.

2. Expand the Libraries folder for this project and note that it includes a JAR file for the SQLite database driver. If it doesn't include this driver, add the SQLite driver that's in the java/db directory of the download for this book.

3. Open the ProductDB class and review its code. Note that it provides all of the methods presented in this chapter, including an update() method.

4. Open the ProductManagerApp class and review its code. Then, run this application. It should let you view and store product data in a database.

Modify the JDBC code

5. In the ProductDB class, modify the getAll() method so it uses column indexes instead of column names to get the data for the row.

6. Run this application to make sure this code works correctly.

7. In the ProductDB class, add a private method that can create a Product object from the current row in the result set like this:

```
private Product getProductFromRow(ResultSet rs) throws
SQLException {}
```

8. In the ProductDB class, modify the getAll() and get() methods so they use the getProductFromRow() method to get Product objects from the current row. Note how this reduces code duplication and makes your code easier to maintain.

9. Run this application to make sure this code works correctly.

Add an update command

10. In the ProductManagerApp class, modify the code so it includes an update command. This command should prompt the user for the product code. Then, it should prompt the user for a new description and price like this:

```
Enter product code to update: java
Enter product description: Murach's Java (5th Edition)
Enter price: 59.50
```

11. In the ProductManagerApp class, add code that gets the specified product from the database, sets the new data in that product, and updates the database with the new data. If successful, this should display a message that indicates the product was added to the row.

12. Run this application to make sure this code works correctly.

Section 6

Advanced skills

The first 5 sections of this book have presented many important skills for developing console or GUI applications that work with files and databases. So far, these applications have only run in a single thread, and they have only used lambda expressions to connect controls with event handlers. In this section, you'll learn more skills for working with lambda expressions. In addition, you'll learn how to work with multiple threads.

22

How to work with lambda expressions and streams

Lambda expressions are the most important feature introduced by Java 8. They're commonly used to connect a GUI control to an event handler as described in chapters 17 and 18. However, lambda expressions are also useful for many other tasks. In this chapter, you'll learn more about how they work. In addition, you'll learn how to use lambda expressions with streams, another feature that was introduced by Java 8. This feature provides powerful new ways to work with collections of data.

How to work with lambda expressions

Lambda expressions, or *lambdas*, allow you to pass the functionality of a method as an argument without having to code a name for the method. As a result, they are sometimes called *anonymous methods*.

Anonymous classes compared to lambdas

Figure 22-1 begins by showing a code example that uses an anonymous class to connect a GUI control for an Exit button to an EventHandler object. If you read chapter 17 or 18, you should be familiar with how this works. In short, an *inner class* is a class that's coded within another class or method, and an *anonymous class* is an inner class that doesn't include a name. In this example, the code creates an object from an anonymous class that implements the EventHandler interface and its handle() method. Then, it uses the setOnAction() method to connect the EventHandler object to the Exit button. Although this is more concise than including a name for the inner class, the syntax is still long and unwieldy.

Using a lambda expression, you can accomplish the same task more concisely as shown by the second code example. Here, the lambda expression specifies the name of the argument that's passed to the method, the lambda operator (->), and the body of the method.

This works because the compiler can infer the rest of the information. It knows that the setOnAction() method accepts an EventHandler<ActionEvent> object, so you don't have to write that code, and it knows that this object must have a handle() method, so you don't have to write that code. As a result, you only have to name the argument that's sent to the method and provide the statements that supply the functionality for the method.

Pros and cons of lambda expressions

The ability to treat functionality as data can result in the benefits listed in this figure. To start, lambda expressions are more concise than anonymous classes. In addition, they allow you to write more flexible methods. This can reduce code duplication, which can make your code easier to maintain.

However, lambda expressions also have some drawbacks as summarized in this figure. As a result, you might not always want to use them. Most of these drawbacks stem from the fact that the Java virtual machine doesn't support lambdas. Instead, the Java compiler rewrites lambdas into "normal" Java code.

This rewriting by the compiler results in three drawbacks. First, lambda expressions can be difficult to debug because you can't step through them with a debugger like normal methods. Second, when a lambda throws an exception, the stack trace can be difficult to understand. Third, methods that use lambdas can sometimes be inefficient compared to methods that accomplish the same task without using lambdas.

How to connect an event handler to a button

With an anonymous class

```
exitButton.setOnAction(new EventHandler<ActionEvent>(){
    @Override
    public void handle(ActionEvent event) {
        System.exit(0);
    }
});
```

With a lambda expression (anonymous method)

```
exitButton.setOnAction(event -> {
    System.exit(0);
});
```

The EventHandler interface

```
public interface EventHandler<T> {
    void handle(T event);
}
```

Pros and cons of lambda expressions

Pros

- They can allow you to write code that's more concise.
- They can allow you to write methods that are more flexible.
- They can reduce code duplication.

Cons

- They don't work well with the integrated debugger.
- They can be inefficient.
- They can result in stack traces that are very difficult to understand.
- They can result in code that's difficult to understand.

Description

- An *inner class* is a class that's coded within another class or method.
- An *anonymous class* is an inner class that doesn't supply a name for the class.
- With Java 8 and later, you can use a *lambda expression*, also known as a *lambda*, to pass functionality to a method as an argument.
- Since a lambda expression works much like a method that doesn't have a name, you can think of a lambda expression as an *anonymous method*.

Figure 22-1   An introduction to lambda expressions

A fourth drawback is that lambda expressions can result in code that's confusing and difficult to maintain. This is especially true if you use lambda expressions in situations where they aren't necessary.

So, when should you avoid using a lambda expression? If you find yourself needing to perform the same task more than once, you probably want to avoid using a lambda expression. In that case, you probably want to store the code in a normal method so that it's reusable.

A method that doesn't use lambdas

To understand how lambdas can be helpful, figure 22-2 shows a method that doesn't use a lambda expression but could benefit from the use of one. This method accepts a list of Contact objects as a parameter, and returns a new list of Contact objects consisting only of the contacts from the original list that have a null phone number.

To accomplish this task, the code within this method creates a new list to store the Contact objects that have null phone numbers. Then, it uses a loop to check each contact in the list that's passed in as an argument. Within this loop, an if statement checks whether the Contact object's phone number is null. If so, this code adds the Contact object to the new list. After the loop, this code returns the new list.

This method has several advantages. First, there's nothing tricky about it. As a result, it's easy to read and understand. Second, because it's is easy to read and understand, it should be easy to maintain.

However, this method also has several drawbacks. First, it's inflexible. For example, what if you want to find all contacts that have a null email address instead of a null phone number? This method can't do it. To do that, you'd have to write a new method that checks for a null email address instead. However, most of the code in the new method would be duplicate code. You'd only need to change the condition inside the if statement.

And what if you wanted to find all contacts that have a null phone number and a null email address? To do that, you'd have to write a third method. Once again, the code in the third method would be almost identical to the code in the first two methods.

At this point, the code duplication begins to make it difficult to maintain these methods. For example, if you need to change the Contact class, you might need to change the code in all three methods to reflect that change. In this situation, it makes sense to use a lambda expression because it can make the method more flexible, which reduces code duplication and makes your code easier to maintain. You'll see how that works next.

The Contact class

```
public class Contact {
    private String name;
    private String email;
    private String phone;

    // constructor and get / set methods here ...
}
```

Code that creates a list of contacts

```
List<Contact> contacts = new ArrayList<>();
contacts.add(new Contact("Mike Murach", null, "800-221-5528"));
contacts.add(new Contact("Anne Boehm", null, null));
contacts.add(new Contact("Joel Murach", "joel@murach.com", null));
```

A method that returns contacts that don't have phone numbers

```
public List<Contact> filterContactsWithoutPhone(List<Contact> contacts) {
    List<Contact> contactsWithoutPhone = new ArrayList<>();
    for (Contact c : contacts) {
        if (c.getPhone() == null) {
            contactsWithoutPhone.add(c);
        }
    }
    return contactsWithoutPhone;
}
```

Code that gets contacts that don't have phone numbers

```
List<Contact> contactsWithoutPhone = filterContactsWithoutPhone(contacts);
```

Code that prints contacts to the console

```
for (Contact c : contactsWithoutPhone) {
    System.out.println(c.getName());
}
```

The output

```
Anne Boehm
Joel Murach
```

Description

- The filterContactsWithoutPhone() method accepts a list of Contact objects, finds all the contacts in the list that have a null phone number, adds these contacts to a new list, and returns this list to the caller.

- The filterContactsWithoutPhone() method is inflexible. If you want to search by different criteria, such as no email address, you need to write another method.

Figure 22-2   A method that doesn't use lambdas

A method that uses lambdas

Figure 22-3 shows how to perform the same task as the previous figure with a method that accepts a lambda expression as an argument. This results in a flexible method that you can use to filter the list of Contact objects in multiple ways.

Before a method can accept a lambda expression as an argument, you need to define the parameters and return type for the lambda expression. To do that, you can use a *functional interface.* A functional interface works like a normal interface except that it can only contain one method.

The first example in this figure shows a functional interface named TestContact that contains one method named test(). This method accepts a Contact object as its only parameter and returns a boolean value.

The second example shows a method named filterContacts() that accepts the functional interface as its second parameter. This works the same as coding a method that accepts any other type of interface as a parameter. So, this method accepts a list of Contact objects as its first parameter and a TestContact object as its second parameter. Within this method, most of the code is similar to the code in the previous figure. However, the condition in the if statement calls the test() method of the TestContact object and passes it the Contact object. As a result, the filterContacts() method doesn't include the test condition. Instead, the calling code can use a lambda expression to supply the test condition as shown in the third and fourth examples.

The third example calls the filterContacts() method and passes it a lambda expression that specifies the test condition. As in previous examples, this example passes the list of Contact objects as the first argument. However, this example passes a lambda expression as the second argument. This expression checks whether the contact's phone number is null. To do that, this code specifies a variable name of c for the Contact object, followed by the *lambda operator* (->), followed by the condition. Here, the condition calls the getPhone() method from the Contact object and checks whether it is null. For now, focus on the concept, and don't worry if you don't completely understand the syntax of this lambda expression. This syntax is explained in more detail in the next figure.

The fourth example shows how to pass a lambda expression that checks whether the contact's email address is null. This shows that the method in this figure is more flexible than the method in the previous figure. If you want, you could code more complex lambda expressions to filter the list in other ways. For example, you could check for Contact objects that have a null or empty phone number by using this lambda expression:

```
c -> c.getPhone() == null || c.getPhone().isEmpty()
```

As a result, you don't have to write multiple methods that perform almost identical operations. Instead, you can write one method that accepts a lambda expression. Then, you can use a lambda expression to pass functionality to this method. This makes the method more flexible, reduces code duplication, and makes your code easier to maintain.

A functional interface

```
public interface TestContact {
    boolean test(Contact c);
}
```

A method that uses a functional interface to specify the filter condition

```
public List<Contact> filterContacts(List<Contact> contacts,
        TestContact condition) {
    List<Contact> filteredContacts = new ArrayList<>();
    for (Contact c : contacts) {
        if (condition.test(c)) {
            filteredContacts.add(c);
        }
    }
    return filteredContacts;
}
```

Code that gets contacts that don't have phone numbers

```
List<Contact> contactsWithoutPhone = filterContacts(contacts,
        c -> c.getPhone() == null);
```

The list after it's printed to the console

```
Anne Boehm
Joel Murach
```

Code that gets contacts that don't have email addresses

```
List<Contact> contactsWithoutEmail = filterContacts(contacts,
        c -> c.getEmail() == null);
```

The list after it's printed to the console

```
Mike Murach
Anne Boehm
```

Description

- A *functional interface* can define only one method.
- A method can specify a functional interface as the type for a parameter. Then, within the method, you can call the method of the functional interface from the parameter.
- You can pass a lambda expression to a method that defines a functional interface as a parameter.
- A lambda expression consists of a parameter list, the *lambda operator* (->), and a body. You'll learn more about the syntax of a lambda expression next.

Figure 22-3   A method that uses lambdas

The syntax of a lambda expression

Figure 22-4 presents the syntax of a lambda expression. This syntax consists of three parts. First, you code a parameter list. This list contains zero or more parameters that are passed to the body of the expression. Second, you code the *lambda operator* (->). Third, you code the body of the expression. This body contains one or more statements that provide the functionality.

The syntax of the parameter list of a lambda is the same as the syntax of the parameter list for any Java method. But, in a lambda, some of the syntax is optional. If the compiler can infer the data types of the parameters, you don't need to declare the data types for the parameters. Also, if there's only one parameter and its data type isn't declared, you can omit the enclosing parentheses.

Similarly, the syntax for the body of a lambda expression is the same as the syntax for the body of any Java method. But, in a lambda, some of the syntax is optional. If the body only contains one statement, you can omit the semicolon at the end of the statement, the return keyword, and the enclosing curly braces.

To show how this syntax works, this figure presents five examples that gradually work from the full syntax to the most minimal syntax possible. The first example shows the parameter list and the function body with the full syntax. Here, the parameter list is enclosed in parentheses, and it contains a single parameter of the Contact type with a name of c. This indicates that this lambda expression passes a Contact object to the body of the expression. In this example, the body is enclosed in curly braces, and the code uses a return statement to return the boolean value that results when the code checks whether the getPhone() method of the Contact object is null. In addition, this statement ends with a semicolon.

The second example simplifies the parameter list by omitting the type declaration for the Contact object. That's possible because the compiler can infer it from the context of the code.

The third example further simplifies the parameter list by omitting the parentheses that enclose the Contact object. That's possible because there's only one parameter in the list, and its type isn't declared.

The fourth example simplifies the body by omitting the curly braces, the return keyword, and the semicolon at the end of the statement. That's possible because there's only one statement in the body. As a result, there's no need to use braces to identify the start and end of the body, there's no need to use semicolons to separate the statements, and there's no need to use the return keyword to identify the statement that returns the boolean value.

The last example simplifies both the parameter list and the body of the function. This is how this lambda was coded in the previous figure, and it's how you typically code a lambda like this. That's because you typically want to code your lambdas as concisely as possible. However, you can always include more of the optional syntax if it makes your code easier to read and understand. In addition, you can't always omit as many parts of the syntax when you work with more complex lambda expressions. For example, if the lambda specifies two parameters, you can't omit the parentheses around the parameter list.

The syntax of a lambda expression

```
(parameterList) -> { statements }
```

The rules for the parameter list of a lambda expression

- The parameter list is enclosed in parentheses and can contain zero, one, or more parameters.
- The parameter list can declare the type of each parameter. However, if the type can be inferred by the compiler, declaring the type is optional.
- If there's only one parameter and its type isn't declared, the parentheses are optional.

The rules for the body of a lambda expression

- The body is enclosed in curly braces and can contain one or more statements.
- If the body contains multiple statements, the curly braces are required and semicolons must be coded at the end of each statement. In addition, if the body returns a value, the return keyword must identify the value to be returned.
- If the body only contains a single statement, the curly braces, the return keyword, and the semicolon can all be omitted.

Several ways the lambda expression from the last figure could be coded

Use the full syntax
```
(Contact c) -> { return c.getPhone() == null; }
```

In the parameter list, omit the type declaration
```
(c) -> { return c.getPhone() == null; }
```

In the parameter list, omit the type declaration and parentheses
```
c -> { return c.getPhone() == null; }
```

In the body, omit the curly braces, return keyword, and semicolon
```
(Contact c) -> c.getPhone() == null
```

Omit as much as possible
```
c -> c.getPhone() == null
```

Description

- A lambda expression consists of a parameter list, the *lambda operator* (->), and a body that contains one or more statements.
- Typically, you'll want to omit as much as possible to keep your lambda expression concise.

Figure 22-4   The syntax of a lambda expression

How to use functional interfaces from the Java API

Lambda expressions are commonly used to perform certain tasks. For example, it's common to need to check a condition and return a boolean value as described in figure 22-3. Because of this, the Java API includes many predefined functional interfaces that you can use to perform common tasks.

Figure 22-5 begins by summarizing three commonly used functional interfaces that are described in this chapter. However, the Java API includes many more functional interfaces. To learn more about them, you can check the API documentation for the java.util.function package.

How to use the Predicate interface

The code examples in figure 22-5 show how to use the Predicate interface to perform the same task performed by the TestContact interface presented in figure 22-3. To start, the Predicate interface defines a method named test() that works much like the test() method in the TestContact interface.

However, the Predicate interface has two advantages over the TestContact interface. First, it's already available from the Java API. As a result, you don't need to write the code to define this interface. Second, the Predicate interface uses generics to specify the type of object that's passed to its test() method. As a result, its test() method can accept an object of any type. By contrast, the test() method of the TestContact interface can only accept a Contact object.

In this figure, the second parameter of the filterContacts() method defines a parameter of the Predicate<Contact> type. As a result, the lambda expressions that are passed to this method can call methods of the Contact object.

Common functional interfaces from the java.util.function package

Interface	Method	Description
Predicate<T>	test(T)	Tests the T object and returns a boolean value.
Consumer<T>	accept(T)	Performs the specified operation on the T object and does not return a value.
Function<T, R>	apply(T)	Performs the specified operation on the T object and returns an R object.

The Predicate interface

```
public interface Predicate<T> {
    boolean test(T t);
}
```

A method that uses the Predicate interface to specify the condition

```
public static List<Contact> filterContacts(List<Contact> contacts,
        Predicate<Contact> condition) {
    List<Contact> filteredContacts = new ArrayList<>();
    for (Contact c : contacts) {
        if (condition.test(c)) {
            filteredContacts.add(c);
        }
    }
    return filteredContacts;
}
```

Code that gets contacts that don't have phone numbers

```
List<Contact> contactsWithoutPhone = filterContacts(contacts,
        c -> c.getPhone() == null);
```

The list after it's printed to the console

```
Anne Boehm
Joel Murach
```

Description

- The java.util.function package provides predefined functional interfaces.
- Many of the interfaces in the java.util.function package use generics to specify the type of objects that they accept and return.

Figure 22-5   How to use the Predicate interface

How to use the Consumer interface

The first code example in figure 22-6 shows the Consumer interface. This interface works like the Predicate interface, but it defines a method named accept() that doesn't return a value. As a result, it's useful for tasks where you don't need to perform further processing on a return value. For example, you might want to print the object to the console. You might want to use data in the object to update a database. Or, you might want to modify the data that's stored in the object.

The second example shows a method named processContacts(). This method accepts a list of Contact objects and a lambda expression for the Consumer interface. Within this method, the code loops through each Contact object and uses the accept() method of the Consumer interface to perform an action on each object.

The next three examples call the processContacts() method with different lambda expressions. The third example calls the System.out.println() method and passes it the name of each contact. As a result, this code prints the names of each contact to the console as shown in the output below the code.

The fourth example calls the setName() method of the Contact object and passes it the name of the same Contact object after the name has been changed to uppercase characters. As a result, this code changes the name that's stored in each Contact object so it contains all uppercase characters as shown in the output below the code.

Finally, the fifth example passes a more complex lambda expression to the processContacts() method. Here, the body of the lambda contains several code statements. As a result, this expression must be coded within curly braces, and each statement must end with a semicolon. However, since the accept() method doesn't return a value, the body doesn't need to include the return keyword.

Within the body, the first statement uses the split() method to split the name into an array that contains a first and last name. Then, the second statement converts the first name so it has an initial cap, the third statement converts the last name so it has an initial cap, and the fourth statement concatenates the first and last names and sets the result as the contact name.

These examples should give you a feel for the power of lambdas. In particular, they show how you can use them to make methods serve more than one purpose by using lambda expressions to supply some of their functionality.

The Consumer interface

```
public interface Consumer<T> {
    void accept(T t);
}
```

A method that passes each object to a method

```
public static void processContacts(List<Contact> contacts,
        Consumer<Contact> consumer) {
    for (Contact c : contacts) {
        consumer.accept(c);
    }
}
```

Code that prints the names of the contacts in the list

```
processContacts(contacts, c -> System.out.println(c.getName()) );
```

The output

```
Mike Murach
Anne Boehm
Joel Murach
```

Code that changes the names of the contacts to upper case

```
processContacts(contacts, c -> c.setName(c.getName().toUpperCase()) );
```

The list after it's printed to the console

```
MIKE MURACH
ANNE BOEHM
JOEL MURACH
```

Code that changes the names of the contacts to their original state

```
processContacts(contacts,
    c -> {
        String[] names = c.getName().split(" ");
        names[0] = names[0].substring(0, 1).toUpperCase() +
                    names[0].substring(1).toLowerCase();
        names[1] = names[1].substring(0, 1).toUpperCase() +
                    names[1].substring(1).toLowerCase();
        c.setName(names[0] + " " + names[1]);
});
```

The list after it's printed to the console

```
Mike Murach
Anne Boehm
Joel Murach
```

Description

- The Consumer interface uses generics to specify the type of object that's passed to the accept() method.

- The accept() method performs an operation on the object that it receives and doesn't return a value.

Figure 22-6   How to use the Consumer interface

How to use the Function interface

Figure 22-7 shows how to use the Function interface. This interface is similar to the Consumer interface, except that it returns a value. At first, this may make the Function interface seem like the Predicate interface. However, the Predicate interface returns a boolean value, and the Function interface returns an object of any type. To make that possible, the Function interface uses generics to specify the type of object that it accepts as well as the type of object that it returns.

The Function interface is typically used to transform an object to a new data type. For instance, the transformContacts() method in this figure uses the Function interface to transform a list of Contact objects to a list of strings. However, the Function interface can also be used to make copies of objects by returning a new version of the object that it receives. For instance, the copyContacts() method in this figure transforms a list of Contact objects by creating a copy of the list that contains new Contact objects that have been modified so the name is capitalized.

Both of these methods accept a list of Contact objects and a lambda expression for the Function interface. However, the transformContacts() method has a Function interface that accepts a Contact object and returns a String object. Within this method, the first statement creates a new list of strings. Then, the code loops through the list of Contact objects and passes each one to the apply() method of the Function object. Next, it adds the string that's returned by the apply() method to the list of strings. When the loop is done, this method returns this new list of strings.

The code that calls the transformContacts() method uses a lambda expression that returns a string that consists of the contact's name and phone number or "n/a" if the phone number is null. To do that, the first statement uses the *conditional operator* (?:) to create an inline if statement that performs the same task as the following statements:

```
String phone;
if (c.getPhone() == null) phone = "n/a";
else phone = c.getPhone();
```

Then, the second statement concatenates the value of the phone variable to the name of the contact and returns the string as shown by the output below the code.

Since the body of this lambda expression contains multiple statements, it uses curly braces to identify the statements. In addition, since this lambda expression returns a value, it uses the return keyword to identify the return value.

The copyContacts() method works much like the transformContacts() method. However, the copyContacts() method has a Function interface that accepts a Contact object and returns a Contact object. As a result, this method returns a new list of Contact objects.

The code that calls the copyContacts() method uses a lambda expression to create a new Contact object from the Contact object that's passed to the lambda expression. To do that, it uses the get methods of the Contact object argument to provide the values to the constructor for the Contact class and it converts the name to uppercase characters. This works similarly to the processContacts() method presented in figure 22-6. However, the copyContacts() method doesn't modify the original list of contacts. Instead, it returns a new list of contacts.

The Function interface

```
public interface Function<T, R> {
    R apply(T t)
}
```

A method that runs a function on each object and returns a string

```
public static List<String> transformContacts(List<Contact> contacts,
        Function<Contact, String> function) {
    List<String> strings = new ArrayList<>();
    for (Contact c : contacts) {
        strings.add( function.apply(c) );
    }
    return strings;
}
```

Code that creates a new list of contact info with a default value

```
List<String> contactPhoneNumbers = transformContacts(contacts,
    c -> {
        String phone = (c.getPhone() == null) ? "n/a" : c.getPhone();
        return c.getName() + ": " + phone;
});
```

The new list of strings after it's printed to the console

```
Mike Murach: 800-221-5528
Anne Boehm: n/a
Joel Murach: n/a
```

A method that runs a function on each object and returns a new object

```
public static List<Contact> copyContacts(List<Contact> contacts,
        Function<Contact, Contact> function) {
    List<Contact> newContacts = new ArrayList<>();
    for (Contact c : contacts) {
        newContacts.add( function.apply(c) );
    }
    return newContacts;
}
```

Code that creates a new list of contacts with upper case names

```
List<Contact> capsContacts = copyContacts(contacts,
    c -> new Contact(c.getName().toUpperCase(), c.getEmail(),
                    c.getPhone())));
```

The new list of contacts after it's printed to the console

```
MIKE MURACH
ANNE BOEHM
JOEL MURACH
```

Description

- The Function interface uses generics to specify the type of object that's passed to the apply() method and the type of object that the apply() method returns.

Figure 22-7   How to use the Function interface

How to work with multiple functional interfaces

Figure 22-8 shows a method called processContacts() that accepts a list of Contact objects and three functional interfaces: Predicate, Function, and Consumer. The Predicate interface accepts a Contact object and returns a boolean value, the Function interface accepts a Contact object and returns a string, and the Consumer interface accepts a string and doesn't return a value.

To start, the method loops through the list of Contact objects and tests each one against the condition defined by the Predicate object. If the Predicate object returns true, the first statement in the if block applies the function defined by the Function object to the Contact object, which returns a string. Then, the second statement passes the string to the Consumer object.

Because the processContacts() method accepts three functional interfaces as parameters, you need to pass it three lambda expressions when you call it. In the first example that calls this method, the first lambda provides a condition that checks whether the contact's phone is null. Then, the second lambda provides a function that accepts a Contact object and returns a string that consists of the contact's name after it has been converted to uppercase. Next, the third lambda provides a consumer that prints its string argument to the console. As a result, this method uses uppercase characters to display the names of all contacts that don't have a phone number.

The second example that calls the processContacts() method works similarly to the first one. However, the Predicate argument gets contacts that have either a phone number or an email address, rather than those with no phone. Then, the lambda expression for the function creates a more complex string that includes the name, email address, and phone number for the contact. To do that, this code replaces "null" with "N/A" to create a user-friendly message that indicates when an email address or phone number is not available.

These examples show how flexible code that uses functional interfaces and lambda expressions can be. The lambda expressions store the functionality needed to process contacts instead of being hard coded in the body of a method. As a result, you can use lambdas to control the condition for finding contacts, the function for converting contacts to strings, and the consumer that processes the strings that are returned by the function.

A method that uses three functional interfaces

```
public static void processContacts(List<Contact> contacts,
        Predicate<Contact> condition,
        Function<Contact, String> function,
        Consumer<String> consumer) {
    for (Contact c : contacts) {
        if (condition.test(c)) {
            String s = function.apply(c);
            consumer.accept(s);
        }
    }
}
```

Code that calls the method with three lambda expressions

```
processContacts(contacts,
    c -> c.getPhone() == null,
    c -> c.getName().toUpperCase(),
    str -> System.out.println(str));
```

The output

```
ANNE BOEHM
JOEL MURACH
```

Another example of calling the method with three lambda expressions

```
processContacts(contacts,
    c -> c.getPhone() != null || c.getEmail() != null,
    c -> {
        String info = c.getName() + ": " +
                "Phone - " + c.getPhone() + " | " +
                "Email - " + c.getEmail();
        return info.replace("null", "N/A");
    },
    str -> System.out.println(str)
);
```

The output

```
Mike Murach: Phone - 800-221-5528 | Email - N/A
Joel Murach: Phone - N/A | Email - joel@murach.com
```

Description

- You can write methods that use more than one functional interface.

- When you call a method that accepts multiple functional interfaces, you code a lambda expression for each interface.

Figure 22-8   How to work with multiple functional interfaces

How to work with streams

Streams provide an efficient and flexible way to perform operations on collections of data. Like lambda expressions, streams were introduced by Java 8. Streams can connect to each other so the output of one stream serves as the input of another stream. If you're familiar with shell scripting or batch file writing, this is similar to a concept known as *piping*, where the output of one command is "piped" as the input to another command.

So far in this chapter, you've learned how to code methods that loop through a list of elements and use a functional interface to filter, transform, or process the list. Now, you'll learn how to use streams to perform the same operations on the fly without coding the method that accepts the functional interfaces. To do that, you can use the methods summarized at the top of figure 22-9. Of these methods, the filter(), forEach(), and map() methods accept lambda expressions for the Predicate, Consumer, and Function interfaces described earlier in this chapter.

How to filter a list

The first example in this figure uses a stream to filter a list and process each element in the filtered list. To do that, this example begins by calling the stream() method on a list of Contact objects. As the name implies, this method returns a stream of elements from the collection.

From this stream, the code calls the filter() method and passes it a lambda expression for the Predicate interface. This lambda expression checks whether the contact phone number is null. As a result, the filter() method returns a new stream that only contains contacts where the phone number is null.

From the filtered stream, this code calls the forEach() method and passes it a lambda expression for the Consumer interface. This lambda expression prints the name of each contact in the list to the console.

When you use the forEach() method, you should know that you can't use it with a lambda expression that throws a checked exception. As a result, if the lambda expression you want to code throws a checked exception, you'll need to use a for loop instead.

The second example shows how to filter a list and collect the filtered elements in a new list. To do that, this code calls the collect() method on the filtered stream and passes it a Collector object that collects the elements from the stream and stores them in a list. To get this Collector object, this code calls the static toList() method from the Collectors class. For this chapter, this is the only type of Collector object that you need. However, the Collectors class provides methods for returning other types of collections such as sets and maps.

In this chapter, all of the examples use the stream() method to use one CPU to process the stream. This is known as *serial processing*. However, if your computer has multiple CPUs and your stream performs intensive processing on each element, the performance of your code might benefit from using the parallelStream() method instead. This method uses multiple CPUs to process the stream, which is known as *parallel processing*.

Two methods that return a Stream object

Method	Description
`stream()`	Returns a Stream object for the collection that allows you to use one CPU to process the stream. This is known as *serial processing*.
`parallelStream()`	Returns a Stream object for the collection that allows you to use multiple CPUs to process the stream. This is known as *parallel processing*.

Common methods of the Stream object

Method	Description
`filter(predicate)`	Applies the specified Predicate interface to the stream.
`forEach(consumer)`	Applies the specified Consumer interface to the stream. You can use this method instead of a for loop, but you can't use it with methods that throw a checked exception.
`collect(collector)`	Adds all of the elements of the stream to the collection that's specified by a static method of the Collector class. Then, it returns the collection.
`map(function)`	Applies the specified Function interface to the stream.
`reduce(identity, accumulator)`	Uses the identity argument to specify the data type and initial value for the return value, applies the operation specified by the accumulator argument to all elements in the list, and returns the result.

Code that uses a stream to filter a list and process each filtered element

```
contacts.stream()
        .filter( c -> c.getPhone() == null )
        .forEach( c -> System.out.println(c.getName()) );
```

The output

```
Anne Boehm
Joel Murach
```

Code that uses a stream to filter a list and collect the filtered elements

```
List<Contact> contactsNoPhone = contacts.stream()
        .filter(c -> c.getPhone() == null)
        .collect(Collectors.toList());

System.out.println("There are " + contactsNoPhone.size() +
                " contacts with no phone number.");
```

The output

```
There are 2 contacts with no phone number.
```

Description

- To get a *stream* of elements for a collection, you can call the stream() or parallelStream() methods of the collection. Then, you can use the other methods shown in this figure to work with the stream.

- These methods are available with Java 8 and later.

Figure 22-9   How to filter a list

You might think that the parallelStream() method would always improve performance for a computer that has multiple CPUs. However, using parallel processing requires significant overhead such as splitting the stream, processing its elements, and joining the streams back together. As a result, the parallelStream() method only provides improved performance when the processing for each element is intensive. Even then, the parallelStream() method doesn't always provide improved performance. That's especially true if the stream can't be split efficiently, or if the processing of each element uses some synchronized functionality. In the latter case, each stream has to wait for the other stream to finish before it can continue. To understand this better, it helps to understand threads, which are described in the next chapter.

How to map a list

Figure 22-10 shows two examples of using the map() method on a stream. This method performs an operation on each element in the stream and returns a new stream based on the result. To specify the operation that's applied to each element, you can supply a lambda expression for the Function interface as the argument for this method.

The first example starts by calling the stream() method on a list of Contact objects. Then, it calls the map() method on the stream and passes it a lambda expression that returns the name of the contact. Next, all of the strings in the new stream are collected into a new list of strings named contactNames. After that, the forEach() method prints the new list of strings.

In addition to implementing the Function interface, lambda expressions that are passed to the map() method must meet two more requirements. First, they must be *non-interfering*, which means they cannot alter the structure of the list or stream. For example, they cannot add an element to the list that's being streamed. Second, they must be *stateless*, which means that they cannot rely on any state variables to perform their action. For example, they can't access a counter variable that's defined outside of the map() method and update its state.

When you work with streams and you provide a lambda expression that calls a single method, you can often use a method reference instead as shown in the second example. This example performs the same task as the first example, but it uses the *double colon operator* (::) to supply a method reference for two of the lambda expressions. However, this only works if the Java compiler can infer the arguments for the method. In this figure, for example, the Java compiler can infer that the getName() method of the Contact object doesn't accept any arguments. Similarly, it can infer that the println() method of the System.out object prints the String object that's stored in the list of contact names.

Code that uses a stream to transform a list of Contact objects

```
List<String> contactNames = contacts.stream()
        .map(c -> c.getName())
        .collect(Collectors.toList());

contactNames.stream()
        .forEach(str -> System.out.println(str));
```

The output

```
Mike Murach
Anne Boehm
Joel Murach
```

The syntax for using the double colon operator

```
ClassName::methodName
```

Code that uses a method reference instead of a lambda expression

```
List<String> contactNames = contacts.stream()
        .map(Contact::getName)
        .collect(Collectors.toList());

contactNames.stream()
        .forEach(System.out::println);
```

Description

- The functional programming concept known as a *map* runs a function on all the items in a stream and creates a new stream based on the result.

- The map() method accepts a lambda expression for the Function interface. This lambda expression must be *non-interfering*, meaning it cannot modify the stream. In addition, it must be *stateless*, meaning it cannot rely on the state of any variable to perform its actions.

- The *double colon operator* (::) provides a way to supply a reference to a method. This method is available with Java 8 and later.

- When you work with streams and you provide a lambda expression that calls a single method, you can often use a method reference instead. However, this only works if the Java compiler can infer the arguments for the method.

Figure 22-10   How to map a list

How to reduce a list

Figure 22-11 shows how to use the reduce() method to summarize the data in a stream. Often, this method is applied to a stream after a filter() or map() method has performed filtering or mapping operations to a stream. In that case, the operation is known as a *map-reduce* operation. This figure shows two examples of a map-reduce operation.

The first example reduces all the Contact objects in a list to a single string that contains the names of all the contacts in the list, separated by commas. To start, this example uses the stream() method to get a stream of elements from the list of contacts. Then, it calls the map() method and returns a string for the contact's name. Next, this code calls the reduce() method to combine the names into a single string.

The reduce() method accepts two arguments known as an *identity* and an *accumulator*. The identity acts as the initial value of the summary operation. In this case, the code specifies that the operation starts with an empty string. The accumulator provides the operation that combines the elements in the stream. In this case, the accumulator is a lambda expression that specifies that the operation should add each name plus a comma and a space to the string that contains the list of names.

This works because the accumulator argument implements a functional interface named BinaryOperator. This interface isn't presented in this chapter, but it accepts two arguments of the same type, and it returns a value of that type. In this case, the accumulator accepts two string arguments named a and b and returns a string. The first argument stores the results of the summary operation so far. In other words, it stores the string that contains all the names that have been concatenated up to this point. The second argument holds the current element in the stream. In this case, it stores the name that's being added to the string of names.

The body of the lambda expression concatenates the two arguments and adds a comma and a space to the end of the string. This process continues until all the items in the stream have been processed. At this point, the code stores the resulting string in the String variable named csv. Finally, the code removes the last comma and space added by the summary operation and displays the comma-separated string of names.

The second example works like the first example, but it shows how to use a map-reduce operation to find the largest invoice total for a list of Invoices. To do that, the code uses the map() method to get the total for each invoice, and it uses the reduce() method to get the largest invoice. To do that, the reduce method supplies an initial double value of 0.0. Then, it uses a lambda expression to supply an accumulator that works by using the max() method of the Math class to get the largest total.

The third example performs the same task as the second example, but it uses method references instead of lambda expressions. This works for the accumulator because the Java compiler is able to infer that you want to pass two double values to the max() method and return a double value. Since this code is concise and easy to read, it's a good illustration of when it makes sense to use the double colon operator to specify a method reference.

Code that reduces a list of Contact objects to a single string

```
String csv = contacts.stream()
        .map(c -> c.getName)
        .reduce("", (a, b) -> a + b + ", ");

csv = csv.substring(0, csv.length() - 2);       // remove last comma and space
System.out.println("All contacts: " + csv);
```

The output

```
All contacts: Mike Murach, Anne Boehm, Joel Murach
```

Code that gets the largest total from a list of Invoice objects

```
double maxInvoiceTotal = invoices.stream()
        .map(i -> i.getTotal())
        .reduce(0.0, (a, b) -> Math.max(a, b));

System.out.println("Max invoice total: " + maxInvoiceTotal);
```

The output

```
Max invoice total: 3425.82
```

Code that uses method references instead of a lambda expressions

```
double maxInvoiceTotal = invoices.stream()
        .map(Invoice::getTotal)
        .reduce(0.0, Math::max);
```

Description

- The functional programming concept known as a *map-reduce* operation uses a map() method to perform a map operation followed by a reduce() method that performs a summary operation.

- The reduce() method accepts two arguments, an *identity* and an *accumulator*.

- The identity argument specifies the initial value of the summary operation. In addition, the reduction operation returns this value if the stream is empty.

- The accumulator argument accepts a lambda expression for the BinaryOperator interface. This interface accepts two arguments of the same type, performs the specified operation on them, and returns a value of that type.

Figure 22-11   How to reduce a list

Perspective

In this chapter, you learned the basic skills for working with lambda expressions that can make your code more concise, flexible, and easier to maintain. Along the way, you learned how to use some of the functional interfaces provided by the Java API. However, there are many more functional interfaces available from the Java API. To learn more about them, you can refer to the API documentation for the java.util.function package.

This chapter also introduced you to the basic skills for working with streams. For example, you learned how to filter, map, and reduce a stream. Along the way, you learned how you can sometimes use the double colon operator to use method references instead of lambda expressions.

Summary

- A *functional interface* is an interface that only defines one method.

- With Java 8 and later, you can pass a *lambda expression*, also known as a *lambda*, to any method that accepts a functional interface as an argument. This allows you to treat functionality as data.

- Since a lambda expression works much like a method that doesn't have a name, you can think of a lambda expression as an *anonymous method*.

- A lambda expression consists of a parameter list, the *lambda operator* (->), and a body.

- The Java API provides many functional interfaces including the Predicate, Consumer, and Function interfaces.

- With Java 8 and later, you can use *streams* to process collections of data.

- To stream data from a collection, you can call the stream() method to use one CPU to process the stream. This is known as *serial processing.* Or, you can use the parallelStream() method to use multiple CPUs to process the stream. This is known as *parallel processing*.

- To process each element in a stream, you can use methods of the stream such as the filter(), forEach(), collect(), map(), and reduce() methods.

- You can use the filter() and map() methods followed by the reduce() method to summarize data. This is known as a *map-reduce* operation.

- With Java 8 and later, you can use the *double colon operator* (::) to supply a reference to a method.

Exercise 22-1   Code a method that accepts lambda expressions

In this exercise, you'll use a lambda expression to reduce code duplication when searching a book catalog.

1. Open the project named ch22_ex1_BookCatalog in the ex_starts folder. Then, review the code for this application and run it to make sure it works correctly. It should print lists of books filtered by title, category, and format like this:

```
BOOKS BY TITLE:
[Java Programming, Java, Paperback]
[Java Programming, Java, Electronic]

BOOKS BY CATEGORY:
[Java Servlets and JSP, Java, Paperback]
[Java Servlets and JSP, Java, Electronic]
[Java Programming, Java, Paperback]
[Java Programming, Java, Electronic]

BOOKS BY FORMAT:
[MySQL, Database, Paperback]
[Java Servlets and JSP, Java, Paperback]
[Java Programming, Java, Paperback]
[Android Programming, Mobile, Paperback]
```

2. Open the BookManager class and examine these three methods: getBooksByTitle(), getBooksByCategory(), and getBooksByFormat(). Note that the code for these methods is almost identical, except for the condition at the beginning of the if statement.

3. In the BookManager class, import the java.util.function.Predicate interface.

4. Add a single method named getBooks() that accepts a Predicate<Book> object as a parameter and uses its test() method in the condition at the beginning of the if statement.

5. Open the BookManagerApp class and replace the old calls to the methods of the BookManager class with three calls to the new getBooks() method. To do that, you'll need to pass a lambda expression as an argument to this method. For example, here's the lambda expression to test the title of a book:

```
b -> b.getTitle().equals("Java Programming")
```

6. In the BookManager class, delete the old methods that are no longer being used. Note how this reduces code duplication and increases the flexibility of your code.

7. Run the application and test it to make sure it works correctly. It should print the same list to the console as in step 1.

8. In the BookManagerApp class, modify the lambda expression that gets books by title so it prints all books that have a title that contains the word "Java".

9. Run the application again to make sure it works correctly.

Exercise 22-2   Use streams to process a list

In this exercise, you'll use streams to process the list of books shown in the previous exercise.

1. Open the project named ch22_ex2_BookCatalog in the ex_starts folder. Then, review the code for this application and run it to make sure it works correctly. It should print a list of books like the one shown in exercise 22-2.

2. In the BookManagerApp class, replace the calls to the printList() method with code that prints the books by creating a stream for each list and using the forEach() method to print each book to the console. To do that, use a method reference for the println() method.

3. Delete the printList() method to make sure that it's no longer being used.

4. Run the application again to make sure it works correctly.

5. At the beginning of the main() method, add a statement that gets a list of Book objects like this:

    ```
    List<Book> bookList = new BookCatalog().getCatalog();
    ```

6. In the BookManagerApp class, modify all statements so they use streams to filter the list and print it to the console instead of using the method of the BookManager class.

7. Delete the BookManager class to make sure it's no longer being used.

8. Run the application again to make sure it works correctly.

9. Add code that streams the book list, filters the stream so it only contains books in the DATABASE category, and maps the stream so it only prints the title and format of each book like this:

    ```
    DATABASE BOOK TITLES:
    MySQL (Paperback)
    MySQL (Electronic)
    SQL Server (Electronic)
    Oracle SQL and PL/SQL (Electronic)
    ```

10. Run the application again to make sure it works correctly. It should add the database book titles to the list of books shown in exercise 22-1.

23

How to work with threads

When you run an application in Java, the application runs in one or more threads. So far in this book, all of the console applications have run within a single thread. However, all of the GUI applications have run in two threads: one to run the main() method and another to display the GUI and listen for its events. In this chapter, you'll learn how to develop applications that use multiple threads to perform separate tasks. For example, you can use one thread to retrieve data from a database while another thread makes a complicated calculation. Then, the application can alternate between the two tasks so it runs more efficiently.

An introduction to threads

Before you learn how to develop applications that use two or more threads, you need to understand how threads work and when you would typically use them. You also need to be familiar with the classes and interfaces you use when you work with threads, and you need to understand the life cycle of a thread. That's what you'll learn in the topics that follow.

How threads work

As figure 23-1 explains, a *thread* is a single flow of execution through an application. By default, Java applications use a single thread, called the *main thread*. This thread begins executing with the first statement of an application's main() method and continues executing statements in sequence until the main() method exits. The application may create additional objects and call additional methods, but the flow of control is always sequential, one statement at a time.

In some cases, single-threaded execution can be inefficient. For example, imagine an application that performs two independent tasks. To accomplish the first task, the application must read data from a file, and this task spends most of its time waiting for file I/O operations to complete. As a result, the second task must wait too, even though it doesn't require any I/O operations.

The first diagram in this figure shows how this application might work when executed as a single thread. First, the application performs the first task. In this case, the *CPU (central processing unit)* is idle while it waits for the I/O operations required by this task. When the first task is complete, the application runs the second task.

The second diagram shows how this application could benefit from being split into two threads, one to perform each task. Here, using two threads allows the two tasks to overlap, so the second task is executed while the first task waits on I/O operations. The result is that the two tasks finish sooner than they would if they were executed as a single thread.

Applications that perform several tasks that aren't dependent on one another benefit the most from *multithreading*. For example, the second task shown in this figure can only be overlapped with the first task if the second task doesn't depend on the results of the first task. If the second task depends on the results of the first task, some overlap may still be possible. However, the two tasks must communicate with each other so they can coordinate their operations.

Typical uses for threads

In addition to showing the basics of how threads work, figure 23-1 lists three of the most common uses for threads. The first is to improve the performance of I/O operations. Any application that performs extensive I/O can benefit from multithreading. That's because I/O operations are thousands of times slower than CPU operations. So any application that reads data from a disk spends almost all of its time waiting for that information to be retrieved.

How using threads can improve performance

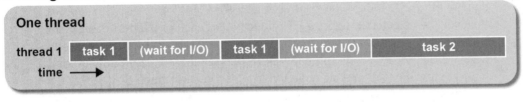

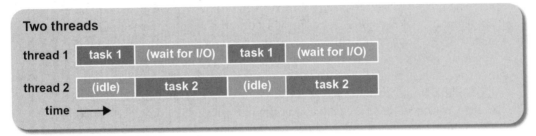

Typical uses for threads

- To improve the performance of applications with extensive I/O operations
- To improve the responsiveness of GUI applications
- To allow two or more users to run server-based applications simultaneously

Description

- A *thread* is a single sequential flow of control within an application. A thread often completes a specific task.

- By default, a Java application uses a single thread, called the *main thread*. However, some applications can benefit by using two or more threads to allow different parts of the application to execute simultaneously.

- On a computer that has just one *CPU (central processing unit) core*, the threads don't actually execute simultaneously. Instead, a part of the operating system called the *thread scheduler* alternately lets each thread execute. Because this happens so quickly, it gives the appearance that all of the tasks are running at the same time. As a result, this can make an application work more efficiently.

- Most modern CPUs have multiple cores and can run multiple threads at the same time, even though there is only one CPU.

Figure 23-1   How threads work

To give you some perspective on this, you should realize that the actual amount of time that the CPU spends waiting for I/O to complete is much greater than what's indicated in figure 23-1. In fact, since each of the blocks that show task 1 executing are about one half of an inch long, the blocks that show the CPU waiting for I/O would probably need to be about the length of a football field to show the wait time accurately. That's about how much slower disk operations are than CPU operations.

The second reason for using threads is to improve the responsiveness of applications that use graphical user interfaces. For example, when a user clicks a button, he or she expects the application to respond immediately, even if the application is busy doing something else. A GUI application automatically runs in a thread that handles the events that occur when the user interacts with the GUI. Then, it updates the GUI accordingly. However, if the application needs to perform a task that may take a long time, this task should be performed in a second thread.

The final reason for using multithreading is to allow two or more users to run server-based applications simultaneously. For example, Java *servlets* automatically create one thread for each user. As a result, when you write servlet code, you must make sure that the code is thread-safe. (To learn more about web programming in Java, you can read *Murach's Java Servlets and JSP*.)

Classes and interfaces for working with threads

Figure 23-2 presents a class and an interface that you can use to create and work with threads and summarizes the key methods they provide. As you can see, the Thread class implements the Runnable interface. Because the Runnable interface declares a single method named run(), the Thread class must implement this method. The Thread class also provides two key methods for working with threads: start() and sleep(). You'll learn more about these methods shortly.

In addition to the methods shown here, you should know that, like other classes, the Thread class inherits the Object class. That means it has access to all of its public and protected methods. In particular, it has access to methods that can be used to coordinate tasks that may overlap. Because the use of these methods is beyond the scope of this book, they aren't presented in this chapter.

To create a thread, you can use one of two techniques. First, you can define a class that inherits the Thread class. This class should override the run() method so it contains the code to be executed by the thread. Then, you can instantiate this class to create a thread.

Second, you can define a class that implements the Runnable interface. To do that, this class must implement the run() method. Then, you pass an instance of this class to a constructor of the Thread class. This creates a thread that executes the Runnable object by calling its run() method.

If these two techniques seem confusing right now, don't worry. They'll become clearer when you see examples later in this chapter. For now, you just need to know that the Thread class defines a thread, but the code that's executed by the thread can be provided by any class that implements the Runnable interface.

An interface and a class that are used to create threads

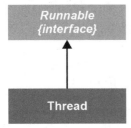

Summary of these classes and interfaces

Class/Interface	Description
Thread	A class that defines a thread. This class implements the Runnable interface.
Runnable	An interface that must be implemented by any class whose objects are going to be executed by a thread. The only method in this interface is the run() method.

Key methods of the Thread class and Runnable interface

Method	Class/Interface	Description
start()	Thread	Registers this thread with the thread scheduler so it's available for execution.
run()	Runnable, Thread	An abstract method that's declared by the Runnable interface and implemented by the Thread class. The thread scheduler calls this method to run the thread.
sleep(long)	Thread	Causes the current thread to wait (sleep) for the specified number of milliseconds so the CPU can run other threads.

Two ways to create a thread

- Inherit the Thread class.
- Implement the Runnable interface. Then, pass a reference to the Runnable object to the constructor of the Thread class.

Description

- After you create a Thread object, you can call its start() method so the thread scheduler can run the thread. Then, once a thread is running, you can use the sleep() method to cause the thread to wait while other threads run.
- The advantage of implementing the Runnable interface is that it allows the thread to inherit a class other than the Thread class.

Figure 23-2   Classes and interfaces for working with threads

The life cycle of a thread

Figure 23-3 shows the life cycle of a thread and explains each of the five states a thread can be in. To create a thread, the programmer writes code that defines a class for the thread and instantiates a Thread object. When the Thread object is first instantiated, it is placed in the New state, which means that the thread has been created but is not yet ready to be run.

When the application is ready for the thread to be run, it calls the thread's start() method. Although you might think that this causes the thread to begin execution, all it really does is change the state of the thread from New to Runnable. Once it's in the Runnable state, the thread joins a list of any other threads that are also in the Runnable state. Then, a component of the operating system called the *thread scheduler* selects one of the Runnable threads to be executed.

Note that there isn't a separate state for the thread that's running. The thread that's running is in the Runnable state, as well as all other threads that are eligible to be running. Also, the thread scheduler may at any time decide that the thread that's currently running has been running long enough. Then, the thread scheduler interrupts that thread and lets one of the other threads in the Runnable state run. This doesn't change the state of either thread.

A thread enters the Blocked state if a condition occurs that makes the thread temporarily not runnable. For example, a thread enters the Blocked state when it is waiting for an I/O operation to complete. The thread automatically returns to the Runnable state when the I/O operation completes. A thread that's in Blocked state can't be selected for execution by the thread scheduler.

The Waiting state comes into play when threads need to coordinate their activities. For example, if a thread can't continue what it's doing until another thread completes, it can enter the Waiting state. Then, when the other thread it is waiting on completes its task, it can notify the waiting thread to stop waiting and enter the Runnable state again. Because of the complexities of implementing this coordination between threads, you won't learn how to coordinate threads in this chapter.

Finally, when the run() method of a thread finishes execution, the thread enters the Terminated state. Once a thread has entered the Terminated state, it remains there until the application ends.

The life cycle of a thread

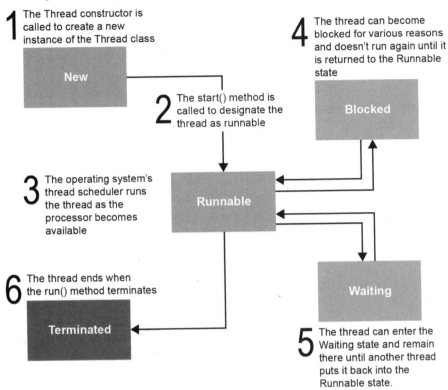

1 The Thread constructor is called to create a new instance of the Thread class

New

2 The start() method is called to designate the thread as runnable

3 The operating system's thread scheduler runs the thread as the processor becomes available

Runnable

4 The thread can become blocked for various reasons and doesn't run again until it is returned to the Runnable state

Blocked

5 The thread can enter the Waiting state and remain there until another thread puts it back into the Runnable state.

Waiting

6 The thread ends when the run() method terminates

Terminated

Thread states

State	Description
New	The thread has been created (its constructor has been called), but not yet started.
Runnable	The thread's start() method has been called and the thread is available to be run by the thread scheduler. A thread in Runnable state may actually be running, or it may be waiting in the thread queue for an opportunity to run.
Blocked	The thread has been temporarily removed from the Runnable state so it can't be executed. This can happen if the thread's sleep() method is called, if the thread is waiting on I/O, or if the thread requests a lock on an object that's already locked. When the condition changes (for example, the I/O operation completes), the thread is returned to the Runnable state.
Waiting	The thread is waiting and allowing other threads to access the object. It remains in the waiting state until another thread notifies it to stop waiting and re-enter the Runnable state.
Terminated	The thread's run() method has ended.

Description

- All threads have a life cycle that can include five states: New, Runnable, Blocked, Waiting, and Terminated.

Figure 23-3   The life cycle of a thread

Two ways to create threads

In the topics that follow, you'll learn two ways to create a thread. But first, you'll learn more about the Thread class, which you must use regardless of how you create a thread.

Constructors and methods of the Thread class

The first table in figure 23-4 summarizes some of the constructors you can use to create Thread objects. The first constructor creates a thread from a class that inherits the Thread class. The second constructor creates a thread from any object that implements the Runnable interface.

The third and fourth constructors let you specify the name of the thread that's created. By default, threads are named numerically (Thread-0, Thread-1, etc.). Since you don't typically refer to threads by name, the defaults are usually acceptable.

The second table in this figure presents some of the methods of the Thread class. You can use these methods to get information about a thread and to control when a thread runs.

The Thread class

`java.lang.Thread`

Common constructors of the Thread class

Constructor	Description
`Thread()`	Creates a default Thread object.
`Thread(Runnable)`	Creates a Thread object from any object that implements the Runnable interface.
`Thread(String)`	Creates a Thread object with the specified name.
`Thread(Runnable, String)`	Creates a Thread object with the specified name from any object that implements the Runnable interface.

Common methods of the Thread class

Method	Description
`run()`	Implements the run() method of the Runnable interface. This method should be overridden in all subclasses to provide the code that's executed by a thread.
`start()`	Places a thread in the Runnable state so it can be run by the thread scheduler.
`getName()`	Returns the name of a thread.
`currentThread()`	A static method that returns a reference to the currently executing thread.
`sleep(long)`	A static method that places the currently executing thread in the Blocked state for the specified number of milliseconds so other threads can run.
`isInterrupted()`	Returns a true value if a thread has been interrupted.

Description

- By default, the threads that you create are named numerically (Thread-0, Thread-1, and so on). If that's not what you want, you can use the constructor of the thread to specify a name.

- The sleep() method throws an InterruptedException. Because this is a checked exception, you must throw or catch this exception when you use the sleep() method.

Figure 23-4   Constructors and methods of the Thread class

How to extend the Thread class

Figure 23-5 shows how to create a thread by extending the Thread class. Here, the IOThread class defines a thread that simulates an I/O operation, and the ThreadApp class contains the main() method that's run when the application starts.

The IOThread class starts by inheriting the Thread class. Then, it overrides the run() method to provide the code that's executed when the thread is run. Within this method, the first statement prints the name of the thread. Then, the run() method uses the static sleep() method to place the thread in Blocked state for 2000 milliseconds (2 seconds). After 2 seconds, the thread is returned to Runnable state so the thread scheduler can resume its execution.

Because the sleep() method can throw an InterruptedException, that exception must be either caught or thrown. This exception indicates that some other thread is attempting to interrupt the current thread while it is sleeping. How you deal with this exception depends on the application. In this case, the application simply ignores any attempts to interrupt the thread by catching the exception but not providing any code to process it. Normally, "swallowing" an exception like this is not a good programming practice. In this case, however, it's appropriate.

If you use the sleep() method, you should also realize that it doesn't guarantee that the thread will start running after the amount of time you specify. Instead, it simply guarantees that the thread will be returned to the Runnable state after that amount of time. It's up to the thread scheduler to decide when the thread will resume execution. Because of that, you shouldn't use the sleep() method for applications that require precise timing.

The ThreadApp class contains the main() method for the application. Within this method, the first statement calls the currentThread() method of the Thread class and assigns the Thread object that's returned to a variable named t1. Then, the second statement uses the println() method to display a message that indicates that the thread has started. To include the name of the thread in this message, this code uses the getName() method to get the name of the current thread.

The third statement creates the IOThread object and assigns it to a Thread variable named t2. Then, the fourth statement starts the thread by calling its start() method. This places the thread in the Runnable state so the thread scheduler can run it. The fifth statement prints a message indicating that the main thread has started the second thread. And the sixth statement prints a message indicating that the main thread has finished.

The first three lines of the output shown at the bottom of this figure are printed by the main() method, which runs in a thread named "main". Then, the next two lines are printed by the thread that's created from the IOThread class named "Thread-0". The first line is printed at the beginning of the run() method to indicate that the thread has started, and the second line is printed at the end of the run() method to indicate that the thread has finished. This output shows that the main thread can continue executing while the code in the second thread executes. In other words, the statements in the main() method don't have to wait for the statements in the run() method of the second thread to finish.

A procedure for creating a thread from the Thread class

1. Create a class that inherits the Thread class.

2. Override the run() method to perform the desired task.

3. Create the thread by instantiating an object from the class.

4. Call the start() method of the Thread object.

A class named IOThread that defines a thread

```
public class IOThread extends Thread {
    @Override
    public void run() {
        System.out.println(this.getName() + " started.");
        try {
            Thread.sleep(2000);         // Sleep for 2 seconds to simulate
                                        // an IO task that takes a long time
        }
        catch(InterruptedException e) {}
        System.out.println(this.getName() + " finished.");
    }
}
```

A ThreadApp class that starts a thread

```
public class ThreadApp {
    public static void main(String[] args) {
        Thread t1 = Thread.currentThread();
        System.out.println(t1.getName() + " started.");

        Thread t2 = new IOThread();    // create the IO thread
        t2.start();                    // start the IO thread
        System.out.println(t1.getName() + " starts " + t2.getName() + ".");

        System.out.println(t1.getName() + " finished.");
    }
}
```

Sample output

```
main started.
main starts Thread-0.
main finished.
Thread-0 started.
Thread-0 finished.
```

Figure 23-5   How to create a thread by extending the Thread class

How to implement the Runnable interface

Figure 23-6 shows how to create a thread by implementing the Runnable interface. Although this technique for creating threads requires a little more code, it's also more flexible because it lets you define a thread that inherits a class other than the Thread class.

If you compare this code to the previous figure, you'll notice that the IOTask class differs from the IOThread class in two basic ways. First, the IOTask class implements the Runnable interface rather than extending the Thread class. Second, the first statement within the run() method of the IOTask class calls the static currentThread() method of the Thread class to get a reference to the thread that's currently executing. That way, the getName() method can be used to get the name of this thread.

In the main() method, you can't create a Thread object directly from the IOTask class. Instead, you have to create a Runnable object from this class and pass it to the constructor of the Thread class. That's shown in the third statement of the main() method.

A procedure for creating a thread using the Runnable interface

1. Create a class that implements the Runnable interface.

2. Implement the run() method to perform the desired task.

3. Create the thread by supplying an instance of the Runnable class to the Thread constructor.

4. Call the start() method of the Thread object.

An IOTask class that implements the Runnable interface

```java
public class IOTask implements Runnable {
    @Override
    public void run() {
        Thread ct = Thread.currentThread();
        System.out.println(ct.getName() + " started.");
        try {
            Thread.sleep(2000);    // Sleep for 2 seconds to simulate
                                   // an IO task that takes a long time
        }
        catch(InterruptedException e) {}

        System.out.println(ct.getName() + " finished.");
    }
}
```

A ThreadApp class that starts a thread using the Runnable interface

```java
public class ThreadApp {
    public static void main(String[] args) {
        Thread t1 = Thread.currentThread();
        System.out.println(t1.getName() + " started.");

        Thread t2 = new Thread(new IOTask());    // create the new thread
        t2.start();                              // start the new thread
        System.out.println(t1.getName() + " starts " + t2.getName() + ".");

        System.out.println(t1.getName() + " finished.");
    }
}
```

Sample output

```
main started.
main starts Thread-0.
main finished.
Thread-0 started.
Thread-0 finished.
```

Figure 23-6   How to create a thread by implementing the Runnable interface

How to synchronize threads

So far, the threads in this chapter have executed independently of each other. Threads of this type are known as *asynchronous threads*. Now, you'll learn how to work with threads that access the same fields within a class or object and must be synchronized. Threads of this type are known as *synchronous threads*.

Whenever you create an application that uses multiple threads, you need to think about any *concurrency* issues that the application might face. Concurrency issues result from conflicts that can occur when two or more threads attempt to access the same class or object at the same time. In that case, concurrency problems such as lost updates can result. To prevent concurrency problems, you can design classes that might be used by multiple threads so they're *thread-safe*.

How to use synchronized methods

One common way to create a thread-safe class is to add the synchronized keyword to any methods that aren't thread-safe, as shown in figure 23-7. Here, the InvoiceQueue class defines an object that allows a thread to add or remove an invoice from a list of invoices.

Within this class, the declaration for the add() and remove() methods include the synchronized keyword. As a result, when a thread calls one of these methods, the Java virtual machine *locks* the object until the method finishes executing. Once the object is locked, no other thread can obtain a lock on it until the synchronized method ends and the lock is released.

Note that it is the object itself that's locked, not the synchronized method. As a result, when a thread calls a synchronized method, other threads are prevented from running any of the object's synchronized methods, not just the method called by the first thread. However, other threads aren't prevented from running unsynchronized methods. That's because an object's lock isn't checked when an unsynchronized method is called.

When to use synchronized methods

As a general rule, if an application uses multiple threads that may access the same class or object, any methods that access the fields of that class or object should be synchronized. This prevents two threads from accessing the same fields at the same time. In figure 23-7, both the add() and remove() methods work with the field named invoiceQueue that stores the list of invoices. As a result, both of these methods should be synchronized. However, the print() method doesn't access any fields, so it doesn't need to be synchronized.

Although both the synchronized methods in this example modify the invoiceQueue field, you should realize that methods that access, but don't modify, a field should also be synchronized. That way, another thread can't modify the field while the first thread is accessing it.

The syntax for creating a synchronized method

```
public|private synchronized returnType methodName([parameterList]) {
    statements
}
```

A class that contains two synchronized methods

```
public class InvoiceQueue {
    private ArrayList<Invoice> invoiceQueue = new ArrayList<>();

    public synchronized void add(Invoice invoice) {
        invoiceQueue.add(invoice);
    }

    public synchronized Invoice remove() {
        if (invoiceQueue.size() > 1) {
            return invoiceQueue.remove(0);
        } else {
            return null;
        }
    }

    public void print() {
        System.out.println("This method doesn't need to be synchronized.");
    }
}
```

Description

- *Asynchronous threads* execute independently of each other. *Synchronous threads* need to be coordinated if they could access the same field within a class or object at the same time.

- *Concurrency* refers to a state when multiple threads use the same class or object at the same time. Whenever this happens, concurrency problems such as lost updates may occur.

- When you code a class that multiple threads may use, you need to make sure that the class is *thread-safe*. This means that multiple threads can use it safely without causing concurrency problems.

- The synchronized keyword *locks* the class or object and guarantees that only one thread at a time can execute any of its synchronized methods. Any other thread that attempts to run any synchronized method for the class or object is blocked until the first thread releases the lock by exiting the synchronized method.

- A thread can run an unsynchronized method even if the class or object is locked by a synchronized method. This can potentially cause problems if the unsynchronized method accesses the same field that's used by a synchronized method.

- It's a best practice to use synchronized methods whenever two or more threads might execute a method that accesses a field of the class or object.

Figure 23-7   How to synchronize threads

Perspective

In this chapter, you learned the basic skills for working with threads. Threads are a complex topic, so this chapter could only provide a brief introduction. Frankly, threading is one of the most challenging topics in this book. So don't be too worried if you don't understand every detail of how it works. As you learn more about different types of Java programming, you'll learn more about working with threads in those environments. For example, you'll learn more about threads if you learn more about GUI programming, web programming, or Android programming.

Summary

- A *thread* is a single sequential flow of control within an application that often completes a specific task.

- A *multithreaded application* consists of two or more threads whose execution can overlap.

- A single core processor can only execute one thread at a time, and the *thread scheduler* determines which thread to execute.

- Most modern processors have multiple cores and can run more than one thread at the same time. In this case, the thread scheduler determines which threads to run, and which core to run them on.

- *Multithreading* is typically used to improve the performance of applications with I/O operations, to improve the responsiveness of GUI operations, and to allow two or more users to run server-based applications simultaneously.

- You can create a thread by extending the Thread class and then instantiating the new class. Or, you can implement the Runnable interface and then pass a reference to the Runnable object to the constructor of the Thread class.

- You can use the methods of the Thread class to start a thread and to control when a thread runs.

- *Asynchronous threads* execute independently of each other.

- You can use *synchronized methods* to make sure that two threads don't run any synchronized methods of a class or object simultaneously. When a thread calls a synchronized method, the class or object that contains that method is *locked* so other threads can't access any of the synchronized method.

- It's generally considered a best practice to synchronize any methods where there's potential for two threads to access the same field of a class or object at the same time.

Exercise 23-1   Extend the Thread class

In this exercise, you'll create an application that extends the Thread class to create one thread that prints odd numbers from 1 to 10 and another thread that prints even numbers from 1 to 10. The output from this application should look something like this:

```
main started.
Thread-0 started.
Thread-1 started.
main finished.
1
3
5
2
4
7
9
Thread-0 finished.
6
8
10
Thread-1 finished.
```

1. Open the project named ch23_ex1_Counter in the ex_starts folder. Review the code for the Main class and note that it prints a message to the console that indicates when the main thread starts and finishes.

2. Add a class named CounterThread that extends the Thread class.

3. Add an instance variable for a starting value and a constructor that sets that starting value like this:

```
private final int startingValue;

public CounterThread(int startingValue) {
    this.startingValue = startingValue;
}
```

4. In the CounterThread class, add a run() method that prints every other number from the starting value to 10 to the console and displays an appropriate message when it's finished.

5. In the CounterApp class, add code to create and start two instances of the CounterThread class. The first should use the ODD constant to specify the starting value, and the second should use the EVEN constant to specify the starting value.

6. Run the application two or more times to make sure it works correctly. The output may vary each time you run the application.

7. Depending on the speed of your system, it's possible that one thread will finish running before the thread scheduler switches threads. In that case, it may look like the two threads are running in sequence rather than in parallel.

8. Add a statement to the run() method of the CounterThread class that calls the Thread.sleep() method to make the thread sleep for one second between each number. See if this changes the order of the output when you run the application.

9. Run the application two or more times to make sure it works correctly. The output may vary each time you run the application.

Exercise 23-2   Implement the Runnable interface

In this exercise, you'll create an application that's similar to the one that you created in exercise 23-1. However, in this exercise, you implement the Runnable interface instead of extending the Thread class.

1. Open the project named ch23_ex2_Counter in the ex_starts folder. Review the code for the CounterApp class and note that it prints a message to the console that indicates when the main thread starts and finishes.

2. Add a class named CounterThread to the project that implements the Runnable interface.

3. Follow steps 3 through 9 from the previous exercise.

Appendix A

How to set up Windows for this book

This appendix shows how to install the software that we recommend for developing Java applications on a Windows system. This software includes the Java Development Kit (JDK) and either the NetBeans IDE or the Eclipse IDE. Then, this appendix shows how to install the source code for this book, which has been formatted to work with NetBeans or Eclipse.

As you read this appendix, please remember that most websites are continually updated. As a result, some of the procedures in this appendix may have changed since this book was published. Nevertheless, these procedures should still be good guides to installing the software. And if there are significant changes to these setup instructions, we will post updates on our website (www.murach.com).

How to install the JDK and NetBeans

Figure A-1 shows how to install the Java Development Kit (JDK) and the NetBeans IDE. For convenience, you can install them as one package. To start, click on the Download button for NetBeans with JDK to download the exe file for the setup program from the Java website. Then, navigate to the folder that contains the setup file, run this file, and respond to the resulting dialog boxes.

Since the Java website may change after this book is printed, we've kept the procedure shown in this figure somewhat general. As a result, you may have to do some searching to find the current version of NetBeans and the JDK. To start, you can search the Internet for the download for Java SE. Then, you can find the most current version of the JDK and NetBeans for your operating system.

By the way, all of the examples in this book have been tested against the early access release of JDK 1.9. Since Java is backwards compatible, these examples should continue to work equally well with future versions of the JDK. In addition, most of the examples in this book don't use new features of JDK 1.9. As a result, they work equally well with JDK 1.8. Of course, the examples that illustrate new features of JDK 1.9 won't work with Java 1.8, so as soon as JDK 1.9 is officially released, you should use it.

The download page for Java SE

`http://www.oracle.com/technetwork/java/javase/downloads`

How to install the JDK and the NetBeans IDE

1. Go to the download page for Java SE. If necessary, you can search the Internet to find this page.

2. Click on the Download button for NetBeans with JDK and follow the instructions for your operating system.

3. Save the setup program to your hard disk. For Windows, this program is an exe file.

4. Run the setup program and respond to the resulting dialog boxes. When you're prompted for the JDK folder, use the default folder. For most Windows systems, the JDK should be stored in the C:\Program Files\Java folder.

How to start the NetBeans IDE

- In Windows 7 or Windows 10, go to NetBeans IDE in your Start Menu and run the program. If necessary, you can search the Start Menu to find the program.

- In Windows 8, go to NetBeans IDE in the Apps list and run the program.

Notes

- Java SE 9 is due to be released in July 2017. Until it is released, you can use Java SE 8 with this book.

- For more information about installing the JDK, you can refer to the Oracle website.

- For more information about installing NetBeans, you can refer to the NetBeans website.

Figure A-1   How to install the JDK and NetBeans

How to install the source code for this book

Figure A-2 shows how to download and install the source code for this book. This includes the source code for the applications that are presented in this book. In addition, it includes the source code for the starting points and solutions for the exercises that are presented at the end of each chapter.

When you finish this procedure, the book applications, exercise starts, and exercise solutions should be in the folders shown in this figure. Then, you can review the applications that are presented in this book, and you'll be ready to do the exercises in this book.

Note, here, that you use the files that are in the netbeans folder if you're using NetBeans as your IDE, and you use the files in the eclipse folder if you're using Eclipse as your IDE. You will only use the files in both the netbeans and eclipse folders if you're experimenting with both IDEs.

The Murach website

www.murach.com

The folder that contains the NetBeans projects

C:\murach\java\netbeans

The folder that contains the Eclipse projects

C:\murach\java\eclipse

The subfolders

Folder	Description
book_apps	The applications that are presented throughout this book.
ex_starts	The starting points for the exercises at the end of each chapter.
ex_solutions	The solutions to the exercises.

How to download and install the files for this book

1. Go to www.murach.com, and go to the page for *Murach's Java Programming (5th Edition)*.

2. If necessary, scroll down to the FREE Downloads tab. Then, click on it.

3. Click the Download Now button for the exe file, and respond to the resulting pages and dialog boxes. This should download an installer file named jvp5_allfiles.exe.

4. Use Windows Explorer to find the exe file.

5. Double-click this file and respond to the dialog boxes that follow. This should install the files for this book in folders that start with C:\murach\java.

How to use a zip file instead of a self-extracting zip file

- Although we recommend using the self-extracting zip file (jvp5_allfiles.exe) to install the downloadable files as described above, some systems won't allow self-extracting zip files to run. In that case, you can download a regular zip file (jvp5_allfiles.zip) from our website. Then, you can extract the files stored in this zip file into the C:\murach folder. If the C:\murach folder doesn't already exist, you will need to create it.

Notes for other versions of the JDK

- If you're using JDK 9 (Java SE 9) or later, you should be able to compile and run all of the applications in this book.

- If you're using an earlier version of the JDK, you can still view the source code, but you won't be able to compile and run applications that use the features of Java introduced with later versions of the JDK. To solve this problem, you can download and install JDK 9 as described in figure A-1.

Figure A-2   How to install the source code for this book

How to install Eclipse

If you want to use NetBeans as your IDE for this book, you don't need to install the Eclipse IDE. However, if you're going to use Eclipse or you want to experiment with both IDEs, you can use the procedure shown in figure A-3 to install Eclipse. This figure also shows how to start Eclipse and select the workspace directory where your projects are stored.

If you're going to use Eclipse, you may also want to read the Eclipse PDF for this book. This PDF shows you how to use Eclipse instead of NetBeans for all of the NetBeans procedures that are shown in the book. You can find this PDF in the eclipse folder shown in the previous figure.

The URL for the Eclipse download

`http://www.eclipse.org/downloads`

How to install the Eclipse IDE

1. Go to the download page for Eclipse. If necessary, you can search the Internet to find this page.

2. Find the download for the installer for the current version of Eclipse (Eclipse Neon.2 at the time of this printing), and download the version for your operating system. For Windows, this program is an exe file.

3. Run the installer and respond to the resulting dialog boxes. When a list of the packages you can install is displayed, select "Eclipse IDE for Java Developers". When you're asked to selected an installation folder, accept the default.

How to start Eclipse

- In Windows 7 and Windows 10, go to Eclipse Java in your Start Menu and run the program. If necessary, you can search the Start Menu to find the program.

- In Windows 8, go to Eclipse Java in the Apps list and run the program.

The dialog box for selecting a workspace directory

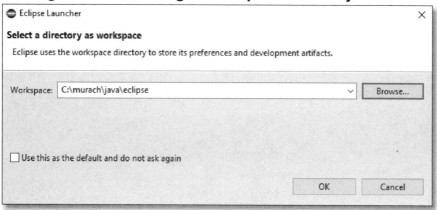

How to select the workspace directory

- When you start Eclipse, you typically select the *workspace* you want to use from the dialog box shown above.

- When Eclipse is running, you can switch to a different workspace by selecting the File→Switch Workspace command. This restarts Eclipse and selects the new workspace.

- Once you have selected a workspace, it appears in the Workspace menu. This makes it easy to switch between workspaces.

Notes

- If you want to use NetBeans as your IDE, you don't need to install Eclipse.

- If you want to use Eclipse with this book, be sure to read the Eclipse PDF that shows how to use Eclipse instead of NetBeans throughout this book. You'll find this PDF in the eclipse folder shown in the previous figure.

Figure A-3   How to install Eclipse

How to install SQLite Manager

Figure A-4 shows how to install the software that you'll need for working with the database chapters in section 5 of this book. Although several management tools are available for SQLite, we recommend SQLite Manager for this book, which is an add-on for the Firefox web browser. If don't already have Firefox on your system, you start by installing Firefox. Then, you install the SQLite Manager add-on for Firefox.

The download page for Firefox

`www.mozilla.org/download`

How to install Firefox

1. Find the download page for Firefox. The easiest way to do that is to search the Internet for "Firefox download".
2. Follow the instructions on that web page to download the installer file.
3. Find the installer file on your system and run it.
4. Accept the default options.

How to install the SQLite Manager add-on

1. Start Firefox.
2. Press Ctrl+Shift+A to open the Firefox Add-ons page. Or, select Tools→Add-ons from the Firefox menu bar. (If the menu bar isn't displayed, you can display it by right-clicking on the toolbar area of Firefox and selecting Menu Bar from the popup menu.)
3. In the search box, search for "SQLite Manager".
4. Click the Install button for SQLite Manager.
5. Click the "Restart Now" link to restart Firefox.

How to add the SQLite Manager icon to the toolbar

1. Right-click in the toolbar area of Firefox and select Customize from the popup menu.
2. Drag the SQLite Manager icon from the Additional Tools and Features panel up into the toolbar and drop it.

Two ways to start SQLite Manager

- Click the SQLite Manager icon in the Firefox toolbar.
- Press Alt+T to access the Tools menu and select the SQLite Manager command.

Note

- SQLite is used as the database for chapters 20 and 21 of this book. If you aren't going to use any of the programs, exercises, and solutions for those chapters, you don't need to install SQLite Manager.

Figure A-4   How to install SQLite Manager

Appendix B

How to set up Mac OS X for this book

This appendix shows how to install the software that we recommend for developing Java applications on a Mac OS X system. This software includes the Java Development Kit (JDK) and either the NetBeans IDE or the Eclipse IDE. This appendix also shows how to install the source code for this book, which has been formatted to work with NetBeans or Eclipse.

As you read this appendix, please remember that most websites are continually updated. As a result, some of the procedures in this appendix may have changed since this book was published. Nevertheless, these procedures should still be good guides to installing the software. And if there are significant changes to these setup instructions, we will post updates on our website (www.murach.com).

How to install the JDK and NetBeans

Figure B-1 shows how to install the Java Development Kit (JDK) and the NetBeans IDE. For convenience, you can install them as one package. To start, click on the Download button for NetBeans with JDK to download the dmg file for the installer program from the Java website. Then, navigate to the folder that contains the installer file, run this file, and respond to the resulting dialog boxes.

Since the Java website may change after this book is printed, we've kept the procedure shown in this figure somewhat general. As a result, you may have to do some searching to find the current version of NetBeans and the JDK. To start, you can search the Internet for the download for Java SE. Then, you can find the most current version of the JDK and NetBeans for your operating system.

By the way, all of the examples in this book have been tested against the early access release of JDK 1.9. Since Java is backwards compatible, these examples should continue to work with future versions of the JDK. In addition, most of the examples in this book don't use new features of JDK 1.9. As a result, they will work with JDK 1.8. Of course, the examples that illustrate new features of JDK 1.9 won't work with Java 1.8, so as soon as JDK 1.9 is officially released, you should install and use it.

The download page for Java SE

`http://www.oracle.com/technetwork/java/javase/downloads`

How to install the JDK and the NetBeans IDE

1. Go to the download page for Java SE. If necessary, you can search the Internet for "Java SE Download".

2. Click on the Download button for NetBeans with JDK. For Mac OS X, this is a dmg file.

3. When the download is complete, find the dmg file in the Downloads folder and double-click on it to run the installer program. Then, respond to the resulting dialog boxes. If you're prompted for the JDK folder, use the default folder.

Notes

- Java SE 9 is due to be released in July 2017. Until it is released, you can use Java SE 8 with this book.

- For more information about installing the JDK, you can refer to the Oracle website.

- For more information about installing NetBeans, you can refer to the NetBeans website.

Figure B-1   How to install the JDK and NetBeans

How to install the source code for this book

Figure B-2 shows how to download and install the source code for this book. This includes the source code for the applications that are presented in this book. It also includes the source code for the starting points and solutions for the exercises that are presented at the end of each chapter.

When you finish this procedure, the book applications, exercise starts, and exercise solutions should be in the folders shown in this figure. Then, you can review the applications that are presented in this book, and you'll be ready to do the exercises in this book.

Note, here, that you use the files that are in the netbeans folder if you're using NetBeans as your IDE, and you use the files in the eclipse folder if you're using Eclipse as your IDE. You will only use the files in both the netbeans and eclipse folders if you're experimenting with both IDEs.

The Murach website

www.murach.com

The folder that contains the NetBeans projects

/murach/java/netbeans

The folder that contains the Eclipse projects

/murach/java/eclipse

The subfolders

Folder	Description
book_apps	The applications that are presented throughout this book.
ex_starts	The starting points for the exercises at the end of each chapter.
ex_solutions	The solutions to the exercises.

How to download and install the files for this book

1. Go to www.murach.com, and go to the page for *Murach's Java Programming (5ᵗʰ Edition)*.

2. If necessary, scroll down to the FREE Downloads tab. Then, click on it.

3. Click the Download Now button for the zip file for the book applications and exercises. Then, respond to the resulting pages and dialog boxes. This should download a zip file named jvp5_allfiles.zip to your hard drive.

4. Move this zip file from your Downloads folder into your Documents folder. Then, double-click on the zip file to extract the book_apps, ex_starts, and ex_solutions folders for this book into the murach/java folder.

A note about right-clicking

- This book often instructs you to right-click, because that's common in Windows. On a Mac, right-clicking is not enabled by default. However, you can enable right-clicking by editing the system preferences for your mouse.

Notes for users of other versions of the JDK

- If you're using JDK 9 (Java SE 9) or later, you should be able to compile and run all of the applications in this book.

- If you're using an earlier version of the JDK, you can still view the source code, but you won't be able to compile and run applications that use the features of Java introduced with later versions of the JDK. To solve this problem, you can download and install JDK 9 as described in figure B-1.

Figure B-2   How to install the source code for this book

How to install Eclipse

If you're going to use NetBeans as your IDE for this book, you don't need to install the Eclipse IDE. However, if you're going to use Eclipse or you want to experiment with both IDEs, you can use the procedure shown in figure B-3 to install Eclipse. This figure also shows how to select the workspace directory where your projects are stored.

If you're going to use Eclipse, you may also want to read the Eclipse PDF for this book. This PDF shows you how to use Eclipse instead of NetBeans for all of the NetBeans procedures that are shown in the book. You can find this PDF in the eclipse folder shown in the previous figure.

The URL for the Eclipse download

http://www.eclipse.org/downloads

How to install the Eclipse IDE

1. Go to the download page for Eclipse. If necessary, you can search the Internet for "Eclipse download".

2. Find the download for the current version of Eclipse (or Eclipse Neon), and download the version for your operating system. For Mac OS X, this download is stored in a tar file.

3. In the Documents folder, double-click on the downloaded tar file. That will download the Eclipse Installer.

4. Double-click on the Eclipse Installer to start it. Then, respond to the dialog boxes that are displayed. When a list of the Eclipse packages is displayed, select "Eclipse IDE for Java Developers". If you're asked to select an installation folder, accept the default.

5. When the installation is complete, click on the Launch button to start Eclipse.

The dialog box for selecting a workspace directory

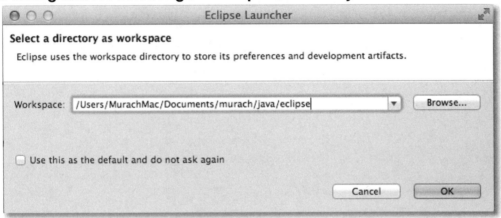

How to select the workspace directory

- When you start Eclipse, you typically select the workspace you want to use from the dialog box shown above. A *workspace* stores information about how to configure Eclipse, including which projects to display.

- When Eclipse is running, you can switch to a different workspace by selecting the File→Switch Workspace command. This restarts Eclipse and selects the new workspace.

- Once you have selected a workspace, it appears in the Workspace menu. This makes it easy to switch between workspaces.

Notes

- If you're going to use NetBeans as your IDE for this book, you don't need to install Eclipse.

- If you want to use Eclipse with this book, be sure to read the Eclipse PDF that shows how to use Eclipse instead of NetBeans throughout this book. You'll find this PDF in the eclipse folder shown in the previous figure.

Figure B-3   How to install Eclipse

How to install SQLite Manager

Figure B-4 shows how to install the software that you'll need for working with the database chapters in section 5 of this book. Although several management tools are available for SQLite, we recommend SQLite Manager for this book, which is an add-on for the Firefox web browser. If don't already have Firefox on your system, you start by installing Firefox. Then, you install the SQLite Manager add-on for Firefox.

The download page for Firefox

www.mozilla.org/download

How to install Firefox

1. Find the download page for Firefox. The easiest way to do that is to search the Internet for "Firefox download".

2. Download the version of Firefox for your computer.

3. In the Downloads folder, double-click on the downloaded file. Then, double-click on the Firefox icon in the window that's displayed. This should install and start Firefox with its Start Page displayed in the first tab.

How to install the SQLite Manager add-on

1. Start Firefox.

2. Select Tools→Add-ons from the Firefox menu bar. Then, scroll to the bottom of the page and click the See More Add-Ons button.

3. In the search box for the Add-ons, search for "SQLite Manager".

4. Click the SQLite Manager icon, and then click the Add to FireFox button.

5. Click Restart Now to restart Firefox.

How to add the SQLite Manager icon to the toolbar

1. If the bookmarks toolbar isn't displayed, select View→Toolbars→Bookmarks Toolbar to display that toolbar.

2. Select View→Toolbars→Customize to display the Customize page.

3. Drag the SQLite Manager icon from the Additional Tools and Features panel up into the bookmark toolbar and drop it.

4. Click Exit Customize to exit from the Customize page.

Two ways to start SQLite Manager

- Click the SQLite Manager icon in the Firefox toolbar.
- Select Tools→SQLite Manager.

Note

- SQLite is used as the database for chapters 20 and 21 of this book. If you aren't going to use any of the programs, exercises, and solutions for those chapters, you don't need to install SQLite Manager.

Figure B-4   How to install SQLite Manager

Index

H

I

S

100% Guarantee

When you order directly from us, you must be satisfied. Our books must work better than any other programming books you've ever used...both for training and reference...or you can send them back within 60 days for a prompt refund. No questions asked!

Mike Murach, Publisher   *Ben Murach, President*

Related Book

Next stop: Android programming

With your core Java skills in place, you're ready for Android programming. Our book uses Android Studio and an app-based approach to get you going quickly! Soon, you'll be turning your own ideas for apps into reality.

Books for programmers

Murach's Python Programming	$57.50
Murach's Beginning Java with Eclipse	57.50
Murach's Beginning Java with NetBeans	57.50
Murach's Android Programming (2nd Ed.)	57.50
Murach's Java Programming (5th Ed.)	59.50
Murach's Java Servlets and JSP (3rd Ed.)	57.50

Books for .NET developers

Murach's ASP.NET 4.6 Web Programming w/ C# 2015	$59.50
Murach's C# 2015	57.50

Books for web developers

Murach's HTML5 and CSS3 (3rd Ed.)	$54.50
Murach's JavaScript and jQuery (3rd Ed.)	57.50
Murach's PHP and MySQL (2nd Ed.)	54.50

Books for database programmers

Murach's SQL Server 2016 for Developers	$57.50
Murach's MySQL (2nd Ed.)	54.50
Murach's Oracle SQL and PL/SQL (2nd Ed.)	54.50

*Prices and availability are subject to change. Please visit our website or call for current information.

We want to hear from you

Do you have any comments, questions, or compliments to pass on to us? It would be great to hear from you! Please share your feedback in whatever way works best.

 www.murach.com

 1-800-221-5528
(Weekdays, 8 am to 4 pm Pacific Time)

 murachbooks@murach.com

 twitter.com/MurachBooks

 facebook.com/murachbooks

 linkedin.com/company/ mike-murach-&-associates

 instagram.com/murachbooks

What software you need for this book

- The JDK (Java Development Kit) for Java SE (Standard Edition).
- The NetBeans IDE or the Eclipse IDE.
- SQLite Manager (only necessary for chapters 20 and 21).

You can download this software for free and install it as described in appendix A (Windows) or appendix B (Mac OS X).

The downloadable files for this book

- Complete source code for the applications presented in this book, so you can view the source code and run the applications as you read each chapter.
- Starting points for the exercises presented at the end of each chapter, so you can get more practice in less time.
- Solutions to the exercises, so you can check your work.
- A PDF file that shows how to use Eclipse with this book.

All of this code is included in both NetBeans and Eclipse formats.

How to install the source code for this book

1. Go to murach.com.
2. Go to the page for *Murach's Java Programming (5th Edition)*.
3. Follow the instructions there to download the zip file that contains the source code for the applications and exercises for this book.
4. Unzip all files. This creates the java folder.
5. If necessary, create the murach folder on your hard drive.
6. Copy the java folder into the murach folder.

For more information, please see appendix A (Windows) or B (Mac OS X).

www.murach.com